SAINT IGNATIUS LOYOLA

Saint
Ignatius Loyola

Letters to Women

HUGO RAHNER S.J.

HERDER AND HERDER

This English translation by Kathleen Pond and S. A. H. Weetman

is based on the first German edition of

"Ignatius von Loyola, Briefwechsel mit Frauen"

published by Herder, Freiburg, 1956

Second impression published 1960 by Herder and Herder Inc.

7 West 46th Street, New York 36, New York

Library of Congress Catalog Card Number: 59-14554

© by Herder KG 1960

Made and printed by Herder Druck, Freiburg, West Germany

TO THE MEMORY OF

HER IMPERIAL HIGHNESS

ARCHDUCHESS MARIE THERESE OF AUSTRIA

INFANTA OF PORTUGAL

1855—1944

CONTENTS

vii

CONTENTS

PART TWO

GOD'S CAVALIER

Correspondence with Noble Ladies

PART THREE

BEGGING FOR THE KINGDOM OF GOD

Letters to Benefactresses

CONTENTS

PART FOUR

THE INEXORABLE COMFORTER

Letters to Spiritual Daughters

CONTENTS

CONTENTS

PART FIVE

FATHER IN CHRIST

Letters to the Mothers of Fellow-Jesuits

CONTENTS

PART SIX

FRIENDSHIP IN GOD

Correspondence with Women who were his Friends

CONTENTS

FOREWORD

In the early hours of the morning of July 31st, 1556, Ignatius of Loyola died in his humble room next to Santa Maria della Strada in Rome. Four hundred years have gone by since then, swallowed up in the darkness of the past. But the portrait of this great man and saint of the sixteenth century is being more and more irradiated with light, as the scholarship of our own time discovers and makes available the historical facts of his life. Only now is it possible to present Ignatius as he really was. The dead man begins to speak again.

He speaks above all in his letters. We cannot therefore commemorate his death in a better way than by raising up from the grave of historical documents the immortal, living Ignatius, who was a saint of God because he always remained human in Christ.

The silent Ignatius reveals to us the secret fullness of his heart not only in his *Spiritual Exercises,* his mystical diary and his memoirs, but also in his letters, especially in his hitherto almost unknown correspondence with women of his time. We present it for the first time in this book as a compact whole. It was in this unexplored territory that we wished to discover the unknown Ignatius.

The book is dedicated to a truly royal lady who many years ago took an affectionate interest in the planning of it. In her person were united the houses of Habsburg and Braganza, whose ancestresses were once favoured with letters from the great Ignatius.

I wish to thank my dear fellow-religious, Father Burkhart Schneider S.J. and the fathers of the Historical Institute of the Society of Jesus at Rome for their unwearying help.

Hugo Rahner S.J.

NOTES ON THE ILLUSTRATIONS

PLATE I *(facing page 32)*. Queen María of Hungary and Bohemia, Govern-
or of the Netherlands, the second youngest sister of the Emperor Charles V.
The portrait, inscribed KUNIGINNE MARIA, shows her wearing the white
widow's cap and dates from *c.* 1550. The artist is unknown. Vienna, Kunsthistorisches Museum. See *Jahrbücher der kunsthistorischen Sammlungen des
allerhöchsten Kaiserhauses,* xiv (1893), 146. For other portraits of Queen
María see O. Rubbrecht, *L'origine du type familial de la maison de Habsbourg*
(Brussels, 1910), 134–8.

PLATE II *(facing page 33)*. Queen Catherine of Portugal, Infanta of
Spain, youngest sister of the Emperor Charles V (1507–78). Portrait by
Antonio Moro (1519–75). Madrid, Prado (No. 2109). See V. von Loga,
Antonis Mor als Hofmaler Karls V. und Philipps II. in *Jahrbücher der kunst-
historischen Sammlungen des allerhöchsten Kaiserhauses,* xxvii (1809), 99–104;
O. Rubbrecht, *loc. cit.,* 138 et seq. For other portraits of Queen Catarina see
M. Bataillon, *Études sur le Portugal au temps de l'humanisme* (Coimbra, 1952), 272.

PLATE III *(facing page 96)*. The Infanta Juana of Spain, widow of the
Heir Apparent of Portugal, Regent of Spain (1535–73). Portrait by Antonio
Moro. Madrid, Prado (No. 2112). For other portraits of Princess Juana see
J. M. March, *Niñez y juventud de Felipe II* ii, (Madrid, 1942), 120; 445 et seq.

PLATE IV *(facing page 97)*. Conclusion of the autograph letter of the
Regent Juana to Ignatius, Valladolid, May 28th, 1556. In the general archives
of the Society of Jesus at Rome: *Epp. Ext.,* 25, fol. 119ᵛ. Published in *Mixt.,*
v, 336. The text of the Spanish original is as follows: ". . . activéis y supli-
quéis á S. S., y lo tratéis tanbién de my parte, si os pareçiere, y que de la
vuestra lo encaminéis con la pudençia que Dios os a dado, de manera que se
haga con brevedad; que por esto os e querido dar este trabajo, sabiendo la
voluntad con que vuestra caridad lo hará. Yo no lo escribo á S. S., por
averlo tratado con su nunçio. La brevedad deste negocio os encomiendo
mucho, porque lo deseo terriblemente, y conviene asy, para que esto se
efectúe mejor. Os ruego mucho os accordéis en vuestras oraciones de enco-
mendallo muy de veras á nuestro Señor, y tanbien os pido que en este
tiempo os acordéis de my.

De Valladolid á xxviii de Maio   La Prinçesa"

PLATE V *(facing page 144)*. Margaret of Austria, Duchess of Parma, natural daughter of Charles V (1522–86). Portrait by Antonio Moro. Berlin, Staatliche Museen. There is another portrait at Parma. See I. Drei, *I Farnese, grandezza e decadenza di una dinastia italiana* (Rome, 1954).

PLATE VI *(facing page 145)*. Letter of Margaret of Austria to Ignatius, Parma, January 16th, 1554. Written by her secretary (probably the one who was called Armenteros, cf. *M.Borg.*, v, 19) and signed by the Duchess herself. In the general archives of the Society of Jesus at Rome, *Epp. Ext.*, 25, fol. 99ʳ. Published in *MI* I, v, 700. Text of the Italian original:

"Reverendo M(aestro) Ignatio, La lettera vostra ci è stata di molta consolatione per havere inteso di vostra salute, et conosciuto per essa, che l'affectione ci havete portata, non è diminuita per si lungha assentia, ne vi sete scordato in li nostri molti travagli pregare Dio benedetto, per noi, di che vi restiamo con infinito obligo, et vi preghiamo a volere continuare in le vostre orationi, et se di qua possiamo cosa alcuna, per voi o per la compagnia vostra, sempre ci troverete prontissima, a farvi ogni piacere, et cosi vi ci offeriamo che Dio N. S. vi contenti. Di Parma il di xvj di Gennaro 1554.   Margarita d'Austria."

PLATE VII *(facing page 208)*. Eleonora de' Medici, Duchess of Florence, consort of Duke Cosimo I (1517?–62). Portrait by Agnolo Bronzino (1503–72). Florence, Uffizi. There is a similar portrait at Berlin, Staatliche Museen. See E. Heyck, *Florenz und die Medici* (Bielefeld-Leipzig, 1909), 118; H. Schulze, *Angelo Bronzinos Werke* (Strasbourg, 1910); F. Cereceda, *Diego Laynez en la Europa religiosa de su tiempo*, i (Madrid, 1945), 145.

PLATE VIII *(facing page 209)*. Letter from the Duchess Eleonora of Florence to Ignatius, Florence, July 27th, 1555. Written by her secretary and signed by the duchess. In the general archives of the Society at Rome, *Epp. Ext.*, 46, fol. 101ʳ. Published in *Mixt.*, iv, 738 et seq. Text of the Spanish original: "Muy Rdo Padre. Yo scrivo al Señor Conde de Montoro que por mi respecto y intercessión favorezca con su santidat á Francisco Mudarra para que se la haga merced de perdonarle, ques pretende de ser buen xpiano, y desear bivir como tal, y por no ser con él muy larga me remito á V. R. que de mi parte le informará del negocio, y dirá lo que el dicho Mudarra pretende, y el deseo que yo tengo se le haga por mi medio esta merced, por parescerme cosa de mucha misericordia. V. R. le dará mi carta y le informará de todo de mi parte, como tengo dicho, y me abisará de lo que se hiziere. Nuestro Señor guarde vuestra muy Rda persona. De Florencia 27 de Julio 1555.
De V. R.   La Duquesa de Florencia."

PLATE IX *(facing page 256)*. Autograph letter of Vittoria Colonna, Marchioness of Pescara (1492–1547) to Ignatius, Viterbo, January 21st, 1542. In the general archives of the Society of Jesus at Rome, *Epp. Ext.*, 25, fol. 16^r. Published in *MI* I, xii, 362 et seq. Text of the Spanish original:
"Muy manyfyco y Rdo Señor in X° Padre, muchas gratyas le doy del trabajo y fatyga che por nuestro común Señor y por my ha tomado con Maestro Andrea y más de acerme conoçer al bueno humyl y santo Don Antón su sobryno. Y porque dél mesmo sabrá il todo no seré más prolyxa dexando que las obras y el obedezerle en quanto me mandare le muestren my voluntad. Y nuestro Señor Dyos cumpla sus deseos acá por arra y señalde complyrlos del todo adonde ellos tyenen su fyn. De Santa Cataryna de Vyterbo á los xxi de Henero.

A lo que mandare su merced la Marquesa de Pescara.
On the back (fol. 16^v) is the address: Al muy Rdo Padre don Ignygo in X° honorando."

PLATE X *(facing page 257)*. Juana of Aragon, Duchess of Tagliacozzo, consort of Duke Ascanio Colonna (1502–75). The portrait, painted in 1518, is by Raphael (1483–1520); the decorative details are by Giulio Romano, Paris, Louvre. See G. Vasari, *Vita di Giovanna Romano,* ed. Milanesi (Florence, 1880), v, 525 (English edition of the *Lives of the Painters* in Everymans Library).

PLATE XI *(facing page 320)*. Autograph letter from Catarina de Badajoz, maid of honour to the Duchess Giovanna Colonna (1526–53), Naples, March 23rd, 1539, in the general archives of the Society of Jesus at Rome, *Epp. NN.,* 65, I, fol. 247. Published in *Mixt.,* i, 17–9. Text of the Spanish original (including the corrections and mistakes made by Catarina):
"R^{do} y Noble S^{or},
Despues de besadas las manos de V. M. hagole saber como ha Dizisiete meses que estoi en (Roma) Napoles y sempre con desseo de saber de V. m. y de todos (essos) essos señores y siervos de ihu xpo en cuyas oraciones de contino me encomiendo que a v. m. no me atrevo; que si no temiesse de enojarle de contino yria enpos de v. m. como la cananea enpues de ihu xpo, Señor mio. De todo lo que en otro tiempo me mando no he puesto nada en olvido; porque en cierto sus palabras no son de olvidarlas, mas sienpre me hallo descontenta y tengo la muerte delante los ojos. Suplico a v. m. me haga merescedora de me escrevir que es lo que deva de hazer en los demas este padre le podra ynformar. Marco antonio besa las manos a v. m. y le he dado a su padre y besa las manos a v. m. De Doña Ysabel ni se si es biva ni muerta. Al Señor Maestre Fabro y al Señor Don Diego y al Señor

Estevan de Guia les beso las manos, y les suplico me sean buenos abogados para con v. m.; que yo haunque pecadora siempre soy esclava de v. m. y de essos Señores, y en mis debiles oraciones nunca dexo rogar a nro Señor que les conserve en su sanctissimo servicio; y quedo rogando a dios su R^{da} y noble persona guarde y prospere en su sancto servicio para consuelo y salvacion de muchos.

De Napoles a xxiij de Marco de MDxxx viiij.

La que en dios y en la virtud y sancta doctrina de v. m. confia

su humilde esclava Cathalina de badajoz."

PLATE XII *(facing page 321)*. The sick Ignatius and the women of Manresa (1522). Picture by an unknown artist of the seventeenth century, now much painted over. At Manresa, in the possession of the Marquis of Palmarola. Photograph by Leonard von Matt, Buochs (Switzerland). In the medallion over the bed is the inscription *S. Ignatius de Loyola languens;* in the cartouche at the lower edge of the painting the words *Haec omnia evenerunt 22 Iulii anno 1522.* In the picture to the right of the bed stands Don Pedro de Amigant; his wife, Angela de Amigant, *née* Segui, hands the sick man some refreshment; beside her stand her two sons Francisco and Luis de Amigant, behind her Brianda Paguera, Micaela Canyelles and Inés Clavera. For the history of the picture see Creixell, i, 119 et seq., 287; Larrañaga, i, 190.

PLATE XIII *(facing page 400)*. Autograph copy of the words of the vow made by Isabel Roser on her admittance to the Society of Jesus on December 25th, 1545, in the general archives of the Society at Rome: *Cod. Ital.,* 59, fol. 11. Hitherto unpublished. Text of the Catalan original, with Isabel's errors (the original is somewhat mutilated at the right-hand edge, and we have placed the parts supplied in square brackets):

"yo ysabel roser viuda sota escripta promet y fas vot solene a nre. S. deu omnipo- tent en presencia dela sacratiss [ima] verge maria senyora mia y del glorios sant ieronim y [de] tota la cort celestial de paradis y davant tots los que aci [son] presens y a vos reverent pare Mro innacio preposit [de la] compania de jesus S. nre. en lo loc de deu tenint por pobresa segons que per v. r. me sera man-[d]ada y castedat y obediencia segons la forma del vivre que per v. r. me sera [mandada]. fet en roma en la iglesia de sant maria dela est- [rada] el dia de la nativitat de jesu crist senyor nostre lany m[il] cinc cents y quaranta cinc yo ysabel roser viuda."

PLATE XIV *(facing page 401)*. Ignatius' draft of a letter to Miguel de Torres, Rome, May 3rd, 1547: *MI* I, i, 488–90. Original in the general archives of the Society at Rome, *Cod. Hist. Soc.,* 1 a, fol 73^v. The contents concern the settlement of the dispute with Isabel Roser (cf. page 289 et seq.). The page here reproduced begins with the words "lagrimas de la Sra. Roser"; but there are many additions, erasures, and corrections in Ignatius' own hand, intended with the help of special signs to make it easier for the secretary to write the fair copy. We put these additions in brackets. The Spanish text is as follows:

" . . . lagrimas de la Sra. Roser era [antes] propitio [a ella] mas que ahora conozce que nosotros tenemos razon. Porque V. M. [vea y pondere quanto] credito se deve dar [a los que asi hablan facilmente dire una miseria o cosa tan baxa acaecida sobre esta demanda.] Un dia el dottor Ferrer sobrino della Sra Roser diziendo mucho mal [de mi] [de Mtro] Ignacio y de la casa nuestra delante del mismo juez y de Mtro Gasparo y de don Sylvestro el nuestro el qual don Sylvestro respondiendole que se acordasse de lo que havia dicho que le seria bien demandado, el qual [Ferrer despues de muchos coloquios] con el temor que tuvo [se desdixo y] confesso dos vezes [delante de los mismos] que el habis mentido [mentia *erased*] en lo que havia dicho. De todo esto mirando la charidad que nos obliga a todos procimos no querriamos que V. M. [diese parte destas cosas] [lo mostrasse *erased*] a nunguno si no fuesse en dos casos: en el primero quando alguno stuviesse scandalizado de nosotros, en el 2º para en defension de la verdad guardandando [siempre] el mayor servicio de dios [nro Señor] en todo. Quien por la su infinita ect. [bondad a V. M. con toda su casa y familia conserve y aumente siempre en su mayor servicio alabança y gloria]."

This draft is, on account of the additions made in Ignatius' own hand, of such interest for the understanding of the Saint's character and method of work, that we append a translation, in which the additions are also placed within square brackets. In the first part of the letter Ignatius had spoken to Miguel de Torres of the court of arbitration before which Isabel and her nephews had called Ignatius because of their demands for money. Cardinal Carpi and the representative of the Cardinal-Vicar of Rome had to pronounce judgment. The latter, Ignatius reports, had been much impressed by the tears of Señora Roser. This is where our text begins:

"At the sight of Señora Roser's tears he was [at first] favourably disposed [towards her], but now he recognizes that we are in the right. But that you may [see and judge what] credit those persons deserve who talk thus so readily, I will relate what a mean and low thing happened at the judicial enquiry. One day Dr. Ferrer, Señora Roser's nephew, brought up [against me] [against Master Ignatius] and against our house many evil accusations, in the presence of the same judge and of Master Gasparo *(de Dotti)* and our Father Don Silvestro *(Landini)*. Don Silvestro retorted that he did indeed remember what that man had said, namely that he was right in bringing the action. He [Ferrer, after much beating about the bush] became frightened [and took everything back] and confessed twice [before the same witnesses] that he had lied [was lying *erased*] in what he had said. Having regard to the obligation of charity that we have towards all our neighbours, we would not have you [say anything] [show this *erased*] to anyone, unless it were in two cases: firstly, if anyone should be scandalized at us; and secondly, in defence of the truth, having regard [always] the greater service of God our Lord in all things. May he in his infinite etc. [goodness ever preserve you with all your house and family and make you advance in his greater service, in his praise and glory.]"

PLATE XV *(facing page 464).* Doña Leonor Mascarenhas, governess of King Philip II of Spain and of his son Don Carlos (1503–84). Portrait by an unknown artist. Madrid, convent of Franciscan nuns, *Santa Maria de los Angeles la Real.* The inscription around the frame of the picture (not reproduced here) reads: *Doña Leonor Mascareñas Haia del Rey Don Felipe Secundo y del Principe Don Carlos su Hijo Fundadora del Mon [asterio] de S. Maria de los Angeles la Real de Madrid.* See for the history of the picture J. M. March, *Niñez y juventud de Felipe II* (Madrid, 1941) i, 129, 354 et seq.

PLATE XVI *(facing page 465).* Draft, in Ignatius' own hand, of a letter to Doña Leonor de Vega Osorio, Vicereine of Sicily, Rome, August 11th, 1548. In the General Archives of the Society at Rome, *Cod. Hist. Soc.,* 1 a, fol. 109ᵛ. Published in *MI* I, ii, 189 et seq. Here too the corrections have been added by Ignatius in the margin and indicated by special signs. We have placed these additions in square brackets. Text of the Spanish original:

"Doña Leonor

La suma gracia y amor eterno de Chro. nro. Señor a V. S. salude y visite con sus sanctissimos dones a gracias espirituales. Despues que el sabado pasado escribi a V. S. de las dificultades que me avian puesto sobre las gracias de las cuentas ect, el domingo seguiente a los 5 de agosto able al papa con much oportunidad y la victoria es de V. S. a maior gloria divina. Porque despues que le di alguna cuenta de la Compania y hablando del señor de Vega y de V. S. [lo que me parecia] y Su Sᵈᵃᵈ alabando a VV. SS., y a todo mi juizio con mucho buen affecto, toque el puncto, es a saver, si Su Sᵈᵃᵈ avia revocado las gracias concedidas a V. S. sobre las cuentas ect· Su Sᵈᵃᵈ me responde y con un impetu gracioso que jamas las avia revocado y de nuevo las confirmo echando su bendicion en cruz. Yo luego vesandole otra vez el pie le hable tanbien sobre los quatro lugares para hazerse casas de niños huerfanos [y que la suplicacion abiamos de hazer poner] [*here there are some words crossed out and illegible*] en sinatura que Su Sᵈᵃᵈ mandase expedir: a lo qual asimismo se ofrecio de muy buena voluntad. Despues tornando a hablar al Card. Crescencio [y Su S. R^{ma} ofreciendose mucho] la suplicacion se ha dado a un referendario, creo se expedira presto segun que la cosa esta bien dispuesta a maior glora divina. En la mucha gracia de la S^{ra} doña Ysabel, de los SS. sus hermanos con toda la casa V. S. me mande tener mucho por encomendado en el S^{or} nro. Quien por la su . . . 11 de agosto 1548."

The editors of the *Monumenta* (*MI* I, ii, 190) have omitted the Spanish text of the postscript. It reads as follows:

"Illmo [*or* nro.] Sor Bernardino de la † [*i.e.* de la Cruz] se manda mucho de buen animo encomendar en V. S. y asimismo en el S^{or} Jo. de Vega."

SOURCES OF THE ILLUSTRATIONS

Alinari, Florence: Plates VII and X.

F. Bruckmann, Munich: Plate V.

Prado, Madrid, Laboratorio fotográfico: Plate III.

Mas, Barcelona: Plates II and XV.

L. von Matt, Buochs, Switzerland: Plate XII (by permission of the owner, the Marquis of Palmarola, Manresa, Spain).

Kunsthistorisches Museum, Vienna: Plate I.

The remaining illustrations (plates IV, VI, VIII, IX, XI, XIII, XIV, and XVI) are from the General Archives of the Society of Jesus at Rome, Borgo Santo Spirito 5, and have been reproduced by kind permission of the authorities.

REFERENCES TO SOURCES

We have placed all references to sources in the notes at the end of the book, in order to make the text itself more legible.

GENERAL INTRODUCTION

Porque la escritura queda y da siempre testimonio.

"The written word remains and bears perpetual witness." Ignatius of Loyola wrote these words when, in December 1542, he sent to the members of his Society his carefully considered views concerning the nature and importance of correspondence.[1] Their truth is proved by the example of Ignatius himself, man and saint of the sixteenth century, who is so well known and yet still so unknown. We have still, wholly or in part, about 7000 letters of Ignatius. These written words remain and bear witness in all ages to the saint's greatness, both human and spiritual. Only he who has taken the trouble to read and study the twelve volumes of Ignatius' letters in Spanish, Italian, or Latin, is qualified to say anything about the character of this man, which is so difficult to understand. We are forced by them to the almost paradoxical conclusion that Ignatius, who was no literary man, who all his life handled the pen with difficulty, and who hid himself behind the awkward sentences of his *Spiritual Exercises* and the rough-hewn phraseology of the Constitutions of the Society, only in his letters becomes alive, with that humanity without which there is no holiness in the Church of God made Man.

The attempt has often been made to make the spiritual stature and the permanent significance of Ignatius' achievement intelligible by a selection from his letters.[2] Hitherto such selections have been made principally from his "spiritual" letters. Now every anthology is one-sided, and even though the spiritual letters form by far the most valuable part of the saint's correspondence, his nature is perhaps more immediately revealed to us in the innumerable letters which the circumstances of his everyday life, the unspeakably wearisome business of ruling the Society, and the necessities of his fellowmen compelled him to write: life, in fact, as it came to him every day, and not the few rare hours in which he wrote letters of spiritual direction to chosen souls. Nobody has so far dared to attempt to include these letters with the rest of Ignatius' *Correspondence*.[3] We also possess five more large volumes of letters which Ignatius received from all parts of the world in the years 1537–56, the so-called *Epistolae Mixtae*. It belongs as it were to the metaphysics of letter-writing, that everything that is written only comes to life through the echo it produces, or through the question that finds its

1

answer in a letter. Letters are always dialogues. This is especially so in the case of a man like Ignatius, who in his whole life never wrote a line for its own sake, and who could be induced to break his habitual silence only by a question that needed answering, by a soul in distress, by the claims of friendship, and by an infinitely patient charity.

To get to know the whole Ignatius, one would therefore have to begin anew the task of editing his letters. For that purpose the inexhaustible riches of his correspondence would have to be arranged in groups according to the subject-matter: divided, say, into the letters of spiritual direction in the strict sense, in which he was a master, though a laconic one; into the political letters, which this "worldly saint" wrote from his other-worldly standpoint to kings and great men for the shaping of earthly affairs; into the letters of ecclesiastical reform written to popes and cardinals; and into the letters on administration to his fellow-religious, which he despatched to all parts of the world. Only thus would the figure of the great Ignatius become alive again for us men of to-day, and we should gain admittance to the treasures contained in these letters, which the editor of the latest Spanish anthology, Ignacio Iparraguirre, has rightly called an *epistolario plurifacético*, a many-faceted collection.[4] The present book intends to follow this principle. We have chosen from the total correspondence of Ignatius a clearly defined group: his correspondence with women of his age. Nor do we offer a selection, but all the letters which Ignatius wrote to women and received from them. This numerical completeness does not therefore omit even those letters which are apparently unimportant; for only in the triviality of such letters can the living, everyday holiness of Ignatius be understood. The text of the letters is accompanied by a detailed historical commentary. In this way alone is it possible to comprehend these letters as it were *in situ naturae,* in their context of everyday needs; and only thus does each letter retain its inimitable air of genuineness. This is true hagiography.

The fact that we have made St. Ignatius' letters to women of his time the subject of this book needs detailed justification. Why publish these particular letters? Does not everyone who has the remotest acquaintance with the founder of the Jesuits know that his letters on church reform, on the government of the Society, and on the politics of his century are far more numerous and of far greater historical importance? Ignatius will always remain essentially a "man's saint", and the spiritual guidance of men, students, prelates and laymen, always held the first place for him and his Society. Is it then worth the trouble to pry uninvited, as it were, into Loyola's correspondence with women? Anton Huonder wrote in his book on Ignatius: "There are among the saint's correspondence also some letters to women, especially to religious or those towards whom he had obligations. But they are few." It was, we

2

openly confess, in a sense by way of contradiction to these words that we first undertook to write this book. The hagiographic ideal that inspires us is more comprehensive. Huonder made Ignatius into the "soldier-saint"; and to that the leading authority, Pedro de Leturia, rightly objected.[5] We would like to think that Ignatius was more "human", and this humanity must be shown if we are to realize the heroic spiritual greatness of the saint – a saint who precisely in the realm of the heart, of friendship and of earthly ties and relationships, displays the heavenly purity of his undivided love for God. For this very reason we resolved to seek the complete, real and unfalsified Ignatius in his correspondence with women.

If we consider merely the number of the letters, Huonder's judgment may indeed stand. We possess to-day in the volumes of the *Monumenta Historica Societatis Jesu* 6,813 letters and instructions of Ignatius. Of these, it is true, a large part exists only in so-called *regesta* (dated lists of contents), and even in those letters that we possess in their entirety there are many which Ignatius' secretary Juan de Polanco wrote on behalf of the General of the Society and then handed to him for approval and often for signature. To these are added in the volumes of *Epistolae Mixtae* 956 letters which were addressed by his correspondents to Ignatius personally, among them about 200 from laymen. In comparison with these the correspondence with women can indeed be called scanty. What is still preserved of it, in letters and answers of which the full text exists, amounts to only 139 documents. There are besides twenty lists of contents of letters to women in the *regesta*.[6] A critical examination of the surviving letters further shows that a comparatively large number of such letters have been lost, as they were kept for only a short time in Ignatius' files and then destroyed as being of no historical importance; or else they disappeared in course of time without trace from among the papers of the recipients or their heirs. So we have to-day only a compact group of 139 letters, of which Ignatius wrote eighty-nine to women and received fifty. They form the contents of this book.

But by this purely statistical method we cannot discover the real nature of Ignatius. We should not merely count his letters. We should study them; and this study is the real justification for their publication. We have had two aims in view. Firstly, these letters constitute a veritable biography of the saint and give us a more concrete understanding of his innermost thoughts than any number of psychological reflections. Secondly, their contents, taken as a whole, give us access to a hitherto almost unknown territory in the history of the spiritual care of women at the beginning of the ecclesiastical reform in the sixteenth century.

These letters are then first of all a biography of St. Ignatius. They cover his career from 1524 to the year of his death, 1556. The earliest of the "Pil-

3

grim's" letters are addressed to the humble housewife Inés Pascual, his motherly benefactress in the decisive Manresa period; his last letter is the inspired farewell message to one of his most faithful admirers, Doña Leonor Mascarenhas, the highborn governess of King Philip II of Spain and of the unfortunate Don Carlos. In between rises the sharply ascending curve of Ignatius' life and work. From the cave of Manresa to the simple room in Rome, where he was spiritual director to the whole world; from the ancestral castle in Loyola to the courts of the princes of his age; from Lisbon to Flanders; from the Emperor's daughter to the middle-class housewife; from the hidden spiritual distress of a nun to the great plan for Church reform – this great mind embraces them all. All becomes living, tangible, colourful and familiar in these letters to women of his time.

We have arranged them in six groups, in order to simplify our summary of the riches they contain.

The first chapter shows us the letters which Ignatius wrote to royal ladies. Here is that Iñigo de Loyola who had once at Arévalo served as a page to Queen Germaine of Aragon and had gone into raptures over the little Infanta Catherine of Castile. There he acquired that delicate courtly manner which he never lost; and, as General of the Society, he soon established connexions with influential princesses, whom as "Courtier of Heaven" he invited, with the inimitable gesture of a now spiritualized good breeding, to share in God's work.

The second chapter contains the letters which Ignatius exchanged with ladies of noble birth. Here he is indeed "God's Cavalier", who moves in such circles with perfect assurance. The women of his own feudal family, the ladies of the houses of Spanish grandees and of the Italian aristocracy, became automatically, if one may so express it, his correspondents, with that instinct of solidarity which even in Ignatius, that scion of ancient Basque nobility, never died. Here we can truly comprehend the nature of this saint: he returned from solitude, heroically endured for God, to his own world, to lead it also back, silently, courteously, and skilfully, to the lofty regions of the divine.

The third chapter shows us Ignatius, as it were, laboriously scaling those heights. His paths were steep and wearisome; he remained all his life the "Pilgrim" until his death on the way to the longed-for Jerusalem, the Kingdom of Christ on earth, which, ever subject to new attacks, is to be defended and extended among men. Therefore Ignatius was throughout his life the "beggar for the Kingdom of God". For his king, who was to him an earthly king, he went with the hat of a beggar through the world. He sought the help of men to the same extent as he relied upon God's help; and it was from the women of his time that he got the most abundant help, from the early years of his

4

own spiritual development to the period of the Society's magnificent expansion. The letters to his benefactresses bear grateful witness to this.

The fourth chapter, by the number and contents of the letters in it, forms the real highlight of this correspondence. It contains the letters of spiritual direction and those addressed to women who subjected themselves to Ignatius in religious obedience, or even wished under his guidance to form a female branch of the Society of Jesus. In him they found their master. They knew that they might turn to him in every spiritual difficulty; but they had to learn too that Ignatius was an "inexorable comforter". With them we discover how slowly this master of the spiritual life himself progressed. At the beginning of his conversion he was still prepared to write detailed letters of spiritual direction, as for example to the Benedictine nun, Teresa Rejadella. With the years he became more and more laconic. Experience and disappointments (it really began with the strange events during his ministry in Alcalá) caused Ignatius' native Basque taciturnity to reassert itself; he became more reserved, almost shy, and in his spiritual correspondence with women kept himself within firmly drawn limits. In this connection Huonder for once makes a shrewd remark: "In spite of this reserve and his powerful, masculine style – indeed, because of them – but above all on account of his virtues, pious women felt strongly drawn towards Ignatius."[7] So this chapter lets us follow dramatically, letter by letter, the spiritual struggle that Ignatius had to wage against those women who wished to join him as members of his new Society.

The fifth chapter takes us down from the precipitous heights of the "inexorable" Ignatius to a region of gentler slopes – the human heart. This saint is indeed never merely the soldier of God, the imperious general, the unapproachable man. His companions who knew him best always remarked on the "motherly" strain in him, his cheerfulness and the smiling radiance of his countenance. For them he was simply the "Father", just because he could be so motherly – the eternally insoluble paradox of the saint. And since Ignatius, as father of his fellow-religious, knew what every member of the Society owed to his mother, he was linked with the mothers of his sons, whether enthusiastic, anxious, or sad, by a bond which found expression in a few letters of deep sincerity. The women who were favoured with these letters knew that their sons had found a Father in Christ, who could give them love and a home, even when for the love of Christ he had to defend against an unenlightened mother-love, the hardness and uncompromising nature of the divine vocation to the religious life.

Finally the sixth chapter leads us from the heights of Ignatius' spirituality to the delightful plains of human friendship, "friendship in God", to which only he can descend who is at home upon the heights. The great heart of this saint was ever open to human friendships. He called his first companions, with whom he founded the Society, his "dear friends in our Lord". When he lay on his death-bed, men all over the world mourned a friend who was utterly sincere and reliable. It is part of an unfalsified picture of Ignatius that, with a small number of women, too, he was linked in what can only be described as friendship in God. It found expression in the letters of this last chapter. Among them is included the previously mentioned farewell message to Doña Leonor Mascarenhas, which even Pedro Ribadeneira, who is otherwise silent about almost all Ignatius' relations with women, gives word for word in his life of the saint. Everything in these letters is irradiated with the mellow kindness of a mature spirit, giving friendship without talking overmuch about it.

We can however get more biographical material of deeper psychological significance from this correspondence. Letters are always evidence of a person's real nature; they contain and reveal their writer, whether he will or no. This is especially true of Ignatius, who all his life found letter-writing such a labour. Each word wrung with difficulty from his pen is carefully weighed and considered. When we look at the drafts of his letters to women, which are still preserved in the archives of the Jesuit General, their innumerable corrections remind us of Ribadeneira's words in his memoirs of Ignatius: "He was so careful in the drafting of letters, especially to persons of high rank or when dealing with important questions, that he spent much time in revising what he had written. He read and re-read his letters, examined every word, crossed out and corrected wherever he thought necessary. Then he had the letter copied out several times. He regarded the time and labour that this involved as well spent." We may seek then in vain, even in his letters to women, any words that flowed spontaneously from his pen, or that were not the subject of careful thought. With Ignatius there are no intimacies, no unguarded moments, even in the final sentence of a letter, or in the briefest note. Should anyone expect anything sensational in this correspondence, let him lay aside this book at once. In this respect, Ignatius is magnificently disappointing. He was, as his intimates testify, a sworn enemy of "empty chatter". His letters are like his talk: "The Father speaks at all times with so much deliberation, that all his words remain as they are uttered and require no alteration." Thus Luis Gonçalves da Câmara, who was daily with him, informs us. But to him who has discovered the man Ignatius behind the laconic form and cold rigidity of the letter, treasures are opened up, "though they may often be hidden in a hard or incorrectly constructed sentence, even in a marginal note". Love has no need of grammar.[8]

One can better understand the distinctiveness of this correspondence and of its author in another way: by comparing it with letters written to women by Ignatius' contemporaries. In the years after 1540, when the newly elected General was counting by night with his secretary the letters in his files, Michelangelo in that same city of Rome was carrying on with his friend Vittoria Colonna a correspondence that has become immortal. But what a difference in language, in thoughts, in the longings expressed! Ignatius had no more time to compose sonnets, although even at the end of his life he remembered with an indulgent smile the *motes,* the rimed epigrams which he once wished to lay at the feet of the lady of his heart. He, as we shall soon show, called Vittoria Colonna to other work. In these same years at the beginning of the reform of the Church, Ignatius often met the young Philip Neri, who soon became his close friend. Letters from Philip, too, have been preserved; but they are in all not more than about thirty, for Philip shared with Ignatius his shyness of the written word. Unlike Ignatius, however, the writer of seven thousand letters, he did not feel within him the call to overcome this shyness so heroically. It is vastly entertaining to unfold Philip's letters and to read them beside those of Ignatius, to see the merry Italian beside the stiff Spaniard, to enjoy the often comical ideas of the one as compared with the almost uncannily controlled correctness of the other. Then we must look at another collection of letters and read them together with those of Ignatius: the correspondence of St. Teresa, especially her letters to the ladies of noble Spanish families, to whom Ignatius also wrote: Mendoza, Medinaceli, Cerda, Alba, Osorio, and the rest of them. Ignatius' carefully worded epistles pale beside the entrancing brilliance of these letters. The editor of the German edition of Teresa's letters praises in them just what we miss in those of Ignatius: "They are of marvellous elegance and delicacy, of an almost magical richness of expression." The gay chatter of the Carmelite has passed into the classical literature of Spain; whereas the letters of the Basque who founded the Jesuits are masterpieces only in God's sight. But Teresa, Philip and Ignatius were canonized together.[9]

We are taken a step further in the study of the saint's psychology when we compare his letters with the letters to women written by his disciples and closest collaborators. There is his secretary, Juan de Polanco, to whom he confided everything and who drafted or wrote for him many letters to women, adapting himself with astonishing skill to his master's style. How utterly differently Polanco writes when he sends what one may call a private letter! On his father's death, for instance, he sent to his mother a letter of condolence, which might rather be called a little treatise, in which quotations from Scripture and the Fathers of the Church are piled one upon the other. Ignatius never wrote thus. It is the same with the letters of Pedro Ribadeneira to ladies of his family or of the Spanish nobility. They are full of learning, ardent emotion, elegantly turned Spanish, even those to his own mother, or

7

when he writes to the Duchesses of Infantado or Arcos. These features are still more noticeable in the letters to women of St. Francis Borgia (Francisco de Borja), who could never hide the fact that he was once a duke and a viceroy. With these gifted writers among his sons Father Ignatius, whose literary efforts were laborious and, as it were, wrung out of him, is not to be compared: herein, too, he is incomparable.[10] His letters reveal him at a level deeper than the literary or the scholarly, even than the religious. They can afford to be so commonplace, because their writer is so other-worldly. They have no need to teach holiness with words, because behind each word there is a saint; a shy man, a man without literary skill, but a man of courage and a man gifted with an ear for the "inner language" of which he tells in his mystical diary. This is why his words still find an echo, even when the human sound has died away. We shall soon be reading a letter which a girl of sixteen wrote to the great Ignatius, which contains an expression that might be applied to the whole of this correspondence: "I have forgotten nothing of what you said to me before; for indeed no one can ever forget your words." The Spanish editors of the *Cartas de San Ignacio* have drawn a masterly portrait of him from his letters: "All that is written in these letters is open and straightforward and without any undue exaggeration. The man who wrote them is a very humble man, yet one who never forgets himself. He is master of his passions and of the first movements of the soul. He has a sure and stable judgment and a penetrating eye for the deep places of the heart. He is a very shrewd man, one who knows his fellow men and who is in touch with all that is noble, great, and flourishing in Europe. His letters are in their very brevity full of the majesty of simplicity. They are irradiated by that aristocratic and exquisite knowledge of the world which was peculiar to the Spaniard of noble birth at that time." Another authority on Ignatius' letters, however, adds that they are also filled with that down-to-earth, sound knowledge of men, which alone can enable one to master life, nor do they scorn the innumerable irritating trivialities, by which even the lives of saints are beset. This is the Ignatius who is brought to life in the letters which follow.[11]

One might, however, object to the publication of these letters on the ground that they apparently contribute nothing essential to the understanding of important historical events, being the product of casual circumstances and often disappointingly trivial. As experts are aware, a vast amount of work still remains to be done in the field of the history of spiritual direction. Each new contribution is welcome, if based on a sound knowledge of sources. The publication of these letters with a detailed historical commentary may therefore provide material for a judgment on the spiritual direction of women in the sixteenth century, superseding the largely general and

8

colourless presentation we have hitherto been given of this section of pastoral history. It is not our intention to refute the spiteful and scantily documented attacks which Miguel Mir and Paul von Hoensbroech saw fit to make on the spiritual direction of women by the Jesuits and their founder. Even in the serious writing of history the treatment of this subject is unsatisfactory, or needs many corrections, such as are possible only after diligent consultation of the sources. We have in mind E. Gothein, L. Koch, A. Huonder, L. von Pastor, and nearly all the lives of Ignatius that have appeared up to the present. Even what we ourself have previously written by way of historical explanation of Ignatius' letters to women will be corrected in many points, generally enlarged upon and explained in this book.[12]

In order more fully to understand the historical significance of this correspondence, it is first necessary to give a general picture of Ignatius' experience and teaching in this matter of the spiritual care of women. There is now no doubt – even though earlier lives of the saint, from Ribadeneira's on, have been largely silent on the subject – that Ignatius of Loyola had his first, still uncrystallized experience of pastoral work in connection with women. It would be as easy as it would be questionable to see in this merely the after-effect, transposed to the religious level, of the obscure "affairs with women" (*cosas de mujeres*) which Ignatius had as a young officer. If we take his confessions literally, we must likewise be prepared to believe what he himself dictated concerning that sacred hour at Loyola, which was the very beginning of his spiritual experience: "As he lay awake one night, he saw clearly a vision of our Lady with the child Jesus. The sight filled him, for a considerable time, with extraordinary solace. And he was filled with such abhorrence for the whole of his past life, especially for his sins of the flesh, that it seemed that all the ideas which had formerly occupied his mind were now vanished. From that hour, therefore, until August 1553, when these lines were written, he never again – even in the least degree – gave his consent to sensual temptations. Because of this effect, it may be said that this vision came from God, although he himself dares not to say so with certainty." He who can relate with so much tact and restraint the secret movements of his soul and who practised lifelong self-examination, as Ignatius did, must be accepted as a witness, even in his own case. The severe purity and noble self-discipline of this man forbid any apparently sensitive, but actually clumsy, probing into his psychology, such as Georg Lomer, for instance, has attempted. Ignatius' experiences in the spiritual direction of women do not lend themselves to such abuse.[13]

The fact remains: no sooner had Ignatius settled after his conversion at Manresa, there to begin his new and heroically improvident life for God, than there gathered around him pious female admirers, middle-class housewives and ladies of the country nobility, whose names live on in the beatification documents of the strange "Pilgrim" of Manresa. At their head stands the widow Inés Pascual, who remained till her death attached to Ignatius in a motherly way. There is also the matron of the hospital of Santa Lucia, Jerónima Clavera; there are the ladies of the De Amigant family, who lovingly tended the worn-out Ignatius; there are Miguela and Anna de Canyelles, Brianda Paguera, Catalina Molins. There is the female mystic, whose name is unknown, who wished for the "Pilgrim" a vision of our Lord. They were the first to whom Ignatius made known the ideas from which sprang the *Spiritual Exercises;* and as his disciples these women acquired, according to the earliest biographical sketch of Ignatius, "a deep understanding and taste for divine things". In these early days of his spiritual ministry, however, Ignatius also experienced something which was to be often repeated, until he gained the mature clarity of his later years: malicious gossip arose in the little town of Manresa about this spiritual converse, and evil tongues promptly gave the name *Iñigas* to the women of Iñigo's circle. The gossip died down only when the "Pilgrim" set out for Barcelona and the pilgrimage to Jerusalem.[14]

Even in the Catalan capital, during the few weeks (February and March, 1523) that he was waiting for a ship, Ignatius became acquainted with several women who were important for the subsequent developments in his life, especially Doña Isabel Roser, who was to meet him again in Rome after twenty long years. In the two years of his studies in Barcelona, to which Ignatius devoted himself on his return from Jerusalem (1524–6), so that he might later on be better able to help souls, a group of women formed itself about him, to whom he ministered, and whom he persuaded to take an active interest in his charitable work. Here already, then, Ignatius was groping after methods of spiritual direction for women, for which he later found the classic form in Rome. The nobility of Barcelona, says one of the old writers, assembled in his poor garret at Widow Pascual's house. Besides Doña Isabel Roser, there was her gifted friend Isabel de Josa, and with them the ladies of the capital's nobility, Doña Estefanía de Requeséns, Doña Guiomar Gralla y Desplá, Doña Leonor de Zápila, Isabel de Boxados – all of whom we shall meet again in Ignatius' correspondence. In Barcelona the Latin student made his first attempt to promote the reform of lax nunneries, a task that required careful handling. In all this he had but one desire: with all the enthusiasm kindled by the divine illumination at Manresa, he wished to help those souls in whom he found the capacity for the love of God, for the inner life, for works of charity. This capacity he found more in women than in men. All that he undertook was, however, still very immature – full, as it were, of pastoral romanticism. He had brought back from Palestine a box with earth and flowers for pious Sister Antonia, portress of the Hieronymite convent, and he had innumerable spiritual conversations with this nun. His attempts to reform the Convent of the Angels resulted in his receiving a sound thrashing from the disappointed gallants who frequented the place. Ignatius never forgot that beating, and we shall learn from his letters how he later, with the support of the Pope and the King of Spain, undertook anew the reform of the Catalan convents. In Barcelona too he made the acquaintance of the saintly Benedictine nun Teresa Rejadella in the Convent of Santa Clara, to whom he was to write his finest letters. The nuns and ladies of Barcelona never forgot Ignatius.[15]

We are probably not wrong in supposing that Ignatius also had some painful experiences in his dealings with ladies belonging to high society. In any case, when he entered the University of Alcalá in March 1526 he had formed a resolve: he would thenceforth devote himself principally to the spiritual care of simple women and tell them something of the lofty matters of which he treats in his *Spiritual Exercises*. What Ignatius experienced at Alcalá in this connection forms the strangest chapter in the history of pastoral ministrations. He has told us something of it in his dictated memoirs; but the main facts we learn from the documents of the three ecclesiastical trials which he had to undergo on account of these spiritual activities, on November 19th, 1526, on March 6th and on May 10th, 1527.

There we meet more than twenty women of the people: widows, artisans' wives, servant-maids, so-called "praying women" or *beatas*,[16] women too of dubious occupation, a students' wench, young apprentice-girls – in short, life itself, ordinary, everyday, sinful and devout. Only two ladies of quality are among them, Doña María del Vado and her daughter Luisa Velásquez, who, as Ignatius himself relates, "had quite a special reverence for the Pilgrim". One of the chief witnesses was the *beata* Beatriz Ramírez, who sometimes brought the poor student a bunch of grapes or a piece of bacon; gave him a mattress and bedclothes, and begged material from two rich ladies to make him a new gown. Beside her in the witness-box stood a weaver's widow, Mencia de Benavente. She had a niece, María de la Flor, who admitted in court: "I used to be very wicked, keeping company with students; I was one of the lost." To all these women Ignatius expounded in long conversations ideas from his *Spiritual Exercises*; he spoke to them earnestly about the Ten Commandments, of mortal sin, of the daily examination of conscience. Simply and sincerely he explained to them the words of the Gospel; but he tried also to convey to them something of the struggle between good and evil. The effects were astonishing and strange, and soon gossip was rife in the town. The prostitute wanted to go off into the desert like another St. Mary of Egypt, the two ladies Vado and Velásquez disappeared one day – against Ignatius' advice – on a begging pilgrimage to Jaén in Andalusia; girls swooned away, so deeply did they take Ignatius' words to heart. Only the matter-of-fact Mencia de Benavente stated in court that in her case the fainting-fits were only an "hysterical" manifestation. Ignatius himself hints at these remarkable phenomena in his evidence: "During his stay in Alcalá he also occupied himself in giving the Spiritual Exercises and instruction in the Catechism. In this, to the glory of God, he had some success. A considerable number of persons had converse with him, and attained great knowledge and happiness in the spiritual life. Others again had to deal with various temptations. There was, for instance, a woman who wished to chastise herself with the discipline, but was unable to do so, as if her hand were forcibly held back – and many other similar cases, so that much talk was occasioned in the town." From April 18th to June 1st, 1527, Ignatius was in prison, until all these matters had been thoroughly investigated. The prisoner was visited by Doña Teresa Enríquez de Cárdenas, friend of the late Queen Isabella the Catholic, and famous throughout Spain, who because of her ardent devotion to the Blessed Sacrament was called *la Loca del Sacramento*. Perhaps she already knew Ignatius of Loyola from the old days at Arévalo or at King Ferdinand's court; but the "Pilgrim" had long since cut himself off from that world, and declined all legal aid and all patronage.

He never forgot his experiences as spiritual director to lower-class women and refers to them again in his later instructions on the subject. Henceforth he knew the narrow and dangerous boundaries between true and false piety, and the difference which prudence requires between the spiritual care of simple and of educated women. We may quote here a piece of advice which Ignatius wrote in the last years of his glorious maturity to his fellow-religious in Portugal, as the fruit of his life's experience: "I would not enter upon spiritual conversations with women who are young or belong to the lower classes of the people, except in church or in places which are visible to all. For such women are easily won, and through such conversations, rightly or wrongly, evil talk arises. Usually such women are rather superficial and do not persevere in the service of the Lord our God. According to their degree of devotion, they are converted over and over again, when the flesh or when weariness demands, or even for the sake of money for their immediate necessities. . . . In all spiritual conversations, I would rather aim at one single degree of real progress that is beyond suspicion, than a hundred, if I should thereby expose myself to any danger. A scandal, whether true or false, injures us more than the loss of half of all the spiritual progress that God achieves through us."[17]

Ignatius, however, rises above his own defeats. So he never forgot the

12

pious women of Alcalá, especially the two who appeared as chief witnesses at his trials, the *beata* Ramírez and the widow Mencia de Benavente. His great son, Blessed Peter Faber, knew how to give a special pleasure to his master Ignatius in Rome. In the same letter, dated October 27th, 1541, in which he relates his visit to the daughter of the Duke of Medinaceli, Catalina de la Cerda, he tells of his meeting with the two women in Alcalá. The *beata* Ramírez, he says, was now satisfactorily settled in a home, where she was spending her old age in prayer. She was indeed now too weak to live according to the counsels which Ignatius had once given her, and to take under her care the women of the university town; but if the reverend Father Ignatius should command it, she would still take this cross upon her and walk the streets in search of lost souls; she would do everything that Ignatius advised her to do, and she expected from him a few lines of spiritual comfort. That was the effect that this master of the spiritual life had upon this simple woman after fifteen years. Even in the great days of his spiritual successes in Rome, Ignatius thought of the women in Alcalá, and as late as 1546 he gave the learned Doctor Miguel de Torres the commission not only to greet the noble ladies of the house of Borja, but also to visit the old *beata* Ramírez and the widow Benavente.[18]

The unfortunate experiences at Alcalá completed in Ignatius a process of clarification. When he went to Salamanca in 1527, in order to continue his studies there, he had become, in matters concerning the spiritual care of women, a different man. On the way, in Valladolid, he did indeed make the acquaintance of another woman; perhaps he already knew her in Alcalá. She was Leonor Mascarenhas, with whom he maintained a friendship till his death. In Salamanca itself he was consulted by a *beata;* he had spiritual talks with an anchoress walled up beside the church of St. John; and in Salamanca, too, he was visited by a noblewoman of the city. In those weeks of enforced recollection, however, Ignatius became clear in his mind about his future aims: from now on he would not only study more thoroughly and not let himself be distracted by any pious undertakings; he would do more. He would go to the University of Paris, where he did not know the language of the country, and so could not act as spiritual director to women; he would win recruits for the great work he planned for the Kingdom of Christ. In Paris we first recognize the future saint, the man who sought to win *men* for God. He accepted indeed with heartfelt thanks the help of his female admirers in Barcelona; but in all the seven years of his studies in Paris we know of only one benefactress of the new Society, whose surname is not mentioned, and to whom Ignatius sent a letter from Venice.

In the spring of 1535 the graduate of Paris came to stay for the last time in his native town. He was already a celebrated spiritual director, as he

13

was to be later in Rome, although not yet a priest. He gave a mission in Azpeitia, where rumours still circulated about the wicked doings of the former officer. For that very reason he concerned himself with the moral reform of women. He brought order into his own undisciplined family; he helped the poor tertiaries of his native town in their lawsuit with the Loyolas; he thundered authoritatively from the pulpit against priests' concubines. So thorough was his conversion of loose women, that it was still talked of in Guipúzcoa fifty years later. Among them was a notorious beauty named Magdalena de Mendiola, also called Sendo. Like Ignatius himself, she made a penitential pilgrimage to Rome and Jerusalem; and in 1539 Ignatius gave her a letter to the Loyola family, with delicate tact helping this Basque Magdalen to acquire that good reputation of which the documents for Ignatius' beatification tell us.[19]

In November 1537 Ignatius entered the Eternal City. It was the beginning of the period when the Society was founded, the years of the great work for souls, of the drafting of the Constitutions. The experience, too, which he had gained in the spiritual direction of women was tested again and clarified. He was to suffer much till he had reduced it to definite rules. The words which the master addressed to his companions in the first months of their work in Rome sound like a *Leitmotiv*: "We must keep watch over ourselves and never enter into spiritual conversations with women, unless they be ladies of noble rank." Grounds for such prudence soon became evident, and Ignatius in dictating his autobiography emphasized the need for restraining the pastoral adventurousness of his first disciples: "Some time afterwards, Master Francis [Xavier] heard a woman's confession and visited her several times to speak with her on spiritual matters. A little while later it was found that the woman was expecting a child; but the Lord ordained that the guilty man should be discovered. Jean Codure had a similar experience with one of his spiritual daughters, who was caught in the company of a man." The distinction that Ignatius here and later often makes, even in his Constitutions, between women of the lower classes and ladies of higher rank, seems offensive to our modern social feelings. In this Ignatius is thoroughly the child of his age and background, and we must not lose sight of this limitation, if we are to understand his whole correspondence. Nevertheless, in his work for souls at Rome he became in truth all things to all men (and women); here he united as it were Barcelona and Alcalá. A group of ladies of the highest rank soon gathered round the General Ignatius; and at once the zealous apostle of souls set these same ladies to work in the unremitting task of caring for the poor, lost women and girls of the unholy Holy City, whose hearts were yet so ready for the love of God.

First there were the noble ladies. Heading the list was Faustina de' Jancolini, the "first benefactress of the Society of Jesus", who in 1539 bequeathed her house and lands to the companions of Ignatius, in a will that was, it is true, encumbered with conditions incapable of fulfilment. There was Donna Lucrezia de Bradine; there was the little companion of the Duchess Colonna, Catalina de Badajoz, whose confessor Ignatius was; and her mistress, Juana de Aragón, Duke Ascanio's consort, was one of the first ladies to whom Ignatius acted as adviser. A few years later, the much sought-after spiritual director was to attend Charles V's young, unhappily married daughter, Margaret of Austria, in the Palazzo Madama. The latter's dominating mother-in-law, Girolama Orsini, and the daughter of the reigning pope, Costanza, Countess of Santa Fiora, were devoted to Ignatius. The city fathers of Parma applied to the Countess Costanza to persuade her to put in a good word with the Pope for the recognition of the new Society. Even shortly before his death Ignatius had to defend himself against the rumour that the Society owed its establishment to the "patronage of women" *(favor de mujeres)*, especially to that of Margeret of Austria. This rumour had certainly no foundation in fact; but one thing is sure. Ignatius accepted with a magnificent gesture the favour and the gifts of these ladies for his works of charity and pastoral ministry; and the best proof of this is a list of women who under his direction formed the "Compagnia della Grazia", the pious society for the support of the "House of St. Martha", which Ignatius founded for the prostitutes of the City. There are illustrious names in this list. Vittoria Colonna, Marchioness of Pescara; Catarina, Countess Carpi, the wife of Bonifazio Gaetani, Duke of Sermoneta; Elena Orsini; Doña Leonor Osorio, wife of the imperial ambassador, Don Juan de Vega. Ignatius made use of their services with the humble and at the same time royal liberality of a man dedicated to God's work, in the spirit of the words he once dictated to his secretary Polanco concerning the question of patronage: "He who rejects the opportunity of using worldly patronage for religious purposes has clearly not learnt to direct all things towards one goal: the greater glory of God."[20]

That was the reason, and indeed the only one, why the General, in the midst of his never-ending labours, still found time and patience to continue to be spiritual director to the ladies of Roman society. A few examples from his correspondence illustrate this fact. Donna Giulia Orsini placed her quietly situated villa at his disposal when he gave Dr. Miguel de Torres the Spiritual Exercises. Giulia Colonna wished to sell him her house on the Piazza Margana, and on the very eve of his death Ignatius was discussing this matter with his companions. On the road which his brethren had to travel as mendicants, the houses of Elena Orsini and the Countess Carpi had been noted with forethought. At the request of his friend Pedro de Zárate,

Ignatius occasionally visited the noble Madonna Costanza Salviati. What we read of the regrettable story of Costanza and Giovanna Conti is a kind of miniature of this burdensome part of Ignatius' duties. He was great even in little things.

The large number of penitents attracted by the Fathers of the Society was soon looked askance at in Rome, and the fact that they were mostly such aristocratic ladies was considered unedifying and scandalous. In 1547 Ignatius' former friend, the priest Don Giovanni da Torrano, lodged a complaint with Pope Paul III against the methods of the Fathers in hearing women's confessions. In the same year the Dominican Fra Teofilo da Tropea submitted to the Inquisition a not very well-informed libel against the "priests who allow themselves to be called the Society of Jesus, who are also called Reformati, Theatines, Illuminati or Ignatians". It read: "They have brought great shame upon the two ladies Giovanna and Costanza Conti, having betrayed the secrets of their confessions, as may be more exactly learnt from the ladies themselves." The document was pigeonholed, but the bad feeling lasted for several years. Only in the last year of Ignatius' life did a formal reconciliation take place. Pedro de Zárate, then in Flanders, acted as mediator, and sent Ignatius a safe-conduct, a letter of introduction to hand to the Conti ladies. Ignatius had to pluck up his courage. At first he excused himself to Zárate, saying that it was just carnival-time, "and then we never go into the streets, so as not to come in contact with all the buffooneries". But after that he dared to tread the difficult road. He did not go with empty hands. Zárate had sent him a present from the far North, calculated to delight the heart of pious ladies: some rings made from the horn of the "great beast", said to be a wonderful remedy against epilepsy and other complaints. On March 31st Ignatius wrote to his friend: "I visited Madonna Costanza Conti and gave her the letter and the horn rings. Madonna Giovanna had just gone out. Master Polanco can give you further details." The secretary, who was present whenever Ignatius visited ladies, according to the rule laid down by Ignatius himself, lets us share in the grim humour of the situation, as the two ventured into the Conti house, for he wrote on the same day: "At first I expected only coolness and an icy reception; but lo and behold! Ignatius himself admitted that he had never met the Lady Costanza in such a good mood and so friendly. I offered her one of the horn rings, but she at once helped herself to two of the best, and I gave them to her straightway." The reconciliation was now quite complete.[21]

These things may be trifles, and Ignatius regarded them as such. But of such is the life of a saint composed. After all, in this way he was performing a great work, by giving some meaning to the spoilt and idle lives of these ladies, some imagination and understanding for the needs of the poor, for which they remained grateful to their beloved master.

This is shown in his labours for the poor and often uprooted women of the Eternal City: he bestowed all his pastoral charity on them, and in the homes which he founded for them the highborn ladies humbly served. First of these foundations was the House of St. Martha for fallen girls and wives who were in moral danger. "Rome was then encrusted with the filth of prostitution", says Ribadeneira himself in his life of Ignatius. There had indeed existed since 1520 the House of St. Mary Magdalen on the Corso, founded by the "Oratory of Divine Love"; but the fallen women who found a refuge there had to live together as a religious community. Ignatius was more far-seeing: from 1542 onwards he was continually occupied with the thought of a socially more effective way of caring for these women: there should be a house in which prostitutes willing to reform could be re-educated for a regular position in the world, above all for a proper marriage, without being compelled to the often reluctantly chosen life of the cloister. His keen vision saw besides another evil: many women who plied an immoral trade in the city were unhappily married. To restore a healthy society, it was therefore necessary to have a house in which these women could regain their self-respect and thus gradually be brought back to their husbands. In this too Ignatius, with his enlightened, modern approach, sought to pave the way for new methods in the pastoral care of women. At the beginning of 1543 he had his plan drawn up. First he needed financial support and ecclesiastical backing. This was where the Pope and Ignatius' lady penitents came in. He called into being the "Compagnia della Grazia", and on February 16th, 1543, Pope Paul III approved the new foundation in the Bull *Divina summaque*. Among its promoters were to be found all the rank and nobility of Rome. The list of ladies who signed their names we already know. There were at first, it is true, difficulties about finance; but then awoke the real Ignatius. "If no one will be the first, then they shall follow me, for I myself am the first." It happened that at that time, while the foundations of the small house in process of erection for the Jesuits beside the church of Santa Maria della Strada were being dug, some ancient marble sculptures from the Hecastylon of Pompey came to light. Ignatius had them sold for a hundred golden *scudi* and bought with them a house by the Arco di Camigliano, in the immediate vicinity of the Piè di Marmo, which he called after St. Martha. Then he drew up statutes for the new foundation. The principles which he therein develops result in these documents being among the finest in pastoral history. "The whole foundation of Christian society rests in the first instance upon the peaceful and honourable conduct of married people. In these our unhappy times, however, we see how in respect of this very Sacrament of matrimony there reigns so much disorder, and bad example flourishes like a weed. Married women live without fear of God, and without blushing in the sight of man they live separated from their husbands in open sin. And the same sinful life is led by a great number of unmarried women." It was to be the business of St. Martha's to bring back these women, especially the so-called *cortegiane onorate,* the elegant *hetaerae* of the city, to the discipline of married life, or, without forcing them to enter the cloister, to prepare them for marriage. Therefore Ignatius laid down in the statutes for the married women of St. Martha's: "Whenever the husband gives an assurance that he will resume married life with her, she is bound to return to him in peace, love, and conjugal loyalty." For the unmarried inmates the principle to be followed was: "The unmarried women shall be quite free either to marry or to take the veil."

The House of St. Martha flourished. Ignatius was proud of it, and his reports on the progress of his foundation were sent even to India, to his beloved companion Francis Xavier. At the end of 1543 there were already nearly eighty inmates; but in May 1545 there were only thirty-eight, for many had been sent forth, completely transformed, to lead respectable lives in the world. In 1548 the number of those who had been brought back to God's path at St. Martha's during the previous four years was over a hundred. We shall hear much in the correspondence about the labours and joys that Ignatius experienced with this home. The spirit which animated it was worth all the cares, disappointments, and persecutions it brought upon its founder. The women, who perhaps for the first time encountered there real love and kindness, were devoted to their master Ignatius. Again and again the beloved Father had to come and preach to them. Among Ignatius' papers a little note has been preserved, the back of which that indefatigable letter-writer afterwards used as rough paper for drafting another letter: it is an invitation sent from St. Martha's for him to preach there: "Most reverend Father in Jesus Christ, salvation and peace! I with all my daughters beg and implore Your Reverence please to preach us two sermons to-morrow, one in the morning, the other in the evening, so that we may have some little consolation. Nothing else. We your daughters all cast ourselves at Your Reverend Paternity's feet and kiss your venerable hand. Your unworthy daughters of St. Martha." It is not then to be wondered at, that towards the end of 1546 a number of women in the home determined to remain in St. Martha's permanently and to form a religious community, consisting of those who of their own free will decided to so do. Ignatius fully approved of this development, and he carried with his own hands into the *clausura* a simple wooden cross that is still preserved. Cardinal Ranuccio Farnese confirmed the foundation in the name of the Pope on February 21st, 1547.[22]

18

This House of St. Martha, however, like all the other works of Ignatius, who was so much ahead of his time, met with violent opposition. The Spanish Franciscan Fray Valentino Barbarán preferred a complaint to the Pope, which in the opinion of Cardinal Crescenzi, who had been commissioned by Paul III to conduct the enquiry, "had neither rhyme nor reason in it". It contained the statement that the Jesuits "would like to reform the whole world, and have drawn up statutes, according to which all adultresses were to be banished from Rome". Moreover, Fray Barbarán had said in conversation that all Jesuits living between Perpignan and Seville ought to be sent to the stake. So it was in connection with St. Martha's that Ignatius sent him, through a friend, the famous retort: "Tell the Reverend Fray Barbarán, I wish that he and all his friends and acquaintances, not only between Perpignan and Seville, but throughout the whole world, may be seized and consumed by the fire of the Holy Ghost."

This was not, however, the only attack upon the House of St. Martha. We shall later hear in detail what a scandal was raised by the pontifical postmaster Mattia di San Cassiano against the house of refuge near the Arco di Camigliano, because Ignatius was harbouring there the mistress of that distinguished gentleman. The documents of this case have been preserved, and we can read in them the degree of calumny of which the enemies of Ignatius and his Society were capable. The postmaster was not ashamed to assert, in the presence of the Pope and many prelates, that this House of St. Martha was nothing less than the seraglio of the priests of the Society of Jesus, who visited it for the purpose of gratifying their lust. Ignatius insisted firmly in this case upon a judicial enquiry, and the affair ended in a peaceful reconciliation.

The House of St. Martha became a model for many other foundations of a similar kind, in which Ignatius and his sons took a keen interest. At the saint's death in 1556 there were St. Martha's homes in Florence, Bologna, Modena, Trapani, Messina and Palermo. Even in Valladolid an attempt was made to imitate the institution under the patronage of Prince Philip. Several times the General had to warn the Fathers not to venture too far in this department of the pastoral ministry, and to withdraw tactfully when possible from the spiritual care of "penitent women".

Yet another work of the indefatigable apostle of Rome's women must be mentioned here – it is an excellent example of the breadth of vision of his pastoral ideals. Ignatius had obviously gained a profound knowledge of the spiritual background of the women who were being looked after in St. Martha's – the questionnaire he drew up for new entrants suggests this – and therefore he knew that the best kind of spiritual care is protection. So in 1546 he represented to the Pope, in a memorandum now unfortunately lost, the need for a home in which young girls whose morals were in danger, having been removed from their evil surroundings, might be educated and protected. Soon a pious society was formed for this purpose, the *Compagnia delle Vergini Miserabili*. Not long afterwards a house was established near Santa Catarina dei Funari, in which girls saved from moral ruin found a home. The General's secretary at the time, Father Bartolomeo Ferrão, wrote concerning it to Rodríguez in Lisbon on April 12th, 1546: "In all these things our Father has taken no little trouble upon himself, to say nothing of the task of getting young girls out of the houses of the courtesans and finding them homes in religious establishments, which have been set up here in Rome by order of His Holiness, so that these girls may not be seduced by the enemy through bad example, but may be removed from danger." This home, too, by its success brought him much happiness.[23]

The prudent and experienced General, moreover, gave an example, in this decidedly difficult kind of pastoral work, of his ability to retire at the right moment from undertakings he had himself initiated. More important tasks lay ahead of him. In this he followed the advice he once gave to Father d'Achille: "One cannot do all good works at once", and that other message he sent to Father Gian Lorenzo in Modena, who was much too heavily burdened with the spiritual direction of women, saying that he was quite right to be glad if the pious women let others attend to their spiritual welfare. If this happens, "all the better; then you have more time to devote yourself to God's service in other fields, and there will be no lack of such work". Thus did Ignatius himself act, for after 1547 he sought quietly to detach himself from the work of St. Martha's and St. Catharine's, once they were firmly established. This signifies, in a man in all things so well-balanced, no final break; the spiritual care of women was to go on by all means, within the limits decreed by prudence and by consideration for the importance of other works. Thus there follows in his letters after 1547 an abundance of pastoral advice to the Society in answer to the numerous urgent questions which arise from this kind of ministry. In the closing years of his life he enunciated this principle, which sounds like an echo of that first wise counsel given at the beginning of his Roman apostolate: "The Father emphatically recommended reserve in dealing with women, even when they seem holy and, indeed, are so: but especially if they are young or pretty, or of the lower orders or even of bad reputation. This was not only to avoid danger to oneself, but also because of the scandal to others and the gossip of the people, who are always more ready to suspect and slander religious and servants of God than to speak in their defence." On July 28th, 1553, Ignatius issued precise instructions to all Jesuits concerning the manner of hearing women's confessions, and they end with the advice, to deal quickly with the ladies, especially when they were "devout". This sounds hard, but it was meant kindly. For this same Ignatius could upon occasion defend boldly the rights of female penitents against excessive rigorism. The holy prior of Venice, Andrea Lippomani, Ignatius' friend since the far-off days of the pilgrimage to Jerusalem, thought it scandalous that many noble ladies confessed so frequently to the Jesuits, and would have liked to see it absolutely forbidden. Ignatius was of quite a different opinion; the confessions were short, it is true, but as long as everything was in order it was wrong to give them up altogether. All was for the greater glory of God. In Venice another difficulty arose over this matter: the Signoria forbade every priest under thirty-six years of age to hear women's confessions, and this prohibition caused the Fathers no little embarrassment. Ignatius defended freedom of conscience, citing the privileges of his Society, but nevertheless advised prudent submission, although some ladies of the noble family of Cornari imagined they could only confess to Jesuits. An even more awkward problem was that of pastoral visits to ladies. We shall learn something of this in the correspondence. Ignatius had sharply to reprove many of his sons for somewhat indiscreet visits of this kind. Father Adriaenssens in Flanders was warned not to celebrate Mass in the bedroom of a sick female penitent. Father Leernus in Modena received a directive, not under any circumstances to have anything to do with the ladies' religious guild. Spiritual exercises for women should be given only in church, save in the case of specially noble ladies, but even then a companion must always be present. All this was very prudent, for in Italy they were particularly careful about the avoidance of any scandal. In this connection the history of the Society tells an illuminating story. In Naples, Father Francisco Araldo occasionally paid visits of a pastoral nature to noble ladies, as he did one day to Beatrice Carafa, sister of the future Pope Paul IV. "This cardinal's sister, who was almost eighty years old, flared up in anger and shouted: 'Get out! Will you bring ruin on my house? Get out of here!' And after that, Father Salmerón forbade such visits." It is, however, indicative of Ignatius' delicate tact that he would mitigate this Italian rigorism to suit Spanish conditions. Shortly before his death, the General issued to Father Juan de Vitoria in Burgos the following instruction: "As for visits to ladies, we are prepared to believe that in this matter more can be permitted than in this country. Nevertheless, we are of opinion that they are not seemly and not in accordance with the spirit of our Constitutions, save in the case of ladies of rank, or if it concerns a matter important for the service of God, or when a visit is made in time of sickness. Otherwise one may follow the manners and customs of the country in this respect." That even in Spain the Jesuits had to be careful is shown by the impassioned attack which the Dominican Melchor Cano launched against the Society. It may be that Father Araoz in particular was rather too zealous in his spiritual care of the ladies belonging to the grandee families in Valladolid and Salamanca, with whom he got on so well; for he writes on one occasion: "Here there are so many ladies whose dearest wish is that the Society may found houses; I have just received a letter on the subject from Valladolid, written on the orders of a highborn lady. Oh, how many good souls the Lord has upon earth!" It is then understandable that one of the Dominican's accusations was as follows: "They take pleasure in familiar conversations with pious women and even visit them often in their homes under the pretext of converting them or helping them, or of leading them to higher things." The Duchess of Alba industriously and maliciously repeated this in Naples, to the General's sorrow. It was no doubt in this connection that he uttered the well-known words: "From such conversation comes nothing usually but smoke or flame"; but that did not in any way alter his principles.[24]

A brief chapter from Ignatius' teaching on the spiritual direction of women is of such interest as social history that we would not wish to pass it over. It is the saint's attitude towards the question of women's fashions, which constantly cropped up in the confessional and when advising ladies. From Venice and Naples came requests from Jesuits who had become unsure of their moral theology: what was one to say to the follies of women's fashions, to jewelry and make-up? The answers that the secretary Polanco sent on the General's orders illustrate the wise moderation, but also the Christian severity, with which Ignatius wished these questions to be dealt. For instance, Father Galvanello was indignant that the women of Morbegno in the Val Tellina appeared in church without head-coverings. Ignatius calmed him: such things could not be changed by making a fuss, but by persuasion; besides, they were just local customs, and surely one could not see a sin in every question of dress. Of a rigorism equal to Father Galvanello's was Father Tavoni in Padua, who would have preferred to send away fashionable ladies without absolution. He received the somewhat laconic instruction: "One cannot exclude all ladies from confession because of their follies in dress, merely because they indulge in a little vanity in costume and hairstyle. No general rules can be given in this matter. It is true that, granting the fashion, grave sins may be committed here too by evil intention or by excess. Look up the summaries of moral theology and in individual cases do as God directs you." Father Araldo in Naples had scruples especially concerning ladies' make-up. The answer that he received from Rome is so characteristic of the mean between pastoral clemency and the demands of asceticism, that it is here quoted in full: "As for the painting of the Neapolitan ladies, you can look up the subject in the handbooks of moral theology under the word 'Cosmetics'. If the women make up their faces with the express intention of doing wrong, it is a grave sin. If they do it because it is their husbands' wish, you can declare them free of guilt; but it will be well to persuade them to tell their husbands not to insist any longer on such follies. But if they do it from mere vanity, in order to look pretty, and have no evil intentions, making-up is no grave sin. Yet it is indeed a great imperfection, and it usually leads to sin, even if it is not grave sin. So even if they can be completely absolved of guilt, it appears more fitting for confessors of our Society not to hear the confessions of these ladies any more, if the advice already given has been of no avail. Say explicitly to such a lady, that if she intends to continue in this imperfection, you will have no more to do with her; that she may go and look for a confessor elsewhere. For the rest, discretion must teach you in these and other special cases whether you ought to proceed in this manner. One cannot in such cases lay down a rigid rule, that leaves no room for exceptions." A few months later a similar instruction was sent to Father Alberto Ferrarese in Venice: "We have heard through a report from Father Rector that you have declared war on the fashions and hairstyles of the Venetian ladies. You are quite right; for if we show approval of them in this matter, the ladies quickly seize upon it as a pretext, and so offend God. Nonetheless, when it is a question of local custom and where they do not fall into grave abuses that are contrary to common morality; when, moreover, there is no intention or incitement to sin, you ought not to talk straightway of grievous sin. Indeed, when a lady does it only to please her husband, it need not even be a venial sin. . . . For the rest, it might be that your zeal for the good cause could play you false; and so it would be as well for you to abide by Father Rector's judgment in such cases. With him you can discuss matters that you see and hear of outside the confessional. Be neither timid nor scrupulous!"

News reached the General's office from many cities about the success of this ascetic training for ladies. From Lisbon Father Cypriano Suárez reported in May 1553 that many noblewomen had pledged themselves to reduce their expenses on rich clothing – which even St. Paul allowed – and to give the money to the poor. Of a pious society formed by the Neapolitan ladies, the chronicle of the Society observes: "This congregation of women approached the Lord's table once a month, and the ladies gave instruction in Christian doctrine to their servants. They forbade themselves the use of cosmetics and other so-called aids to beauty, with which the ladies in Naples were wont to disfigure their faces: and they did not allow a woman with a painted face to join them, no matter how hard she pleaded for admittance." A year later there is a further entry about this same society: "None is admitted who has not said farewell to the practice of vanity, especially the abuse of painting the face red and white; and it became manifest that in this way almost as much was done for the reform of women's morals as by preaching."[25]

Even when in reading all these instructions one bears in mind the historical limitations to which Ignatius also was subject, it remains clear that here spoke a remarkably broad-minded director, a saint who for the sake of souls had again become "worldly". The women whom he advised personally, or through his sons, realized this; they found in him what the men about him also praised as one of his greatest qualities, namely his tact in the personal direction of souls, his wise way of calming troubled consciences, and above all his skill in smoothing over quarrels and lawsuits. No wonder that Ignatius was always called in when there was a matrimonial disagreement to clear up or when the way was to be smoothed before a projected marriage. We shall read of many such cases in the correspondence: his anger at the marriage of his great-niece Lawrencia to the son of the former duke, Father Francis Borgia; his anxiety about the marriage of little Isabel de Vega; his intervention in the matrimonial quarrels of the Duchess Colonna or Madama Margaret of Austria. Ignatius was unwillingly involved in these often painful family affairs of the aristocracy: to him they turned as a last resort, for what did not Ignatius succeed in bringing to a happy conclusion? The friend of ordinary folk felt happier when it was a question of mending broken marriages among the people. It was his achievement when in September 1541 he organized a great celebration in the little church of Santa Maria della Strada, of which he wrote a glowing account to Peter Faber. A well-to-do Jew had been converted to the Catholic faith and at his baptism was simultaneously married to his former mistress. . . . Two cardinals took part in the celebration, as well as Margaret of Austria, the ambassadors of Spain and Portugal, and many other noble personages. "Now the concubine is become a lady", wrote Ignatius joyfully. "Master Laynez preached, Master Salmerón baptized the man and took his hand and that of the newly converted woman and joined them. May unceasing thanks be given to God the Lord!"

Another matrimonial case in Naples was the subject of Ignatius' correspondence for a whole year: that of Don Nicolà, an official of the papal chancellery. His wife had absconded to Naples. Ignatius asked his fellow-religious there for exact information, so that he might promote the case at Rome – as though he had nothing else to do. The news from Naples was discouraging, and in his answer to Father Oviedo Ignatius wrote laconically: "We have read through everything that you wrote about the wife of Master Nicolà. The conclusion of it all is that the woman is a little crazy." Then affairs took a usual turn and Ignatius must have smiled as he announced, two months later :"Master Nicolà is consumed with longing for his wife's return, and says he is ready to fulfil all the required conditions. So it would be a good thing if this reconciliation could be brought about." And it was.[26]

We need not wonder, therefore, that this eminently reasonable Ignatius, who lived right in the middle of things and who could see so penetratingly into the feminine soul, had a marked aversion for allegedly mystical favours claimed by pious persons. Not that he rejected on principle everything in this field as false or suspicious; since Manresa, he had himself had enough experience of that dark region of the soul where the gift of the Spirit can be so close to the trickery of the senses, and he collected his experiences in that section of the *Spiritual Exercises* in which he gives such wise rules for the "Discernment of Spirits"; but Ignatius considered prudence and tact to be the essential conditions of a mature and balanced judgment. Let one example suffice. Half the world was then talking about the stigmatic Jacoba Bartolini of Bologna; even Queen Catherine in Lisbon wished to have detailed information on this remarkable case. In the diary of the Portuguese Father da Câmara we are told what Ignatius thought of it: "It was about the year 1544 that there arose in Italy a woman, a native of Bologna, who lived in the reputation of great spiritual gifts and holiness. After long exercise in the contemplative life, during which extraordinary things occurred, she withdrew to the mountains near Bologna, in order that, remote from the world, she might give herself entirely to the life of perfection. There she converted many highway robbers, murderers, and other outcasts who came to her, and brought them to repentance, confession, and the Sacrament of the Altar, which was administered by some priests of irreproachable reputation, who lived near by for this purpose. What astonished all Italy, however, was that the woman had an open wound in her right side, as St. Francis had; and indeed, blood flowed from the wound. This wonder became so well known, that people flocked to see it. Even two Portuguese Jesuit fathers, who were on the way back from Rome, made a short detour, so that at least one of them might see the miracle. When they returned to Portugal in 1551, they told me of it with such enthusiasm that I did not gainsay them, although I am usually very unwilling to credit such cases when they occur in women. I considered the matter to be important, and told the queen of it, with the result that she absolutely insisted on knowing more about the woman. When I shortly afterwards went to Rome for the first time, I got into conversation about the case with Father Ribadeneira. He told me that at the time when this woman's fame was at its height, a certain religious came to Rome, a man of mature age, great virtue, and experienced in prayer. He had been this woman's confessor for a long time in Bologna. As he was on very friendly terms with Father Ignatius, the latter invited him to dinner at our house. At table the priest related wonder after wonder concerning the holiness and the virtues of the woman, but especially about the wound in her side; and he said he had seen with his own eyes and made quite sure that blood indeed flowed from the wound, as was generally said. To all this

25

our Father answered in only a few words of no significance, merely nodding at the priest's account. When the religious was gone, Ribadeneira asked our Father what he thought of this wound and of the other things. At first Ignatius replied to him also with vague expressions: 'All is well, all is done by God's grace', or something similar, but Ribadeneira insisted that he should say more definitely what he thought. So Ignatius spoke with greater explicitness: 'Our Lord alone can, and usually does, let his graces and gifts work in our inmost soul; but the Devil can effect nothing save upon the outward senses. Occasionally God permits such things to happen'. So it was here. For at the very time that Ribadeneira told me this, the wound in the side had disappeared and all the miraculous events had come to nothing."

As with the stigmatic of Bologna, so it was too with the celebrated nun Magdalena de la Cruz; in this case also Ignatius behaved, as it were, with inflexible tact, and here also the miserable outcome of that pseudo-mystical imposture proved him right. Ribadeneira has summed up Ignatius' position in the following words: "He advised us, more by this example than by what he said, to be on our guard against the credulous acceptance of the genuineness of relations which certain spiritual and devout persons claim to have had. This not only because of the possibility of deception, which is always likely in such things, since such women take dreams and figments of their imagination for visions; but also because of the loss of confidence in him who has given her his approbation, when once the deception has been discovered."[27]

We could speak more of the extensive work that Ignatius did during his later years in Rome for the spiritual direction of nuns, and of the principles he based on his experience, but an exact account of them will be given in the chapter of his correspondence that contains the letters to his spiritual daughters.

Our portrait of this inspired spiritual director of women has now been drawn in its essential outlines. We have had a glimpse into a part of the work of the saint of Loyola, who was so great a saint because for God's sake he became again so worldly. We must, however, expressly insist: it was only a part of his great work for God, a small part. Because the impression may be given, now that we have collected the historical proofs of his pastoral work for women and thus prepared the way for the understanding of the following correspondence, that Ignatius was primarily concerned with ministering to women – just because of this, it is necessary to retain the correct historical perspective and not to forget that we have learnt to see Ignatius from one particular angle only. The whole Ignatius is incomparably greater than the work he performed for the souls of women. That in spite of all hostility and discouragement he undertook this work – this, too, makes him great in the Kingdom of God. His written word remains.

26

PART ONE

THE COURTIER OF HEAVEN

Correspondence with Royal Ladies

Introduction

THE royal ladies with whom Ignatius corresponded either belonged to the House of Habsburg or were closely connected with it politically or through marriage. In order to understand the human and historical significance of these letters, it is necessary first of all to sketch briefly the relations which the founder of the Jesuits had with the male wearers of the Habsburg crowns: for it will become clear that Ignatius owed his influence over the princes of this family largely to the friendly terms on which he stood with the ladies of the imperial House. Thus his correspondence with these princesses, although it was concerned with the things of God and the inner life, has also an immediate importance for the history of Habsburg politics.

At the outset it must be clearly stated: Ignatius was never in the confidence of the head of the family, the Emperor Charles V. The secret mistrust with which the Emperor regarded the sons of the officer of Pamplona is symbolic of the clash between the old and the new order in Church and State. It was the same with the newly founded order of the Capuchins ten years earlier. Charles entreated Pope Paul III in a letter dated December 4th, 1535, not under any circumstances to permit "a certain sect, calling themselves Capuchins", to enter the kingdom of Spain, for such innovations "were always more productive of scandal than of edification". It is true that the Emperor soon saw his mistake; but he remained rooted in the old, medieval order of things. Neither had the humanistic attitude of his Flemish advisers, such as Granvelle and Viglius van Zwichem, any understanding for the tempestuous ideals of the new Society. It may be too that a number of painful experiences with the Jesuits made him inaccessible. There was, for instance, the protest which Father Bobadilla made in June 1548 against the Augsburg Interim, to the Emperor's great annoyance, and which caused Charles to banish the Jesuits from the Empire forthwith; and there was the frigid letter in which the Emperor gave permission for his vassal, Duke Francis Borgia, to enter the Society. "The Emperor has certainly not taken much notice of the Society of Jesus", summarily observes the General's secretary Polanco. Ignatius took considerable trouble to overcome this imperial coolness. Thus he once in a letter dated February 24th, 1551, respectfully reminded His Majesty, then in Augsburg, of his own loyalty and merits and those of his noble ancestors in the service of the crown. The most interesting document illustrating Ignatius' attempts to gain the ear of the Emperor, towards whom his loyalty was unswerving, is a letter of the March 3rd, 1554, which the General drafted, polished, thought over – and then never sent. We insert it here, because it introduces us to the complicated world of courtly relationships in which the Emperor's sister and daughters played, as we shall see, an essential part; because, moreover, it expresses that half spiritual, half political idea of the relation between Church and State which is reflected in many of Ignatius' letters to royal ladies.[1]

The sovereign grace and eternal love of Christ our Lord be with your Majesty, with his most holy gifts and spiritual graces.

Since the Providence of God, our Creator and Lord, has placed Your Majesty in such a position and office, and given you so much zeal that you regard matters of universal good and of God's glory as your own, and since his glory has raised up, in Your Majesty's time, this humble Society of ours by whose ministry he is served and I hope will be served increasingly in your realms and in other parts of Christendom and beyond the bounds thereof – it seemed to me in our Lord that, since a great obstacle to this work has arisen, it was fitting to have recourse to Your Majesty, whose every thought, I am persuaded, goes straight to God's service. I therefore humbly beseech Your Majesty that you would deign to listen to certain details which will be submitted to you by us, and that you would make provision as should seem to you to be for God's greater glory.

We all hold ourselves as a thing very much your own, as we are in our Lord, yours and the King of England's[2] as we are likewise at the disposal of the most serene Princesses, your daughters, of the King of the Romans and the Queen of Portugal, Your Majesty's brother and sister, not only as your vassals which we are for the most part, certain of us coming from families well known to Your Majesty, but as under a deep obligation for the kindness and goodwill which God our Lord and the author of all good inspired you with for the furthering of this Society in its early days.

May it please him to give us all his abundant grace that we may know his most holy will and fulfil it perfectly.

Rome, March 3rd, 1554

To the Emperor Charles V

Nothing is more significant than the fact that it was this letter which lay undispatched in Ignatius' drawer. No subsequent communication passed between these two leaders of the last struggle for the religious unity of the West. When Ignatius was dying, the weary Emperor was preparing for his last journey to Spain. Only there, in the stillness of Jarandilla and Yuste, did his old friend Francis Borgia by conversing with him open his mind to the true ideals of Ignatius of Loyola. Borgia has related the contents of these conversations in a moving letter to the General Laynez.[3] In it he always refers to the Emperor by the pseudonym "father of Mateo Sánchez"; by Mateo Sánchez is meant, as we shall learn later, the Emperor's daughter, the Infanta Juana. From this it appears that this last act of reconciliation between Charles V and the Jesuits was due to the Princess Juana, who was on terms of close friendship with Ignatius.

From the secretary Polanco's correspondence with Father Salmerón in Naples we know more of the details of this forgotten episode at the close of Charles's life. A galley from Spain arrived in Naples, and amongst the political rumours was another to the effect that the Jesuit Borgia was spending hours with the old Emperor at Yuste. The Vicereine of Naples, the Duchess of Alba, one of the leaders of anti-Jesuit gossip, was furious, and said that wherever she went the Emperor's dislike of the Society was quite well-known. On enquiring at Rome, Father Salmerón, who was worried at all this, received the reply: "It is true that Father Francis Borgia was with the Emperor. The latter sent for him and spoke at length with him. One of our fathers who is just come from Spain knew all about the falsehoods which had been told to the Emperor concerning us; and he said that the Emperor struck himself on the forehead with the flat of his hand and exclaimed in anger at his lying informants: 'So they have deceived even me!'"

The Duchess of Alba, however, was filled with the spirit of Fray Melchor Cano.[4] What that spirit was we know well enough: the passionate and bellicose Dominican saw in the Society of Jesus a sort of precursor of Antichrist. In one of his letters to Juan de Regla, the confessor of Charles V at Yuste, he wrote in the summer of 1557: "It is not a bad joke that the Marquis of Tavara laments the fact that His Majesty has refused to make the Exercises!"[5]

Ignatius had very good reasons for singling out Philip and the Princess Juana for special mention in his letter to the Emperor. For it will soon be seen that he had more success with the next generation of the imperial family, with Philip and his two sisters, and through them with their Austrian relatives in Vienna. The careers of Ignatius and Philip II touched one another in a remarkable way at a number of points. When the Emperor's son was born at Valladolid on May 21st, 1527, Ignatius was studying at Alcalá; and he was there when the explosion took place at the fireworks in honour of the birth of an heir apparent, in which one of his enemies got burnt. At Alcalá or Valladolid Ignatius made the acquaintance of the lady who more than any other prepared the way for his influence at court: Doña Leonor Mascarenhas, the Prince's governess. It was while under her care in 1535 that Philip, then eight years old, met Ignatius personally on his return from Paris; and decades later the king remembered this meeting. When in 1586 he saw the painting which Sánchez Coello had made from Ignatius' death-mask, he said that it was a good likeness, only in 1535 the beard had been longer.

So it is not surprising that in the twelve volumes of St. Ignatius' letters we find a large correspondence with Philip, which begins in July 1545 and goes on till the saint's death. With often touching interest Ignatius followed all the events, personal and political, in the life of his "natural sovereign", from the death of his first wife to the memorable journey to England, over the return of which country to the Faith Ignatius rejoiced in vain. "I feel a sincere and heartfelt reverence and gratitude towards Your Highness", he wrote in July 1548, "and these sentiments have long been imprinted on my heart and remain ever with me." With King Philip then Ignatius might realize his ideal of co-operation between the Society and the Crown, which he had no longer felt able to suggest to Charles V. Monastic reform in Catalonia, the Council of Trent, the cessation of Jesuit-baiting in Spain, the advancement of the Roman College, the admission of the Jesuits to Flanders: these were the questions which Ignatius discussed with the King, and it is most important to emphasize at the outset that Ignatius had only purely spiritual matters to discuss with his princely correspondents and with the ladies of the House of Habsburg, and only concerned himself with politics when they served the kingdom of God. The finest of his letters to the king is that of February 18th, 1549, a spiritual homily of deepest wisdom. The great St. Teresa was the only other person who spoke thus to Philip.[6] Ignatius found it much easier to co-operate with King Ferdinand, the Emperor's brother, than with the ever-mistrustful Charles. We possess nearly two dozen letters exchanged between Ignatius and the court of Vienna. Ferdinand was indeed, in contrast with his brother, very Spanish; and there are among the usual coldly official letters in Latin also some written in Spanish by the King-Emperor's Spanish secretary, Juan de Castillo. There is no doubt that Ferdinand's niece and daughter-in-law María, Philip's dearly loved sister, favoured the participation of the Jesuits in the work of reform[7].

We are not then wrong in stating that Ignatius gained access, as it were, to the inner counsels of imperial policy through his friendship with the women of the House of Habsburg. At the very beginning of his career, before his conversion, there was – if the findings of recent research prove

KVNIGINNE · MARIA

QUEEN MARIA OF HUNGARY AND BOHEMIA
see page 38

QUEEN CATHERINE OF PORTUGAL
see page 45

correct – his knightly veneration for the lady of his heart, the little Infanta Catherine, immured with her crazy mother in the dark castle of Tordesillas, who charmed the page Iñigo de Loyola. As Queen of Portugal she was to be one of his chief helpers in God's work. There were also the two infantas, daughters of the Emperor, to whom Ignatius and his first disciples were introduced by the ever-faithful Leonor Mascarenhas; and if Ignatius was never able to overcome the mistrust of the powerful "Aunt María", the much respected Queen María of Hungary and Governor of the Netherlands, Charles V's sister, he was all the more successful with the Emperor's natural daughter Margaret of Austria, whom María had brought up, and whom, as her confessor, he influenced most of all the Habsburg ladies. The most remarkable thing in all Ignatius' relations with women of royal birth is the fact that the daughter of Charles V, the Infanta Juana, Regent of the Spanish kingdoms, was actually made a female member of the Society. A Habsburg princess is the only Jesuitess in the Church's history.

To these ladies of the imperial house can be added two other princesses with whom Ignatius corresponded and who were closely connected by family or political ties with the Habsburgs. They are the Duchess Eleonora of Florence and the Infanta Isabel of Portugal.[8]

Before we enter the world of these letters, so earthly, so colourful, so confused politically and so simple spiritually, the world of the "courtier of heaven" (for this Ignatius was, even after he became General), it may be of interest to describe briefly his relations with other princesses of his time, although they do not find expression in his actual correspondence.

Chief of these high-ranking ladies who enthusiastically supported Ignatius and his work was the sister of the Infanta Juana, Charles V's eldest daughter, the Infanta María. Through her governess Doña Leonor Mascarenhas she came to know the Jesuits, and Father Araoz was always the one she most esteemed. On September 14th, 1548, she married at Valladolid her cousin Maximilian of Austria, was regent of Spain with him for a time, went in 1551 to Vienna and became empress, to return quietly and wearily to Spain after the death of her beloved husband. Like some good spirit, her figure moves through the world of Ignatius' letters. She was the Jesuits' undaunted patroness in Vienna. It is due to her that Maximilian's wavering attitude in the religious question did not result in apostasy. "For the sake of her, who as Charles V's daughter is unshakable in her Catholicism, Maximilian all his life avoided going over openly to Protestantism, and preferred to continue in the vague imaginings of his own mixture of the two religions." This fact was of course of decisive importance for the destinies of Europe; but it could be even more clearly proved from Jesuit sources how great was the part played by the Empress María. In the chronicle of the Society we read: "The Queen of Bohemia, who afterwards became empress, regarded the Society with much favour, and so King Maximilian was also well disposed towards them, and the great lords at court followed his example." Only a few days before his death, Ignatius wrote to Pedro Ribadeneira in Flanders: "The Queen of Bohemia is especially well disposed towards us and sincerely attached to the Society." In this María was like her sister Juana.[9]

It is significant, too, how the marriages of Philip of Spain find their echo in Ignatius' letters. The congratulations which Ignatius sent him on his first marriage with María of Portugal arrived too late: the young bride was already dead when the letter reached Valladolid. But soon there were rumours of a second marriage. There was in Portugal another Infanta María, daughter of King Manoel's third marriage to Eleanor, the sister of the Emperor Charles V, who later at her brother's command married Francis I of France. Araoz kept his General at Rome well informed: "I heard in confidence from a person of high rank that the Prince wishes to marry the Infanta of Portugal, the Queen of France's daughter, and that the Duke of Gandía [later St. Francis Borgia] is to be appointed Master of the Household." This was embarrassing for Ignatius, since Borgia had already secretly become a Jesuit. However, he was not absolutely against the idea when he sent an answer on April 6th, 1550. Then the project hung fire, and the Prince's lengthy hesitation of over two years earned for the unfortunate Infanta the title of "the forsaken bride". "Complete silence", says a letter to Ignatius in October 1553, "envelops the Portuguese marriage question." Understandably so; for in the meantime the magnificent possibilities of a marriage with the English Queen Mary Tudor had opened up for Philip and for the policies of his imperial father. The forsaken María remained unmarried and bore her fate with "a sovereign courage".[10]

When Philip of Spain was betrothed to the Queen of England on October 30th, 1553, the world held its breath. Great things seemed about to be realized. By the death of King Edward VI on July 6th, 1553, his Catholic half-sister Mary, the daughter of the unfortunate Catharine of Aragon, had succeeded to the throne. Ignatius knew already on August 5th, of the English king's death, and full of joyful hopes he wrote: "May the Lord God deign to have mercy on that kingdom!" For "now the great gate opens, to re-admit the Kingdom of England into the bosom of Holy Church". His letters in these months are exultant in tone. Meanwhile Philip's marriage plans became publicly known in Rome; in the General's curia events were followed with almost feverish interest – the splendid voyage to England and the sumptuous wedding on July 25th, 1554, at Winchester. Ignatius regretted only that political wisdom did not allow Father Araoz to be sent to England with the prince. There is a good deal of understandable Spanish patriotism in Ignatius' recommendation to all his brethren in Spain to pray for England's return to the Church. He sent a personal message of congratulation to Philip, "the King of England". "Angels and men rejoice at England's homecoming." In a letter to Cardinal Pole Ignatius with courtly precision observes the etiquette which required Queen Mary always to be mentioned first, that is, before her consort. His apostolic heart was overflowing with a thousand projects. But then the tragedy began. The Emperor Charles V had in his will of June 6th, 1554, shared out the world with an imperial gesture: the expected child of the English marriage was to inherit not only his mother's throne, but also the Netherlands; the Spanish grandson Don Carlos was to have the other dominions. Alas! Don Carlos was a madman, and the no longer youthful Mary, whose most intimate affairs were discussed in whispers throughout Europe, produced no heir. In May 1555, Cardinal Pole announced to Ignatius the glad tidings of the approaching birth of a child – it proved to be an hysterical pregnancy, a state into which the unhappy woman, stared at by all the world, had worked herself. Soon the chronicler of the Society records the collapse of all hopes: "It was observed that the queen was not with child at all, and therefore that it did not please God to give England a son by this excellent queen."[11]

There is another royal lady whom Ignatius knew and who was also involved in Charles' and Philip's matrimonial policies – Jeanne d'Albret, daughter of the famous Margaret of Valois and of that King of Navarre against whose superior forces Ignatius of Loyola had fought in vain at Pamplona in 1521. Jeanne had been singled out since 1537 by her parents and the Emperor to become the wife of Philip, and this marriage would have meant more for the Emperor's French policy than the recovery of Pamplona; but the plan came to nothing. Later Jeanne was to become the mother of Henry IV. The half-heretical court chaplain of the Navarrese princesses was the Abbé de Clairac, Gérard Roussel, Bishop of Oloron in Béarn. Ignatius knew him from his Paris days. In 1553 it was said in Rome that this equivocal prelate was to be made a cardinal at the request of the princesses. Ignatius fought a skilful and well-planned action against this "friend of the Queen of Navarre", and thereafter there was no more talk of a cardinal's hat.[12]

Altogether the General had a great deal of trouble with the ladies of the royal house of France, who were so capricious in matters of religion. One day in February 1556 there came a modest request from Father Broët in Paris that a share in the spiritual riches of the Society might be granted to the younger Margaret of Valois, King Henry II's rather odd sister. This was not altogether unreasonable, for Margaret had helped the Fathers a lot in Paris; but to crown it all, the same letter also asked a similar privilege for Her Grace the Duchess of Valentinois – in other words, for Diane de Poitiers, the celebrated mistress of the two kings, Francis and Henry. This was too much. On April 3rd, 1556 Ignatius with Roman politeness caused the following reply to be dispatched: *Si risponderà un' altra volta*.[13]

Much more important in the General's eyes was the conversion of Princess Renée of France, daughter of King Louis XII, who was married to Duke Hercules of Ferrara and there, as a disciple of Calvin, was trying to practise and to spread the new doctrine. Much has been written about the spiritual tragedy of this intelligent and eccentric woman; yet the sources for the history of her dramatic conversion, contained in the volumes of Ignatius' correspondence, have hitherto been hardly or never used. From his chamber at Rome Ignatius followed with burning interest all the phases of the struggle waged by Father Pelletier, whom he had sent to Ferrara, for the soul of this obstinate lady. Pelletier's report of the duchess's penitent return to the Church on September 24th, 1554, sounds like a fanfare of victory; and Ignatius hastened to announce the news to Spain and Brussels and above all to Francis Borgia, cousin of the duke on the side of his mother, Lucrezia Borgia. Ignatius did not live to learn that the success was only apparent.[14]

Finally, another unfortunate princess must be mentioned, whom Ignatius, through the members of the Society, was able to help. She was the widowed Queen of Poland, Bona, daughter of Gian Galeazzo Sforza of Milan and Isabel de Aragón of Naples. Her bitter quarrels with her son, King Sigismund August, had awakened in her a longing for her Italian homeland. In June 1555 Father Salmerón set off with Bishop Lippomano of Verona on a diplomatic mission to Poland on behalf of Pope Paul IV. Ignatius gave him good advice as to his behaviour at court; Salmerón for his part sent his beloved master humorous accounts of the north: "He who has once travelled through this land has done penance for all his sins and gained a plenary indulgence into the bargain!" In Warsaw, however, the otherwise so skilful Jesuit had no success: the queen could not be persuaded to found a college. She desired but one thing – to get home to Italy, preferably to Naples, where in 1517 she had celebrated her wedding in the presence of Vittoria Colonna and her niece Juana de Aragón, whom Raphael had painted. Now all was changed. Vittoria was already dead, and Ignatius Loyola had been the comforter of her last years. Juana was unhappily married to Vittoria's brother Ascanio Colonna, and Ignatius had tried to mend the marriage. We shall hear later of all these matters. Now God's Cavalier wanted to help, too, the last unhappy lady of the House of Sforza, and when the arrival in Naples of the Queen of Poland was due, he sent instructions to Father Vignes on December 8th, 1555, that he should attend the queen. Bona Sforza died a lonely death in Bari soon after Ignatius.[15]

The letters which Ignatius wrote to royal ladies introduce us to this amazingly rich world of courtly relationships. From them, it is clear that Ignatius remained all his life what he was as a page in Tordesillas and Arévalo – a man of perfect tact, who never forgot his courtly manners nor lost his gentlemanly bearing, when the lady "was more than a countess or a duchess". But it is clear, too, that Ignatius was wholly a man of the spirit, who spoke to these ladies only of the things of the next world, or enlisted them in the service of the one great work that to him seemed important on earth: helping souls.

Queen María of Hungary

THERE was one important member of the imperial house who was loved and not a little feared by all the family: "Aunt María" as they called her, Charles V's second youngest sister. She is first among the Habsburg ladies whose correspondence with Ignatius we shall speak of, for Aunt María was, even in the Society of Jesus, very much respected and feared.

María is well known to students of history, for she was one of the partners in the famous double wedding of 1515, on which the power of the Austrian dynasty was based. As consort of King Louis of Bohemia and Hungary, widowed since 1527, she knew all her life the importance of her inheritance for the House of Habsburg, and therefore she was always in the centre of all discussions on family policy. To get on the wrong side of Aunt María was to be halfway to losing one's case; causes that she promoted were already half won. From 1530 till the abdication of the Emperor Charles on October 25th, 1555, she was Governor of the Netherlands. Well has she been called a Charles V in petticoats, and even Brantôme said she was "somewhat mannish". The portrait of her in old age, in the Vienna National Library, confirms this description. One can see that this woman knew exactly what she wanted, and that she would make short work of any opponents. Among all the ladies with whom he corresponded, Ignatius certainly had no tougher antagonist.[16]

The Netherlands, which María ruled in her brother's name, were in the middle of the century the trouble-spot of the Emperor's vast dominions. This was all the more so since Philip's English marriage, when, according to the Emperor's will of 1554, the Netherlands together with England were to be the kingdom of Mary Tudor's expected child. Moreover, Spain felt a threat to her faith from her northern possessions, and the innovators must be opposed by force of arms if the Catholic faith in the whole Empire was to remain unshaken. Queen María tactfully tried to steer a middle course, being completely under the influence of the all-powerful Antoine Perrenot de Granvelle, Bishop of Arras and afterwards cardinal, who as a Renaissance prelate somewhat late in time had no understanding for denominational or ascetic questions. The secretary Viglius van Zwichem shared his opinions. Philip II regarded his aunt's political indulgence in the Netherlands with

38

mistrust; indeed, it appears from the account of the Venetian ambassador that aunt and nephew almost hated one another. María and her brother, on the other hand, agreed well; and later María retired with him to solitude in Spain, where she soon followed him in death.[17]

Ignatius, too, had cast his eyes upon Flanders, whence many excellent recruits had already joined the Society. If the Faith in the north was to be defended, it was of decisive importance to gain a foothold there, especially in Louvain, the intellectual centre. This was, it is true, easier to reflect on than to accomplish; but Ignatius did not content himself with reflections. One of those masterly diplomatic campaigns now began which are so typical of his tactics. For six years he tried to storm the Flemish fortress, apparently in vain. Success came at last only when Ignatius in Rome lay on his deathbed.

As early as 1550 Ignatius began to think seriously about the question of his Society's official admission to Louvain and the establishment of a college there. At first he wanted to send a petition to the Emperor, then at Augsburg; but as this question immediately concerned the Regent María, and as she was under the influence of Granvelle and Viglius van Zwichem, who were not at all favourable to the Jesuits, the Nuncio Pighino advised against the plan; but Ignatius did not let himself be put off. The Flemish Father Adriaenssens was commissioned to put out feelers at the regent's court. She asked the theological faculty of Louvain for an opinion. Their report was most favourable. Nevertheless, María gave a negative answer. In its wording we hear the typical argument of the humanist Viglius: there were already enough colleges and religious in Louvain. Besides, some surprise had been caused at the court of Brussels by the rumour that some ladies of the nobility had become Jesuitesses. "Jesuit" was then at the regent's court a kind of reproach for a religious hypocrite or devotee. It was reported at Rome that the Queen would have none of them. Ignatius insisted that she should be told the truth; he was disturbed to hear that the secretary Viglius had said Brussels was swarming with Jesuits, male and female.[18]

Meanwhile King Ferdinand had received the petition originally intended for the Emperor. He added a long letter of recommendation to his sister, and Otto, Cardinal von Truchsess for his part also wrote to the regent. With these documents, Father Adriaenssens came back to Brussels in 1551 and handed the letters, together with a recommendation from the theological faculty of Louvain, to the influential Viglius. The latter gave him a good dinner, many fair words – and a fresh refusal. Only if the Pope himself wrote personally to the Emperor, said Viglius, something might be done. This was like a battle-cry for Ignatius; now he set half the world moving. The Pope wrote to the Nuncio, the Nuncio spoke to the Emperor, who in turn promised to have the matter seen to by Granvelle; but in Flanders they turned a deaf ear. Ignatius expected this, and wrote as much to Father Jay in Augsburg: no progress would be made before "my Lord of Arras" and Queen María had been won over. It was incidentally in this connexion that Ignatius was not too proud to remind the Emperor – what would he not have done in this affair! – of his ancestors' faithful services. At the same time another request was sent to Ferdinand that he might again recommend the Jesuits to his sister. Then Ignatius himself made ready for the general assault. On March 26th, 1552, he dispatched a petition, written in Latin and Spanish, to Her Sacred Majesty the Queen Regent, in which he described the nature and purpose of his new Society, and asked for approval for the foundation of a college at Louvain. Simultaneously he ordered Father Salmerón, then attending the Council of Trent, to go to Innsbruck, there to promote with the Emperor in person the cause of the Louvain college.[19]

Sacred and royal Majesty,
Most merciful Lady,

When a few years ago in the city of Rome, this Society of the Name of Jesus, whose protector indeed is His Eminence Cardinal Carpi, was instituted and confirmed by the Apostolic See, it so pleased God the Greatest and Best, that very many men, both learned and devout, leaving their own countries and giving up their worldly goods and their property should devote themselves to Almighty God in the Society. Later very many studious young men presented themselves, of good disposition and giving great hope, coming from various parts to embrace the discipline of the Society in which under the banner of Jesus they practised a spiritual warfare. For the whole Society was instituted for this purpose, that those in it who were admitted to profession, promising obedience to the holy Apostolic See should promote the general salvation of souls, and should do this by preaching the word of God publicly, by performing works of Christian charity, and also (as often as they were sent to do this) by making known the faith of Christ among the infidels; and, finally, by resisting the attacks on religion by heretics, each one to the best of his ability in accordance with the talent received from our Lord.

Such things, indeed, cannot be rightly performed except by those who are not only pious but learned in sacred theology, and Divine Providence has brought it about that there should be certain most illustrious and religious princes, besides very many other men, godfearing, noble and high-minded, all of whom being of the same mind and having an affection for the students of the Society, set up and generously founded for them certain colleges in many famous places, as for instance in Catholic universities in different parts, where, while many of them are living there, they can at one and the same time be formed to honest and truly Christian morals, and be trained in solid study of theology with faith and care. Of these colleges some, of course, are in Spain, one in Portugal, several in India, two in Sicily, and one also in Rome, Bologna, Padua and Venice.

For the rest, from the very beginning of this Society's foundation there have not been lacking in it studious youths who have been giving the labour of many years to learning in various places and in particular in the very flourishing university of Louvain. There some of them are making so much progress in learning by the grace of Christ, that when their studies there are happily ended, they will then provide labourers for tilling the Lord's vineyard, and those not useless ones. Certain of them continue to devote their energy to those studies.

In the meantime it has pleased God's goodness to stir the minds of certain good men and move them to help those students who are poor. There are some, therefore, who desire to see instituted in the celebrated university of Louvain as elsewhere, a college of the Society of Jesus. For this purpose, moreover, someone might be willing generously to offer and apply to this purpose whatever wealth or even property he himself possessed. This, however, cannot in any sense come about without the kind consent and pious favour of your sacred Majesty. This, therefore, Ignatius of Loyola, a Spanish priest, General of the aforesaid Society, implores, asking with all due respect and humility that your sacred Majesty would deign to consent that such a college be founded close to the most celebrated university of Louvain and also that property may be assigned to this purpose, and the income paid yearly, as much as the liberality of good friends shall provide, up to, indeed, the value of a thousand ducats.

If your sacred Majesty will grant this favour, it is unquestionably a good work and you will have done something very pleasing to the Lord Jesus. Thus you will then have placed even more in your debt this whole Society which up to this time hitherto has received your favours in other respects and in many ways, and as long as it lasts will never cease to pour out its prayers to God, both for the safety and health of Your Sacred Majesty and for the happy estate of all your realms.

Rome, March 26th, 1552

To Mary of Austria, Governor of
Flanders and Queen of Bohemia

41

Both campaigns, that in Brussels and that in Innsbruck, ended in complete failure. To the petition addressed to Queen María no answer at all was vouchsafed, and it disappeared among the state archives, to be rediscovered only in 1840. Salmerón, who had reached Innsbruck on April 2nd, 1552, departed again only two days later for Trent, without having accomplished anything. For Tyrol was then full of the alarms of war, and on April 6th, the Emperor rode secretly and by night out of Innsbruck with Granvelle – his celebrated flight before Maurice of Saxony. Polanco was imbued with Spanish-Imperial patriotism and also with sorrow for the failure in Flanders when he wrote in the chronicle of the Society at this historic moment: "Just at this time Maurice was besieging the city of Augsburg with his army, which had been got together by the French King and was paid with French money."[20]

Even this, however, could discourage the iron-willed General only for a moment. In December 1552 he consoled his Flemish brethren with hopes of better political conditions. Then he began his campaign anew, this time with his tactical base in Spain. The political and religious destinies of the Netherlands had assumed European importance now that Philip's English marriage was under discussion, and they were of immediate interest to the prince who was soon to sit beside Mary Tudor on the English throne. Father Araoz in Spain was now mobilized. He was to ask Philip to write to Queen María, Granvelle, and the States-General; and the matter was to be pressed energetically, for hitherto nothing had been achieved under María's regency because, as Ignatius says, "certain men sit in her Council who are not filled with good and wholesome doctrine"; but the prince was not to write to the Emperor himself, for Philip had already done a good deal for the colleges in Sicily, and besides His Majesty was "not exactly friendly towards a certain man or men". Who these men were was clear to the initiated, and one of them was no doubt Ignatius himself. These letters must be written, adds Ignatius with a wry smile, in good ink". It is then all the more remarkable that the shrewd General should listen to his almost equally shrewd Araoz (who, as he himself wrote, "had his finger on the pulse" of Philip's Flemish policy), advising him against such ponderous methods. The question of the Jesuits' establishment in Louvain might, he said, be dealt with when Philip, as *seigneur naturel* of the Netherlands, was there in person. After some hesitation, Ignatius decided at least to send to the Emperor a petition in the same words as that to Queen María, Charles having meanwhile retired weary and out of temper to Flanders. It was then that he also drafted that fine letter to the Emperor which he never dispatched.[21]

The scene of battle now shifted in the last phase of the war to Brussels itself. There literally all the influential noblemen at court were pressed into service in order to make the obstinate regent change her mind. Cardinal Pole received from her handsome but meaningless promises. The Abbot of Liesse, Louis de Blois, tried his luck with Viglius, but without success. About this time President Viglius wrote down his opinion of the Jesuits in a memorandum. As he wrote, the painful memory came to his mind of Father Bobadilla's appearance at the Imperial Diet in Augsburg, when the Emperor flew into a passion against the new Society. Viglius wrote: "One ought to study their Constitutions more thoroughly." He was right in this, for the rules of the Society were not published until 1558. "Secondly", he continued, "I see that they have no house or monastery in which they live as a community. Rather are they fully at liberty to move and wander about, without companions or witnesses, like Bobadilla, who sat at table with all the world and was always discussing the latest news. And lastly, it is not good that they cannot be recognized by a religious habit, but at most by a certain humility which they affect." No encouragement was likely, then, from this quarter. The Dominican Pedro de Soto, the Emperor's confessor, was asked to intercede with Charles, "for we know hardly any man", wrote Ignatius, "who so zealously promotes Christ's cause and has so much authority with His Imperial Majesty". Soto spoke to the Emperor. The latter sent him to María, who graciously listened to him and promised to speak to the Emperor. Nothing happened. Soto observed that neither of them had any understanding for the aims of the Society.[22]

Even now Ignatius did not give up. He was well informed about the rumours coming from Brussels that the Emperor was thinking of abdicating and was going to hand over the government of Flanders to his son Philip. "Then, it is said, that lady would soon go", he wrote to a friend in Flanders. Meanwhile Philip II had arrived in Brussels, and on October 25th, 1555, the famous abdication ceremony took place, at which Queen María also took leave of the Netherlands in a tearful speech. It was almost with a sigh of relief that Ribadeneira wrote a few weeks later from Brussels: "María can now do no more and will do no more." With Philip there were also in Brussels the lords of his suite, who in Spain had been favourable to the Jesuits, especially the allpowerful Ruy Gómez, whom the court wits on account of his influence aptly named "Rey (King) Gómez", Gonzalo Pérez and the Count of Feria, brother of the Jesuit Antonio de Córdoba. When the Count spoke to Philip in favour of the proposed college at Louvain, and referred to the Regent María's opposition, Philip answered: "It no longer matters what the Queen thinks or does not think." A new wind was blowing in Brussels, and Ignatius knew how to take advantage of it.[23]

At an audience on February 14th, 1556, Ribadeneira presented a new petition in Ignatius' name, accompanied by a letter to Philip written by Ribadeneira: "Although we have several times addressed petitions to Her Majesty Queen María, she was misinformed by those who do not know our Society, and so rejected them all." In June Ribadeneira was able to inform his master in Rome that the King had put the new petition among his private papers, in the box marked: "To be dealt with promptly." From Spain the Regent Juana wrote warmly in favour of the Jesuits. Her sister, Queen Maria of Bohemia, arrived in Brussels on July 16th, to take leave of her father. Ribadeneira spoke with her; the Queen, glowing with enthusiasm, interceded with Philip and the obstinate Viglius. This fitted in well with the General's plans, for on July 20th, 1556, ten days before his death, he had sent instructions to Flanders that the Queen of Bohemia, who was so well disposed towards the Jesuits, should be asked to intervene on their behalf. It was Ignatius' last order.[24] He never lived to hear of the victory in Flanders. On the eve of his death, the faithful Ribadeneira, together with Count Feria and the rector of Louvain University, Ruard Tapper, was invited by Viglius van Zwichem to a momentous dinner-party. Success was assured. On August 15th and 20th, Philip signed the document that granted the Jesuits permission to settle in the Netherlands. Father Nadal was afterwards firmly convinced that this victory was due to the prayers of their Father, glorified in death. The two princesses, the Emperor's daughters Juana and María, received from the grateful Society the honour of sharing in its spiritual privileges.[25]

But María, good Aunt María, who was always courageous and somewhat stubborn, went with her beloved brother into solitude in Spain. On October 18th, 1558, she died in Cigales, only three years after her mad mother and three weeks after her imperial brother. She was forgotten by the world, but not by the sons of her bold antagonist Ignatius. In their letters written during this year of Habsburg deaths we sense, as it were, a whole world in dissolution. "Pray, Reverend Father, to God for the souls of the Emperor Charles and his sister, Queen María; and for the Queen of England, whom the Lord has called to himself. May he give them all eternal life, and may he protect the kingdom of England, that it may continue in the Catholic faith." So wrote the General Laynez to Father Bobadilla, whom Charles had once banished from Germany; and Father Francis Borgia, the former duke, gave Queen María her finest epitaph: "God removed this royal lady from wars and the cares of government and placed her in a lonely corner to die, that he might give her everlasting life."[26]

Queen Catherine of Portugal

WHEN we look at the majestic severity and the once beautiful features of Queen Catherine of Portugal, worn by age and the cares of government, as they are depicted by Antonio Moro in the Madrid portrait, we can hardly believe that this is the woman who was the exquisitely pretty Infanta with the good looks of her father, Philip the Fair. Catherine, born at Torquemada on January 14th, 1507, after her father's death, was the youngest daughter of Joanna the Mad. She grew up with her mother and spent her dreary youth sharing the latter's prison in the gloomy castle of Tordesillas.

Only once did a ray of sunshine illumine her young life. What happened has been described for us by an eye-witness. It is like some charming fairy-tale or a story from the chivalrous romances of Amadis of Gaul, which the page Iñigo de Loyola once read with passionate interest. When young King Charles in 1517 made his first journey to Spain, to enter upon the inheritance of his unfortunate mother, he visited the mad Queen in December at Tordesillas. He was shocked at the gloomy surroundings in which his little eleven-year-old sister was growing up. On her mother's orders she went about in a dress of grey woollen cloth, wore a leather cloak against the cold, and a linen cap. At the child's request a window had been made in the wall, through which the lonely little girl could watch the ships on the Douro, the horsemen on the road, and the children playing noisily outside the castle. Her brother at once began to think of a remedy; the assembled grandees in Valladolid were, moreover, loudly clamouring for the young Infanta.

In the retinue of the Duke of Nájera, who upheld in the Cortes the principle of unconditional loyalty to the hereditary right of the House of Austria, there was no doubt his officer Iñigo de Loyola. The family of Oñaz y Loyola was then particularly interested in the outcome of the Cortes' deliberations, for Ignatius' brother Martín García was at this time in Valladolid, trying to obtain royal permission to create an entail on his property. This in fact he received on March 5th, 1518 in the name of Queen Joanna and her son Charles. It is besides highly probable that Ignatius had already been more than once in Tordesillas in the suite of the Grand Treasurer Juan Velásquez, while King Ferdinand was still alive and visiting his insane daughter in the company of his consort, Germaine de Foix.[27]

45

King Charles knew with what passionate mother-love Joanna was attached to her youngest child, who for ten years had been her only happiness. He therefore thought of a romantic plan to free the Princess from the prison of Tordesillas without her mother's knowledge. In the night of March 12th–13th, 1518, he caused his sister to be abducted from the castle, with the help of a gentleman of the bedchamber who was in the secret; two hundred mounted men were waiting at the bridge over the Douro to escort Catherine to Valladolid. There the little Cinderella was clothed in royal garments, and the following day she looked on in delight from a high balcony while knights jousted in her honour. "I saw her", says our informant, "as she stepped on to the balcony from the apartment of her sister Leonor, accompanied on the one hand by the Seigneur de Trazeguies and on the other by Madame de Chièvres. The Lady Anne de Beaumont bore the train of her gown, which was of violet satin, heavily embroidered with gold. On her head she wore a veil in the Castilian manner."

The dream was soon over. Her unfortunate mother in Tordesillas raved and refused all food until her beloved child was brought back to her. Catherine disappeared once again for more than six years within the gloomy walls of the palace. Her enchanting image, however, remained in the memory of Iñigo de Loyola; the Infanta Catherine was henceforth the lady of his heart, of whom he was thinking when three years later on his bed of pain at Loyola recollections of his chivalrous past filled his mind. Even in his latter years he dictated the following words concerning her: "Among the many vain thoughts that crowded upon him, one in particular had taken possession of his heart, so that he remained sunk in reverie for two, three, or four hours on end, without being aware of the fact. He imagined what he would do in the service of a certain Lady, how he could contrive to reach her place of residence, what fine speeches he would make to her and what deeds of heroism he would perform in her service. So absorbed was he in these thoughts, that he did not perceive how impossible of fulfilment they were. For the lady was not of ordinary nobility, not merely a countess or a duchess, but her estate was far higher than these."[28]

This was in August and September 1521, a few months after the cannon-ball had shattered Ignatius' leg on the citadel of Pamplona. Meanwhile great things had been happening at Tordesillas. No doubt Ignatius received an exact account of them, principally from his former fellow-page, Alonso de Montalvo, who visited his friend immediately after he was wounded and while he was still at Pamplona. The Infanta Catherine was in the greatest danger. On August 29th, 1520, the Comuneros had occupied the castle of Tordesillas, in order to secure the queen and the princess for their political ends. But on the 5th December the royal troops had reentered it, and on

April 23rd, 1521, they inflicted the decisive defeat of Villalar on the Comuneros, without, it is true, being able to bring help to Navarre, which was
gravely threatened, and whence the Duke of Nájera had withdrawn all
available troops as reinforcements against the Comuneros. Actually, then,
Ignatius of Loyola was wounded in the desperate battle for the citadel of
Pamplona in order that the victory which freed the royal ladies at Tordesillas
might be won. From that same August 1521 dates the written justification
which Catherine sent to her brother in Flanders, a moving account of the
distresses which the courageous Infanta suffered in her mother's palace-
prison. At the beginning of 1522 the removal of the queen and her daughter
to the loyal city of Arévalo was being seriously considered. There dwelt the
widow of the Grand Treasurer Velázquez, Ignatius' motherly friend,
Doña María de Velasco. We relate all this only in order to depict the living,
historical background to Ignatius' wandering fancies when he thought about
the "lady of his heart". Henceforth indeed Catherine's path and his were to
lie in different directions: Ignatius was slowly to become, through suffering
and the grace of God, the saint we know –but the Infanta whom he worship-
ped in secret entered at the end of 1524 upon her sorrowful journey to
Portugal, where she was married to King John III. In her suite was Doña
María de Velasco. This much-tried lady, towards whom Ignatius had a deep
obligation of gratitude, remained loyally by her mistress till 1540. At her
death she bequeathed to the queen, always a keen collector of relics, a
particularly valuable treasure which had once been given to her by Queen
Isabella the Catholic in person – a piece of silver from Judas' purse. The two
ladies may well have spoken together of the former page, who had in the
meanwhile founded an order. Certain it is that news of Ignatius and his
companions had already reached the court at Lisbon; and soon the Portuguese ambassador in Rome was reporting the ambitious plans of these
graduates of Paris.[29] The king and his consort were at once enthusiastic, and
in April 1540 Catherine received for the first time, in an audience lasting
an hour, one of the erstwhile page's spiritual sons, Master Simon Rodríguez.
At the end of June the future Apostle of India, Francis Xavier, presented
himself to her. Xavier sent an interesting account to Ignatius of his reception
at court. The queen introduced him to her two surviving children, the heir
apparent Prince John and the Princess María, and told him about the seven
children whom during fifteen years of marriage death had taken from her –
the last queen of the stricken House of Aviz bore her grief heroically. Then
Catherine made Xavier tell her of Ignatius' new foundation, of his ideals and
of the presecutions which he had to endure at Rome.

From this time began a lively correspondence between Lisbon and Rome,
between the General of the Jesuits and the one-time object of his chivalrous

aspirations; but now all was in the service of God. It is well known how the king and queen, filled with enthusiasm for Ignatius' work, opened the missions of East Asia to the Society. Its initial success in Portugal under Simon Rodríguez was also due to the queen's patronage, Ignatius therefore took a keen interest in all her affairs great and small.[30] The marriages arranged between Madrid and Lisbon in December 1542, after careful preparation by her, were of world importance. Catherine's daughter María married Philip, heir to the Spanish throne, and Philip's sister Juana was promised in marriage to the Portuguese king's heir, John Emanuel. When one thinks of the tragedy that resulted from these two marriages, one cannot read without emotion what Ignatius wrote to the Portuguese sovereigns on March 8th, 1543: "These marriages, which have met with such general approval, are indeed, rather the work of God than of man, and they will confirm the two kingdoms in peace and security." God knows, even saints can make mistakes. This is what Ludwig Pfandl wrote of these two marriages: "The bride was, indeed, closely related to her prospective husband. Philip's father and María's mother were brother and sister. María's father and Philip's mother were also brother and sister. Philip was to become the son-in-law of his aunt, the husband of his cousin and the brother-in-law of another cousin. María became the daughter-in-law of her uncle, the wife and sister-in-law of her cousins. The bride and bridegroom had scarcely completed their sixteenth year, and so two immature children were to contract a union that was a glaring example of inbreeding; but all this was not taken into consideration. The unnatural connection was even to be made double by the betrothal at the same time of Doña Juana, Philip's sister, to the Portuguese heir apparent, Prince John."[31] The House of Aviz indeed needed a saint's prayers, and many times did Ignatius appeal to the Society to remember the royal house of Portugal.

Catherine took Father Miguel de Torres as her confessor and performed the Spiritual Exercises under his direction. Her attachment to the Society is apparent from the moving expression of sympathy which Peter Faber addressed to her mother after the Princess María's early death. "The love and affection which the princess showed towards the Society of Jesus was a proof whose daughter she was." It was then all the more painful for Ignatius when, to the great vexation of the queen, and largely owing to Father Rodríguez' unwise behaviour, a crisis arose in the Portuguese province, and a number of members left the Society. Ignatius at this juncture made a point of offering his services to the queen, in order to be assured of her continued benevolence.[32] We know already that Catherine was a passionate collector of relics. Blessed Peter Faber had brought her from Cologne some relics of St. Ursula's eleven thousand virgins, which added to the precious store in which she already had one of Judas' pieces of silver. When Simon Rodríguez was called to Rome, the queen commissioned him to procure for her, through the good offices of the General of the Society, relics from the Roman shrines. No task could have been more welcome to Ignatius at this difficult time. At once he applied to Pope Julius III, who, acting through Cardinal Bernardino Maffei, granted him permission to take relics from any church he wished and to send them to Portugal. The document giving Ignatius this permission is still preserved: "We, Bernardinus de Maffei, Cardinal Priest of the title of St. Cyriacus in the Thermae, hereby declare and make known: Our Holy Father Pope Julius III has at our request *vivae vocis oraculo* granted permission to the Very Reverend Father Ignatius of Loyola, General of the Society of Jesus, to remove personally or through his representative, all relics that he wishes, from any churches whatsoever, and to send them to Portugal or to any other place that shall seem good to him. In testimony whereof we have signed this document with our own hand and confirmed it with our seal. Given at Rome on the June 16th, in the Year of Our Lord 1551, in the second year of the reign of the said Holy Father. Bernardinus Cardinal Maffei." Ignatius, with his correct and sometimes rather exaggeratedly legalistic way of thinking, attached the greatest importance to such documents, if they concerned a matter which, as in this case, might have been misconstrued by others. From July 1551 till March 1552 he was busy collecting bones of saints. On March 12th, 1552, he sent them by the new Visitor to Portugal, Father Miguel de Torres, to the queen in Lisbon. The heir-apparent, too, who had recently become the Emperor's son-in-law, was to have a share of them. The General's continued anxiety over the crisis in the Portuguese province is apparent in the latter part of the letter accompanying the relics. The following year, however, he was to be comforted by the reports of his brethren on the queen's unshakable attachment to the Society of Jesus.[33]

My Lady in our Lord,

The sovereign grace and eternal love of Christ our Lord be with Your Majesty, with his most holy gifts and spiritual graces.

When he was here in Rome last year, Master Simon (Rodríguez) took some trouble to procure leave from His Holiness to bring away some relics for Your Majesty and the Prince; and although His Holiness willingly gave leave, as Master Simon left Rome, this favour did not actually take effect. As, therefore, this seemed to me to be a matter in which Your Majesties would be served to the glory of God our Lord, I begged the Pope once again to give this permission, and, having received it, I myself, with others of this house, went to bring away all that could be had. Your Majesty may dispose of all as it seems to you best in our Lord, for the Prince's Highness will be satisfied, as to the share that falls to him, with the division that Your Majesty makes, according to the intention of His Holiness.

I shall not write at greater length, nor shall I offer my person and those of this humble Society again, for the continual service of Your Majesty in our Lord, for it is now so many years since we have considered ourselves, as is most fitting, and as Your Majesties, I believe, consider us, a thing entirely yours in this Lord of ours. May his infinite and sovereign goodness deign to give us all his abundant grace so that we may always know his most holy will and perfectly fulfil it.

Rome, March 12th, 1552

To Her Highness, the Queen of Portugal, Lisbon

To maintain his good relations with the Queen of Portugal was always a matter of importance to Ignatius. For her part Catherine, with all her youthful memories of the dark years with her insane mother at Tordesillas, was deeply grateful to the Jesuits for having undertaken the spiritual consolation of the poor mad queen. We still possess the letter dictated by Catherine's filial piety, in which she thanks Father Borgia for his visits to Joanna the Mad.[34]

In the very year of his death, Ignatius gave Father Gonçalves da Câmara detailed instructions concerning his behaviour towards the king and queen, especially as owing to the king's sickness the whole weight of government fell upon Catherine. As regent for her grandson Sebastian, who had inherited the tainted blood of the mad Joanna, she had summoned Father Gonçalves to court to educate the young king.[35] From the beginning of Sebastian's reign in 1568 the old queen was on bad terms with her unfortunate grandson. The Jesuits too were involved in the dispute, which was at length decided by the Pope in Catherine's favour; but Ignatius had by then been long dead, and Catherine, who died in 1578, did not live to see Sebastian's terrible end. Only the historian can see what tragedies resulted from that marriage of Catherine's children, which Ignatius had praised as the work of heaven. The knight of Loyola's fair princess became one of the tragic figures of the House of Habsburg. "Her son, the heir apparent John Emanuel, who married Prince Philip's sister, died before his second wedding anniversary.

Shortly after his death, the widow bore his son and successor Sebastian, whose eccentric character and terrible end seem more like fiction than fact. He disappeared without trace on a crusade to North Africa, undertaken with careless heroism; but his people celebrated him in legend and song, and waited a whole lifetime for his return. Catherine's daughter, the Infanta María, was the first wife of Philip of Spain and the mother of Don Carlos, whose birth she survived by only a few days. Don Sebastian was half mad, Don Carlos completely so. In the veins of both fermented the fatal blood of the insane Joanna."[36]

Such was the tragic life-history of the charming Infanta of Tordesillas, who was the subject of Ignatius' daydreams during his convalescence. When we stand before Catherine's tomb in the splendid church of Belem near Lisbon, our thoughts turn towards that of St. Ignatius in Rome, gleaming in baroque magnificence; and oppressed by the facts of history we cannot but admit that "God's ways are not our ways".

The queen's epitaph is as follows:

Here lies buried Catherine, daughter of King Philip of Castile, consort of King John III of Portugal, the pious, the fortunate, the victorious. She was a woman of great courage, unsullied piety, and singular prudence. The incomparable example of a queen.

Princess Juana of Spain

OF all the ladies of the imperial house, those who played the greatest part in Ignatius' life were the two daughters that Charles V's beautiful but short-lived wife Isabel of Portugal bore him. They were the Infantas María, born at Madrid on June 21st, 1528, and Juana, also born at Madrid on June 24th, 1535. María was to go to Vienna as consort of the Emperor Maximilian II; and even though no letters of Ignatius to her have been preserved, he owed much to her sincere affection for the Society. His relations with Juana were of greater significance. We must therefore concern ourselves more closely with this royal personage, because Juana was the only one of all the women connected with Ignatius who was made a permanent member of the Society.[37]

The little Infanta was four years old when she lost her mother in 1539. Her brother Philip was twelve, María eleven; and the dying Empress had entrusted the children to the care of her friend Leonor Mascarenhas. Their imperial father directed the careful upbringing of his children from afar. The main credit for their formation, however, was due to those ladies who were in charge of the household, which was constantly on the move from Valladolid to Toro or Arando de Duero. They were women who were already acquainted with Ignatius of Loyola, such as the daughter of the Count of Oropesa, of whose interest in Ignatius Peter Faber tells us. It is no wonder then that Father Araoz on his first journey to Spain in 1540 was invited to preach before the Infantas at Valladolid. Five-year-old Juana, it is true, probably did not understand much. Two years later, however, the princesses' court chaplain, Mosén Juan Aragonés, came to know Blessed Peter Faber and decided to join the Society of Jesus. That was, so to speak, a big event for the new Society, and Ignatius was informed of the matter in detail.[38]

At eight years old, so contemporary accounts tell us, the Infanta could understand Latin and play several musical instruments. She was, too, already the object of her father's matrimonial policy; for when her brother Philip's marriage pact was signed, she was, as we have seen, promised to the Portuguese heir apparent John Emanuel, two years her junior. What importance was attached to this event in Ignatius' curia at Rome we have likewise noted. At the same time Araoz wrote to Ignatius from Almeirim, where the marriage

52

pacts were agreed upon: "The queen [Catherine] is a gift of God, and the heir apparent is very well disposed". In reality John Emanuel was a sickly child of six, who had been unable to talk till he was four. Here, then, the dynastic tragedy was already beginning, and little Juana had need without knowing it of the prayers and words of spiritual consolation that Ignatius occasionally sent her through Leonor Mascarenhas.[39]

At first, the Infanta's youth passed peacefully enough. Her interest in the spiritual sons of the former page increased. Thus on November 13th, 1551, Araoz was called upon to preach at Toro. Again it was Leonor Mascarenhas, together with the two ladies-in-waiting to the Infanta, the daughters of Duke Francis Borgia (who had meanwhile become publicly known as a Jesuit), who kept that interest alive. Ignatius in Rome always found time enough to follow all these developments. In September 1552 he reported to Gaspare de Dotti: "Father Borgia preached before the Infanta Juana, the Emperor's daughter, who will soon be Queen of Portugal. And she has even made some spiritual exercises already." For the understanding of the things that were to come it was necessary now, before her marriage, to make sure of Juana's conversion to a deeper spiritual life. Her leader along this path was no doubt Father Francis Borgia, whose own conversion had taken place beside the corpse of Juana's mother, and who now placed his experience of courts and his aristocratic delicacy of feeling at the service of God in the seventeen-year-old Infanta's court. It is particularly noted in the records of the Society how Borgia waged war against the ladies' card-playing, and how Juana handed over to him all her worthless novels.[40]

The wedding, which was afterwards celebrated with royal pomp at Lisbon, took place at Toro on January 11th, 1552. Juana felt utterly forsaken in Portugal with her sickly sixteen-year-old husband. All the greater then was her joy when Father Borgia came to stay in Lisbon from August 31st to October 5th, 1553, and made the princess's court into a veritable convent.[41] For the entertainment and edification of the ladies, Borgia invented a card game of the virtues and a kind of lotto with the privileges of our Lady.

Father Bustamente, who was very pious, did not fail to inform Ignatius of this in a letter of interminable length: "If it will be of service to Your Paternity I will send you a set of these cards; I think it would be a good recreation for the most reverend cardinals, which would not be injurious to the soul." He had come to the wrong man with such suggestions. Bustamente's modest request for approval of these pious pastimes brought in reply a letter from the secretary Polanco, obviously inspired by the General, to the effect that in any case some of the cardinals would not care for these religious playing-cards; but Father Francis need have no scruple in continuing to employ this means of being "all things to all men", as God had given him a special talent for getting on well with persons of rank. When the cards actually arrived in Rome, Polanco answered (and Ignatius did not delete the sentence): "They are an eloquent proof of the energy with which Father Francis follows up his ideas."[42]

The religious idyll of Almeirim ended tragically. On January 2nd, 1554, the heir apparent's feeble life was extinguished, and eighteen days later Juana bore her son, the future King Sebastian, who inherited through her his grandmother's insanity. With almost precipitate haste the Infanta left Portugal, which she had never loved, and returned to Valladolid.

A new phase of her life now began. On July 12th, 1554, the Emperor appointed his daughter as regent of Spain for the period during which Philip would be absent on account of his ill-conceived marriage with Mary Tudor. It was an historic moment, the uncanny suspense of which Ignatius also sensed. If he had already been filled with emotion by the rich gifts which Juana had destined for the Society in the will she made before her son's birth, he now saw in Philip and in the sister who so much resembled him the guarantors of the progress of all his spiritual undertakings. "I am much comforted", he wrote in July 1554 to Father Nadal, "by the good dispositions of the prince and the princess his sister, and I hope that His Divine Majesty will deign to employ their help in his service, for the common good."[43]

The five years of her regency in Spain form the climax of the young widow's life. She was the true daughter of her imperial father. Even when one allows for the courtly style of contemporary accounts, it appears that the Regent Juana was one of the most beautiful women at the Spanish court; but more than that, she displayed a truly masculine intelligence and strength of will. She was the born ruler, filled with an almost stubborn consciousness of her position, wont to command, unyielding in all questions which involved the royal authority and the preservation of the Faith. Philip could be satisfied with her. Her correspondence as regent and her letters to her father in Yuste are undeniable proofs of her political skill. Only a year before her death a companion of the Venetian Antonio Tiepolo thus described the Infanta: "This princess is now about thirty-six years old, of great charm, delicate features, brown hair and a pale complexion, tall and slender – a dazzling vision. Her behaviour is queenly, and she has moreover intelligence and understanding. To me it seems that she resembles her brother Don John of Austria in charm and goodness of heart." Something of what the Italian saw in the Infanta the court painter Antonio Moro has succeeded in capturing in his portrait of Juana, which to-day hangs in the Prado at Madrid.[44]

The painting indeed betrays something more. It is borne out by the

54

documents and by graphological study of her handwriting, which we can admire in the letters written to Ignatius, with its magnificently careless strokes, imperious yet with a concealed uncertainty. Her spirit was overshadowed not only by the brief tragedy of her marriage, but by the whole burden of her descent from families intimately related by blood. Thus in her letters to Ignatius we read again and again of her illnesses. It has been asserted that this granddaughter of Joanna the Mad was herself insane for years. This is an error. We do indeed hear once in 1568, that Juana's mental balance was disturbed for a time; but she kept till her death not only her beauty, but also her sound political judgment and her royal bearing.[45]

This statement is of importance for the right understanding of a feature of her life which was to bring her into the closest contact with Ignatius and the Jesuits. When in 1557, the Venetian ambassador in Flanders reported with some surprise that this beautiful princess led a kind of monastic life, he was describing from hearsay what was in fact the truth, though a closely guarded secret: the daughter of Charles V was a member of the Society of Jesus.[46] How this came about, and for what reasons the Emperor's daughter, regent of the Spanish kingdoms, sought admittance to the Society, we must now explain.

It was quite understandable that the Infanta on returning from Portugal should have had thoughts of renouncing the world. Visits to her slowly dying grandmother in Tordesillas strengthened this inclination. We know that the princess wrote to Father Borgia from Portugal, asking him to place himself at her disposal, as she must on her return, in spite of her deep mourning, take over the regency. Scarcely had she reached Valladolid than she began lengthy discussions with her spiritual adviser Borgia "concerning the manner of ruling without forgetting to attend to the spiritual life". "The regent's palace is more like a convent", wrote Father Bustamente in April 1555 to Ignatius. For Father Borgia himself, indeed, his sojourn at the regent's court was like banishment; but Ignatius charged him under obedience with the care of the Infanta's soul, in spite (as was expressly noted) of his somewhat imperfect theological training. It is delightful to read, in the letters which Ignatius received and Polanco included in his history of the Society, how the court ladies amused themselves with the pious card-games of their aristocratic confessor; how the regent daily prayed the Rosary of the Holy Name for Borgia, or sent food and sweetmeats to the Jesuits in Valladolid and Simancas. These Borgia one day repaid, on his return from the deathbed of Queen Joanna, by giving her a piece of bread with some pork, which he had begged on the road; and the regent accepted it with greater joy than if it had been a conquered city.

55

The princess had certainly at an earlier date, probably after her husband's death, made a vow to enter the Franciscan Order at a suitable opportunity.[47] While she was regent, there could, of course, be no question of this. It does not appear that she had obtained from the Roman Penitentiary a dispensation to exchange this vow for an equivalent one. Be that as it may, the idea of joining the new Society of Jesus grew in her mind with astonishing rapidity during the summer months of 1554, doubtless under the influence of Borgia and Araoz. It will be seen later in another connexion that, unlike Ignatius, Father Araoz, who had become rather too much at home in the society of aristocratic ladies, considered a female branch of the Society to be desirable, and had encouraged several women with hopes of establishing one. He too was especially dear to the Princess, and on the feast of St. Sebastian (the name-day of the son she had left behind in Portugal) he preached in her presence on the virtues of princes. He would certainly not have been the one to dissuade her from such thoughts. Father Francis Borgia informed Ignatius in Rome of the regent's decision. After all that the General had experienced ten years before with similar projects of pious ladies, we can imagine the shock that this news – which had its political implications – caused him.[48] A lively correspondence now began, in which the Infanta always appeared under the pseudonym of Mateo Sánchez, so that the devout audacity of the Spanish regent might not become known. In October 1554, Ignatius summoned a conference of the most sagacious of his fellow-religious, to discuss with them the possibility of accepting Mateo Sánchez as a member. From the document in which the results of this meeting are recorded, one senses the embarrassment of the fathers in Rome. A refusal of the obviously very definite request of Her Highness was simply impossible. On the other hand, the nineteen-year-old widow was naturally still so much a possible subject for the Habsburg matrimonial policy that no irremovable obstacle to marriage, such as the taking of religious vows, could be considered. So the fathers decided to give Mateo Sánchez permission to take the vows of a scholastic in the Society of Jesus, according to the provisions laid down in the fifth part of the Constitutions. The peculiarity of this form of vows, newly introduced by Ignatius and only after lengthy opposition, consists in the fact that though they are permanently binding vows of poverty, chastity, and obedience, only the individual who makes them is bound by them, while the Society reserves to itself the freedom to release from them for just causes. This interpretation, primarily intended for Jesuits still undergoing training, very opportunely relieved the General from his embarrassment in this particular case: he did not have to refuse his royal petitioner, and yet her acceptance could if necessary be revoked.[49] A memorial contains the result of these deliberations.

IHS

Information about the acceptance of a person into the Society and of the manner of procedure.

Dr. Nadal, Dr. Olave, Dr. Madrid, P. Luis Gonçalves and Master Polanco have taken counsel together by order of our Father Master Ignatius, to treat of the manner of admitting Mateo Sánchez into the Society by virtue of a bull from the apostolic Penitentiary which commutes the simple vow of the religion of St. Francis into ours. If, on the one hand, we regard our constitutions which forbid such an admission, and the privileges of our foundation bulls, we cannot be forced to accept such a charge. On the other hand, understanding that three persons of like condition were admitted in the early days of the Society, and in view of the terms of the above-mentioned bull,[50] we have resolved on the following:

That this person be admitted, and that the admission might be fittingly made in the way in which the scholars of the Society are received, on probation, it being made clear to the said person that for two years (and longer if it seem good to the superior), it is usual to be on probation, and that until this period has elapsed our constitutions do not impose any obligation to take a vow of any kind. If anyone, however, makes a vow of his own free will before this time has elapsed, in conformity with the Society's constitutions he should make it in this form:

My God and my Creator, eternal Father and Lord of all things, I, N., although in all things I find myself most unworthy to appear and present myself before your divine Majesty, yet looking to your infinite mercies and with the desire of serving you (through the help of your most holy grace) always and without end, I hereby make a vow and promise to your most sacred and divine Majesty, in the presence of the most glorious Virgin Mary and of the whole court of heaven, to enter the congregation of the Society of Jesus and to live and die therein. In this order I promise perpetual poverty, chastity and obedience, interpreted according to the constitutions of the said Society. I beseech your divine mercy to accept me as a pleasing sacrifice through the blood of Christ our Lord, and to vouchsafe to grant me the grace to accomplish what you have deigned to make me desire and offer.

In such a place, on such a day, month and year.

Whoever makes such a vow is a religious of the Society, as may be seen from the sixth part of the constitutions.

It further seemed that it should be explained to this person that such vows have full force and vigour just so long as the superior wants to keep in the Society the person making them, and no longer. If this person is admitted in this form, on probation for two years, during which there is no obligation to make a vow, if, nevertheless, a private vow is made, after the probation of two years the obligation of the initial vow must be fulfilled by entering the Society in the ordinary way.

Similarly the above-mentioned fathers were of opinion that whosoever the person may be, since they are admitted to the Society with such a special privilege and on that alone, they should keep the admission under the seal of secrecy and as in confession, because, if it came to be known, it might be taken as a precedent, so that some other person of like condition would trouble the Society for a similar admission.

As to the rest, this person shall not have to change their dress, or residence, nor to give any demonstration whatever of what it is sufficient should be kept between themselves and God our Lord. The Society, or someone from it, shall have the obligation of the care of this person's soul, in so far as it is demanded by God's service and the comfort of that soul, to the glory of God our Lord.

Rome, October 26th, 1554

To Father Francis Borgia

Thus it came about that the daughter of that Emperor who was never favourable to the Jesuits became a true member of the Society of Jesus. The immediate preparations still took a few months. In November 1554, Ignatius had to ask the Pope for commutation of the regent's previous vow to join the Franciscans, without, of course, mentioning her real name. At the same time he hastened to write once more to Spain, saying that although Mateo Sánchez could be accepted, this must remain an absolute exception[51].

When all the formalities were completed, Ignatius could send in a formal letter to the Regent at Salamanca the actual permission to enter the Society. With perfect tact and diplomatic skill, the princess was informed of everything necessary, without an uninitiated reader's being able to learn the real nature of the letter's contents.

My Lady in our Lord,

The sovereign grace and eternal love of Christ our Lord be always with us, to our continual help and favour.

From a letter from Father Francis Borgia I have understood what a great service it would be to you that we should comply with the pious and holy desires of a certain person. Although there was no small difficulty in the matter, we put such difficulty second to the will we all have and should have to serve Your Highness in our Lord.

Because Father Francis will speak of the details of which Your Highness will wish to be informed, since I have confidence in whatever he will say on my behalf, I shall say no more, but humbly beg Your Highness to consider us all as a thing very much yours, since we are so in our Lord.

I beseech the divine and sovereign goodness that he give us all his abundant grace that we may always know his holy will and accomplish it perfectly.

Ignatius

Rome, January 3rd, 1555

To the Princess, Salamanca

It was in this case more than the customary Spanish politeness, when Ignatius asked the regent to regard the whole Society as her own property; for the royal lady Jesuit henceforth took full advantage of the offer. Like an echo of this letter are the words she used when spending the night at the Jesuit house in Simancas, when on one of her visits to her dying grandmother: "I regard all houses of the Jesuits as my own." We do not indeed know when and with what formalities the princess's vows were made, a sign of the secrecy with which all was performed, doubtless thanks to Father Borgia.[52]

From now on the regent felt herself a full member of the Society, with all the duties and claims that this involved; and she could make claims too. Her co-operation was often of decisive importance for the prosperity of the works undertaken by the Society in Spain, where its progress was more rapid than elsewhere. With royal self-assurance Juana intervened to stop the persecution of the Jesuits that had broken out in Saragossa, where a mob was going about with banners and smashing the windows of the "Ignatians". The regent's letters to the archbishop and to the viceroy at Saragossa are among her most caustic political documents; and how respectfully yet inflexibly she defended the Jesuits against the attacks of the great Dominican Melchor Cano!

Murmurs began to arise in Spain and especially in court circles against the "Jesuit government" of Valladolid, and there were those who looked forward to the return of the Emperor and his son, who would no doubt soon put a stop to Juana's "jesuitical practices". All the greater then was the princess's joy when Father Borgia in his long talks with the Emperor at Jarantilla and Yuste persuaded the world-weary monarch to take a more favourable view of the new Society. In 1556 Borgia was able to report to Ignatius from Simancas that the regent had promised to be their advocate, on the return of her father and brother to Spain, so that "certain matters" might be ordered more satisfactorily. By "certain matters" are meant no doubt Ignatius' efforts to gain a foothold in Flanders.[53]

Now Ignatius began in his characteristic way to make use of Juana's services, as he always did with the women he had won for the Kingdom of God, each according to her position in life. The General took the princess's vocation seriously. Hardly a letter reached Spain in which Borgia or Araoz and other fathers were not informed of the regent's services or asked to report on them. Thus the attention of the princess was to be tactfully drawn to the needs of the Roman College; or again, she gave 3000 ducats towards the founding of a college at Valladolid. To the Emperor, still in Flanders, and to her sister, Juana wrote with her own hand letters in favour of the Louvain foundation. Ignatius employed the regent's good offices, as he had formerly those of her brother, in promoting his long-cherished project of reforming the Spanish nunneries. In order to gain an audience with Pope Paul IV, elected on May 23rd, 1555, and mistrustful of Ignatius and his Society, the General got the princess, through Borgia, to give him some simple message of a devotional character to carry to the Holy Father and to ask for a polite letter of introduction to the Pope.[54] It is, indeed, amazing for what apparent trivialities the regent's help was invoked, as, for instance, when she undertook the settlement of a sordid dispute about an inheritance for Father Doménech in Valencia; or when Ignatius asked her to write to the Pope concerning canonical difficulties respecting Don Antonio de Córdoba's property. In his review of the state of the Society at the beginning of 1555, secretary Polanco, secretly aware of the Infanta's peculiar position with regard to the Jesuits, writes: "The Princess Regent of Spain has such an affection for the Society that one can think of no other person of high or low degree who has more. She shows it by favouring our cause in every way, and this she does with quite especial love and with sincere confidence in the fathers of this Society."

We can understand then that Ignatius could write in the last year of his life, having in mind the daughter of his imperial señor natural who had become his own daughter: "This is an infinite consolation to us." Juana, too, always showed herself a grateful daughter of such a father. The best evidence of this is the letter of recommendation for the Society of Jesus which the regent sent Pope Paul IV through the Spanish ambassador in Rome. It was certainly too with Ignatius' wishes in mind that Juana by her influence prevented

Father Borgia's elevation to the cardinalate.[55] A proof of the seriousness with which Ignatius and his successors took the princess's membership of the Society, despite its unique and secret nature, are the repeated reports to Rome on her progress in virtue. In these letters about the princess the pseudonym Montoya is used. Thus in October 1558, Borgia wrote to the General Laynez: "She grows daily in the spiritual life and in pious submission to the Society; I think she is one of those who fully understand the nature of the Society, and she has in truth a good will for all our affairs." The novice-master of Juana's favourite novitiate at Simancas bears witness to the same: "Her Highness said she regarded everything belonging to the Society of Jesus as her own." A few years before her death Borgia wrote to Father Nadal: "Montoya is just as well disposed towards us as ever, nay more so."[56]

Perhaps the gossips were not far wrong when they called the regent's courts jesuitical and described her palace as a convent. With such descriptions may be compared the utterance of a pious and thoughtful Jesuit who – somewhat later, it is true – made the bitter remark that the College in Valladolid was "more like a state chancellery than a religious house". Not all Jesuits were saints like Francis Borgia, who found the "Egyptian air" of the court hard to breathe. Evil tongues did not spare even him, and went as far as to accuse him of immoral relations with the regent. It cannot be denied that the former duke, who combined diplomatic skill with other-worldly asceticism, became daily more and more indispensable to the Princess, striving after eternal things in the midst of innumerable cares of state. She prevailed upon him, in spite of his initial refusal, to undertake the executorship of the dead Emperor's will, according to Charles' wishes. Scarcely a day went by on which either he or Araoz was not called upon to give advice. Ignatius observed these developments with anxiety, for he saw both the apostolic freedom and the independence of the Society's government thereby endangered. The best thing to do was to recall the two Jesuits;[57] but now Ignatius was to see what it meant to have allowed an emperor's daughter to join the Society. When Juana complained, he hastened to write a reassuring letter to the princess, to the effect that there could be no question of transferring the two fathers without express approval of the regent. Ignatius' actual letter is lost. The princess's joyful answer, sent on February 7th, 1556, is all the more revealing. Certainly the General in Rome, used to obedience, had never received such a letter, at once so full of piety and yet so royally presumptuous in its demands.

Most reverend Father,

Father Nadal gave me a letter of yours at which I greatly rejoiced. What you say in it gives me double reason for favouring the Society, since you do not want Father Francis' departure to take place without my consent. For this I am extremely grateful to you; it is the greatest satisfaction you can give me, since I could not but feel deeply the loss I should thereby sustain. Certainly it seems to me that I should not do what I ought if I allowed him to go, because things here are developing in such a manner that a man of his sort will reap a great harvest here and is more necessary than he is anywhere else. I feel the same about Dr. Araoz and thus I have commanded them under no circumstances to go away.

I well believe that when you know this and the satisfaction you are giving me thereby, you will not want things to be otherwise and thus I beg this of you. Because, however, these two fathers cannot go anywhere without my leave, you must give me authority over them, so that what they are ordered may be done through holy obedience; in this you will give me very great pleasure.

Because I know how careful the whole Society is to commend to God their Majesties and us, I do not want to ask this again, except that you will remember me specially, that it may please our Lord to make me his (true) servant.

The Princess

Valladolid, February 7th, 1556

To the Reverend Father Ignatius, General of the Society of Jesus,
   from the most illustrious Princess of Portugal,
   Regent of the Kingdom of Spain

A classic example of the difficulties into which Ignatius could get through the regent's devout imperiousness is the story of the marriage of Father Borgia's stepbrother. We must treat this case rather more in detail, because we owe to it a second letter from the regent to Ignatius, and also because this court tragedy was later to be the cause of King Philip's dislike of the Jesuits, which for a time made life in Spain positively dangerous for them. Don Pedro Luis Galcerán de Borja, born in 1528, had, after a stormy election and thanks to the intrigues of his family at court, been elected Grand Master of the Order of Montesa. Then, in the palace of the Infanta, he got to know a Portuguese lady, Doña Leonor Manuel, Juana's principal lady-in-waiting. Leonor was very dear to the princess and had till then gladly joined in all the religious devotions of that remarkable court of Valladolid. Don Galcerán de Borja for his part had, doubtless under the influence of his stepbrother, made the Spiritual Exercises of St. Ignatius. But now it was the voice of love that spoke; and the Infanta would not have been a woman if she had not attempted to arrange a marriage – an activity she usually enjoyed. The chief obstacle was that Don Galcerán, as Grand Master of the Order of Montesa, had taken a vow of celibacy and consequently could be released therefrom only by the Holy See. There is no doubt that the relations between the lovers at the regent's court had already led to malicious talk. It was high time for the Crown to use all its influence to bring about an early marriage. The request for a dispensation went indeed by the regular channels from the princess through the nuncio to Rome; but the experienced regent cannot have had much hope that it would be speedily dealt with by the Roman courts. Therefore the daughter of Ignatius tried another way. She knew that her Father in Christ was accustomed to the skilful and expeditious settlement of such affairs. So on May 28th, 1556, a messenger was despatched to Rome with two letters: one from the impatient lover himself, desiring to be released from his vow, the other from the regent in person to Ignatius with the command – once more expressed piously yet brooking no refusal – to take the matter up, the prompt settlement of which she desired "terribly" *(terriblemente)*.[58] To make the situation clear, we print first the letter of the eager Grand Master.

Very reverend Lord and most illustrious Father,

For Your Paternity to receive me as your son, no merit is great enough. If there were any sufficient, it would be my being Father Francis' brother, and a very great sinner, and I am not certain which of these two things would move Your Paternity most. The reasons which move me are so many that I shall not begin to relate them, but beg Your Paternity to count me as one of your number in obedience, love and reverence, for in this our time, and I say this without any wish to flatter, there is no one more devoted to God's honour than you.

The knight of my Order who brings this letter comes to you on account of the business that Her Highness has written to Your Paternity about. The intercession for which I humbly ask is not with the Pope, but that Your Paternity should do me the kindness of recommending the matter to our Lord – that if he is to be served in this new vocation, he will permit it, and if not, not: for even this detachment remains easy for me, now I have once done the Exercises. I beg Your Paternity to

63

give me your blessing and to remember me, for my troubles, and difficulties, both as regard body and soul indeed need this.

May our Lord guard Your Paternity's very reverend person, so that the fruit in all Christendom which is thus each day multiplied through you may increase.

Your Paternity's obedient son and servant who kisses your hands,

Simancas, May 28th, 1556   Grand Master Peter Borja

To Ignatius Loyola, from
   Pedro Luis Galcerán de Borja

Such was the lover's petition, modest indeed, and filled with an almost anxious expectation. Quite different is the precisely worded letter of the Spanish regent to Ignatius.

Most reverend Father,

You will already have learnt that negotiations are being made for a marriage between the Grand Master of Montesa, brother of Father Francis, and Doña Leonor Manuel, of whose qualities and good parts and of how much I desire to favour them, you will already have been informed by Father Francis and the Provincial.[59] Both hold you and the whole Society in great affection, and therefore, I shall speak no further of the matter here. Since all the rest is arranged, and from the result great service to our Lord is hoped for as a means of quietening certain passions, as you must already know, all that is wanting is His Holiness' dispensation for the Grand Master, whose name is Don Pedro de Borja, since he is a Knight of the Order of Montesa and St. George. And although I am certain that His Holiness, when he is informed of the just reasons there are for this, will readily grant it, and the nuncio is petitioning for it on my behalf and himself hopes for a most favourable answer, I ask that you, in all earnestness, as my devotedness to you deserves, should entreat His Holiness about the matter, doing so on my behalf also if you think fit, and that as far as in you lies you act with the prudence God has given you to the end that the thing be done quickly. This was the reason I wanted to entrust this to you, knowing the willingness with which your Charity will do it.

I do not write expressly to His Holiness, since I have treated of the matter with his nuncio. The urgency of this business I commend much to you, because I have a terrible desire for it, which is a good thing for thus it may be carried out the better. I ask you earnestly to remember to commend the matter fervently to our Lord in your prayers, and I also ask you at this time to remember me.

The Princess

From Valladolid, May 28th, 1556

To Father Ignatius of Loyola
from Princess Juana, Regent of Spain

The letter of his impatient spiritual daughter reached the world-weary Ignatius when he was already weakened by his final illness. Whether he ever made any approach to Pope Paul IV, or achieved anything with that notorious enemy of Spain, we do not know. Certain it is that several years went by after Ignatius' death, and the dispensation was still not granted. Soon Father Francis Borgia had to bear the whole burden of Juana's impatience instead of the dead General. With a sigh he wrote in March 1559 to the new General, Laynez: "Were it not for the salvation of souls and the edification of my neighbour, I would not write two lines in this affair, let alone whole letters." For Don Galcerán de Borja had in 1558, obviously with the regent's foreknowledge, found a strange solution to his problem. He made short work of the matter by availing himself of the dispensation which Pope Paul III had granted in 1543 to the Order of Calatrava, permitting its members to contract marriage, on the ground that that Order was an offshoot of the Order of Montesa. Philip II was furious at this, and let the full weight of his displeasure fall upon Father Borgia, who, hitherto favoured by Juana, was now being gradually eclipsed by the more versatile Father Araoz. With truth has an historian said of this question of the Grand Master of Montesa's marriage: "By his example the Grand Master of Montesa opened the way for as many knights of his Order as wished to take to themselves wives, and there were many such." Only in 1588 did Sixtus V grant ecclesiastical permission for the conversion of the Order into a secular order of knighthood. In 1560 Doña Leonor bore a son, who, it is true, died shortly after; but the father had a brilliant political career before him, and no less a person than Cervantes composed verses in his honour.[60]

This matrimonial affair, the history of which reveals so much of Juana's character, was settled only in the year when Philip II finally returned to Spain and the regency of his sister came to an end; but the very fact of the princess's withdrawal from the political stage raised the problem of her religious vocation in a more acute form. What, in view of the vows she had taken, was she now to do? One thing was certain: even now she could not openly admit that she belonged to the Society of Jesus. To bury herself in a convent was not her intention, nor would that have suited Philip's policy. His politically experienced sister must be ready at any time to fit in with his plans. So Juana remained at court, which had meanwhile been set up at Madrid. She also remained under the spiritual direction of the Jesuits. After Borgia's fall from favour and his retirement to Lisbon and Rome, Araoz, who had long been indispensable, became the spiritual leader of her household, which grew more and more like a convent.[61] Ignatius was forced to admit, in the last year of his life, how dear Araoz had become to the princess, and realized that there could be no question of his recall. Father Araoz, who was related to the founder through Ignatius' sister-in-law Magdalena de Araoz, had made an excellent beginning as an ascetic and apostolic religious under the saint's direction. Now that Ignatius was dead, he allowed himself to be gradually transformed by the palace air of Valladolid and Madrid into a somewhat self-willed Jesuit, who caused his superiors a great deal of trouble. Whoever in the last ten years of the princess's life desired any favour from her, sought to get it through her spiritual director. "There is nobody at court," writes a Jesuit father, "who does not wait upon him: dukes, counts, and the lords of the Council." General Laynez must have read with some anxiety the rather vain report of Father Duarte Pereira: "Many lords and gentlemen, as well as the princess's master of the horse and a number of her pages, besides the Countesses Olivares and Ribagorza, come to us for confession."[62]

Meanwhile Borgia had persuaded the pious Infanta, evidently mindful of her former Franciscan vow, to execute in 1577 a plan which had already been discussed during Ignatius' lifetime. Next to the palace of Madrid, her birthplace, she founded a convent of discalced Poor Clares, *Nuestra Señora de la Consolación*. The people at once named this royal foundation *Las Descalzas reales*. To this convent Juana devoted all her affection and her princely generosity. The first superioress came from Gandía, from the ducal nunnery of the Borja family – Ana de Borja, half-sister of Father Francis, who took office under the name of Juana de la Cruz. She was of the same age as the princess and a woman of royal disposition. For fourteen years this daughter of St. Francis of Assisi waged war with King Philip against rigid adherence to the principle of admitting only ladies of noble birth and the liberal interpretation of religious poverty in Juana's foundation. The princess herself had now given up all idea of entering the cloister. Adjoining her convent she did, indeed, have some rooms fitted up, to which she was wont to retire for spiritual meditation. There too she occasionally received visits from the great St. Teresa, who showed the noble ladies, with their playing at being nuns, what true poverty was, and nevertheless delighted them with her gay chatter. The princess's Franciscan daughters never ceased to wonder at so much natural amiability in a woman blessed with the revelations and sufferings of a mystic. "God be praised", they said – and it was also no doubt a consolation for Juana, who had never wholly embraced the religious life, "he has let us see a saint whom we can all emulate. She speaks like us, sleeps and eats like us, and is quite natural in conversation."[63]

Accounts of Juana's subsequent life tell us that she now and then stayed with King Philip, went to Aranjuez, coursed the hare with the little archdukes Ernest and Rudolph, and was able to devote herself undisturbed to her beloved music. We relate this to illustrate, as it were, the ascetic fate of her Jesuit vows, and to show how wise Ignatius was to leave Juana a way out.[64] Nor was her part in Habsburg matrimonial politics finished. At the end of her regency she was just twenty-four years old, beautiful, fond of ruling, and in every way an emperor's daughter; but even for that period, what we read of Philip's plans for his sister's marriage from 1560 onwards is astonishing. At one time the prospective husband was the French King Charles IX; then, if we may believe the whisperings of the diplomats, the son of the Duke of Florence. Without regard for kinship or difference of age, marriages were suggested for her with the archdukes Ferdinand and Charles, her cousins, and even with her youthful nephew Rudolph, to whom she had played the part of a mother in Madrid. The climax of this uninhibited matrimonial policy was, however, the apparently serious project of marrying the princess to her nephew Don Carlos, Philip's pathological son. We will not enquire how far these plans, which were transmitted to Vienna by Adam von Dietrichstein, the imperial ambassador in Madrid, were successful, nor if Juana herself really promoted them for dynastic reasons or even out of an unrestrained passion for ruling. Be that as it may, it was said at court that it was necessary to give the half-mad prince a wife who knew how to rule and who could make up for his deficiency by her intelligence. We can see from the careful account that Nadal wrote to Borgia that this political tragedy within the Spanish royal family was also discussed by the fathers with much anxiety.[65]

History tells us that nothing came of all these projects. Juana continued her half-religious, half-courtly way of life till her death. Her spiritual director Borgia meanwhile became General of the Jesuits. Again and again he asked for news from Madrid of the illnesses of his daughter in Christ and of her retired life among the *Descalzas reales*. In his spiritual diary he carefully notes the prayers he said for Juana. When the news of the victory of Lepanto set Spain aflame with rejoicing, the former regent asked the messenger pertinent questions on the strategy of the battle. Soon afterwards the battle of life, too, was over for her. On September 7th, 1573, the emperor's daughter entered into eternal life, the only female Jesuit in the Church's history.[66]

The Infanta Isabel of Portugal

IGNATIUS' relations with the royal family of Portugal (those, that is, which had no direct connexion with ecclesiastical policy) were not confined to his sending of relics to the one-time lady of his affections, Queen Catherine. Another event, this time of the most painful nature, compelled him to send a letter to the royal palace at Lisbon. It was the affair of Don Teotonio de Braganza's vocation, which almost developed into a scandal for the young Society of Jesus. The Dukes of Braganza, "whose house is the first after the Royal Family in the Kingdom of Portugal", were related many times over to the reigning dynasty. At the time of King John III, his younger brother, Duarte, Duke of Guimaraens, was married to Isabel, daughter of Duke Jaime of Braganza. Isabel's brother Teodosio inherited the ducal title, while her younger brother Teotonio thought of devoting himself to the Church, as did so many younger sons of noble families.[67] In 1549 the seventeen-year-old youth was studying at Coimbra, and there he was attracted by the Society of Jesus, whose Portuguese province had, to Ignatius' great joy, flourished exceedingly under the leadership of Simon Rodríguez. Teotonio was always, it appears, given to eccentric behaviour; for in the middle of the night he climbed over the wall of his college and ran away to join the Jesuits, whereupon violent protests were made by the ducal family, especially by the Infanta Isabel. However, the king and Queen Catherine (who was so friendly with Rodríguez) were too just to employ against Teotonio the force which his sister demanded. The young nobleman remained in the Society. His fellow-religious at Coimbra and Evora were delighted with the kinsman of royalty and his striving after virtue. They praised him in a letter to Rome as their "true duke and brother, who more than anyone else is a model for others". To this Polanco, the Society's historian, was later to add resignedly: "Ah, would that things had remained thus!"[68]

The admission into the Society of a man of such high birth was, like that of Duke Francis Borgia or Don Antonio de Córdoba, an event that stirred the courts of Europe. Ignatius was obliged, in a letter to Flanders of January 12th, 1552, to deny the rumours circulating at the court of Queen María, governor of the Netherlands, that the Jesuits kept promising young men in the Society against the will of their parents. In it he himself relates the story of Don

Teotonio in the following words: "In recent years a young man of the highest nobility in the kingdom of Portugal, the son of the Duke of Braganza, a family which in that country ranks next to the royal house, felt a serious and persistent call to join our Society. Therefore he climbed one night over the wall of the college where he lodged and betook himself to our fathers in Coimbra. When they took him in, his kinsfolk, as is usual in such cases, were beside themselves, and set everything in motion to get the young man out of our house. They importuned the king to command that the young man should go elsewhere, in order the better to think over the ordering of his life; but he firmly refused to leave the house of the Society, fearing the dangers that awaited his vocation outside, and our fathers defended him before the king with such Christian reasons, that all the efforts of his family remained unavailing. So the young man, whose name is Teotonio, is still a member of the Society."[69]

On account of his somewhat weak health, Teotonio continued his studies at Salamanca. At the Portuguese court they were not at all pleased with this "Castilian" exile of the duke's son. One suspects the truth: Teotonio was an ardent partisan of Simon Rodríguez, who had meanwhile become involved in a tragic difference with Ignatius. Letters were exchanged between Ignatius and Teotonio, who wrote from Salamanca and later from Alcalá. At the beginning of 1553, Rodríguez himself came to Alcalá. Now began, as Polanco expresses it, "the tragedy of Master Teotonius". Rodríguez went back to Portugal of his own accord, "on medical advice", and against the General's wishes; Teotonio also went back to Portugal after some hesitation, interrupting his journey to Rome (undertaken by desire of Ignatius) at Barcelona, so as to "protect his dear Rodríguez". In vain Ignatius invited him in two friendly letters to come to Rome; generously he even relieved Teotonio of the duty of obedience; but the disobedient young nobleman had in the meantime settled himself comfortably at Villaviciosa, seat of the Braganzas, with his mother. Ignatius learnt from Father Mirón in a detailed account, dated January 2rd, 1554, of Teotonio's bad behaviour. But the patience of the father with his undutiful son, expressed in charming little letters, was unconquerable. All at once Teotonio declared himself willing to go to India or Brazil under obedience, nay, even to Rome; on April 18th, 1554, he appealed to Ignatius: "Help me, I pray, out of this abyss!"

Meanwhile, Ignatius had already acted. In a truly moving letter he again ordered Teotonio to come to Rome. He may have suspected what lay before him, for on the same day he wrote to the Portuguese provincial: "I will burden myself with him here in Rome, as long as you are rid of him." In fact Teotonio, on Father Borgia's advice and without taking leave of the court at Lisbon, now set off from Corunna with Philip's wedding party for

England, whence he rode through Flanders and Germany to Italy. The provincial Mirón had to bear the consequences in Portugal. The duchess, Teotonio's mother, and the Infanta Isabel, whose passionate nature clearly resembled her brother's, were furious at this too severe test of obedience to which their dearly loved son and brother was being subjected. "The Infanta is after all these events not at all so zealously in favour of the Society", wrote Father Mirón on August 2nd, 1554, to Ignatius. From Polanco's chronicle we learn of another reason: the Braganza family feared that it and the Portuguese court would be exposed to ridicule if Teotonio, already known everywhere as an *enfant terrible*, went to Rome.[70]

Ignatius, who was genuinely looking forward to the arrival of this difficult son of his, was to suffer a disappointment even before the latter reached the Eternal City. Father Simon Rodríguez, who with infinite trouble had been brought to order again, had shortly before left Rome for Venice, with the intention of making a pilgrimage to Jerusalem, or at least, as in the happy days of 1537, of devoting himself to contemplation in some Lombard hermitage. Then news reached Ignatius that Don Teotonio had met his beloved Rodríguez in Venice. From his letters we can see what a shock it was to Ignatius; it was just such a meeting that he had at all costs wished to avoid, and he had therefore delayed Teotonio's journey as long as Rodríguez was still in Rome. At once he wrote to the Jesuit superior in Venice: "We do not know what the pair of them are up to." Master Simon was obviously having a bad effect on the young man's attitude towards the Society, which had been improving since April; Teotonio was to be directed gently but firmly to proceed to Rome. But Don Teotonio had his own ideas about obedience. It needed three more letters from Ignatius – already, heaven knows, more than occupied with other things – to persuade the young religious to set out for Rome. On September 22nd, 1554, Ignatius wrote an affectionate letter; four days later a command under obedience was sent post-haste to Venice, which in turn was followed by an explanation to the effect that the command was not binding under pain of sin. On October 3rd Teotonio left Venice, and he reached Rome on October 14th.[71]

Polanco specially mentions in his chronicle that Ignatius gave his undutiful son an affectionate reception. At first, Teotonio's behaviour was encouraging; then in February 1555 he was slightly ill, and already unfavourable comments were being made at the Portuguese court about the poor brother's harsh treatment. He found his theological studies difficult, a fact which was also known in the ducal home at Villaviciosa. Teotonio's brother, Duke Teodosio, wrote a ceremoniously polite letter to Ignatius on the subject, in which we sense all the noble family's displeasure. "I consider that my brother is of a religious disposition, that he is a friend of our Lord and of every virtue. It is true that he is less suited for study; but his inclination for prayer is all the greater." Apparently the Duke's sister, the Infanta Isabel, also wrote to Ignatius at the same time in her brother's favour. At the great farewell ceremony which took place in the royal palace at Lisbon in honour of twelve Jesuits about to leave for India, the Infanta wept tears of emotion and said: "How gladly would I see Teotonio among you!" In women, tears and anger often follow close upon one another: that Ignatius knew. So, while he prudently answered the duke's letter by return of post, he carefully put that of the Infanta away in a drawer for the time being. In her case, as the answer would go straight to the royal palace, it would have to be thought over several times. To the duke, Ignatius said that everything was being done for Don Teotonio, especially were efforts being made to help him in his studies, in spite of his inclination to prayer. Whether he would make progress or not could not yet, indeed, be stated with certainty. This sounded very cool. Ignatius had in the course of long talks with Teotonio soon discovered what spirit really prompted him, and pressed him to make a clearcut decision. In February 1555, he was already able to write to the Infanta Don Luis of Portugal: "Teotonio is well. He has decided either to be a good religious or to leave the Society of Jesus." It was at this time that Teotonio with many tears begged the General's pardon for all his faults and renewed his vows. All seemed to be well again, and in August of the same year Ignatius had a remarkable conversation with young Teotonio about the humility of an aristocrat entering the Society.[72]

It was in vain. How seriously Ignatius took Teotonio's case appears from the fact that at the beginning of July 1555, he asked twelve of the most respected fathers in Rome to enquire into it and to test the young man's vocation. We still have the written report which Fathers Salmerón and Miona handed to Ignatius. It is as follows: "Having regard to the disposition of mind in which Don Teotonio was at the beginning of July, when the undersigned spoke to him, we declare that we conscientiously consider Teotonio, if he do not alter and improve, to be unsuitable for the Society of Jesus. And this we confirm with our signatures. Dated July 25th, 1555."[73]

Towards autumn, notes Polanco, "Don Teotonio's spiritual restlessness began anew." Resignedly, Ignatius had to inform Father Mirón in Lisbon that Teotonio was a hopeless case. He described in detail (clearly so that the court might know of it) what this strange religious had been doing during the summer holidays. Now Teotonio wished to leave the Society, because he "had not found in the Society of Jesus that perfection which he expected". He was continually making exceptions and requiring privileges; he had two or three infirmarians to look after him; he wished to make excursions for a fortnight at a time; he needed organ music to calm his nerves; he did not study and had faith only in Master Simon Rodríguez. On September 1st, another list of scandals was despatched to Portugal. Teotonio was leaving the house of his own accord whenever he wished and having dealings with the Portuguese ambassador Alonso Lancastre, who was driven to despair by the impulsive young man and feared for the good name of the royal kinsman. On the evening of the day when Ignatius wrote this report, there took place at the door of the Roman College a truly disgraceful scene, a description of which he did not fail to add to the letter. The rector, Father Olave, had had the door guarded, but the returning Brother Teotonio used force, and loudly abused the rector with these words: "You are not my superior, and I am no longer a Jesuit. I will not stick it another hour with you!" Beside himself with rage, Teotonio of Braganza bit one of the doorkeepers in the arm and struck another in the eye so that it bled.

Ignatius remained calm. Don Teotonio must choose another way of life. On September 3rd, the news was sent to Portugal that Teotonio was totally unfitted for the Society, and that "no further hope existed that he would give up his headstrong judgment and self-will". Teotonio, now much chastened, agreed after a good deal of persuasion from the ambassador to this solution[74]. On September 9th, the unsuccessful Jesuit left Rome. "God has delivered us from a great burden by the departure of this *hombre de cuestas*", wrote Ignatius with relief to the Portuguese provincial. But at the same time the diplomatic saint left the final decision about Don Teotonio to the King of Portugal, who on September 4th, was informed of the whole tragedy in a personal letter from Ignatius. "For Your Highness is not only King and Lord, but the Father of this lowly Company." To Duke Teodosio of Braganza the tone of his explanatory letter was somewhat colder. In it Ignatius, the Spanish hidalgo, dared to write: "The noble blood of Don Teotonio should have called him to a life of perfection."

Now at last Ignatius remembered that he still had a letter from the Infanta Isabel to answer. On the same September 3rd, his studied reply, masterly also in its skilful wording, was despatched to the princess.[75]

JESUS

My Lady in our Lord,

The sovereign grace and eternal love of Christ our Lord be with Your Highness, with his most holy gifts and spiritual blessings.

Up to the present I have not replied to a letter I have from Your Highness, in which you greatly recommended to me the studies of Don Teotonio and what was best suited to his peace of soul and spiritual consolation, because I desired before writing to see what effect would be produced by the measures that were taken here to that end. It is true that although many measures of every kind, some gentle, others severe, have been employed, such as we felt in our Lord might be suitable, we have not achieved what we sought, as Your Highness will be able to learn from our Father Provincial in the Kingdom of Portugal. This grieves us the more, as we have so much love for Don Teotonio and desire to serve Your Highness and your illustrious House to the glory of God's Majesty.

Don Teotonio will leave soon for Portugal, that plan seeming good to the ambassador and to myself, so that the king may examine his affairs and decide what is best. In whatever state of life he adopts, however, I and our whole Society will always hold him in affection and shall try by our prayers and what other means we can to help him to serve God our Lord and save his soul, for apart from the fact that charity moves us to this and apart from the considerable trouble and time spent over him up to the present (although I do not know how much he appreciates it) the respect for and desire of serving Your Highness and the Duke your brother, which we all have in our Lord, obliges us to this.

May Christ our Lord grant us all his light and grace so that we may always know his most holy will and fulfil it perfectly.

Rome, September 3rd, 1555   Ignatius

To the Infanta Dona Isabel, Duchess
   of Braganza

Teotonio departed in the company of Brother Andrew Fernández, to whom Ignatius gave exact travelling instructions which were also forwarded to the Portuguese king. Simon Rodríguez received a command to have nothing to do with Don Teotonio. After this remarkable scholastic had left, things came to light which thoroughly justified Ignatius' treatment of him. Teotonio had all this time being secretly keeping his two former servants in Rome, to attend to his private correspondence; and he had besides provided himself with a banking account of 500 ducats. He was soon, moreover, to bring embarrassment to his family, who were still full of ill will towards the Jesuits. In Lyons, where Fernández parted from Teotonio, the inconstant young man suddenly decided to go to Paris instead of to Portugal, and there to complete his theological studies. The last news Ignatius received of him was that Teotonio was said to be in Paris, but nothing further was known about him. Ignatius therefore wrote to the superior in Paris, Father Broët, that Don Teotonio was under no circumstances to be treated as a Jesuit.[76]

In Villaviciosa and Almeirim they were on the whole pleased about Teotonio's dismissal, for his theological studies at Paris opened the way to a brilliant ecclesiastical career for the young nobleman. The Duke of Braganza was petty enough to demand back from the Jesuits the 250 ducats that Teotonio had once given to the college at Coimbra, in order to pay for his brother's studies in Paris. At the court of the Regent María in Flanders excited whispers were once more circulating against the Jesuits, who had expelled such a highborn gentleman. Ignatius heard no more of all this; from the complications of this affair, too, he had been removed by death. The Infanta Isabel soon calmed down and she remained well disposed towards the Jesuits. Only the Marquesa de Elche, Don Teotonio's other sister, was bitter against the Society on account of her brother's dismissal.[77] It must also be mentioned that María, daughter of the Infanta Isabel, as consort of the great Alexander Farnese, did much for the Jesuits. Teotonio, too, later became a sincere well-wisher to the Society, after he had been made Archbishop of Evora – as was almost inevitable for a Braganza – in succession to Cardinal Enrique. What Ignatius of Loyola did not succeed in doing, St. Teresa attempted in letters of profound spirituality: to bring the divine peace into the soul of the ever-restless Braganza. Teotonio died on the 29th July 1602.[78]

Margaret of Austria

THE Habsburg princess on whom Ignatius exercised the most immediate influence was Margaret of Austria, the illegitimate daughter of Charles V, who later as regent of the Netherlands and mother of Duke Alexander Farnese helped to bring about the victory of the Society of Jesus in Flanders, which Ignatius had sought to achieve through Aunt María, and for which he had been labouring on the eve of his death. The relationship between Ignatius and Margaret is perhaps one of the best documented examples of the influence that the hidden power of a truly Christian spiritual direction can have even upon politics. For there is no doubt that Margaret rose to that degree of intellectual and political importance which an unbiassed judgment of history must accord her only through the influence of her confessor Ignatius. By nature and through the unhappy experience of her marriage, Margaret was a woman whom even a spiritual director of genius could hardly find an attractive penitent. "She displayed some markedly masculine characteristics, was self-willed and domineering, ungovernably proud and difficult to lead. She was distinguished neither by intelligence nor feminine charm, and liked to play the part of a misunderstood, injured, ill-treated woman." Thus Ludwig Pfandl judges her, perhaps a shade too harshly. Out of this unmanageable clay, Ignatius formed a great figure.[79]

Margaret had the opportunity to show this greatness only, it is true, after Philip II had appointed her governor of the Netherlands. The prudent and yet royally self-confident manner of ruling, which contemporary accounts of the years 1559–67 praise in her, has its roots no doubt in the firm spiritual foundation laid by Ignatius' skill as a confessor. When we read what her own secretary wrote to the king's private secretary about her, we can almost detect a note of that now supernaturalized ideal of loyal service to the king, which the erstwhile officer Iñigo de Loyola expressed in his letters to Philip: "Madame would die a hundred deaths in the service of God and the King. She has enough courage and strength of will to do so. For she loves the king and desires nothing, but to obey him."[80]

It is true that Margaret had a hard road to travel before she reached these heights. It is almost as though the time and circumstances of her birth linked her in some way with Ignatius. During the same war against France as that

75

in which Ignatius at Pamplona received the wound that changed the course of his life, the young Emperor Charles V was from October to December 1521 in the Burgundian castle of Oudenaarde, on the Netherlands front. In the service of the captain of the castle was a pretty maid, Johanna van der Gheynst, daughter of a tapestry-maker from the village of Nukerke. Margaret was the offspring of the Emperor's passing love-affair with this servant-maid. She was carefully brought up at Brussels under the guardianship of Aunt María, and the Emperor always acknowledged her as his daughter. Margaret herself and her contemporaries saw no shame in her illegitimate birth, nor did she, with her marked self-consciousness, ever forget her descent. Fifty years later the Belgian court historian Famian Strada S.J. endeavoured to gloss over her obscure origin; but that was only "a charming fairy-tale quite in the style of a courtly Jesuit father".[81]

After all that we have read about Charles' daughter Juana, it need not surprise us that the illegitimate daughter, too, played at an early age an important though subordinate part in the Emperor's matrimonial projects. In 1533 Margaret was sent to Italy, and from then on was allowed to call herself "de Austria". In February 1536, the magnificent wedding of the fourteen-year-old girl with Alexander de' Medici took place in Naples. Only a year later Alexander was murdered. Two new suitors at once appeared for the hand of the young widow, who brought as dowry the favour of the all-powerful Charles. Alexander's successor Cosimo de' Medici was unsuccessful in winning the Emperor's approval, and had by imperial command to content himself with Leonor of Toledo, daughter of the Spanish viceroy of Naples. (This lady, too, we shall meet in Ignatius' correspondence.) For in that very year the friendship of the reigning Pope, Paul III of the house of Farnese, was absolutely necessary to Charles V, therefore the second of Margaret's suitors was given preference: Ottavio Farnese, son of that Pierluigi whom Paul III as cardinal had begotten in 1503. On November 4th, 1538, there took place at the Vatican palace, with a display of refined luxury, the marriage between the grandson of the reigning pope and the natural daughter of the reigning emperor.[82] Only two weeks later, in the same palace and before the same Pope, appeared Master Ignatius of Loyola with his companions, in order to place themselves wholly in the service of the papacy, according to their vow of 1534, and after the final collapse of the Jerusalem project. These two events of November 1538 are, as it were, a symbol of the changing times: Renaissance and Reform stood face to face with one another.[83]

Ignatius did not then know that the bride of sixteen, forced at her father's command to marry the immature Farnese, would soon be his penitent and one of his most valiant helpers in his apostolic labours for the moral reform of Rome. First, the young wife had to go through a veritable hell. "It is a miserable marriage", wrote a cardinal at this time, "which has been concluded between Ottavio and his wife. They live together like cat and dog. The Pope and all his family are much put out over it." Charles V wrote sharply to his daughter, urging her to submission and wifely obedience. Margaret replied by using expressions "such as a Christian and still more a lady of her rank and an emperor's daughter ought not to use, and which the devil has put into her". A first-class scandal seemed to be in prospect: a serious quarrel threatened to break out between the two heads of Christendom because of the matrimonial squabbles of their illegitimate offspring. But then Margaret gave in. What had happened? History has been able only vaguely to indicate that here the influence of several members of the Society of Jesus, finally approved by Paul III in 1540, had been at work. The earliest records of the Society alone can give us a more detailed account of this historically important transformation.[84]

It was no doubt a piece of luck for the newly founded Society of Jesus when in 1540, at the express wish of the Pope, the Frenchman Father Jean Codure was appointed confessor to Madama (for thus the Romans called the Emperor's daughter). It was a good choice. Codure, who was, it is true, to die at thirty-three on August 29th, 1541, was, as a contemporary account testifies, "a venerable Father, a man of blameless life and burning with spiritual zeal", for whom Paul III had a real friendship. The Pope gave this priest the task of taming the Emperor's daughter, who was such an embarrassment for the Farnese family, and yet so necessary to them. Diego Laynez followed Codure in this office, and from 1542 it was Ignatius himself who had to visit the Palazzo Madama every week, where he also took over the spiritual direction of the ladies of the ducal court.[85]

In his biography of Ignatius, the historian Gothein aptly wrote: "Margaret was the first princess who took Jesuits as her confessors; the members of the Society in all parts of the world read with satisfaction of the implicit trust which the Emperor's daughter had in Ignatius and of her special request to him to baptize her twin sons. The prudent woman who later steered the ship of state with so much skill in the face of threatening storms was the first pupil of the Jesuits."[86]

When Ignatius once in a letter to Margaret praised her "characteristically Habsburg" devotion to the Blessed Sacrament, it was no mere courtly compliment: he himself had taught his spiritual daughter this devotion, together with the practice of regular confession . . . The young woman responded to his solicitude for her spiritual welfare with an unswerving loyalty to her master and the work of his Society, which she had supported to the utmost of her ability in its difficult beginnings. The story of Ignatius and

Margaret belongs to the Society's earliest history, the *Fioretti,* as it were, of the Jesuits: *Nuestra Madama* she is often called in Ignatius' letters. While Father Codure was still alive, Madama at his request gained from the Pope a number of religious privileges. Years later, Ignatius had to deny that even the bull of foundation of the Society of Jesus was due to Margaret's influence with the Pope. Versed as he was in the rules and niceties of court life, Ignatius may well have found it hard sometimes to keep his balance upon the polished marble of the Palazzo Madama. Ribadeneira, who was also a frequent visitor at Madama's house, tells the following characteristic anecdote of Ignatius: "One day, in the house of Madama Margarita, the Emperor's daughter, Ignatius met a knight of the Order of Santiago and promised him that he would be his advocate in some affair or other. Afterwards he regretted this promise. In relating this, he added: 'For eleven or twelve years now I have to the best of my memory said or promised nothing that I would subsequently regret'."[87]

Another occurrence dating from these years has also become classic in the traditions of the Society. "At the time when Ignatius was confessor to Madama Margarita de Austria, daughter of the Emperor Charles V, in the earliest days of the Society and the time of its bitterest poverty, that lady sent two or three hundred ducats at once to our Father, that he might distribute them among the poor. Although Ignatius well knew that it was the giver's intention to relieve our own poverty, he took not a farthing for the needs of the house, but caused the money to be distributed among the religious houses and pious foundations of Rome, in such a way, moreover, that he could afterwards have accounted for every penny." One other event may be mentioned here, because it too forms part of the Society s traditions, as an example of the Founder's attitude towards persons of rank. "Our Father was accustomed, whenever he entered into private conversation with a person of high station, to tell the latter plainly and in detail about his imprisonments and his persecutions and the cause thereof. He did this in order that such persons might be fully aware of the truth and therefore would not lend an ear to others, who might through jealousy give an untrue account of these matters. Thus he acted in the case of Madama de Austria and several cardinals."[88]

Now began some years of apostolic co-operation between Ignatius and Madama; and in this work for others the young woman's soul was healed. She could no longer do without the advice of a confessor, and so Laynez went with the duchess in September 1541 to Lucca to meet her imperial father. Back in Rome, Margaret was the indefatigable Ignatius' indispensable support in the founding of a house for catechumens; and her name headed the list of noble ladies who helped to found and develop the House of

St. Martha for fallen and morally endangered girls. Ignatius specially relates how on one occasion Madama, deeply moved, acted as godmother to a converted Jew; and he regarded her courageous labours in the house for catechumens as important enough to write about them to Francis Xavier in India. She and Doña Leonor de Vega, wife of the imperial ambassador at Rome, of whom much will be said later, were his main supporters. It was not only for the Society's charitable works that this was important; Ignatius was fully aware that the cultivation of Madama's friendship was necessary not only for his good relations with the Spanish ambassador and therefore with the Emperor, but also for the continued favour of the Pope. "In the bosom of the family she detested, Margaret developed into an attentive observer and ardent admirer of her imperial father. Juan de Vega was often the guest of the Pope, together with her and her husband Ottavio Farnese."[89]

One can then hardly blame Ignatius if he occasionally with tact, restraint, and complete lack of self-interest made use of Madama's intervention with the Pope. In the summer of 1543, the papal court was staying at Bologna and Rimini. In Rome, the House of St. Martha for fallen girls had just been established with the help of the wealthy Pietro Codacio, a canon of Lodi near Milan, who had belonged to Ignatius' "Company" since 1539; and the final execution of the bull of foundation had now to be obtained. For this purpose Codacio went to Bologna. In his travelling-bag he carried a letter from Ignatius to Madama, the contents of which show us the kind of task Ignatius laid upon his penitent. In Codacio's company there apparently travelled also a Dominican, otherwise unknown to us, who had probably been in trouble with the Inquisition for suspected heresy. Certainly nobody in Rome had more understanding for such unfortunates than Ignatius, who had once been examined so strictly in theology by the Dominicans at Salamanca. He had, as the letter shows, taken up the case of this religious with generous zeal, and had unhesitatingly taken advantage of his exalted connexions to interest the Emperor's daughter in the matter.[90]

Even the postscript to this letter is significant: Ignatius did not forget to add news of the health of a lady who also worked nobly with him for the House of St. Martha, the Countess Carpi, wife of Bonifazio Gaetani, Duke of Sermoneta, of the same family as Ignatius' close friend, Cardinal Rodolfo Pio de Carpi, Cardinal Protector of the Jesuits. One can see how the circle of his Roman friends, all related to one another, served for him but one end – to help souls.

JESUS

Your Excellency,
Most illustrious Lady in our Lord.

The sovereign grace and eternal love of Christ our Lord be with Your Excellency.

As Master Peter Codacio, Canon of Milan, is the one who is looking after all our affairs and the new home for fallen women, he is going to the Curia to obtain execution of the bull of foundation necessary for them when some pressing need arises in that house and company. Taking advantage of this opportunity, he himself, and a father of the Order of St. Dominic who is travelling in his company is bringing a letter from me, enclosing a series of recommendations by persons whose opinion I deem it right and honourable to defer to and whom I could not or dare not refuse without hurt to my conscience. I therefore thought I would write this to Your Excellency to the greater glory of God.

In the first place, God our Lord has given this father the grace (as I see it) that his great trial and trouble should have come to Your Excellency's knowledge. As one of the most important works of mercy among those which are spiritual is to comfort a soul much distressed and in tribulation, I can only plead with and humbly entreat Your Excellency for that reason, since I know by personal experience that Your Excellency is anxious to perform, and wholly given to, all works of mercy in our Lord.

Moreover, in order not to show myself insistent in entreating and imploring in a matter which might not seem to you possible, just and worthy, and to avoid the inconveniences of a refusal, in addition to having examined the matter before our Lord, I have spoken very seriously to several learned men and penitentiaries, and to all of them it seemed a meritorious thing and worthy of a favourable reception, chiefly because the poor man has been in prison three years for his sin, and has done considerable penance for the space of eight or nine years. Now he comes here with leave of his superior and it would seem with the approval of learned men of his Order, so that by his rehabilitation he might comfort his soul by offering the Holy Sacrifice. Nevertheless, according to the custom followed here to avoid scandal, it would be understood that he should not celebrate in the same place where the sin was committed, but elsewhere, either in public or privately, as his superior and the Order may judge to be to the greater glory of God our Lord. In this way and with this reservation His Holiness will be more easily and more willingly disposed to release him from his penalties and comfort his soul.

As in this and in all the rest, I refer you to Master Peter Codacio as if he were I myself, I will conclude, praying and humbly begging God our Lord that your Excellency may be guided and governed in all things by the divine and everlasting Goodness.

Your Excellency's most humble and constant servant in our Lord, Ignatius.

The Countess of Carpi has recovered from her illness although not completely. Unceasing thanks be given to the Giver of all life, spiritual and bodily, to his greater service, praise and glory.

Rome, August 13th, 1543

To Her Excellency, my Lady in our Lord,
Madama Margarita de Austria

The Pope's joy over the improved conjugal relations in his grandson's palace can be imagined. What Famian Strada was later to write about Margaret in these years (that is, until 1545) is no courtly fairy-tale; and a modern biographer of Madama is wrong when he says: "The zealous Jesuit evidently loved to lay the colours on thick, for the greater glory of his Society and its founder." Strada's words are: "Margaret's piety was great. Ignatius of Loyola gained great influence over her in Rome. She chose him as her spiritual adviser, and confessed to him oftener than was then usual in aristocratic circles. He led her to cultivate an ardent devotion to the Most Holy Sacrament of the Altar."[91]

No doubt Ignatius also spoke to her of the duties of a wife. On August 27th, 1545, Margaret gave birth to twin boys. The Pope had sent her four musicians from the Vatican to entertain her while in labour. He was delighted at the news of the birth of his two great-grandsons, sent rich jewels to Margaret and two hundred *scudi* to the midwife. The first twin, Carlos, died after a few months; but the second, who was at first baptized privately as Giovanni Paolo, was the future hero of Lepanto and governor of the Netherlands, Alexander Farnese. The five-volume biography which has lately been written as a worthy monument to Alexander's historic greatness, says nothing of the exact circumstances of his birth. No less a man than the founder of the Jesuits administered that first private baptism to the little Alexander. The importance Ignatius and his companions attached to this happy event appears from the fact that Pedro Ribadeneira at the request of

81

the founder had to send a detailed report of it to Fathers Araoz and Faber, then in Spain at the court of Princess Juana. We add here this eye-witness account, although it is not a letter from Ignatius himself; for it was without doubt written on his instructions, and it describes better than any other testimony the cordial relations of the saint with the Emperor's daughter.[92]

The sovereign grace and eternal love of Christ our Lord be always with us to our continual help and favour.

Last Thursday, which was the seventeenth of this present month of August, the divine will was fulfilled and Madama gave birth to two sons. Now because I know that you will be very glad in our Lord to learn the details of this birth, and as the matter is of so much edification, with the aid of God our Lord and to his honour and glory, I should like to narrate certain of the events briefly in the present letter.

Firstly, on Thursday, as I say, at 8 o'clock in the morning, they came in great haste to fetch Master Ignatius at the request of Madama. He went to the palace and she made her confession to him, afterwards hearing Mass and communicating. By the grace of God our Lord she was in such dispositions that Master Ignatius who was present says that on receiving the Most Holy Sacrament she was so full of tears, that they ran down in great abundance not only from her eyes, but from her nostrils and face – so much so that it moved those present to great devotion. Then, immediately she had received the Holy Sacrament, the thing seeming more divine than natural, when the creatures in her womb felt the presence of their Creator and Lord whom the mother had received, those babes leaped for joy in her womb. Certain pains, but not severe, began to come upon her and she remained thus, half in pain, half sleeping, until the hour of Vespers. Afterwards, when the great pain began to come upon her, Master Ignatius went away to the chapel to engage in prayer, and while he was there all the ladies of the court came to engage in prayer, too, and thus they all waited together. At this Doña María de Mendoza came to look for Master Ignatius, to ask him to pray very fervently, for the pains were then very severe. After they had been in the chapel an hour, someone came to say that Madama had just given birth to a son and a little while after came another to say she had now given birth to a second son. Afterwards the ladies went away and Master Ignatius remained alone in the chapel. When he had spent some time in prayer, he came to Madama's anteroom. While he was there she sent to say that the babes should be baptized. When they came to baptize them, they learnt that the midwife, when removing part of the body of the first had baptized him, on account of the danger there was, and he was called by the name Giovanni Carlo. The second they wanted Master Ignatius to baptize. Thus when there were present Signor Ottavio, the Duchess of Castro and other ladies, the said Signor Ottavio bringing the water for the baptism and answering the responses, Master Ignatius baptized the infant and he was called Giovanni Paolo. The gratitude of Signor Ottavio, the Duchess of Castro and the other ladies to Master Ignatius was so overwhelming that it was a matter for wonder, for they attributed the happy issue of the birth to his prayers. Master Ignatius was there from the morning until the birth, and in the room where Madama was no one was allowed to enter, except the Duchess of Castro, Doña María de Mendoza and Lope de Guzmán, her husband, who is Madama's Lord Chamberlain, Master Ignatius and two of Madama's other serving ladies.

After the birth Master Ignatius came home, returning again to the palace at the hour of supper. Madama, in the great devotion she has for him, wanted him to recite a Gospel over each of the babes and so he did. Thus now, in the opinion of those who best understand the matter, all three, mother and children, find themselves very well.

May it please the most holy Trinity that the pleasure and joy shown at this birth on earth may be shown among the angels in heaven and, indeed, much greater joy when it is revealed to them that the babes are predestined and their names written in the book of life.

For the love and reverence of God our Lord, I commend them much to your assiduous and devout prayers and most holy sacrifices, that their lives may be entirely given to God's most holy service, praise and glory. May he in his infinite and supreme goodness deign to give us his abundant grace that we may know his most holy will and fulfil it perfectly.

Your unworthy servant in our Lord,

Pedro de Ribadeneira

Rome, August 29th, 1545

To my beloved fathers in Christ our Lord
Master Peter Faber and Licentiate Araoz

Soon afterwards Madama and her lady-in-waiting María de Mendoza, who was also Ignatius' penitent, resumed their charitable work for the Jesuits. In a matter of decisive importance for the stability of the Society, Margaret was able to be of assistance to her spiritual father. King Ferdinand I was firmly resolved to give the bishopric of Trieste to Father Jay. Ignatius regarded this as nothing less than a threat to the Society and its ideals, and set heaven and earth in motion to induce the Pope to protest. Madama and the ambassador Juan de Vega succeeded in persuading the Pope to act and, together with Ignatius, wrote personally to the King of the Romans; and the *Te Deum* that the Jesuits sang when the king desisted from his plan was absolutely sincere.

The cordial relations between the saint and his spiritual daughter were expressed in a journey which Ignatius undertook to Tivoli in October 1548, in order to establish peace between the town and the Castel Sant' Angelo, also called Castel Madama. The reasons for the surrender in this case of the duchess, who was usually not at all easy to deal with, are contained in a letter written at the time: "Madama raises no difficulty at all in any matter which Master Ignatius considers just and honourable."[93]

The confessor was pleased with his penitent. He mentioned to Laynez that Madama had made a pilgrimage to Loreto and there had reverently received the Blessed Sacrament. Margaret for her part took an enthusiastic interest in the great works which the Society was initiating throughout the world. She was, as a letter of the period states, "devoted whole-heartedly to the Company of Jesus"; and in September 1550, Polanco could write to Borgia in Spain, when the misfortunes we are about to relate had already come upon Margaret: "This daughter of the Emperor has an uncommon affection for the Society of Jesus."[94]

Madama indeed needed the spiritual help of her confessor. With the death of the Farnese Pope Paul III on November 10th, 1549, political disaster overtook the hated family of his descendants. Margaret and her husband Ottavio had to retire in February 1550 to Parma and Piacenza, and the war for the possession of these two duchies, so decisive for Charles's Italian policy, broke out. Ottavio had succeeded to the dukedom on the death of his father Pierluigi on September 10th, 1547. He now stood between his imperial father-in-law and the successor of his papal grandfather, Julius III.[95] For a man like Ignatius, this sudden political change was no reason to alter his loyalty to Margaret. As if nothing had happened, on August 16th, 1550, he sent to the banished duchess in Parma one of those letters couched in that courtly language of which he was a master. He had already sent many such letters to Madama, though she had not received them. He added special greetings to Alexander, now fifteen years old. One has to bear in mind the recent tragic collapse of the splendour of the house of Farnese when one reads the simple opening sentence: "Your Excellencies have now left Rome for that city which belongs to you. . . ."

JESUS

My Lady in our Lord,

The sovereign grace and eternal love of Christ our Lord visit and bestow on Your Excellency his most holy gifts and spiritual graces.

Your Excellencies have now left Rome for that city which belongs to you, but the continual desire which, by the grace of God is ever with me, has not left nor will it leave my soul – namely, that his divine and sovereign goodness may direct and prosper all your affairs and the Duke Octavius and Don Alexander, as is most fitting for your sovereign happiness and for God's service and glory. This is the best consolation that can be hoped for from a person of my frailty – yet it seemed to me good in our Lord to pay my respects to you with this brief letter and to tell you that I greatly rejoiced in his divine Majesty to learn that in bodily health Your Excellencies are very well. I hope in him who is our true salvation and our life that he has also given you and will give you spiritual health, which is what matters most. This we shall continually beseech him for.

I know that Your Excellency will be glad to have news of us, as we so completely belong to you with a love that goes far beyond the general desire of charity we have for all. We are well and the affairs of the Society in God's service are everywhere increasing and prospering.

May it please the infinite and sovereign goodness of God our Lord to increase in all his creatures his honour and glory and give us all his grace always to know his holy will and perfectly to fulfil it.

Always Your Excellency's humble servant in our Lord,

Ignatius

Rome, August 16th, 1550

To my Lady in our Lord, Madama Margarita de Austria,
Duchess of Parma and Piacenza

Meanwhile the great struggle between Duke Ottavio and the Emperor continued. The opinion of it that prevailed in Rome and at the imperial court may be judged from a letter written by Pope Julius III on March 31st, 1551, to the Emperor: "I find it intolerable that a miserable worm, Ottavio Farnese, rebels at the same time against the Emperor and the Pope." Although an armistice was concluded after two years, Alexander's mother still had to defend Parma for a long time, while the Emperor occupied Piacenza[96]. These, the darkest years of her life, were illumined by a letter which Ignatius wrote to her, full of wisdom, consolation and profound spirituality. He evidently knew that Madama would understand it.

85

IHS

My Lady in our Lord,

The sovereign grace and eternal love of Christ our Lord be always with your Excellency, with his most holy gifts and spiritual graces.

I was much consoled in our Lord with the visit of Master Adrian on Your Excellency's behalf, receiving as a very great favour this token of the wonted remembrance and special charity which he who is infinite and sovereign charity has given Your Excellency in regard to our Society. He himself is the author of the joyful wish we all feel deep in our soul always to be at Your Excellency's service to the glory of his divine Majesty. His infinite wisdom knows how often I bring the memory of Your Excellency before his most holy presence, desiring that he may preserve his gifts in Your Excellency and increase them for his greater service and praise, and that from all these trials which he has permitted, there may result the fruit which his divine goodness alone can draw, for the greater perfection of Your Excellency's soul in this life and the earning of a special and everlasting crown in the other. There he has stored up for us for ever our supreme and most blissful good without any admixture of trouble or any wretchedness – he who acquired this for us at the price of his blood and his life.

May it please him in the meantime to give us a deep knowledge of the most sweet rulings of his Providence, through which both in prosperity and in adversity we are always provided with opportunities to help us in obtaining our everlasting happiness and bliss.

In this house and college we are well; and both here and in other parts God our Lord marches before us and makes use of this humble Society which is wholly at Your Excellency's service and always will be so to the glory of his divine Majesty. May it please him to give us all his abundant grace so that we may always know his most holy will and perfectly fulfil it.

Ignatius

Rome, November 17th, 1553

To Margaret of Austria

It may be noted, in this and the preceding letter, how Ignatius reports to the Duchess of Parma on the worldwide progress of his Society. Clearly Margaret took a particular joy in it, and such words found an echo in her own royal mind, which soon would no longer have to confine itself to the petty cares of governing Parma. "God our Lord marches before us": these are words which none understood better than the mother of Alexander Farnese, and which none had a better right to say than the officer of Pamplona.

But saints are always men who in the least can discover the greatest. Ignatius taught his penitent to do likewise and to put this teaching into practice in apparently trivial works of charity. Thus only four weeks later he could again turn to the Duchess of Parma concerning a question in which, with his inexhaustible patience, he had undertaken to act as mediator; for everyone in Rome knew who was the most successful advocate with Madama. It was a wretched dispute about property, which had arisen through the building of an extension to the Palazzo Madama at Rome. A certain Master Nerli thought his rights of ownership were threatened, and begged Ignatius to intercede with Margaret.

My Lady in our Lord,

The sovereign grace and eternal love of Christ our Lord be with Your Excellency with his most holy gifts and spiritual graces.

Through Master Adrian I sent you a letter recently. The present is only to oblige Master Giovanni Battista Nerli, a gentleman of Florence, who is writing to Your Excellency about a certain house at the back of your palace, which he says by right is his. He would not care to go to law, but asks that his right should be clearly recognized, and thus be defined without the costs, difficulties and loss of time which lawsuits usually bring with them. I know Your Excellency is so little partial to having anything which is not yours by a very good right, that my request may be excused, and on this account I said that I would write to oblige him. As Master Giovanni Battista is a poor gentleman, I shall be pleased if I can serve and help him in this somewhat difficult matter. It seems to me that what he asks, which is that it be ordered that justice be done speedily, will be no less to the service of Your Excellency than to his profit.

Because I think that Your Excellency will be informed about this matter from other sources, I shall not enlarge upon it more, relying on those who are dealing with it more in detail. I shall say no more, except that I ask God our Lord, by his infinite and sovereign goodness, to give us all his abundant grace so that we may know and perfectly accomplish his holy will.

Rome, December 17th, 1553   Ignatius
To Madama, Parma

Fortunately the duchess's brief reply has been preserved among the General's papers. It was dictated to her secretary and then signed in her fine, masculine handwriting – there is a tremble in it after all the distresses she had undergone. At the same time we detect, beneath the formal phrases of the official style, all the affection that Margaret felt for the confessor of her Roman days, whom she had not forgotten.

Reverend Master Ignatius,

Your letter has given us much consolation, since it gave me news of your health and I have learned from it that the affection you bear us is not diminished by so long an absence, nor have you failed to remember to pray to the blessed God for us in our many trials, for which we are infinitely in your debt and we beg you kindly to persevere in your prayers. If we can do anything for you or your Society, you will always find us very ready to do you any favour, and in this spirit we are always at your disposal. May God make you happy.

Margarita d'Austria

Parma, January 16th, 1554

To the most reverend and to us very dear
Master Ignatius in Rome

A year later Ignatius had to trouble Madama again. She had, indeed, disappointed him a little through her inaction in the matter of founding a college at Parma. Now it concerned another affair. We shall have occasion to speak of it more in detail when discussing the correspondence of the saint with the Duchess Eleonora of Florence. It was the question of the religious vocation of a young Roman, Tarquinio Rainaldi, who had entered the Society on April 18th, 1553, at the age of twenty. His ambitious father, a lawyer, seeing in this a dishonour to his family, did everything possible to make his son renounce the project. To protect Tarquinio from his father's importunity, Ignatius sent him in July 1553 to Florence, where the father, who had followed him, made a last attempt with the help of the Duchess Eleonora to make his son return to the world. Ignatius was inexorable, and sent the young scholastic in 1554 to Valencia in Spain, where he could carry on his studies undisturbed. The influential father now desisted for a while; then, among other attempts which he made, turned in his distress to the Duchess of Parma, whose word, as was well known, counted much with Ignatius. Margaret then wrote to Ignatius, without looking further into the case, asking him to recall the brother from Spain. In this instance, however, she had come to the wrong man. When it was a question of a recognized vocation, the General was of a politely adamantine inflexibility. In this case he did indeed do everything to reassure the father and the two illustrious advocates; but only as far as his conscience and his regard for the freedom of his government of the Society allowed. The letter in which Ignatius answered the Duchess of Parma is a model of his diplomacy based on firmly held principles. Margaret never again approached Ignatius with such requests.[97]

IHS

My Lady in our Lord,

The sovereign grace and eternal love of Christ our Lord be with Your Excellency with his most holy gifts and spiritual graces.

In the past few days I have received from the hands of the Comendador Puente a letter from Your Excellency, in which you show that you would be served if a student of our Society, Tarquinio Rainaldi, who is at present in Spain, could be brought to Rome for the consolation of his father who greatly desires this.

Although the Comendador told me that the reply he would give Your Excellency would be sufficient without my writing, it did not seem to me that I ought to omit to reply by letter, if only to have an opportunity of greeting Your Excellency by that means, although with the continual remembrance we make of you in our prayers, I know that Your Excellency is, indeed, visited by this your house and Society, as the love we all have for Your Excellency's service to the divine glory obliges us.

Turning to what Your Excellency requests in your letter, you will see from a brief report which I enclose here and from the copy of a letter from Tarquinio to me what are the facts of this affair. I have, however, written and given letters to another, elder brother of Tarquinio, who is going to Spain, so that the Rector of our college in Valencia where he is studying may allow Tarquinio to speak with his brother alone – and if he should want to come back to Rome with him, let him come immediately.

I know for certain that Your Excellency, if you were in possession of a knowledge of the facts as I am, would not pursue the matter further if you were in my place – because to order Tarquinio to come to Rome against his will, when he fears and dreads the grave danger to his soul, would not be so much pity and compassion for the father as cruelty to the son. And since I know for certain that Your Excellency only wants what is for the greater glory of God our Lord, I know that you do not want this nor would be served by any such thing.

In this house and in the college in Rome, we are in tolerable health and here and everywhere God our Lord is leading forward this humble Society of his, which thing, since the Society is all Your Excellency's in him, I know that you will rejoice to hear.

I will say no more now, except to ask God's supreme goodness to deign to give us all his abundant grace, so that we may always know his most holy will and fulfil it perfectly.

Ignatius

Rome, August 3rd, 1555

To Madama, Duchess of Parma

Report on Tarquinio Rainaldi

Tarquinio will be about twenty years of age. He entered the house of the Society of Jesus in Rome on probation after long deliberation. His father made a certain amount of difficulty and therefore it seemed advisable to grant the young man what he had been wanting, namely to leave Rome and be assigned to Florence.

When his father learnt that he was in Florence, he went there, and through the intermediary of the Marchese de Marignano, and taking advantage of the Duke's favour, they removed him from the college and took him to the palace where the Marchese and Tarquinio's father, having him alone for a short time, made every endeavour, both themselves and through others, to deter him from his purpose and deprive him of the habit of the Society and dress him in secular attire. The young man, however, was so steadfast that all attempts were in vain. They were thus all much edified, saying that such a vocation must be from God, and the father, giving Tarquinio his blessing, returned alone to Rome.

After some time the father made new difficulties, asking for his son to be sent to the college in Rome and promising not to trouble or hinder his vocation, which promise he even made to the Duchess of Florence and the Cardinal de Medici. Relying on this promise, the young man was transferred to Rome and when he had been in our college there some months, his father by divers means again tried to influence him, as is evident from the copy of the letter from Tarquinio I am enclosing.

It was then that the young man again asked to be given leave to go away from Rome and he was sent to Spain, where he is pursuing his studies.

Now his father is pitying himself once more and it is, in fact, clear that he would like to take him away from religion for his human designs and so goes seeking all the means he can to this end.

Tarquinio's return shall, however, be allowed if the father should ask Your Excellency for it.

Rome, August 3rd, 1555   Ignatius

To Madama Margarita

Less than a year passed before Ignatius died in his little cell beside Santa Maria della Strada. The faithful Polanco, who knew better than anyone who stood highest in the saint's affections, wrote personally to the Duchess of Parma to inform her of his death. Madama was grief-stricken and wrote to thank Polanco in the following words:[98]

I have learnt from your letter of August 12th, that it has pleased God to summon the good soul of Master Ignatius from us and take it to himself. I have been deeply grieved by this not only from a personal sense of loss of so loved and sincerely affectionate a friend, but also because of the loss which has befallen this holy Society of Jesus. That this loss is very great I am quite certain and with good reason; after all he has been of your fellowship. But I know also that I myself am not in a position to comfort the Fathers, for I cannot say anything that your Reverences do not know much better than I. Then I am mindful, Reverend Fathers, of how the Fathers of the Society readily find their comfort in their inmost hearts, since they accept adverse things from the hand of God as fortunate. I can only tell you, therefore, that you can depend upon my assistance in everything as far as lies in my power and that you will find me always ready to further your interests and do whatever I can for you in all things. Accordingly I beg you not to hesitate to address yourself to me on any question which may arise and to remember me in your holy prayers. This will always give me the greatest satisfaction. And this we ask in the conviction that it will also be acceptable to God our Father.

Parma, August 21st, 1556   Margaret of Austria

When Diego Laynez had taken over Ignatius' office, he wrote specially to Madama de Austria to announce his election and began his letter, sadly yet proudly, with praises of the dead Ignatius.

Margaret did not forget her holy confessor even in the days of her greatness, which were soon to dawn. From 1559 to 1567 she was regent of Flanders, and then she returned to Italy, where she was solemnly received by the General Francis Borgia, and where she kept up for many years a cordial friendship with that wild fellow Nicholas Bobadilla, whom Ignatius too had loved. She gave him a rosary of agate, and the two of them must often have spoken together of their Father in Christ, Ignatius. On January 18th, 1586, Margaret died at Ortona. Her body was first buried at Loreto, where she had once to the delight of her confessor Ignatius received Communion so devoutly, "like a true member of the House of Austria". Bobadilla was the last of the founder's generation who prayed at her tomb. She found her last resting-place beside her unloved husband in the Benedictine church at Piacenza.[99]

Duchess Eleonora of Florence

FOR Ignatius, who since his Venetian days had been deeply aware of the need for ecclesiastical reform in Italy, Florence was, after Rome, the city whose spiritual conquest he most desired to effect. The earliest possibility of founding a college in the ducal city on the banks of the Arno occurred in July 1546, and Ignatius reported this to Diego Laynez, then attending the Council of Trent. The reason why the prospects seemed to the strategist of Santa Maria della Strada to be so good was that he believed he could count not only on the favour of Duke Cosimo but even more on that of the Duchess Eleonora. Thus it came about that this unusual and in a sense truly great woman is among the princesses with whom Ignatius corresponded.[100]

The portrait of the duchess painted by Agnolo Bronzino still hangs in the Uffizi at Florence; and whoever has been impressed by the severe magnificence of the Palazzo Pitti can feel something of the spirit of the woman who built it. We have met the Duchess Eleonora already. Duke Cosimo de' Medici, forced by the imperial policy of Charles V, had, instead of wooing the Emperor's daughter, to be content with the daughter of the Viceroy of Naples, Don Pedro de Toledo, Marquis of Francavilla. It is true that this bride, belonging to an illustrious Spanish family of which the Dukes of Alba were also members, was not to be despised. Eleonora was descended on both sides from those Spanish grandees, about whose exclusive and aristocratic manner of life, based upon vast wealth, Ranke has so unforgettably written. This was the world that Ignatius knew so well, and in which he moved with such inimitable assurance. In June 1539 the Medici wedding took place. In 1549 Eleonora bought the Palazzo Pitti and together with the Boboli Gardens made it into the ducal residence, which henceforth became the intellectual centre of Florence. It was she who introduced a routine at court exactly regulated by Spanish ceremonial, whereas her husband still retained something of the old republican attitude of the Medici. She it was, too, who gave Florentine politics an unequivocally Spanish and Habsburg orientation; and it was with a sure insight that Charles V in his great political testament of January 18th, 1548, thus described the situation in Florence: "I have promoted the interests of the Duke of Florence, and he is devoted to us, being besides closely related to us through the house of

Toledo." Through her granddaughter Maria de' Medici, Eleonora became the ancestress of Louis XIV and therefore of nearly all the princes of Europe.[101]

From her exchange of letters with Ignatius, well-versed as he was in the caprices of aristocratic ladies, it will be clear that the Duchess of Florence was one of his most difficult correspondents. It may be that her non-royal birth and the compulsion exercised by imperial policy in the matter of her marriage produced in Eleonora a kind of overcompensation in the form of an excessive consciousness of her own dignity. Ignatius knew that in this particular point one had to stick strictly to etiquette when dealing with Her Highness of Florence. The duchess was a real Spaniard – imperious and secretive at the same time, of extreme self-mastery and reserve, yet full too of deep passion. The confessors whom she asked Ignatius to send her were to find her a difficult penitent. Her religious life was not all it should be. In a contemporary Florentine diary Eleonora is thus described: "The duchess was virtually never seen to go on foot, so proud was she. Nor did she let herself be seen on horseback; but she generally appeared publicly in a litter, as if in a reliquary; that is to say, one half of the litter was open, and in the other half she could be seen. It was a marvellous thing to behold such a proud woman. She was never seen to visit churches or other holy places, as her high station demanded – even if it were only for the sake of good example." Alfred von Reumont describes her similarly: "Eleonora of Toledo was melancholic and in her later years suffered from ill-health. She was a faithful wife and a loving mother, more thrifty than was fitting, so that her considerable private fortune, estimated at 40,000 ducats, was continually increasing. She was charitable; but it was remarked with disapproval that she spent considerable sums of ecclesiastical revenue in this way. Her main recreation was gambling, at which she always wanted to be the winner."[102]

The new Society had its best advocate at the duchess's court in her father, who was Viceroy of Naples from 1532 to 1553. He had already invited Father Bobadilla to Naples in 1539 to oppose the dangerous reforming ideas of Juan Valdés. The Marquis of Francavilla was positively enthusiastic about the success of Father Araoz, who preached at Naples in the spring of 1543. So in 1546 Ignatius sent the newly ordained Father Juan de Polanco to Florence, in order to see how the land lay. The learned and still somewhat over-zealous Polanco thought he could not do better than begin by reforming the ducal court, and at once aimed at the highest objective: the duchess herself. The prudent Ignatius must have felt a little uncomfortable when his ardent disciple wrote on December 15th, 1546, from Pisa: "The duchess told me to send her in writing what I had to say. And I did so. Please God

94

the words I wrote may work upon her soul. For if this woman were converted, she would become, I believe, the cause of a more general increase of virtue in her State."[103]

In his memorandum to the Duchess Eleonora, Polanco gives a sort of "mirror for princes", adorned with quotations from the *Ethics* of Aristotle and from Suetonius, and with references to the example of the emperors Trajan and Titus. The climax of the homily is an admonition to keep a less splendid court, which he boldly justifies by saying that the wealth of princes comes from the sweat of the poor. The duchess was intelligent and Christian enough not to take this exhortation amiss: after all, she had asked for it. It was even reported at Rome that she had been sincerely pleased with it. Ignatius was less satisfied with this apostolic sermon to the court. A severe letter to Polanco brought the would-be Jesuit Savonarola to his senses, and this letter contains, written in the Founder's own hand, the celebrated words: "We have the reputation among some persons who do not trouble to find out the truth, especially here in Rome, that we would like to rule the world." As Polanco had besides rather imprudently become involved with the members of the old Savonarola party, Ignatius recalled him to Rome. To the duke he sent a diplomatic letter, in which the General defended his impetuous Polanco with almost touching chivalrousness.[104] The more circumspect Diego Laynez was sent to Florence, where he arrived on June 18th, 1547. Now began the minor tragedy of the duchess's affection for the Spanish Jesuit, who became with every month more indispensable to her, but whom with his great gifts Ignatius regarded as being called to higher things than comforting the soul of the Medici princess.

At the beginning, it is true, things were difficult. Laynez first devoted his attention to Don Pedro de Toledo, then to one of the older ladies-in-waiting to the duchess, and began quietly to spread the idea of founding a college. The duke was not keen. "These new things are always dangerous," he said, and believed that the Jesuits made it their special business "to alienate wives from their husbands." The duchess, however, was "aglow with eagerness to help". It was soon to appear that the glow did not last. For a time it seemed that the ducal pair wished to found a college at Pisa; but Laynez had to write with disappointment that Their Highnesses were too much occupied with hunting and fishing, and that he seldom saw them. This complaint, that the duchess did not make any particular use of Laynez' presence, was to be repeated later. "That is not to be wondered at; it is the way of the world", he wrote resignedly. Ignatius did not lose patience. The visit which Duke Francis Borgia (then already secretly a Jesuit) made in December 1550 with a great retinue to his kinswoman the duchess had as its real motive to promote the idea of founding a college.[105]

Ignatius found time to write himself about the matter to the duchess's secretary, Cristóbal de Herrera. He knew the pious moods of a Spanish noblewoman better than the unimaginative Laynez. It is delightful to read in his letters to Florence the precise instructions as to the scholastics' behaviour at court in the presence of the duchess. They were specially ordered to speak only Spanish with her and to keep their heads uncovered. Ignatius, great in all little things, asked the superiors in Florence for details of the way in which they had kissed the duchess's hand and spoken with her. Above all, he warned them, they were not to get on the lady's nerves. Once again Laynez, together with Borgia, now on his way back from Rome, recommended the projected college to the duchess. And when at the beginning of 1552 the plan was about to be realized, the glad tidings of this victory travelled as far as Asia to Francis Xavier, who, however, never lived to receive the letter.[106]

The foundation was indeed a very modest one, and extreme poverty reigned in the new house of the Society. Ignatius could not refrain from remarking to Laynez in Florence two years later, with pointed reference to the duchess, that the Princess Juana had acted far otherwise when she made a will before the birth of her son and gave five hundred pieces of gold for each of two foundations, one in Jerusalem, the other in Peru; and he dared to add that the poverty of the college in Florence was obviously quite unworthy of such mighty princes. But in Florence it was as so often later: the duke, always a little prejudiced against the foundation, said: "The Jesuits have enough money themselves." When Father Louis du Coudray asked Ignatius if they might accept money from the duchess in spite of their vow of poverty, Ignatius replied drily that of course they might, provided no scandal were given. Eleonora herself had a bad conscience in the matter. When Father Salmerón waited upon her on behalf of Ignatius, she said to him with disarming humility: "It would really be better if I gave money to you, instead of squandering it in play."[107]

It was in this poverty-stricken house that in July 1553 dwelt Tarquinio, the young scholastic from Rome, whom we have already mentioned because the Duchess Margaret of Parma took up his case. This fact itself indicates that the modest affair of an unimportant Roman youth's vocation had grown into a court scandal. Tarquinio's father was a lawyer who enjoyed considerable esteem among the prelates of the Eternal City. His son Tarquinio had on completion of his classical and legal studies decided to devote his life and his talents wholly to the service of God, and had joined the Jesuits as a novice on April 15th, 1553. The disappointed father regarded his belonging to such a new order as a disgrace to the family, and in his blind paternal love attempted everything to bring Tarquinio back to the world

THE INFANTA JUANA OF SPAIN
see page 54

AUTOGRAPH LETTER FROM THE REGENT JUANA TO ST. IGNATIUS

see page 64-65

again. To protect the son from his father's importunity, Ignatius sent the young man to Florence. Enraged, the father promptly followed him, and succeeded through the good offices of the Marquis of Marignano, Gian Giacomo de' Medici, brother of the future Pope Pius IV, in getting an audience with Duke Cosimo and stating his complaint to him.[108]

What now followed is rightly called by Father Laynez a tragicomedy. The scene took place in the Palazzo Pitti, probably in August 1553. The *condottiere* of Marignano and the duke managed to entice the young Jesuit into the palace. There he was forcibly stripped of his cassock, and one of the soldiers of the ducal bodyguard made sport with it. Tarquinio had to don military costume, and the father sought by flattery and threats to move him to return to his family; but the young man stood firm. For a day and a night he was detained in the Palazzo Pitti, but in vain. Cesare Rainaldi had to return to Rome beaten.

Now the duchess's feminine diplomacy was exerted upon Ignatius. It is no discredit to her good-nature that she took the part of the grief-stricken father and pleaded in favour of a middle course which she had devised with him: Tarquinio might remain in the Society, but he should at least continue his studies in Rome, to comfort his father. Then he would not be further molested. On September 16th, 1553, a letter, written in no uncertain terms, was sent by the duchess to Ignatius, recommending the General to give way entirely to the wishes of Don Cesare Rainaldi. What would Ignatius do? Should he throw away the favour of the Duchess of Florence for the sake of a novice? There are moments in the life of this saint when the sheer folly of the supernatural breaks through and yet finds a way out of the entanglements of this life which can only be described as the highest wisdom. It was such a moment when Ignatius held in his hand the letter from the lady in the Palazzo Pitti. At once he sat down and drafted an answer, "a masterpiece of Christian prudence, which reveals the writer's profound knowledge of the human heart."[109] Young Tarquinio's vocation, which was recognized to be genuine, was not to be interfered with, and the wishes of the duchess and his father were to be met as far as conscience allowed.

My Lady in our Lord,

By a letter from Your Grace of the sixteenth of this month, I see what is asked and required of me in respect of Tarquinio, scholastic of our Society, and I do not doubt that Your Grace's piety and tender heart will have sympathized with Master Cesare Rainaldi, his father according to the flesh, which he has shown he loves in his son more than the spirit

97

or spiritual profit, since he is using very great diligence to turn him aside from the way in which God our Lord had set him for his service; and the wish he now expresses of his being moved to Rome might very well be with that intention. Therefore, since I respect (as I should do) Your Grace's letter and since it gives me some opportunity of assuring myself of the young man's constancy and also of obtaining fulfilment of certain promises which his father made us, I shall do what you want about Tarquinio, provided that he has the courage to come, and trust that God our Lord will give him strength. I would beg Your Grace in matters of this kind not to interpose your authority lightly, for it might be the cause of some soul's leaving God's service and being lost for ever. That, I know, is very far from Your Grace's holy intention. It is, indeed, better not to give way to the importunity of those who treat matters without much fear or love of God even in things which bring no little burden to one's conscience, and since I and our whole Society are Your Grace's, it has seemed to me that I ought not to refrain from giving this advice, as one who sincerely desires in Your Grace the service of God our Lord, with his supreme and eternal gifts.

May it please the divine goodness to give us all his abundant grace, so that we may always know his most holy will and perfectly fulfil it.

Rome, September 23rd, 1553   Ignatius

To the Lady Duchess in Florence

Ignatius could, in words of perfect courtesy, speak his mind quite openly to the duchess. Tarquinio did in fact return to Rome, while the father made a written promise not to place any further obstacle in the way of his son's vocation, and the Duchess of Florence made a similar promise. We shall soon learn that the young novice's steadfastness had made a great impression on her. She admitted herself, in this case, beaten by Ignatius. This is all the more significant, since the verdict of one of the best authorities on Eleonora remains true, namely that she was an imperious woman who stood by her opinion unyieldingly, and that when once she had made up her mind, he who succeeded in persuading her to change could indeed be called fortunate. Yet the story of young Tarquinio was not over. During the sickness of the last year of his life, Ignatius had time to correspond with the young brother in Spain, and expressly exhorted him not to forget his parents: "Write to your father now and then and show yourself a good and obedient son in all which does not conflict with the service of God."[110]

98

Meanwhile Father Laynez, whom the Pope had sent to Florence at the express wish of the duchess, had become more and more indispensable to her. It was almost the same as with the Regent Juana in Valladolid and her confessor Father Borgia: the duchess's demands were so emphatic that Ignatius in Rome was often seriously embarrassed in his government of the Society. Laynez was after all the best man he had in Italy. He was required in Rome, Venice and Genoa needed him; but the obstinate duchess felt it almost as an affront that Laynez' recall was even contemplated. In the summer of 1553, the Signoria of Genoa had urgently asked for Laynez, and the duchess had to the General's astonishment approved his departure for September; but in a letter to Ignatius (now lost) in August 1553 she withdrew this permission. Ignatius' position with regard to the Genoese was now exceedingly awkward. He employed the good offices of the duchess's uncle, Cardinal Juan Álvarez de Toledo, to try and persuade her to relent, and himself took great pains to keep the peace with her. At last Eleonora gave her confessor leave of absence for two months. Ignatius did not neglect to ask Laynez and the Genoese government to write the duchess a specially polite letter of thanks. Laynez stayed longer at Genoa than was arranged, and Ignatius was almost driven to distraction at the thought of the difficult lady in the Palazzo Pitti. In May 1554, he thought it advisable to yield. Laynez returned to Florence. It was high time, for a letter from that city had informed Ignatius of a remark of the duchess's: "If Father Laynez does not come back soon, it will be the end of the whole college."

In the early summer of 1554, a marked cooling-off of the duchess's enthusiasm for Laynez was noted in Ignatius' curia. It appears that he was not altogether sorry at this.[111] For there were more important tasks in Rome for a man like Laynez. Some time afterwards, he was to undertake a journey to Germany at the Pope's request. Together with Father Nadal he was to act as theological adviser to Cardinal Morone, whom Pope Julius III had deputed to attend the Imperial Diet at Augsburg. We can still detect in Ignatius' correspondence the burning anxiety that filled him at the beginning of the year 1555, so heavy with destiny for the German Church. In a circular letter written by himself, he exhorted all his fellow-religious in Italy to pray for Germany; and it was a consolation to him that the Pope had with confidence appointed two of his best men to this legation, which it was hoped would be of decisive importance. What could the petty spiritual problems of the duchess in Florence signify in comparison? Nevertheless, even Ignatius had a kind of respectful fear of this lady, and so he did not neglect to add, in the letter to Laynez which conveyed the Pope's command: "The sojourn in Germany will, they say, last four or five months. His Holiness will himself write to the duchess to calm her; but it is absolutely necessary for us Jesuits to obey His Holiness first."

Scarcely had Eleonora learnt of this than she recognized only too well how indispensable her Father Laynez was. On January 21st, 1555, she wrote a letter to Ignatius, unfortunately lost, to the effect that Laynez' departure for Germany in the company of the Cardinal Legate was at all costs to be prevented.[112] On February 2nd, Ignatius, his patience strained to the utmost, despatched his answer to Florence. This time the General found himself between the Pope and the duchess; and it was now merely a question of expressing to the latter in a diplomatic way that the Pope's commands were of more importance than her pious ideas.

IHS

Illustrious Lady in our Lord,

May the sovereign grace and eternal love of Christ our Lord be with Your Grace, with his most holy gifts and spiritual blessings.

From a letter from Your Grace dated January 21st, I have gathered that it would be to your service if Master Laynez might be prevented from going to Germany – and this because of certain fruit to God's service which might come from his preaching and contact with souls if he remained where he is, and particularly because Your Grace (whom we all so rightly desire to serve in our Lord) shows that it would please you not a little, I should be very glad in that same Lord of ours if all that Your Grace asks for God's greater glory could be done.

It is true, however, that the Pope himself personally appointed Master Laynez and another of our Society to accompany the Cardinal Legate and the embassy it was decided to send to the German Diet, and, in addition to the fact that that mission is of such a nature that in it the very great and universal good of religion is aimed at, for it will help to bring back that nation to the Catholic Church, we cannot and ought not to refuse obedience to the Vicar of Christ our Lord; it is therefore necessary to accept the order given to us. It is true that for the moment it is doubtful whether the embassy will go to Germany or not, and if it does not go, the problem is settled. If it does go and the Pope still wants Master Laynez to go to Germany, it is said that he will not be detained there more than three or four months. Thus if his departure cannot be avoided, we shall order that he return to Florence as soon as possible.

As to what concerns me, and Master Laynez himself, Your Grace already knows that the latter is under your orders – thus, provided the

Pope does not will otherwise, he will do what Your Grace commands, as I also desire always to do in our Lord. May it please God's infinite and supreme goodness to grant us all his abundant grace, so that we may always know his most holy will and perfectly fulfil it.

Rome, February 2nd, 1555   Ignatius

To the Lady Duchess in Florence

Here even Ignatius had miscalculated. It is almost comic to read how, in his subsequent correspondence, the duchess's reaction to the above letter finds an echo. "Her Highness protested with great warmth." She wrote herself to the Pope and to several cardinals and went to the greatest trouble to keep Laynez in Florence; but it was all useless. The Pope and Ignatius remained adamant. On February 18th, 1555, the Cardinal and Father Nadal left Rome; Laynez joined them at Florence. On March 24th, they reached Augsburg. Then it almost seemed that providence took pity on the "forsaken" woman in the Palazzo Pitti. On March 23rd, the Pope had died, and when the news arrived in Augsburg it meant the end of Cardinal Morone's legation. He at once set out again with Laynez for Italy. So the obstinate duchess had her way after all, and soon her confessor was restored to her. Another Pope was to die and Paul IV to be elected before Laynez was finally got away from Florence.[113]

The fight for her confessor was not the only occasion on which the duchess made claims upon the General's superhuman patience. In the early summer of 1555, she gave him an opportunity to exercise heroic love of his enemies. Since May of that year, Paul IV had occupied the throne of St. Peter. He was that Cardinal Carafa, inveterate foe of Spain, with whom Ignatius had not been on very friendly terms ever since his Venetian days, and at whose election, as he himself admits, every bone in his body trembled. During this pontificate, to intervene on behalf of a Spanish cleric accused of heresy by the Inquisition was a bold thing to do. Ignatius did it, and the Duchess of Florence courageously supported him. The case was that of a rich priest, formerly well thought of at the Roman Curia, Francisco Mudarra, with whom Ignatius had become acquainted at the very beginning of his Roman period. At that time Ignatius had warned him against the suspect preaching of Fra Agostino Mainardi, who had expounded the Lutheran doctrine of grace in Lent 1538 in the church of Sant'Agostino at Rome, had broken with the Church in 1540 and later died, a Protestant pastor, at Chiavenna. But Mudarra's Spanish friends turned the tables on Ignatius: it

101

was not Fra Agostino but Ignatius who was the heretic. He has himself given us an account of the matter in his autobiography: "At that time Mudarra and Barrera began the persecution, by declaring that the Pilgrim and his companions had left Spain, Paris, and Venice as fugitives. In the end they both admitted in the presence of the Governor and the Legate that they had nothing to say against them concerning either their morals or their doctrine." Ignatius, indeed, in order thoroughly to destroy Mudarra's accusations, which in those early months in Rome were particularly harmful, went personally to Pope Paul III at Frascati. For years no more was heard of Mudarra.[114] Then in the summer of 1554, Ignatius heard that he had had to flee from Rome, because the Inquisition was concerned about the orthodoxy of his teaching. He had, in fact, been suspected of heresy for years. Leaving his rich possessions and losing his benefices too, he went to Florence and placed himself under the protection of the Duchess Eleonora, well known for her love of all Spaniards. It was no doubt a painful surprise for Ignatius when he was asked to put in a good word with the duchess for the unfortunate Mudarra. Now the moment was come when he could help his former opponent. As early as November 1554, Ignatius intervened on Mudarra's behalf, and on February 9th, 1555, he asked the duchess for letters of recommendation, simply on the ground that "I am sorry for the poor man." He would do anything "to prevent Mudarra from going over to the Lutherans." On April 13th, 1555, he urged the duchess to write personally to the new Pope, Marcellus II, from whom Ignatius might expect any favour. But the Pope died after only a few weeks, and Ignatius could not entertain the same hopes of his successor, Paul IV. Especially in the case of Mudarra was the greatest care necessary. However, the duchess acceded to Ignatius' request, and with remarkable prudence wrote in the first instance to Giovanni Carafa, nephew of the new Pope, who bore the title of Count of Montorio. At the same time, on July 27th, 1555, she sent a note to Ignatius, commissioning him to inform the papal nephew of the case in greater detail by word of mouth.[115]

The letter is, like all of hers, dictated by a very marked sense of princely dignity, and it commands in a regal manner. The original is still in the Society's archives; and the signature, in the Duchess of Florence's own hand, shows in its somewhat uncontrolled extravagance – compare it with the calm simplicity of Madama's – more of the character of this woman than the contents and style of the letter.

Very Reverend Father,

I am writing to the Count of Montorio that on account of the respect he has for me and at my request, he should plead with His Holiness for

Francisco Mudarra, that he would grant him the favour of pardoning him, since Mudarra claims to be a good Christian and desires to live as such. In order not to write to him at great length, I rely on Your Reverence to inform him of the matter on my behalf, and to say what the said Mudarra is asking for, telling him of the desire I have that he should do him this favour at my request, since it seems to me a thing of great mercy. You will give him my letter and inform him of everything on my behalf, as I have said, and will advise me of what is done. May our Lord guard your very reverend person. . . .

The Duchess of Florence greets Your Reverence.

Florence, July 27th, 1555

To the most reverend Father Master Ignatius,
General of the Society of Jesus, in Rome

On September 10th, 1555, Ignatius received a long letter from Mudarra, in which the latter expresses his warmest thanks for Ignatius' intervention. How he must have rejoiced to read: "My desire has always been and always will be to live and die in the communion and faith of the Holy Catholic and Roman Church." Father Luis Gonçalves notes in his diary: "Our Father went to great pains to liberate Mudarra from the hands of the Inquisition. This Mudarra was at the beginning the Society's most violent opponent; and he had fled from Rome with the loss of all his benefices, which were considerable, while the Inquisition confiscated many thousands of ducats which had belonged to him." Ignatius even applied to the Viceroy of Sicily, Juan de Vega, with the request that he would write a petition in Mudarra's favour to the Pope; and Father Doménech, who was rather dilatory in forwarding the request to the viceroy, was afterwards sharply reprimanded. Only two weeks before his death, Ignatius was using his influence on behalf of his erstwhile adversary. He was always magnanimous towards his enemies. Mudarra's further career is unknown to us.[116]

Meanwhile the duchess's pen-and-ink war for her precious Laynez continued. At the beginning of 1555, singing his praises in a letter to Cardinal Cristóforo del Monte, she said that he could not possibly be allowed to attend the Imperial Diet in Germany, for had he not to hear her daughters' confessions regularly? But after Paul IV's election Ignatius found a good pretext to enable Laynez, indispensable also to him, to come to Rome. He could get the duchess's permission to visit Rome, on the ground that he considered it necessary to kiss the new Pope's feet, not mentioning any other reasons. Hardly had he arrived in Rome than the duchess impatiently made repeated requests for his return. With truly heavenly meekness Ignatius bore the ill-humours of the great lady, who vented her displeasure on the unfortunate rector of the house in Florence, and treated Father Nadal with marked coldness when he went out of his way to pay his respects to her on his return from Germany. The Pope, however, would not let Laynez go; and it is certain that Ignatius, despite all diplomatically polite efforts by himself and others to change the Pope's mind, was really very glad. He felt that a less prominent Jesuit would do for the chaplaincy in the Palazzo Pitti. So, on October 13th, 1555, he sent the duchess one of those politely worded but inflexible letters that are characteristic of Ignatius. Instead of Laynez, he suggested to Her Highness the name of Father Diego de Guzmán.[117]

JESUS

May the sovereign grace and eternal love of Christ our Lord be with Your Grace, with his most holy gifts and spiritual blessings.

I learn from letters from the Rector of this college and by the verbal report of Master Jerome Nadal, who on his way back from Germany to Rome presented his respects to Your Grace, how much you would be served if Master Laynez were to be sent to you. Since, however, he had an obedience from the Pope not to leave Rome, I tried to get the matter brought to the attention of His Holiness, and this the Cardinal of Santiago and Cardinal Carpi did. Since the Pope did not refuse, interpreting the request as granted, I sent Master Laynez on Friday last, to get formal leave of His Holiness, but it was refused, as Laynez will write to Your Grace. A further attempt has been made through the Cardinal de Santiago with, however, the same lack of success.

My fervent wish would be, in all that lies in me, for Your Grace's greatest service and consolation, to the divine glory. Thus, if there should be an opportunity, I shall not fail to try once more for this permission for Master Laynez to go to Florence. In the meanwhile, the best thing I could think of that could be done to further the same end was to send Don Diego de Guzmán to reside in Florence and serve Your Grace. This I have arranged and he will shortly arrive in that city.

May it please him who is the true consoler to comfort Your Grace's soul with his Holy Spirit and his grace, he who is the Creator and Lord of virtue and steadfastness, in all the trials with which he tests Your Grace's virtue and constancy, as is his wont with his chosen ones, so that they do not acquire so much liking for the small and passing good things of this world as to neglect and lose the very great and eternal ones of heaven.

May God's supreme goodness deign to give us all his abundant grace, so that we may always know his most holy will and fulfil it perfectly.

Rome, October 13th, 1555   Ignatius

To the Lady Duchess, in Florence

Polanco in his chronicle of the Society does not omit to mention the duchess's blazing anger. She protested against the sending of Father Guzmán. But now Ignatius was at the end of his patience. It was Guzmán or nobody. Eleonora was perhaps particularly touchy on account of the then imminent birth of her son. Be that as it may, Ignatius' joyful congratulations on the occasion of "the Most Illustrious Lady's happy delivery" soon followed. At the same time he gave Guzmán directions as to how he should treat the duchess on his arrival. "We shall soon see if the anger of the lady, for whose special service you have been sent, will calm down," wrote Ignatius on November 9th, 1555, to the new confessor, just arrived in Florence.[118]

The "anger of the lady" did soon calm down. Ignatius had advised Guzmán to go to the duchess only when she sent for him, and in general to keep himself tactfully in the background. In December the news from Florence sounded better; a more favourable wind was blowing at court. It was then that Ignatius asked Father Laynez' young nephew, Juan de Mendoza, who was on his way to Rome to join the Society, to go and kiss the duchess's hand while in Florence, without making any other request. He did this in order to mollify the duchess, still smarting at the loss of her favourite Laynez.

It was not long before the new confessor, too, won the favour of Eleonora. He became so dear to her that one day, temperamental as ever, she said: "If Father Diego has to go, then all other Jesuits can depart at once with him." In fact, the barometer of princely favour, which Ignatius in Rome watched so carefully, was again rising.[119]

It is true that good Father Guzmán did not find things easy. The duchess was still passionately addicted to gambling. She made daily good resolutions, which were at once forgotten. One day she said to Father Diego: "Pray for my conversion, even against my will!" The conscientious spiritual director was often driven to despair and, as he complained to Ignatius, would have preferred not to stay in Florence. His reason for this was, he said, that a moral theologian had assured the duchess that it was no grievous sin to lose at play 2000 ducats in a single night, although many people in Tuscany were starving. What did it signify that Eleonora occasionally sent a few hares or a wild boar to the Fathers in their poverty-stricken college, after she had been hunting? But Ignatius had only one reply to all this: persevere, and try to persuade the duchess to endow permanently the college that meant so much to him. To Father Louis du Coudray he wrote: "Give Her Highness a slight hint." After all, the duchess was very well disposed towards the Jesuits. Since Tarquinio Rainaldi had so bravely defended his vocation in the Palazzo Pitti, she had given every encouragement to those young men about her who had decided to enter the Society. There was, for instance, Cristóbal Truxillo, son of a Spanish couple in the duchess's household. At court they called him her "little favourite", and she herself once said: "I will make a great man of the world out of him." Now he wished to become a Jesuit. The duchess admired his zeal, and the remark she made in this connexion, to the astonishment of her court, was at once reported to Ignatius in Rome: "I would give 20,000 ducats to become a Jesuit myself, if I were a man!"[120] It is characteristic of the financially astute duchess that she could reckon the value of her spiritual emotions in ducats.

There is no evidence of any correspondence with Eleonora during the last year of Ignatius' life. When on July 31st, 1556, Ignatius entered into eternity, Polanco announced his death in a somewhat cold and official letter to the duchess in Florence. The matter of the Florentine college was taken up by Laynez, as Ignatius' heir: the duchess, who had not forgotten him, was as attached to him as ever. On October 24th, 1556, he sent a detailed letter to Father Guzmán in Florence concerning the main lines to be followed in the spiritual direction of Her Highness. The duchess, says Laynez from bitter experience, possesses indeed rare gifts, but she is a victim of the demon of gambling. He should make her devote one hour a day to spiritual exercises and employ her great wealth for pious purposes. Many a letter was despatched to Florence from the General's office in Rome. The duchess was even prepared to let the General Congregation of the Jesuits meet, if necessary, in Florence, when Paul IV's hostility to Spain at first prevented its coming together in Rome.[121] In November 1560 she went to Rome for the Jubilee and confessed at Christmas to Father Laynez. Years before she had promised him that she would endow the college at Florence. She had also made proposals to the successor of Ignatius which had both political and ecclesiastical implications: she wanted her seventeen-year-old son Juan to be a cardinal. Laynez has left us an account of this conversation, and the ambitious mother's oft-repeated question is: "Shall we get a cardinal's hat for Juanito?" He did get it, on January 31st, 1560, together with the Pope's young nephew, Charles Borromeo.

So the relations between the duchess and the Jesuits, now governed by

Laynez, were satisfactory, although the actual purpose of Ignatius' and his successors' inexhaustible patience and diplomacy, namely the establishment of the college in Florence on a secure footing, was still unfulfilled. When Laynez fell ill shortly after Ignatius' death, Polanco wrote in connection with his recovery: "The kindness with which the illustrious lady expressed her joy at the recovery of our Vicar General is a sign of her good dispositions – let us hope that she will direct her energies towards a good work, namely to the assistance of the college in Florence." It is perhaps not superfluous to mention that Fathers du Coudray and Guzmán were once called upon to ask the duchess for some of the powder which she had formerly offered to Father Laynez for the relief of the stone, as well as for Alexandrian rose-honey and mineral water. They were remedies against impatience.[122]

But death was already knocking at the door of the Palazzo Pitti. On November 2nd, 1562, Eleonora's favourite son, Cardinal Juanito, died in a hunting accident, for which his elder brother García was probably to blame. Among the people there were rumours – perhaps unfounded – of murder. The duchess, who already in March 1556 had mentioned to Ignatius her forebodings of death, did not long survive this terrible blow. On December 18th, 1562 she, too, departed this life. Laynez wrote from Trent, where he was attending the newly reassembled council, a letter of condolence to Duke Cosimo in the name of the whole Society.[123]

PART TWO

GOD'S CAVALIER

Correspondence with noble Ladies

Introduction

IGNATIUS' correspondence with ladies belonging to the princely houses of his time has already shown us with what skill and assurance he moved in such exalted circles: it was the fruit of his courtly upbringing at Arévalo, which he now used entirely in the service of the Divine Majesty. That service also brought him in contact, as it were inevitably, with the higher aristocracy, to which after all he belonged by birth. We therefore group together the following letters in one chapter, for they illustrate Ignatius' connexions with the Spanish and Italian nobility. It is true that among his letters to benefactresses and other ladies some are also addressed to noblewomen. Our main aim here is to show how this *caballero – noble caballero* is an essential phrase in the spiritual teaching of a man who in the service of God prized nothing more than the "nobility" of mind of a "nobleman" in the best sense of the word – sought also to win for God's cause the women of a social class, the existence and justification of which were to him, as a child of that feudal age, beyond question.[1]

Ignatius of Loyola, the Basque aristocrat, felt that he belonged wholly to that class, and even in the years of his maturity he could never repudiate it. His family was among the *Parientes Mayores* of Guipúzcoa, who had served the kings of Castile for centuries and had the right of being specially invited by the latter to give counsel and military help. It had, moreover, been a family tradition in the house of Loyola for more than a hundred years to have the sons brought up in the household of some great Castilian grandee. This had resulted in numerous connexions with the families of the counts of Oñate, the dukes of Nájera and through them with other Castilian houses. The Basque nobility had besides their own particular pride: with regard to purity of lineage they considered themselves without equal in all Spain, and it was an honour for any Castilian family to be related to them. The Venetian ambassador Andrea Navagero, for instance, who in 1528 on his journey from Spain to France travelled through the province of Guipúzcoa, writes of Ignatius' homeland: "There are here countless peasant houses in which dwell the greatest aristocrats, and these believe – and all Spain regards it as true – that the real nobility is to be found here. One cannot flatter a grandee of Castile more highly than by saying that his family takes its origin from this

111

region. Most of the grandees themselves are of this opinion. And indeed it is well known that the noblest families of Spain derive their origin from these parts."[2]

Ignatius, too, was brought up to think in this way. That is the reason why at the beginning of his conversion he regarded it as so important to forget house and lineage, in order to divest himself ruthlessly of feudal pride by going about as a miserable pilgrim, begging and doing penance. It is also the reason for his not very successful attempts to begin his work for souls at Alcalá by being spiritual director to women of the lower classes. How different were his first successes at Barcelona, where, with a feeling as it were of class solidarity, a group of pious ladies from the highest social circles of the Catalan capital formed at once around Ignatius! We shall hear more of these ladies later. Although Ignatius, with the delicate instinct of one whose life had been spiritualized, kept away from such circles during the remainder of his career, he felt among them less inhibited, more responsive – in fact, he belonged there. This is apparent even in the letters he wrote to these ladies, in spite of all the ruthless self-criticism with which he laboriously penned each word. So it came about that at the very outset of his real lifework in Rome he gathered about him a select number of ladies of the aristocracy, whom he occupied in the service of God. The list of Roman ladies who served the House of St. Martha for fallen girls shows this even as early as 1543. In it figure the proudest names of Rome: the Countess Catarina Pio di Carpi, the Duchess of Sermoneta, Vittoria Colonna, Elena and Claudia Orsini, the Duchess of Castro, the wife of Pierluigi Farnese, even the daughter of the reigning Pope, the Countess of Santa Fiora.[3]

In those years, too, Ignatius was in close touch with ladies of the higher aristocracy of Spain; letters were sent to and fro; passionately yet prudently he wished to win them for some task in the kingdom of his Master that should fill their often purposeless and idle lives. Many of these letters are lost to us, and we know of them only through indications contained in the General's voluminous correspondence. The loss which is most to be regretted is perhaps that of the letters which Ignatius wrote to Doña Catalina de Velasco, the daughter of the Grand Treasurer Juan Velázquez de Cuéllar, in whose household Ignatius was educated. What remains of his correspondence with noble ladies is contained in the following chapter.[4]

The austere tone of these letters (the irrelevance of which to his more important work is only apparent) will be self-evident from their text and from the historical introduction. Here, too, Ignatius remained true to himself in every line, and did not forget for a moment that he was writing to these women purely and solely for the love of God. For that very reason it is astonishing how wide was the scope of Ignatius' truly chivalrous readiness to serve. He had time and patience for all, from the tiresome requests of Spanish ladies for dispensations from fasting to the world-stirring matrimonial quarrels of the Duchess Colonna; from the women of his own family to the distant Marchioness Jacqueline in Flanders. He knew how to reply with the most exquisite politeness, and with an inbred feeling for what was correct in the delicate matter of titles. Without being too insistent, he always, in answering the most trivial questions, came round in the end to the things of God, with which his heart was filled. Hence the admirable tactfulness of his language, with which he maintained his aloofness. What St. Teresa once wrote of herself applies also to Ignatius in his correspondence with women: "The Lord has blest me with such independence, he has given me such a disregard for all visible things, that I allowed myself as much freedom in my relations with these great ladies – in whose service I might have deemed it an honour to be – as if I had been of the same standing as they."[5]

Women of the House of Loyola

WHEN Ignatius wrote letters to women of the great noble families of Spain and Italy, he was, as we have seen, moving in the circles among which he himself had grown up. It is fitting therefore that we begin this chapter with the letters he addressed to women of his own family.

Indeed, not much has remained of the little that Don Iñigo, entirely given up to the service of the Divine Majesty, thought worth writing to his family. In fact, on August 26th, 1552, he rather unwillingly wrote in answer to the Duke of Nájera, who wished to have the heiress of Loyola, Ignatius' great-niece Laurencia, as a wife for a kinsman of his, that he had forgotten his own family once and for all, as he had forgotten the world; and that for a good ten years he had not written to any member of the house of Loyola. This was, indeed, a lapse of memory on Ignatius' part, for he had, as we shall see, sent a letter to his sister Magdalena in May 1545. All the same, it is true that he wrote home but seldom; that, however, by no means implies that he had forgotten the ties binding him to his own kin. We still possess a series of letters which Ignatius wrote to the head of the family in the castle of Loyola. In the first, dated June 1532 from Paris, and addressed to his brother Martín García, he even said he had been wishing for six years to write home oftener, but the things of God had kept him from doing so. Nor did he forget to send polite greetings to the lady of the house. From Rome he announced the news of his first Mass at the crib of the Christ-child – two months later, it is true, and still unaware of the death of his brother, to whom the letter was addressed. At the end of September 1539 he was able to inform his nephew with humble pride of the Pope's oral approval of his new Society, "which we have decided to call the Society of Jesus". By the same post went a letter to his niece Doña María de Vicuña and greetings to his beloved sister Magdalena and her son. The letter is, according to ancient custom, addressed to the head of the house of Loyola, together with his humble greetings to the lady of the house, Juana de Recalde. We can see, then, that even such a man as Ignatius did not forget his family.[6]

Let us first with due respect make mention of his mother, who in her youngest son gave the world a saint, but who could have influenced only the earliest years of Ignatius' life. She was Doña Marina Saenz de Licona, daughter of Doctor Martín García de Licona, who had considerable influence at the court of Henry IV of Castile, and who was heir to the rights and properties of the extinct family of Ladrón de Balda in Azcoitia. The marriage agreement of the lady with Don Beltrán Yáñez de Oñaz y Loyola dated July 13th, 1467, still exists, but we do not know when Ignatius' mother died. It must have been before 1498, when her eldest surviving son Martín García married Doña Magdalena de Araoz, and the latter became mistress of the castle of Loyola. That being so, Ignatius could have had only a few childhood memories of his mother. But the foundations laid by a pious mother in early childhood are more than a memory. We know from reliable witnesses that Ignatius' mother was remarkably firm in her faith, and she is especially praised for her obedience towards the hierarchy of the Church – and we must not forget that the Borgia Pope Alexander VI was then reigning. She zealously attended with her children the services in both churches of which through her father and her husband she had the patronage, Azpeitia and Azcoitia. We may imagine how Doña Marina often prayed with her youngest son; and how he, protected by her love, enjoyed a feeling of well-being in the great, smoky kitchen of Loyola, which, according to the good old Basque custom, was also the living-room of the family.[7]

Before we turn to the woman who took the place of his mother for the growing Ignatius and who won his undying affection, we must briefly mention another lady of the house of Loyola who undoubtedly made a deep impression on the boy. She was María López de Emparán y Loyola, cousin of Ignatius, whose mother Catalina, sister of Ignatius' father, had married the heir of the Emparán family, head of the most powerful house in Azpeitia. Cousin María not long afterwards became an anchoress in the hermitage of San Pedro de Elormendi, in Loyola territory. Ignatius often visited her there, and in 1535, when the widely venerated anchoress was already dead, his gratitude erected a monument to her by settling the sordid legal dispute between the Loyolas and the Franciscan nunnery which had developed out of the hermitage.[8]

The lady by whom Ignatius was brought up, and to whom the first extant letter to a woman of his own family was written, was the wife of his brother Martín García, who after the heroic death of the eldest brother, entered upon the inheritance in Oñaz and Loyola, and later created an entail on these rich properties which was confirmed by the Emperor Charles V. Ignatius was seven years old when his brother's wife came to Loyola. Magdalena was the daughter of Don Pedro de Araoz, Inspector General of the troops to the Gran Capitán Fernández de Córdoba, in whose army the eldest Loyola had fallen in battle two years before. As maid of honour to Queen Isabella the Catholic, she was so beloved at court that on her wedding

115

day the queen gave her jewels and the beautiful painting of the Annunciation for which Magdalena fitted up a chapel in the castle and before which Ignatius often prayed. This deep devotion to the Virgin Mother is reflected in all his relations with women. One of the best authorities on Ignatius' early life says with justice of this devotion to the picture in the castle chapel: "In the life of the author of the *Exercises,* Doña Magdalena's picture of our Lady had the first place, long before those of Olaz, Aránzazu and Montserrat."⁹

Meanwhile Magdalena was called to play a much more important part in the education of the future saint. It was she who, having experienced at the court of the Catholic queen the soaring flight of Spanish piety, now introduced the more refined religious and moral spirit of Castile into the hitherto somewhat too rustic and soldierly life of Loyola. Thus it came about that the recently published Spanish translation of Ludolph the Carthusian's *Life of Jesus* and the *Legends of the Saints* by Jacobus de Voragine were to be found in her possession when her brother-in-law Ignatius asked for books, as he lay wearily on his sickbed at Loyola after his wounding at Pamplona.

As the lord of the castle, Martín García, was from July to September 1521 still in the field, the task of nursing the wounded man fell entirely upon the excellent Doña Magdalena and her two already grown-up daughters, María and Magdalena. Many years later the lady of Loyola had to pay the surgeon Martín de Iztiola ten ducats for the operation on Ignatius' shattered leg. Magdalena's care for her brother-in-law not only brought him bodily recovery but also gave a decisive impulse to his inner conversion. The impression that his sister-in-law made on him is made clear to us by a little incident related many years later. Ignatius once told a Belgian novice that a picture of our Lady, before which he was wont to recite the Hours of the Blessed Virgin, reminded him so much by its beauty of his sister-in-law Magdalena that it disturbed him in his devotions, and he forthwith stuck a piece of paper over the face. ¹⁰

Magdalena bore her husband four sons and four daughters. Ignatius always took a heartfelt interest in their careers. Magdalena's son Millán became a Jesuit, and her daughter Catalina, wife of Don Juan Martínez de Lasao, later expressed to the General of the Society her sincere joy at its growth. We can then understand what Ignatius meant when he greeted the lady of the house so warmly in his letters. Magdalena's husband died on November 29th, 1538. The news was, as we have seen, slow to reach Rome. Ignatius was then fully occupied with the greatest task of his life, the foundation of the Society. It is understandable that it was not until September 24th, 1539, that he found time to send a letter of condolence to his sister-in-law. The widow was all

116

the more in need of consolation because Don Beltrán, her eldest son and successor to the property, was squandering the inheritance and thus imperilling her own settlement.[11]

The grace and love of Christ our Lord be always with us to our favour and our help.

Knowing that it was the good pleasure of God our Lord to take away from these present sufferings the companion whom he gave you for a certain time in this life, I then did the greatest thing I could do for anyone, namely, I said Mass for his soul at an altar where, each time Mass is celebrated there, a soul is released from Purgatory. We ought not to weep when he rejoices, nor to grieve when he is glad, but to look to ourselves that we may attain the same goal, so living in this life that in the other we may live for ever. I know full well, indeed, that you are completely convinced of this because I have always known you to be a God-fearing woman.

Now it remains for me to ask you, for the service of God our Lord, to help us with your good works and with your prayer in an important undertaking upon which for the glory of God we have embarked, for we feel in this so unworthy. I refer to the letter which I have written to your son Beltrán. I hope that he will be guided in all things by you; for I am certain that he, who in other times knew how to squander both what he had and what he had not, will now be generous in anything he can, for such a devout, righteous and holy matter.

I will conclude, praying God's divine Majesty that he may dispose of us all as is best for his service in all things and that we may in everything give thanks for ever and ever.

From Rome, September 24th, 1539   Poor in goodness,
                                                                            Iñigo

To my sister in Christ our Lord,
    Doña Magdalena, the Lady of Loyola,
    Azpeitia

Soon after receiving Extreme Unction on September 29th, Magdalena died. On October 30th, 1539, Father Araoz, Magdalena's cousin, wrote from Saragossa to inform Ignatius of her death; so she never read her brother-in-law's letter. Ignatius answered Araoz in words of deep emotion. But Doña

117

Magdalena's fairest epitaph is the sentence which Ignatius wrote to her: "I have always known you to be a God-fearing woman."[12]

There were other women in the wide family circle with whom Ignatius was on terms of friendship. Magdalena's son Beltrán had in 1538 married Doña Juana de Recalde, daughter of Don Juan López de Recalde, Inspector-General of the Spanish army. To her, too, as mistress of the house, Ignatius sent his respects. We shall later see what a painful surprise it was to Ignatius when the son of Duke Francis Borgia married Juana's daughter Laurencia, the heiress of Loyola.[13]

Another woman connected with the family exercised a truly motherly influence on Ignatius as a page and young officer: María de Guevara, mother-in-law of the Grand Treasurer Juan Velázquez de Cuéllar, in whose household Ignatius spent a good ten years of his youth. She was related to Ignatius' mother through the counts of Oñate. Through her, while in Arévalo, he came in contact with the Franciscan piety of the great days of Cardinal Ximenes de Cisneros. Doña Maria watched with anxiety her protégé's early escapades. Tradition relates that she once said to him at that time: "Iñigo, you will give us no peace until you get your leg broken!"[14]

When a few years later Ignatius, with a shattered leg, was being carried on the long road from Pamplona to Loyola, the sad procession called at the house of the lords of Echeandía at Anzuola. The lady of the house was Doña Magdalena, Ignatius' beloved sister. She was married to Don Juan Beltrán de Gallaíztegui, Lord of Ozaeta, and had a son called Beltrán. Ignatius paid another visit, this time of gratitude and farewell, to his sister at Oñate, when he was riding to Montserrat after his recovery. Later, too, he remained warmly attached to her and her son, and from time to time sent them greetings. In the spring of 1545 Ignatius received a letter from his sister, who sought spiritual consolation from her now famous brother. Ignatius answered her with words of sincere advice, and sent her through her cousin Araoz a quantity of heavily indulgenced rosaries.[15]

IHS

The sovereign grace and love of Christ our Lord be always with us to our continual favour and help.

During the last few days I received a letter from you and since I could see in it your good desires and holy affection for God's greater glory, I rejoiced much at this in our Lord. May it please him through his infinite and sovereign goodness continually to increase in you the love for him above all things, setting not in part, but in everything, all your love and affection on that same Lord of ours, and for his sake loving all creatures, frequenting persons whose conversation and work is for the glory of his divine Majesty. You should also go often to the Sacrament of Penance and receive the most holy Eucharist every time you can, so that God may unite your soul to him through true hope, and increase of lively faith and most necessary charity without which we cannot be saved.

To this end, as the soul desirous of serving her Creator and Lord in all things should seek all the good means possible to her, it seems to me that I should help you with one such means. Believing, then, that they will be received with that reverence and respect with which the things of our Creator and Lord ought to be revered and respected, I send you twelve rosaries, which have many blessings attached to them, and three more which have different indulgences, together with three others which contain all the blessings attached to all the rosaries already mentioned – as you will see from a memorandum which I am sending you with this letter through the Licenciate Araoz – with the conditions required to enjoy such great treasures as are contained in them. Since you will thus receive a special grace, it will be a joy to me in our Lord if you will keep me informed of the spiritual profit you experience from them, to the greater glory of his divine Majesty.

I ask you kindly to remember me to all those who love you in our Lord and would probably be glad to be remembered by me, greeting them on my behalf in his divine Majesty. May he in his infinite and sovereign goodness deign to give us his abundant grace so that we may know his most holy will and fulfil it perfectly.

Poor in goodness,
Iñigo

From Rome, May 24th, 1545
(Held back until June 10th)

To my sister in our Lord,
Doña Madgalena de Loyola, in Anzuola

In 1551, long after Doña Magdalena's death, Don Beltrán de Gallaíztegui wrote his uncle Ignatius a well-phrased letter containing greetings from his wife, Doña Isabel de Recalde, a sister of the lady of Loyola. Of the latter he says: "The lady of Loyola castle has two daughters of fourteen and eleven, who have turned out very pretty." From his letter too we gather how proud the whole family was of its Ignatius. Don Beltrán praises God "that He has given our family such a man, whose learning and exemplary life oblige us to imitate him." When in 1571 the General Francis Borgia, accompanied by Father Polanco, was riding past the house of Magdalena Gallaíztegui in Anzuola, he dismounted from his mule and on his knees kissed the walls within which his master Ignatius had once been tended by his sister.[16]

The later history of Ignatius' birthplace is the effect of the genealogical complications caused by the female succession in the house of Loyola. Ignatius' great-nephew, Don Martín García de Loyola, the last male scion of this ancient race, won fame and riches as a commander in the conquest of Peru. He married a princess of Inca blood, Beatriz Sayre de Goya Tupac, and died a soldier's death in Chile in 1598. The daughter of this marriage, Ana María de Loyola y Goya, married in Spain a great-grandson of Francis Borgia, duke and Jesuit. She was never able to enter into her inheritance in Guipúzcoa, as other relatives contested her claim in a lawsuit that dragged on for many years; but her granddaughter, Teresa Enríquez y Loyola, Marquesa de Alcañices, at last became mistress of Loyola and gave Ignatius' birthplace to the Queen Mother of Spain, Mariana of Austria, who in 1682 handed it over to the Jesuits. Soon the ancient walls of the Casa Solar of Loyola were hidden beneath the baroque magnificence of church and college.[17]

Women of the House of Borja

WHEN the spiritual sons of Ignatius first began their work in Spain, and Father Araoz landed at Barcelona in 1539, the viceroy there was the Marqués de Lombay, Francis Borgia. No one at that time could have imagined that this grandee, so close a friend of the Emperor Charles V, would, after the death of his wife and when his numerous children had been provided for, enter the new Society. Even when that happened, the understandably delighted General could not have foreseen that he would become related to the illustrious house of Borja through the marriage of Don Juan de Borja, Francis' son, with his great-niece Laurencia, heiress of Loyola, which was celebrated on August 7th, 1552. Let it be said at once that Ignatius was very displeased at this marriage; for there at once arose evil gossip at the court in Valladolid and in the palace of the King of Portugal to the effect that the old General of the Jesuits had engineered a match so advantageous for his family. Father Araoz, who knew better than any how to deal with such situations, pacified the angry uncle in a long letter dated November 25th, 1552. With a certain irony he pointed out how skilfully the Jesuit-duke had now provided for this son of his, who had hitherto lacked a position. For – as Ignatius must know – the Loyola inheritance was a rich one, even if the name of Borja had a more aristocratic sound. Juan de Borja had brought more blue blood than money into this marriage. At the Portuguese court in Almeirim, Father Francisco Enríquez defended his General in an audience, saying that the match was more in Don Juan de Borja's favour than in that of the house of Loyola, "for only the greatness of the inheritance and the nobility of the bride have brought about this alliance, which might have attracted other illustrious and highborn gentlemen, whereas Don Juan de Borja could not call an acre of ground his own."[18]

Apart from this painful episode, Ignatius was on excellent terms with all members of the Borja family. As early as September 1546 he asked Doctor Miguel Torres to visit in his name "every male and female relative of the Lord Duke". When Duke Francis had put his house in order and announced to all the world that he belonged to the Society of Jesus, Ignatius could write in a solemn letter to the new Duke of Gandía, Don Carlos – and we cannot read without emotion these resounding words of a Saint,

121

when we think that the family he so praises had sprung from the sins of Pope Alexander VI and King Ferdinand the Catholic; "For many years I have had your whole family inscribed in my heart, and my only wish is that our Lord Jesus Christ, too, may let it be written in the Book of Life."[19]

It was through the daughter of St. Francis Borgia, Doña Isabel, that Ignatius first entered into correspondence with the women of the house of Borja. Born at Medina del Campo in 1532, she had the Empress Isabel herself in person as godmother. In October 1548, her father married her to Don Francisco Sandoval y Rojas, Count of Lerma. Ignatius sent his heartiest felicitations on the occasion. The count was on his mother's side the great-grandson of that Doña Teresa Enríquez de Cárdenas, who had once visited Ignatius in prison at Alcalá. He was later to be one of the most influential courtiers of Philip II. Isabel was for some years maid of honour to the mad Joanna at Tordesillas. When her father was in Rome in 1550, and the world was in amazement at the Jesuit vocation of the former viceroy, the new member of the Society expressed the wish to his General that the latter would write some words of spiritual counsel to his beloved daughter. Ignatius was at once willing to do so. Pope Julius III had just renewed for him the same indulgences on rosaries that Paul III had granted (as we shall see later) to the Vicereine of Sicily, Leonor Osorio, whom Ignatius much respected and who had died shortly before. "God's Cavalier" therefore presented the noble lady and her husband with some rosaries.[20]

IHS

My Lady in our Lord.

May the sovereign grace and eternal love of Christ our Lord visit Your Ladyship with his most holy gifts and spiritual graces.

Although it is a new thing for me to write to Your Ladyship, to obey the Duke who has ordered me to do so is not new, nor is the desire to serve Your Ladyship in the Lord of all, and to present you before his divine and sovereign goodness in my unworthy prayers, as one who has a very special and very right affection in our Lord for all that very illustrious and blessed House.

I also wanted to give testimony to Your Ladyship that the Duke, by the grace of God, is very well, and that every care is taken that he should preserve his bodily health which he employs so well in God's service and by his grace will continue so to employ.

I also send Your Ladyship blessed beads with the same indulgences that were given to Doña Leonor Osorio who is in glory. And because our Holy Father Julius III has confirmed all the privileges which his predecessor granted us, the Duke wanted me to send one of these rosaries to Your Ladyship and another to the Count, for I cannot but desire that God, the author of all spiritual good, should confer on Your Ladyship an abundance of his very special favours and graces.

And because I think that you have both recognized that the whole ·of this little Society continually offers itself for your service, I excuse myself from offering it to you here. I merely ask the divine and sovereign goodness to deign to give us all his abundant grace, so that we may always know his most holy will and fulfil it perfectly.

Rome, January 1st, 1551   Ignatius

Doña Isabel was not to use the rosaries Ignatius had given her for long. After she had given birth to the heir her husband desired – this was the Duke of Lerma who acquired an evil reputation under Philip III – she had only a few more years to live. She died from a heart attack on March 21st, 1558, at the age of twenty-six. Her father was staying at Valladolid at the time, and was just on his way to the palace of the Regent Juana. It was then that he received a supernatural indication of his daughter's death. While talking calmly to Juana he said, as if casually, "Pray, Your Highness, for the soul of Doña Isabel, who was so devoted and so dear to you, for I have just learned that she has left us suddenly for the next life."[21]

On the same day as the above letter was despatched to the Countess Lerma, Ignatius wrote similarly to another daughter of St. Francis Borgia, the Marquesa Juana de Alcañices. Born in Madrid in 1535, she was the last of his children for whom he made provision by an excellent marriage shortly before his departure for Rome – a happy event which he duly reported to Ignatius. Juana married Don Juan Enríquez de Almanza y Rojas, Marqués de Alcañices. Her husband belonged to the great family of the Almirantes of Castile. Juana was a celebrated beauty, and the poet Pedro de Lemos dedicated to her one of those fashionable epigrams called *motes,* such as Don Iñigo de Loyola had once wished to compose for the lady of his affections. The amount of Juana's dowry was the reason why she was preferred to Isabel, the daughter of the Viceroy of Sicily, Juan de Vega. More will be said of this later.[22]

Let us here at least mention briefly that soon after the date of Ignatius' letter to Doña Juana, a great misfortune fell upon the Enríquez family, when Don Juan's sister Ana Enríquez, the friend of St. Teresa, was imprisoned by the Inquisition for sympathizing with the Lutherans. Ignatius must have

123

remembered how an ancestress of hers, Teresa Enríquez, had visited him in the prison of the Inquisition. The members of his Society, especially Francis Borgia, later gave the unfortunate woman solace and help.

On April 2nd, 1552, Juana was able with great joy to greet her father in Valladolid after his ordination. Father Bustamente informed Ignatius in detail of the meeting. Some months after the letter to Doña Juana, a comprehensive dispensation from fasting, for which Ignatius had asked the Roman Curia, was sent to Juana's mother-in-law, the Marquesa Elvira de Rojas.[23]

The third lady of the house of Borja to whom Ignatius wrote a letter was St. Francis Borgia's sister, Doña Luisa de Borja y Aragón, wife of Don Martín de Gurrea y Aragón, Count of Ribagorza and later Duke of Villahermosa. Born in 1520 at Gandía, she was Francis' favourite sister, brought up with him in the house of their uncle the Archbishop of Saragossa, Juan de Aragón. After her marriage, therefore, Luisa continued to have her home in the kingdom of Aragón. Her palace in Pedrola was later to be the refuge of the Jesuits, when the mob of Saragossa drove them from the capital. Her marriage with Don Martín, who was only sixteen at the time, did not turn out well. For five years, from 1547 to 1552, Count Ribagorza was with the army in Flanders; and on his return from the wars he brought a mistress with him, who not till two years later, and after energetic protests on the part of the injured wife, retired to the Dominican convent in Saragossa. Then the husband went off to England with Prince Philip on the latter's wedding voyage. Francis Borgia consoled his sister with affectionate letters.[24]

Luisa and her husband, Francis reported to Ignatius as early as 1546, were remarkably well disposed towards the Society of Jesus. It was therefore a keenly felt disappointment that her brother never told her anything of his decision to become a Jesuit. When the count was at home for a year, between the war in Flanders and the voyage to England, the couple felt a great desire to invite to Saragossa their famous Father Francis, then about to travel to the Portuguese court at Prince Philip's command. For that the permission of the General of the Society was necessary. With the count's official petition to Ignatius there went to Rome also a note from the Countess Luisa, in which she expressly stated that her request was in no way dictated merely by earthly affection. Prudently they did not send their letters direct by post to Ignatius, but had them brought to him in his room by Cardinal Bartolomeo de la Cueva; for they knew how friendly the General was with this prelate of the ducal house of Albuquerque. He it was who shortly afterwards, together with Michelangelo, drew up the first plans of a great Jesuit church in Rome. So Countess Luisa got a personal reply addressed to her, and in fact soon had the consolation of being able to greet her priest-brother, for whom on the occasion of his first Mass three years before she had embroidered that beautiful chasuble which is still to be seen at Loyola.[25]

IHS

My Lady in our Lord.

The sovereign grace and eternal love of Christ our Lord be with Your Ladyship, together with his most holy gifts and spiritual graces.

A letter from you, together with one from the Count, was given to me by His Eminence Cardinal de la Cueva, who for his part carried out Your Ladyship's command in respect of ordering Father Francis de Borgia to go to Saragossa. I do not doubt that your desire for his presence is more spiritual than natural love, although Your Ladyship seemed to fear that I should suspect only a natural sister's love on your part, and tried in the beginning of your letter to disabuse me of that suspicion. I am quite convinced, in the divine Majesty, that as Your Ladyship is Father Francis' sister in the flesh, so you are also, and very much so, in the spirit and desire of God's glory which does not seek its own consolation and satisfaction, but what is best suited to the helping of souls and that God our Lord and Creator may be served and glorified in them.

I shall write to Father Francis that he is to do what Your Ladyship orders, and even though it is not commanded in virtue of obedience, let Your Ladyship not doubt that he will do it. I really think that he will already have gone to Portugal at the command of the King, or will go there soon, but it will be for a short time only. I am writing to him by this same post and would have sent the letters a month or two earlier, if I had had someone to send them by.

As to the rest of Your Ladyship's letter, about the devotion and frequenting of the holy Sacraments that there is in that city, much thanks for this should be given to God our Lord as the author of it and of all good.

In the matter of the prayers that Your Ladyship asks me to make and in all the rest that you command me for the glory of God our Lord, I shall obey with a right good will, as is, indeed, my duty.

Thus I conclude, asking God's goodness that he will deign to give us all his full grace, so that we may always know his most holy will and perfectly fulfil it.

Your illustrious Ladyship's most humble servant in our Lord,

Rome, August 20th, 1553   Ignatius

125

Countess Ribagorza came to resemble her brother in her striving after Christian perfection. She was especially renowned for her love of the Blessed Sacrament and for her solicitude for the spiritual care of the Moorish "new Christians" living on her estates. (It was the same district in which Ignatius, when still a knight, had wished to stick his dagger into a Moor for the love of the Virgin Mary.) Her state of mind is best expressed in the will which she drew up before her husband's departure for England. Her son, Duke Fernando of Villahermosa, married in 1582 Johanna, the daughter of the Bohemian chancellor, Wratislaw von Pernstein, and at the wedding in Saragossa the Empress María and her little page Aloysius Gonzaga were present.

Duchess Luisa lies buried with her husband in the same grave at Pedrola, and the inscription thereon says: "As they loved one another in life, so in death they are not divided." Her portrait, by the Fleming Rolan de Mois, still hangs in the palace of the dukes of Villahermosa at Madrid. The people called her "the Holy Duchess". The prayer that Ignatius once promised her bore fruit in her soul.[26]

Finally there is still one woman in the ducal family at Gandía for whom Ignatius had the deepest respect, the venerable Aunt Juana. She was the sister of Duchess Leonor, St. Francis' wife. Her parents were of the highest aristocracy of Portugal, Don Álvaro de Castro and Isabel de Meneses Barreto. Juana always used her mother's surname. When her sister married, she came to live with her brother-in-law's family, stayed with them from 1539 onwards in Barcelona, and there got to know the Jesuits. The first mention of this lady in Ignatius' letters occurs towards the end of 1545, when Juana was using all her influence for the founding of a college at Gandía. Ignatius refers to her as "our sister". There was a special reason for this title. Doña Juana had become acquainted with Father Araoz, and the latter wrote to Ignatius in January 1546, that Juana "would much like to travel to Rome to see Ignatius". It will be shown later that this desire was the effect of the much-envied example of a woman whom Juana already knew in Barcelona as an ardent admirer of Ignatius, Doña Isabel Roser, and who in the meantime had been admitted to the obedience of the Society in Rome. With this idea in mind, Juana decided in 1546, to found at Gandía a convent of ascetic women under Jesuit direction. Father Oviedo pleaded urgently in favour of the scheme. The General, alarmed, categorically decided against it. Instead, Juana caused him joy by richly endowing the new college at Gandía and by paying for the studies of two scholastics in Alcalá or Salamanca. Delightedly Father Oviedo wrote to Ignatius: "When one sees the generosity of this lady and her love for the Society, one must love her in the Lord Jesus Christ."[27]

Doña Juana shared at Gandía the banishment of the ducal pair from court; they had fallen into disgrace on the marriage of Philip to María of Portugal. Here a new task offered itself to the courageous woman when her sister, Duchess Leonor, died on March 27th, 1546. She now took the place of a mother to the duke's children and shared all his anxieties concerning the marriage of his numerous daughters. When, as we have seen, the last daughter Juana left her father's house, and the duke solemnly revealed to his sister-in-law that he was a Jesuit and now wished to admit the fact before all the world, Juana's task in the Borja household was finished. Moreover, the royal favour once more shone upon the house of Borja, and the request came to Doña Juana from Valladolid to enter the court of the Regent of Spain, the Infanta María, and her husband Maximilian of Austria. The royal pair, who had received on their marriage the title, confirmed by Charles V, of "King and Queen of Bohemia", then resided at Valladolid, and in December 1550, when Maximilian had to return to Germany and leave his wife alone, Queen María was pregnant. Juana departed for Valladolid.[28]

Shortly before this, a long petition from her for a dispensation from fasting had been sent through Ignatius to the Roman Curia. The answer of the Penitentiary was too indefinite and not comprehensive enough for the evidently rather scrupulous lady. She complained to her brother-in-law, who at that time, just after his first mass at Loyola, was staying in his hermitage at Oñate in the Basque provinces. From there Francis wrote to Ignatius: "The brief of the Penitentiary to Doña Juana was too niggardly, for the dispensation from fasting and permission to eat meat were not given. Juana is at the moment in Valladolid on account of a royal birth." To this request Francis added another, to the effect that Ignatius would also send his sister-in-law, who was now so influential at the regent's court, a document granting her a share in the spiritual benefits of the Society of Jesus. To avoid all difficulties arising from his recently made vow of poverty, the Jesuit-duke adds specially that the expenses of both documents should be charged to the account of the new Duke of Gandía, Carlos.

Meanwhile an archduke had been born at Valladolid. He was given the name Ferdinand, and Juana took care of him like a mother. It is no wonder that the General, ever anxious to keep up good relations with the great, set about procuring from the Penitentiary a new and clearer dispensation. On June 1st, 1551, it was despatched to Valladolid, together with the document conferring a share in the spiritual benefits of the Society and a polite letter to Juana. It is amusing to note that Ignatius, usually so well-versed in questions of title, is here guilty of a slight error, for in his letter he calls the Infanta "Queen of Hungary" and not "Queen of Bohemia". He does not forget to ask Juana to kiss her Majesty's hands. He already knew from his

127

friendship with the royal governess Leonor Mascarenhas what could be achieved through the influence of a pious lady at court.[29]

IHS

My Lady in our Lord.

The sovereign grace and eternal love of Christ our Lord be with and visit Your Ladyship with his most holy gifts and spiritual graces.

During these last few days, I have learnt that you have been called to the court of the Queen of Hungary and that you were setting out for that country, and that, with that charity which he who is sovereign and perfect charity has always shown for this humble Society of ours, you wanted to take one of our members with you. At all this I have rejoiced in our Lord and desire that the most holy and kindly Providence of God our Lord may set Your Ladyship in the place where you may be most useful with your gifts to his honour and glory. This I hope he has done in this matter of going to the Court of Her Majesty, whose hand I beg Your Ladyship to kiss for me as on behalf of a man of prayer very devoted to her in our Lord, and as one who is daily offered new occasions of God's service, as the Duke will have written you more in detail.

Here I send Your Ladyship a document which contains the communication of the suffrages and merits of the whole Society, for since it is under such a deep obligation to Your Ladyship, it is right that it should make you a special sharer in everything in it that is pleasing to God.

I also send you a fuller dispensation, in order not to give any room for scruple over what it contains, in accordance with what the Duke commanded.

I will not say more now, except may it please the divine and sovereign goodness to give us all his abundant grace, so that we may always know his most holy will and perfectly fulfil it.

Rome, June 1st, 1551   Ignatius

To Doña Juana de Meneses

The little archduke, whose birth Juana had attended, died after only a year. Queen María soon afterwards set out for Vienna. Francis and his sister-in-law begged her to support the work of the Jesuits in Austria as much as she could. Aunt Juana returned to Gandía. There she died on August 15th, 1564, as Araoz informed the General Laynez. According to her wish, uttered many years before, she was buried in the college church of Gandía.[30]

Women of the House of Colonna

CULTURAL relations between Spain and Italy in the sixteenth century formed an intricate network of paths crossing one another; and thus Ignatius, the great reformer of the Church, met also the two women who were the glory of their age, the one on account of her mind, the other because of her beauty. They were both of the illustrious house of Colonna: Vittoria, sister of Ascanio Colonna, Duke of Tagliacozzo, and the latter's wife Joanna. In biographies of these two famous women their relations with the founder of the Society of Jesus have hitherto hardly been mentioned. Therefore let us first state what the archives of the Society have to say about them.

It may be new even to those who have made a study of Vittoria Colonna to hear that the poetess was on the friendliest terms with Ignatius of Loyola. Here we will presume that the main facts about the great woman's life are known and concern ourselves only with the circumstances which towards the end of 1544 brought her into contact with the General of the Jesuits. Vittoria, born in 1492, the daughter of the Constable of Naples, Fabrizio Colonna, married on December 27th, 1509, in the castle on the island of Ischia, Don Ferrante de Ávalos, Marquis of Pescara, who died in battle on the imperial side in 1525. The widow withdrew once more to the castle of Ischia, a favourite residence of the family, at that time the home of the gifted Costanza de Ávalos, whom Charles V so much esteemed. Vittoria's marriage and all the subsequent events of her life show how faithful the Colonna family was at this period to the Spanish-Imperial cause. In the years following 1532, Vittoria attended the lectures on the Bible given by the Spaniard Juan Valdés in nearby Naples, where he had gathered round him in his splendid house on the Riviera di Chiaia a brilliant circle of ladies educated in the school of Humanism. She had little to do, however, with the heretical tendencies of the already suspect Valdés, which were becoming increasingly obvious. In 1534 she got to know in Rome the famous Capuchin Ochino, whose fiery Lenten sermons even the Emperor attended. The climax of Vittoria's political and social career was reached when she, together with her sister-in-law Joanna, gave a magnificent reception in the Emperor's honour at Rome in April 1536. She was already celebrated as a poetess throughout Italy; but she had become more and more disillusioned with the world. Her friend Cardinal Pole opened her eyes to the burning question of a real reform of the Church; and restlessly seeking the peace of God she travelled in the years 1537–40 from one place to another, staying in Rome at the Palazzo Colonna, then in Orvieto, Arpino, or Ferrara.[31]

There, at the brilliant court of Duke Hercules and his French wife Renée, the friend of Calvin, Vittoria stayed from May 8th, 1537, till February 1538. It was the time when Ignatius' companions, coming from Paris, were preaching and tending the sick in Northern Italy, until they should have the opportunity to take ship for Jerusalem. Vittoria, too, was then seriously considering a plan to make a pilgrimage to the Holy Land in company with a Capuchin and a group of pious women. Then two strange figures appeared in Ferrara and took up their abode in a miserable hospital. They were Ignatius' friends from Paris, Claude Jay and Simon Rodríguez. Many years later Rodríguez wrote in his memoirs of those days how the stern and surly matron of the hospital, following her usual custom, even subjected the newly arrived strangers to an examination for syphilis, which was then everywhere rampant, before she would give them lodging; and how they both submitted to this humiliating procedure and then, by nightly prayer and severe fasting, converted the mistrusting woman to a different opinion – these men were saints indeed.

The strange news even penetrated into the ducal palace, for the Marchioness of Pescara soon learnt that these men were graduates of Paris who wished to go to the Holy Land. She also wanted to do so; so she hastened to the matron of the hospital and heard her enthusiastic words of praise, and thus it came about that Vittoria Colonna became acquainted with the two Jesuits. The first wave of the spiritual movement that Ignatius had stirred up had reached the soul of this great woman.[32]

Now she had the same experience as Ignatius. Neither she nor Ignatius and his companions ever reached Jerusalem. The Marchioness did indeed obtain from Pope Paul III on March 13th, 1537, permission to go on a pilgrimage, just as Ignatius and his companions did on April 27th of the same year; but in a letter of June 12th, 1537, to Cardinal Hercules Gonzaga, Vittoria complains that "at the moment there is no possibility of getting to Jerusalem". If the political confusion of the year 1537 had not prevented Vittoria and Ignatius from going on a pilgrimage to the Holy Places, they might have sailed together in the same ship from Venice. God ordained otherwise. Their destination was Rome, their destiny to reform the Church. In October 1541 Vittoria retired to the convent of Santa Catarina at Viterbo, and the three years she spent there were decisive for her spiritual life. It was there that she received the letter of August 22nd, 1542, in which Ochino told her of his apostasy from the Catholic Church. Vittoria was shaken to the depths of her soul, and the scandal resounded throughout the Church.[33] But her soul, burdened as it was with all the frightening problems of ecclesiastical reform, had also its consolation; shortly before, she had met in Viterbo the cousin of the extraordinary man who was the master of those who had so impressed her at Ferrara, namely Father Antonio Araoz. He visited her in Ignatius' name and spoke to her of the things of God and of the Church. Vittoria felt it at once – here was the true reform in action. Personal contact with the General of the Society was thus established.

Vittoria's conversations with Father Araoz did not indeed concern only the work of reform, but also sordid family quarrels which had broken out between her and her outrageous brother Duke Ascanio, and more especially the latter's broken marriage with Joanna Colonna. In connexion with this matter Araoz had already been to Naples and Ischia. The noble lady therefore felt it her duty to write a personal letter of thanks to Ignatius in January 1542, and to tell Araoz when she met him all the latest news about her brother's matrimonial difficulties.

In the superscription of this letter she calls Ignatius "Don Ignygo". We can hardly be wrong in supposing that this almost familiar mode of address is an echo of the conversations that Vittoria had had with Araoz, Ignatius' cousin. The General kept the note carefully and before filing it wrote thereon with his own hand: "1542. Viterbo. The Marchioness of Pescara."[34]

Most illustrious and reverend Father in Christ.

I give you most grateful thanks for the trouble and toil you have taken for our common Lord and for me in relation to Master Andrea, and still more for introducing me to the good, humble and holy Don Antón, your nephew. And because you will know everything from him, I shall not write at greater length. I think my deeds and my obeying in whatever you order me to do, sufficiently show you my goodwill. May God our Lord fulfil your desires as an earnest and sign that they will be completely fulfilled there where they have their end.

From St. Catherine at Viterbo January 21st, (1542)
Wholly at your reverence's disposal
The Marchioness of Pescara

To the most illustrious and reverend
    Father in Christ Don Ignygo

131

After her deep disappointment with Ochino, whose subsequent career in Zürich, Geneva, and Germany she followed with sorrow, Vittoria's growing sense of the need for a true reform of the Church brought her to Rome. At the end of 1544 she took an apartment in the convent of Sant' Anna de' Funari. We know from her biography about the hours she spent there in conversation with her friend Michelangelo, who was also disillusioned with life. But there was in Rome another great man, Ignatius, whose spiritual attraction was felt by Vittoria. To him she could best express her grief at Ochino's apostasy. When Ignatius about this time mentions in one of his letters "a person of great charity", who had interceded with him for Ochino, Vittoria Colonna was certainly meant. Ignatius did indeed, after long consideration, in the same letter of December 12th, 1545, to Father Jay in Dillingen, encourage the latter to attempt Ochino's conversion. Apart from this, the conversations between Ignatius and Vittoria concerned the reform of the Church – not in unrealizable plans and vague longings, but, as Ignatius' way always was, in practical works of simple charity. Vittoria joined the ranks of those women who under the Master's direction took up the work of looking after catechumens, prostitutes and orphans. In the list of patrons of the House of St. Martha for fallen girls we find her name: "The Illustrious Lady Marchioness of Pescara". In a letter of that time it is related how Vittoria once found accommodation in the House of St. Martha for a rich girl of her acquaintance whose morals were in grave danger.

Vittoria was also concerned with a fact which she had learned from her experience with Ochino and Valdés; that true reform must begin with good sermons, filled with sound Catholic doctrine. The sons of Ignatius seemed to her specially suited for this work. In a report sent to Spain in May 1545, it states that she had asked Ignatius himself to preach, but he was already too much occupied with his Spanish sermons. "The Marchioness of Pescara, who lives at Sant' Anna, thereupon asked Master Ignatius, and repeated her request often and insistently, that he would send someone from our house to preach at Sant' Anna. And so Master Salmerón went and spoke to them, to the great satisfaction of the Marchioness and all who heard him."[35]

Thus Vittoria Colonna during the last two years of her life was at home among those who put into practice their ardent love of the Church their Mother. With her humanistic friend Lattanzio Tolomei, to whom Ignatius in person had given the Exercises in 1539, she must often have spoken of her longing for God, as she did with Michelangelo. The spirit with which Ignatius' saintly penitent Leonor Osorio filled the house of her husband, the imperial ambassador Juan de Vega, was for Vittoria like a heavenly blessing. She once wrote to her brother Duke Ascanio: "One of the favours God has shown us is the fact that we have here in Rome such a good ambassador, Don Juan de Vega." Does not the beautiful sonnet which she composed at the end of her life in honour of the great martyr of the early Church, Ignatius of Antioch, contain some echo of her reverence for the living Ignatius and his ardent love for the name of Jesus? When Vittoria Colonna died a holy death on February 25th, 1547, the sorrowing Michelangelo wrote: "Death has taken a great friend from me." Ignatius could have written the same.[36]

Before we turn to Vittoria's sister-in-law Joanna, whose fate Ignatius sought to direct, it may be of interest to mention four other ladies of the Italian nobility who were related to the house of Colonna. The poor pilgrim Ignatius hardly thought, when on his first landing in Italy shortly before Easter 1523, he had a fainting fit at the gate of Fondi and was kindly taken in by the lady of that city, Countess Beatrice Appiani, wife of Vespasiano Colonna, that he would ever come into social contact with these aristocratic circles. Later he was told with what piety Isabella di Capua, Ferrante Gonzaga's wife, had received the sacraments at Loreto with her son. It is Ignatius the Reformer who writes of Isabella: "There is someone who can restore much, and in many places." He took an even more heartfelt interest in Isabella Gonzaga, wife of the Marquis Francesco del Vasto, a nephew of Joanna Colonna on the side of his mother, María de Aragón. She pressed Ignatius to let her have as preacher Father Salmerón, so beloved among the aristocracy of Naples. Often the General remembers her in his letters. Ignatius' last conversation at supper before his death concerned the purchase of a house which belonged to Giulia Colonna, and which he wished to acquire for the Roman College.[37]

All these ladies, however, were outshone in beauty and political importance by Joanna Colonna, consort of Duke Ascanio. She was the most beautiful woman of her century. Her sister-in-law Vittoria had written a sonnet in her honour:[38]

To thee Heaven gave with full hands;
My star was niggardly, and my sun turns
From thy paradise its gaze upon itself.

Joanna has become famous for all time through the wonderful portrait of her that Raphael painted for Cardinal Bibiena in 1518, the year in which she was betrothed to Ascanio Colonna. The Cardinal, who played such an inglorious role in the history of the papacy, presented the picture while legate in France in 1518 to King Francis I, that connoisseur of women, and it hangs to-day in the Louvre. Contemporary poets delighted to lay their works at the feet of the woman who was called throughout Italy *Diva Signora*. A modern historian of the house of Colonna says of her: "Joanna was in her time renowned for her gifts of beauty and intellect. Many men of letters employed their pens to sing her praises; Ruscelli published a collection of poems entitled *Temple of Fame of Donna Giovanna di Aragona*." Filonico Alicarnasso wrote her life, and the unpublished manuscript still lies in the Vatican Library.[39]

Her origins were Spanish; and loyalty to Charles V's Italian policy determined her whole life. She was the daughter of Duke Ferdinand of Montalto and his wife Castellana, of the house of Cardona. Her father was an illegitimate son of King Ferrante I of Naples, of the royal house of Aragon, and therefore Joanna always gave herself the proud suffix "di Aragona". Born in 1502, she was betrothed to Duke Ascanio Colonna in 1518, and the magnificent wedding took place at Naples in 1521, when Vittoria Colonna attracted much attention by her almost regal elegance. Joanna's marriage was no doubt influenced by the same political considerations as that between Vittoria and the Marquis of Pescara: the powerful family of Colonna was thus to be irrevocably attached to the Spanish policy in Naples, where in 1516 Joanna the Mad and her young son Charles had been proclaimed rulers of the kingdom. Let it be said straight away: the marriage of Joanna to the rough and avaricious warrior Ascanio was from the beginning an unhappy one. It was a consolation for her that she could always retire to the castle of Ischia, and that the lively intellectual life of Naples provided her with some compensation.[40] Joanna's inseparable friend during these first years of disillusionment was her sister-in-law Vittoria. A circle of humanistic poets and scholars assembled at Ischia around the lady of the castle, Constanza de Ávalos.

Joanna bore Ascanio six children, three daughters and three sons: Fabrizio, Prospero and Marcantonio. The daughters were called Vittoria, Agnese and Girolama. After the birth of Marcantonio on February 26th, 1535, Joanna withdrew again to Ischia, having tried again in vain to live with her husband in the Colonna castle at Marino. The latest history of the family remarks on this first breach: "Ascanio's behaviour was such, and his extravagance so great, that the estrangement between the pair became obvious to all. Though it never actually came to a judicial separation, they lived as though separated."[41]

It seems quite just to assign the principal blame to Ascanio. Her husband's lengthy absences, lasting for years at a time, estranged Joanna from him. Ascanio took part with Vespasiano Colonna in the shameful attack on Rome of September 20th, 1526, and a year later played a leading part in the infamous sack of the city. The family historian adds that Ascanio became

134

odious to his wife through his immoderate extravagance and his sudden fits of anger, which found expression in acts of violence. Such was the state of things after the birth of Marcantonio.

From Ischia Joanna attended at Naples Juan Valdés' lectures on the Bible, which in 1539 were being more and more recognized as heretical. It was through this that her first meeting with a Jesuit was brought about.[42] The history of the Society notes expressly that Joanna Colonna assisted at Valdés' lectures. At the end of September 1539, in order to meet this danger and at the same time to clear up the duchess's matrimonial affairs, which were gradually becoming a cause of scandal, Ignatius sent to Naples at the Pope's request the zealous but somewhat eccentric Father Nicholas Bobadilla. From a letter which Bobadilla sent to Duke Hercules of Ferrara on July 4th, 1539, it appears that the idea of this apostolic journey to Naples and Ischia was due to the insistent request of Duke Ascanio himself. We may be sure that Vittoria Colonna in her anxiety was the prime mover in the matter, for she had made the acquaintance of Bobadilla at Ferrara in 1538. In his autobiography Bobadilla notes: "Master Nicholas was sent to the island of Ischia to restore conjugal harmony between Donna Joanna of Aragon, the Duchess of Tagliacozzo, and her consort Ascanio Colonna. He devoted himself to this task with the aforesaid lady till Easter 1540, to the satisfaction of the Pope and the Lord Ascanio." Among the papers left by Father Bobadilla was later found an account, admittedly not very exact, of the Jesuit's opposition to Valdés during his lectures on the second Epistle to the Thessalonians before the noble ladies of Naples. The fiery Bobadilla is said to have sprung up in the middle of Valdés' ingenious speech and cried out to the horror of his audience: "You lie, you lie, you lie!" As a matter of fact, we do not know that Joanna's religious convictions suffered in any way through her contact with Valdés. All the more did Bobadilla have to discuss with the duchess a painful quarrel, apparently about rights of inheritance, with her sister María de Aragón, wife of Alfonso de Ávalos.[43]

In 1541 there broke out between the Colonna and Pope Paul III a dispute over questions of taxation, to which the people gave the name of "the Salt War". Joanna had recently come to live in Rome, but left the capital again before things had reached their worst and took refuge once more at the domestic hearth of her aunt in Ischia, whence she wrote on April 18th, 1541, a letter of entreaty to the Pope, whose troops were then investing the Colonna castle at Paliano in a disorderly siege. She was thus trying to effect in her own way what Vittoria Colonna attempted in her sonnets to Paul III. The Pope, who was pleased with Bobadilla's immediate success in Ischia, was following the duchess's matrimonial affairs with anxious attention. Soon another son of Ignatius had to go to Naples on this difficult mission.

This time it was a more skilful messenger – Araoz, who was to experience for the first time the difficulties of being spiritual director to ladies of the nobility. After his return from Spain at the beginning of September 1540, he was sent by Cardinal Cervini in 1541 to Naples, to carry out the visitation of an abbey there. At the same time he went also to Ischia, but what he did there we do not know. One thing only is certain: he had no success. Therefore, on returning from his second journey to Spain, he travelled again to Naples on April 15th, 1543. Duke Ascanio was also staying there at the time.[44]

Ignatius gave him a letter for Ascanio, inviting the husband to discuss his questions of conscience seriously with Araoz. "Build your nest in heaven", he admonished him. In the earthly nest of the Colonna there was indeed nothing but discord. Araoz must certainly have spoken also with the angry wife at Ischia. Joanna now knew who in Rome was most sincerely concerned at the tragedy of her marriage, and who was behind all these visits by Jesuits: it was Ignatius himself. After Father Araoz' departure she therefore felt obliged to send the General of the Society a note of thanks. It is dated September 1st, 1543. The original is still in the archives of the Society and bears in the hand of an unknown secretary the following inscription: "From the wife of Ascanio. Of no historical importance." But when we consider all that has been said so far, and are thus able to read between the lines, we shall be of a different opinion. Joanna writes of the progress in virtue and of the graces which have been granted to her through Araoz. It is apparent that she was even now willing, as often in the past, to mend her broken marriage.[45]

Most Reverend Father,

Since I am grateful for the progress in virtue and the graces which God our Lord has bestowed through the present coming and work of Father Antonio (de Araoz), for what he has done, indeed, has put and is putting everyone under an obligation, I did not want to fail to write to you. I will merely present my respects to Your Paternity again, thanking you for all I already owe Your Reverence. May our Lord bless you. From Castel del Ova,[46] September 1st, 1543

At Your Very Reverend Paternity's disposal,
Joanna Aragón de Colonna

To the most reverend Father Don Ignatius,
reverend Father in Christ

The success of this visit lasted indeed but a short time. Joanna's dislike of her husband was too deep-rooted. Ascanio's meanness became more and more evident as he curtailed the household expenses of his wife and of her growing children. In the biography of Joanna by Filonico Alicarnasso it is specially stated that the duke was tempted by Satan because of his inherited riches, with the result that he had endless quarrels with his consort. We know too from other sources that he was at loggerheads with his relatives over questions connected with the family property, and that his daughter Vittoria had lost several prospective husbands because Ascanio was niggardly about her dowry. A few years later, when his sister was dead, he haggled with Cardinal Pole over a sum of 9000 ducats, which Vittoria had left for the poor in England.

To add to their troubles, the couple had cruel bereavements to bear. In 1545 their firstborn son Prospero died. Two years later their son Fabrizio fell in the struggle between the Emperor and the Farnese family for Parma. So Joanna had left to her only her dearly loved Marcantonio who from then on passionately espoused his mother's cause against his father.[47]

Such was the state of affairs at the end of 1548. The duchess herself had gradually wearied of all this interminable wrangling. She discussed the matter with the Cardinal of Naples, Gian Pietro Carafa, and begged him to get Ignatius to send one of his sons again, not only for the care of souls in Naples, but evidently also for her own consolation. The cardinal brought Ignatius a letter written by the duchess, in which she asked that Master Laynez or Master Salmerón might visit her. That was in January 1549. Ignatius was just then very ill and prevented from writing. He was also at the same time full of anxiety about the great mission of Fathers Salmerón, Jay and Canisius to Germany. Salmerón was already in Verona, Laynez was about to leave for Sicily, where he was to build up the local province of the Society at the request of the Viceroy, Juan de Vega. The grateful Joanna, who had a great respect for Ignatius, procured ships in Naples for the Jesuits' voyage to Palermo.

Great things were under way. What signified in comparison with such works the spiritual needs of the Duchess Colonna? But Ignatius knew that here, too, the things of God and the reform of the Church were involved. He therefore again sent Father Bobadilla to Naples, as he was already familiar with the duchess's affairs, together with a letter of comfort.[48]

My Lady in our Lord.

The sovereign grace and eternal love of God our Lord visit Your Grace with his best gifts and spiritual blessings.

It is a great occasion of happiness and spiritual joy to those who desire the glory and service of God our Creator and Lord, to see any persons whatsoever zealous in his service, and more so when they are persons of rank through whom God's honour can be more widely extended. Thus it has certainly been an occasion of much happiness and rejoicing for me in this same Lord, to see the devotion to his word and to his ministers, and the desire for the comfort of souls which Your Grace shows in one of your letters which has been sent to me to-day by His Eminence the Theatine Cardinal (Giovanni Pietro Carafa, afterwards Paul IV). It would, however, be a much greater joy to me still if, as I greatly desire in our Lord all Your Grace's spiritual service and conso-lation. I could effectively do what you ask me so earnestly in your letter about Master Laynez. From another letter, however, received this same day, I learn that he is already embarked for Palermo, and therefore this would not be possible. As to some other person of our congregation whom Your Grace suggests should be invited, Master Salmerón, since he is in Verona at the instance of certain persons to whom our whole Society is under great obligation, cannot be withdrawn from that city. Your Grace will, however, be served in this matter, because Master Bobadilla, for many years devoted to the spiritual service of Your Grace and a person of much learning and goodness, has been sent to Naples and will be employed in giving consolation with the Lord's word and serving souls, insofar as grace is given to him by the Author of all good, Jesus Christ, our God and Lord. I beg God to preserve and increase in Your Excellency his very abundant grace for the greater glory and praise of his holy name. Amen.

Rome, January 18th, 1549   Ignatius

Again, there can be no talk of success. It almost seems as if only the skill of Ignatius himself could tackle this desperate case. Before it came to that, however, a new problem began in 1550 to complicate Joanna's matrimonial difficulties. The dislike of Marcantonio (who had meanwhile grown up) for his father had developed into political opposition, which by 1555 had become a poisonous campaign of hatred and calumny. The mother was entirely on her son's side. Historians say that the actual causes of this quarrel can no longer be ascertained. It appears, however, that Ascanio's loyalty to the Emperor had begun to waver, whereas Marcantonio and his mother were attached body and soul to the Spanish party.[49] From Ascanio's letters, preserved in the archives of the Colonna family at Rome, we learn that already in 1550 the duke was complaining bitterly that the Pope and the Emperor were on the side of Joanna and Marcantonio, who had called him "a public rebel and robber".

Nevertheless, Joanna was not free of all blame. With her pride in her Aragonese descent and her domineering character, she was not the one to find a peaceful solution to these political and matrimonial quarrels. The accusations which husband and wife threw in one another's faces became more and more violent. One of the recent historians of the Colonna no doubt apportions the blame justly when he says: "Joanna had once been a very beautiful woman and as such celebrated by the poets, among them Ariosto himself. With the years, she had become arrogant and given to intrigue, and it is not surprising that she was often aggresive towards Ascanio, when the radiance of her beauty was no more. On the other hand, we can well understand why she wished to live apart from her husband and declared herself entirely on the side of her son Marcantonio, who had rebelled against his father, for Ascanio had accused her to her face of being a whore." In the lawsuit which Marcantonio and his mother later brought against Ambrogio Felici, Ascanio's faithful agent, the duke was accused of the worst political and moral crimes: of siding with the French against the Emperor, of coining false money to pay his debts, of indulging in unnatural vices and of attempting to take the duchess's life by physical violence. The scandal had by then reached its climax. The whole world was talking of the Colonna marriage. Pope and Emperor were furious. It was time to call in Ignatius.[50]

For years the General of the Society had not left Rome, except to make a short excursion to Tivoli or Frascati. Now, after a conversation with Duke Ascanio in Rome, he decided to travel to see Joanna. The duchess was then staying at Alvito in the kingdom of Naples, a little mountain town east of Sora, crowned by a proud *rocca*, the castellated seat of the Count of Alvito, head of the Neapolitan family of Cardona, to whom Joanna was related through her mother, Castellana de Cardona and her sister-in-law Antonia de Cardona. It was in this mountain solitude that Joanna had hidden herself, and hither Ignatius, with his zeal for souls, had to follow her. Without hesitation he set out.[51]

It was at dawn on November 2nd, 1552. Let us hear the account of the faithful Ribadeneira, who adduces this story as evidence of Ignatius' "greatness of heart": "In November of the year 1552, Ignatius set out on a journey into the kingdom of Naples in the company of Master Polanco and of

139

the lay-brother Juan Pablo Borrell. On the morning of the day fixed for their departure, it was raining in torrents. Father Polanco said to Ignatius that it would perhaps be more advisable to put off their departure till the morrow, so that he might not come to harm because of the pouring rain. But our Father answered: 'We leave at once. For thirty years I have never let myself be put off by rain or wind, or by any inclemency of the weather, from beginning punctually at the appointed time any work in the service of God our Lord'. So they set out at the hour appointed. Ignatius was travelling for a reason of the greatest importance: namely to restore peace and matrimonial concord between Donna Joanna of Aragon and Don Ascanio Colonna her husband. The two had been living separated for many years; and neither the Pope nor the Emperor nor other great princes had so far been able to reconcile them. Our Father, however, brought the matter to a succesful conclusion where others had failed. That lady did indeed come to Rome to resume married life with her husband, as she had promised our Father; but certain cardinals and other persons of rank put their fingers in the pie and spoilt everything."[52]

This account of the success and failure which Ignatius had to record at Alvito needs, it is true, some corrections. As the whole excursion lasted from the 2nd to the 12th November, and as Ignatius took the opportunity, at the request of his friend Cardinal Mendoza, to do some pastoral work in Ceprano, we may reckon that his stay with Joanna was of two and a half days' duration. What passed between Ignatius and the duchess during that time? One thing is certain: the embittered woman did not by any means surrender at the first assault. She felt the request that she should return to her unloved husband to be not merely unreasonable but positively dangerous, for she had to fear his acts of violence. That, she thought, would be tempting Providence; and therefore she intended to submit only if Ascanio would guarantee, legally and in writing, her financial and social position, especially with regard to the dowries of their two daughters, Vittoria and Girolama. The final result of the long discussion was a half-affirmative, half-negative answer.

So Ignatius rode back on his mule through the mountains to Rome, disappointed and pensive. Joanna's affairs left him no rest. On his return, therefore, he at once sat down at his desk in order to write for the perplexed duchess a long memorandum containing all the reasons for submission. This was indeed (he wrote) contrary to his usual custom; but he hoped she might in consequence still change her mind in accordance with his advice. It is significant how Ignatius appeals to the noble blood and the high-mindedness of the duchess. But we are hardly making a false judgment if we think that the saint, despite all the scriptural passages he quotes, overesti-

140

mated Joanna's urge for perfection. All the more effective on that account are the reasons connected with matrimonial politics – if we may be permitted the expression – which Ignatius, skilled in feminine psychology, puts forward. We can regard this lengthy document, which it took Ignatius a great deal of trouble to write, not only as a proof of his greatness of heart and his wisdom, but also as an indication of the importance attached in Rome to this affair, of which, as Ignatius said, the whole world had been talking.[53]

JESUS

My Lady in our Lord.

Although I have advised Your Grace by word of mouth of the means of agreement with Señor Ascanio, which I feel in our Lord would be more in conformity with his divine will and which becomes Your Grace more than anything else, drawing upon the affection which God's infinite goodness has given me for your service and your complete perfection, I shall not fail (although this is contrary to my custom) to set down in writing the reasons which move me to this, so that looking at them and pondering over them from time to time with the good and holy intention that God our Lord has given you, and principally with his grace, Your Grace will be able to change your present opinion and disposition.

I say, then, my Lady, that the best means I can find, all things considered, is that Your Grace should arrange, with a generous mind and trusting in the Lord, to go to Señor Ascanio's house, putting yourself entirely in his power, without seeking for other security or making any other conditions, but freely, as a wife is normally, and ought to be, in the power of her husband; and the reasons which move me to this are as follows.

1. Because if the concord has to be made entire and perfect, there is no other way of doing so except by gaining the love and whole heart of Señor Ascanio, and this will not come about if you go with conditions and seeking for guarantees, as between enemies, but through your showing love, humility and confidence in him, as a husband, and this is done in the way mentioned above.

2. This way would show more perfection of humility in you than the other. And in truth, if one of the two parties does not give way and humble itself, no agreement can come about, for then, indeed, the heart remains unappeased. And if one of the two has to give way and humble him or herself, it is much more reasonable that the wife should be distinguished in humility than the husband. How much less excuse

141

has she before God and men if through her not humbling herself, the union which there should be between her and her husband is frustrated.

3. This would also be an act of greater strength of mind and magnanimity which becomes Your Grace's noble birth and generous heart, for in it you would show that you did not fear even the danger of death which some would be afraid of, and this is where great hearts are usually to be recognized; on the contrary, courageous persons are not wont to seek so many cautions and guarantees.

4. This would be a means — and the more difficult it is, the more heroic — for Your Grace to overcome yourself and subdue the feeling of aversion in respect of Señor Ascanio if you have had or have any, and consequently would be of most excellent merit before God our Lord, if you were to do it for his divine love. Thus Your Grace ought to prefer this way, as the more perfect, even though some other and easier means should present itself.

5. It would be a work of greater perfection and consequently more pleasing to and more in conformity with the counsels of Christ our Lord. If he is such a lover of peace among all people, even strangers, that he wants oblations and sacrifices left aside until they are reconciled to each other, how much more does he will this among those whom he joined in matrimony, of whose union he says in his Gospel, let not man separate those whom God joins together, that they will be two in one flesh and that the one, in order to make his life with the other, should leave father and mother, etc.

6. It will be more in conformity with the laws which God's Majesty has laid down for holy matrimony. Such laws the Scriptures declare to us in many places, saying that the head of the woman is the husband and that wives should be subject to their husbands, taking as example Sarah, who calls her husband her lord.

7. This would be an act of greater confidence in God our Lord, who rejoices that we trust his Providence about ourselves. It would not be tempting his divine Majesty, since it appears to prudent and learned persons that this confidence would be very praiseworthy and, moreover, a thing involving no risk or very little.

8. It would be a work all the more pleasing to God as by it the devil is deprived of the weapons by which he attacks his divine Majesty. These are many, both from Your Grace's side and from that of the opposing party, when one considers your present state, which would to God our Lord were not seen so clearly.

9. It would be a work of greater charity in regard to Señor Ascanio, to try to win him by this way (as I am persuaded in our Lord you would

win him) and bring him back to a state more secure for his salvation, in which he would live more in God's grace and service. You would thus put him under an obligation by this very virtuous act also to try to be more outstanding in all Christian virtues.

10. It would further be a great charity to him, not only that Your Grace should relieve him of domestic cares, governing his household as he desired, but that you would also give him peace and contentment of spirit and a good old age, from which he is not far distant, for he is already sixty. He would thus end his life in love and union with his wife and children.

11. This way of reconciliation would also provide the most speedy and best solution for your illustrious daughters, and you would win the heart of Señor Ascanio with such an act.

12. Even Señor Marcantonio would be more completely reconciled with Señor Ascanio, since his reconciliation depends on that of Your Grace, and consequently all the difficulties which he probably now has would cease.

13. Your Grace would also remove the occasion of many passions and sins and difficulties from your servants and those of Señor Ascanio; and also from the friends and supporters of both parties, giving to all a great occasion of consolation in the Lord.

14. There would be given to all wives a very praiseworthy example of behaving with the submission, humility and charity which is due to their husbands.

15. By an act of so much virtue and nobility of mind, Your Grace would give great edification and a reason for praising God our Lord to all those everywhere, both small and great, who have had so much to talk and gossip about in the matter of this separation.

16. If Your Grace's reputation and honour are to be taken into account (as is quite right), I hold it as certain that you will enhance it by this very magnanimous procedure – for honour properly speaking is the reward due to virtue. Thus the more this reconciliation is effected with a most generous and perfect act, the greater the honour that would be due, and given, to all good people. The more this case of yours is publish-ed and known throughout the world, the more the reputation of Your Grace's magnanimity will be spread abroad, to your greater glory both in heaven and on earth.

17. Your Grace's good and noble heart should also be moved by the fact that by this act the honour of Señor Ascanio, which Your Grace and all your children also ought to hold as your own, would be greatly enhanced and promoted.

18. For if Your Grace thinks of your temporal advantage you may take it for certain that this way is the right one, because thus Señor Ascanio is given into your hands and will now be your slave. Hence it follows that besides endowing your daughters, he will pay the debts and will for the future make provision for Your Grace's necessary expenses, for you will be the mistress of all he has and will have control of it all, as I understand from him. I am certain that it would be a great relief to Your Grace not to have to burden your friends further in this respect.

19. By this means, moreover, Your Grace would be relieved of certain expenses, for part of the retainers you have to guard you in your house can then be dismissed.

20. For as to the safety of Your Grace's person, this is the best way of all, as far as I can see, for by it this wound there is in your soul will be completely healed, the goodwill of Señor Ascanio will be gained, the occasion of Your Grace's being annoyed by him will be removed and consequently the ground of all fear, for no one is afraid of one who loves, and he cannot fail to give love when he sees that Your Grace trusts him and honours him in such a way. Thus all his strength will be in defence of Your Grace and not against you.

21. Even though he should persist in his ill-will (which I consider to be impossible if Your Grace acts as I have said) it is a thing most unlikely that he would do anything against your person; for he would fear, if not God, the Pope, the Emperor, his son and the whole Spanish nation. He would see that this would be to act to his own undoing both in his reputation and in his estate and life and all he had. All the less would he risk this with Your Grace's humbling yourself to him, as we have said, and obeying him in what is due.

22. If one looks to Your Grace's contentment and peace, this is the most sure way of obtaining it, for it removes fear and lack of confidence and suspicion and alarm, which you would necessarily have if you were to keep away from your husband's protection, not giving yourself to him and placing yourself entirely in his hands.

23. Moreover, the way to quiet and peace of mind for Your Grace is to remove from yourself so many occasions of annoyance that you now have, for you would dwell in your palace with spiritual and temporal comfort.

24. Moreover, if one looks to the ease or difficulty of this reconciliation, it is certain that the way I suggested is much easier than any other, without so much negotiation, circumvention and intermediaries.

25. If one considers speediness, by this means the matter is ended to-day and whenever Your Grace wants to end it. By any other way, I do not know when it would end.

144

MARGARET OF AUSTRIA, DUCHESS OF PARMA

see page 75

Reuerē m' Ignatio, La lettera vra ci è stata di molta conso=
latione per hauere inteso di vostra salute, et conosciuto per essa, che
l'affectione ci hauete portata, non è diminuita per sì lungha assentia,
ne ui sete scordato in li nostri molti trauagli pregare Dio benedetto,
per noi, di che vi restiamo con infinito obligo, et vi pregsiamo a'uolere
continuare in le vostre orationi, et se di quà possiamo cosa alcuna,
per uoi ò per la Compagnia vostra, sempre ci trouerete prontissima,
à faruj ogni piacere, et così uj ci offeriamo che Dio n. s. vi,
contenti. Di Parma il di. xvj. di Gennaro. 1554.

Margarita
d'Austria

a m̃ Ignatio

LETTER FROM MARGARET OF AUSTRIA TO ST. IGNATIUS

see page 88

26. Lastly, Your Grace should consider that this is the opinion of those who are most devoted to your service in Christ our Lord and that it is right to take the opinion of others rather than oneself when one's own cause is in question.

Rome, Mid-November, 1552   Ignatius

It may in fact be assumed that Joanna did, after long hesitation, return to her husband in Rome for a while. When this occurred, and whether she was influenced by Ignatius' admonitions, can no longer be stated with certainty. As late as August 14th, 1553, in a letter to Araoz (who was still very interested in Joanna's matrimonial problem), Ignatius wrote: "The lady from Naples is ready and resolved to live with her husband again. She would, indeed, prefer it if he came to Naples to live there with her for a time, or even went with her to Spain." In any case, then, the success of the memorandum was not immediate. We still possess the will which Ascanio drew up on December 17th, 1552. In it he disinherits his own son Marcantonio "because prompted by a diabolical spirit, he has committed many deeds of ingratitude against his father. He has even dared to enter into an immoral relationship with the wife of the testator, at a time when she, contrary to all conjugal duty, was disobedient, hostile and rebellious towards her husband."[54]

The brief reconciliation, if it ever took place at all, was rudely interrupted by a fresh political catastrophe in the house of Colonna. It was not for nothing that Ignatius in his memorandum had appealed to the patriotic feelings of the duchess when he tried to reconcile her to her husband by referring to the Pope, the Emperor and the Spanish nation. This agrees fully with what we read in his letter to Araoz of Joanna's plan to go with Ascanio to Spain for a time. The duke's political loyalty had, indeed, long been suspect; and it was obviously the intention to get him away from the anti-Spanish surroundings of Rome and Naples. Nothing came of this either. The quarrel between Marcantonio and his father continued. Even the chronicle of the Jesuits has something to say of it. Perhaps Ascanio was careless; perhaps, even, he had a clear conscience – in short, at the end of 1553 he was arrested while in Neapolitan territory by troops of the Viceroy Cardinal Pacheco and imprisoned in the Castel Nuovo at Naples. Probably he was thought guilty of treasonable dealing with Siena, where the French were then trying to establish a military strongpoint against the imperial power; or else he was believed to be involved in a conspiracy with the Prince of Salerno, who was the driving power behind the riots which had broken out in Naples against the Spanish Inquisition. The commandant of the Castel Nuovo at the time was Juan de Mendoza, who soon afterwards without the permission of Philip II entered the Society of Jesus.[55]

Ignatius had apparently had a long and intimate conversation with Duke Ascanio before the latter's departure from Rome, in which not only the matrimonial question but also the political attitude of the Colonna was discussed. One can imagine the two old soldiers as they talked together for hours on end, one with his leg injured by a French cannonball, the other under the suspicion of being at that very moment in league with those same French against the Emperor. Ignatius was therefore very much shocked by the news of Colonna's arrest. His one object now was to save at least the soul of this man for God, this man whom he had once advised to "build his nest in Heaven". So on October 14th, 1554, he wrote a moving appeal to Juan de Mendoza to treat the prisoner in a manner befitting his station: "God is trying him severely in his latter days, that he may be the better prepared for his heavenly fatherland. I have spoken quite confidentially with Don Ascanio, and he said to me that he would never become 'French' like the Prince of Salerno, that his house had always been loyal to the imperial cause and would remain so as long as he lived." Mendoza's reply to Ignatius is also preserved, and it appears from it that his imprisonment was for the proud Colonna a time of recollection: "Don Ascanio is a princely gentleman in his behaviour and appearance, and he is well pleasing to God."

This was enough to make Ignatius write a truly heartfelt letter of comfort to the man for whose marriage he had taken such trouble. He was, indeed, convinced of Ascanio's political innocence because of a written report which the latter had sent him from prison, in which the Duke of Termoli, Vincenzo di Capua, testified to Colonna's guiltlessness. But all Ascanio's powerful connections were of no avail. He remained a prisoner in the Castel Nuovo till his death. When death relieved him of all his earthly troubles is not quite clear; it was probably in 1557. Certainly he was still alive when the new Pope, Paul IV, launched his bull of excommunication against Marcantonio and his father on May 4th, 1556. It is understandable, in view of the Carafa pope's passionately anti-Spanish policy, that the ban of the Church should fall upon Marcantonio; the son of the Duchess Joanna was soon to march in the Duke of Alba's army against Rome, in order to bring the obstinate Pope to reason by force of arms. But that Duke Ascanio should also be included in the excommunication can only be a proof, though a belated one, of his political steadfastness.[56]

Joanna herself had been living since the summer of 1555 with her daughters in the Palazzo Colonna at Rome. Her situation was desperate: her husband was in prison, her son in the camp of the Pope's enemies. No wonder the duchess was closely observed, and her presence in Rome was regarded, as it were, as a guarantee against Marcantonio's anti-papal activities. In October 1555, Bernardo Navagier, the agent of the Signoria of Venice, was already able to report: "The Pontiff has had the secretary of the Duchess of Tagliacozzo, wife of Don Ascanio Colonna, arrested; and he has confiscated all her papers." Joanna now knew what to expect. Her only escape lay in flight. During the night of December 31st, 1555, Joanna, her daughter and her daughter-in-law disguised themselves as peasants from the Abruzzi. Wearing a false beard, she made her way through the streets of Rome to the Porta San Lorenzo, where the papal police, after having been heavily bribed, let the party pass unhindered. Horses had been held in readiness, and the three ladies then rode swiftly through the mountainous country till they came to the safety of the castle of Tagliacozzo.

The following morning all Rome was in an uproar. The Pope was beside himself with rage; and the Venetian envoy ordered an express messenger to ride northwards, that he might be the first to report this political sensation. What must Ignatius in his narrow cell have thought? For certainly the Pope knew about his relations with the wife of Ascanio. The flight of the duchess was the first battle Paul IV lost in his struggle against the Spaniards. It was perhaps some satisfaction to him when, on September 14th, 1557, he signed the Peace of Cave with Philip II, that the Spanish King coolly and calculatingly sacrificed the interests of the Colonna family, whose properties in the Campagna were in the hands of the Pope's nephews. But here too an abrupt reversal of fortune took place. After the Pope's death in 1559, the glory of his family suddenly collapsed, the Colonna properties were restored, and on June 4th, 1560, Duchess Joanna was able to celebrate a truly triumphal entry into Rome.[57]

Ignatius had already been dead for four years. His successor Laynez wrote to Joanna: "Although I have for many years, like the whole Society of Jesus, had a special desire to serve Your Excellency, now that desire is even greater, since I have taken over the burden of office laid down by our Father Ignatius of blessed memory, who was always so devoted to Your Excellency and to your illustrious house." The duchess was always grateful to the Jesuits for their services. With Francis Borgia, Laynez' successor, she was on terms of sincere friendship. She and her son Marcantonio founded in 1566 the noviciate of St. Andrew on the Quirinal, which in the following year was hallowed by the virtues of St. Stanislas Kostka. Joanna's daughters, about provision for whom Ignatius had so much concerned himself in his memorandum, were as devoted to the Jesuits as their mother. Girolama, who married Duke Pignatelli of Monteleone, gave evidence in Ignatius' process of beatification in 1606; Vittoria, wife of García de Toledo, Marquis of Villafranca, became vicereine in Catalonia and Sicily and everywhere promoted the work of the sons of Ignatius. Joanna lived to see the triumph of her son Marcantonio in the battle of Lepanto. On September 11th, 1575, she followed her unloved husband into eternity. Her grave at Paliano bears the inscription: "Joanna of Aragon, granddaughter of King Ferdinand of Naples, sister of the Duke of Montalto; a noble lady, a loving wife, praiseworthy in her chastity."[58]

Let us conclude this sad story of the house of Colonna, in which Ignatius was so intimately concerned, on a happy note. At the time of Bobadilla's first visit to Naples for the purpose of mending the duchess's marriage, there was in her household a little Spanish girl of thirteen, Catalina de Badajoz. It was at the beginning of spring in the year 1539. Catalina, who was later to win literary fame in her native land, had evidently met Ignatius already in the first month after his arrival in Rome, in November 1537; indeed, she had as early as 1536 got to know the two brothers Diego and Esteban de Eguía, who had been friends of Ignatius since Alcalá, and had in April 1536 received from Pope Paul III permission to go on the pilgrimage to Jerusalem. In Rome, Ignatius had taken a touching fatherly interest in Catalina, and had given the clever, precocious child his spiritual counsel. Therefore in March 1539, she wrote Ignatius a charming letter in a style of childlike seriousness. She made a few mistakes which she neatly crossed out, and addressed Ignatius rather stiffly as "Your Grace", while using the correct title "Don" for the priest Diego de Eguía and the half-Italian "Maestre" for Father Faber. The unidentified Spanish lady in Rome named Isabel must already have belonged to Ignatius' circle of acquaintances.

Catalina entrusted her letter, written so carefully that it almost looked like an engraving, to a cleric who was travelling to Rome – not Bobadilla as has hitherto been supposed, for not till March 14th, 1540, did he return to Rome, whence he was to have set out with Rodríguez for India. Instead of Bobadilla, who was sick, Francis Xavier undertook the historic voyage to the East. Ignatius was no doubt delighted with the letter. The original is still among the yellowing papers of the Society's archives: Ignatius kept it carefully and thus preserved for us a document which shows with rare directness what an impression his personality had made upon this child.[59]

Reverend and illustrious Father,

After kissing Your Grace's hands, I want to let you know that I have been in Naples seventeen months and always with the desire of having some news about you and all those gentlemen and servants of Jesus Christ. To their prayers I continually commend myself, for I do not

148

dare to do so to Your Grace. If I did not fear to annoy you, I would forthwith follow you as the Canaanite woman did after Jesus Christ my Lord.

Of all you formerly told me to do I have forgotten nothing, for indeed, your words are not such that one forgets them; but I am always unhappy and I have death before my eyes. I beg Your Grace to do me the favour of writing to me as to what I have to do. As to the rest, this Father (i.e. Bobadilla) will be able to give you information.

Marcantonio kisses Your Grace's hands and I have handed him over to his father. The latter, likewise, kisses Your Grace's hands.

Of Doña Isabel, I know not whether she be alive or dead.

As to Maestre Faber, Don Diego and Señor Esteban de Guia, I kiss their hands and beg them to be good advocates with you on my behalf – for I, although a sinner, am always the handmaid of Your Grace and of those gentlemen, and in my poor prayers I never fail to ask our Lord to preserve them in his holy service. I remain, asking God to guard and prosper your reverend and noble person in his holy service, for the comfort and salvation of many.

She who trusts in God and in Your Grace's virtue and holy teaching, your humble handmaid,

Naples, March 23rd, 1539   Catalina de Badajoz

Of Catalina's later career we know only that she returned to Spain and there became celebrated at the university of Alcalá for her humanistic learning and her Latin poems. She died at Guadalajara in 1553, aged twenty-seven. Alonso García in his fulsome epitaph wrote of her as follows: "Such was Catalina de Badajoz, who, when not yet fully twenty-seven years old, was snatched away in the bloom of life by a cruel and all too early death and thus caused irreparable sorrow to the Muses. Alas, on that day what a fountain of the spirit ceased to flow, which had sprung up to the glory of eloquence! What springs of poetry has Fate at one blow quenched! Let Cicero praise as he will his Cornelia, mother of the Gracchi; let him stand amazed at Lelia, Mutia and Licinia – never will Alcalá be so ungrateful to thee, O Catalina de Badajoz, as not to dare to compare thee with those women of old."

Catalina has endeared herself to us more by her childish letter to Ignatius than by this humanistic epitaph.[60]

149

Doña Catalina de Zúñiga, Marchioness of Denia

WE have already mentioned several times the gloomy palace of Tordesillas in which the life of the mad Queen Joanna slowly ebbed away. The master of the household to the unhappy queen was Don Luis de Sandoval y Rojas, Marquis of Denia and Count of Lerma, who succeeded his father in the same office in 1535. His son Francisco de Lerma married, as we already know, Isabel, daughter of St. Francis Borgia. The mutual relationships of the Spanish aristocracy are truly of bewildering complexity; but Ignatius, who had been at Tordesillas too, was well versed in them. The marquis' wife, Doña Catalina de Zúñiga y Avellaneda, was a cousin of the celebrated tutor of Philip II, Don Juan de Zúñiga, and his wife Estefanía de Requeséns, who had been Ignatius' benefactress in Barcelona. On her mother's side she was the granddaughter of the *Loca del Sacramento*, Doña Teresa Enríquez de Cárdenas, whom the grateful Ignatius never forgot. One of her brothers was the famous Cardinal of Seville, Gaspar de Zúñiga, who brilliantly represented the Spanish Church at the Council of Trent.[61]

Denia, the family seat, was near Gandía, and thus it was that the couple became great benefactors of the college which had been founded there by St. Francis Borgia when duke. For this reason the latter did not fail to visit them at Tordesillas in 1552, after he had become a Jesuit. He was not merely performing his polite duty as a relative; the soul's salvation of the ailing queen was also involved. On this occasion Doña Catalina, with whom were living also her daughter-in-law Countess Francisca de Paredes, her unmarried sister Teresa de Zúñiga and her brother Don Guttiere de Cárdenas, discussed her spiritual problems with her Jesuit kinsman. As was often the case with these noble ladies, she had scruples about the obligation of fasting. There was a custom in the Spanish Church of releasing oneself rather conveniently from that obligation by a generous offering of alms. Through Borgia the ladies' request to be allowed to do this was forwarded to Ignatius in Rome; and again the General had to hobble on his stick to the Pope, who granted the dispensation orally, though he was sick at the time. On August 24th, 1552, the document, duly drawn up, was sent off to the three ladies at Tordesillas.[62]

Ignatius of Loyola, Master General of the Society of Jesus.

To all the faithful in Christ, who shall read these present letters, eternal salvation in our Lord.

Since our most holy lord, Julius, by divine Providence the Third Pope of that name, in response to the verbal petition of the most illustrious lady the Marchioness of Denia and of the Lady Teresa, her sister, and the Countess of Paredes, her daughter, together with Don Guttiere de Cárdenas, her brother, has to-day granted to us, who humbly petitioned him for this favour, the faculty of commuting the fast, on the days prescribed by the Church, into alms, which must be at least of two ducats, it has seemed good to us to confirm this dispensation by these letters signed with our hand and the seal of the Society.

At Rome, the 9th of the Calends of September, 1552

Ignatius of Loyola

Three years later an event of greater historical importance occurred at Tordesillas: the Emperor's mother died. On Good Friday, April 12th, 1555, the Jesuit Francis Borgia, having been sent for by the Marquis of Denia, assisted at the queen's deathbed and gave her Extreme Unction. The ladies of the house of Denia prayed at her bier before the body was transported to the royal vault at Granada. The Marquis of Denia informed the Emperor Charles in Brussels of the "truly Catholic death" of his mother. The chronicle of the Jesuits thus relates the peaceful end of that tragic life: "The manner of the queen's death was a consolation for all her realms, and it was announced to the Emperor Charles, to King Philip of England, to the Queen of Portugal and the other princes, who had all been so much concerned about Queen Joanna and had sincerely wished that the manner of her going home might be thus."

In addition, Francis Borgia wrote on May 19th, a personal letter to the Emperor in which he conveyed to Charles the last words of his dying mother – we cannot read them without emotion when we think of the unhappy fate that was hers: "Her Highness's last words, only a few hours before her death, were: 'Jesus crucified, stay with me!'" So the sad story of Tordesillas, where Ignatius had once served as a page, ended in the radiance of that peace which it was permitted to a son of Ignatius to bestow.[63]

Doña Catalina de Mendoza, Countess of Melito

IN those days, for anyone who was familiar with the little world formed by the proud aristocracy of Spain, the name of Mendoza stood for something. There was no family whose ramifications were more widespread, whose influence in Church and State was greater; their possessions were enormous. For the success of the spiritual tasks which Ignatius set his sons in Spain, it was therefore important to stand well with the Mendozas. For many years a bond of real friendship had existed between him and a prince of the Church who had made the name of his house famous throughout Europe: Cardinal Francisco Mendoza y Bobadilla. As Archbishop of Burgos he is generally referred to in the Society's papers as "Cardinal of Burgos". At nineteen, Francisco was already lecturer in Greek at Salamanca, and it was then that he visited Ignatius, a prisoner of the Inquisition. Neither ever forgot that meeting; and the cardinal later used all his influence at the papal curia and at the imperial court in favour of Ignatius' Society. The cardinal's brother, Andrés Hurtado de Mendoza, Marquis of Cañete, was Viceroy of Peru. The viceroy's son afterwards became a Jesuit, and that too was an advantage for the Society, just as was the entry into it of that other Mendoza, who, when commandant of the Castel Nuovo at Naples, suddenly went off to join the Jesuits and thus raised such a storm that Ignatius had to write a personal letter to King Philip to calm him.[64]

There was another branch of the same family, the head of which, Diego Hurtado de Mendoza, bore the title of Count of Melito. He was married to Doña Catalina de Silva, and to inherit his fabulous wealth there was only his daughter, Ana de Mendoza. This heiress, with her yearly income of 100,000 ducats, was the Doña Ana, Princess of Éboli, later so famous in Spanish history. Her parents were, as the records of the Society abundantly show, on excellent terms with the Jesuits from 1550 on. The Count of Melito in particular generously undertook to pay for the building of the Jesuit church in Alcalá, and was prepared to spend twelve thousand ducats on it – a sum which he hoped to raise partly by drawing on his wife's resources. Besides this, he supported the Fathers with all the weight of his family's influence when they were involved in a dispute with Archbishop

Siliceo of Toledo. "The Count already feels himself to belong to our Society" notes the chronicler.[65]

Don Diego made the Spiritual Exercises several times and one day asked Ignatius for a Latin edition of them for himself and Prince Philip. In this letter he wrote: "The countess recommends herself especially to Your Paternity's prayers, through the intercession of which she hopes that God will fulfil a wish of hers. She implores you urgently (for piety is ever insistent) that Your Paternity will make us partakers in all the sacrifices and merits of the holy Society of Jesus, through the merits of Jesus Christ our Lord." At the end of the letter the father also recommends his daughter Ana to the General's prayers. So it came about that a saint prayed for the very unsaintly Princess of Éboli. She had good need of such prayers, for soon afterwards she was betrothed at the age of thirteen to Ruy Gómez de Silva, the celebrated favourite of Philip. Perhaps the approaching wedding threw the Count of Melito's finances into some confusion, for the chronicle of the Society remarks somewhat disappointedly: "Of all the promised ducats for the church in Alcalá, there is now nothing more to be seen." That did not prevent Ignatius from writing out in due form the document conferring a share of the Society's spiritual riches upon his benefactors. We can see from this document how and with what well-chosen words the General drew up such a proof of the Society's favour of which many have already been mentioned.[66]

Communication of all the good works of the Society to the Count of Melito and to his wife

IHS

Ignatius of Loyola, Master General of the Society of Jesus.

To the most illustrious Lord Diego Hurtado de Mendoza, Count of Melito, and to his noble wife, health in the Lord.

Although in the Catholic Church, since it is the mystical body of Jesus Christ, compacted and fitly joined together, all the members – according to the testimony of the Apostle – should be solicitous each for the other throughout the whole structure, so that each member individually communicates to all the others his good offices and good works according to the measure of grace infused in him by the head, Jesus Christ, it is nonetheless admitted that such communication is all the richer and more abundant when the bond of love that binds the parts with one another is closer and more solid. For this reason it seemed good to St. Paul

153

insistently to demand that the prayers of the faithful be applied to himself. It is clear, then, that a special union of this kind is of great efficacy and usefulness.

Since, therefore, your most illustrious Excellencies are linked to this insignificant Society of ours by a special religious affection and also no common measure of beneficence, we, mindful, indeed, of our poverty in that we are not sufficient to think anything of ourselves as of ourselves – but also of the measure of the gift of Jesus Christ, from whom is all our sufficiency, however little it is, and desirous of truly repaying your charity both in affection and in deeds – we confer on you with a special communication and out of the deep affection of our heart, a share in all and each of the spiritual good works which, by the grace of God's goodness, are undertaken in this Society of ours, day by day, whether privately or publicly, and whether for the special advantage of one of our members, or for the common benefit of our neighbours, namely, prayers, suffrages, meditations, Masses, preachings of the word of God, religious instructions, the administration of the sacraments, any of the works of mercy, fasts, pilgrimages to shrines, and finally any pious works whatsoever, whether for the soul or the body.

At the same time we humbly beseech the God and Father of our Lord Jesus Christ, that from the inexhaustible treasury of the merits of his Son, supplying and enriching our poverty, you may be made full sharers in all the works which up to this time in this same Society out of his goodness, have been found pleasing in his sight and will be so found in the future; and having enriched you by every blessing of his grace in this life, may he at length reward you with the crown of eternal glory. Amen.

Ignatius

Given at Rome, June 1st, 1552

Through the marriage of their daughter Ana to Ruy Gómez, the gates of royal favour were opened to the Count and Countess of Melito. In 1554 Don Diego was appointed Viceroy of Aragon. The news that reached Rome of his court at Saragossa was highly edifying. The Viceroy with his whole suite attended the sermons which Father Strada gave before large congregations in the church of our Lady of the Pillar. During Lent the servants of his household took it in turns, one each day, to receive the sacraments. But the Archbishop of Saragossa, Fernando de Aragón, an illegitimate grandson of King Ferdinand the Catholic – and the people of Saragossa insisted on having such scions of their own royal house for their bishops – was hostile to the Jesuits, and we have heard already about the attack on them which broke out soon afterwards.[67]

It was a great comfort to the Fathers to have the protection and help of the viceroy and his wife. Ignatius was duly appreciative of this. In July 1554 he sent the viceroy a detailed report on the state of the Society throughout the world. In return he received from time to time fresh accounts of the pious practices in Doña Catalina's house. When a French nobleman was imprisoned at Saragossa under suspicion of being a spy, although in fact he was only a pilgrim on his way to Santiago de Compostela, the Viceroy and his wife set him free, in memory of the former pilgrim Ignatius of Loyola. Meanwhile the marriage of their daughter Ana had taken place. Ignatius was informed in detail about this too, and he must have read with a frown what the court gossips in Valladolid were saying: "It is said here openly that this marriage was arranged by Father Araoz." Because of the marriage, the Viceroy was for a time so much in debt that the Jesuits were prepared to pay back the money already given by him for the church in Alcalá; and in spite of Ignatius' requests, they did not dare to approach Mendoza for a contribution towards the Roman College.[68]

In 1555 Count Melito was made Duke of Francavilla by Philip II, who had attended the wedding of Countess Ana, and the title of Count of Melito was transferred to his son-in-law. This too is duly noted by Polanco, well versed in all these personal affairs of the aristocracy. Ignatius sent the following message to Saragossa: "I pray for the whole illustrious family. May God give health especially to the gracious lady Ana, as we heartily wish it for her, in the service of God." When we read this sentence, we cannot but consider what part this Princess of Éboli was later to play in Philip's life. Her proud consciousness of being descended from the illustrious house of Mendoza, as it found expression in her later letters, was to cause St. Teresa in her Carmelite convent at Pastrana some painful moments. It is not always saints who write letters to saints.[69]

Jacqueline de Croy

In the years 1548–50, Ignatius waged a little paper war with a lady belonging to the nobility of the Spanish Netherlands, the conquest of which for the Society of Jesus cost him much labour. She was Jacqueline de Croy, daughter of Henri de Croy, Comte de Porcéan, Seigneur d'Archot, and wife of Antoine de Glymes, Lord of Bergen-op-Zoom, who since 1533 had borne the title of Marquis de Berghes by the grace of Charles V. When she wrote to Ignatius she was already widowed. Her territories lay in the district surrounding Bergen, north of Antwerp, where the *Markiezenhof*, the family's residence, is still to be seen. Two of her brothers were made bishops by the Emperor Charles: one, Charles de Croy, became Bishop of Tournai at the age of seventeen in 1525, the other of Cambrai in 1519. Both, as the chronicle of the Jesuits notes in many places, strongly disapproved of the new Society, and Ignatius often speaks in his letters of the anxiety these two prelates caused him. On that very account, his co-operation with the Marchioness Jacqueline was to be all the more cordial.[70]

This lady, who was solicitous for the spiritual welfare of her subjects, found it a great consolation in her widowhood that she had in Bergen a zealous parish priest whose parish was, as the chronicle of the Society says, "like the primitive Church in miniature". He was Nicholas Floris, a native of Gouda. For this reason he is usually called Goudanus. Born in 1517, he so distinguished himself as a student at the university of Louvain that he was called by everyone there "the Pearl of Louvain". In March 1545 he joined the Society of Jesus, whose members, still without a house of their own, were studying at Louvain at that time and exercising a powerful attraction on the best minds. Ignatius early recognized the strategic significance of Flanders and rejoiced at the addition to the Society's numbers. But for that very reason it was important that he should bring these untrained Flemish Jesuits to Rome, that they might there be sent to school and become familiar with the spirit and the proper form of the Society.

Nicholas Floris had retained the living of Bergen after joining the Jesuits. Then in January 1548 came the summons to Rome. By the same post came also a letter from the General to the marchioness, in which he endeavoured to make clear to her the need for taking such a step. This was very necessary, for Jacqueline fought like a lioness for her revered parish priest. To make his departure more acceptable to her, Ignatius had evidently expressed himself in such carefully chosen words that Jacqueline believed one year's stay in Rome would see an end of the matter. Therefore she had sent at the beginning of the year by way of answer to Ignatius a letter of protest, in which she urged with some insistence not only that the presence of her favourite parish priest was a source of comfort to her in her widowhood, but also that his absence would seriously endanger the progress of religion in her territories. But she could do nothing about it. Goudanus went to Rome. Jacqueline lived for a year in the hope of having him back again soon.

In the meanwhile Ignatius took care to make the period of waiting seem shorter. In a letter to Flanders dated as early as April 30th, 1548, Polanco wrote that the Chancellor of the University of Louvain, Ruard Tapper, had calmed the marchioness, saying to her: "Leave the matter to God, who will guide the General of the Jesuits in the right way."[71] On July 3rd, Ignatius sent two letters, one to the marchioness's chancellor and one to the chapter of Bergen, who had also insisted on Goudanus' early return. In August the Jesuits in Louvain received instructions as to how they were to reply tactfully to the marchioness's complaints. The year 1548 was drawing to its close, and the impatiently waiting marchioness thought it was time to remind the General of his undertaking. Ignatius had promised in his first letter that he would never leave the people of Bergen in the lurch. Jacqueline interpreted this without further thought as meaning that the cure of souls in her marquisate could belong only to Goudanus. From her letter one understands what the Jesuits in Louvain must have said to her: that there were much greater tasks in the Church for such a gifted man as Master Nicholas than to be parish priest of Bergen. The lady, however, argued skilfully, and the idea on which she based her argument was fundamentally the same as that which filled the mind of Ignatius when he thought of the Netherlands: she reminded him of the danger to these people from the "reformers" and from the moral degeneration of the Catholic clergy.[72]

The grace of our Lord Jesus Christ be always with you.

The letter, reverend Father, which I received from Your Reverence on the departure of Master Nicholas Goudanus, your confrère, has encouraged me to write these further lines to you, since your first letter gave me confidence that what it was not possible to obtain by my former letters will at least be procured by this. For you promised – it is to be

157

hoped they still remember, Your Reverence – that you would never fail the people of Bergen; on the contrary that you would strive to bring it about by your good works and prayers and those of your brethren that God would continue and bring to completion his work in my people, who are after all his people.

You said, indeed, that you had called Master Nicholas away so that he who had chosen you as a father on earth in place of God and had promised that his whole way of life should be established according to your good pleasure, might have a deeper knowledge of spiritual things and the graces granted to him by Almighty God and thereby might come to a more perfect practice of the spiritual life and be adequately prepared for bringing in a richer harvest into the Lord's storehouse.

Accordingly I beseech Your Reverence through the Lord Jesus, that now at length, mindful of your promise, you deign to assign Master Nicholas here for the good of my people and their more fruitful salvation.

You will perhaps say that he is to be prepared for greater things than for spending his entire labours merely upon the people of Bergen. This, too, I myself say. Nor should I strive so much to obtain him from you, if the city of Bergen and that alone were my care. But I would, indeed, ask you how many thousands do you think there are in these lands of mine who do not know the difference between right and wrong. Then, too, there is (a grief which touches me closely) the exceeding carelessness and incompetence of the shepherds who, a thing exceedingly to be deplored, feed themselves rather than their flock. Nor can I find any other remedy for this evil than that others should sometimes come in to teach the people in their stead, for which office in the opinion of all my people there is no one more suitable than your Master Nicholas. I implore you to deign to accept their point of view and satisfy our pious wishes and those of my citizens and subjects. Such wishes, indeed, are not so much my will as that of God, who perhaps has willed it that he should be asked for these things through me, namely, that someone should come to the help of his flock – when learned doctors have been sought even from Rome.

But why do I detain Your Reverence with so many words when you are so exceedingly busy? I do not doubt that you will do this, in that loving kindness which you show towards all and chiefly to those who are afflicted and widows, among the number of whom God has willed to place me, and especially to those whose principal grief is that the faith, and a life worthy of the Christian faith should be so neglected everywhere. Oh that I may be counted among the number of such afflicted, as

158

I ought to be. May God the greatest and best keep your reverend Paternity safe for a long time. From our Castle at Gouda, December 3rd, 1548.

Your Reverence's most devoted daughter in Christ

Jacqueline de Croy

To the most reverend Father and Lord in Christ, Don Ignatius of Loyola, General of the Society of the name of Jesus, in Rome

Now there occurs another of those cases which give us a vivid realization of what Ignatius understood by the" greater glory of God". While fully understanding the pastoral needs of Flanders, he had to deny the marchioness's request. The testing and the vocational training of a Jesuit, he wrote, especially when he was as promising as Master Nicholas, needed more time. When one thinks of the short period of training which Peter Canisius or Francis Borgia had, this remark of Ignatius sounds like an excuse; evidently he had in the meantime realized that Goudanus' gifts might be better employed in a more important place. For were not the most urgent appeals coming at that time from Germany? There a graduate of Louvain, with a theological and humanistic training, could be of more use than in Flanders, where hostility towards the Jesuits was already showing itself at the court of the Regent Maria.

Illustrious Lady in Christ.

May grace and true peace which is in Christ Jesus ever abound in our hearts. Amen.

I have received your second letter, written on December 3rd, concerning the pious care of those under you and the fostering in them of those things which pertain to religion. I understand your loyal anxiety, not only do I desire but I even hope that God, the author of such a Christian attitude and such good desires, will, indeed, fulfil them. For it may be conceded that there are few – would that it were not necessary to admit it – who being both faithful and prudent give themselves as the Lord's servants to taking care of his sheep; but it is even rarer I think that God should grant us someone of such exceptional solicitude as yourself, and he will not fail to provide the right fellow labourer. I wonder, indeed, that he has not done so already.

159

Concerning Master Nicholas, since he has been summoned for this purpose, namely, that through certain tests (which in accordance with the constitutions of our Order are by no means brief) he might be both better known to us and he himself might be more certain of his own mind, before things are settled and he makes profession, it would be neither reasonable nor fair to bring him to profession without such tests and on these grounds Your Excellency will not wish to oppose the measure.

As far as I am concerned, he to whom all things, even our inmost hearts, are known, knows what desires of the salvation and progress of souls he has given to me and how eagerly I would go into the whole of Germany and Flanders and particularly to the inhabitants of Bergen and to other subjects of Your Excellency. If therefore God would give the opportunity and the strength, I would lend myself to the work as far as in me lies. In the meantime it will be for Your Excellency's goodness and charity to have confidence that God will give me, who desire it so much, understanding of what at any particular time will be to his greater glory, and pleasing to him, and more useful to the common good, in the matter of the direction of those things which are committed to our care and which I am charged to follow out on their human side. This, I think will certainly not displease Your Excellency. I pray Jesus Christ our salvation and that true consoler and teacher the Holy Spirit to be ever present with you, with the communication of all spiritual gifts.

At the house of the Society of Jesus   Ignatius

Rome, January 14th, 1549

The zealous marchioness did not give up. Perhaps in her Flemish simplicity she interpreted too literally the Spanish General's diplomatic politenesses. In several letters to Ignatius during the year 1549, now lost, she repeated again and again the same request. From Louvain, too, came reports to the General in which the return of Goudanus was represented as urgently necessary.

Nicholas Floris had meanwhile been tested enough, and he was regarded as sufficiently capable to take part in the legation which Pope Paul III intended to send to Poland shortly before his death. Ignatius had already discussed the matter with Cardinal Marcello Cervini of the title of the Holy Cross. That was, indeed, something different from the work of a parish priest in Bergen.

So the General in his answer to the Marchioness defended himself by invoking the authority of the Pope, and postponed Goudanus' return "for the present". In the diplomatic language of Rome that was equivalent to saying: "He will not come back."[73]

IHS

Illustrious Lady in Christ.

May the grace and peace of our Lord Jesus Christ always remain, and increase, in our hearts.

Since both by the accounts of others, and from what is evident from your own letters, the piety and singular modesty of Your Excellency and your care and holy solicitude for the glory of God and the salvation of souls, in particular of those specially committed to you, is clear to us, we have not the least doubt that you will always continue to bear the same will and the same feeling towards us. For how can there be any division between those who are joined in the acceptable and perfect will of Almighty God – which we are both seeking? It not seldom happens, however, that those who earnestly strive after something holy and pleasing to God disagree among themselves, when different good works are envisaged on one side and the other. Those, however, who earnestly seek what is most pleasing to God, when they have understood the matter, cannot fail to be united in heart over it.

It is true that you have put forward the plea that Master Nicholas, our brother, is useful to the people of Bergen. When, however, you understand it to be the mind of the sovereign pontiff, that is, of the Vicar of Christ, that Master Nicholas should transfer himself to some other part of the Lord's vineyard, which, as it is more destitute of labourers, is in greater need than that which Providence and your care tends day by day, I think that you will find it possible to bear this not only with a calm, but even with a joyful mind.

When the Cardinal of Holy Cross spoke to me about Master Nicholas and another of our brethren who were to be sent by the Sovereign Pontiff to the King of Poland, I did not delay to show Your Excellency the letters from which it was clear that it would be very useful, indeed, that he should be sent there. It is, however, possible, for his setting out for Poland to be postponed but it could not nor ought it to be altogether prevented, especially in our case by us to whom it is absolutely unlawful to refuse, through the very constitution of our Society, any mission

161

imposed upon us by the Vicar of Jesus Christ. If, therefore, Master Nicholas has not been able to be sent to you as soon as we should have wished, that will have to be attributed to the will of God, which is wholly to be obeyed in the person of the Sovereign Pontiff and not to our will, for we should most willingly have satisfied your holy desire and devotion so far as it might be in our power. In all things which happen we shall be more than ready to serve in Jesus Christ our Lord you and all your undertakings.

May things go well with Your Excellency. May Christ Jesus, the most generous fount of all good things deign to give you of his abundance, that not only in your self alone, but in all your subjects, you may always promote his glory, honour and worship.

Rome, October 8th, 1549   Ignatius

On reading this letter, the resolute marchioness must have held her hands to her head. She could not follow all this diplomatic verbiage. Her Goudanus' time of training now seemed to be really over; had she not heard that Master Nicholas had already left for Venice, where he was engaged in teaching while waiting to depart for Germany? Jacqueline could not understand such things. What was the point of Nicholas' giving lessons to Italian boys, when in Bergen they were crying out for Flemish sermons? So she did not give in. One cannot but admire the words she addressed to her obstinate opponent Ignatius: "If you persist in refusing, I too, shall persist – in entreating."

The grace of our Lord Jesus Christ be with us all. Amen.

Although, most reverend Master Ignatius, I send frequent letters to your Reverence, you have not yet sent me a favourable answer. Nevertheless, relying both on the fact that the matter under consideration is a holy one and on your humanity, I trust that you will grant my request which I have begged your Reverence for repeatedly and which I ask for, indeed, with all my heart, and that you will now at length grant that which you seemed in your most recent letters sent to us to be postponing to some more suitable opportunity. Surely you will deign to send back to us Master Nicholas Goudanus, whom you called away from here so that you might have full assurance as to the man's piety and learning, and that, according to the rules and practice of your institute, this servant might now be sent out as a fully qualified worker for the Lord's harvest.

These were the reasons, as far as memory now serves me, which were put forward as the cause of his recall. From Bergen, as if in the midst of his course, he was snatched away two years ago, and that to the grief of many and would that it were not at the expense of devotion. Now, however, you will not be able to plead any such excuse, either that you had not sufficient personal knowledge of him or still less that his absence was necessary according to the rule and practice of your institute, for he has spent two whole years there. We therefore beg that you will order him to return here, where he can teach and instruct an ignorant people. We hear, however, he has been recalled to the Venetians where in our opinion, and not perhaps wrongly, he can give very much less fruit than in Bergen, inasmuch as he is extremely skilled in our tongue. I do not know who brings it about that so far as I am concerned the memory of this man can never be obliterated, but my heart always urges me (moved as I hope by the impulse of God) not to cease from entreaties until I have obtained him from you. If you persist in refusing I, too, shall persist in entreating. Indeed, I hope that God who ceases not to urge me to entreat you, will set the same mind in you as in myself, that Master Nicholas, who up to this time has done your will both in Rome and now in Venice, and whom we can thus by no means doubt to be so disposed that whenever you order him to move, he will obey most willingly, may by your will return here.

Pardon, I pray you, Reverend Father, my importunity in writing and entreating. To a person in need, as men are wont to say, shyness is useless, particularly before him who may be able to help and may wish to do so, on account of his goodwill. May the Lord Jesus preserve Your Reverence safe for many years and according to his accustomed mercy, may he deign to prosper your holy enterprises undertaken by you for his Church.

Bergen, the Calends of July

Your humble daughter in Jesus Christ

Jacqueline de Croy

Bergen, July 1st, 1550

To the most reverend Father and Lord in Christ, Don Ignatius of Loyola, General of the Brothers of the Name of Jesus, in Rome

When Ignatius read the marchioness's elegant French signature at the foot of the letter which her chancellor had translated into Latin, he may well have thought that at last he would have to write in clear and straightforward language to this "humble daughter". At the beginning of the Holy Year 1550 he had taken the trouble to send the marchioness a solemn Jubilee Indulgence, by way of consolation for the loss of Goudanus. For as regards the latter, affairs had now reached a point where his return to Bergen was simply out of the question. He was occupied in the first half of 1550 with the building up of the new college at Venice, in which connexion Ignatius had warned him on April 26th against the dangerous books of Erasmus of Rotterdam. On July 25th Nicholas was allowed to make in Venice the solemn profession of a Jesuit – a high honour for the marchioness's protégé; for apart from Ignatius and his first nine companions, Goudanus was only the eighth of the chosen few whom Ignatius, very strict in this matter, considered worthy to make their profession.

Meanwhile the General had received a letter from the new Duke of Bavaria, Albert V, asking for more professors for Ingolstadt. As Fathers Jay and Salmerón had been removed from there in August, Ignatius sent Goudanus, at the request of Pope Julius III, to take their place. This news must somehow be made palatable to the Marchioness of Bergen. The following letter was the last shot fired in this paper war.[74]

IHS

Illustrious Lady in Christ.

May grace and true peace which is in Christ Jesus be always preserved and increased in us. Amen.

I have received Your Excellency's letter, written on July 1st, in which you ask that Master Nicholas, our brother, with his persevering devotion and, as I am persuaded, no little love for helping the multitude entrusted to him by God, should be sent back to Bergen. Although I see clearly Your Excellency's holy desire and also my own wish to give you satisfaction in this respect, yet, nevertheless, that which we both desire clearly does not come about. I think, then, that God is certainly preventing this for other reasons, perhaps less clear to us. Quite recently, indeed, Master Nicholas was ready to travel to Poland, but Pope Paul III of holy memory was taken away by death and so the journey was cancelled and Master Nicholas was sent to Venice, both that he might help the beginnings of the college lately erected there, that he might be useful to the people, for he had already learnt the Italian tongue in that very famous city, and also that since he was later to set forth into Germany, he might thus have part of the journey accomplished.

164

When, however, Your Excellency's letter reached me, already, at the entreaties of the new Duke of Bavaria who said that he had a theological college in readiness, the Sovereign Pontiff had decided that Master Nicholas should be sent to Ingolstadt and should replace another of our theologians whom he had called away from there. Accordingly about the middle of August he left Venice setting out for Germany, where he will have, indeed, a very full harvest and where there is a great dearth of labourers of this kind, so that no little fruit may be hoped for, both in the people and in scholastics, and perpetual fruit, indeed, through the college erected there.

In the meantime, however, it grieves me that it is not possible, as I have said, to satisfy such a holy desire and devout request on the part of Your Excellency. I hope, however, that out of your charity and goodwill you will accept this willingly and that as from God, so from his Chief Vicar, you will accept all things with an even mind. God who is rich and mighty will know best when the time is ripe how to fulfil the desires which he himself has poured into Your Excellency for his honour and the salvation of souls, be it through Master Nicholas or some other instrument, no less suitable.

I greet Your Excellency in our Lord Jesus Christ. May he deign richly to confer his grace upon us all that we may be worthy always both to know and to fulfil his most holy will.

I hope Your Excellency has taken advantage of the jubilee indulgences which I have obtained for you and all others whom you wish them extended to.

Rome, September 15th, 1550   Ignatius

To Jacqueline de Croy, Marchioness of Bergen

The marchioness had suffered an honourable defeat. She bore no grudge against Ignatius and his sons. Now she could at least follow from Bergen the apostolic career of her beloved Master Nicholas; and she greeted with great joy the founding of the college at Louvain in 1556. In 1552 Goudanus was working at Vienna, and in 1557 he attended the conversations with the Protestants at Worms. From August 1558 till the spring of 1559 he was allowed for the good of his health and to the comfort of the good marchioness to work in his never-forgotten parish of Bergen.

With all her solicitude for her Flemish subjects' spiritual welfare, Jacqueline had become old and ill. However, she continued to keep up a correspondence

165

with Ignatius' successor Laynez. On October 23rd, 1558, she wrote to the General of the Jesuits: "I am now about seventy years old, and for six years I have been almost continuously bedridden." It was the greatest joy of her latter days, for which she thanked him in her letter, that Laynez had at the request of the faithful Goudanus granted her and her two sons a share in the spiritual benefits of the Society of Jesus. The old marchioness had now only one more small wish: she desired the same favour for her daughter Anne of Bergen. And she had also one very great worry: the religious disorders, the beginnings of which she had once described to Ignatius, were threatening to invade her marquisate. Her eldest son, the Marquis John of Bergen, was indeed in the favour of Philip II, had been with him in England and wore the Golden Fleece; but as Governor of Hainault under the regency of Margaret of Austria he joined in the Prince of Orange's demand for calling the States General and soon became suspect in the eyes of the Privy Council on religious grounds. The same suspicion fell upon his wife, the young Marchioness of Bergen. Jacqueline's younger son Robert of Bergen had been Bishop of Liége since 1557, but resigned his high office in 1563, as Margaret stated in a report to Philip. It is not certain when the old marchioness died, and whether she lived to be a witness of these events.

Goudanus reached the climax of his wanderings when, at the command of Pope Pius IV, he undertook his historic mission to Mary Stuart in Scotland. Perhaps when he was speaking with the Queen of Scots he thought of his little parish in Bergen and of the faithful Marchioness Jacqueline. In any case, the unhappy lady learnt to know in Father Goudanus a true son of St. Ignatius. In 1574 she wrote to Father Edmond Auger: "I offer my simple and unworthy prayers up to God, that he may keep your holy Company in that same service, in which I too by his grace wish to live and die."[75]

PART THREE

BEGGING FOR THE KINGDOM
OF GOD

Letters to Benefactresses

Introduction

By his sudden conversion in 1522, Ignatius of Loyola had turned his back on the world of riches and nobility, to become in entire and heroic poverty a pilgrim on earth, penniless, with only a bold trust in God to help him on his way. One must be poor in order to understand the riches of the God who became poor: that was the first lesson he had learnt, as all the saints have learnt it. But it meant from the beginning that henceforth Ignatius was dependent upon the charity of others; and so the same power of grace that impelled him to beg for Christ's sake opened the hearts and hands of generous men and women. For the understanding of his whole life, this fact must be borne in mind: Ignatius, the erstwhile rich nobleman, desired with all the passion of his mighty spirit to be poor, and he did indeed live as a mendicant till the completion of his studies in Paris and Venice in 1536. It was in such a frame of mind that he looked upon the pious ladies in Manresa and Barcelona, the sea-captains of his voyages to Italy and Palestine, and the rich Spanish merchants in Flanders, as commissioners appointed by his Heavenly Father, from whose hands he expected and accepted with sublime simplicity the money necessary for his daily life and his studies. The counterpart to this attitude, however, was a characteristic which distinguished the noble heart of Ignatius from the very beginning of his conversion: a truly passionate gratitude.

This ascetic link between poverty and gratitude found its expression on a higher plane after Ignatius came to Rome in 1537 and founded his Society there. Holy poverty was as a matter of course a requirement of Christian perfection for his new community. We know from his spiritual diary how hard he strove to express this ideal in the constitutions of his Society. As the work of that Society became world-wide in its extent and the number of its members greater, the difficult problems involved in reconciling poverty with ownership grew more pressing. The studies of new members and the consequent necessity of founding colleges, schools and universities, were impossible without those well-considered regulations which Ignatius afterwards embodied in the Constitutions. At the outset, however, he was with his spiritual sons in the same position as he himself had been at the beginning of his studies in Barcelona: in the social conditions of the time,

169

the Society could carry on its work only by the generous help of benefactors. Cities, princes, or rich private persons must be found to establish and maintain colleges; and one of the main concerns of the General of the Society till his death was to prepare the way carefully for such foundations and to bring them to a successful conclusion. When, however, such a task had been accomplished, Ignatius' great heart opened in profound gratitude.[1]

In this work of helping first Ignatius the pilgrim and later Ignatius the General of the Society of Jesus, women play an essential part; and to the imperishable gratitude which the saint tendered to these ladies who helped to further the high ideal of his life we owe the letters that appear in this chapter.

It is not then by accident that the earliest of Ignatius' letters that we possess are addressed to the first benefactress of his poverty, the worthy Inés Pascual in Barcelona, who from the time of their meeting on the road between Montserrat and Manresa looked after him like a mother. Most of these letters, however, date from the years after 1550, when the Society in Italy and Spain really began its work of education and scientific study, and Ignatius could enlist in the service of God a number of generous benefactresses. These letters take us into the very centre of the General's lifework, into his everyday existence, rich in joys and in disappointments. It was by his letter-writing and his invincible patience that the man of God mastered life. This correspondence brings Ignatius to life for us at his best: in his expressions of gratitude.

In these letters to the women who supported him with such abundant generosity as only women can show, Ignatius is filled with what one might almost call a helpless gratitude, and to express the needs of his heart he finds words that do not otherwise come easily to his laconic style. It is always hard for him to say "No" outright. He exhausts himself in his readiness to comply if possible with all the wishes of these ladies – and they did indeed pester him with their pious importunity. But when the time for gratitude came, there was no restraining him. His companions knew this, and Ribadaneira once wrote: "Among all the virtues that our Father possessed was one by which he was especially distinguished: the virtue of gratitude. In that he was simply wonderful. It was of the utmost importance to him that he should as far as possible equal in generosity and even surpass his pious admirers and the benefactors of the Society. He kept them informed of its progress, he sent them invitations, he visited them, helped them in whatever way he could; he even undertook for them special commissions which were quite against his inclination, merely in order to please them."

We still possess a letter which Ignatius wrote to Simon Rodríguez in Portugal on March 18th, 1542, in which he develops a veritable theology of gratitude. As late as 1555 the following lesson was given in writing to a party of members leaving Rome: "When I judge it in comparison with God's goodness, ingratitude is a characteristic which, in the eyes of our Creator and Lord and in those of his creatures who are worthy to receive divine and eternal glory, is most to be abhorred. It is the greatest of all imaginable sins, for it is a disregard of the blessings, graces, and gifts that we have received; it is the foundation, origin and source of all sins and of all evil. On the other hand, how loved and honoured in heaven and on earth is gratitude for all the blessings and gifts that we have received!" Here we can look into Ignatius' innermost heart; we hear in these words – and in all the letters that follow – the prayer he teaches us in the Spiritual Exercises: "I beg for an inward recognition of all the great blessings that I have received from God, so that I may with a wholly thankful mind love and serve His Divine Majesty in all things."[2]

Ignatius' finest expression of gratitude towards the benefactors of the Society is contained in the chapters of the Constitutions which deal with its obligations towards founders of colleges. In the original draft of 1547 Ignatius wrote a sentence on the subject which illustrates both the clumsiness of his pen and the overflowing gratitude of his heart. "Beginning with the gratitude so pleasing to God our Lord", he wrote, "both towards the divine generosity, from which all good things come, and also towards his servants, through whose hands the good things come from above; having regard to the good and holy intentions of the founders and benefactors of those colleges which are founded or endowed for the scholastics of the Society, out of the love of God and the eternal salvation of souls; finally, having regard likewise to the pious reverence which the founders in God show to this lowly Society; it is our duty to take pains – in the same love and veneration towards our Creator and Lord – in some way to repay or respond to that pious reverence and love which these founders and benefactors show to us, who are but the unworthy servants of those who labour to serve our Creator and Lord in every way."

This very monster of a sentence, in which is compressed all Ignatius' vigour, is followed by an exact enumeration of the obligations of gratitude which the Society undertakes towards its benefactors. The final text of the Constitutions is more succinct: "It is a genuine obligation for us to respond, as far as in us lies, to the pious reverence and beneficence of those whom the divine Goodness uses as instruments for the foundation and endowment of colleges of our Society." Ignatius then adds those excessively precise regulations that govern the annual ceremony of presenting a blessed candle to the founder or foundress. Here we catch a breath of that aristocratic, feudal world from which Ignatius came, and to which most of his benefactors

171

belonged. The candle must bear the arms of the founder's family; it must after his death be given to his next of kin; it must be specially sent to a founder who happens to live in another town; and it must burn at the requiem of a dead benefactor. In all this, Ignatius is quite the child of his age, when the greatest importance was attached to such ceremonies; and we shall see in the letters what little tragedies sometimes arose therefrom. Even here he shows a prudence born of experience: all these marks of gratitude are for "actual" founders only, that is, for those to whom belongs the merit of having established a fully endowed foundation. In the history of the founding of the college at Ferrara we shall see the classic example of such difficulties.

The hitherto unpublished list of benefactors and foundresses, which still lies in the archives of the Society, bears witness how seriously Ignatius and his sons took this duty of gratitude. More eloquent, however, are the letters which now follow.[3]

Inés Pascual

THE first woman who met the pilgrim Ignatius of Loyola after he had entered upon his new life for God was the widow Inés Pascual. We owe the earliest letters of Ignatius to the cordial relationship that existed from the first between the still somewhat romantic Knight of Holy Poverty and the practical housewife of Manresa.

On March 25th, 1522, Ignatius, clad in rough sackcloth, came limping down from the holy mountain of Montserrat through the valley to Manresa. The pilgrim himself gives us the reason for the choice of Manresa: "Now, he did not go along the direct road to Barcelona, for there he would have met many people who would have recognized him and treated him with honour; but he turned aside in the direction of a little town called Manresa." We know of what historic importance in the realm of the spiritual life this in itself unforeseen détour became.

Ignatius was nevertheless recognized and honourably treated by someone, though in quite another sense. It was the pious widow Inés Pascual, whose son Juan many years later in the first process of Ignatius' beatification gave evidence of his mother's experiences. In spite of the garrulousness of the aged witness, whose many contradictions can be pointed out, we may believe his account in its essentials. Juan relates: "My mother was coming back from a visit to the Holy House of Our Lady of Montserrat with two of her kinsmen, named Juan Torres and Miguel Canyelles, and three women, Paula Amigant, Catalina Molins and the matron of the hospital, Jerónima Clavera, who were all widows. When they reached the hermitage of the Holy Apostles, which is situated a little below the monastery, she met a young man dressed as a pilgrim, of low stature, with a pale face and reddish hair, whose manner was so grave and modest that he hardly raised his eyes from the ground; and he limped with the right foot. The man asked my mother if there was in the neighbourhood a hospice in which he might lodge for a few days. Being struck by the noble yet friendly air of the pilgrim, she looked at him more closely and felt moved to piety and devotion. She answered that the nearest hospice was three miles away and that she herself was going thither and if he were willing, she would be of use and service to him, to the best of her ability. The pilgrim was pleased with my mother's offer and decided to follow her."[4]

Inés Pascal belonged to a class with which the feudal lord of Loyola had till then probably never been in close contact. Her maiden name was Pujol, and she had first been married to a moderately well-off citizen called Juan Sacristá. Of this marriage was born her son Juan. Early becoming a widow, she next married Bernardino Pascual, who dwelt in Barcelona. As this marriage, also of short duration, was childless, the inheritance and name of Pascual passed to Juan Sacristá; and to him we are indebted for most of our information about the relations between the "pilgrim" and his mother. The widow Pascual had a house in Manresa, but she also owned a modest house and a shop in Barcelona at the corner of the Calle de Contoners (Wool-weavers' Street), near the church of Santa María del Mar. Her brother, Don Antonio Pujol, was a respected cleric, master of ceremonies and confessor to the Archbishop of Tarragona, Pedro Folch de Cardona. Such then was Ignatius' first and never-forgotten benefactress. On the evening of the first day that he spent in the hospice of Santa Lucía for the poor at Manresa, the widow Pascual sent him a boiled fowl for supper.[5]

This beginning of his spiritual labours at Manresa is in a sense typical of all that was to follow. Worldly honours, from which Ignatius fled, now pursued him under the form of the devotion of the women whose spiritual welfare he felt himself obliged to promote. The worthy widows in whose company he entered Manresa soon no doubt found out about his origin and his virtues and noised them abroad. The first account of Manresa in the Pilgrim's Book is as follows: "People related great things of him, and this opinion arose in consequence of the occurrences at Montserrat; indeed, the rumours grew at once to such an extent that they exceeded what was true. He was said to have given up vast revenues, and much else of a similar kind was related of him." One can guess from this to whom Ignatius was referring. He meant the worthy women of the little town, some of whose names appear in the Manresa beatification process: Juana Ferrer, Michaela Canyelles, Brianda Paguera and others.[6]

These, however, were soon joined by ladies belonging to the local aristocracy who lived in Manresa – Ignatius in the Pilgrim's Book expressly calls them "ladies of fashion". One of them was Ángela de Amigant; she and her husband Pedro de Amigant were ancestors of the Marquis of Palmerola, whose family archives have preserved so much information about Ignatius' early days in Manresa. He himself tells us how these women nursed him in his first serious illness in the Amigants' house at Manresa: "When the Pilgrim had somewhat recovered from the fever and was no longer hovering on the brink of death, he began loudly to entreat certain ladies of fashion who were come to visit him, that if they again saw him in danger of death they were to remind him in a loud voice that he was himself a sinner and should remember the offences he had committed against God." When in the winter of 1522-3 he again fell seriously ill, he was nursed to health in the house of the well-to-do Juana Ferrer; Ignatius met her again later in Rome in the suite of the Portuguese envoy. It was to some degree a presentiment of something which all his life Ignatius could not avoid, and to which each of the letters in this collection bears witness, when he wrote of these early days in Manresa: "Even then many noble ladies had a great reverence for him."[7]

Already at Manresa, too, Ignatius learned what he was to know throughout life: that such relationships easily gave rise to idle talk and malicious gossip. Thus it was at the beginning of 1523, when accusations against him and the widow Pascual were spread about, so that her priest-brother Don Antonio Pujol had to come and straighten things out. In the company of the latter and young Juan Sacristá, Ignatius left Manresa and went to Barcelona. His departure caused bitter tears at Manresa, especially in the house of the pious Doña Angela de Amigant.

Inés Pascual received the Pilgrim joyfully in her house in the crowded Old Town at Barcelona. Her son Juan's little room, which she placed at Ignatius' disposal, was now and henceforth on all his visits to Barcelona his home, the scene of his penances and his mystical consolations. On three occasions Ignatius stayed here: first for just over three weeks in February and March 1523, then when he was attending Latin classes from Lent 1524 to March 1526, finally for about three months up to December 1527 before his departure for Paris. The dark bedchamber in Inés' house was his new Manresa. In 1582 old Juan Sacristá-Pascual, deeply moved, gave evidence concerning his conversations with the pilgrim Ignatius, who constantly exhorted him to keep the Commandments, especially those of filial love and fidelity in marriage, a state which Ignatius urgently advised him to enter upon. Juan had listened to the nightly prayers of the mysterious lodger and often heard him say in a whisper: "O my God, how infinitely good thou art, for thou bearest with a man who is so wicked and corrupt as I am."

During Ignatius' first sojourn in Barcelona the same things happened as in Manresa, but on a higher social level, where he felt more at home. A circle of ladies belonging to the highest society of the Catalan capital at once formed about him. "The noblest of Barcelona", Juan Pascual calls this group of Ignatius' pious female admirers, with all the pride of a weaver who is honoured by such visits.[8]

One of these ladies, Isabel Roser, was later to play a decisive role in the

175

life of the Founder of the Jesuits. How another, whose generosity made possible Ignatius' theological studies in Paris, became acquainted with him, was related in evidence many years later by the Carmelite nun Estefanía Countess of Rocaberti: "Leonor Zápila, a noble lady of this city of Barcelona, great-grandmother of the witness, told how Ignatius entered her house one day to beg for alms. As he appeared to her to be a person of gentle birth, his face being nobly formed and his hands shapely, she said to him in a tone of reproach: 'I am sure you are something of a scamp, since you go about the world in that garb. You would do better to go home again, instead of wandering around the countryside like a good-for-nothing.' My great-grandmother states that the holy man took this reproach with much patience and answered her humbly, thanking her for her admonition and admitting that she had spoken well, for he was indeed a good-for-nothing and a great sinner. When she heard this and saw the humility with which he said it, her heart was touched, and she felt such respect for Father Ignatius that she gave him alms and provisions of bread, wine and other things for his voyage; and from that hour she regarded him as a saint."

Let us mention here the other aristocratic ladies of Barcelona whom we meet in Ignatius' letters to Inés Pascual. The dark little house in the Woolweavers' Street had never seen so many noble visitors. Among them were Isabel de Josa, of whom we are to hear a great deal more, and Doña Aldonza de Cardona, of that ducal house which even Ignatius in his Pilgrim's Book calls by far the noblest family among the grandees of Catalonia.[9] Another great lady who belonged to this group was Doña Estefanía de Requeséns, wife of Don Juan de Zúñiga y Avellaneda, who was King Philip's tutor; Don Luis Requeséns, a son of Estefanía, was later one of the victors at Lepanto. In the Calle de la Puerta Ferissa stood the beautiful palace of the Gralla y Desplá family, the mistress of which was Doña Guiomar Gralla, whose husband Don Miguel had received his patent of nobility from Joanna the Mad and her son Charles at Brussels in 1512. She, too, was a sincere admirer of the strange pilgrim Ignatius.[10]

With Doña Zápila's provisions, Ignatius now set out for Rome. Thence he travelled by way of Venice to the Holy Land. In Jerusalem he sat down and filled three folio pages with an account of his travels written in his beautiful handwriting. It is significant that he did not write to one of the noble ladies, but to the humble widow Pascual. If we still had this account, it would be our first letter of Ignatius, and it would be priceless. Unfortunately the document, long kept as a relic in the widow's family, is now lost.

In Lent 1524 Ignatius returned after innumerable adventures to Barcelona, where he already had many friends. He had decided to learn Latin, that he might one day help souls as a priest. Again he stayed with Inés Pascual, this time for two whole years. It was she who made the Pilgrim, who still indulged in ascetic excesses, exchange his rough sackcloth for a clerical cassock. As her guest, he was also able to use the library of her learned brother, Antonio Pujol. The room in which he conned his Latin vocabularies was also the parlour where he received aristocratic ladies and the headquarters of his crusade for the reform of the lax nunneries of Barcelona.[11]

The widow was often away for months, as she had to look after her property in Manresa. Besides, during these first weeks of study the Pilgrim had been joined by a companion, Callisto de Sa from Portugal, who wished to emulate Ignatius in his penitential exercises at Manresa and in making a pilgrimage to Jerusalem. While Callisto and Inés Pascual were in Manresa, the latter wrote to Ignatius in Barcelona to say that one of the women belonging to his circle in Manresa had died, and that the malicious talk still continued. Ignatius at once replied in the first of his letters that we possess. The text of this document, preserved only in a copy, is obscure in some places and in one quite illegible. The date 1525 has been added by a later hand, but the letter certainly belongs to the year 1524. As regards its contents it is important as enabling us to form a judgment about Ignatius' spiritual teaching: it shows us more clearly than the scanty indications in the Pilgrim's Book how Ignatius spoke to the pious women of those early days, and moreover we see that in his spiritual teaching too the pilgrim's garb had now been exchanged for the cassock, so that even in this first letter the later Ignatius, with all his harmonious balance between Nature and Grace, is already apparent.[12]

May the grace and love of Jesus Christ our Lord be always with us.

It seems to me fitting that I should write to you, on account of the desire I know you have of serving the Lord. I can well imagine you must be feeling distressed, both on account of the absence of that blessed servant whom it has pleased the Lord to take to himself, and also because of the many enemies and obstacles in the Lord's service that you have in Barcelona. Moreover, there is the enemy of human nature who never ceases his temptations. For the love of God our Lord, however, I beg you to see that you always put such good desires into effect, shunning the obstacles, for if you pay no heed to it, temptation will have no power against you. What you must do, then, is always to put the glory of the Lord before all things and all the more so when the Lord does not command you to do things which might cause suffering or harm to your person, but rather wants you to live in him in joy, giving the body whatever things are necessary for it. Let your speaking, thinking and conversing be in him and of the things necessary for the body to this end, putting the Lord's commandments before all else, for this he wants from us and commands. He who considers this will find the . . . greatest trouble and pain in this life to be . . .

A pilgrim who is called Callisto is in Barcelona. I should very much like you to talk over your affairs with him, for in truth it is possible that in him you will find more than there appears.

Thus for the love of our Lord let us make an effort in his service since we owe him so much, for we shall much sooner tire of receiving his gifts than he will in bestowing them.

Pray to our Lady to intercede between us sinners and her Son and to obtain for us in our labours and toil that our weak and sorry hearts may be changed into strong and joyful ones, to his praise.

The poor pilgrim,
Iñigo

IHS

To my sister in Christ our Lord, Señora Pascual
December 6th, 1524 (1525)

After his period of study at Alcalá and Salamanca, whither he had gone in March 1526 and where he underwent such strange experiences in his spiritual direction of women and in the prisons of the Inquisition, Ignatius returned once more to Inés in Barcelona for three months, from October to December 1527. Both his plans and his urge to work for souls had in the meantime become more sober and practical. This, however, altered nothing in his grateful friendship for the Pascual family. The gentleman from Loyola was at home in the Woolweavers' Street, and to that address many of his letters were sent. At the beginning of the new year Ignatius set out on a new adventure that was part of his now less extravagant schemes – he went to the University of Paris. This time he did not begin his journey as on that former occasion when he departed for the Holy Land; then he had to be forced by long spiritual arguments to eat ship's biscuit. In this respect, too, Ignatius had now so to speak become reasonable. The sources note particularly how solicitously and abundantly the pious women of Barcelona, above all the motherly Inés Pascual, stocked him with provisions. The Pilgrim even had in his pocket a bill of exchange duly made out for 25 gold *scudi*.[13]

This and much else about Ignatius' journey to Paris and his stay there, about his debts, his letters and his plans, we learn from old Juan Pascual's report of 1582; with the not always trustworthy loquacity of an old man he poured forth all he could still remember of the revered Pilgrim. He often confused dates; and when he talks of a lady-in-waiting to the Empress named Beatriz de Melons (actually she was called de Melo), said to be a cousin of Ignatius, it is another of the old man's mistakes. Beatriz de Melo was in fact related to the Viceroy of Catalonia, Francis Borgia, and his wife, and had known Ignatius for several years through Leonor Mascarenhas. Peter Faber calls her "a lady heartily devoted to Ignatius". As the Empress Isabel was in Barcelona in 1533, Ignatius may then have written to Beatriz from Paris, if indeed the old man is not also mistaken in this. Be that as it may, we cannot refrain from quoting a part of this valuable document (which is written in Catalan), because it is of the greatest interest for the understanding of the relationships which Ignatius formed at that early date:[14]

"Six years later he set out for Paris in order to study there, and he took leave of my mother, my family and me, and of all Barcelona with many tears on both sides. My mother, to the best of her ability, gave him everything necessary for the journey, and the above-mentioned ladies did likewise. During the time of his studies in Paris, there was with him Father Ramón Pasqual Català, of the Order of Preachers, who had lived here in Barcelona at the Convent of St. Catherine. Him I call upon to witness that during the four or five years of his stay in Paris my mother sent him annually bills for 100 ducats for books and other expenses, and for his board and lodging. As, however, he was very charitable, he used it all for the poor. To my mother and me he often wrote with great affection and gratitude, and he said that God had given her to him, like that other widow who supported Elias, so that he might spend his life in poverty, without the help of kinsfolk or revenues, in the divine service, while the love of his family and homeland had wholly left him. He also wrote that he wished to go to Rome, in order to travel to the Holy Land; he wrote about his intentions and his plans, that we might pray for him to God, saying that we should most likely not see him again on earth, but only in Heaven, as he hoped.

"After the end of his pilgrimage and his return to Rome, he wrote to me an account of his whole journey with its experiences, and he told me of his joy at knowing that my mother and I were still alive. He also wrote to Doña Beatriz de Melons, a holy noblewoman, lady-in-waiting to the Empress Isabel, consort of the Emperor Charles V and mother of King Philip II, who was married to a daughter of the King of Portugal. He wrote to the said lady-in-waiting (she was his first cousin, the daughter of a sister of his mother) about the obligation of gratitude which he had towards my mother Agnes (Inés) Pascual, the widow who had so long looked after him and supported him in her house. She was to repay in his name this debt of gratitude, as far as she was able, to the widow's brother, or son, or kinsfolk. The lady was very pleased with this letter, and formed a great friendship with my mother. She made so much of the letter that she would not be parted from it for a moment.

"Now, just when she received the letter she was at Barcelona with the Empress Isabel. When they were returning to the court at Valladolid, she did not depart without taking my mother with her. The latter travelled with her, and I also; but we stayed only two months at Valladolid, for a sickness which befell my mother compelled her to return home, much to the lady's sorrow. Immediately after her return to court, the lady had by her influence procured for my mother's brother, Antonio Pujol, the Abbey of St. Michael de Coja in Catalonia. But he enjoyed it only for seven months. The rumour went about that the monks had killed him, but I do not believe it."

Let us go back to Ignatius' leavetaking from Inés Pascual. On February 2nd, 1528, Ignatius arrived in Paris after long journeying on foot through France in the winter. The first disillusioning experience of the no longer youthful student, who was a complete novice in money matters, was that a fellow-Spaniard robbed him of the beautiful gold pieces he had obtained for his pious admirers' bill of exchange. Before Lent was over, the Pilgrim was heavily in debt. For this reason alone, quite apart from the chivalrous feeling of gratitude that distinguished him through life, it was necessary to keep up his correspondence with Barcelona. So on March 3rd, 1528, a letter was sent off to his spiritual mother in Barcelona, not a very long one, characteristic of the later Ignatius in its sober matter-of-factness, but full of interest in the familiar domestic affairs of his former landlady; he asks about a friend's letter, he brings in a bit of advice for his room-mate Juan Sacristá, and does not forget either to send greetings to the lady next door in the Woolweavers' Street[15].

May the true peace of Christ our Lord visit and protect our souls.

Having regard to the great goodwill and affection that you have always had for me in God our Lord and have shown by what you have done for me, I thought I should write you this letter so as to let you know about my journey after I left you. Favoured by the weather and in perfect health, by the grace and goodness of God our Lord, I arrived in this city of Paris, where I shall continue my studies until it please the Lord to ordain otherwise, on the second day of February.

I should very much like you to write to me if, and what, Fonseca replied to the letter you wrote, or to know if you spoke to him.

Commend me much to Juan and tell him always to be obedient to his parents and to keep the feast-days; if he does so, he will have long life upon earth and still longer in heaven.

Commend me much to your neighbour – her presents have arrived here; the affection and goodwill she bears me in God our Lord are always present to my mind. May the Lord of the world reward her. Through his infinite goodness may he deign ever to dwell in our souls, that his will and good pleasure may always be fulfilled in us.

Poor in goodness   Inigo

Paris, March 3rd, 1528

To my sister in Christ our Lord, Señora Pascual

It must not be supposed that Ignatius relied solely on the regular arrival of gifts from his pious lady friends: during the following three years he went himself to Flanders and once even to London to beg from the rich Spanish merchants; but in 1533 his need was especially great. On March 13th, he had passed his examination for the licentiate in philosophy, having obtained the baccalaureate in 1532. The licentiate gave him the right, after further examination and an inaugural lecture, to be called Master *(Magister)*. As this cost money, Ignatius postponed the ceremony till March 1535; but to the gaining of the licentiate itself there was attached a custom for students who could afford it, which Ignatius in his autobiography calls "taking the stone". We no longer know exactly what this was; probably a convivial entertainment which a new licentiate was expected to give for some of his fellow-students. For this at least one gold piece was needful; and Ignatius had not got one. On the contrary, he had to provide for a group of companions who had meanwhile gathered round him. In short, money was necessary. To whom could he turn more hopefully than to the pious ladies of Barcelona, who all these years had kept in touch with Ignatius through the letters of Inés Pascual and through the oral accounts of occasional visitors? In the spring of 1532 a Catalan doctor called Benet had come to Paris and brought a letter with him. In his manner of answering it Ignatius already displays remarkable diplomatic skill. First he sent the good widow a reply to all her questions: and only later, after a well-calculated interval, a letter asking for money – the eternal request of all students. In it he does not refrain from exaggerating a little – let it be recorded in all reverence – when

181

he writes to Barcelona: "This Lent I became Master, over which I spent on unavoidable things more than I was authorized or was able to."

This letter is really only part of an elaborately planned campaign for money. At the same time he sent letters to Doña Eleonor Zápila and Isabel Roser. The latter was not actually asked for money, for she herself was at the time in financial difficulties. Inés Pascual was asked to organize the other ladies, Isabel de Josa, Aldonza de Cardona and the Pilgrim's special devotee Doña Guiomar Gralla y Desplá, into concerted action. One cannot read without a smile how Ignatius specially draws attention at the end of the letter to the fact that the bearer had to return at once to Paris; but the skill which Ignatius devotes to seeing that his everyday wants are supplied is overshadowed by the love of the Pilgrim and ennobled by the spiritual counsels contained in his letter for the widow and her son Juan.[16]

The grace and love of Christ our Lord be always with us to our favour and help. It is now a year since I received a letter from you, through Dr. Benet (God grant him glory) when he brought me alms and provisions from Barcelona. I learnt from your letter and from the information I was given, of the great diligence which you have been giving to my affairs, doing so with that perfect devotedness you have always shown towards me. And now you further offer to devote yourself to them with great diligence and solicitude for the future. It would seem that not only have you made me indebted to you for the past, but you even want me to be under an obligation to you in the future. May it please God our Lord that that true Lord, for whose love and reverence you do it, may repay you.

Although I have written to you in another letter in reply to that which you sent me, I thought I would write you this, not only on account of your great good will, but because my studies have cost more than has been the case up to the present, for this Lent I became Master, over which I spent on unavoidable things more than I was authorized or was able to. I have thus remained at the end of my resources and it will indeed be very necessary for God our Lord to help us. I am therefore writing to La Zápila who in a letter she wrote me offered herself wholeheartedly to help me generously saying that I should write to her for what I needed.

I am writing also to Isabel Roser, but not about this request, because she wrote me a letter in which she said I was not to be surprised if she no longer sent me help as she would have liked to do, on account of the many necessities in which she found herself, and I believe this to be the case. I would even venture to say that she has done more for me than she really could and thus I owe her more than I shall ever be able to repay. It seems to me that you ought not to speak to her with the idea of letting her know about any need of mine lest she should be sad at not being able to provide for it.

When I left there, the wife of Mosén Gralla made generous offers to me to give me all the help she could and she has always done so. I likewise received offers from Doña Isabel de Josa and Doña Aldonza de Cardona who have also helped me generoulsy. I am not writing to these three, in order not to show myself importunate, but ask you to recommend me much to them; as to Doña Gralla, I still think that when you tell her about me she will certainly want to participate in the alms given to me. In this as in all other questions I shall consider whatever you do as best, and I shall remain contented for I am continually in your debt and for the future I shall always be under an obligation to you.

The person who is bringing this will inform you at greater length about everything here; and in all things I have as much confidence in him as in myself. As to Juan, your son, my old friend and true brother in the love of our Lord who will judge us for ever, I should very much like you to write and tell me how he is getting on, for you know that I cannot do otherwise than rejoice at his good and grieve at the contrary. May it please God our Lord to give him grace, so that he may know himself fully and feel his divine Majesty in his soul, so that captivated by his love and grace, he may be detached from all creatures in this world.

I make an end, asking God our Lord, of his infinite goodness, that he give you both in this life such things as he gave to that blessed mother and her son, St. Augustine.

Remember me warmly to all those about you and all whom I know and love in Christ our Lord.

From Paris June 13th, 1533

The person who was to bring this letter has stayed behind for a certain business, but he sent me the man who will give you this letter; he must, however, return here straight away.

Poor in goodness   Iñigo

To Inés Pascual

From this time on we do not know much about the relations between Ignatius and his motherly benefactress. He did indeed write to the lady-in-waiting Beatriz de Melo 1533 on behalf of Inés Pascual. Two years later, in March 1535, Ignatius actually took his examination for the degree of

Master, having previously on August 15th, 1534, with his six companions, made at Montmartre that vow which was to determine the course of his life. At the beginning of April 1535 he left Paris. Now were fulfilled in him the words which he had written to Inés Pascual at the beginning of his university career, and which show us how Ignatius undertook all his long studies only in the service of an ideal that had become ever clearer in his mind since the revelations of Manresa: "I will stay here in Paris and devote myself to study until the Lord has other work for me to do." Now he knew what God wanted him to do. Ignatius went to Rome.[17]

Only from afar had the simple widow followed the progress of her protégé. No doubt, however, she was kept informed of it by Doña Isabel Roser. Ignatius never forgot his generous spiritual mother in Barcelona. When the first Jesuits came to Spain, they received instructions to call at the Woolweavers' Street. On April 9th, 1548, Inés died a holy death. Father Araoz attended her on her deathbed, after he had to her great comfort said Mass in her room. At Ignatius' beatification process, on September 8th, 1595, Ángela Sacristá-Pascual, Juan's widow, deposed as follows:

"The witness remembers that at the death of her mother-in-law Father Araoz, nephew of Father Ignatius, of the same Society of Jesus, was present in Barcelona. On account of the obligation which all members of that Society felt towards the said Inés Pascual, and especially because of benefits which Father Ignatius had received from Inés Pascual, Father Araoz, by express permission of Don Jaime Cazador, Bishop of Barcelona, erected an altar in Inés Pascual's bedroom where she lay sick, and on this altar he said Holy Mass. The witness was present. After hearing this Mass, Inés Pascual held the crucifix in her hands, and as Father Araoz pronounced the blessing, she gave up the ghost most devoutly and holily. After her body had been buried in the chapel of St. Martin in the Augustinian church, Father Araoz wrote to Father Ignatius and informed him of Inés Pascual's death. But only a few days later he received a letter from Ignatius, and the witness has herself seen this letter; it was written in Spanish and its contents were more or less as follows: 'Before you put pen to paper, I already knew that Inés Pascual was in Heaven.' From that all understood that Father Ignatius had said these words in a spirit of prophecy."[18]

Doña María in Paris

AMONG the letters which Ignatius wrote to the women who helped him in his studies and in the establishment of his Society, there is one curious document: the recipient remains unknown to us. This is the only such case in the whole of Ignatius' correspondence with women, apart from that of the anchoress in Salamanca, of whom more will be said later. We are reminded of the mystically gifted woman at Manresa, who was, indeed, as Ignatius notes in the Pilgrim's Book, "so famous throughout Spain that even the Catholic King once sent for her to seek her advice about something"; but whom we to-day cannot identify in spite of all researches.

For three hundred years there lay in the Jesuit college of Querétaro in Mexico a copy, or it may possibly be the original of a letter to a "very dear María in Paris", which Ignatius sent from Venice on November 1st, 1536. Of the genuineness of the document, first published in 1903, there is no doubt.[19]

Since December 1535 Ignatius had been in Venice, where he completed his theological studies privately, waiting for his companions of Montmartre, who were still studying in Paris. They were due to arrive in Venice in February 1537, and thence to travel to the Holy Land. On his departure from Paris in April 1535, Ignatius had entrusted the care of his disciples to Master Peter Faber, who was not particularly experienced in money matters. To study cost money in Venice too, and Isabel Roser helped Ignatius from Barcelona to purchase the necessary books. But a greater anxiety for him was that concerning his friends in Paris, who needed money for their final examinations and even more for their journey to Venice; and, at the most modest estimate, for nine men that meant a considerable sum. So Ignatius applied direct to Paris, for he could not call upon his benefactresses in Barcelona for that. Not without an effort he wrote to the Spanish Dominican Gabriel Guzmán, who lived in Paris as confessor to Queen Eleanor, sister of the Emperor Charles V, and with whom Ignatius was on very friendly terms. One feels from this letter that begging did not come easily to him; but since he *was* begging, he would do the thing thoroughly. He knew in Paris a rich Spanish lady (probably belonging to the suite of the imperial ambassador) who had already helped him and to whom he wrote at least twice from Venice in terms of some urgency. There can be no doubt that this lady had been the object of Ignatius' pastoral ministrations and had been advised by him in serious questions of conscience. He therefore felt quite justified in appealing directly and almost sternly to her conscience. The "very dear María in Paris" did not perhaps read the letter with much pleasure.[20]

JESUS

The grace and love of Christ our Lord be always with us to our continual help and favour.

I wrote you another letter earlier than this one and I know that you have received it, though you have not replied. It clearly seems that you are more in my mind than I in yours: I think you have the same reason to remember me in the true love and charity of that Lord who is to save us as I have to think of your peace of conscience in the service and praise of his divine Majesty. Giving as much thanks as I can to him, I find myself well in bodily health, waiting for Lent to leave my studies to embrace other and greater work of more momentum and value.

Because time is brief and we desire to have Faber and some of his friends with us, and I want to be digging and toiling in this vineyard of the Lord, since you have sometimes done things for me and have had certain great desires of doing more, now I ask you as a favour for the love of God our Lord that you busy yourself now the time for their departure has come, both as regards your own power to help them and by speaking to certain persons who may wish to share in this meritorious work, so that they may leave Paris and come here. It is a question of a project so holy and well-founded but so laborious as to be, indeed, a pilgrimage. I hope that God our Lord, besides the fact that your soul is prepared and disposed for such works of charity, will put in you the complete will to employ yourself in them.

I conclude, asking God through his infinite and sovereign goodness to give us grace to know his most holy will and fulfil it perfectly.

Wholly yours in our Lord. Iñigo

November 1st, 1536

JESUS. To my sister in Christ our Lord, my dear María, in Paris.

186

One thing is certain at any rate: the letter reached Paris too late, for Ignatius' companions had already set out for Venice on November 15th, 1536,
under the leadership of Peter Faber, contrary to the original plan, which
was that they should not start till January 1537. It is almost symbolic that
the mysterious Doña María in Paris should remain unknown to us: henceforth,
after the companions had reassembled at Venice, the new community took
on a more definite character, Ignatius' plans began to be realized, his pastoral
work was more consciously directed towards men rather than women. His
studies, Paris, his Basque homeland – all lay behind him. He was to call again
upon the services of his pious women only when it was a question of furnishing the newly-built house of his Society – of founding colleges and works
of charity and securing the influence of the great ones of this world for
the greater glory of God.[21]

Donna Maria Frassoni del Gesso

THE letters that follow all belong to the years after 1550; for only then, after the drawing up of the Constitutions and when the number of members was growing rapidly, was the Society's apostolate directed more and more towards teaching in colleges, which had to be newly founded. These establishments were, however, even according to the well-considered rules about poverty in the Constitutions, entitled to live on assured revenues; and the prudent Ignatius never ventured upon new foundations until financial security gave hopes that they would prosper. Here there opened up fresh possibilities of harnessing the readiness to help of pious lady admirers in the service of souls. Actually, all the women with whom Ignatius corresponded henceforth can be included one way or another among such benefactresses. In this chapter, however, we have selected a number of women whom Ignatius always considered as classic examples of foundresses of colleges. They are mainly ladies of the higher ranks of Italian society, who by founding colleges helped the saint to carry on the apostolate that he had begun in the North Italian university towns even before he finally established himself at Rome.[22]

In a very real sense the original model of a college foundress was for Ignatius and his successors the woman to whose munificence the Society owed the foundation of a college at Ferrara. She was Donna Maria Frassoni del Gesso.

This noblewoman was born in 1504, the daughter of Count Jacobo Frassoni and Catarina dei Biondi. She married in 1524 Lanfranco del Gesso, who in the course of a brilliant political career had become *Fattor Generale,* or prime minister to Duke Hercules of Ferrara. He died while still quite young in 1550, leaving Donna Maria a childless widow. She, wealthy and highly influential at the court of the duke and his consort Renée of France, and later of his daughter-in-law, the Archduchess Barbara of Austria, had taken an interest in the Jesuits from the first. In 1573, the General Everard Mercurian was to greet her as the woman to whom the whole Society of Jesus was indebted, "because you have always been a mother to us".

Ferrara had been since the duke's marriage to Renée of France, who was early suspected of Calvinism, a danger-spot from the point of view of the Church in Northern Italy; and Ignatius had very soon cast his eye upon that city. He had indeed stayed there for a short time after his journey to Jerusalem in February 1524, on which occasion he distributed all that was left of his money to the importunate beggars and thus earned the justly merited acclamation: "A saint, a saint!" From the end of 1537 till April 1538, Ignatius' companions Rodríguez, Bobadilla and Jay were sent by him to work there. No less a person than Vittoria Colonna, who had been at Ferrara since 1537 and wished to go from there on a pilgrimage to the Holy Land, had introduced the Jesuits to Hercules II.[23]

The deep impression which these apostolic men made determined the future course of events. The duke, who was the son of the once notorious and later, as Duchess of Ferrara, pious Lucrezia Borgia, and who was not opposed to the reform of the Church, formed a genuine friendship with the disciples of Ignatius and with their Master himself. He entered into a correspondence with Ignatius in Rome, and his influence proved useful in 1540, when the Society obtained definite papal approval. In 1543 Ignatius could already write of "traditional gratitude". In August 1547, Claude Jay was again sent to Ferrara, as it was hoped that he, being a Frenchman, would have a salutary influence upon the Duchess Renée, whose faith was in doubt. Ignatius gave him characteristically prudent instructions as to his behaviour at court; and soon Father Jay, as he reported to his Master in Rome, found himself involved in a depressingly large number of moral-political problems, which the duke and his *fattore* set him to solve. Here we meet for the first time the influence of the wife of the Minister of State, whom we will from now on call, as did the Ferrarese, simply the *Fattora*. She wished that the Jesuit might, like Ignatius in Rome, take up the spiritual care of fallen girls. In September 1549, however, Father Jay had to go to Germany, and on June 1st, 1550, the Minister of State died suddenly.[24]

From this time on the childless Donna Maria was the main promoter of the plan, which Ignatius had proposed to the Duke, of founding at Ferrara a college of the Society of Jesus for the instruction of youth. The Duke, indeed, wanted to make the Jesuits undertake another activity as well: that of being spiritual directors to the convent of Santa Maria della Rosa, which, as he wrote to Ignatius, had been founded by Lucrezia Borgia, *"Madonna mia madre"*. Politely but firmly, Ignatius declined any sort of responsibility for nunneries; but he pushed forward all the more insistently with the plan of founding a college. He next sent Father Broët to Ferrara, again with the French duchess in mind; and when Broët was ordered to Paris in June 1552, he sent a third Frenchman, Father Jean Pelletier, who entered Ferrara at the head of a party of seven Jesuits from Rome on June

5th, 1552. At that time Ignatius had already written to the *Fattora,* but the letter survives only in a summary.[25]

It was of great advantage to the Jesuits in Ferrara when Francis Borgia paid a state visit to the duke and duchess, to whom he was of course related through his great-aunt Lucrezia. Because of this, the court took part fervently in all the religious services of the Jesuits. The sermons of Father Pelletier were listened to with especial keenness because of his French pronunciation; and on St. John's Day 1552 the *Fattora* with the whole court was able to arrange a suitable celebration on the occasion of his solemn profession.

Although the premises in which the school had to begin were decidedly modest, 120 pupils at once applied for admission. Therefore the rich and independent widow spared no effort to get a new building erected. She began to save money, dismissed redundant servants and gave generously to the Fathers. With nine female members of her household she made the Exercises. At the departure of Father Broët she was inconsolable. A letter of complaint, no longer extant, was sent to Ignatius; but Paris seemed to the General to be more important than the spiritual comfort of the *Fattora.* He gave her the choice: either Pelletier or nobody. The relations between Pelletier and the *Fattora* of Ferrara were soon to develop into something of a minor tragedy.[26]

Ignatius tried to meet the lady's wishes as far as possible. Thus in August 1552 he allowed her majordomo, Bartolomeo Castaldo, to become a Jesuit and yet to continue in his office during his mistress's lifetime, "if he does as the Duke of Gandía did", that is, if his membership of the Society remained secret for the present. The *Fattora's* motherly solicitude was sometimes too importunate, as when, towards the end of that year, Ignatius had politely to decline the gift of some alum, which was then very costly. On the other hand, Father Pelletier was occasionally asked to allow the *Fattora* to mother the Jesuits a little. As early as November 1552, Ignatius had to calm her – she was evidently very easily worked up – and assure her that rumours of the recall of Pelletier, who had already become indispensable, were false.[27]

Meanwhile plans and site for the new college, together with the necessary funds, had been procured by the indefatigable *Fattora.* Ignatius was delighted and promptly decided to do what in other cases he did only after mature deliberation: he made the foundress of the college in Ferrara a participant in all the spiritual merits of the Society. Pelletier would have had him do more, and perhaps the *Fattora,* too, had expected more; be that as it may, Pelletier, zealously devoted to his mistress, asked the General's curia in Rome for special letters patent, solemnly declaring Donna Maria to be the foundress of the new college. But Ignatius never let himself be hurried into anything and damped Pelletier's ardour with the reply: first the foundation with an assured income, then the letters patent. A letter from Ignatius in January 1553 fully satisfied the *Fattora* and was also some consolation to her after all the rather painful misunderstandings she had lately had to put up with in dealing with Father Giovanni Viola, who had been appointed by Ignatius on December 10th, 1552, as his personal representative for the Society's establishments in Northern Italy.[28]

JESUS

My Lady in our Lord.

May the sovereign grace and eternal love of Christ our Lord be ever with us to our help and favour.

I have, indeed, not replied up to the present to your Ladyship's letter of December 10th. I will do so now, thanking your Ladyship for the great charity and devotion with which you help that work of God our Lord in Ferrara and for the good intention you have to help it for the future. I do not doubt but that God our Lord will make you share in all the good that shall be done in it. Moreover, through the same charity and beneficence of your Ladyship, it seems to me to be our duty that we give you a share in all the graces and merits of the said Society throughout the world, a thing we are wont to do for our principal benefactors, so that in all our brethren do and suffer, wherever they may be, your Ladyship shares in the merit of it, in so far as we are able to communicate this to you personally. If you wish for letters patent to this effect, I will send them.

About the site (of the college) and the project of seeking another place, I am writing to our fathers to defer to Your Ladyship's opinion, and unless you are willing, Master Jean Pelletier shall not leave Ferrara, nor anyone else under my authority, except Don Battista (Viola), who, in his capacity as my deputy will from time to time have to visit other colleges but his more permanent residence will be in Ferrara.

No more, except to recommend myself much to your Ladyship's prayers and to beg our Lord to grant us all grace always to know and follow his holy will.

Ignatius

Rome, January 7th, 1553

To my illustrious Lady in our Lord, Madonna Maria del Gesso, wife of the Secretary of State in Ferrara.

191

Polanco notes in his chronicle of the Society that Madonna Maria in Ferrara received this letter and the conferring of a share in the spiritual benefits of the Society of Jesus "like a precious treasure, with expressions of profoundest gratitude". At the beginning of 1553 she really needed such comfort, for it was to be for her a year of bitter spiritual trials and bodily sickness. She was besieged on all side by her kinsfolk, who saw their aunt's great fortune already in the hands of the Jesuits. The *Fattora's* nerves were not good and she suffered from a weak heart. No wonder that she sent for the faithful Pelletier almost every day. Because of this no doubt quite innocent but certainly imprudent conduct on the part of her spiritual director, there arose the minor tragedy which cast a shadow all through that year on Ignatius' correspondence with Ferrara. As early as April, he instructed Father Viola, his representative, to try to moderate the *Fattora's* desire to converse with the Jesuits. A letter of May 6th, 1553, shows us that similar instructions had already been sent to Pelletier himself. On June 3rd, he received definite orders from Ignatius, who had evidently heard a good deal of talk about what was going on in Ferrara: save in the case of the *Fattora's* serious illness, he was not to visit her more than twice a week. But when was the *Fattora* not seriously ill? Even the more prudent of his fellow-Jesuits found much that was blameworthy in Father Pelletier's too great complaisance.

Ignatius had now had enough. In August he assured the *Fattora* through Pelletier of his prayers and of his unchanging gratitude for all her kindness. To Pelletier, however, he caused Polanco to send on September 2nd, 1553, the following letter:[29]

"As for your visits to the house of the Minister's widow, our Father's opinion is as follows: We servants of God must always be careful about two things, namely to have a clear conscience, and to stand well in the eyes of those for whose edification we work. As regards the first, our Father is perfectly assured of the good and pure intentions both of Your Reverence and of the lady herself. Concerning the second point, we must consider 'what may be good, not only before God, but also before men' (2 Cor. 8:21).

"Our Father therefore thinks that one must in this case be more than ordinarily circumspect, at least more so than Your Reverence has been hitherto; for indeed it has been brought to his notice from different quarters that such frequent comings and goings at that house have no very edifying effect, but rather the contrary. The testimony of your own good conscience is no longer enough – with regard to that, all are agreed as to its integrity – but it is necessary also effectively to remove every possible appearance of anything wrong, even in the eyes of those who wish to

192

calumniate us. And if our Father in this respect saw that Your Reverence did not willingly submit to his direction, he would without doubt unhesitatingly recall you from Ferrara.

"Your Reverence must then observe three points in this matter. Firstly, you must go to that lady's house at most twice a week, as you have already been told. Secondly, you must endeavour to make yourself more and more unnecessary by introducing to her Father Filippo [Leernus], that he may hear her confession occasionally and converse with her. This is in order that the lady may relinquish any irregular inclination towards you, should such exist, even a spiritual one. Thirdly, Your Reverence must never under any circumstances or any pretext go alone to that house, but always in the company of a fellow-religious, as the custom of the Society demands, so that the one may always keep the other in view."

Pelletier tried tactfully to teach his penitent these rules of conduct. But the moment was singularly unpropitious. At the beginning of 1554 the *Fattora* really did fall gravely ill. Her heart trouble was so serious that the physicians considered any mental excitement dangerous. The Jesuits in Ferrara at once reported this to Rome. Now Ignatius feared that the fulfilment of his strict instructions to Father Pelletier might injure the sick woman, to whom he was after all under such a deep obligation of gratitude. So he forthwith wrote a letter to Pelletier, to the effect that in his relations with the *Fattora* he should leave everything as it was for the time being. To the lady herself, however, he despatched on January 20th, 1554, a letter full of profound thoughts on the meaning of suffering, written as only Ignatius could write, with a simplicity and an economy of words born of experience.[30]

IHS

My most illustrious Lady in our Lord.

The sovereign grace and eternal love be with Your Ladyship, with his most holy gifts and spiritual graces.

Having understood by letters from our fathers that your Ladyship has been visited by God our Lord with some bodily sickness, and is also suffering in soul, it seems to me that I ought to pay you a brief visit with a letter, since it is not possible for me to do so in another way. I would remind you that the providence of our most loving Father and most wise physician only acts in this way those whom he loves much; and the sooner after the present life he wills to lead [us] to participation in his eternal bliss, the more does he purge [us] with such trials in this

193

world, in which he does not will that we should be able to be quiet or lie down to sleep in comfort with our self-love, for he is wont, indeed, to purify his elect not only with the yearning for heaven, but also with the trials of earth. These serve, indeed, for the increase of our glory, if we accept them with the patience and thanksgiving with which we should accept the gifts of His fatherly love, which is the source of both trials and favours. If there is any way, indeed, of freeing ourselves from trials and afflictions of spirit in this world, it is the forcing oneself to conform one's will wholly with that of God, because if our heart possesses him entirely, since we cannot lose him except of our own free will, it would not be possible for anything to befall us which would occasion us much distress, because all affliction arises from losing or fearing to lose what one loves.

I write to our brother, Master Jean [Pelletier], that although he has many new occupations added to those he already had, he should not fail to visit Your Ladyship as he was wont, for in truth it is through Your Ladyship that he is in Ferrara and it is for your satisfaction and consolation that I am thinking of keeping him there permanently, so far as it is in my power, and God our Lord gives him life.

I say no more except to commend myself much to your prayers and I beg God our Lord to grant us all the grace always to know his most holy will and to fulfil it perfectly.

Wholly Your Ladyship's in our Lord,   Ignatius

Rome, January 20th, 1554

IHS. To my illustrious Lady in our Lord, Madonna Maria del Gesso in Ferrara.

When this letter reached the sickbed in the *palazzo* of the *Fattora,* a strange thing happened: the lady at once recovered. In the family tradition of the counts Frassoni this occurrence has been made into a kind of miracle. In reality the fact was at once simpler and stranger. Polanco has described it in the following words:

"When Ignatius conveyed his respects to the *Fattora* in a letter – it was at a time when her life was feared for, as she could take no food but a little broth – she experienced such consolation on reading this letter that she immediately felt better. She regained her appetite for food, and in a short while her strength and health were restored."[31]

194

The best medicine the letter contained was no doubt the statement that Father Pelletier could remain in Ferrara, for thereby the prosperous continuance of the college was assured. The indefatigable convalescent was already thinking of buying a more favourably situated house for it. Scarcely had she recovered than she sent an almost extravagant letter of thanks to her Most Reverend Father in Christ, Ignatius.

JESUS MARIA

May the grace and peace of our Lord Jesus Christ always remain and increase in Your Reverence's soul.

Most reverend father in Jesus Christ.

The visit Your Reverence has paid me by your letter has given me new life, for it has taken away the worry that was the cause of my illness – a palpitation of the heart. In this respect the doctors have told me on many occasions that the disease might be mortal if I did not guard against worry. This seemed to me a very difficult thing, since I know that this world promises nothing other than anxiety and trouble, and, since my soul is sick inwardly, avoiding worry is well-nigh impossible. So would things have been, if the good God had not given me relief through my spiritual father. In him I find great comfort through the great confidence I have in him.

Your Reverence can see from this how great is my debt to you. To place my life and fortune and all my strength at Your Reverence's disposal to the praise and glory of the giver of all good gifts is a very poor return. With all my heart I ask you to pray for me, that I may make this a fact.

All is well with Father Jean. His college has greater success every day and is making rapid strides in our Lord's service. It is a benefit and a great blessing for our city, which would not have come about without the very great labours of Master Jean. We still have the hope that one day we shall be offered a better place for the college more suitable than that house about which enquiries were first made. Nevertheless, the question of that house, or some other, will not be lost sight of and we still hope that the matter will be satisfactorily settled one day. For this purpose we are already with foresight setting aside a sum of money in the hope that the Lord will allow that plan which is most pleasing to him to meet with sure success.

Reverend Father, I ask you again, for the love of God, to be good enough to help me and to bless my sorely oppressed soul so that it may find the strength to go forward along the path of God's good pleasure. I will say no more.

Ferrara, February 15th, 1554

Your Reverence's unworthy daughter and servant,

Maria del Gesso

To the most reverend father in Christ, Master Ignatius, General of the Society of Jesus, at Santa Maria della Strada, near San Marco, in Rome.

During her illness Donna Maria had already written to Rome on January 1st concerning a matter, which could win over Ignatius entirely. This was the financial stability of his most promising but also most difficult undertaking, the Roman College, for which Ignatius had called upon the services of everybody, especially the rich ladies of his acquaintance.

The *Fattora* at once sent a bill of exchange to Rome, payable to the banking house of Baltassare Olgiati & Co. There the Jesuits could borrow, at the usual rate of four per cent, the money they needed, which they declared themselves willing to pay back to the *Fattora*. For this welcome tiding-over in his greatest need, Ignatius caused his secretary to write a letter full of gratitude to his benefactress.[32]

My most illustrious Lady in Jesus Christ.

The grace and peace of Christ our Lord.

I have received a letter from Your Ladyship dated the first of this month and enclosed in it another one for the heirs of Master Baltassare de Olgiati. I thank Your Ladyship with all my heart on behalf of the whole college as well as for myself. And certainly, your great kindness in giving us this gift makes it possible for us to continue the college for some months; and because we are already so much indebted to Your Ladyship, it is a real joy for us to be so still more, trusting in God our Lord that he himself will be the most generous rewarder of all Your Ladyship does for us, for in his divine service.

I presented the letter to the person to whom it was addressed and they offer to do very willingly what was suggested therein, and this coming week will put it into execution.

I will say no more, except that our Father and all of us with all our hearts recommend ourselves to Your Ladyship's prayers. May Jesus Christ, the salvation and life of all, keep you safe in body and soul. Amen.

Rome, February 17th, 1554

To the wife of the Minister of State

Meanwhile Donna Maria's letter of February 15th had arrived in Rome. Ignatius acknowledged it immediately in a letter now lost. Shortly afterwards a big parcel from Ferrara was delivered at the door of the General's curia, together with a letter from the *Fattora* dated December 18th of the previous year. Ignatius was at a loss how to express his thanks and at the same time protest gently against such an excess of motherly kindness. In his answer of March 13th he speaks somewhat laconically of "some things sent as a gift". Perhaps the former officer felt it did not become him to give a detailed list of these charitable gifts. In any case, we know from Polanco's letter of thanks, sent two days later to the *Fattora,* what the parcel contained: "Shirts, scarves, caps, handkerchiefs and socks". With charming playfulness Ignatius wrote by the same post to Father Pelletier: "May God reward the *Fattora* by clothing her with true and solid virtue!"

The solid virtue after which Donna Maria strove under the guidance of the indispensable Pelletier consisted in a great desire to bear her cross willingly. Ignatius knew this, and so the following letter too was a carefully thought out lesson on Christian mortification. It was, moreover, a masterstroke of psychological insight on Ignatius' part when at the end of it he authorized the *Fattora* to moderate in a motherly way the zeal of Father Pelletier, who was overworked. This difficult problem had now lost all its bitterness.[33]

Most illustrious Lady in our Lord.

The sovereign grace and eternal love of Christ our Lord be always with us to our help and favour.

These last few days I have replied to Your Ladyship's letter of February 15th. I afterwards received another letter from you of December 18th, which came together with some things sent as a gift and alms by Your Ladyship, very greatly appreciated by us in our Lord, for we see in

197

them the great devotion and charity by which you were moved to send them. God, for whose love every well-ordered gift is given and received, will be Your Ladyship's most generous rewarder on behalf of us and all his poor.

As to the disposition Your Ladyship desires to feel to be more prepared for the cross, in his own good time God our Lord will surely readily grant you this; until that time comes patience will be necessary. Of this there can be no doubt, since we have the promise of his eternal truth, that he will not permit that we be more tempted or tried than what we are able to bear: thus, he who looks to God's most sweet Providence, deservedly trusts that all things will work together for his good and holds it as certain that God's supreme goodness acts always with equal love, whether he chastises or caresses his little children. He always acts for their greater good. We are, therefore, able to conform our will very confidently with God's will, resolving to content ourselves with whatever he sends us. Thus in the time of need patience will not be wanting to bear our trials not only without murmuring, but even with thanksgiving, persuading ourselves that both adversity and prosperity are a gift from God our Lord, as they are, indeed, especially in the case of those who are devoted to God's service.

With regard to our brother Master Jean's overworking himself, my wish is that this should be moderated and I have written to him accordingly, and when he does otherwise he acts against our wishes and instructions, a thing I hope he will not do. To be sure, good will often mean that the servants of God exceed what is reasonable and for this have need of a word of caution and Your Ladyship does well to give them one now and again.

I say no more except that we commend ourselves heartily to Your Ladyship's prayers.

May God our Lord deign to grant us all his grace always to know his most holy will and to fulfil it perfectly.

Rome, March 13th, 1554

To the wife of the Minister of State, Ferrara

Subsequently Ignatius often sent kind messages to Ferrara: "May Jesus Christ comfort Her Ladyship", or: "May our Lord God grant her perfect health in this world and salvation in the next"; but he was always careful never to become the object of her too maternal solicitude.

In the summer of 1554 the hundred gold *scudi* which the *Fattora* had lent were punctually repaid. Donna Maria wanted to pay herself the four per cent which the banking firm of Olgiati demanded. Ignatius, however, would not allow this, remarking that the good lady must not be bothered by such trifles, and besides the four per cent would not be subtracted from her heavenly reward.

At the end of March the new house was in fact purchased. Duke Hercules lent 1000 Ferrarese *lire,* but the greater part of the price was paid by the *Fattora.* Her kindness was inexhaustible. At the end of her life, it was reckoned that she had spent 70,000 gold *scudi* on the erection of the church and college of the Society of Jesus in Ferrara. On May 30th, 1554, a description of the new establishment went like a cry of jubilation to Rome. The *Fattora,* who was then just fifty years old, was at the peak of her generous activity towards the new Society.[34]

The grace and peace of our Lord Jesus Christ always increase and remain in Your Paternity's soul, Father.

My very reverend Father in Jesus Christ.

Although at present we find ourselves weak financially, God's Majesty has given us so much courage and good will that through his grace we have bought a new house for the college. This has been arranged in exchange for five thousand pounds in the currency of Ferrara, part being already paid over and part has been raised with the goodwill to pay it back in due time, when God our Lord shall bless us with means to do so. The house is near the palace of the Duke and near the square in the centre of the city. It is very suitable for a college; firstly it has a very fine and beautiful church and has very good accommodation for the activities of a college. The garden borders on that of the Hospital of St. Anne from which it gets good fresh air. On the twenty-fifth of the present month I solemnly took possession of the house in the name of God. I felt wonderful satisfaction seeing them depart from the houses of men and enter the house of Jesus Christ, and observing the Reverend Father Master Jean who could now harvest the fruits of all his labours, for I have written to Your Paternity on other occasions, how much he has toiled. Your Paternity knows that he only wants to help souls to persevere in the service of the Lord God, and to provide what is necessary, as in the matter of buying the house, and [knows] what all that has cost him in reflection and words and in unwearying initiative.

Your Paternity must now help us before the Lord God with your prayers to bring it about that here and throughout the world the affairs of such groups of men may prosper to the honour of God and the salvation of souls. I also beg Your Paternity to say Mass just once for the soul of my consort, so that, if he is suffering at all, the eternal Father may deign to free him for the love of Jesus Christ. And even though I need it, I do not remind Your Paternity to pray for me, because I am certain that you do that through your kindness; and through the favours Your Paternity has shown me you have proved to me that you love me in Jesus Christ and desire the good of my soul.

My Venerable Father, if it is in my power to do anything for you, deign to command me as your servant and daughter because it is to me a holy duty to revere and obey you through Jesus Christ until the hour of my death. With this I conclude, asking your blessing through Jesus Christ.

Your Paternity's unworthy daughter and servant, Maria del Gesso

Ferrara, May 30th, 1554

To the most reverend Father, Father Master Ignatius,
General of the Society of Jesus, at Santa Maria
della Strada, near San Marco in Rome

This joy was, however, mingled with bitterness, and only Ignatius' knowledge of the human heart was able to smooth over certain difficulties which had arisen. The question was: how to honour the *Fattora* suitably as the real foundress of the college. The usual ceremonies consisted in the presentation of a certificate and a lighted candle. Political considerations, however, were involved. On such an occasion one could not ignore His Serene Highness the Duke. The question was debated for a long time at Rome; and finally suggestions for a solution, full of Ignatian diplomacy, were despatched to Ferrara. Pelletier was to try and persuade the *Fattora* to be satisfied with the title "Foundress by Merit" *(Fondatrice per via del merito)* or, as it says in another letter, "Anonymous Foundress" *(Fondatrice in occulto)*. Each of these solutions relied ultimately upon the *Fattora's* goodness. It was agreed that to her, as the real foundress of the college, belonged all the merits and honours prescribed in the Constitutions; but the founder's candle was to be presented to the Duke alone. As a true "handmaid of Christ", the *Fattora* certainly attached no importance to outward signs; on the other hand, the Jesuits had to be sure of the favour of the duke[35].

The truly noble lady was quite satisfied with this solution and on May 30th wrote a letter of thanks to Ignatius, which is now lost. At the time,

Ignatius lay seriously ill; but as soon as he could, he gave expression to his never-failing gratitude in the last letter that we possess of his correspondence with Donna Maria del Gesso.

IHS

My most illustrious Lady in our Lord

The sovereign grace and eternal love of Christ our Lord be always with us to our help and favour.

To Your Ladyship's letter of May 30th, I have not replied until now because I was ill. Although I am still not completely better, I did not want to fail to write you these few lines not so much to thank Your Ladyship for your very great benefits, because this I leave to him for whose love and reverence you have conferred them, namely Jesus Christ, God and our Lord, but to show you that I am not unmindful of them and to ask God in his generosity to deign, according to his power and infinite goodness, to give you eternal rewards. I especially rejoice at the contentment Your Ladyship shows at our having our own house and having it from your hands, and I hope it will be a sure beginning of some great service for God our Lord.

The Mass Your Ladyship asks me for I have not been able to say personally through being still in bed; but I shall not fail, provided God gives me the health, to do what you ask me. In the meanwhile I have entrusted this to another priest whom I have made a sharer in the same favour that His Holiness bestowed on me for helping souls. Accordingly his prayer, you may be sure, has the same efficacy, especially for Your Ladyship, who in many ways has a special share in all our prayers.

Again Your Ladyship will please us by recommending us to God our Lord, for not only in temporal matters but also in spiritual we need your help.

May God our Lord grant us all grace always to know his most holy will and to fulfil it perfectly.

Yours servant in our Lord,   Ignatius

Since our Father Master Ignatius cannot write with his own hand, I, John of Polanco, have written it in his name.

Rome, June 23rd, 1554

IHS. To my illustrious Lady in our Lord,
    Maria del Gesso, in Ferrara

201

The name of the *Fattora* often turns up again in Ignatius' letters. Till his death he prayed for her health; at a time of great need he once again appealed for her help for the Roman College; and he allowed Father Pelletier to remain at Ferrara. The *Fattora* in turn did not let herself be outdone in gratitude by Ignatius. She sold a large estate in order to help her beloved foundation at Ferrara. With increasing years, however, she was not too easy to deal with, and, like other benefactresses with whose peculiarities Ignatius had patiently to contend, as a foundress she had her whims. A letter to Pelletier in October 1555 shows the General both resigned and prudent: "As for the rest, one must just sympathize with her and take care that she is always comforted and satisfied."[36]

Only once did Ignatius get angry: in May 1556 the pious *Fattora* tried to induce her Jesuits in Ferrara to sing solemn Vespers. Ignatius at once protested and ordered that she must be absolutely prevented from even making such a request in Rome. This was a few weeks before the death of the saint. The *Fattora* was also seriously ill at this time and it was not until December 26th, 1556, that Laynez sent her a heartfelt letter of consolation on the death of Father Ignatius. He sent the General's loyal fellow-worker a rosary and the picture of St. John the Evangelist which Ignatius had had for many years standing beside his crucifix.

The *Fattora* lived to see the brilliant development of the college at Ferrara and the consecration of the magnificent church of Il Gesù, where in her presence St. Charles Borromeo celebrated his first Mass on February 5th, 1580. On March 4th, 1590, she died, and she was buried beside her husband in the Jesuit church. A marble tablet to the right of the high altar still bears witness that she was once called by Ignatius himself Foundress of the College of the Society of Jesus at Ferrara.[37] The inscription reads:

Jesus – Maria

Maria del Gesso, a lady of exemplary piety,
called by our Father Ignatius himself
"Foundress of this College of Ferrara."

In the Year of our Salvation 1590, the 86th of her age,
on the fourth of March.

Donna Costanza Pallavicini Cortesi

In the marshy and, in summer, fever-ridden plain of Lombardy lay the other ducal capital of the Este, the ancient city of Modena. There the founding of a Jesuit college took as it were, under Ignatius' direction, a medical form. In the centre of this remarkable affair there again stands a charitable woman, to whom Ignatius was always gratefully devoted, though he often had to contradict her. This was Donna Costanza Pallavicini Cortesi, known to the whole city as *la Cavaliera,* which was the name Ignatius also used for her.

Tragic discord cast a shadow over the beginning of the Jeuits' work at Modena. The young, zealous Father Salmerón got involved through his sermons from April to August 1543 in a violent dispute with the bishop, later the celebrated Cardinal Morone, concerning the Catholic teaching on grace and good works, and had to leave Modena. (Fifteen years afterwards, at the Inquisition's infamous trial of Morone, this was made the principal accusation.) On account of this, the new Society, having at first been received with enthusiasm, was not looked upon at Modena with much favour.

In 1551 Father Silvestro Landini began to preach there. He was, indeed, a sick man, though of tremendous energy, so that the new Bishop of Modena, Egidio Foscarari, a Dominican (who in 1548 had, as *Magister Sacri Palatii* in Rome, examined and highly approved of Ignatius' book of the *Exercises*), exclaimed in enthusiasm: "A second St. Geminianus is come to Modena!" He even wished to make Father Silvestro, under holy obedience, act as his confessor.

Landini began, following as it were his Master's classic procedure, with sermons in the convent of female penitents, which was then being reformed by the bishop. We shall hear later remarkably edifying things of this house and the Pezzani ladies who conducted it. [38]Here there sat at Father Landini's feet a noble widow, the *Cavaliera,* who occupied herself with the fallen women, led a life of piety with frequent reception of the Sacraments, and set a good example to the aristocratic ladies of Modena. With her help, Landini founded a kind of women's society for the purpose of tending the sick poor, settling quarrels between women, and protecting girls who were in moral danger. His preaching started something like a eucharistic movement in the whole city. The bishop, full of enthusiasm, wished to band together the noble ladies, under Landini's direction, into a community on early Christian lines for active works of charity, and the *Cavaliera* was to be at the head of it.

Such was the situation in Modena when the name of the *Cavaliera* first appears in Ignatius' correspondence. It was in June 1552; and in December he sent her a letter of greeting, unfortunately preserved only in the *regesta*. The reason for the letter was the same as usual: in Modena, too, there had been since the beginning of 1552 plans for founding a college, and for that in Ignatius' experience the assistance of a motherly hand was of great advantage. Duke Hercules, Cardinal Morone and many noblemen of Modena were prepared, somewhat hesitantly, to contribute;[39] but while the men talked, the *Cavaliera* began to act. She declared herself willing to support ten of the Jesuits. She would be personally responsible for the household equipment and the bed linen.

On September 26th, 1552, it was possible to open a college in a house that was exceedingly unpretentious and quite unsuitable for the purpose. Mindful of Salmerón's painful dispute, Ignatius had given detailed instructions to the fathers he sent to Modena. The rector was Father Cesare de Aversa, who was not yet twenty-five. Singing the *Te Deum,* the ten Jesuits entered the house which Ignatius was soon to refer to as "that hole". *The Cavaliera* in her motherly kindness had indeed provided everything as far as she was able; and the poverty-loving rector was almost alarmed at the profusion of furniture, wine and flour that Madonna Costanza had procured. It was utterly impossible to accommodate the hundred pupils who at once applied for admission. When Father Landini shortly afterwards had to leave for Corsica on the Pope's orders, his friends' sorrow was indeed great; but he himself sang a *Nunc Dimittis* of relief.

The circumstances under which the Jesuits lived were indescribable. In the hot and marshy air of the low-lying plain all the teaching staff fell ill in the summer of 1553. The state of the whole house was pitiable. No sooner did Ignatius hear of this heroically endured hardship than he became angry and took steps to remedy the situation. An order at once went out to Modena and to his representative Father Viola at Bologna either to rent another house or to close the newly opened college.[40] One may well imagine that this must have hurt the *Cavaliera,* whose truly maternal solicitude was fully recognized at Rome: the house she had furnished with such touching enthusiasm was to be closed down! No doubt Ignatius realized this, so he wrote to the *Cavaliera* on August 26th, 1553, the following letter:

My Lady in our Lord.

May the sovereign grace and eternal love of Christ our Lord be with Your Ladyship with his most holy gifts and spiritual graces.

Understanding that God our Lord has visited all our brethren together with bodily sickness, and that not only do they not serve your ladyship but of necessity they give you trouble, I have written to the Rector of the College of Bologna who, on the advice of the physician (which would be to take them away from Modena) will remove them with Your Ladyship's kind permission and that of the other gentlemen who are benefactors of this College, whom I do not want to seem to go against, my desire being to please and serve you in the divine Majesty. As soon as the fathers are well, they or others will then be able to return to your service and that of the city.

I will say no more except to recommend myself much to Your Ladyship's prayers and beg the divine wisdom to direct you all and make you always to know and accomplish his most holy will.

Rome, August 26th, 1553

To the Cavaliera Cortesi

It will be seen that for Ignatius the Modenese foundation had become mainly a medical question. On his orders, the rector of Bologna, Father Francesco Palmio, had to discuss with qualified physicians the suitability of the house in Modena from the hygienic point of view. The personal physician to the Duke of Ferrara said it was more like a wild beast's den. Moreover, in spite of the *Cavaliera's* eagerness to help, the college was by no means established on a secure basis; and Ignatius declared that only in such a case would he send qualified teaching staff to Modena. Incidentally, he did not neglect to send the ducal physician's report about the "wild beast's den" to the Bishop of Modena.[41]

To settle matters in Modena effectively, and not by correspondence only, Ignatius sent there the Flemish Jesuit Father Philip Leernus, a very useful man in practical everyday affairs. From information supplied by this incorruptible witness, Ignatius learnt the full seriousness of the situation. Father Palmio was at once ordered from Bologna to Modena, and with his help the Jesuits succeeded in renting a more healthily situated house, in which the work of the college could continue.

It appears that the pious *Cavaliera* regarded all this as evidence of a lack of the spirit of sacrifice on the part of the fathers, and pursued a policy of passive resistance against the move. So another letter had to be written to the lady, who was, after all, a person who had to be taken into account.[42]

My Lady in our Lord,

May the sovereign grace and eternal love of Christ our Lord be with Your Ladyship with his most holy gifts and spiritual graces.

Through letters from our fathers I have understood what the doctors think and experience proves about that house where the fathers have been living in Modena up to the present, and we have reached the conclusion that with a good conscience we cannot and ought not to allow them to remain there. Because to be prepared for any illness and for death itself in God's service and the help of souls is only right and fitting, but this is no longer the case when it is a hindrance to that work, as in the present instance. Of this Your Ladyship will well be able to judge, realizing how little the good of the city and also its devout people can be served by our fathers when they all begin to fall sick. I therefore ask Your Ladyship to put aside your resistance to the change of residence and thus the servants of God will rather be helped by your accustomed charity towards them. And although they remain few in number, they will serve the common good more if they are living in reasonable and healthy conditions, than if they were dead or all or almost all unwell, as they are now.

For all other matters I refer you to our dear brother, Don Francesco Palmio, and I shall therefore be all the more brief in this letter. I heartily commend myself with this whole house to Your Ladyship's prayers.

May the divine and supreme goodness deign to grant us all his grace to know and follow his holy will.

Ignatius

Rome, October 7th, 1553

Ignatius' representative Father G. B. Viola now appointed Leernus rector, and the former rector, Father Cesare de Aversa, was recalled to Bologna. This was, as it were, the ascetic side of the medical problem. Father Cesare was himself a sick man, subject to anxiety and always enveloped in melancholy, and because of this he had with exaggerated severity imposed too much strain on the health of his fellow-Jesuits. For having done so, Ignatius rebuked him; but otherwise the General was pleased that Father Cesare now lived in the more salubrious city of Bologna. He must on no account go again to "that hole" in Modena, Ignatius ordered him. But here once again the latter had not reckoned with the pious unreasonableness of his bene-factresses. The "devout persons" of Modena complained, and the *Cavaliera,* who was in any case upset by the recall of the very capable Master Adrian de Witte, a Flemish scholastic, sent on November 5th, 1553, a kind of protest to Ignatius against his action.[43] From his answer it is apparent that, even now, the General was not put out and that he was in no way inclined to yield an inch.

My very illustrious Lady in our Lord,

The sovereign grace and eternal love of Christ our Lord be always with us to our help and favour.

I have learned from Your Ladyship's letter of November 5th, that some people were displeased at the departure of our dear brother Don Cesare. I am edified by the good affection from which this proceeds, although the reasons for which I had instructed our father commissary to make the change, were well-founded for I saw how very unwell Don Cesare was and how often he had a relapse. At present he is in Bologna, rather unwell. If, therefore, I were to write to the father commissary to send him back to Modena, in the desire I have to please and serve Your Ladyship, I do not think the result would be what we are all aiming at, namely that God our Lord should be better served and the souls of those who are spiritually in contact with us, be comforted. I shall therefore write to the father commissary to do what he sees to be best, and I do not doubt that Your Ladyship will be in agreement.

Master Adrian [Witte], indeed, if his health permitted, I should be glad to send back [to Modena], for it is only on that account that I am obliged to withdraw him.

I say no more for the present except to commend myself most since-rely, with our whole house, to Your Ladyship's prayers. God our Lord grant us all his grace always to know and follow his most holy will.

To the Cavaliera Costanza Pallavicina Cortesi

Rome, December 2nd, 1533

Even Ignatius, however, did not always reckon with the weaknesses of his fellow-Jesuits. Father Cesare, to whom had been sent an impressive list of his mistakes, did nevertheless return to Modena at the invitation of his devout friends. The misunderstandings which arose because of this were soon resolved by the death of the melancholic Father de Aversa.

The year 1554 was for the college at Modena one of ill-success, in spite of every effort. The initial enthusiasm for the Jesuits in the city had evaporated, even in the case of the bishop. The prosaic Fleming Leernus expressed his opinion thus: "If we leave Modena again, only thirty or forty women at most will mourn our departure." The bishop, a Dominican, even believed that when Ignatius was dead, his whole Society would dissolve, and the words of the Psalmist were applied to the Jesuits: "I have seen an end of all perfection" *(Omnis consummationis vidi finem)* (Ps. 118:96).

This news produced only a smile in the General's curia. Polanco could not resist sharpening his pen and writing to Leernus in Modena: "The foundation of this our Society is Christ, who remaineth for ever, and not our Father General, who, indeed, will one day help us from heaven as he has helped us upon earth. It is true certainly that if all our colleges were in the same state as that in Modena, we should indeed be seeing the end of all perfection."[44]

Only the *Cavaliera* remained loyal to the Jesuits. Not all the means she employed to come to the assistance of the college were, it is true, desirable. She endeavoured, for example, to have small children admitted. This moved Father Polanco to make the ironic remark that at Modena it was becoming usual to send children who could not yet write to follow lessons on Cicero and Virgil.

The kind of exasperating thing that the General in Rome had to put up with is shown by the request which came to him from the *Cavaliera* that he would allow her servant's little boy to be admitted to the college, although the child could not form one letter of the alphabet. The number of pupils declined again, and Ignatius took advantage of this to recall to Rome for further training a young Jesuit employed at Modena, Giovanni Lorenzo de Patarinis. The rector, Leernus, was actually glad of this, for the young graduate exercised a marked influence on the pious women of the city by his handsome figure and engaging features – it was all quite respectable, of course, but in view of his youth prudence was advisable. At once the *Cavaliera,* saddened by his departure, set about asking for a substitute; and Ignatius, ever ready to oblige, sent her a Jesuit called Stefano Baroelli, who not only was well versed in moral theology and an experienced confessor, but also knew some Hebrew. Baroelli brought with him on his arrival in Modena the following letter from the General to the *Cavaliera.*[45]

ELEONORA DE' MEDICI, DUCHESS OF FLORENCE AND HER SON FERDINAND I.
see page 93

LETTER FROM THE DUCHESS ELEONORA
OF FLORENCE TO ST. IGNATIUS

see page 102-103

IHS

The sovereign grace and eternal love of Christ our Lord be always with Your Ladyship with his most holy gifts and spiritual graces.

With regard to Your Ladyship's letter in which you write that it would be a great kindness to you if I could send you another father in place of Master Giovanni Lorenzo, I am doing what you ask, sending Master Stefano, the bearer of the present letter. I wanted him to bring this letter of mine with him so that I might thus take advantage of the opportunity of visiting Your Ladyship by letter. To your service in our Lord Jesus Christ I am greatly devoted, and also desirous that God's generosity may always increase and preserve the gifts of his grace in Your Ladyship.

To recommend to you what is being done in Modena and our fathers who are there, seems to me unnecessary, because Your Ladyship's great charity to them makes such a request superfluous.

I will merely ask Your Ladyship to recommend us in your prayers to God our Lord. In his divine and sovereign goodness may he grant us always to know his most holy will and perfectly to fulfil it.

Rome, November 10th, 1554

To the Cavaliera Cortesi

The whole of 1555 was filled with difficulties concerning the building of a new and healthier college. Again it was the pious ladies of Modena, Barbara Pezzani, Laura Pallavicini and others, who under the leadership of the *Cavaliera* generously contributed. The *Cavaliera* gave 100 gold *scudi*, the others together 300 Ferrarese lire. "The Lord be with them", wrote Father Nadal.

The *Cavaliera* gave the example, too, in every kind of piety. "We have large congregations in the church, for the Signora Cavaliera sets the tone here in Modena, and the other ladies follow her", stated a report to Rome. As late as November 1556, when St. Ignatius was already dead, the *Cavaliera* was working with Cardinal Morone to establish the college at Modena on a permanent footing.[46]

Donna Margherita Gigli

It is remarkable that, even before the founding of the Society, the first sermons which Ignatius' companions preached in the North Italian cities in the years 1537-8 proved to be such a favourable starting-point when later the real work of the Order began, because on that earlier occasion they had made a deep impression on some pious and high-minded women. This was the case in Ferrara, as we already know, and also in Bologna; as if here too Ignatius himself had, as it were, unwittingly blessed the ground in advance by his presence and his virtues. On the journey from Genoa to Venice, Ignatius arrived frozen and ill at the gates of Bologna, having endured "the greatest bodily hardship of his life", the crossing of the Apennines, on whose steep slopes he had often had to crawl on hands and knees. This was at the beginning of December 1535. "As he was about to enter Bologna, he had to cross a little wooden bridge. In doing so he fell off. When he picked himself up, covered with mud and soaking wet, he provoked many who were there to laughter by his appearance. In the city he began to beg for alms, but he got not a penny, although he traversed the whole town."

Ignatius had originally intended to lodge at the Spanish college of San Clemente, and from there to complete his theological studies at the university. Isabel Roser sent him money from Barcelona; but it was too cold and foggy at Bologna, and soon Ignatius lay sick in hospital with his old complaint of gallstones, which all his life he thought to be a stomach disease. So at the end of December he went to Venice.[47] He had not, however, forgotten Bologna, for he knew the world-wide importance of that university city, for which, as for Salamanca and Paris, he had apostolic plans. At the end of October 1537 he sent there a strange pair chosen from among his companions: Francis Xavier, the saint, and Nicholas Bobadilla, the gifted eccentric. They began the work of reform with street sermons and hearing confessions. "The fragrance of their labours is still to be felt there", said Diego Laynez later; "it was a beginning which grew and is still growing." Already in those days the two Jesuits made the acquaintance of two ladies belonging to the highest society of the city: Donna Violante Gozzadini and Donna Margherita Gigli. With both of these Ignatius later corresponded, and Donna Margherita became in Bologna what the *Fattora* was in Ferrara, "the most loving mother of the Society of Jesus", as she is described in an unpublished document.[48]

Donna Margherita Gigli, often also called "del Gigli", was married to a nobleman, Giovanni Francesco Fantuzzi, who died leaving her a widow with a daughter named Elena. She had a brother, Monsignor Tommaso del Gigli, usually called "Giglio". In 1550 the latter was living in Rome as administrator of Cardinal Alexander Farnese. Later he became Bishop of Sora and then of Piacenza, where he died in 1578. A bond of sincere friendship was soon formed between Ignatius in Rome and this pious prelate. In 1549 Monsignor Giglio had already gone to some trouble to obtain from the sick Paul III the bull of privileges for the Society of Jesus, which was published on October 18th, 1549. In matters of Canon Law, too, he was a wise counsellor and mediator for the General of the Society. As deputy for the Vice-Chancellor Cardinal Alexander Farnese, Monsignor Giglio also signed the letters patent allowing Ignatius to take relics from the Roman churches for the Queen of Portugal. So the good lady in Bologna had already heard quite a lot about the great Father of her never-forgotten Master Francis Xavier. Margherita had besides another brother, Don Giovanni, whose younger son Leone del Giglio entered the Society as a scholastic at Florence in 1552, and from there wrote well-worded letters to Ignatius in which *inter alia* he gave accounts of the illnesses of the Duchess Eleonora of Florence. There was further a nephew, still quite small, whom his aunt would very much have liked to send to the college at Bologna as a boarder, but Ignatius was altogether against it. They should not, he said, make a little Jesuit out of him; and he could be accepted only as a half-day pupil at most. Lastly, in Donna Margherita's house lived her daughter Elena, in whose marriage plans Ignatius was to take as keen an interest as in all the other trivial problems of Donna Margherita's household.[49]

In 1540 the apostolic labours of Father Claude Jay so much affected the people of Bologna and caused such a rush to go to confession that the doors of Santa Lucia had to be closed. In 1546 the young priest Don Francesco Palmio, even before his actual entry into the Society, continued this work; and Ignatius' former companion at Paris, Alfonso Salmerón, delighted the Bolognese by his sermons full of scriptural learning. This must have been the occasion when Donna Margherita began to take an active interest in the priests of the new Society, for in her will, which she submitted to the General Laynez on April 1st, 1559, she writes that it was fifteen years since she had been by God's grace in the service of the Society of Jesus. In fact, the chronicler of the Society notes that in 1547 a few well-to-do friends of the Fathers had obtained two small houses near the church of Santa Lucia, in order to make them into a dwelling for the Jesuits; and this, he adds, was done "at the instigation of some pious ladies who are devoted to us".

Here too, as in Ferrara and Rome, the work of the Society began with the care of morally endangered girls, which was taken over by a guild of women, the "Congregation of Love".[50] The Jesuits' success was amazing; by 1550 the little community numbered fourteen men. In the church of Santa Lucia a special celebration was held on the first Sunday of the month in honour of the Blessed Sacrament, and the number of communicants rose perceptibly. Retreats were given for ladies; and vocations among young women increased, as the chronicler of the Society says, "to the astonishment of the older nuns". What the same chronicler reports of the moral improvement in Bologna – which would have delighted Savonarola himself – illuminates the social history of the period of transition from Renaissance to Reformation. "Many of the married ladies, even from among the nobility, now went frequently to confession and communion. Everyone was edified by their new manner of dress and behaviour: pearls and silken garments and chains of gold, all the baubles and tinsel, were now laid aside. In Bologna of all places this was a good thing, because that city was notorious for extravagant spending on such vanities. The new behaviour of the ladies therefore pleased their husbands very well. The latter at once felt relieved of that all too well known pressure upon their purses, which they had hitherto had to endure on account of the pompous attire of their wives. And so it came about that the men themselves began to preach to their wives that they might devote themselves zealously to the spiritual life."[51]

In Bologna, however, it was as everywhere else in the Society's beginnings: the house was very poor, and the Fathers had scarcely enough for their daily needs. There was already a rumour that the General wished to recall the Jesuits from Bologna on this account. At the same time, however, the long-cherished plan for founding a college began to take concrete shape. The question that faced Ignatius was therefore: should the Jesuits give up in Bologna altogether, or begin even more intensively? Donna Margherita was among the friends who had been enthusiastic for a college from the beginning. On hearing the rumour of the possible recall of the Fathers she wrote to her brother in Rome, who at once hastened to Ignatius with the lady's letter. This brought her on May 31st, 1551, the answer which follows. From the address: "To a sister of Monsignor Tommaso Giglio", we may presume that the letter was conveyed to his sister by the prelate himself.[52] The tone of it is distinctly cool. Ignatius had evidently been touched on a raw nerve by the complaints from Bologna – namely his ideal of holy poverty, the subject of so much meditation; and he feared no doubt at the same time that he would be hindered in his freedom of action by such insistent complaints.

IHS

May the sovereign grace and eternal love of Christ be always with us to our help and favour.

I have seen a letter from Your Ladyship and have taken comfort from it, for I can see the spiritual intention and love of perfection and imitation of Christ our Lord which is shown in it. As to the end of this letter, however, which urges me not to move our fathers from Bologna on account of the poverty which they experience, I want to say two things, both very true. One is that although it came into my mind to remove our fathers from there for a similar reason, in the meantime, on thinking the matter over, I saw that it would be a greater service of God if we did our duty where we have colleges already. The other thing is, that in spite of what has been written, none of our fathers who are in Bologna has complained to me or shown in any way that he was suffering need of necessary things.

It is true that, besides the two students sent to Vienna, and another who has come here to Rome, we have thought fit that Francesco Palmio or Master Paschasius [Broët] should be assigned to Ferrara for a time with another student. For that purpose we are sending provisionally six other brethren from here until final provision is made for Ferrara from elsewhere.

After this explanation, I do not see that my answer need have anything more added to it, unless to recommend myself much to Your Ladyship's prayers and to beg Jesus Christ our Lord to grant us always the grace to know his most holy will and to fulfil it perfectly.

Ignatius

From Rome, May 30th, 1551

At the end of 1551 it became possible to open a college at Bologna. Schoolrooms were fitted up in the house adjoining Santa Lucia: 130 pupils formed the nucleus, and Father Francesco Palmio was rector. At the same time social work for the poor continued, and the ladies of the "Congregation of Love" helped enthusiastically with the collection of clothes, flour and bread. Visits to poor homes were carefully organized.

All this meant an intolerable burden of work for Father Palmio. Donna

Margherita, who was worried at this, could look on no longer, and again she wrote to Monsignor Tommaso Giglio a report which she did not dare to send to Ignatius personally. She asked that one more Jesuit at least might be sent for the immediate relieving of the rector. Shortly afterwards, however, she plucked up courage and made the same request to the General himself. The answer that Ignatius sent to Donna Margherita on Christmas Eve 1552 is once more characteristic of him. The fulfilment of her wish was not merely promised for practical reasons – providing it were possible – but represented as the rendering of an agreeable service to Monsignore and his honoured sister. As it was impossible at the moment for Ignatius to accede to her request, the lady was referred to the Provincial in Florence, Father Laynez.[53]

JESUS

The sovereign grace and eternal love of Christ our Lord be always with us to our help and favour.

From a letter from Your Ladyship I have understood (as also from Monsignor Giglio's account) how desirable it would be to send another priest to accompany Master Don Francesco. And certainly I desire this both for the need of it and also for the satisfaction of Monsignor Giglio and of Your Ladyship, who are seeking this with so much charity. I hope at the first opportunity not to fail in what is at present impossible without noticeably inconveniencing other places. If you could also write to the Father Provincial who is in Florence perhaps he might possibly be able to make some provision if he can do so without neglecting the greater service of God. This I know that both Your Ladyship and also all of us are seeking.

Offering myself, then, to Your Ladyship's service in our Lord with a very good heart, I will not say more, except that I pray God our Lord to grant us all abundant grace always to know his most holy will and to fulfil it perfectly.

Wholly your Ladyship's in our Lord,   Ignatius

From Rome, December 24th, 1552

To my illustrious Lady in our Lord,
Madonna Margherita Gigli de Fantuzzi, in Bologna

This letter suggests that the cordial friendship of Ignatius for Monsignor Tommaso was being extended more and more to Donna Margherita as well. Thus it was that Ignatius, overburdened as he was with affairs that were really more important, was drawn into the little family tragedy in which Donna Margherita's kinsfolk were divided against one another. Her daughter Elena Fantuzzi was now of marriageable age; but she continued to live quietly with her mother. Her good uncle in Rome evidently wanted his niece to enter a convent, or else to make a marriage suitable to her rank as soon as possible. He could think of no better course than to make enquiries through Ignatius of the Jesuits in Bologna.

Patiently Ignatius wrote on May 12th, 1554, to the rector, Father Palmio: "Monsignor Giglio has a niece there, the daughter of his sister, who has not yet been able to make up her mind whether to become a nun or to marry. Her family greatly desires Your Reverence to see to it that she come to a decision, either to enter some convent – and that would be incomparably better for her, as she could thus devote herself entirely to God, as is her duty – or to choose the married state. . . . If, however, Your Reverence be of opinion that it is better for her to remain in her present state for the time being, then encourage her in it and inform us by return of post, that we may give an answer to Monsignor Giglio; or better still, let Your Reverence write to him; he and all of us desire only what is best."[54]

The mother was against her daughter's entry into a nunnery – that goes without saying. Ignatius acted as mediator between the mother, who wished to keep her child with her, and the uncle, who, in accordance with the then current view about a young girl's state in life, knew only two alternatives, convent or marriage. Ignatius won the first battle: Elena was able to remain with her mother for the time being. To this victory we owe the letter which Ignatius sent from his sickbed to Donna Margherita on July 28th, 1554 – the very day on which Polanco recommended him to the prayers of the Jesuits in Bologna. He was able to report that he had talked Uncle Tommaso out of the convent idea.[55]

The sovereign grace and eternal love of Christ our Lord be with Your Ladyship with his most holy gifts and spiritual graces.

Although last month and this I have been rather unwell, as I still am, I have not failed to do what Your Ladyship asked me in regard to Monsignor Tommaso de Giglio, your brother; and it seems to me that he is pleased and fairly satisfied that Madonna Elena, Your Ladyship's daughter, remains in her present state of life so long as Your Ladyship lives. He was merely trying, as he declared to me, to satisfy another person of rank whom he could also have helped. At all events, so far as it depends on him no pressure at all will be used in this matter.

215

For the rest I desire with all my heart to be remembered in Your Ladyship's prayers and those of your daughter whom I am always most ready and willing to serve in our Lord, and I beg God's supreme goodness to grant us all grace always to know his most holy will and perfectly to fulfil it.

Ignatius

Rome, July 28th, 1554

Margherita de Fantuzzi in Bologna

Who the "other person of rank" was, of whom Monsignor Tommaso spoke to Ignatius, cannot now be known with certainty. Probably it was that noble kinsman of Elena's father, Ottaviano Fantuzzi, who found his niece's position so scandalous that after a year he went to Rome to tell Ignatius what he thought. A report of this somewhat stormy interview in the parlour of the General's curia was sent to Bologna on July 13th, 1555:

"Fantuzzi was very insistent and demanded that our Father should write to Palmio, telling him to make every effort to make Elena either marry or enter the cloister. Otherwise (he said) it was a cause of scandal, and the occasion of gossip against Father Palmio too; it was a danger to Elena's soul, and a Dominican had said that to live in such a state was a mortal sin, for which the Jesuits would have to do penance."

The opinion about this case held by those nearest to Ignatius is also of interest to the social historian; they had advanced far enough to admit that another way of life besides the alternatives "nunnery or marriage" might be Christian too, and have a purpose. Polanco writes: "Among us here it is agreed that Elena's action is not only permissible but positively meritorious." Father Palmio then had the task of writing a letter to the indignant Signor Fantuzzi to calm him down, the text of which was subsequently criticized by Ignatius, who sent the Rector the following communication: "Your letter to the Gentiluomo Fantuzzi is very good; but the last part, in which you admonish him to let Elena be as she is, is not so well done." So the unmarried daughter stayed with her mother till her early death, which was communicated to the General Laynez by the grief-stricken Donna Margherita on April 1st, 1559.[56]

Meanwhile in Bologna conditions in the cramped house next to Santa Lucia had become so intolerable that a plan for a new building by the church of Sant' Andrea was being considered. The person who was most keen to help was Monsignor Giglio, who to the gratification of Ignatius

216

travelled specially to Bologna to get things going. The pious ladies, however, were not at all pleased, because they had got used to the beautiful services of the Jesuits in Santa Lucia. Margherita and her friend Donna Violante Gozzadini wrote a kind of protest to Ignatius on March 15th, 1555, in the name of many other ladies, and asked that at least a few of the Fathers might be allowed to stay in the house at Santa Lucia. Ignatius' answer was a little cool; but he nevertheless allowed himself to be induced to compromise by the pious insistence of the ladies.[57]

CHRISTUS

The sovereign grace and eternal love of Christ our Lord be always with us to our help and favour.

By a letter from Your Ladyship of the fifteenth of last month, I have learnt of the wish of yourself and your husband, the illustrious Madonna Violante, and other persons, that some of our Society should remain permanently in the house near the church of Santa Lucia. And in truth, on account of the obligation which gratitude and charity impose on us, that we should try and give pleasure to people to whom we are so much indebted, I should very much like to be able to do what Your Ladyship writes. For the present, however, it seems to me quite impossible, unless we want to fail in both cases, dividing the fathers who are all necessary in one place. I have therefore written to our fathers that they come to Santa Lucia at least once a week, or wherever else Your Ladyship may deem most fitting for your spiritual consolation and service.

And because I know that Your Ladyship only wants what is most pleasing to God our Lord I hope we shall all be of one mind in our Lord. May his grace always increase in us all that we may always know his most holy will and fulfil it perfectly.

Your Ladyship's most humble servant in our Lord,

Ignatius Loyola

From Rome, April 6th, 1555

To my very noble Lady in our Lord, Madonna Margherita Gigli de Fantuzzi, in Bologna

Ignatius must have smiled when he heard shortly afterwards that the plan for a college near Sant' Andrea had come to nothing, and that the Jesuits were staying at Santa Lucia, where a new house had been bought and

217

was being adapted, and this with the help of a gift from Monsignor Tommaso of a hundred gold *scudi*. Ignatius' gratitude was worthy of such generous assistance. With fatherly solicitude he followed developments in Bologna. Things were now going forward slowly *(pian piano)* in Bologna too, he wrote on December 28th, 1555, to Father Palmio; and on the same day he sent a letter to Monsignor Tommaso and his sister with hearty greetings for Christmas and the New Year. The brother and sister were addressed as founders, and the college at Bologna was referred to as their property in perpetuity. It is true that there was here, as in Ferrara, some disagreement over the question: Who in the legal sense was entitled to the position and honours of founder? In May of the year of his death Ignatius, matter-of-fact as ever, wrote to the Rector of Bologna: "The intention of Monsignor Giglio's sister is, it seems to us, very holy. However, who is or is not founder can only be decided when it has been established that others have not given more than she."

The year of St. Ignatius' death saw favourable developments in Bologna. As he lay dying, he may well have thought with affection of the college in that city at whose gate he had once fallen in the mud of the town ditch; for according to reliable accounts he appeared at the moment of his death to the sorrowing yet happy Donna Margherita. Be that as it may, this report plays an important part among the documents for the saint's beatification; and in one of the most voluminous manuscripts there is a particular and detailed examination into the virtue and credibility of Donna Margherita Gigli. "Behold, Margherita," Ignatius is alleged to have said to her, "as you see, I am no longer on earth; I commend to you the sons of our Company."[58]

Certainly it seemed like a miracle to the faithful band at Santa Lucia. "Despite all our poverty, the amount we receive in alms always suffices. We are convinced that Ignatius' death has blessed us." From 1556 the sub-minister at Bologna was young Tarquinio Rainaldi, who had once so bravely defended his vocation in the Palazzo Pitti and who now, back from Spain, was continuing his theological studies. Father Palmio also appointed a committee of twelve ladies, who promised to see that necessary expenses were met; and of Donna Margherita it was said that "she helps not only with promises but with deeds". Monsignor Tommaso gave a further sum of 300 gold *scudi* and continued to maintain with Father Laynez the same hearty friendship that he had once had with Ignatius. His generous sister did the same. On April 1st, 1559, she made her will and sent a copy to the General in Rome. In it this noble lady, who had been the friend of men like Francis Xavier and Ignatius Loyola, wrote the following words:

"Lately on Good Friday, as I saw my Lord Jesus Christ offer himself on the Cross for me, I too, out of love for him offered myself entirely to the

Divine Majesty with all that I possess. On that day I made my will. Therein I leave all that I possess or that shall hereafter come into my possession to the College of Bologna. And I desire to persevere till the end of my days in the service of, and in the sacrifice of myself for the Society of Jesus, as I have already done by the grace of the Divine Majesty for fourteen or fifteen years. I therefore beg Your Reverence to number me among the faithful friends of the Society and among those who greatly love it. Pray for me, that I may become a good handmaid of the Lord, and that my efforts may be pleasing in the eyes of God's Majesty."[59]

Madonna Violante Gozzadini

AMONG the penitents on whom the mystical virtue of St. Francis Xavier made the deepest impression when he worked in Bologna from November 1537 onwards was another noblewoman, Donna Violante Gozzadini. She was a close friend of Margherita Gigli. We have already met her on the occasion when the devout ladies in 1546 asked Ignatius to send some of his priests to do pastoral work in Bologna.

Donna Violante, of the noble house of the Casali, was born in 1498 and married Camillo Gozzadini, who had been made a knight by Pope Julius II in 1506. Five children were born of this marriage; but the early death of her husband in 1531 left the widow burdened with many obligations in her beautiful *palazzo* in the Strà Castiglione, in the Old Town at Bologna. Her son Cesare became a priest, and her daughter married a rich nobleman. Another son, Tommaso, died while travelling at Worms; and in December 1554 her dearly loved youngest son Don Camillo was seized with a mortal sickness.[60]

Ignatius, who in 1550 had already written a polite letter to Madonna Violante (preserved only in the *regesta*), heard with deep sympathy of Camillo's illness. On December 1st, 1554, he promised the inconsolable mother his prayers; but on December 15th Polanco, on behalf of Ignatius who was gravely ill, had to convey to Donna Violante through the Rector, Father Palmio, condolences on the death of her son. Polanco adds a special note to the effect that Father Ignatius would write himself as soon as possible.[61] This he did on December 22nd. Thus it is to his lifelong gratitude towards Donna Violante that we owe one of the most beautiful letters of condolence that Ignatius ever wrote.

Most illustrious Lady in our Lord.

The sovereign grace and eternal love of Christ our Lord be with Your Ladyship with his most holy gifts and spiritual graces.

I have learnt of the sickness of the late Master Camillo and shortly afterwards of his passing from this temporal life to that which is eternal. At both pieces of news, all those in this house and in the college have in our Masses and prayers made intercession and supplication for him to Christ, our Lord and God. To this we are moved not only by the charity which we owe to all men but on account of the special attachment which we owe you because of the many benefits and the charitable disposition of Your Ladyship towards us, which has been so continual and of such long standing.

I hope sincerely that he who is our true health and life, although he did not hear us in granting Master Camillo the present life, after his many trials and dangers and finally death, will do so by granting him in a brief while the life that is eternal and supremely secure and happy, for which he was created and redeemed at the price of God's blood, and to which all our desires and those of others ought rightly to be ordered.

I hope also that that same Father of mercies and God of all consolation, who by this visitation has shown how much he loves Your Ladyship and with what confidence he treats you as a valiant daughter and his true servant, will have granted you so much inner light, that you clearly see all the benefits his divine and supreme goodness gives to those whom, strengthened by his holy sacraments, he removes in faith, in hope and in love from the wretchedness of this world, to transport them to the bliss of heaven. I also hope that God will have given Your Ladyship so great a conformity of your will with the divine will, that you are not too deeply grieved at being deprived of any human consolation that you would have had with the presence of your son, because of your happiness that he should be in such a good estate and safe in our most blessed fatherland, the goal we all seek where we shall rejoice together in the sight of our supreme and infinite Good for all eternity. May it please God each day to take possession more and more fully of the heart of Your Ladyship and to unite it more closely to himself and turn it towards his holy kingdom, notwithstanding the little opportunity Your Ladyship has ever to fix your heart on anything but God alone.

I will not say more nor offer myself to Your Ladyship's service anew, for you know that for a long time past we have been and are all yours in Our Lord. May it please him to make us always to know his most holy and perfectly to fulfil it.

Ignatius

From Rome, December 22nd, 1554

To Madonna Violante, in Bologna

But the letter of December 12th, in which Father Palmio announced the death of young Camillo, contained also more complicated matters. "The highborn Lady Violante", he wrote, influenced by the mortal illness of her son, was about to make a will. As her priest son and her only daughter were already well provided for, she was thinking of leaving all the rest of her money for the founding of the projected college in Bologna, while the two surviving children were to have only a life-interest. Evidently Donna Violante had long been talking of bequeathing her property to the Jesuits, for the Rector reported that the other relatives of the rich widow were getting anxious, and that gossip was rife in the city; the Fathers were being spoken ill of and it was said that they were "emptying the pockets of poor widows". The enemies of the Jesuits and their preaching, which was directed against the luxury and immorality of the upper classes, were besides very active at Bologna, and innumerable calumnies were circulated. One of these about this time took the form of a cartoon representing a Jesuit with a wolf's face, wearing a biretta and standing in the pulpit, while at his feet sat the pious ladies with sheep's heads, looking reverently up at him.[62]

It was a difficult position for Ignatius: on the one hand, there was the great need of the house, on the other, the reputation of his sons. He sent word to Palmio that he should for the present neither advise nor prevent anything in the matter of Donna Violante's will, that God himself would guide the noble lady to do that which was to his greater glory. Soon more urgent warnings were despatched to Bologna. The Jesuits must not give any assistance whatever in the drawing up of the will – but neither must they hinder a work that was good in itself, despite the murmurs of certain persons!

The conclusion to this distressing story was that Donna Violante died in October 1556, without having made a will in favour of the Society of Jesus. In Rome they breathed a sigh of relief. Violante had appointed her priest son as sole heir, but when dying she had whispered to him: "I make you father and protector of the College at Bologna." Polanco, who conducted the correspondence in this affair, noted with dry humour in the chronicle of the Society: "We have had not a single penny"; but he added that the whole of Bologna was greatly edified.[63]

From Ignatius' correspondence with Madonna Margherita Gigli we know of the consternation caused among the pious women of Bologna when the Jesuits were going to move from Santa Lucia to Sant' Andrea. Donna Violante also protested energetically to Rome. But whereas Ignatius wrote an answer to Donna Margherita on April 6th, 1555, he had to postpone replying to Donna Violante until May 25th, on account of illness, although that determined lady was not satisfied with the joint letter she had sent with Margherita Gigli on March 15th, but had written separately to Ignatius on April 2nd.[64] Even then the saint's patience was not exhausted. Shortly after his recovery, he wrote to her on May 25th:

JESUS

The sovereign grace and eternal love of Christ our Lord be always with us to our help and favour.

I have not replied earlier than this to a letter of Your Ladyship's of April 2nd, partly because I have not been well, partly because of my many occupations. Knowing Your Ladyship's great charity, I hope that you will take it all in good part.

With regard to leaving some of our fathers at Santa Lucia, where some members of the Society have been up till now, during the time the others are obliged to be at Sant' Andrea, we have considered if that would be possible, desiring to please Your Ladyship and some other persons who were wanting the same thing. We do not think, however, that such a division of our forces would be feasible, for various reasons which it would take long to explain to you. Accordingly we cannot think of anything better than to charge our brother Don Francesco Palmio to take care to send you for the feasts, or, indeed, during the week, a father from the college, to satisfy the devotion of the persons to whom the fathers are under a special obligation in our Lord, who cannot conveniently go to our new church. This should have almost the same effect that Your Ladyship shows you desire and for which you write that someone should remain at Santa Lucia.

Since from the outset Your Ladyship has been so favourable to and such a benefactress of the Society, and desirous that all in it should be for God's greater service, I do not doubt that you will be satisfied with this decision which we judge to be fitting for the good of our Society and God's greater glory necessary at this particular time.

For the rest, we are all sincerely devoted to Your Ladyship's service to the glory of God our Lord. We recommend ourselves much to you and beg the divine goodness to grant us all grace always to know his most holy will and to fulfil it perfectly.

Ignatius

From Rome, May 15th, 1555

To Madonna Violante Gozzadini, in Bologna

As we know, the Jesuits finally remained at Santa Lucia – and it was partly because so many letters of protest had reached Ignatius. Donna Violante lived to mourn with her friend Margherita the death of their revered Father in Rome; but she followed him into eternity at the beginning of October 1556. She, too, is called in the chronicle of the Society "the beloved mother of the College of Bologna".[65]

Donna Lucrezia di Storento

SOME projects for new colleges failed, partly owing to the lack or inadequacy of means, partly to the inability of founders to fulfil specific conditions prescribed by the inflexible Ignatius. In most cases these unsuccessful attempts have left no trace in Ignatius' letters to women; but the cares and vexations connected with them make themselves heard more or less distinctly in many of his other letters.

There was, for instance, the foundation planned by a rich lady in Naples, Madonna Belotta Spinola, of the famous Genoese family, and her son, Geronimo Spinola. This lady gave the college in Naples 500 gold *scudi,* gave her beautiful house as well to the Jesuits, renounced as a tertiary in Franciscan poverty all the comforts of old age to live as a pilgrim in Rome, Loreto and Assisi. From March 1554, when Belotta came to Rome, up to the time of his death, Ignatius often referred with gratitude to this saintly woman. Thus he commends her in May 1554 to Everard Mercurian in Perugia, when Donna Belotta was on a pilgrimage to Loreto, because "this lady is much devoted to our Society". Sometimes it was even necessary to provide financial support for the benefactress who was now poor; but the letter to Belotta, in which such an alms was enclosed and which Ignatius mentions in a communication to Signor Spinola, has unfortunately not been preserved. Father Salmerón took her under his special protection, no doubt because he knew Ignatius' opinion of her. We still possess some letters from him to Madonna Spinola, whom he calls "reverend mother in Christ". After the death of the Founder of the Society and that of Belotta, which occurred in 1556, a distressing difference arose about her property with Geronimo Spinola, who was himself a Jesuit for a time, but soon left the Society. In 1568 her house in Naples was sold at a price of 2600 ducats for the benefit of the college there.[66]

There was another unsuccessful attempt at founding a college in Southern Italy, and to it we owe a letter, preserved by chance, from the saint to the lady who wished to be the foundress.

Three months before his death, in April 1556, Ignatius was visited one day by a gentleman unknown to him, sent with a letter from a rich noblewoman of San Marco in Calabria, Madonna Lucrezia di Storento. She used to spend the winter in Naples, and there she zealously attended the church of the Jesuit college. Seeing the excellent results of the fathers' work in Naples, the desire came to the pious lady to establish a similar college in the chief town of her estates in the heart of Calabria. Ignatius was indeed aware of the sad state of religious life in Southern Italy, and the colleges he founded with the collaboration of the Viceroy of Sicily in Messina, Palermo and Bivona show how he desired to help, by means of schools, in the restoration of the Faith in those parts, where "Christ had come only as far as Eboli". From Rome Ignatius looked with satisfaction on the large number of young scholastics who were there preparing themselves for tasks which he knew he would never live to see fulfilled. In that very spring of 1556 he was faced with a number of new commitments which he had to undertake at the wish of Pope Paul IV, who was otherwise not particularly well disposed towards him.

For all these reasons Ignatius had become at the end of his life rather cautious in the matter of founding colleges.[67] So he wrote to Donna Lucrezia that the Society could not run miniature colleges of three or four fathers, such as the lady wanted; fourteen men was the lowest number for the staffing of a college. She might, however, apply to the rector in Naples, Father Cristóbal de Mendoza, and ask him for a Jesuit priest to do temporary pastoral work on her estates. On April 24th, this answer from the General was sent off through the Roman agent of Donna Lucrezia. At once the zealous lady applied to the rector of Naples and asked him for a priest and two laybrothers – rather more than Ignatius had suggested. But in Naples there was not at the moment a single Jesuit available for such a remote outpost.

Donna Lucrezia, however, was not to be put off. At once she wrote again to Rome, supported this time by a petition from a gentleman otherwise unknown to us, called Giulio Cesare.[68] On May 17th, 1556, Ignatius answered this double attack with the following letter:

IHS

My most illustrious Lady in our Lord.

The sovereign grace and eternal love of Christ our Lord be always with us to our continual help and favour.

Through a letter from Your Ladyship and another from the most illustrious Master Giulio Cesare, I have gathered that no opportunity was found in Naples of giving a priest to Your Ladyship with two brothers, and that you now wish us to send these from Rome.

God our Lord knows that it would be a great consolation to me to be able to serve and please Your Ladyship, for your devotion and charity showered down upon us put us under the obligation of doing our best to satisfy you. At present, however, on account of the different responsibilities that our Society has assumed recently, and because His Holiness has sent many of us to different places, we have not even the priests we know to be necessary for our own house and church, especially since there are a large number of students who have not finished their studies. For this reason Your Ladyship will kindly hold us excused for the present. We shall all, however, pray God our Lord to supply the spiritual needs of that territory of Your Ladyship's in some other way, and to deign to multiply the labourers to cultivate his vine which has need of them in so many places.

I do not write a special letter to the illustrious Master Giulio Cesare, because this will suffice, since I cannot extend our work, which I should have preferred to do rather than to write.

May Christ, our Lord give his grace to us all that we may always know his most holy will and fulfil it perfectly. Amen.

Ignatius

From Rome, May 17th, 1556

To San Marco in Calabria

This letter gives some indication of the apostolic distress that filled the heart of Ignatius at the close of his life. It was, more so than it had been for a long time in the Church's history, the ever-new situation described in the Gospel: "The harvest indeed is great, but the labourers are few." Nothing came of the college in Calabria, in spite of the goodness and the eagerness to help of Donna Lucrezia.

Aldonza González de Villasimplez

THE history of the beginnings of the Jesuit college in Saragossa takes us into a totally different world from that of the Italian foundations. We shall meet in this correspondence many Spanish women, to whose help Ignatius owed the growth of his Society in Spain. But Saragossa is a special case: here, thanks to the letters which survive, we can see the inner working of various forces, religious, legal, personal and emotional, into which the distant Ignatius in Rome, calmly noting every move, was drawn, and out of which there arose in the end a flourishing college.

In the Aragonese capital of Saragossa there lived till his death in the summer of 1548 Don Juan González de Villasimplez. He was one of the highest officers of the Crown, privy councillor to Charles V and keeper or Conservador of the royal estates in Aragon; he was the father of four children. Juan Luis, the eldest son, succeeded his father in all his offices. There were also a younger son, Melchor, and two daughters, Doña Aldonza and Doña Ana. After the early death of his wife, old Don Juan had become a priest. He was a close friend of Duke Francis Borgia, whom shortly before his death in 1548 he visited at Gandía. He discussed with him the ideals of the new Society of Jesus and "made much progress in spiritual knowledge". The year before he had made a retreat with Father Torres and again with Father Araoz, and on September 2nd, 1547, Ignatius had written him a deeply moving letter. On feeling the approach of death Don Juan had made his will.[69]

He had built a house in Saragossa with a small church adjoining as a kind of private convent for his two as yet unmarried daughters. This foundation, however, was dissolved at the request of the Pope, and the old Conservador had decided to hand over the house and church to the Jesuits. There were at that time only a few of the fathers working in Saragossa; besides, the house was not big, and the Archbishop Fernando de Aragón was from the first unfavourable to the new religious; difficulties were to be expected. In the final draft of Don Juan's will it was arranged that the house and church, as well as an endowment of 1000 ducats and an income of 1000 *soldi* yearly, were to be left to the Society of Jesus for the founding of a college, the right of living in the house till her death being reserved to the daughter Aldonza.

Hardly had the father closed his eyes, and hardly had the family heard of these testamentary dispositions, than the legal battle broke out. Don Luis and Doña Ana launched an attack against their sister, objecting that Ana had at least an equal right. Father Araoz, the Spanish Provincial, advised arbitration. The result was that house and church were given to Aldonza, who felt herself under an obligation, in accordance with the wishes of her late father (whose passionate defender she set herself up to be), to hand the buildings over at once to the Jesuits.[70]

The dead Conservador, who was well versed in canon law, had already persuaded the papal curia to draw up a brief, permitting the establishment of a house of studies for the Society of Jesus in Saragossa. Ignatius, who knew about this, had a presentiment of the coming disputes, and in his name Father Polanco wrote to the new Conservador, Don Luis: "If the heirs make difficulties, our Father in Christ is not desirous of insisting on the foundation of a college, but will regard the bequest as not having been made; for thank God there are still many other places where we can accommodate our students."

Meanwhile the brief asked for by the late Don Juan had arrived at Saragossa. It clearly proved his intention of founding a college, as laid down in the will. This was in August 1548. On September 20th, 1548, Ignatius gave Father Oviedo in Gandía exact instructions in a letter as to how Duke Francis Borgia, the dead man's close friend, might help the Provincial Araoz to settle the distressing affair. The General's curia in Rome (he wrote) had indeed received no actual deed of gift from Saragossa, but the intention of Don Juan to found a college was clear from the wording of his petition to the Pope. The Society, he repeated emphatically, insisted on nothing; but Aldonza's right, as laid down in the will, must be upheld.

Father Rojas in Gandía now consulted the duke on behalf of the Provincial. A legal settlement between the children of Don Juan was devised.[71] Ignatius in Rome arranged for another brief to be drawn up, which ostensibly also permitted the founding of a college, but which at the same time renounced, by way of bringing about a reconciliation, the rights conferred by the will. Clearly this made everything rather vague; Doña Aldonza's rights were increased, while those of the Society were voluntarily diminished.

On January 25th, 1549, Ignatius informed the Duke of Gandía that the brief, which, however, was not actually a solemn bull of foundation, was being despatched that day. The college could be opened, but only under the condition that Doña Aldonza would agree to a settlement with her family,

228

so that the Jesuits would not again be drawn into the affair in any way. Ignatius appears to have written already to Doña Aldonza in this conciliatory vein in a letter now lost to us. Araoz worked actively for a "clearing of the atmosphere" and remained faithful to the policy of a legal settlement.

The family agreed to these proposals.[72] The first extant letter in the correspondence of St. Ignatius on this subject belongs to this stage of the complicated business. Doña Aldonza wrote it on March 29th, 1549, to "The most reverend Father in Christ, Master Ignatius of Loyola, General of the Society of Jesus, by the Church of Santa Maria della Strada, adjoining San Marco in Rome".

IHS

Very Reverend Father,

I am deeply touched that Your Paternity should have had the kindness to seek a means by which I could obtain possession of what is justly mine, without my having to suffer the wrong and prejudice which has been done me up to the present in my not being allowed to live peacefully in my own house. May our Lord, who is able to do so, give Your Paternity the reward for this and make me such that I am able to repay with prayers the charity Your Paternity has shown towards me by the letter you have sent me. As, however, the rights of the Society are, as Your Paternity realizes, so interwoven with my own, my own rights cannot be clearly vindicated apart from those of the Society. If this [further] brief, then, is to have valid force, it must be based on the favour the Pope already granted the Society and myself before the Conservador, my father (may he be in glory) died, through the brief we already have concerning the erection of the College, of which he wanted to defer execution for the present, as Your Paternity says. That brief is all the basis there is, and there is no other charter of foundation except that which, through the request my father and I made, the Pope gave in the brief for the erection of the College. Until this is understood through the charter of erection, for it is not set out in the present brief, according to the opinion of the learned men to whom I have shown the brief Your Paternity has now sent me, my right cannot be recognized. They tell me it would cause additional prejudice to my rights if I were to present this brief without the original one. I cannot, therefore, take advantage of the declaration which I have here, until everything is complete.

These are the reasons which place one who is so wretched as myself, in great need, through the inconveniences which arise daily because I

229

cannot have possession of my house in peace. May our Lord give me his grace to undergo all the trials which come to me through this cause, without offending him, and with quiet and peace of mind. I beg Your Paternity in your Masses and devout prayers to commend me to our Lord, because I certainly need them. If my principal aim in this business were to claim my own rights, I should already have left it all alone in order not to find myself in so many occasions as is the case of not being able to preserve the quiet my soul desires in order to serve our Lord. My chief aim, however, is to promote the interests of the college, as my father – may he rest in peace – left the matter arranged. For this I should like the right of the Society to be recognized, so that my brothers would see the fathers' generosity in not wishing to make use of it until they [my brothers] are satisfied, for it might be that with this they would realize what they ought to do as good Christians. In this, however, as in everything else concerning this business, I defer to Your Paternity's opinion so that, until that is known I shall never agree to anything that runs contrary to what has already been done, without first receiving Your Paternity's decision and consent in the matter. Father Rojas, indeed, has persuaded me that I should try to come to an agreement with my brothers, in consenting to many things they want which are against the founder's intention. He is making things very difficult for me over this. I never felt in my soul that I ought to do so, since this is a thing for the peace of my father's conscience and my own.

I shall take it as a very great favour and kindness if Your Paternity will write me your opinion on this matter so that I may find peace of soul in pursuing it. This would not be the case if I followed the opinion of anyone else, for I have always felt that I ought to strive to forward this business, so that our Lord may be served here in Saragossa by the Society. All the trouble that comes to me through this, I shall consider well employed if God allows me to see this come about. I beseech him to increase his love and grace in Your Paternity's soul and prosper you many years in his service.

Saragossa, March 22nd, 1549

Since I wrote this, Father Rojas, who had gone there to discuss this business with the Duke, has come back from Gandía. He comes with the determination to try and bring about agreement between me and my brothers and has considerable powers from Father Licentiate Araoz for doing all that seems good to him on behalf of the Society. The reply

I have given up to the present is that which Father Rojas has sent to Your Paternity. I am confident that the Society will not do anything against that which is for the peace of my father's conscience. I shall do nothing until I know whether this business of the College has been transacted in conformity with the founder's intention, for, if that is so, I should not wish to oppose it in anything nor feel in my soul that I ought to do anything different, despite the fact that Father Rojas wants to make me weaken in this. He says and gives me to understand that those who have negotiated the matter have not understood it. For this reason it seemed to him that he should now prepare a further, fresh report in order that the matter might be properly understood. If up to the present the business is not understood, with the care my father took to make it as clear as it could possibly be, as those who had a thorough knowledge of the matter, of whom one was Dr. Torres, advised him, I do not think that the business will be clearer with this new report, for all is founded on the assumption that there must be agreement between the Society, my brothers and me. He tries to persuade me to this by telling me that in his view I have no reason to fear that what has been done in Rome will prejudice my right. I, until I see it, cannot believe that in the brief for the erection of the college it is not declared how the Pope made over this house of ours to the Society, giving me the right of residence in it while I lived, apart from the church and choir which are to be for the Society forthwith. As I have gathered from Your Paternity's two letters – the one replying to the letter my brother wrote you and the other that which I received with the [second] brief – the whole business has been done in this sense and they understood it so, except in wanting to divide my right from that of the Society, drawing up another brief. This, since it is not based on that which the Pope had already granted before my father died, has no legal force at all for my rights. I think that, as my brothers are far from doing what reason and justice oblige them to in my regard, until they are convinced of my rights they will make no agreement that will be of any value nor approve anything for the purpose I am pursuing, which is the one I have set out above.

Your Paternity's obedient daughter,
Doña Aldonza González

Saragossa, March 22nd, 1549

To the most reverend Father in Christ, Master Ignatius of Loyola, General of the Society of Jesus, by the Church of Santa Maria della Strada, adjoining San Marco in Rome

Here, it can be seen, speaks the true daughter of the crown lawyer of Aragon. Aldonza had a legal mind. Her sister Ana, however, was also made of the same stuff; she remained irreconcilable, and Ignatius now found himself placed between the two quarrelling women. It was with a characteristically Spanish mixture of inflexibility and diplomacy that Araoz during April 1549 succeeded in establishing peace – more or less – between the children of Don Juan. Ana and her brothers acknowledged the right of the Jesuits to move into the house during Aldonza's lifetime. The Jesuits on their part solemnly renounced this right, and were then in turn expressly asked by the family, to occupy the house nevertheless, and begin the work of the college. From a summary dated May 15th, 1549, we gather that Ignatius had in the meantime had to calm Aldonza, who had been urging that the bull of foundation should be issued as soon as possible. That cost a lot of money, he wrote to her, and if they were in such haste they must send the money in advance; the best thing would be to appoint a legal adviser who resided in Rome.[73]

Before this, however, Ignatius had already sent Aldonza, who almost ferociously defended the Jesuits' rights, a letter expressing his joy at the peace now apparently concluded in her family. He showed himself to be wholeheartedly behind Father Araoz's efforts at reconciliation.

My Lady in our Lord.

May the sovereign grace and eternal love of Christ our Lord be always with us to our continual help and favour.

Although my indispositions and occupations force me to be brief, yet I should like to write these few lines to you to say that among the many things which I have heard about the lawsuit in which you are engaged with your brothers, what gives me most satisfaction is the agreement reached of which you have written to me. Not only, it seems to me, will things be done in such a way that the parties remain without suffering loss, although a loss in temporal things of this sort is slight in comparison with loss of peace and quiet of soul and the possibility of injuring love between brothers and sister, but this agreement seems to me to be a good remedy, and what Dr. Araoz has done, making it possible to bring about such concord, I approve and consider a very good thing.

May it please Jesus Christ our Lord, in whose service we desire for the help of souls, houses and colleges and the rest, that his divine Majesty direct everything as is most fitting, and may he give you and your household his abundant grace so that we may always know his most holy will and fulfil it perfectly.

Your servant in our Lord,
Ignatius

From Rome, May 4th, 1549

IHS. To my Lady in our Lord,
    Doña Aldonza González de Villasimplez,
    in Saragossa

This was not enough. In this affair, which took place as it were in full view of the aristocratic society of Aragon and later occupied the attention of the Regent Juana's court, Ignatius was most anxious to end the legal battle without in any way jeopardizing the good name of the Jesuits. On July 3rd, 1549, therefore, in support of Araoz's policy of reconciliation, he issued a solemn document of renunciation, by which the Society gave up the rights conferred on it by the will of the old Conservador; and it did so unequivocally in favour of Doña Aldonza, who thus was to retain a lifelong right to dwell in the house and a life interest in the endowment fund.

IHS

Let it be known to all those who shall see the present letters, that whereas the Señor Don Juan González de Villasimplez of pious memory, Conservador of Aragón, out of zeal for God's service and the devotion he had to our humble Society of Jesus, with the authority of the Holy See, has erected a college for the said Society at his own expense, setting aside for this purpose, besides the church and the house, a fixed sum of the value of one thousand ducats and a fixed revenue or usufruct of one thousand *soldi* each year, the said Society and I, Ignatius Loyola, as General, in the name of the whole Society make donation, in the best and most complete way I can, of the buildings and also of the said revenue and usufruct to Señora Doña Aldonza González, his daughter, as long as she shall live (after which it shall return to the said Society), and all the rights in connection with the foundation that the Society has through the Apostolic See shall pass to her. To this we are moved, because we judge it to be the course that will best serve God our Lord, as for other devout reasons, for we have understood that this was the will of the said Señor Conservador.

233

And in attestation of the said donation, I have drawn up, in the name of the whole Society, the present letters patent, signed with my name and sealed with the seal of the said Society, in Rome, July 3rd, 1549.

Ignatius of Loyola

That Aldonza's family were satisifed with such a settlement is obvious, for she was thus provided for during her lifetime in a manner befitting her rank. Aldonza for her part, however, felt this extension of her rights to be a diminution of the claims which the Jesuits were entitled to make by virtue of Don Juan's will, and so a slight on her father's memory. She saw that the Jesuits would hardly move into the house while she still occupied it or had rights upon it; but for the time being she gave in.

The quarrelsome brothers and sisters were thus in agreement for a while, and drafted a document signed by all of them, in which they expressed to the Provincial Araoz a wish that he would accept the gift under the conditions named in the act of renunciation.

Araoz was delighted at the solemn surrender which Ignatius had made. "That comes from the head", he said – meaning by that the brain of Ignatius; for now the disinterestedness of the Jesuits was clear to all; but Aldonza was not satisfied. The settlement did not suit the lady at all, wrote Ignatius to Araoz; in July 1549 he even sent a soothing letter to Aldonza, the too zealous defender of the Society's rights.

Aldonza had rightly foreseen that it would be difficult for the Jesuits to move into the house, which was in any case small and still inhabited by herself. The Provincial gave her no grounds for hoping that they would do so.[74] So the saddened lady wrote a resigned letter to the General in Rome, whose "daughter in obedience" she so much desired to be. However, in order to leave nothing undone, she sent Ignatius by the same post a gift of eighty ducats with the request that he would pay therewith the costs of obtaining final papal approval for the founding of the college.

IHS

Very Reverend Father,

Your Paternity will already have been able to gather from my letters the great desire I have in our Lord to see the end of the dispute over this college. To achieve this I have done everything which seemed best fitting and most expedient, my purpose always being to follow Your Paternity's opinion in everything and to wait for your decisions. Thus

234

matters have been done as Your Paternity wrote to me they should be done. Our Lord knows that my purpose has always been to negotiate this business in such a way that, my own interest and that of my brothers being terminated, the Society could then come in and take possession of this church and house during my lifetime, the usufruct of it being left to them immediately. For this I have striven with all my might by every way I could, promising my brothers, whenever the Society should take over possession, the usufruct I have from the share adjudicated to me, for that is what they most desired and wished and the question over which they entered into litigation with me – over and above what has been adjudicated to them by the sentence of arbitration, which is the same sum that the Society will give them after my time, in accordance with the terms of the agreement which has been made. Of this I sent to inform my brothers, since with this the differences between my brothers and sisters and myself would be at an end and all the divisions which there had been between us healed. They, however, must do their part and arrange that the Society shall take possession here forthwith. I wanted to accept this arrangement, taking possession of the house for the time until it seemed to the Society that they should take possession. My brothers replied that they were very satisfied and that they desired this, so that my father's last wishes (may he be in glory) should be carried out, and thus they set it in hand, begging Father Doctor Araoz as the representative head of the Society of Jesus that he would kindly accept it. For its surer accomplishment they and I put it into writing, signing with our hand and names, I promising them by the same document to leave them the usufruct of that share which the Society is giving them after my death, so that they can enjoy it during my lifetime and the Society come in and take possession of this house.

It seems to me that Father Doctor Araoz was not willing to accept this, nor to give me hope that during my lifetime the Society would come here, for it seemed to him that it was not good that I should leave my house, or that the Society should take it, because of my having to leave it. I felt in my heart that the end for which I have laboured so much was not being achieved. Our Lord, who has given me strength to bear this, knows that what was in my mind was none other than this – that it seemed to me, and because of the experience I have of this business I was afraid, that if in my lifetime the matter was not clinched by the Society's taking possession here, after my days difficulties would not fail to arise, as they have not failed to do since my father's death. Moreover, since my brothers and I are now in agreement about this, and say they desire it as much as I do, it seems to me that there would now be a better opportunity of it than ever. The other reasons that move Father Doctor Araoz not to want to accept this I indeed believe are very important, except for ceasing to live in this house, for in whatever place I took a house, I could serve God as in this place and even with considerably more quiet and peace of mind, since, while I have this worry, I shall never have such peace entirely nor shall I live content if I do not see this come to pass in my day. If I thought that solely on account of me the Society was refraining from coming here, nothing would induce me to remain here – rather I am under an obligation [to give up the house], for that is what I promised our Lord, namely, that provided I acquired this house without lawsuits and could possess it freely, I would then offer to make it over to the Society, so that from now on it should be used in God's service, since I desire to see the fruit which I hope in his mercy, there will be in this city of Saragossa. If there is anything which, if I could be certain of it, would quieten my soul, it is the knowledge that it would be for the advantage of the Society in their taking over this house, that I should now remain in it, as Father Doctor Araoz has told me I ought to do, and for this reason alone I shall now remain in it. If it should still happen that the Society should not come here, when the negotiations for the fitting execution of the business are terminated, I have nothing more to hope for, for the reasons I have already given, since the greatest gratitude that could be shown to me would be for the Society to be willing to accept, in view of my intense desire for it. If this does not come to pass, I shall always think that they left on account of my living in my house and thus I shall have additional reason for having to leave it myself.

I beseech Your Paternity that for the love of our Lord you would kindly accept this alms I am sending of sixty ducats and twenty further ducats of those sent to the Lord Duke of Gandía. Instructions have been given to the bank accordingly for the eighty ducats. In this way the erection of the college may be proceeded with and the expenses of the brief which they sent me paid. With this and in no other way, my soul will be at rest, for I am anxious about what may happen if the erection is not carried out speedily and am concerned over the time that must elapse for the completion of this business so that nothing is omitted. Again we cannot expect that the indult which it is necessary to have from Rome for this business of the college will be received soon, even though it is necessary for this to be obtained now. Thereby I shall receive very great contentment and [I hope] time will not slip by, as it did on the other occasion when I provided this money through the merchant Jaime López. Since I now have this opportunity and possibility of being able to provide this money, I beg Your Paternity not to refuse to accept my alms which is given with so much good will. If you will not accept it I cannot but remain vexed, for I say that my soul cannot be at rest or satisfied if this very small alms is not accepted so that the purpose I have in giving it may be achieved.

I received a letter from Your Paternity a few days ago, from which I see how good you are to me, showing me every kindness and favour in order to bring me contentment, as you have done up to the present in all questions of importance. I know well that your own wish is to forward this business and all other things that I desire in God our Lord. May he in his infinite goodness increase and prosper Your Paternity's life in his service for many long years, as is needful for the progress and usefulness of this institute, so that God may be served and praised in it, despite my unworthiness, as my soul desires.

Your Paternity's daughter in obedience who kisses your hands,
Doña Aldonza González
From Saragossa, September 2nd, 1549

The messenger who brought this letter to Rome reached Santa Maria della Strada on October 10th, and already on the next morning he had to leave again. Ignatius did not neglect to give him a friendly letter of comfort for Doña Aldonza.

To my Lady, from my own hand,

The supreme grace and everlasting love of Christ our Lord be with Your Grace and may that supreme grace and God's spiritual gifts descend upon you.

Although we received your letter of September 2nd only yesterday evening, and the messenger has already departed again, yet I must not omit to answer your Grace's letter at once, and if only briefly, I will say, therefore, only this: since I see the good intention and the devout wishes, with which God our Lord so constantly inspires Your Grace, that our humble Society of Jesus should take over that college for the honour of God and the profit of souls, for my part I cannot do otherwise than express my readiness to co-operate with your great devotion and charity. In this sense I am also writing to Dr. Araoz, telling him to take care of the matter to the best of his ability, so that Your Grace may have the benefit of his help and advice. It remains for us, however, to implore

God's Majesty and goodness to guide all things towards the attainment of that goal after which we all strive in God's most holy service. May God reward with a crown of glory and with an everlasting reward all those who have been the most efficacious instruments of his providence in this work.

Your Grace also requested me most urgently to accept as an alms the eighty ducats sent to me and to use them for procuring the bull of foundation for the college in Saragossa. To this I cannot give you a precise answer at the moment, since I must first enquire into certain details of the matter. Be assured, however, that I will do all that is in my power to satisfy Your Grace in this, as in all things in our Lord. For you must consider all of us ever your debtors in our Lord, who are prepared to do everything, having been surpassed in charity by that which Your Grace has shown us in this matter.

There is nothing more to tell you to-day. I commend myself earnestly to your holy prayers, and I pray the infinite and most high goodness of God our Lord to give us all an abundance of grace, that we may know God's most holy will and always perfectly fulfil it.

Rome, October 11th, 1549

Your Grace's servant in our Lord, Ignatius

It was always difficult in Rome to obtain such a document quickly. Moreover, on November 10th, 1549, Pope Paul III died, so Ignatius had to inform Aldonza on January 15th, 1550, that the completion of the bull, on which she wished the eighty ducats to be spent, was possible only after the election of a new pope. On February 8th, 1550, Julius III was elected, and immediately Ignatius resumed the tedious business of procuring the foundation bull for the college in Saragossa. On June 14th he joyfully told Aldonza that the bull would be ready very soon; on July 16th it was sent off by Polanco with a note to say that Ignatius himself was unfortunately unable to write on account of illness. Aldonza must have read with some emotion the polite words of Polanco: "In his name I kiss Your Grace's hands many times, and we profess ourselves your servants."

In the middle of September the papal document reached Saragossa. Aldonza and her two brothers Luis and Melchor were overjoyed. All seemed now to be settled and at peace; and the letter which Aldonza in this mood of exaltation sent to Rome on September 26th must have appeared to Ignatius more intelligible and to the point than all her previous legal subtleties.[75]

IHS

Very Reverend Father,

I give ceaseless thanks to our Lord for his infinite goodness in having willed to allow me to see things brought to their necessary completion, so that with the bulls I have received for the erection of the college this very good work may be accomplished. Since we had the authorization we needed for the accomplishment of this work, I took the opportunity to discuss the site of the college with my brother, the Conservador of Aragón, putting before him his own obligation in regard to it. Our Lord willed it that I should find him in such good dispositions that he immediately set himself to putting the matter into effect as has been done, for it seemed to him that in this way he was closing the door to all differences or litigation there might be between us, and fulfilling his obligation to strive that this work should be carried out for the repose of our father's soul – may he be in glory. Moved by this consideration my two brothers together used the necessary diligence for matters to be arranged forthwith and were of the opinion that we should go together and ask for execution. For, since we were in agreement in wanting to fulfil our father's wish and to comply with what the Pope had decreed, no obstacle would be put in the way of execution. Thus it was done in the way that seemed most fitting, the matter being put into the hands of the lord archbishop and his assistant. Since we found that they made no objection, we employed a man of business, that no hindrance might be placed in the way of immediate execution. Our learned advisers counselled us to proceed in this way, to avoid any inconvenience that might arise through delay.

In due course Father Doctor Araoz arrived in Saragossa, whom it seemed that the Lord brought here for the conclusion of this business. My brothers begged him to deign to accept this church and house, because they wanted to discharge their consciences by giving effect to their father's wish and obeying the command of the Holy See, for as regards their claims they were satisfied. At the request of both my brothers and myself a notarial act was drawn up by which the Society takes possession of the church and house. This was done with all the solemnity that the occasion demanded and to the great satisfaction of my brothers – so much so, that the Conservador told me that he felt a new happiness in his soul when it was done. We then left the church free for the fathers, closing the doors and windows that we had giving access to it in order that they could hear Mass from their house and I from mine, so that there should be nothing that would disturb them or hinder our Lord's service.

What now remains for the completion of this business is that, as I already wrote to Your Paternity some time ago, I should like them to take the house also, for I was only waiting to see the conclusion of what has now been done in order to let the fathers have it as a residence, for thus I offered it to our Lord, and I cannot do anything different. My soul feels this so deeply that, since I decided it, the desire to put it into execution has gone on increasing. Indeed, I think God will be greatly served by this and I do not want to be the one to hinder it by delaying the matter longer. There are many reasons why I ought to do it. One of them is that if the Society now had a resident college in Saragossa, there would be persons who are influential and devoted to the Jesuit fathers, whose objective would then be to employ themselves in doing good to this college for the increase of the service of our Lord in it. If it is not set up forthwith, they will not believe that there is any certainty for its establishment later, on account of the many difficulties they have seen arising. If they see the Society taking possession now, all these doubts will be removed. The other reason is that, with this establishment the fathers could the better exercise their ministry, having a suitable place for those who might want to come to seek to profit by their teaching and example. I could give many other reasons which make it imperative for me to do what I say and since our Lord has willed to give my brothers the desire to proceed with this, and as they are already set upon it, there is no reason to refuse what I ask, for what might follow from not doing it would be greater difficulties. Because I believe that in this matter Your Paternity will decide what is most fitting for our Lord's service, I have no need to stress the matter further, nor to emphasize how much my soul desires it. This I shall show by the work itself which with all my other actions I beg our Lord to direct that they may be in conformity with his will. May he guard Your Paternity's very reverend person and prosper you in his service for many long years, as I desire.

[In her own hand] I beseech Your Paternity not to fail to show me your accustomed favour, with a line from your hand, so that my soul may not lack comfort.

Your Paternity's most obedient daughter in Christ,

Doña Aldonza González

Saragossa, September 26th, 1550

To the most reverend Master Ignatius Loyola, General of the Society of Jesus, at Santa Maria della Strada, near San Marco, in Rome.

Ignatius could not ignore the touching request that Aldonza had made in her postscript. At once he sent a comforting answer to the daughter of obedience in Saragossa. From this and the previous letter, what Aldonza wanted throughout this dispute is clearly apparent. She did not wish to make use of her legal right to remain living in the house, if this should prevent the work of the college from being started. Ignatius for his part continued tactfully to insist on expressly recognizing this right.

My Lady in our Lord,

The sovereign grace and eternal love of Christ our Lord be with Your Ladyship, with his most holy gifts and spiritual graces.

By a letter from Your Ladyship dated September 14th, I learnt more definitely what I had understood in a general way before about the possession of the college, and that Your Ladyship's brothers helped in this good work with so much devotedness and concord. For all this I gave much thanks to God our Lord, of whose infinite and supreme goodness I hope that, through your holy desires, this work will in time come to be of great service.

As to what you write me about the house, in reference to the promise made to God our Lord, what I can say is, that although I recognize and esteem how much such charity obliges people, I do not want you to be inconvenienced in any way, and this I ask for the love of Christ our Lord. Apart from this difficulty, we shall follow Your Ladyship's good pleasure in everything.

To you, together with all of us, may God our Lord give his full grace so that we may always know his most holy will and follow it out to the full.

Ignatius

From Rome, November 1st, 1550

Anyone who thought that peace had now been established in this family of Spanish lawyers would have been mistaken. Only now did war really break out in earnest, in Rome as well as at Saragossa. There were two men in the Aragonese capital who were not pleased at the arrival of the papal bull – two men and a woman. Archbishop Fernando de Aragón and his Vicar General, the Abbot of Verula, could not bear the Jesuits anyway and now they prevented the publication of the bull by appealing to Spanish canon law. The lady who now took up arms against the members of her own family was Doña Ana González de Villasimplez. She protested loudly and in no uncertain terms that wrong was being done to her, as she was indisputably joint owner of the former private convent founded by her father. Ana now formally began a full-scale lawsuit against her brothers and sister and the Jesuits in the Roman courts. She maintained her own legal representative in Rome, whose complaints filled the whole of 1551. As Ignatius knew the real object of the dispute to be something in itself so disproportionate to the means employed, he wished to avoid litigation altogether; the four Jesuits in Saragossa could be accommodated elsewhere or even withdrawn entirely from a city so hostile to them.[76] Don Luis and his sister Aldonza were much annoyed at this spirit of surrender on Ignatius' part. They now wanted to wage war against their sister Ana with every available means; and the attitude of the Jesuits, who by a kind of legal reservation intended to renounce, not indeed their claims, but any legal proceedings to enforce them was positively distressing.

It was at this time that Don Luis wrote to Polanco in Rome and spoke of his sister in the following by no means loving terms: "The activity of this lady rouses us from slumber; for I believe Your Reverence thought that till now we were asleep." He went on to relate how he and the others had even been summoned before the archiepiscopal court "by this loving sister". But Luis did not give way, nor did Ana. The Conservador even applied to King Philip II. He wrote memoranda to the Pope and to some of the cardinals, and confessed to Ignatius' secretary: "I have written so many memoranda that I shall soon look like one myself."[77] Ana, however, travelled to Rome in person, there to defend her case like a fury.

Ignatius had slowly reached the end of his patience. He had tried in vain to prevent this journey. Many letters concerning this affair were despatched to the Conservador in Saragossa, and Polanco said on one occasion that the case of Doña Ana was Ignatius' topic of conversation every evening. The Jesuits could not bear the burden of this litigation much longer. The Conservador, they said, must appoint a legal representative in Rome who would be a match for Doña Ana's; otherwise it might be that she would win, "which we hope will not be the case". So Don Luis went in June 1552 to Rome, where in a lawsuit that lasted ten months he gained the victory over his sister Ana.[78]

The letters of comfort that Ignatius sent to Doña Aldonza during this distressing time have unfortunately not been preserved. In Saragossa itself Ana's legal battle continued meanwhile unabated. Not till November 1554 could Ignatius state definitely that both parties had at last had enough. "Such things do go on for a long time", observed Polanco ironically. To

Father Alonso Román in Saragossa the General caused to be sent the following instruction: "In the name of our Father Your Reverence is to visit the Señor Conservador and the Señora Doña Aldonza, whose hands we kiss again and again for all the devotion and love they have shown us by their actions."[79]

The six-year-old battle, on which Ignatius had expended so much patience and ink, ended in 1555 like a well-planned comedy. The Jesuits' original objection proved fully justified when at last they were able to occupy the house: it was much too small. They therefore sought another – with success. Now, however, the whole wrath of the archbishop and his vicar-general, hitherto kept in check by the papal protection, broke out, supported by a number of religious, who feared the competition of the newly-arrived Jesuits.

The anti-Jesuit riots at Saragossa form perhaps the most dramatic chapter in the early history of the Society in Spain. On August 13th, 1555, a fifteen-page letter from Father Alonso Román to Ignatius described the details, tragic and comic, of this typically Spanish persecution, worthy of the pen of a Cervantes. Sombre processions of clergy and people went and stood before the house of the Jesuits and there sang the penitential psalms. Dancing groups of boys with devils' masks leapt about in the processions to the accompaniment of noisy music. This loud uproar was not without political significance in the capital of the Kingdom of Aragon. The people eagerly used the occasion for anti-Spanish demonstrations. For the Jesuits were after all mostly Castilians; and their Basque Provincial Araoz and their General in Rome, ever faithful to the house of Castile, were strangers to the Aragonese. "They are just Castilians who want to rule over us!" was the cry in the streets. Father Juan Queralt, who was unexpectedly caught in this holy riot, wrote at the end of a long report to Ignatius: "May it please the Divine Majesty to deliver me out of the hand of Herod and from all the expectation of the people of the Jews; for the Catalans may be unassuming folk, but at least I can now say they are a good people." Here speaks the patriotic Catalan, who was now able to state with satisfaction: such things could not have happened among the citizens of Barcelona![80]

With equal solemnity the Jesuits moved out of their house and through the city gate to Pedrola, where the good Duchess of Villahermosa, sister of Francis Borgia, offered them a refuge. Even in Pedrola the people shouted on seeing them: "Whence come these messengers of Antichrist?" In Saragossa the victorious cry resounded: "The Iniguists have been cast out of Aragon!" The Viceroy, Diego Hurtado de Mendoza, and his wife, who were so friendly towards Ignatius, did all they could to help. The Regent Juana in Valladolid, however, heard of these disturbances in Aragon – which were also of political significance – with furious anger. There are still in the archives of Simancas at least six long letters, written in a regal and commanding tone by the princess who was so closely connected with the Jesuits to all the authorities in Saragossa, especially to the obstinate archbishop, Fernando de Aragón.

The family of the Conservador Don Luis had also to bear the full consequences of this persecution of the "Iniguists". Because of their loyalty and their upholding of the papal bull, they were solemnly excommunicated by the archbishop; and when Don Luis took no notice of this, he was ignominiously thrown out of the cathedral while attending Mass, with the cry, aimed equally at his sister Aldonza: "You, too, are of the same sort!"[81]

For Ignatius, who fully realized the dangerousness of these attacks on the Jesuits, it was a real consolation to hear from the fathers in Saragossa of Doña Aldonza's unshakable loyalty. He did not live to see the period of growing prosperity for the Society in that city, which now began under the protection of the Regent Juana. The whole time of his successor Laynez' generalship was still to be filled with the passionate legal quarrel of Doña Ana against Melchor and Aldonza. On April 5th, 1563, Laynez, who was then at Trent attending the Council, renounced all legal claims of the Jesuits in accordance with the declaration of 1551. It was in vain. Ana once more got the archiepiscopal court to launch an excommunication against the Jesuits and against her family – which was promptly declared null and void at Rome. Only in death did the children of the Aragonese crown lawyer cease to litigate. The Jesuits remained in Saragossa.[82]

The Widow Boquet

WE have many times had occasion to note that Ignatius never forgot his benefactors in Barcelona. As early as 1536 he wrote from Venice to the Archdeacon Jaime Cazador in Barcelona that he "owed more gratitude to that city than to any other place he had lived in". From his student days in the capital of Catalonia he had known a gentleman, Don Juan Boquet, who later as auditor in the royal council at Barcelona played an important part in affairs of state. It was therefore only natural that this gentleman and his wife should keep open house for the Jesuits who came to Catalonia in January 1544. Again it was Father Araoz in particular who became a frequent visitor there. On February 3rd, 1544, he sent a long account to Ignatius of all the strange and wonderful things he had seen in the Boquets' house. The couple, Ignatius read (no doubt with slight astonishment), had an only son, a child of four; and this child was a *monstrum in natura,* a real infant prodigy – although this, adds the writer, "is nothing to God". The child could already speak Latin excellently, better than his Catalan mother-tongue; he knew the Gospels by heart – and above all, he prophesied wonderful things of the Jesuits. For the matter-of-fact Ignatius all this was doubtless a mere curiosity. More important to him was the news that the worthy pair received the sacraments every week and had founded a kind of guild of weekly communicants.[83]

In the Boquet family too they often spoke of Isabel Roser, whose enviable lot it had been since 1543 to be permitted to live in Rome under obedience to the General of the Society. Don Juan Boquet was therefore very distressed to hear the rumours that came from Rome about a quarrel between Ignatius and Doña Isabel. He wrote and told his revered friend what anti-Jesuit talk was current in Barcelona, and what unpleasant letters Doña Isabel's brother had received. Ignatius therefore specially commissioned Dr. Torres, who was returning to Spain, to pay a polite visit to Don Juan and tell him the truth. When the storm had passed, he wrote a personal letter to his friend not only about Isabel's approaching departure, but also about the problem of monastic reform in Barcelona, a work in which Don Juan was also an enthusiastic collaborator.[84]

In the early summer of 1554 the news reached Rome that Don Juan Boquet had died a holy death. On August 16th, Ignatius, mindful of the gratitude he owed to the family, addressed a letter of condolence to the widow, which the Archdeacon Dimas Camps of Barcelona, who was in Rome at the time, took back with him and handed to the bereaved lady. The letter is incidentally an example of those which Ignatius indeed signed, but the writing of which was largely left to his secretary Polanco; hence the almost unctuous tone and the sprinkling of scriptural texts.

The grace and eternal love of Jesus Christ our Lord be always with us to our continual help and favour. Amen.

Among the many signs of the living faith and sure hope we have of eternal life, this is one, and a very certain one – not to grieve beyond measure at the death of those whom we greatly love in our Lord. It is more legitimate for those who think that with the death of the body they are destroyed and that the man who before was alive then ceases to be, to grieve, since, according to their mistaken notion, death is the acme of wretchedness; but [to grieve too much] cannot be legitimate for those who say with Ecclesiasticus that death is better than life, knowing that it is a brief passage from trials and present wretchedness to the rest and glory of eternal life, especially for those who live and die as Christians. Of them, indeed, God orders St. John to write that "blessed are the dead who die in the Lord": whence it is seen that if we ought not to weep over the happiness of those we love, neither ought we to do so over their death which is the beginning of that happiness or at least a sure way to it.

I have said this, my Lady, because, if the death of Don Juan Boquet, beloved in Christ, were an evil, it would be necessary that a great share of the grief over it should come to me, as he was someone whom in Jesus Christ our Lord I loved much. Hoping, however, in the mercy of him who created him and redeemed him with his blood, and allowed him at his death to be helped by the most holy sacraments, so necessary to eternal life, that he may be in the place of the chosen ones, I have no grief, but joy in our Lord, who, as by dying he took away from us the fear of death, so by rising again and ascending to heaven, he showed us what it was and where the true life (to which one passes through death) in the sharing in his kingdom and glory, lies. For this reason I find no subject for grief in his regard.

In regard to Your Ladyship and ourselves, we should not suffer grief either if we knew how to recognize God's providence and love towards us and to have confidence in what the wisdom of this kind

Father of ours who loves our greatest good so much, ordains for us, believing that in prosperity and in adversity, in life and in death, he wills and provides that which is best for us.

Thus it often helps to raise to God the love that stoops to things of earth, if we put away from ourselves what we love on earth, in order that with greater liberty we may turn all our love to God's infinite goodness and heavenly gifts, for we centre our love so much the more on our Creator and our Lord, as there is less occasion to scatter it upon creatures.

However, not to enlarge upon this at length, I will merely say that for our part here, we ask God's goodness to give peace and rest in his holy glory to Señor Juan Boquet and also that he may in his goodness console Your Ladyship and be to you in place of your husband and of all things, increasing in your person and family his very special gifts and graces. May it please His Majesty that we all advance day by day in the way of his greater service, praise and glory. Amen.

From Rome, August 16th, 1554.

The bearer of the present letter (who is a father who is a great friend of ours in our Lord) will give you two *Agnus Dei* which I am sending you by him and he will be able to bless them and will tell you of the graces attached to them.

Ignatius

PART FOUR

THE INEXORABLE
COMFORTER

Letters to Spiritual Daughters

Introduction

THE subject of this chapter really forms the dramatic climax of Ignatius' correspondence with women of his time. Loyola would not have been the great spiritual director who in many of his ideas was in advance of his age, if he had not also known how to deal with all the questions, requests and projects which came to him after the foundation of his new Society from women both lay and religious. Numerous experiences, many of which we are to share in the letters that follow, led him to adopt that very sober attitude which found in the Constitutions of the Society its final expression.

With his keen eye for the grave abuses in the Church of his own age, he recognized that true reform must begin not only in the head, but also as it were in the heart: in the places where women pray and devote themselves entirely to the service of God. He therefore regarded the internal reform of nunneries as a holy task for himself and his sons – and in this he was, so to speak, at war with himself, for such a task might easily have distracted him from more essential pastoral work. This tension must always be borne in mind if we are to understand what we read in these letters, and if we try to follow, from a psychological and pastoral point of view, the slow and often painful process of clarification which Ignatius underwent with regard to this matter of the spiritual direction of women dedicated to God.

Three problems are here involved. The first was the most immediate: was the Society of Jesus to remain open to the development, which had taken place again and again in the history of religious orders up to that time, of founding also a female branch? Secondly, even if the tendency to form a "Society of Jesus" for women were suppressed, should the Jesuits undertake permanently the pastoral care of women belonging to other orders, and thus co-operate in the internal reform of the Church? We shall see how skilfully Ignatius solved this problem. Even then, there remained a third question, and here Ignatius' ideas show him to be in advance of his time: Would it not be possible to devise for prudent and religious women a manner of life that should have a purpose and yet not be limited to the alternatives of "marriage or cloister", then generally recognized as the only ones for women? Here we shall discuss by way of introduction these three problems: they form a hitherto much neglected chapter in the history of the spiritual direction of women.[1]

In the general introduction to these letters, we have already shown how the intellectual power of Ignatius attracted pious women in the first few years after his conversion. They were the "Iñigas" of Manresa, the simple women of Alcalá, and soon afterwards the noble ladies of Barcelona. It was the same during the early years in Rome. We have seen how Ignatius set to work in the service of God the active zeal of the women who revered him. There were many among them who were moved by the inspiring power of the new Society's ideals to entertain the thought of subjecting themselves to the great man by the surrender of their whole life under a vow of obedience. These were women towards whom Ignatius was under a deep obligation of gratitude, and who with feminine intuition thought but lightly of the boldness of their request.

We see the genesis of this idea in a letter that Doña Leonor Mascarenhas, an influential lady at the court of the Spanish king, wrote to Peter Faber, whose enthusiastic devotion to Ignatius she shared: "If I were a man, with all my strength I would follow you and Ignatius!"

What Leonor Mascarenhas only dreamt of, however, Ignatius' energetic benefactress from the days in Barcelona, Doña Isabel Roser, was to realize in fact. She became with two companions the foundress of a female branch of the Society of Jesus – that episode, and the consequences which Ignatius drew from it, will be related in detail. The example of Doña Isabel had, however, kindled a spark in Spain and Italy; for years Ignatius had to defend himself against zealous women who begged and prayed to be admitted to the Society. The otherwise adamant General yielded once, in the case of the Infanta Juana of Spain, who was in fact admitted, although the world at large knew nothing about it. That was an exception, however, forced upon the General by political circumstances. On the whole, in this spiritual warfare against his female admirers, Ignatius disproved the words of his Spanish friend, the lawyer Mateo Murranos; "One day Your Paternity will be compelled to admit the female sex to your Society after all, like other religious orders in the Church."[2]

A related problem was how the Jesuits were to work for the reform and the spiritual direction of nuns belonging to other orders. The more intensive this work was, especially through the persuasive power of the ideas contained in the *Spiritual Exercises,* by means of which such convents were to be reformed, the stronger the desire to complete the reform by actually submitting to the Society of Jesus. The classic example is the story of the convent of Santa Clara in Barcelona. Even if the final step was never taken, the problem of principle remained: To what degree did the spiritual direction of female religious fit in with the spirit and purpose of the new Society? In this matter Ignatius underwent a process of transformation, which we must know about if we are to understand the letters which follow.

In his student days at Barcelona he had concerned himself with the reformation of lax nunneries and had been ill rewarded for his pains. There is no doubt that, ever since then, he felt deeply the urgent need for such reform and that he often spoke of it to his brethren; for during the early years of their pastoral work in Italy, from 1538 till about 1543, they again and again sent detailed reports to Ignatius about reforming such convents. As early as 1539, Rodríguez and Broët at Siena were engaged in this work, and so were Faber and Laynez at Parma in 1540. The letter which Laynez sent to Ignatius on June 2nd, 1540, is particularly significant: "The Lord has opened up a new field for us here, the nunneries", he wrote. The richest, a Benedictine convent, was already reformed, another was in process of reformation, three more had asked for assistance. Year after year Laynez, who after all had really more important things to do, reported to Ignatius on his manifold activities at Reggio (Lombardy), Venice, Padua and Brescia. Jay was working on the same lines at Faenza, and it is note-worthy that many of these tasks were undertaken at the express wish of cardinals – they knew too at the Roman curia where true reform had to begin – as for instance when on the orders of Cardinal Carpi, Broët laboured for five months in 1544 in the convent of Santa Clara at Reggio, apparently the same community that Laynez had already ministered to at Cardinal Cervini's request in 1541. Araoz was also active in the same work each time he was in Barcelona on his three journeys to Spain: the reform of the Catalan nunneries was to be a great preoccupation and anxiety for Ignatius. And it was closely connected with the bold project of Doña Isabel Roser – instead of a questionable reform, why not make quite a fresh start at once with something altogether new, the founding of a female branch of the Society of Jesus?[3]

It was in these early years that Ignatius realized that such efforts, however important and fruitful they might be, were likely to endanger the growing obligations which everywhere presented themselves to the Society. Besides, between 1543 and 1546 the distressing affair of Isabel Roser's foundation played itself out Rome; and it was this which convinced the General that a middle course must be found, enabling the members of the Society – without being either too rigorous or too one-sided – to remain free for the more important tasks of ecclesiastical reform. Wherein lay the "greater glory of God"? How could they hold themselves in readiness to answer the call which might come at any time to go on some mission, by virtue of their vow of obedience to the Pope? This was the question which ever more pressingly weighed upon Ignatius. The purity of the ideals of his new

Society was at stake; and there were present to his mind the words of St. Paul, that the feet of the evangelical man must always be "shod with the preparation of the Gospel" (Eph. 6:15).

As early as 1546, then, we see Ignatius in his first draft of the Constitutions of the Society considering and pondering over the question: which kinds of work, despite their importance and holiness, are nevertheless to be avoided by his sons whenever possible? In the rough draft entitled: "Pastoral works that we do not wish to undertake", dating from 1546, there appear for the first time the words: "The men of the Society do not take any kind of women under their obedience"; and as a second principle: "Let them not be confessors in any convents or other houses of women living in retirement from the world, unless it be occasionally, as when passing through a town, or in the course of a general reform of such convents, at the most, and in either case only for exceptional reasons and with the consent of both sides." While keeping a due distance, he wisely did not wish to close the door entirely to a work so important in itself, but he would open it only with reluctance. We have already mentioned the reason for this, and in the General's letters from 1546 onwards it occurs again and again: his sons were to remain free for more important things. In connection with requests for the reform of a convent in Ferrara, he wrote to Duke Hercules d'Este that the Society must keep itself free "for the greater and more general good of souls". To the senate of the city of Messina he wrote: "We must always stand as it were ready and girt *(star sempre in procinctu)*"; and to Miguel Torres: "We must keep the Society free so that it may be able to hasten unhampered to meet the greatest need, and we must not tie ourselves down to less important tasks." The Spanish lawyer, Mateo Murranos, who was enthusiastic for a female branch of the Society, was told: "We must always stand with one foot raised, so to speak, that we may be able to run freely from one place to another."[4]

When the conflict with Isabel Roser was over, in the spring of 1547, Ignatius felt the time had come to embody all these experiences in canonical form. The Pope himself, who in the previous year had permitted, and indeed commanded the three women to make vows (as will be related), must now be approached and asked to define a limit once and for all. So Ignatius drew up the famous petition to Paul III of May 1547, which the Pope answered favourably on May 20th and which the General thereafter constantly appealed to, until it was solemnly confirmed by the bull of Paul III *Licet debitum* of October 18th, 1549. The text of the petition of 1547 is so important that we give it here in full – a commentary upon it will be provided from Ignatius' letters to those women who were so enthusiastic for the ideals of his Society.[5]

Holy Father,

The General and priests of the Society of Jesus, which has been founded and approved by Your Holiness in virtue of Your apostolic power, appear before Your Holiness as humble petitioners. From the first day of their vocation these priests have recognized with God's grace as their duty, and following upon the approval of the Society by Your Holiness they have put it into practice, to work to the best of their ability in the vineyard of the Lord by preaching and theological instructions, by admonitions and spiritual exercises, and by other works of charity, always free and without encumbrance, "shod with the preparation of the Gospel of peace" (Eph. 6:15), whenever Your Holiness sends them forth under obedience to any part of the world.

These petitioners of Your Holiness now receive from many lands and cities urgent requests to accept the vows and the spiritual direction of nuns and ladies who would fain serve God zealously.

The said petitioners have, however, found by experience, Holy Father, that because of this very thing a great obstacle is raised up to the carrying out of the most important and essential work to which they are called in God's service, such as they are pledged to do according to the constitutions of the Society approved by Your Holiness. As this spiritual direction of women is only just beginning, but appears liable easily to become a hindrance (an at first insignificant obstacle becoming with the passage of time insuperable), the aforesaid priests lay before Your Holiness the following humble petition:

In view of the situation represented above, and in order to be able to live unhampered in accordance with the spirit of their vocation and the constitutions of their lawfully approved Society, the said petitioners ask that permission may be granted that they shall no longer be obliged to undertake the spiritual direction of convents of nuns or female religious, nor that of women who, living together in community, wish to place themselves under the obedience of the said priests; nor finally that of ladies who wish to serve God holily by placing themselves regularly under their direction and following the way of life of the Society.

Let it then be ordained and laid down as a rule that the said petitioners shall be free and exempt from the obligation of accepting the obedience of these women in the sense described, and that they shall be permanently and for ever released from such obligation.

Rome, May 1547.   Ignatius of Loyola

255

All this, then, Ignatius in the Constitutions built into the foundations of his Society, and in the sixth part he wrote, from the experiences that are encased in the letters to follow: "As the men of this Society must be ready at any time to go from one part of the world to another, wherever they may be sent by the Supreme Pontiff or their superiors, they may not undertake the pastoral care of women, still less that of nuns and other such women, in the sense that they permanently *(per ordinario)* carry out the duty of confessors and directors of souls; although this does not prevent their hearing the confessions of a community temporarily *(por una passada)* and for special reasons."[6]

The saint's correspondence from 1547 onwards is full of instructions to avoid or limit, out of prudence and on principle, the permanent spiritual direction of women and nuns. The frequency and urgency of such directives show that this was everywhere a pressing problem, and also how widespread was the desire for reform which the Jesuits encountered among the convents. Ignatius no doubt often had to refuse with great reluctance, but this very fact makes us understand vividly what he meant by "the greater glory of God". We can quote but a few examples from all the abundant evidence available.

From 1547 to 1552, the refusal of such work was always based upon the papal approval of Ignatius' petition or the bull *Licet debitum*. From 1552 onwards, when the Constitutions were completed, every instruction refers simply to the established rule of the Society. Thus, for instance, an order was sent to Louvain on April 30th, 1548, that no vow of obedience was to be accepted from women in confession, for the Pope had forbidden it "at the urgent request of Don Ignatius our Father". Even Catherine Wischaven, the sister of Father Cornelius, who had hitherto acted as housekeeper to the Jesuits, had now to retire to a convent. To Father Diego Mendez in Valladolid Ignatius wrote that working for the *convertidas* was, of course, good (the example of St. Martha's home in Rome was everywhere imitated); but that now the papal brief must always be observed. The convent *Della rosa* in Ferrara, founded by Lucrezia Borgia – Duke Hercules wrote to Ignatius that it had been founded *dalla buona memoria di Madama mia Madre* – was not under any circumstances to be under the direction of the Jesuits. The house of St. Martha in Florence, too, which Father de Coudray wished to make in all respects like the universally admired original in Rome, must be no exception. To Genoa were sent instructions to the effect that all this applied equally to the pastoral care of pious women living in community and looking after hospitals or asylums for the sick or morally endangered women. Father Cesare in Modena was told the same: the spiritual direction of the *convertite* was taking up too much of his time, and he must tactfully see page 131

JOANNA OF ARAGON, DUCHESS OF TAGLIACOZZO
see page 133

(suavemente) withdraw from it. It is significant that such "houses of St. Martha" frequently sought to form themselves into proper convents – the example of Rome, where Ignatius himself had had to transform part of his foundation into a convent, encouraged such developments elsewhere. In the year of his death, the saint instructed Father Michael Botello in Amelia on July 24th, 1556: "To hear nuns' confessions once or twice is not against our constitutions, if we have as our object the reformation and renewal of their spiritual life. If Your Reverence feels unwell, or if you do not seem to be gaining much by this work, you can excuse yourself by quoting the rules of the Society, which forbid us to be regular confessors to nuns." The problem, it will be seen, was with Ignatius till the end of his life.[7]

That is not surprising; for despite his realization that the pastoral ministry to men, the spiritual direction of priests and the founding and running of schools were more important for the reform of the Church, Ignatius was always wise enough to regard the renewal of a true monastic spirit in convents of women as a matter of especial urgency and importance. To complete the picture we shall show that Ignatius, while holding firmly to his principles, nevertheless played a significant role in the reformation of nunneries. Ever since his stay in Barcelona he had been preoccupied with the reform of the Catalan convents. After his experiences in the years 1524 to 1526, he could not but be delighted when in 1539 the zealous Viceroy of Catalonia, Francis Borgia, Marquis of Lombay, took up this problem at the request of the Emperor Charles V and his consort Isabel of Portugal. The Viceroy was helped in his task by the same ladies who had once been Ignatius' benefactresses; and some years later Borgia expressly mentioned in a letter to Ignatius Doña Estefanía Requeséns, wife of the *Comendador* of Castile, Don Juan de Zúñiga y Avellaneda, as "a pillar of monastic reform".

Borgia's efforts were without much success. From 1545 onwards Ignatius therefore addressed himself to the task with all his energy and with delicate diplomatic skill – for it was a matter of political importance too, Prince Philip of Spain being much interested in it. Peter Faber was encouraged and advised to promote the affair at court. In fact, on February 22nd, 1546, Philip despatched a weighty packet; Araoz forwarded it through Ignatius to the imperial ambassador Juan de Vega and the cardinals. It included a letter from Philip to Ignatius himself.

Meanwhile in Barcelona Ignatius' old friend Jaime Cazador had become bishop, Isabel Roser was lending enthusiastic support in Rome, Duke Francis Borgia in Gandía was being plied with searching questions on the situation by Ignatius, and a congregation of cardinals met which delegated the immediate conduct of the reform to Bishop Cazador and an episcopal colleague. Cazador kept Ignatius informed of the course of events; an excellent beginning seemed to have been made, and the General, who had made innumerable *démarches* in connection with this matter, was delighted. Father Araoz was constantly being urged to keep Philip's good intentions alive; and the latter did in fact write to Pope Paul III on August 18th, 1547, a solemn letter on the subject of the Catalan convents. In reply the Pope issued a brief; and this, as Polanco wrote to Araoz on January 23rd, 1548, was done "purely as a favour to Ignatius". It must be admitted that the results were far below the expectations of the zealous reformers; things took the same course as in the case of the convent of Santa Clara in Barcelona, whose history we shall soon hear. But even ill-success could not discourage a man like Ignatius.[8]

The problem of the reform of women's convents added to the already world-wide task of the General from 1548 till his death. Thus he co-operated with the Vicereine of Sicily, Doña Leonor Osorio, to obtain a papal brief for the reform of the nunneries in that island. Father Landini had to carry out a visitation of a convent in Modena; Father Francesco Palmio received detailed instructions as to how he could bring order into a convent at Bologna by dividing the nuns into those who desired reform and those who were incorrigible. Father Bustamente sent Ignatius an account of his labours to reform a nunnery in Granada; from Father Leonhard Kessel in Cologne came edifying reports of the good spirit prevailing in the aristocratic Convent of the Eleven Thousand Virgins; Father Pontius Cogordan worked at the reform of a convent in Provence.

Ignatius had particular trouble with a convent at Messina in the autumn of 1553; the history of its reform developed into a struggle in which Church and State were involved. This was the convent of the Ascension, occupied by fifteen nuns, whose thoughts were by no means directed heavenwards. The viceroy Juan de Vega and the zealous Provincial of the Jesuits, Jerónimo Doménech, started upon the work of reform with almost ruthless zeal, but without consulting Rome, since the Viceroy held that the suppression of such scandals in his territory was a matter entirely under his jurisdiction. The recalcitrant nuns were promptly transferred to other convents, and new candidates were invited to form a fresh community from among the pious women who had been introduced by the Jesuits to a genuine spiritual life; while the convent was at the same time moved out of the noise of the city centre to a more suitable place. When all this was done, the Viceroy and the Provincial felt obliged to inform Ignatius and the Cardinal of Messina, Giovanni Andrea di Mercurio (who lived at Rome) requesting the General now to obtain canonical sanction in Rome for the reform. This was the last straw! The Provincial received a strong reprimand; but the Viceroy could not be treated in the same way, while the whole matter had to be put as delicately as possible by Ignatius and Polanco to the Cardinal of Messina. The General was rightly of the opinion that the high-handed proceedings of the secular power in carrying out this reform had been too severe and even cruel *(cosa cruel)*, and that it was besides indefensible from the point of view of the Society's rules. The chronicle notes further that Ignatius was highly displeased with the unusual position of Father Vinck as "superior" and financial administrator of the new convent. The Provincial must at once see to it that the administration of the establishment be given to persons not belonging to the Society. In principle, however, the arrangement made by the civil power remained, and even the Cardinal of Messina had to come to an agreement with the Viceroy about it.[9]

It was no small matter for Ignatius to concern himself with the many problems connected with the reform of convents. His patience and Polanco's were certainly tried almost to breaking point. There was, for example, the scrupulous Sister Angela in Naples, on whose behalf Father Oviedo repeatedly wrote to Ignatius. This nun had made a vow to transfer to a stricter order than the Benedictines; her confessor had confirmed her in this, but Father Oviedo was of a different opinion – and then the correspondence began. Four times in succession Polanco had to put him off till the following week; then in the General's name he laid the great problem before the Grand Penitentiary, Cardinal Ranuccio Farnese, and at last Sister Angela's mind could be set at rest.

There was a poor maiden at Perugia named Armellina, who could not afford the dowry required to enter a Benedictine convent; Ignatius found time to recommend her warmly to the care of Father Bobadilla. There was Sister María, who had spent some time in the House of St. Martha at Rome and was now returning to Saragossa in her Spanish homeland, but who had lost her documents on arrival: Ignatius had to clear the matter up. At Messina there was Sister Livia Magniera, who wished to leave the Cistercian convent of Santa Maria dell'Alto and become a Benedictine. Ignatius procured for her the necessary papal bull. There was the problem of Madonna Feliciana's private convent in Naples; this lady maintained seven poor maidens in her house, all of them devotees of the Jesuits. When the new college was erected, Feliciana resolutely followed the Fathers and moved into a house the windows of which were immediately opposite those of the Jesuits, whereupon Father Salmerón protested and refused the sacraments to the women until they left the house. Both parties referred the dispute to the patient Ignatius. Madonna Feliciana had to give way.[10]

After all these experiences it is not surprising that Ignatius frequently considered whether there might not be a third solution for these women, even though a female branch of the Society of Jesus was to be rejected and although many of those who turned to him and to the Society were not attracted to any of the existing convents. When Father Oviedo wrote to him from Gandía on June 18th, 1546, about the ardent desire of Doña Juana de Meneses to found a house of women dedicated to God that was to be subject in obedience to the Jesuits, Ignatius gave Dr. Torres, who was then returning to Spain, a memorandum whose contents he was to make known both in Gandía and Valencia, where pious ladies were making similar plans. First of all it clearly stated that an establishment of actual "Jesuitesses" was not contemplated at all: "As regards the question of the foundation of a convent of female religious belonging to and subject to the Society of Jesus, we cannot persuade ourselves that this is advisable. For our Society is still in its first beginnings; it suffers much opposition and lacks members. First of all, it must itself grow in our Lord. Secondly also because the Society has made a special vow to be always mobile, according to the will of the Pope, so as to be able to go from one part of the world to another." Reasons were given why a foundation at Gandía was particularly inadvisable. But then Ignatius went on – and here like a lightning-flash appears an idea that only long afterwards was realized in the Church: "All this brings me to the conviction, that in order to carry out the plans of the Lord Duke and Doña Juana, to win more souls and to serve God our Lord better and more comprehensively in the cause of spiritual advancement, it would be a good and holy means to found a company of women *(Compañía de Señoras)*, which others, too, having been found suitable in our Lord, could then join."

The memorandum on the realization of such a plan, with which this letter was enclosed, has unfortunately not been preserved. No doubt it was about the "union or community of pious women", usually ladies of noble birth, who wished to live a religious life outside the cloister and devote themselves entirely to charitable and social work. How Ignatius imagined it in detail we shall see in the following letters. The three women whom he admitted to his Society in Rome itself at the Pope's command were put by him wholly and exclusively in the service of the House of St. Martha. The new convent of the Ascension at Messina set itself a similar task, as we have heard. The ladies of Valencia, whom Ignatius almost forcibly prevented from joining the Society, devoted themselves to a life of heroic charity, in accordance with the ideas on which the Spiritual Exercises were based. It was the same, as we shall see, with the devout women of Modena, who also wished at one time to be admitted to Ignatius' Society.

It is true that nothing permanent came of these proposals during Ignatius' lifetime. His Society kept to his instructions and henceforth saw its essential task in the pastoral care of men and youths, in cultivating learning and science, and above all in being always ready for missions to any part of the world, which was to be won for Christ. But for the exact understanding of this development it is necessary to learn what were the reasons and the events which moved Ignatius to direct the members of his Society to undertake this form of ministry. They will be found in the following letters.[11]

Isabel Roser

WE have already heard how Ignatius took a touching farewell of the women of Manresa in February 1523, when he set out along the king's highway to Barcelona. There he waited from February 17th till the middle of March 1523 for an opportunity to sail to Rome and thence to the Holy Land. Those twenty days in the Catalan seaport brought him into contact with Isabel Roser, who later played an essential role in the formation of his ideas about the Society's purpose. Isabel Roser (also called Rosell or Rosés) belonged to the noble Catalan family of Ferrer. She was married to the wealthy Juan Roser; but the marriage was childless, and in his latter years her husband was blind. Their beautiful house stood opposite the church of San Yusto y Pastor, and although altered, it is still standing. According to the not very reliable evidence of old Juan Pascual in the first process of beatification, the family was also related to the natural son of the Emperor Maximilian, Don Jorge de Austria, later Archbishop of Valencia. Be that as it may, the Rosers were, in ecclesiastical circles too, among the most influential families of the capital.

Isabel herself later told young Pedro de Ribadeneira how she first became acquainted with the Pilgrim Ignatius in the church of San Yusto y Pastor, where Doña Isabel was attending a sermon with her blind husband. "There I saw our blessed Father, sitting by the altar-steps among the children. I looked at him several times; it seemed to me that there was a radiance about his face, and I heard in my heart a voice which said: 'Call him, call him!' And although I would not believe this to be true at first, I left the church deeply moved. When I got home and told my husband of it, we at once sought out the Pilgrim and invited him to eat with us. He came, and after the meal he gave us a spiritual talk, which made a great impression on us."

The Pilgrim told the pious lady in some detail about his plans to go to Rome and Jerusalem. It may be that Isabel was that noblewoman of whom Ignatius later related in his Pilgrim's Book: "Dismayed, the lady cried out: 'Will you travel to Rome? I know not how those who go there ever return.' She meant that such persons in Rome make little progress in the spiritual life." But Ignatius was not to be dissuaded from his plan, and a brigantine lay ready to sail on which he had already booked his passage. Isabel did, however, succeed in persuading him to go on a larger ship, which was also lying in the harbour. Thus there occurred that minor miracle of Providence which the first Jesuits used to relate to one another, and of which Ribadeneira and others have preserved an account. The brigantine capsized just outside the harbour and sank with all hands. At the very outset Isabel had saved the life of her Ignatius.[12]

It is not, then, surprising that on his return from Jerusalem Ignatius went to discuss his plans for study with Doña Isabel. It was due to her influence that the unlearned Pilgrim found in Master Ardévol a good and strict teacher of Latin; and so the two years from Lent 1524 to March 1526 were passed in the sincere friendship of his pious patroness. The relationship became a very practical one from the moment when Ignatius began his studies in Paris. Isabel in Barcelona was the leader among the noble ladies whom we know already; and it was she who by frequent collections got together the money for the support of the distant student. In the biographical sketch of Ignatius' life, which the Austrian chancellor Albert Widmanstadt published in September 1556, it says of these years: "He was at that time partly supported in his studies by a matron of Spain, partly he supported himself by begging, so that he might not be too great a burden to the same pious matron."

By thus organizing financial help for him, Doña Isabel won Ignatius' undying gratitude; for the student in Paris needed the generous alms of his Catalan friends more and more, not only for himself but also for the support of his companions, who had joined him in 1529 and 1532. It may not always have been easy for Isabel to collect money from the ladies in Barcelona, and to keep interest in Ignatius alive. She herself was occasionally in financial difficulties. Besides, at this time there began to show those traits of her character which later brought her into conflict with Ignatius. She suffered from nervous disorders; calumny abounded; probably, indeed, her relations with Ignatius formed the subject of pious gossip in the town. So it came about that many letters and complaints which have not been preserved accompanied the money to Paris.[13]

When after 1532 Ignatius' plans, which he discussed with his first companions in Paris, took more concrete shape, he found time to answer these complaining letters of Doña Isabel in a lengthy epistle. On November 10th, 1532, an unusually long letter of comfort – for Ignatius – was despatched to Barcelona. It was in one respect especially characteristic: it reveals in almost extravagant words his feeling of gratitude towards his pious benefactresses and confirms that friendship with Doña Isabel which he was to break off so painfully fifteen years later in Rome: "For to you I owe more than to anyone I know in this life" (see p. 265, ll. 24,25). Here speaks that same sentiment

263

of gratitude which Ignatius felt towards Barcelona in general; as he once expressed himself in a letter to the future Bishop of Barcelona, Jaime Cazador: he owed Barcelona more than any other place in the world.

In contrast with other letters, he added to this one a story for the edification and comfort of the pious ladies, which he had apparently heard in Paris, and which was well known in the Middle Ages as the legend of St. Marina. This letter is not only as it were an echo of the spiritual talks which Ignatius used to give the women of Barcelona, but also a valuable document illustrating the development of the ideas which, while he was in Paris, led to the completion of the *Spiritual Exercises*.[14]

May the grace and love of Christ our Lord be always with us.

By Doctor Benet I received three letters from your hand and twenty ducats which you enclosed. May our Lord deign to place these to your credit on the day of judgment and repay them to you on my behalf, as I hope in his divine goodness that he will do in good and sound coinage; I hope also that he will not find me guilty of ingratitude, but will make me worthy to serve and praise his divine Majesty in such matters.

In your letters you tell me that the will of God our Lord has been fulfilled by the recall from exile and departure from this life of Señora Canillas. It is true that I cannot feel grief so far as she is concerned, but rather on our account, for us who are in a place of immense weariness, suffering and calamity; for since in this life I knew her to be beloved and cherished by her Creator and Lord, I can easily believe that she will be well cared for and received and will have no desire now for the palaces, pomps, riches and vanities of this world.

You also write to me of the apologies put forward by our sisters in Christ our Lord. To me, however, they owe nothing – rather, I am permanently indebted to them. If they have put their generosity to good use elsewhere for the service of God our Lord, we ought to rejoice over it. And if they are not doing this because they cannot, it is absolutely true that I should like to have money to give to them, so that they might do much for the service and glory of God our Lord. As long as I live I shall not be able to help owing them something, but I do, indeed, think that after we have left this life, they will be well rewarded for what they have done for me.

In the second letter you write to me of the long drawn out sufferings and illness which you have been through and of the severe pain in the stomach which you still have. In truth, when I think of your suffering state and present pain, I cannot do otherwise than suffer in my soul, for what I desire for you is all the good fortune and prosperity imaginable, that it might be a help to you in the glory and service of God our Lord. When I consider, however, that these illnesses and other temporal misfortunes often come from the hand of God our Lord so that we may know ourselves better and detach ourselves more from the love of created things, and may give more thought to the brevity of this life of ours, and so prepare ourselves for the other that is to last for ever – and when I reflect that God visits with such things the persons he greatly loves – then I cannot feel sadness or grief, for I think that a servant of God comes out of an illness having learnt in some degree how to rectify and order his life for the glory and service of God our Lord.

You also say I must forgive you for not giving me more help, for you have many obligations to fulfil and your resources are not sufficient. There is no need to ask forgiveness – I fear for my own pardon, for I think that if I do not do what God our Lord requires of me towards all my benefactors, his righteous and divine justice will not forgive me – all the more so, if I were to fail in this respect towards you, with all I have received from you. In short, if I do not manage to fulfil what I owe in this respect, I have no other refuge but, when the merits I obtain before God's divine Majesty are counted – merits that are nevertheless gained through his grace – to ask the Lord himself to distribute them among the persons to whom I am indebted, to each one in accordance with the service he has rendered me, and chiefly to you – for to you I owe more than to anyone I know in this life. As I am conscious of this, I hope in God our Lord that he will help me to cancel the debt of my gratitude to you. Think, then, that from this time onwards your goodwill towards me, which is so spontaneous and so sincere, will be received by me with as much pleasure and spiritual joy as all the money you could send me, for God our Lord requires us to look at and love the giver more than the gift and that we should always have him before our eyes, in our soul and in our heart.

You also suggest that I might perhaps write to our other sisters who are my benefactors in Christ our Lord, asking them to help me for the future. I should prefer to decide this on your judgment rather than on mine. Although Señora Cepilla offers in her letter and shows a right goodwill to help me, for the present I do not think I should write to her for help for the studies, for we are not sure of having a year in front of us. If we do arrive at this, I hope that God our Lord will give us understanding and judgment with which we shall be able to do what is best for his service and always accomplish his will and pleasure.

265

In your third letter you tell me of all the malice, jealousy and false accusations that have been levelled against you from all sides. Nothing of this surprises me, nor even would it do so if it were much more, for from the moment when you give yourself to God our Lord, desiring and striving for his glory, honour and service, you are already embarked on warfare against the world, are setting up your standards against it, and disposing yourself to struggle against what is exalted by embracing what is lowly, resolved to accept indifferently things both high and low – honour and dishonour, riches or poverty, to be loved or hated, welcomed or rejected, in short the world's glory or its abuse. So long as they do not go beyond words, we shall not be able to count the insults of this life as much, for all of them together cannot destroy one single hair of our head. Words with double meaning or those which are hurtful and abusive do not cause either more pain – or more inward peace – than what we will to accept. If our desire is to live in absolute honour and glory in the eyes of our neighbours, we shall not be able to be engrafted in God our Lord, nor will it be possible for us to remain indifferent when insults are offered to us. Thus, just as it once pleased me that the world should insult you, so does it grieve me to think that on account of these adversities, you have sought help and remedy for the trouble and suffering they cause you. Would that it might please the Mother of God, provided that patience and constancy remain undiminished in you – considering the greater insults and affronts that Christ our Lord suffered for us – and provided that others do not sin, that greater insults should come upon you, so that you might merit more and more. If, indeed, we do not find this patience in us, we have greater reason to complain of our own sensuality and of our flesh, and of the fact that we are not so mortified or dead in the matter of worldly things as we should be, than to accuse those persons who insult us; for they provide us with material with which we can gain greater treasure than one can acquire in this life and greater riches than a man can gather together in this world, such as a person in the monastery of St. Francis in this very city gained and gathered together. This is the way it came about.

The friars of St. Francis often used to come to a certain house and as their conversation was very pious and holy, a girl, already growing up, who was in the house, grew extremely fond of that monastery and house of St. Francis – so much so that she one day dressed as a boy and went to the monastery to ask the Guardian to give her [i.e. the boy] the habit for he had a great desire to serve, not only God our Lord and the holy Master Francis, but all the religious of that house. He spoke so persuasively that they gave him the habit forthwith, and he remained in the monastery leading a very recollected life full of consolation. Now it happened that one night he and another of his companions stayed in a certain house, with leave of their superior, as they were on a journey. There happened to be a girl in this house and she fell in love with the good friar, or, rather, the devil entered into this girl, and she determined to go in to the good friar as he was sleeping, that he might sin with her. As the friar awoke and drove her from the room, she became so filled with anger that she immediately sought ways and means by which she could cause all the annoyance possible to the good friar, so much so that a few days later the wicked girl went to speak to the Guardian demanding justice – saying that she was pregnant by a good friar of his house, and other things. The Guardian, because the matter was so much talked of in that city, took the friar and put him in the street at the gates of his monastery, bound, that all might see the justice that was being done. He remained like that for many days, rejoicing at the abuse, revilements and insulting words, which he heard referring to his person. He did not justify himself to anyone, but discoursed with his Creator and Lord within his soul, since he was offered the material of so much merit before his divine Majesty. After a certain time had thus elapsed during which he was thus a spectacle to all, when people saw that his patience was so great, they asked the Guardian to forgive him all the past and take him again into his affections and his house. The Guardian, already moved to pity, took him back and the good friar spent many years in that house until the will of God in his regard was accomplished. After he died, when they undressed him for burial, they discovered that he was a woman and not a man, and consequently that very great calumny was lifted from him. Thus all the friars marvelled and praised his innocence and holiness more than they had blamed his supposed guilt. Many of them even now remember more clearly this friar or nun than any of those who lived a long time in their house.

Thus I should prefer to look more to one point in which I had failed than at all the ill that was spoken of me.

May it please the most holy Trinity to grant you abundant grace in all the adversities of this life and in all other things in which you can serve God, as I desire for myself, and to me may he grant no more than that which I desire for you.

Remember me to Mosén Roser, and to all the persons who you feel would like to be greeted by me.

From Paris, November 10th, 1532

Poor in goodness, Iñigo

Post scriptum. In Arteaga as in many persons of Alcalá and Salamanca, I see much constancy in the service and glory of God our Lord, to whom be unending thanks for this. As you ask me, I write to Mosén Gralla in the matter of peace and I am sending the letter enclosed in Pascuala's; I write also to Señora Cepilla.

To my sister in Christ our Lord, Isabel Roser, in Barcelona.

The assistance of his unswerving admirer continued when in December 1535 Ignatius went to Bologna, and then (from the beginning of 1536) to Venice, in order to complete his studies and to await the arrival of his companions from Paris. We know that Señora Roser sent him twelve ducats in Bologna, and also some books. But the life of the Pilgrim now began to take quite a different course: not Jerusalem but Rome was henceforth his goal, and the more he was occupied with plans for his Society, the less time he found to write long letters to Barcelona. Isabel was very worried at the scantiness of the news she received. At last, however, a lengthy bulletin dated December 19th, 1538, arrived at the house opposite San Yusto y Pastor.[15]

This was, indeed, more than an ordinary letter; it was a detailed account of the situation, like a report from headquarters, in which Ignatius related to his faithful friend the persecutions and successes he had met with during the early days of his work in Rome. One can imagine with what pride Isabel read this letter, which made her as it were a fellow-soldier in Ignatius' spiritual battles. The words of heartfelt thanks in this letter drew even closer the bond of gratitude which existed between Ignatius and Isabel. By its detailed accuracy, moreover, it forms one of the most important documents for the early history of the Society; it is due to Isabel Roser that this precious report has been preserved. Perhaps it was while reading it that she first thought of helping Ignatius' little band in Rome, where, as he wrote, "the ground is poor in good fruits and overgrown with evil ones". This discouraging description of conditions in Rome is perhaps due to the fact that fifteen years before she had warned him about the dangers of the Eternal City. This letter, then, is also informative about the history of pastoral work and preaching.

What tended to draw Ignatius and Isabel Roser together was that, just as he had once had to comfort her when she was slandered and calumniated, so later he could tell her of his own experiences in the same line. The disciples from Paris who had come with him to Rome, or who had joined him there, were already beginning in those early days to have a foretaste of the future destiny of the Society. When they opposed the preaching, infected with the errors of Luther, of the Augustinian Agostino Mainardi, malicious talk against them arose in Rome, which, as we have heard, was encouraged by the two Spanish clerics Mudarra and Barrera. The former Rector of the College of St. Ildefonsus at Alcalá, Dr. Mateo Pascual, one of Erasmus' Spanish friends, was also among the enemies of the Jesuits. That just at the same time as Ignatius was endeavouring to procure from Paul III at Frascati the final judgment in this dispute, the three men, who had already been concerned with proving Ignatius' orthodoxy, appeared in Rome as witnesses of the Jesuits' innocence, always seemed to them a dispensation of Providence. They were Juan Rodríguez de Figueroa of Alcalá, the Dominican Matthew Ory from Paris, and Gaspare de Dotti from Venice.

At the end of the letter Ignatius promised his friend that he would send her more frequent news about the further development of his Roman plans. Unfortunately nothing more has been preserved; but this one report compensates for everything else. As the date of the letter shows, it was written six days before the celebration of Ignatius' first Mass at the Crib in St. Mary Major. Now Doña Isabel knew that for Ignatius Rome had taken the place of Jerusalem.[16]

The grace and love of Christ our Lord be always with us to our help and favour.

I can well believe that you have been a little worried and no less surprised at my not having written you frequently as I wanted and desired to do, for if I were to forget the much I owe our Lord through your hands, with such sincere affection and goodwill on your part, I think that his divine Majesty would not remember me, for you have always done so much for me for his love and reverence. The cause of my slowness in writing has been because we hoped from day to day, or from month to month, to conclude a certain piece of business so that we should thus have more definite news of our affairs here. The business is this – during eight whole months we have experienced the most severe persecution and hostility that we have ever undergone in this life. I do not mean that they have annoyed us in our persons, nor called us before the justices, nor ill-treated us in any other way; but by spreading rumours among the people and by unheard – of statements, they made us objects of suspicion and hatred to the people. This resulted in much scandal – so that we were obliged to present ourselves before the legate and governor of this city (for the Pope had then gone to

Nice) on account of the great scandal caused to many persons. We then began to name some who had turned against us and to call on them to declare the evils they found in our life and teaching before the authorities. And because in some way the thing is more easily understood from the beginning, I will here give you some account of it.

It is more than a year since three of us, members of the Society, arrived here in Rome, as I remember having written to you. Two of us then began to teach without charging fees in the Sapienza College, the one positive theology and the other scholastic theology, and this by command of the Pope. I gave myself up entirely to giving and communicating the spiritual exercises to others, both in Rome itself and outside the city. We agreed upon this together in order to have certain learned or outstanding men on our side, or rather on the side of God, to his honour and glory, for our glory is no other than the praise and service of the divine Majesty. Our aim in this was that among those with worldly interests, we might not find such great opposition and afterwards might be able to preach God's most holy word with greater liberty, for we sensed the earth to be exceedingly dry of good fruits and abundant in bad. After we had gained (by the help of God our Lord) some people to our favour and opinion by these Exercises – and those persons of much learning and great esteem – at the end of four months after our arrival, we resolved that all those of the Society here in Rome should join together. As soon as we were all together, we set ourselves diligently to obtain a licence to preach, exhort and hear confessions. This the legate gave us very willingly, although in this matter very bad reports were given about us to his vicar, so as to prevent, if possible, the issuing of the said licence.

After we had the licence, four or five of us began to preach in different churches on Sundays and feast-days, and also in other churches to explain to the children the commandments, mortal sin, etc. We still continued the two courses in theology in the Sapienza College, and, moreover, the confessions. All the others preached in the Italian tongue and I alone in Spanish. For all the sermons there was a considerable concourse of people and immeasurably more than we thought there would be for three reasons – first, because the time was unusual, for we began when Easter was past, when the other preachers for Lent and the principal feasts had ended, and in these parts it is only customary to preach in Lent and Advent; secondly, because commonly, since they have been through the penances and sermons of Lent, many afterwards, on account of our sins alas, turn more to relaxation and worldly pleasures, than to penance or new devotion; the third reason – because we have no polish that would add elegance or distinction to what we say, and in spite of all this, we are conscious, through many experiences, that our Lord in his infinite and highest goodness does not forget us, and for our sake helps and favours many others, despite the simple and lowly manner of our preaching.

We presented ourselves, then, before the justices. Two of our opponents were also summoned, and one of them found himself when before the judges in a position quite contrary to that in which he thought to find himself. The others, who were named so that they might be summoned, were in so much consternation that, not having the will or the courage to appear, they demanded that the case be heard before another court, and obtained a judgment against us which prevented us from pursuing the case before other judges. As they were rich persons, some with a thousand ducats of revenue, some with six hundred, and some of even greater importance, and all were members of the curia and men of affairs, they stirred up so much trouble with cardinals and many other persons of importance at the curia, that they caused us to spend much time over this business.

Finally, the most important of them, on being summoned, appeared before the legate and the governor and said that they had heard our sermons and lessons in theology and found everything, both in our doctrine and in our life a complete justification for us. Although the legate and the governor held us in much esteem they wanted to smooth the matter over through consideration for these men and also for others. We asked on many occasions, as we felt was only just, that the evil or good there was in our teaching should be declared authoritatively, so that the scandal to the people might be removed; this we could never obtain from them, either out of justice or in the name of the law. From this time onwards, however, with the fear they had of the law, no one dared to say the things against us they had done at first, at least in public.

As we could never succeed in getting them to give written judgment or make a declaration in law about our affair, a friend of ours spoke to the Pope as soon as he returned from Nice, begging him to make a declaration on the matter. The Pope agreed; then as nothing happened, two fathers of our Society went to take up the matter with him again: but he had then left Rome for a residence removed from the city. I went there and spoke to His Holiness alone in his apartment, for the space of about an hour. There speaking to him at length of our proposals and intentions, I told him frankly of all the occasions on which they had taken proceedings against me in Spain and in Paris and also the times I had been in prison in Alcalá and Salamanca. I did this so that no one

271

could tell him more than I had told him and so that he should be the more moved to make an inquiry about us, so that in one way or another sentence should be given or a declaration made about our teaching. Finally, as it was very necessary that we should have a good reputation if we were to teach and instruct, and be in good odour not only before God our Lord, but also before the people, and that the latter should not be suspicious of our doctrine and customs, I besought His Holiness in the name of us all, to provide a remedy for the situation – namely, that our doctrine and customs might be inquired into and examined by whatever ordinary judge His Holiness might appoint: for if they found evil, we wanted to be corrected and punished; and if good, that His Holiness should extend his favour to us. The Pope, even though he had cause for suspicion, reacted favourably to what I told him, praising our talents and the use we made of them for good. He then made us a short exhortation, speaking to us, indeed, as a father and a true shepherd. Shortly afterwards with much diligence he ordered the governor, who is a bishop and the highest magistrate here in Rome, both in ecclesiastical and in secular affairs, that he should forthwith hear our case. He set up a fresh inquiry and dealt with the matter with diligence, and the Pope, returning to Rome, spoke in our favour in public many times and even before fathers of the Society, for every fortnight they are accustomed to go and hold a disputation during His Holiness's meal. A great part of the storm against us has thus been dissipated, and each day things improve so that, so far as I can see, things are going much as we desire for the service and glory of God our Lord. We are already much importuned with requests from some prelates and others to go and do good in their dioceses with the help of God our Lord. We are, however, waiting quietly, hoping for better things to come.

Now it has pleased God our Lord that at last our cause has been judged and a verdict given. In connection with this one thing happened here that was truly wonderful, namely, that whereas it was said about us or published here, that we were fugitives from many lands, and especially from Paris, Spain and Venice, at the very time the judgment or verdict about us was to be given there was found newly arrived here in Rome, the regent Figueroa, who once seized my person in Alcalá and twice instituted proceedings against me, and the Vicar General of the Venetian legate, who also instituted proceedings against me (after we began to preach in the State of Venice), and Doctor Ory, who also instituted proceedings against me in Paris, and the bishop of Vicenza, where three or four of us preached for some short time, and all these gave (favourable) evidence about us. Likewise the cities of Siena, Bologna and Ferrara sent their authentic (and favourable) testimony here; and the Duke of Ferrara, besides sending favourable testimony, taking the matter very much to heart on account of the dishonour that was being done in our persons against God our Lord, wrote several times to his ambassador and to our Society, declaring that he looked upon the matter as his own, for he had seen the good that had been produced in his city and likewise in the other cities where we had been, although we had much difficulty in maintaining ourselves at Ferrara on account of the obstacles there. For this we give thanks to God our Lord that, from the time we began until the present moment, there have never failed to be two or three sermons on each feast; likewise two instructions in theology, other fathers being occupied hearing confessions or in giving the Spiritual Exercises. Now that the judgment is given, we hope to add to the number of sermons and also to our instruction of children; and although the soil be dry and sterile and the storm against us so violent, we cannot truthfully say that work has been lacking, and that God our Lord has not wrought more than our knowledge or hopes can attain to.

I do not enlarge about details, in order not to be too lengthy. Generally speaking, however, God our Lord has given us much happiness. I will merely say that there are four or five who are determined to join the Society and have persevered in this determination for many days and many months now. We do not dare to admit them yet, for this was one point among the others we were reproached for, that we received subjects and set up a congregation or religious body without the Holy See's authority. Thus now, although we do not yet live in common, we are all united in heart about making further progress in the future. This we hope for in God our Lord who will quickly dispose [things] so that he may be best served and praised in all.

Since you have heard how our affairs stand, I ask you for the love and reverence of God our Lord, to have much patience with me, as you also wish, desiring that he deign to make use of us in whatever it may please him to employ us for his greater honour and glory; for certainly at the present time there are things of much importance and weight. I will advise you more frequently of what is happening, and I tell you unhesitatingly that if I forget you, I think to be forgotten by my Creator and Lord. Accordingly I have not taken so much care about fulfilling my obligation to you or thanking you in words, but of this you may be certain, that besides the fact that all that you have done to me (before God our Lord) for his love and reverence lives before him, in all things that his divine Majesty may work through me all the days of my life,

273

and that he makes meritorious by his divine grace, you will have a full share, as you have always helped me and have been so especially generous to me, to his divine service and praise. I beg you to remember me to and recommend me to the prayers of all persons we know who are truly for God, who serve him with fervour and are united in holy converse with Christ our Lord.

I conclude, asking God our Lord by his infinite and supreme goodness, to deign to give us his abundant grace so that we may know his most holy will and way follow it out to the full.

Poor in goodness
Iñigo

While I have been writing this letter the Pope through the governor has ordered provision to be made for children's schools to be opened, in accordance with the prescriptions of the law, so that we may instruct them in Christian doctrine as we began to do before. May it please God our Lord, since the affair is his, that he deign to give us strength for his greater service and glory. To Archdeacon Cazador I send the actual judgment which was here given about us. This he will communicate to you.

From Rome, December 19th, 1538

Things did not go well for Isabel in the following year. Her husband grew more and more infirm, and she herself was harassed by sickness. On October 19th, 1539, there arrived in the harbour of Barcelona the first member of Ignatius' new community, which Pope Paul III had orally approved at Tivoli on September 3rd. This was Antonio de Araoz, cousin of Ignatius' sister-in-law Magdalena. In the house of the Archdeacon Jaime Cazador all Ignatius' friends gathered about the new arrival and heard with enthusiasm the news of the victory over persecution and of the papal approval of the Society. No doubt Isabel was there too when Ignatius' friends met together, although her name is not expressly mentioned in the report which Araoz sent to Ignatius.[17]

On November 8th, 1541, Don Juan Roser, Isabel's husband, died; he was buried with solemn pomp. The widow was now free to carry out her pious project. She thought at first of entering the aristocratic convent of Santa Clara, where her friend Sister Teresa Rejadella shared her hearty admiration for Ignatius. Nothing came of this: ascetically and canonically, the conditions at Santa Clara were too disordered, as we shall be hearing in detail. For that very reason, however, Isabel Roser and her friend Isabel de Josa, in collaboration with the Archdeacon Jaime Cazador, took up the burning question of monastic reform in Barcelona and Catalonia.

Father Araoz had meanwhile returned to Rome, where on Christmas Day 1541 he was ordained priest; and on February 19th, 1542, he made his solemn profession before the General of the Society. On February 23rd he set off again for Spain, there to begin his brilliant career. He took with him a letter from Ignatius to Isabel Roser, which had been written on February 1st. In it, Araoz was recommended to the maternal care of the benefactresses in Barcelona. Moreover, there were some misunderstandings to be cleared up, which arose apparently out of the work of reforming the convents in Catalonia, so long desired by Ignatius. Archdeacon Cazador, who was soon to be Bishop of Barcelona, played a decisive role in settling the matter. Master Lorenzo García was also involved: he had in 1538 been one of the "Iñiguists' " accusers in Rome and was now one of their friends. Ignatius wished Doña Isabel to read the letters connected with this delicate question and then pass them on to the ecclesiastics concerned – another proof of the high value attached by him to her influence in Barcelona.[18]

May the sovereign grace and love of Christ our Lord be always with us to our continual protection and help.

My poor health does not help me or give me opportunity to write at length. May his divine Majesty be blessed, praised and glorified who visits us both in this way and afterwards gives us some breathing space so that we may serve him better.

As I have already written you at length in other letters and promised that one of the Society should go to Barcelona ten days before or ten days after we performed the baptism of a Jewish woman, this father will leave here, on Low Sunday. His journey will take some twenty days from now, either by sea or by land. Since he will not lack dangers, whether by the one route or the other, especially as times are, I ask you keep him in your prayers and in those of my other devout friends; for if he arrives well in body, I hope you will be pleased with him and consoled in our Creator and Lord, for here, among all of us especially, he is esteemed and loved for the many graces and gifts from God's Majesty which are showered down upon him.

Cazador wrote me a letter by which it seems to me that he has not understood the meaning of mine. I therefore send him back his letter with another that Master Lawrence wrote to me. At the same time I am writing him a letter in which I lower and humble myself as much as I can as I always desire to do with all persons, explaining myself, that I may be better understood. After reading all three letters and sealing only that which I write to Cazador, you will kindly make a packet of all three and hand them to him.

Please remember me kindly to all our sisters in the Lord. May God ever grant us his protection and favour.

From Rome, February 1st, 1542

Poor in goodness,
Iñigo

To my sister in Christ our Lord, Isabel Roser, opposite St. Yuste in Barcelona.

In the same year 1542 there matured in the mind of Doña Isabel her plan to place herself entirely at the disposal of her beloved Father Ignatius and to travel to Rome. Tragedy was to come of it.

Peter Faber, who came to Barcelona on his return journey from Spain to Germany in March 1542, had long conversations with Isabel Roser and at once sent a report of them to Ignatius in a letter from Lyons dated March 22nd. From this it appears that Ignatius was already informed of Isabel's plans; at all events, Faber had the following news to give him:

"When I spoke with Señora Isabel Roser, she told me that she would, with some other ladies, get together by Easter a sum of money for the rebuilding of Pietro Codacio's church. She would bit by bit collect more money and so try to help wherever she could. She said she was only waiting for an answer from Master Ignatius, by the hand of the Father who was coming, to know his decision about her future way of life. She declared herself ready to go to Rome, so that she might there serve God our Lord better and without hindrance, if Father Ignatius agreed to this. She would bring with her a sum of about 1800 ducats, to be used as she was directed. Doña Isabel de Josa also could hardly wait to leave Barcelona and travel to Rome. I know not what will come of all this."

The shrewd Faber was obviously somewhat sceptical.[19] Father Araoz thought otherwise. We can hardly be wrong in supposing that the main promoter of these ideas was Araoz; for about him there formed a group of influential women, the chief of whom was the Vicereine, Leonor de Borja, Marchioness of Lombay, wife of the future St. Francis. The Duchess of Cardona also belonged to this group. Isabel must have felt quite at home in this circle of great ladies, for was she not the leader among all these female devotees of the distant Ignatius? When in June 1542 Father de Santacruz informed Ignatius from Barcelona that the Vicereine had wanted to bestow on them a generous gift of money, he added that they had not accepted it, because they were already so well looked after by Isabel, "the mother of the poor".

Slowly a genuine friendship grew up between Isabel and Araoz. From July to October she lived on her country estate near the city. There she received two letters from Ignatius, one written in June, the other in August. Ignatius had in the meantime been informed both by Araoz and by Isabel about his benefactresses' plans for entering the cloister. The Vicereine and the Duchess of Cardona had evidently advised them to join the convent of Hieronymite nuns, for the reform of which Ignatius had once so much exerted self, and the portress of which had received from him the touching gift of a box containing earth and flowers from the Holy Land. But Isabel was determined to place herself under the General's obedience at Rome. Ignatius, despite all the gratitude he felt towards Isabel, must have been alarmed when he heard of such a project. On June 19th, 1542, he sent her a letter telling her to find out whether it was a good or an evil spirit that suggested this design to her. On June 12th he had sent a similar instruction to Araoz – an indication of the embarrassment in which Ignatius found himself. While he still thought that Isabel's plan might really be God's will and would therefore advance her along the road of perfection, he was nevertheless uneasy about it; and he was already wondering what effect this decision might have on other women. So he wrote to Araoz:

"If Isabel Roser has decided to come here, and thinks of making public her intention to travel to Rome, consider if it would not be well for her to give as her reason that she is going to visit the holy places, and that she will afterwards make a pilgrimage to Jerusalem and then return home to Barcelona. One can say all this without offending against the truth. I for my part am inclined to believe that the journey to Rome will be for the advantage of Isabel's spiritual life. But I do not say this in order that you should perhaps further the plan more than you have already been instructed. It is in any case better if Isabel herself makes up her mind one way or the other. If, however, she sets out on this journey, I know not what way she should take, at what time and with what companions she should travel, without causing scandal and offence, were it only subjective. God keep you. Amen."

It was too late, however. The ardently enthusiastic Isabel was already busily engaged in settling her temporal affairs. Her property was made over to her nephew Francisco Ferrer, furniture was sold, articles were packed up and given away, and countless plans for the journey were being made. Already, as we have heard, another lady had announced her intention of doing the same thing – Isabel de Josa, whose closer acquaintance we are soon to make. Man-servant and lady's maid were ready to accompany them. All these preparations lasted into October. Isabel wrote on October 1st, 1542, from her country house a long letter, the verbosity of which is highly indicative of the character and mental state of the energetic widow.[20]

The grace and love of Christ our Lord be always with us to our help and favour.

Very dear Father,

I have received a letter of yours of June 19th, with copy of another you say you sent overland and which you knew had been stopped in France, and in one of your letters a postcript of August 19th informing me that you had received some letters of mine, and that because of the haste that there was for post, and because you had already written to me, it seemed to you that what you had written was sufficient until you heard from me again. I am still in my country villa and am having the grapes harvested, but this year by the grace of God will be the last time. I want to give this property to Master Roser's nephew, to whom it should come after my death and that of the sister of the said Master Roser, with the stipulation that he leaves me in my lifetime a share in the profits and also to my sister-in-law. I yet do not clearly see the time when I shall be free from all this business, although I have a great loathing and very little affection for any of these earthly things, and this solely by the grace of God our Lord.

The project for the Hieronymites, as I have written them, has broken down, because they are not willing to have their convent reformed, and I have grown weary of persisting as the Duchess of Cardona and the Marchioness desired. I am in this city collecting up my things, vacating the house and selling the greater part of the furniture, except a chest or two of linen, either linen for the altar or household linen which I wanted to wash here and send by way of Civita Vecchia. Will you kindly write to me as to whom the linen should be sent, so that it may be disposed of according to your wishes.

I am making plans to withdraw to Santa Clara to [Sister] Rejadella's little cell and this I have told my brother, so that he will not be surprised at the household goods being sold. I shall stay in that monastery until God our Lord shall have provided a good opportunity for the journey, with your permission and blessing, as I have written you, for otherwise I have come to no final decision, because I do not want some enemy of quietude to drag me away to what suits my own will and is not with

Your Reverence's leave and the obedience due to your person as a servant of Christ our Lord. Then, however small the difficulties might be which hindered my project, it would seem to me that my presumption in going away without leave had been the cause of them.

As to what you wrote to me, that I myself can know whether I am moved by a good spirit or a bad one, and that the good always brings strength and quietness, peace and hope, whereas the bad brings fear, restlessness, strife, little faith and much dread, as I have already written to you, it seems to me, and I have the same feeling still to-day, that I desire to forget altogether all my possessions, and I have no feeling of attachment to these things. All that is a great grief to me is that I must be kept here so long with the breaking up of my home; for it troubles me that it cannot be done more quickly, whereas my own thought would be for it to be done before Lent. Then, if God our Lord gives us the blessing of peace, I could travel overland, and it would not trouble me to spend three hundred ducats for the journey, for the going would have to be at my cost. Doña Isabel de Josa has promised me that if I go, she will come, too, and will lend me for my service the mother of Suyent Sillent the seal-maker whom you know here, and I think I shall take a man-servant, the same one who has already been in my house seven years and is Damian's nephew. It is true that he is a youth, and I should like to take some man older and more experienced who would be used to going about the world. Don Diego has told me that Esteban de Guía, his brother, would be suitable and that he has received a letter from Esteban from which it appears that a lady of standing has a good opportunity of going to Rome [with him] and that on that account it seems to Don Diego I ought to write to his brother, so that we could all go together. In this I do not dare to decide to write to him, without previously having the opinion and leave of Your Reverence. I therefore ask and indeed implore you for the love of God our Lord, to whom you also owe a debt of gratitude, and because of my affection and good will and confidence, to write to me most clearly as to what God our Lord has given you to understand about the matter and what male escort I should take so that I may travel for the greater peace, quiet and security of my conscience; and if it is not possible to come overland and I find an opportunity of a good passage to Genoa, I shall not hesitate to put to sea and that with much joy, having your blessing and leave. Here I do not dare to discuss such matters seriously with anyone, because there is no one to advise me either cleric or religious; for I should not have great faith in the advice of brothers or relatives because they are my flesh and blood.

The Licentiate [Araoz] has talked to me a little. He thinks he must follow you in obedience and does not want to say anything to me about the matter beyond what is in the memorandum he showed me a little time ago which Your Reverence gave him on this business. I have written him once again from my villa here on account of the answer he sent me; and for the sake of the Passion of Christ, I beg you again not to fail to give me clear instructions for with your leave I shall go away so happy and so much at peace that it seems to me that nothing in this world will be able to hurt me. If you will give me permission, I shall leave a testamentary order concerning what I have here as revenue, arranging for two thousand ducats to be paid over to me in exchequer bills. . . .

I am so scrupulous that it always seems to me that I take the wrong course. For the love of God our Lord pardon the loquacity of my letter, but I cannot get such peace from anyone else as I can from you.

Of the sisters of Santa Clara I think the Licentiate will give you a fuller account than I can, for I have now been in the villa seven or eight days.

The departure of the Licentiate will now take place soon, unless he cannot get a passage, for he has a great desire to comply punctiliously with obedience. Once already they would have left and taken ship (for which I paid out six ducats), but the galleons in the end did not sail.

To all the brethren present and absent will you kindly remember me in our Lord especially to my dear Millán (of Loyola). I have a letter written for Millán; I do not know if he will have received it. For the love of God do not forget my soul in your Masses, for you see how much need there is of God's help and yours. I conclude, asking God's Majesty that we may know his holy will and follow it out to the full.

> The least and most useless servant,
> Isabel Roser

From the Country House, October 1st, 1542

To my dearest Father in Christ, Master Iñigo of Loyola, General of the Society of Jesus, in Rome

The warning against the deceptions of the evil spirit, with which Ignatius anxiously sought to keep his disciple at a distance, was of no avail. Isabel was firmly resolved to embark on the journey to Rome, and Ignatius was under a perpetual obligation to her for all the charity she had once shown towards him and was now showing towards his companions. Doña Isabel had besides given a temporary home to Ignatius' own nephew, Don Millán de Loyola, before the young man set off for Rome to join his uncle's new Society.

Nothing more could be done. Ignatius could only warn Father Araoz not under any circumstances to travel in the same company as Doña Isabel; for the General had had cogent reasons for recalling Araoz from Barcelona. With him was travelling also Father Diego de Eguía. When Isabel heard about Araoz' recall, she hastened while it was still night from her country house to Barcelona, there to concert counter-measures with the Vicereine and the Duchess of Cardona. Even the Emperor Charles, who was just then staying at Barcelona, was drawn into the matter – one of the earliest examples (there would be many later) of how the General's plans were crossed by the imprudent zeal of women.

But Araoz' recall was not cancelled, although Isabel sent four or five letters to Rome during October, which have not been preserved. It shows how the widow Roser already regarded herself as belonging to the Society; and the letter in which she aired her complaints to Father Ignatius could not have seemed to him a very favourable omen for his future collaboration with Isabel.[21]

IHS

The sovereign grace and love of Christ our Lord be always with us to our continual help and favour.

Very dear Father: These few days I have written you four or five letters. I have already kept you informed of the departure of Father Araoz and Don Diego. They have now been in Pálamos twelve days for, to comply with obedience, they went before I wished, for I realize the great loss they are to this city; in truth it is so great that it cannot be written about. May God forgive you for having taken them away from here, just when they were getting known and the people were going to them, some for confession, some for the Exercises, some for advice. The fruit that was produced was so great, both in the orders of nuns and among secular persons of both high and low degree, that I think that, if they had been here for some time more, it might have been possible for this city, whose need is so great, to have been said to be Christian. Now those who remain, both those beginning a Christian life and those who are established in it, feel their absence so much they every day come here lamenting over the great loss their departure makes. I do not dare tell you what my own feelings are, except that now I feel widowed anew, to find myself so deprived of company that was more angelic than human.

I hope in God our Lord that you will remember that we are all near neighbours and that some persons of quality will write to His Holiness asking him to send them back again, because since they are known here, people are very much devoted to them.

For the love of God our Lord, help us rather than hinder us, and give them back to Barcelona.

To all the brethren in our Lord, both present and absent, I ask you to give my respects. I conclude, asking God our Lord that we may know his most holy will and fulfil it perfectly.

Isabel Roser

In my earlier letters I wrote of my determination to go to Rome and see you before I die. I think my departure will be at the end of this coming February, with your blessing. Here the departure of these fathers is felt very much indeed. God forgive you, for if you knew the fruit they were producing, I do not think you would have ordered them to go. What I feel I cannot write, but I draw strength from the hope of going after them.

From Barcelona, November 6th, 1542

Ignatius must have been a little moved when he read in the postscript to this letter that the aging widow was travelling to Rome only to see him once more before her death. Later, too, on February 15th, 1547, Isabel stated in court that she went to Rome of her own free will, "out of the pious veneration that she felt towards Don Ignatius, and Don Ignatius had in no way ordered her to come".

By April 1543 things were so far advanced that Isabel, with the waiting-woman Francisca Cruyllas and her friend Isabel de Josa, could sail for Rome; and soon they appeared before the door of the house by Santa Maria della Strada. We still have an account of the impression which this meeting made upon Ignatius among the documents of beatification dated 1606, given by a very old nun of the Jerusalem convent in Barcelona, who had heard about it from Isabel Roser herself. "When Father Ignatius saw Isabel, he was highly astonished, put his hands to his head and said: 'God save me, Roser, are you here? Who brought you?' And she answered: 'God and you, Father.'"

From Genoa arrived a whole shipload of chests and boxes, in charge of one of her servants. The ladies were at first lodged in a private house, and the

282

lay-brother Esteban de Eguía, Father Diego's brother, had to wait on them. This was no small matter for the elderly and highborn Eguía, who out of humility had wished to be only a lay-brother. In a report dated May 3rd, 1547, when all was over, we read: "Esteban de Eguía, that nobly born old man, had the duty of looking after her night and day, and he continued in this service for two years. He had to wait upon her, accompany her to church, even to sweep out her apartments, and help her into the saddle whenever she had a mind to go riding." Everything was done for Sister Roser.

Ignatius must soon have felt some anxiety; but Araoz, who had returned to Spain, rejoiced at the successful turn of events. Nearly all his letters to Ignatius contained heartiest greetings for "Sister and Mother Isabel" and the worthy Cruyllas. "Our Lord grant that she may know and feel that perfection and peace which my soul desires for her." The nuns of Barcelona too, he reported, especially Sister Rejadella, were envious of "Sister Roser" and her companions. The example of Doña Isabel was, as we shall see, to start a fashion in Spain.[22]

But how were these women to be usefully employed? An answer was soon found – Isabel had arrived in Rome just at the time when Ignatius was occupied with the plans of a house for fallen girls. On February 16th, 1543, Paul III had established by solemn bull the *Compagnia della Grazia* which Ignatius had initiated to take over the running of the future House of St. Martha. In January 1544 the house was being furnished, and the help of the ladies from Barcelona was very welcome. With Madama and Vittoria Colonna, Isabel too now worked energetically and efficiently at the great task. After all, she was used to associating with ladies of such exalted position. When the pontifical postmaster, Mattia di San Cassiano, raised a storm because the zeal of Ignatius and his female helpers had estranged his mistress from him and induced her to enter the House of St. Martha, Isabel wrote a letter on March 27th, 1545, to Margaret of Austria, who had recently become Duchess of Camerino. Its orthography is frightful, as is that of her letters to Ignatius, which are an odd mixture of Catalan and Castilian; but what she says is extremely vivid and deserves to be printed in full. Madama no doubt read it with patience, out of reverence for Ignatius.[23]

Your Excellency, my Lady,

May the grace and blessing of our Lord Jesus Christ be always with Your Excellency and protect you!

I do not know if you have already heard that I have for some while been living in this convent of St. Martha, for the service of God and the solace of my neighbour. My presence here was urgently desired as being a comfort to the inmates; and they implored me for the sake of Christ's passion not to forsake them and to go and live with them. When I observed their feelings towards me, I longed to fulfil this request, for I thought how God our Lord deigned to send his only-begotten Son for the salvation of souls. And although I myself am so wretched and destitute of virtue, yet I trust in his divine Majesty that he will give me his grace, that we may all serve him. I am, therefore, come to live among them; and, indeed, I am highly pleased to see how they labour in the service of his most high Majesty, how they dwell together in peace and love and practise obedience, so that one can only praise God for it.

But the Devil, who is ever envious and sows the seeds of evil, has taken possession of Signor Mattia [di San Cassiano]. This man causes us much annoyance and behaves with great effrontery towards us. Among other things, he forced his way into our church and dragged the priest (who was just hearing some of the girls' confessions) out of the confessional, saying as he did so innumerable lewd words, which I cannot here write down. And he spoke in the same way of all those who have devoted themselves to the service of this house. Yesterday, Thursday, he came twice to the convent door and called out the portress, shouting all kinds of insults and impudent words, saying it was an affront to him that the woman who had once been his mistress should now dwell in a horrible convent. It would be an easy thing for him (he said) to get her out again or to reduce the convent to ruins. And I see him to be so without fear of God and so shameless before the world, that I fear there will be a scandal; for he goes several times a day to the house of a wicked woman quite near our convent, and this might cause much mischief and scandal. May God forbid that I should have to experience such things for my sins before I die!

As I cannot appeal to anyone, after God, except Your Excellency, I humbly beg for the sake of the five wounds of Jesus Christ that you will do us the favour of saying a few words to His Holiness in defence of this house, that the Pope may intervene in the matter. And would Your Excellency please order the police to keep guard at our gate for most of the night, at least until Easter, so that that unpredictable man may not cause a scandal just in Holy Week.

I respectfully beg Your Excellency to forgive the boldness of my request. I cast myself as your servant and handmaid at Your Excellency's feet, and pray you as my mistress graciously to help me. And so I conclude with a prayer to the Most Holy Trinity, that your life may be prosperous in God's holy service.

From the Convent of St. Martha,
  this day, Friday before Palm Sunday
  Your Excellency's humble handmaid, who kisses your feet and hands,

Isabel Roser

Sister Isabel lived in the House of St. Martha and acted as a kind of Mother Superior, still loyally served by the faithful Cruyllas. She was soon joined by a Roman lady, who had known Ignatius for years and had formerly been a greater admirer of Francis Xavier. Because of her piety she was jokingly called the "Capuchin nun". This was Donna Lucrezia di Bradine. Things seemed to be going well.

Now, however, another question arose, which the zealous disciple had put to her Master at the very beginning; namely, what form her vows and her actual admittance to the Society were to take? Evidently Ignatius knew how to put off a decision as long as possible. Two whole years passed before Isabel, her objective always in view, managed, as it were, to pin him down. The energetic lady had applied to the Pope, to procure from him not only permission to take vows, but also a papal command to Ignatius to accept such vows. She succeeded. This was immediately before Christmas 1545. Isabel's petition to Paul III is as follows:[24]

Holy Father,

I am a poor wretched woman of Barcelona, and I travelled hither two years ago to meet a great servant of God named Master Ignatius of Loyola, with whom I became acquainted twenty-two years ago as a man eager to do penance. I am quite devoted to him. As I am a widow and independent, I wished to seek him out here, that he might lead me to serve God my Lord better. I spoke with him and observed in Master Ignatius as in the other members of his Society exceptional virtue and perfection; so I made a vow to place myself under his obedience and vowed poverty and chastity. . . . Humbly I now pray Your Holiness to grant that I may be admitted to the said Society of Jesus, and to command Master Ignatius to accept my solemn vows, that he may concern himself throughout his life with the salvation of my soul as with that of his own sons, and make me a participant in the merits and graces which Your Holiness has granted to the Society. Humbly I pray also that

285

Your Holiness will give me somebody to accompany me, who will speak to Master Ignatius in the name of Your Holiness, that the latter may give me the favour for which I beg and may fully believe that Your Holiness has granted this my petition. Furthermore, I pray that Your Holiness will grant the same permission to one of my female servants, that we may both be able to take the vow of obedience.

Ignatius was not very pleased about this move of his devotee, as is shown in a letter which he wrote in November of the same year to Rodríguez in Portugal about all the vexations he was having because of Isabel and her companions. It was not surprising. Señora Roser had always been a rich and independent woman; she was now no longer young, and she had little understanding for the spirit of the religious life. It was therefore impossible to re-educate her, nervous and even hysterical as she was, to a life of real poverty and complete dependence under obedience. Besides, as Ignatius had already learned by experience with the ladies who assisted him in his works of charity, a laywoman could be a more effective helper and less hampered in her task than a religious.

All this counted for nothing with Isabel. By Christmas she had, with all the cunning and industry of which she was capable, obtained what she wanted-ed. On the eve of the feast, in virtue of an oral bequest of her late husband, she gave the rest of her property to the Jesuits. Ignatius, who clearly had a presentiment of what was to come, prudently renounced the gift by a declaration before a notary on the following day, and restored it, for the time being at least, to Isabel. This somewhat complicated procedure was not contrary to the vow of poverty which she made, for, as Ignatius was later to emphasize particularly, Sister Isabel's profession was accepted by him only on certain conditions. This appears also from the hitherto un-published text of the vow, which no doubt was drawn up by Ignatius himself, and the original of which, written in Catalan by Isabel Roser with her own hand, is still in the archives of the Society at Rome.

On Christmas Day 1545, the three women knelt before the altar in the little church of Santa Maria della Strada in the presence of their revered Master Ignatius, and pronounced the vows of the Society of Jesus. They were Isabel Roser, Lucrezia di Bradine, and Francisca Cruyllas. Isabel solemnly read the following text:[25]

I, Isabel Roser, widow, the undersigned, promise and solemnly vow before God Our Almighty Lord, in the presence of the Holy Virgin Mary my mistress, St. Jerome and the heavenly court of Paradise and before all who are present – and before you most Reverend Father Ignatius, General of the Society of Jesus, our Lord, as the representative of God: perpetual poverty, according to the limits which are laid upon me by your Reverence, chastity, and obedience to the rule of life laid before me by your Reverence.

Given in Rome in the church of Santa Maria della Strada on the day of the birth of Our Lord Jesus Christ in the year, 1545.

I, Isabel Roser, Widow

Thus was laid, at least in principle, the foundation of an order of female Jesuits. It was a far from welcome Christmas present for Ignatius; but gratitude, added to the obedience which he owed to the Pope, had overcome his objections. Sister Isabel, who cherished a special devotion to St. Jerome, must have felt like the holy widow Paula of Rome. In Barcelona they were proud of her.

There now began an almost comic battle between Ignatius and his spiritual daughter. The final result, however, was of decisive importance for the early history of the Society of Jesus. What Ignatius had feared was to become painful reality during the first weeks of 1546. Father Nadal, who had entered the Society at Rome in the previous October, was scandalized by the fact that Sister Isabel got her food daily from the Fathers' kitchen. Years later, in his lectures on the Constitutions, he related of those days: "When Ignatius at the command of Pope Paul III had taken three women under his obedience, they kept all of us, who were in Rome at that time, continuously busy." The young scholastic Benedetto Palmio told in his autobiography how Isabel in her importunate love imposed herself as nurse upon the sick Ignatius, and how the patient General had to listen almost daily to her complaints and scruples and comfort her.

Finally, however, even Ignatius flared up in anger. Sister Isabel had, without asking anyone, invited two of her Ferrer nephews to come to Rome, in order to find a suitable wife for one of them, Dr. Francisco Ferrer. The two gentlemen came with all haste; for they found it intolerable that their rich aunt had now bequeathed even what was left of her property to the Jesuits. An imprudent letter of the French Father Cogordan to Isabel made the pious "sisters" furious in their turn. Ignatius had great difficulty in smoothing things over. From the spring of 1546, therefore, he resolved that this state of affairs must end. Early in April he told the Pope of his troubles and found a sympathetic hearing. Paul III gave oral permission for the women to be released from the vows which he had not long before ordered them to make.

287

It seems that Ignatius, so prudent in all things and unwilling to appear unduly harsh, continued to think the matter over for a long time – gratitude and prudence were still at war within him. Isabel also became less sure of herself. In May 1546 she hinted in a letter to the Bishop of Barcelona that she would soon return to the Catalan capital – as a Jesuitess, of course. In the summer of 1546, Ignatius' cup was full; he had had enough of his spiritual daughter. He laid the case with some urgency before Cardinal Ardinghelli, and the latter asked the Pope in Orvieto to examine it and give a decision. The answer was favourable. Ignatius, the one-time army officer, moved forward, as it were, to the attack. First he summoned a meeting for September 30th, 1546, in the house of the Spanish ambassadress Leonor Osorio. The atmosphere was decidedly strained, for the discussion at the meeting – evidently under the nephews' influence – took the form of barefaced demands for money. Isabel did not hesitate to present her Ignatius with a detailed list of all the gifts, including their exact value, which she had given the Jesuits in Barcelona and Rome. Sheets, napkins, palliasses and silken vestments appear in motley succession in this Catalan document. The total value in money and goods amounted to 465 gold *scudi*.

Sister Isabel had, however, underestimated the man she was dealing with. Ignatius in turn produced an account, proving in detail that, if reckonings were to be made at all, she owed money to the Jesuits. The session lasted for hours. Neither the tears nor the indignation of the excited woman could move Ignatius. Isabel even tried a kind of pious bribery: she hinted that a gift of 200 ducats to the House of St. Martha would follow a decision favourable to her. The report states: "Master Ignatius answered: 'Whether she gives the 200 ducats or not will not affect my decision, which has been made for God's greater glory'."

On the same evening Ignatius drafted in his room a letter of renunciation to his former benefactress. The next day, on October 1st, 1546, the letter was completed; and Father Nadal, on Ignatius' behalf, had to hand it solemnly to Sister Isabel.[26]

To Isabel Roser, venerable Lady,
my mother and sister in Jesus Christ.

It is true that for God's greater glory I should like to satisfy your good desires and have you under the bond of obedience, as up to now you have been for some time. In that way I should be able to exercise the care necessary for the surer salvation and greater perfection of your soul. Nevertheless, since I do not find within my power the strength

I desire for this because of my continual infirmities and the being occupied in matters for which I have a primary obligation to God our Lord
or to his Vicar on earth, and, moreover, since according to my conscience, it is not fitting for this little Society to have special charge of
women bound to us by vows of obedience, as six months ago now I
explained at length to His Holiness, it has seemed to me for God's greater
glory that I should withdraw and separate myself from this care of
having you as a spiritual daughter under obedience, having your rather
as a good and pious mother, as you have been to me for several years
now for the greater glory of God our Lord. Accordingly, for the greater
service, praise and glory of his eternal goodness, as much as I can (always
excepting all higher authority) I hand you over to the most prudent
judgment, ordinance and will of the Sovereign Pontiff so that your soul
may be tranquil and comforted in all things to God's greater glory.

Ignatius

In Rome, October 1st, 1546

Ignatius must have breathed a sigh of relief when Nadal returned from
his mission. Solemnly, four times in succession, he had had to read the
letter aloud to Isabel in the presence of witnesses. Even Ignatius must have
realized, however, that war against a pious woman is no child's play.
Indignant, and harassed moreover by sickness, Doña Isabel left the House
of St. Martha and took up residence in the home of a Catalan fellow-countryman called Juan Bosch, which was to be for more than four months the
headquarters of Ignatius' opponents.

On November 3rd, 1546, Isabel and Francisca Cruyllas received the papal
brief by which their vows were commuted to vows of obedience to the
diocesan bishop; but the three nuns continued to share in the spiritual
merits of the Society of Jesus during their lifetime. Lucrezia di Bradine entered
another convent in Rome and later one in Naples. The pious Francisca
Cruyllas submitted humbly and with much weeping; she later became a
nun in the great Hospital of the Cross at Barcelona.

Isabel, however, had no intention at all of retreating from the battle-
field. Her tears and complaints made a deep impression on Cardinal Carpi
and the papal Vicar General. Great excitement prevailed in pious circles
concerning the case. "O Rome, how canst thou endure such a thing?"
exclaimed a lady in the house of the Spanish ambassador Juan de Vega. In
fact, Isabel and her two nephews succeeded in bringing the matter before a
spiritual court. The documents in the case still exist. Dr. Francisco Ferrer, in

the name of his injured aunt, summed up the complaint against the Jesuits in the following curt sentences: "These Jesuits are rogues. Ignatius wished to steal all my aunt's fortune; he is a hypocrite and a thief."[27] The decision of the judges, as was to be expected, was a victory for Ignatius all along the line. Sentence was pronounced against Isabel, and she signed the following declaration: "I, Isabel Roser, widow, of Barcelona, herewith declare that I have not given any money or other property to the priests of the Society of Jesus in Rome in response to any demand or request or importunity. If I have given anything, it was purely for the love of God and of my own free will. And those calumnies which circulate among the people, to the effect that I have ever done or said anything contrary to the above, are untrue. I, the widow Roser, confirm this with my own signature. February 12th, 1547."

Thus the war ended. Ignatius hastened to act upon the lesson he had learnt. In May 1547 he petitioned Pope Paul III to free the Jesuits for all time from the spiritual direction of women who, living together as a community, wished to place themselves under the obedience of the priests of the Society of Jesus. The story of Isabel Roser had lasting results.

Isabel remained a few months longer in Rome; for malicious talk about the legal complications in which she was involved had already reached Barcelona, and it therefore seemed advisable to wait till her own temper and that of others had calmed down. In a letter to Juan Boquet in Barcelona, Ignatius wrote: "Señora Roser is soon leaving here, and under what circumstances she is leaving God knows! I would rather have had it otherwise. The Devil has sown tares here."

It is significant for the mysteries of feminine piety and for Ignatius' skill as a spiritual director that, before her departure, Isabel made a long and sincere confession to Ignatius in the church of Santa Maria della Strada. They parted from one another in peace, in spite of everything. Having hardly reached Barcelona she sent to her still beloved Master a touching letter with a request that he would forgive her for all the trouble she had caused.[28]

Most reverend and virtuous Father,

May the love and charity of Jesus Christ our Lord be in our souls.

Considering my great wretchedness, my imperfections and my lack of all things, I did not venture to dare to write to Your Paternity. Yet since I am so much in your debt for the very many spiritual benefits received from Your Paternity and from all others in your house, and for the many labours and much toil and fatigue you have suffered and undergone for me, I beg you for reverence of the Passion of Jesus Christ our Lord, and by his precious blood, to forgive me, and thus in this letter I humbly ask your pardon, confessing my imperfection and my wretchedness, not knowing how to draw profit from the virtue of humility and patience. Rather do I confess my lack of mortification, and when I once more considered all that had happened, I came near to losing courage. The mercy and goodness of God our Lord, however, is so great that he has not regarded my sins and weaknesses, rather like a most loving Father he has guarded me and brought me to this city to care for small orphans, for those we now have in the house are twenty-nine, not counting those that have been placed in service, and through the lack of the necessary formalities for the bull and indults there is no one to care for them except Mosén Caselles. May our Lord grant them someone to concern himself with them for in truth they need this very much.

May our Lord fill you with his grace, and although I do not deserve that Your Paternity should remember me in your Masses and prayers, your charity will [I know] extend to this. Thus I beg this of you and I ask the same of your sons for, although I am such a wretched sinner, I do not forget to pray to God, whenever I see him in the hands of the priest, for Your Paternity and those of your house, and I bear you all no less love and affection than formerly. God our Lord is my witness of this. I conclude, kissing Your Paternity's hands and praying God's Majesty that he would let us live and die in his holy love and service.

Your Paternity's unworthy and useless servant,
Widow Isabel Roser

From Barcelona, December 10th, 1547

What follows is like a transfiguring sunset glow after all these storms. In spite of old age and sickness, Isabel remained true to the ascetic ideal she had learnt from Ignatius. At first she adapted a small house as an orphanage and looked after the children; but Ignatius in that last confession had evidently advised her to enter the Franciscan convent of Holy Jerusalem at Barcelona. This was one of the few convents that in earlier days had pleased Ignatius by its faithfulness to the rule. There, on the feast of the Epiphany 1550, Isabel took the veil. Her co-operation in the great work of the Society of Jesus now took the form of prayer and sacrifice. From there she sent on February 5th a letter full of joy and holy peace to her beloved Ignatius.[29]

May the most sweet Jesus our Lord be always praised, served and loved. Amen.

Since I have received such great benefits and favours from Your Paternity and because I am certain that you will be glad to hear from me, I give you news that the orphans are well provided for and have a good administrator to look after them. Nevertheless, I did not want to have no share in the matter and so I decided, with God's help, to give them one thousand pounds of revenue at the rate of fifty pounds each year. The rest of my resources I am dividing between the hospital I have erected here and various Christian persons, and in establishing the poor relatives of Mosén Roser, and other poor people ashamed of their poverty with a sum apiece as a help to marrying their daughters. I will allow Francisca Cruyllas a sum for life so that she is not in need and can serve the sick in hospital.

By the grace of my Lord Jesus Christ I am not in my home, which I have shut up because I determined to retire to a religious house, as I told Your Paternity when you heard my confession in the chapel of our Lady of the Wayside. Although the time I said has lengthened, my intention has not changed and God's Majesty out of his wonted mercy has brought me into this holy monastery of Jerusalem, although I am altogether unworthy of it. The Most Reverend Lady Abbess is Sister Isabel Durala. She kisses Your Paternity's hands for she is very devoted to you. I entered and took the habit on the day of our Lady of Good Hope a year ago. We are fifty-two nuns, with so much love and charity among us that it is a matter for thanksgiving to God our Lord. The black veil I received on the day of the three Kings. We have already sent for Father John Queralt and other fathers who belong to the Society here in Barcelona. I do not know if they have already written you about this. . . . I have asked leave to write to Your Paternity, begging you by the wounds of Jesus Christ our Lord, not to forget me in your Masses and prayers, and to charge the other members of the Society to do the same. I assure you in very truth that each day that I hear Mass, when the priest holds our Lord in his hands, I make supplication and pray for you and the whole Society. Although I am so unworthy and such a great sinner, I hope in God's wonted mercy that he will do me the favour of hearing me and thus I shall please him.

Although this letter deserves no reply I venture all the same to ask for one, which would be a great consolation to me.

To Father Master Miona and all the fathers of the Society, it remains for me to send my greetings. Please forgive my writing you so often and at such length. I always forget myself.

May our Lord God give us grace that we may serve him in this life and in the next enjoy the contemplation of His Majesty. I remain, kissing Your Paternity's hands,

Your Paternity's affectionate and devoted
Sister Isabel Roser

From the Convent of Holy Jerusalem,
February 5th, 1550

To the most reverend and virtuous Master Ignatius of Loyola, General of the Society of Jesus, in Rome

The saint's answer, dated September 3rd of the same year, has unfortunately not been preserved. Through the Fathers in Barcelona, Ignatius kept in touch with his friend. Isabel was now ill and infirm with age and had to be carried into church on a chair. Constantly she told her fellow-nuns about Ignatius, and many years later the aged Sister Angélica Jovells bore witness that the tears of emotion, which flowed from Isabel's eyes as she talked, were "heartbreaking".[30] Once more the aged Isabel Roser looked back to her Roman days, as on April 20th, 1554, her last letter to Ignatius was written.

JESUS MARIA

May the divine love of Christ our Lord give us his grace that we may serve him with a pure heart.

Most loving Father:

I do not know how I dare, both on account of the very great benefits and favours received from you and the Society and because of my ingratitude and lack of appreciation, to write you asking you for pardon. Since, however, I am so certain of your charity and kindness, and for reverence towards the wounds and precious blood of Jesus Christ our Lord and God, through whom I ask pardon, it will not be refused me. In this faith I live and through the mercies which his divine Majesty grants me, when I am such a great sinner and worthy of hell, I know that in your Masses you do not forget me. Through his grace I feel such an utter abhorrence for the world that I have forgotten both my kindred and my estates, so that I never think of setting foot in the latter, except to be with the little orphans. I live in the house near this monastery to keep myself quiet and free from much talking except with these mothers. The most Reverend Lady Abbess and the Mother Vicar are so full of charity that I am frequently asked to go in and see them and on this with the grace of God our Lord I am determined because that is what I need.

I made the orphans a certain gift and one morning, the feast of our Lady of Good Hope, three hours before daybreak, accompanied by the children I entered this holy cloister. My brothers and relatives had no suspicion of it, but their tears did not move me to compassion. This grace I have not deserved on account of my sins and imperfections. It was a great mercy of my Lord and God obtained through the intercession of Your Reverence's Masses and prayers. These I beseech you not to fail to continue until the end of my days, that God may give me grace to live and die in his holy love as a true religious. Be certain that, unworthy and wretched as I am, I pray many times a day for Your Reverence and the whole Society. My Lord Jesus Christ has given me a Reverend Mother Abbess so devoted and affectionate towards Your Reverence and the whole Society, that it is always a great consolation to me. We often see letters telling us what the Lord is working in the Indies through the fathers of the Society, the Abbess has these letters read in the refectory and bids all pray God our Lord for the whole Society. When I told her that I received the Holy Sacrament every Sunday and that Your Reverence praised [this custom], she said to me: "Although our rule does not order it, for your consolation and mine let those sisters who desire to do this through devotion do likewise." Thus we began, her Reverence and five or six, and now by the grace of our Lord we are sixteen to twenty. Praise be to God.

I think the Reverend Mother Abbess is writing to you and I, therefore, refer you to her letter. Only for charity's sake, I ask you to write me a letter, as to what I have to do to serve my Lord Christ better. My chest is troubling me and my whole body is full of pains, so that I cannot walk except from my chair to the choir and when it is absolutely necessary go to the parlour at a late hour, with someone to help me come down. Thanks be given to God's Majesty for the favour he does me in chastising my body for it was the cause that the soul failed to serve its Creator and Redeemer. May he be always praised and continually served.

Pardon my loquacity, Father, but it is a great relief to me to give you an account of what has happened and I assure you that very frequently my soul communes with yours. Might it please God's goodness that my soul might resemble yours. Then I should be content.

I make an end, but I make no end to the request for something written in your hand for the greater quiet of my conscience.

To the Father Master Laynez, to Fathers Salmerón and Miona, I would like to be remembered and to all the others. I kiss Your Reverence's hands and ask your blessing. I conclude, asking our Lord Jesus Christ that we may accomplish his holy will in this life and see each other in glory in eternity where may we praise his divine Majesty for ever.

Your Reverence's very affectionate and unworthy servant
Sister Isabel Roser

From the Convent of Holy Jerusalem, April 20th, 1554

To the most reverend and dear father in Christ our Lord, the General of the Society of Jesus, our Ignatius of Loyola

At the end of the same year, Isabel died a holy death. On January 28th, 1555, Ignatius wrote to Araoz: "We have already received the news of Mother Roser's death, and we have lovingly said our office for her. *Requiescat in pace!*"[31]

295

Isabel de Josa

THE other lady from Barcelona who joined Isabel Roser in the Roman adventure was Isabel de Josa. She too was one of the group of aristocratic helpers who supported the student Ignatius in Paris with gifts of money. Ignatius names her with gratitude in the letter to Inés Pascual of June 13th, 1533.

Isabel de Josa belonged, as we learn from the documents concerning Ignatius' beatification, to one of the noblest families of Barcelona. She married Don Guillém de Josa and had a son of the same name, who in May 1535 married the daughter of the Bishop of Barcelona, Don Juan de Cardona, of the famous ducal house. Because of this, Isabel was on terms of close friendship with Doña Aldonza de Cardona, who was also one of Ignatius' admirers. We know that in 1539 she was a widow and head of the pious confraternity of the Precious Blood, which met regularly at her house. In the same year she met the young Antonio Araoz, who at once sent Ignatius an enthusiastic account of all the profound discussions he had been having with her and Aldonza de Cardona about miracles and revelations, describing Isabel as a woman of sensibility and a skilful talker. He wrote:

"Doña Isabel de Josa has been a source of great consolation to me. She talked to me – as she likes to do – with her usual kindness about her spiritual life from her youth onwards. In the presence of several witnesses she bore witness to the esteem in which she holds you; and she showed herself much pleased by all that had happened [at Rome]. We discussed many questions with one another, as for example, how Satan can transform himself into an angel of light; and in this connection she told me that she did not think much of revelations and was rather incredulous about them. I agreed with her on this subject as far as I possibly could; but then I embarked on a different theme, and I hope I satisfied her. At all events, she asked me on her knees and with marked humility for my blessing, in the presence of many persons of distinction."

All these women were united in a common admiration for Ignatius: "They revered him like an apostle", old Juan Pascual was to testify many years later. Isabel de Josa, however, surpassed her companions in one respect, which in those days made her remarkable: not only did she speak and write excellent Latin, but she was also familiar with scholastic philosophy, especially with that of Duns Scotus, called because of the acuteness of his mind *Doctor Subtilis*. She was, therefore, the pride of the pious society of Barcelona, and it was said later that she once gave a public lecture. She was compared with Plato's Diotima and also, on account of her virtue, with the Roman widow Paula, the friend of St. Jerome.[32]

That this clever woman decided to travel to Rome with Isabel Roser in order to join the Society of Jesus was no doubt felt by Father Araoz to be a special triumph. Towards the end of 1542, plans for the journey were so far advanced that Isabel thought it was now her duty to write a letter to the Master in Rome. It is not dated, but almost certainly it was sent at the same time as Isabel Roser's letter of November 6th, 1542. It was not without feminine vanity that "Sister Isabel" (as she signed herself) wrote this epistle in elegant Latin; but in the General's office they were highly delighted. Such a letter, in which the soul is even spoken of as *forma corporis,* deserved to be read to all members of the Society. Thus the first Jesuits heard in an edifying encyclical about the plans of the ladies from Barcelona.[33]

Most reverend Father,

Through the grace of God I have seen your letters which have reassured me about your health. Being, indeed, a lazy and negligent person, I have not written until now, excepting a signature which I once appended to a letter of Doña Isabel Roser, my sister in Christ. From that you can see that although we may have two bodies, nevertheless, we feel we have only one soul. For, indeed, the soul is rather where one loves than where it informs a body. Therefore, I declare that it is my wish, by God's help, to progress further in those things which I have already begun, if this is pleasing to God. I was delighted to learn from your letters that you will be equally glad if we proceed to Rome together. This, I think, will be as soon as possible, if God grants us health. We shall travel in the company of a gentleman who is completely devoted to Your Paternity and has already received his instructions from Father Licentiate Araoz; he is himself a Doctor and distinguished for his learning. I will not say more, except, indeed, that I am unwilling to put things into writing, because I desire to see Your Reverence. This, therefore, only as a token of my reverence; I kiss Your Paternity's hand,

Sister Isabel Josa

To Father Ignatius Loyola

Isabel did in fact arrive in Rome with her friends in April 1543. It is, however, noteworthy that in all the documents concerning the plan to take vows and its execution her name does not appear. Evidently Isabel de Josa was more reasonable and did not join the new community. In December 1545 she was certainly still in Rome, for Araoz at that time sent her special greetings; but he called her "Señora" in contrast with "Sisters" Roser and Cruyllas. We hear too that the learned woman once expounded the philosophy of Scotus before some of the cardinals. From this fact, it seems, later developed the story, which we meet in the beatification documents of Ignatius, that Isabel even preached before the Pope. The only other thing we know about her is that she died soon after 1570. She was, as the same documents state, a woman of high repute for learning and virtue.[34]

Sebastiana Exarch

THE news of the admittance of the women from Barcelona into Ignatius of Loyola's new Society continued to spread in Spain. In Madrid at the house of Doña Leonor Mascarenhas, in Gandía among the Borgia ladies, even in the Portuguese court, the subject was eagerly discussed. Ignatius was at that time in correspondence with his friend Juan de Castro, the Carthusian monk of Val de Cristo near Segorbe, where he had visited him in 1535. Unfortunately, the whole of this correspondence is now lost. A lady in Valencia had seen the letters Ignatius sent to the monk, and she had got from them a desire for a fuller spiritual life. She was the wife of a rich citizen called Don Francisco Exarch, and her name was Sebastiana. Although not long married, this spiritually ambitious woman felt the matrimonial state to be a hindrance on the way to God. Since she had heard from the Carthusian about the distant Ignatius, she had had but one idea: from one year to the next she waited for the coming of one of the great man's sons, that she might discuss with him the spiritual problems that weighed upon her.

In 1544 Father Araoz came from Barcelona, still full of enthusiasm about the plans of Isabel Roser and her companions, to spend a short time at Valencia. We are doubtless right in supposing that Araoz first inspired Doña Sebastiana, eager for spiritual stimuli, with the idea of following in their footsteps. But Araoz had to depart suddenly, and on July 1st, 1544, Father Diego Mirón replaced him. Doña Sebastiana was delighted. She became his penitent, and the Jesuit, still somewhat inexperienced as a spiritual director, soon allowed himself to be persuaded to let her perform all the Spiritual Exercises. This was simply too much for the good lady. She could not expect that her husband would understand her. He was a decent Christian man, who had supported the Jesuits on their first arrival in Valencia, but otherwise had little time for his wife's spiritual aspirations. She therefore believed that the only thing for her to do on completing the Spiritual Exercises was to make a vow of perfect obedience to her confessor without her husband's knowledge and thus, she thought, be admitted in a real sense to the Society of Jesus.

Good Father Mirón was highly embarrassed: the spiritual zeal of his penitent seemed almost uncanny. Moreover, he knew exactly how Ignatius in Rome thought about such things. On July 16th, 1545, he sought Ignatius' advice in a long letter, which does indeed praise the good intentions of Sebastiana, but admits in moving terms the helplessness of the writer. Besides, the Jesuits had been warned to use care in Valencia concerning this very matter; for Doña Sebastiana was not the only woman who cherished such projects. We shall soon hear more about her friend Juana de Cardona. In Valencia, too, lived the widowed Duchess of Gandía, who had to be handled very carefully. She was the stepmother of Duke Francis Borgia. Of the former consort of King Ferdinand of Aragon, Germaine de Foix, who was spending the sad evening of her days at Valencia as dowager Duchess of Calabria, Father Mirón had to report to Ignatius that she was not very fond of the Jesuits. The former page, who had so often had to wait on Germaine, presumably did not take it to heart. More important, however, was what he was told a year later. The saintly Bishop of Valencia, Thomas de Villanueva, in a conversation with Father Araoz, also criticized the pastoral methods of the Jesuits, especially in that they gave women the Spiritual Exercises to perform "in profound secrecy and silence", after the manner of the suspect *Alumbrados*. Araoz added that the mistrust of the Archbishop dated from the time when Ignatius stayed at Valencia in the summer of 1535, and apparently even then gave retreats to women.[35]

All precautions were, however, in vain. Doña Sebastiana wrote on the same day as Mirón a long letter to Ignatius, the climax of which was the expression of a wish to be admitted to the obedience of the Society of Jesus.

Very reverend Lord and Father in Christ.

It is already five [years] since it pleased the Lord to move my soul to serve him more than I have done till now. This came about through certain letters which came from Rome, written if I am not mistaken to Father Don Juan de Castro. It pleased the Lord to inspire me with longing to do something over and above what I could accomplish in actual fact, notwithstanding the state in which the Lord has placed me, which is to be married. Certainly if at this time the Lord God had given me the state of liberty, by his grace I should have done what His Majesty counselled, which is, to sell what I have and give to the poor and throw myself at Your Reverence's feet and beg you to allow me to follow you. My soul, indeed, had only one desire and hope, to go to Christ with the help of your holy example. Thus, in the faith and hope that someone of the holy Society would come to these parts, I have lived all this time. In truth, however, I could not say living, because it has not been a life with Christ, but rather like that of a little lost sheep without a shepherd, living only with the desire – but how great a desire – that the Lord would send the Very Reverend Father Araoz, who went to Portugal, and of whom it was said that he was to reside at the court of the Prince of Spain, here. Praised be the Lord, because when he came the desire of my soul increased more, through his teaching and example. His departure was so sudden that there only remains the fragrance of his charity. I was as a poor orphan bereft of all good until God through his mercy willed to send me a new, most salutary remedy for my soul, through the coming of Father Master Mirón. To him I addressed myself with very good heart and with genuine faith that God could not but have mercy on my soul through the teaching and charity I received from his holy soul. Thus I have set him as intercessor between God and myself.

My soul, however, feels deeply that that is not sufficient for God's service – although we cannot serve him as he deserves, at least we should do the little we can and with all our strength. I feel, indeed, and this is a fact, that he is an unfaithful servant who does not do all that lies in him, even to dying with Christ on the cross, and more, if more were possible, sincerely desiring that God will give him the grace of suffering this. Such a man feels that he has done nothing and is a useless and un-profitable servant. I have sufficient trust in the goodness and mercy of our Lord Jesus Christ, and in the humility of his servants, to have the courage to importune Your Reverence. Because you are the spiritual father of Master Mirón, you are also my superior and so I can give you an account of my life as your least little daughter, humbly begging you to listen.

It was only a very few days since these Fathers came here – I think it would be three or four. I had a great desire to see them, thinking thereby to serve the Lord more. I saw them and suddenly the next day – I think it was Saturday – I went to confession to Father Master Mirón. It was already more than three years since the Lord through his mercy gave me the grace of communicating every Sunday. Feeling the benefit of this and knowing the great need of my soul, I asked Father Mirón with great earnestness for the Exercises. I was so importunate and persisted for so long that out of charity he was forced to give them to me. It has pleased the Lord to enlighten the eyes of my soul, so that I realize what a lost and degenerate creature I was then. I lifted up my heart to God, giving myself wholly to him, asking him to open the way for me so that his holy will might be done in me. Remembering that the Lord was obedient unto death, even the death of the cross, I offered myself to him to be under the yoke of obedience and to renounce my own will all the days of my life, considering myself as dead in his sight and the sight of men, and reminding myself that the same Lord says that the grain of wheat first has to die before it bears fruit and after it is dead it will bring forth much fruit. I never ceased to recommend myself in my poor prayers to our Lord God that he would inspire me with what would be for his greater service.

I felt continually that I should make my obedience into the hands of my Father Master Mirón; I twice offered this resolution to God before opening my mind to the Father although when he came into this city I gave him a hint of this, but he dutifully put it aside. Afterwards, strong in the confidence which the Lord gave me, I asked it of him with great insistency, having great faith in our Lord that he would give me the grace of Master Mirón's granting me this privilege. He, however, would not grant it me telling me that I was married, that this was a thing I could not do, and that his counselling me was sufficient.

My soul could not be at peace because of the longing the Lord gave me – which grew in it. I was continually considering what greater service I could do for God than divest myself of my own will and renounce myself so that the Lord should live in me. In the supposition that other married ladies had acted in this way, I did not cease to ask Master Mirón for it with great insistency and finally begged him to not fail in charity to my soul but to grant my request, so that I could carry out with merit the commands which he would give me before God, and since I naturally would not fail to satisfy the obligations arising out of my marriage, the Lord would thus be better served.

Seeing my importunity and the faith which the Lord had given me in this matter, Father Master Mirón told me that he would not do it without leave of Your Reverence and a brief from the Pope, although I had heard it said that one from the archbishop was sufficient. Therefore, prostrate before God and Your Reverence, with all the reverence and humility I can, I beg you to grant me this permission for my Father so that he may be able to receive this poor offering which I make to God from my unworthy soul. For the love of our Lord I ask you not to consider the wretchedness of my state in being a woman but rather the mercy the Lord has shown me in willing to place desires for him in a vessel so wretched and of so little worth as mine. Consider that as the Lord makes no exception of persons, so he leads all, both single and married, straight to him. I hope, then, in God, my Lord and Father, that a soul so much God's servant as is that of Your Reverence, will not refuse this charity to mine, in which the Lord has placed so great a desire of serving him.

Furthermore I ask that this should be without my husband's knowing it, not because he is not a great servant of the Lord, but because God has not given him understanding for this, and, in order not to disturb his soul, I have not wished to tell him anything about it, for it can be done without him. I know that the Lord is so good that, although he has obliged me to the yoke of matrimony, not for that will he fail to give me grace to be able to serve him perfectly.

I ask you, my Father and lord, through the sweet passion of our Lord Jesus Christ, that you do not reject my first humble request, to admit me into the holy Society of Jesus, whom my soul desires to serve and follow all the days of my life.

Doña Juana de Cardona, to whom I stand in place of a mother and who is a person by whom the Lord will be greatly served, writes to Your Reverence for permission for us to wash the corporals. Through the love of our Lord I ask Your Reverence to send this permission together with the other. I prostrate myself at your feet, urgently asking you to grant my request as quickly as possible. Thus my importunate requests will become silent. Your Reverence's charity in these wishes of mine as in all other things will be moved by what is best for the Lord's service. I humbly kiss your hands, asking you to give me your holy blessing and receive me as your subject and daughter and to pray to God for me, as I do for you in my poor prayers. Certainly, for longer time than I can remember, our Lord Jesus Christ has shown me favour and mercy. To him I pray for Your Reverence; may he make you holy and count you in the number of his apostles, he who liveth and reigneth with the Father and the Holy Spirit. Amen.

Your Reverence's very humble daughter and servant who kisses your hands.

Doña Sebastiana Exarch

From Valencia, June 16th, 1545

This imploring letter arrived when Ignatius was in the middle of his troubles with Isabel Roser. So the answer that Dr. Torres took with him to Valencia was just a laconic refusal, with an indication of another way into which the striving after perfection of these ladies might be directed, namely the women's society of which we have already heard.

We know no more of Doña Sebastiana's subsequent history. Only once does the chronicle mention her husband as a promoter of the college at Valencia. No doubt he had in this the support of his wife.[36]

Juana de Cardona

THE lady for whom, as we heard, Doña Sebastiana Exarch took the place of a mother, wrote Ignatius two of the most tearful letters that the General ever received from a woman. She was Doña Juana de Cardona, who belonged to the ducal family of that name, a woman of sensibility and typically Spanish, with a tragic life history. Some years before, her still youthful husband had been murdered in Valencia; and she had in her burning desire for vengeance made it the object of her life to demand justice from the king. For years she followed the court on its wanderings from Valladolid to Seville, from Monzón to Madrid. As she was doing so, her noble mind had already learnt the nothingness of all earthly things; and a meeting with the Jesuit Peter Faber at Madrid in 1541 first showed her a Christian way to overcome the tragedy of her life.

When her friend Sebastiana wrote that long letter to Ignatius in June 1545, Juana had been back in Valencia with her children for two months and had had her first decisive meeting with Father Mirón. "This woman is a person of great talent, practised in mortification and far advanced in the service of the Lord", Mirón informed Ignatius. Juana was with all the impetuosity of her character at once filled with enthusiasm for her friend's plan to join Ignatius' Society. They wished, said Mirón, to vow such perfect obedience that it would be like the founding of an order. If there were three or four of them, they wished to occupy one house as a community. "They are regularly besieging me, and they attach so much value to obedience that one can only say: 'God grant that many real religious may feel only half as keen as they are!'"

Juana, too, made Father Mirón give her the Exercises; and she experienced their effect as a complete spiritual conversion – as she confessed with deep emotion to Ignatius: "Then came my dear Father Mirón, and the Lord changed me completely. Since then I have wept, wept unceasingly; for I had forgotten how to weep." The letter was despatched to Rome with that of Doña Sebastiana on June 16th, 1545.[37]

Very Reverend Lord and Father in Jesus Christ,

As the Lord in these parts has sent us these servants of his and disciples of yours for the salvation of our souls, I, as having more need than any other, straightway came to place my soul in the hands of my Father Master Mirón. Although I did not realize it immediately, from the first hour the Lord stirred up in me very great charity with greatly increased faith, so much so that I began to desire that all my operations should be ordered and guided by that father. As I knew that the fathers gave certain exercises, which were of great benefit to the salvation of one's soul, I begged Father Master Mirón to give them to me. At first he refused. Rather he made me desire them for a long time until, seeing my tears and the way God made me feel, constrained by charity he granted me them and gave them to me in Passion week. Then the Lord gave me to feel those things in my soul by which I had offended him and made me desire to remedy them. He enlightened my mind and showed me the true way I was to take. I felt in my heart that the Lord had sent Father Mirón to me in place of himself, since we are not worthy to treat with his divine Majesty except through third persons who are his greater servants, as we can see by the blessed St. Paul who was sent to the prophet Ananias.

For the strictest obedience, even were it to sacrifice my children, the great faith which the Lord has given me would strengthen my weakness and conquer maternal love so that I could do this thing very easily, considering all that I might be commanded to do by holy obedience as true service in the sight of the Lord. Since he obeyed even unto death and the death of the cross, we ought to take up his cross and not to stop until we die with him. And as the cross we can take is this abnegation of ourselves and making over our will to that of him whom he has freely given us as his third-party servant, it is only right to put all one's efforts into acquiring this obedience and not to fear the enemy or his temptations, even though the world and our own vanity and weakness help him, for the Lord permits this to try us. I trust very greatly in his divine goodness that all this will be for his greater service.

When my Father saw the way in which the Lord was giving me to feel the perfection of obedience, accompanied by the other two vows, poverty and chastity, and saw the abundance of my tears, because I was prevented from entering the Lord's service to the full extent of my capacity, and when he knew of my past life, and how much I had offended him each hour, he considered that since in what remained to me of life I could make some return to the Lord, not as I ought but as far as I was able, (for I was giving him all I had), he granted my request, on condition that Your Reverence was willing to grant it me with a dispensation from the Holy Father. It will be easy to procure this, and I have very great confidence in our Lord and in Your Reverence's charity that you will not refuse me your consent.

Thus I beg Your Reverence when you have read this letter, to consider me prostrate at your feet with all the humility and tears I have and am capable of, begging this of you before the Lord for charity's sake that I may serve the Lord better until my death. And since charity never failed in Your Reverence towards anybody, it will not fail towards me.

Thus I beseech and ask you to receive me into this holy Society and religious institute of the most holy and sweet Jesus, for since my childhood, as soon as ever I began to think, this most holy name of Jesus was imprinted on my inmost heart, and I never knew how to call upon the Lord in my troubles except by this most sweet name of Jesus, and on his most sacred Mother by her holy conception. I always hoped by these means to obtain great favours. His most holy Majesty has shown his will, for until now, when there are servants and religious of his holy name, he has not given me to understand how I had to serve him and not offend him. Although he has been giving me very great longings for a considerable time now, everything was frustrated until my Father Master Mirón of the holy Society of my Lord Jesus arrived in these parts. I had not been back here in Valencia two months, having been away six years, following the court on account of law-suits I had there, and my small children, and troubles which were too much for a woman's strength.

Among other things, that which most worried me and hindered me in the service of our Lord was that of my widowhood and the cause of it, because they killed my husband in this city of Valencia, of which he and I were natives. With this suffering I left the city to seek justice and with this suffering I returned here to sell all I had and go away, returning to it no more. With the arrival of my Father, the Lord changed things in such a way that now I weep – I weep constantly, though I had forgotten how to weep. Thus, indeed, God's work in me and that of his and Your Reverence's true servants, ought now to be firmly established. You are God's most loyal servant and my lord and Father and head and governor of this holy Society and of all of us who desire to belong to it. May Your Reverence then give to my soul this sure foundation presenting it through the hand of Father Master Mirón with the strength of God. Let my soul like his be subject to Your Reverence's obedience. I would leave the world, my children, relatives and friends and all I possess from my rank. I would renounce myself and all things for the all, and, counting myself as dead, rise again in the Lord's service. Let not Your Reverence fear my woman's weakness, because, when the Lord sets his hand, he makes the weak strong; and when he removes his hand, the strong become weak. I trust in the Lord that he will create in me a new and clean heart, and a right spirit within me; and that even though the Lord may hide himself from me, he will not hide me from himself, nor turn aside his holy inspirations, but will rather send them with joy and grace of the Holy Spirit to all his servants and to all those of us who desire to be the servants of his servants.

Again placing myself on my knees before Your Reverence and setting my tears in your sight, I beg you as humbly as I can that you grant me this and give me your blessing. Pray to the Lord for me, that his holy will may be done in me, for from to-day onwards Your Reverence has an obligation for this since I take you as my true Father and lord on earth.

In order not to weary Your Reverence with a longer letter, I conclude with my hand what I desire will not finish until death. I shall always pray to the Lord for your holy life that by it you may lead many to eternal life.

Thus may it please the most sweet Jesus.

From Valencia, Your Reverence's most humble servant,
Doña Juana de Cardona
June 16th, 1545

No doubt Ignatius read this touching letter, from which he could see the transforming effect of his book of Exercises, with heartfelt emotion. He always had a delicate understanding for true nobility of soul. Besides, he had before him at this time a similar letter requesting admission to the obedience of the Society, which the sister-in-law of the Duke of Gandía, Juana de Meneses, had written. She was also a friend of Juana de Cardona. The answer which Ignatius sent to Juana has unfortunately been lost. We know for certain, however, that it was in the negative. Ignatius had to force himself to be firm.

But the noblewoman of the house of Cardona had a Spaniard's pertinacity. As impetuously as she had once conducted her case in the courts of justice she now pursued her goal in a spiritual battle with Ignatius. Firstly she had to make the necessary preparations for her withdrawal from the world. In May 1546 she went to Madrid, there to arrange provision for her children. The daughter entered the cloister, the son was a student at Salamanca. Her advisers in all these difficult questions were Araoz and especially Faber, whom she met again in Madrid and whose departure for Rome she deeply regretted. On May 22nd, 1546, Araoz reported to Ignatius from Madrid: "I have just been speaking to a lady whom Father Faber knows well, Doña Juana de Cardona. She is determined to follow our Sister Roser, and it will be difficult to keep her from doing so. She is now going to visit Doña Leonor Mascarenhas in Alcalá in order to discuss the matter with her too." We see here again clearly how Ignatius' female devotees in Spain almost instinctively sought one another out, that they might direct all their efforts to the realization of the much-envied Señora Roser's ideal.[38]

It was high time for Ignatius to intervene. In November 1546 he gave Father Miguel Torres, who was leaving for Spain, a detailed memorandum on the subject of a female branch of the Society of Jesus. Among the reasons for his attitude enumerated by Ignatius, the fourth most clearly reveals the General's way of thinking. Once, in the days of his own conversion, on the sickbed at Loyola, he had among his other far-reaching plans considered the following: "How would it be if I too did what St. Francis and St. Dominic did?" Later, in Rome, sobered by experience, he saw what difficulties the orders of those two saints had to contend with because of their female branches. No doubt, too, he remembered the sordid dispute he had had to settle for the Tertiaries at Azpeitia in 1535. Therefore he wrote in his memorandum: "As far as we can judge in our Lord, what really matters is to keep the Society free to move unhampered in order to meet essential demands, and we must not tie ourselves down to unessential things. Moreover we must, if we wish to progress along the way of the Lord, think first of ourselves and look after ourselves. For although we are not worthy to loose the shoestrings of the blessed St. Francis and St. Dominic, yet we observe how their orders are much burdened and troubled by the constant complaints of their houses of nuns – indeed, we see this daily at the Roman curia. Therefore we have formed the opinion that in the future our Society might be involved in such disputes and scandals, if we were to undertake the spiritual direction of women and accept their obedience. Even with regard to the three women whose direction we have undertaken at the special command of His Holiness, we hope soon to gain the favour of being freed from them again."[39]

Torres was entrusted with the mission of communicating the contents of this memorandum to the women in Valencia as well as at the ducal court of Gandía. Besides this he apparently brought a personal letter from the General to Juana de Cardona, now lost, which undoubtedly contained a decided refusal. One might have thought that the question was now settled.

308

By no means. Juana had meanwhile broken completely with the world, made over all her property to her children, and retired in holy poverty to a hospital, to devote herself to the care of the sick. She would have liked most of all to go to Rome. Her ascetic enthusiasm was already considering a plan to accompany the Jesuits even as far as India. Again she made the Spiritual Exercises under Father Mirón's direction; and again she plucked up all her courage to write a second letter to Ignatius – she could not refrain from particularly mentioning the envied example of Isabel Roser. She did not, of course, know that the latter too had meanwhile had to leave the Society of Jesus.

Very reverend Lord and my dearest Father in Christ,

The grace and peace of the Holy Spirit be in our souls. Amen.

He who asks with true faith, even though he is refused, does not cease his request on that account. That is how I shall act, my dearest Father and lord, for, although I have written to Your Reverence many times and have now received your reply yet not for what it says do I lack confidence in your charity. Rather my desire has kindled more and my faith increased so much that it makes me feel within myself that, just as our Lord, when many were pressing upon him in the crowd, felt someone touch the hem of his garment, so my dearest Father and lord, you will feel me coming to touch yours.

As a pledge of this longing I begged my Father Master Mirón to give me the exercises again, and so he gave them to me once more with much charity. Neither during the exercises nor apart from them, in temptation and lack of consolation, or in desolation and darkness, did I, or do I, feel in the Lord that he was calling me to anything else but to live beneath the standard and under the protection of the Society of the name of Jesus. Thus my heart is ready, my dearest Father and lord, my heart is ready, humbled and prostrate at your feet, from where it will never rise, crying out like the Canaanite woman, until I be granted salvation for my soul. My soul is my true daughter, and I do not ask with less need or hope with less faith than the Canaanite.

For this reason I have left my property to my other children, and dispossessed myself of all, relatives and friends, separating myself from them – and I should like to be even more dispossessed of them – for they are only friends of the flesh and enemies of the soul. I am living wholly in retirement, serving the poor of Christ, beginning to possess the treasure of poverty, being indifferent to all things, in order that the Lord's will may be fulfilled in me through Your Reverence.

If you want me in Rome, I will set out to-day. If I am not worthy to be seen in your presence and receive your blessing, and you order me to go to the Indies or remain here or whatever Your Reverence may order me, I shall obey you even unto death. A woman who has gone more than a thousand leagues for the sake of disordered passion, seeking justice, will not hesitate to go many thousands more, even for as long as life is left to her, on pilgrimage, seeking mercy, with love and for the love of him who is the Lord of my love and of all things. I have left all things in order to gain all. And since your heart, full of charity, has opened to receive others, my dearest Father and Lord, do not Your Reverence close it against receiving me, although I am an unworthy servant of the servants of Jesus. Trusting in our most sweet Lord and in your kindness I shall await Your Reverence's reply, which I beg you, as humbly as I can, may be as soon as may be possible.

In order not to weary you more, I make an end, begging our Lord to guard you, with all those in the Society, and make you advance in his holy service.

From Valencia, at the close of the year 1546

Unworthy servant of the servants of Jesus,
The poor widow,

Doña Juana de Cardona

One thing the heroic Juana did not foresee, when in her letter she declared herself ready to spend all the remaining days of her life in pilgrimage: on March 13th, 1547, God called her to himself. Father de Oviedo sent Ignatius a detailed account of her death. Juana had taken up her abode in the hospital for the poor and was there leading a life of prayer, making "admirable progress in the way of the Lord". She nursed the sick, kissed their wounds and begged food for them at the gates of the city. She may indeed with justice be described as a Spanish Madame de Chantal: by her begging she even obtained alms and food from her husband's murderer. She was truly a saint. Oviedo concluded his report to Ignatius with the words: "I verily believe that she is already praying for us all now in Heaven."[40]

Guiomar Coutinho

Twice already we have suspected Father Araoz of giving too much encouragement to feminine plans for following Isabel Roser's example in Spain. The suspicion is confirmed by a letter which this overzealous apostle of the ladies sent to his Master from Evora in Portugal on the 3rd March, 1545. At the royal court there lived a lady-in-waiting of noble family, probably belonging to the house of the Counts do Redondo, Guiomar (a feminine form of Jerome) Coutinho by name. It was of her that Araoz wrote, and his letter is so characteristic that we will quote it verbatim:

"I believe Your Reverence has already heard of a lady of great talent and nobility, who dwells here in the palace, much loved and esteemed by the members of the royal family and aunt of our Father Don Gonzalo Silveira. She is unmarried. She is most lovingly devoted in our Lord to Your Reverence and to the whole Society, and she proves this by continual works of charity. She is as well disposed towards us as if she had so to speak already made her profession; she regards herself as belonging to the Society and would like to be recognized as a member. She would already have written to Your Reverence herself; but although the virtue with which our Lord has blessed her and her good example would have been more effective advocates, she nevertheless bade me to write to Your Reverence instead of her. She has a sincere wish that Doña Leonor Mascarenhas and she, together with other women, may found a house, subordinate to our Society, in which they may live permanently. It appears to me that she will succeed in persuading Doña Leonor.

"These projects are very praiseworthy. A letter from Your Reverence would not only comfort her very much but also encourage her to advance yet further in the service of the Lord, according to her wishes. Here in this kingdom she is as it were another Isabel Roser of Barcelona and another Doña Leonor of Castile. If I did not love all these ladies equally in our Lord, and if I did not want to avoid comparisons between them, I would have much more to say. The lady of whom I speak is Doña Guiomar Coutinho. She shows herself generous and attentive to the wants of the Fathers, not only in this place but everywhere. May God the Lord reward her, and may he bless and help us always. Amen."[41]

311

Several times Ignatius sent the lady his respects through Rodríguez, the last time as late as August 1546, when in Rome the problem of Isabel Roser was coming to a head. Evidently Araoz in Spain had no inkling of this. He maintained cordial relations with the lady-in-waiting who regarded herself as a Jesuitess and occasionally sent her one of the pious tracts which Duke Francis Borgia had published in Valencia, perhaps the *Spiritual Eyesalve* or the *Mirror of Christian Virtues*. In fact, he was already nursing a plan to found in Castile a proper convent of female Jesuits. Thus he reports to Father Faber: "The Countess of Osorno would like Doña Guiomar to come and live in Castile; they would then go together to Guadalupe, and they wish me to go with them. But I have so many Guadalupes that I doubt if that will be possible"[42]

All these plans fortunately came to nothing, for Ignatius had already, as we know, issued a statement of his principles. Doña Guiomar remained at court and continued in all possible ways to help the Portuguese Jesuits, who under Simon Rodríguez' leadership were enjoying an almost meteoric rise. Doña Guiomar was not always easy to get on with, it is true. In 1548 Father Juan Aragonés had to report many a vexation of which Her Ladyship was the cause. He made great efforts to retain her friendship and was soon able to announce: "Doña Guiomar is now reconciled again." During these years the lady-in-waiting felt an ever-growing reverence for Father Rodríguez. It was no friendship at first sight, and as late as March 8th the latter wrote to Rome: "Slowly, very slowly we are becoming friends." From the same period dates a letter of Guiomar to Ignatius which is no longer extant. In acknowledgement she received from the General in January 1549 a letter "with compliments".[43]

Down to the year 1552, Ignatius received several letters from his Portuguese disciple giving a running commentary on the development of that province of the Society. But then there broke over the Jesuits of Portugal the great storm in which minds were divided concerning the person of the Provincial Simon Rodríguez. Doña Guiomar was one of the passionate partisans of Rodríguez, for whom she had an almost boundless admiration. It now became apparent to what extent she regarded herself as a member of the Society. She wrote to Ignatius, in whom she saw the leader of all Rodríguez' opponents, a man forsaken by God. Her letter, trembling with indignation, was full of exaggerations. It was not true that half the province had been dismissed, as she asserted; and what she related about the houses at Evora and Coimbra were real "atrocity" stories. One thing is certain: Ignatius had never before received such a letter.[44]

312

IHS

I have written several times to Your Reverence how our Lord has favoured this Society called of Jesus in this Kingdom of Portugal, but as the devil saw the fruit that was being produced thereby he set all his forces to destroy it.

It happened in this way:

According to the statements of those who have left the Society, and as we as outsiders can see for ourselves, some of the inmates of this house have written to you stating what they would like done. Your Reverence indeed knows what has happened, but the sequel is this – the house will cease to exist and the common people will finally be strengthened in the view which they have long been prone to, that this whole business of the Society of Jesus is something that will not last, for since such effects followed, the cause naturally seemed to be bad.

Already nearly half of those who were in the Society have left, and many in high position, who were formerly capable of giving great service to God's Church. Others are on the point of leaving, according to report, and each day some leave the Society solely on account of what they saw happening to Father Master Simon and what is said of him each day. His deposition from office has appeared more like hatred than charity, since they have openly attacked his reputation both inside the House of the Order and outside – a man who has worked so hard for the Society and trained them with so much love and care. This is a great scandal for all who hear it, for this Father is a man of virtue as is known to the whole court. Now it is clear that Master Simon himself has the virtues which he wanted to produce in his sons and that the sons lack such virtues.

It is certain that such unheard of things in such a new Society, are very scandalous, and it seems as if the end cannot be far off. May our Lord keep it [that is, the Society] in his care, because it is reported that the brethren are drawn away from their studies and sent to a monastery to dig, and if they refuse, they take their food away; and they force both the sick and the healthy to work, heaping thousands of insults upon them – a thing never seen in the Society and very scandalous. Many, or almost all have left, and go around saying things about those in the Society, which discredit it in the opinion of those who up till then have thought well of it.

In the College of Coimbra things are happening which do not bear repetition. I can only tell you that those there have lost the reputation they had, and there are very few who think well of them, a fact which gives great sorrow to those who had a certain love for the Society. Moreover, Your Reverence should know that on the day on which they deprived Master Simon of his office and gave it to Father Mirón, which was the day of the Exaltation of the Cross, a thunderbolt from heaven fell on the tower of the College of Coimbra and demolished part of it. This was regarded as mysterious. They, therefore, demolished the Society's tower, and I regard it as a judgment on what has been done and is being done daily in the Society.

I am wholly convinced that there was little charity shown in depriving Master Simon of his office. This caused so much talk that I cannot repeat it. Not even would the civil authorities have treated a Moor so cruelly; and if Your Reverence saw him, I believe that you would be greatly grieved, and would recognize the goodness of such a good son, when you saw the patience and calm with which he has suffered everything, according to the accounts of those who have seen it all. It seems to me that he was the only person who realized what was happening and yet he defended the men whose faults he saw. I am confident that he will have better pay in Heaven than what he has received from his sons on earth, and from Your Reverence for whom he has suffered so much. When this happens among religious to whom all looked for an example, it is no good recommendation for the world.

What I ask Your Reverence is, for the love of our Lord, to provide a remedy for so much evil because you have been the occasion of it. Truly, I do not know how the infamy of depriving Father Master Simon of his office can be put right, and how one can further restore Your Reverence's reputation. May our Lord be in our souls.

Doña Guiomar Coutinho

Lisbon, October 1552

Ignatius calmly put this abusive letter away. We know that soon afterwards he received with charity his almost rebellious yet ever-beloved companion Rodríguez, when the latter came penitent to Rome, and that he calmed the tempest in Portugal with perfect tact. But Doña Guiomar did not stop there: she wrote a violent letter of complaint against Ignatius to the papal legate in Lisbon, Cardinal Giovanni Ricci di Montepulciano. The General only instructed the Fathers in Lisbon not to do anything about it. So the story of the Portuguese lady-in-waiting who wished to become a second Isabel Roser ended in peace and quiet. [45]

Jacoba Pallavicino

FROM June 1539 to September 1540, Peter Faber and Diego Laynez were working at the request of the Cardinal Legate Ennio Filonardi in Parma, capital of the dukedom which belonged to the Pope's family, the Farnese. Here they made the acquaintance of a noble lady, Jacoba Pallavicino da Scipione, the widow of the Marquis Gian Girolamo Pallavicino, who was murdered by his relatives in 1536. This wealthy woman lived during the summer on her estates near Cremona, during the winter in her palace at Parma. In January 1540 Laynez was able to report to Ignatius that young Master Doménech had given retreats to four ladies of the aristocracy as well as others. Two of them were Jacoba Pallavicino and her friend Giulia Zerbini, a woman inclined to mysticism, who, it was claimed, took no food and lived only on Holy Communion; but who ended up as a victim of diabolical illusions.

Peter Faber, who was usually in a state of spiritual exaltation, reported on Madonna Jacoba in very sober terms. "A lady named Jacoba, a widow without children, with an annual income of 500 gold *scudi* besides her dowry, is resolved to place all her property and herself entirely at the disposal of some pious work, which I am to designate more particularly. When, five or six days ago, this lady heard that I had to leave for Spain, she hastened weeping to Donna Laura Pallavicino, the wife of Count San Vitale, who is one of the noblest ladies of the city and a kinswoman of the Pope. With tears she prayed this lady to prevent my departure; and she asked her to write to the Lord Cardinal of Santa Fiora, in order that by command of His Holiness I might remain in Parma." This is, even before the actual approval of the Society's foundation, the first example of how the influence of pious women interfered with Ignatius' apostolic plans. In fact a letter was sent by the senators of Parma to Costanza Farnese, daughter of the Pope and mother of the above-named Cardinal of Santa Fiora, Guido Ascanio Sforza, but without any effect. Jacoba, however, remembered clearly thirteen years later that she had heard "God's call" through the mouth of those two Fathers.[46]

For ten years efforts were made at Parma to get Ignatius to send Jesuits to

315

minister in that city. Behind all such efforts were Madonna Jacoba and her friend Giulia Zerbini. Their spiritual adviser was a zealous priest of Parma, Gian Battista Pezzana, who was especially noted for his ministry to repentant women. On January 23rd, 1546, Ignatius had very politely to refuse a request from the Senate of Parma for Father Laynez to be sent there. The following year Pezzana joined the Jesuits, and in 1548 he received a sharp reprimand from Ignatius because he had, together with Giulia Zerbini, caused the Senate to send another petition. The pious women evidently gave Ignatius no peace. In 1549 the repentant women of Parma, who were looked after by Donna Jacoba, asked for a priest of the Society of Jesus as spiritual director. Again Ignatius had to say no. To Pezzana he sent detailed instructions as to how he should guard himself against such importunity.[47]

From 1550 Madama Margaret of Austria herself resided in Parma. This gave a new impetus to the women's spiritual zeal. Ignatius was at this time so ill, that he was seriously thinking of retiring from the office of General. A renewed petition from the Senate dated October 1550 therefore remained long unanswered. Madonna Jacoba knew about this. So on December 10th, she sat down to write a letter to Ignatius with the express request that he would not delay too long in giving an affirmative answer. Cleverly she referred to his good relations with Madama before mentioning to the General the subject of her dearest wish. This was nothing less than to be admitted to the obedience of the Society.[48]

My most reverend Father in Christ, to whom I owe the utmost obedience.

Since it has pleased our blessed Jesus Christ who is infinite goodness to give me sufficient opportunity to come to know true Christian living and since he has given me the desire for this, I beseech Your Reverence to ask all your holy Society to pray for me, so that with my life and possessions I may do all that is according to the pleasure of the blessed Jesus Christ our Lord and of your holy Society.

With this letter of mine I ask Your Reverence for God's mercy and yours and that you will not abandon me so that my poor soul does not stray. I also ask that of your mercy you will deign to send me a religious of the Society to be a father to me and whom I have to obey, and who will have authority to incorporate me in your holy Society, for I will do all he bids me.

If Your Reverence tells me that I am not worthy, the blessed Jesus Christ, our Master, has taught us that sinners are called as well as the righteous, and with his holy help, from a sinner I hope to become his good servant.

I know well, indeed, that it would be good for Her Excellency Madama to ask you whatever our Lord Jesus Christ prompted her heart to ask you. She says she will do not only this but other and greater good works. It is sufficient for me to know that Christ our Lord wills that your Fathers should come, and does not wish that princes should be able to hinder your good work.

I, however, am alone, a widow, and I have a house, and God will surely not fail to support us with his help. I ask Your Reverence on my bended knees, however, to deign to listen to me if you do not want those who have good desires to be lost in body and soul. Through the lack of help in spiritual things, both may well be lost. This is the reason I have to-day sent you a warm and fervent entreaty and with a strong and valiant heart have written my request, hoping in God and Your Reverence that you will not fail me. I ask you for a favourable answer before too long since I am weak and foolish, but I do, indeed, desire the salvation of my soul and that of many others more than my own well-being. With this, asking you for your blessing, as your daughter, I recommend myself to you.

The servant of Jesus Christ and Your Reverence
Jacoba Pallavicino da Scipione

To the most reverend Master Ignatius, servant of Jesus Christ our Lord, General of the Society of Jesus, in Rome.

From Parma, December 10th, 1550

The General's answer was sent off by return of post – for four years past he had been saying "no" to all such applications. From yet another petition by the Senate of Parma dated October 26th, 1550, asking special assistance for the house of penitents, we can see clearly that it was primarily the ladies who were behind these determined requests. The senators declared their deepest devotion to Ignatius and said: "Here in Parma there are not a few persons who have a profound affection and love for Your Reverence." As a proof of this, the letter contained the signatures of twelve ladies, among which is that of Jacoba Pallavicino da Scipione.

From 1552 onwards efforts in Parma were directed towards the project of a college; and this was far more important than the house of penitent women. Jacoba took up the plan with ardent zeal, for which she was

317

commended by Ignatius. She wanted to place the foundation on a firm footing by endowing it with her property; but she still attached the highest importance to combining the work of the college with that of ministering to fallen women. Once again Ignatius patiently refused. By way of consolation Father Elpidio Ugoletti was allowed to go to Donna Jacoba at Cremona, together with a young Flemish brother called Peter. The pious Father Elpidio had some scruples about undertaking this mission, and had to be specially reassured. The negotiations for the foundation of a college were resumed with great keenness on Jacoba's estate at Cremona.

The times were bad, for meanwhile war had broken out for possession of the Duchy of Parma. Jacoba had to pay her contribution towards the expenses of the campaign. Nevertheless, she was highly delighted at the compliment paid to her zeal by Ignatius. She felt herself already so much a member of the Society of Jesus, setting forth all her plans to found a house of female Jesuits, that at the end of the letter which she now sent to Ignatius she signed herself with disarming piety as "Jacoba, of the Society of Jesus".[49]

IHS

Reverend Father in Christ Jesu and my superior whom I must always honour and obey.

Through the grace and goodness of Almighty God, our Lord, Father Don Elpidio Ugoletto, Father Rector of the College of our Society in Parma, has come here. I do not know how to express the joy and satisfaction and gratitude I feel for the good Your Reverence has brought about in sending me this servant of God and of your Society, who is a truly holy man, to procure my salvation and peace of soul and body.

Now we spoke together and arranged, provided it were pleasing to Your Reverence, to set up a college of your order in Parma, to which I would give one thousand *scudi* when the College should be erected. But because of the wars and the very great troubles arising therefrom, I can only do so by giving from now onwards fifty *scudi* each year instead of the sum of one thousand *scudi* at one time so that it will take twenty years to complete the said sum. If by good fortune God gives us the grace of setting up a college here in Cremona, I will to begin with give fifty *scudi* of this sum this year, but this would mean that the payment must in any case be eventually paid back to the college in Parma. From the rest of my property, I mean that which my husband left me as a memorial, when the war contribution and that for home difficulties have

318

been met, I could make an initial payment of six hundred *scudi* for the establishment of a convent of nuns, governed by your Society, and placed under your rule and constitutions and obedience. They would only be able to dispose of this foundation sum for their needs in food and clothing in such a mode and form as should be determined by the Society. Their remaining resources they must dispense as obedience shall command. Of these nuns I intend to be one, but because I feel responsibility for a niece I have, I intend that out of the revenue and interest on this money, if I do not marry this niece during my life-time, the said nuns shall be obliged to marry her and give her a dowry in such a mode and form as my will shall say and as Father Master Don Elpidio will explain to you. Therefore, I entreat you on my bended knees that you deign to accept me and dispose of me as the father of a family does with a prodigal son, remembering also that it is more than thirteen years since I was called by God through the voice of Master Peter [Faber] and Master James [Laynez] of your holy Society. True shepherds gather up their sheep and do not let them wander away to strange shepherds. I shall never change in my purpose and if ever you shall hear me say the contrary of what I write to you at present, it will be false. I shall always remain a true and unfaltering servant of Christ, Jacoba Pallavicino of the Society of Jesus, and shall obey in the very least thing that shall be enjoined on me by the head of the Society and by all of you together. With this I recommend myself to Your Reverence's prayers with those of all the holy Society. Your Reverence's useless servant in Christ.

Jacoba of the Society of Jesus

I affirm what is written above as if written with my own hand.

From Cremona, June 2nd, 1553

To my most reverend father in Christ, Father Master Ignatius, General of the Society of Jesus, in Rome

This letter was too much even for the patience of Ignatius. At once he despatched a letter to Father Ugoletti on June 24th, protesting strongly; and on the same day a polite but coldly unequivocal letter of refusal to Madonna Jacoba, unfortunately preserved only in the *regesta*. Such plans, he said, were against the rules of the Society, once and for all. The Fleming Peter described on July 3rd the impression this letter made: the Signora had been much agitated by the General's reply, saying that she had really

319

expected an affirmative answer this time. From Peter's gentle allusion, doubtless quoted from Jacoba: "After all, there have already been women in the obedience of the Society of Jesus!" it is clear that the ghost of Isabel Roser still haunted the conversations at Cremona.

The storm, however, was soon over. On July 9th, before his departure from Cremona, Ugoletti was able to report: "Madonna Jacoba wishes in any case to found a college, and this without any other condition. We leave Her Excellency somewhat comforted in mind." Wherein this comfort consisted, Madonna Jacoba had already told her revered Father Ignatius in a letter two days before. The persistent lady could not indeed refrain even here from asking to be allowed at least to place herself under obedience to a confessor belonging to the Society. In principle, however, she was ready to submit to every wish of the General.[50]

The affection which I bear to your holy Society in my zeal to serve Jesus Christ, brings to my mind as I contemplate the holy Gospels that I am like the wife of Zebedee, who wished her children to stand one on the right hand and one on the left. Now remembering our Lord's answer, it seems to me, when I read Your Reverence's letter, that I am now reading the reply of that Lord. Therefore, I ask you on my bended knees to pardon my very great presumption. I place myself, indeed, always under your obedience, which I promise you always to observe and to give myself to all the inspirations of the Holy Spirit. To-day I still think it my duty to make a vow to be a nun and to establish a convent of nuns. I think that this vow can be dispensed or changed by you as my spiritual father. In this case I would only reserve the sum of three thousand *scudi* for the marriage of my niece and the expenses of my upkeep; with the rest I shall always do that which you charge and order me.

Master Elpidio's departure has been a great grief to me, for it seemed to me that the father was being cut off from the daughter and the son from the mother, when I consider his holy ministrations and loving admonitions which have bound me to him so closely in Christian love, so that, if it were not a hindrance to him I should follow him in body as I follow him in spirit. He dissuaded me, however, from doing this. I only hope in God that Your Reverence will one day bind me to Christ. . . . I beg and implore you to accept me, if only because as Master Baptist [Pezzana] told me in Rome many other women are under your obedience, promising what I have promised. Therefore I, too, would take a vow of poverty, chastity and obedience to you or some other Father of your holy Society, who has authority over me on your behalf

AUTOGRAPH LETTER FROM CATARINA DE BADAJOZ TO ST. IGNATIUS

see page 148-149

ST. IGNATIUS AND THE WOMEN OF MANRESA

see page 174

and, after you, on behalf of whosoever shall be your successor. . . . If on the other hand Your Reverence should still be of the opinion that my being under your obedience will not be profitable, I will do whatever you decide by God's inspiration. I shall stand at the door and knock and ask with humility and expect that Christ will deign to make his servants hear me. Thus I shall find it will be opened to me and I shall be comforted at all that shall be enjoined upon me, holding it as certain that what will be done will be for my good. I ask you to deign to pray and to have prayers said to the Lord our God for me and so I commend myself to your holy prayers and again ask your blessing.

Please show this letter also to Don Sigismund, my brother. I recommend him to your holy prayers.

Your Reverence's useless servant in Christ, daughter of your obedience,

Jacoba Pallavicino of the Society of Jesus

From Cremona, July 7th, 1553

To the most reverend father in Christ, Father Master Ignatius of Loyola, General of the Society of Jesus, at Santa Maria della Strada, by San Marco, Piazza Altieri, Rome.

Jacoba did not know when she wrote this letter that Ignatius was at that very time occupied in once again setting out for her the reasons for his refusal.

Everything ended peacefully. On January 22nd, 1554, Jacoba wrote a letter to Ignatius containing some pious wishes and giving him a message for her priest-brother Don Sigismondo, then in Rome. Ignatius answered her, and this letter is the only one of his to her that has been preserved in its entirety.[51]

My lady in our Lord

The sovereign grace and eternal love of Christ our Lord be with Your Ladyship to our continual favour and help.

I have received a letter from Your Ladyship dated 22nd January last, and I have carried out what you asked me in the way of praying for you and giving orders that prayers be said in the house so that the good and holy desires which God our Lord gives Your Ladyship may be fulfilled.

As to Signor Sigismondo, your brother, in whatever we can serve him and according to our profession help him in confession and other spiritual matters, we will do so all the more willingly since, because he is Your Ladyship's brother, we are the more obliged to do so in Christ Jesus our Lord.

Prayers will also be said for Signora Himelia, that God our Lord may be her guide and direct all her affairs, and those of Your Ladyship, to his greater service and glory.

We all most heartily recommend ourselves to Your Ladyship's prayers; and we pray God's supreme goodness to grant us all the grace always to know his most holy will and perfectly to fulfil it.

From Rome, February 17th, 1554

To Donna Jacoba Pallavicino, Cremona.

Nothing came of the plan to found a college at Parma up to the time of Ignatius' death, in spite of all the promises of the Duchess Margaret and the efforts of Jacoba. In 1575 Ignatius' faithful disciple died.[52]

The Pezzani Ladies

ONE would have thought that all attempts to found a convent of women under the rule and obedience of the Society of Jesus would have been out of the question after the experiences of 1546 and the bull *Licet debitum* of October 18th, 1549. This was not so in Italy. Even after 1550, Ignatius had from time to time to quash such projects.

The Dominican Egidio Foscarari zealously promoted the social and charitable work of the noble ladies of Modena, as we have read in the correspondence between Donna Costanza Pallavicino Cortesi and Ignatius. It is noteworthy that the plan which Ignatius had proposed in 1546 at Valencia and Gandía, to form the ladies into a kind of women's guild, had already been realized at Modena. The house of penitents in that city was conducted by Jeronima Pezzani, a friend of the *Cavaliera*. In her work for fallen girls she was supported by a group of worthy middle-class women, while a rich citizen named Giovanni Castelvetro provided the necessary funds. No doubt the Bishop's vow had made a deep impression on the devout women. As moreover the House of St. Martha at Rome was regarded in Modena as a shining example, and as good reports had been received about the superioress thereof, Isabel Roser of Barcelona, the suggestion naturally arose that Ignatius should once more be approached and his permission sought for the penitents' home to be transformed into a proper convent of Jesuitesses.

So a solemn petition was sent to Ignatius in the names of Donna Jeronima and Signor Castelvetro, asking him to obtain from the Pope permission to establish such a convent. Ignatius, while delighted at the progress of charitable work among the fallen women, was alarmed at the news that the zealous Jeronima and her fellow-workers had already made a vow to become religious under the direction of the Jesuits. Once more the only answer was an unequivocal no. "He simply declined to accept the vows of Jeronima Pezzani as superioress and those of the other women, who had vowed obedience to Father Ignatius", notes Polanco in the chronicle of the Society.

Whether the audacious women of Modena already knew of Ignatius' decision when the following letter was despatched, we do not know.

In a word, they affectionately and confidently announced to the General the *fait accompli* of their affiliation to the Society.[53]

My lord in our Lord,

I, Jeronima Pezzani, unworthy superior of the penitents of Modena, make perpetual vow of poverty, chastity and obedience, with the sisters mentioned below.

Before the most holy and undivided Trinity, Father, Son and Holy Spirit, before my Lord Jesus Christ and his holy and blessed Mother ever a virgin, and the court of heaven, we place ourselves under the obedience of your reverend lordship, superior and father of the Society of Jesus at Rome, most illustrious throughout all the world. Receive us in the love of the heart of Jesus and do not let us go astray, because without your Lordship we are forsaken by all men. It is in the first place our most reverend lord bishop who urges us to make this request for he has already placed himself under Your Reverence's obedience. We know that you will not refuse us this favour.

From Modena, January 18th, 1552

I, Hieronima Pezzani, your unworthy servant sign hereunder.

I, Sister Paula, sign.   I, Sister Magdalena, sign.
I, Sister Isabel, sign.   I, Sister Caterina, sign.
I, Sister Angelica, sign.   I, Sister Lucia, sign.
I, Sister Maria, sign.

The fact of his refusal to accept this over-hasty admission of themselves to the Society did not affect the friendship between Ignatius and these ladies. The work in the house of penitents went on quietly as though it were a convent. Father Cesare de Aversa eagerly undertook the spiritual direction of the women – too eagerly, it was soon thought at Rome. The nuns, if we may so call them, looked after the sick Jesuits, giving them better food and washing their linen; and with all the visits of a pastoral or amicable nature that went on, there was between their houses a continual coming and going.

Ignatius discouraged this devotedness of the ladies, particularly as Jeronima liked to refer to an alleged statement of his that his sons had a special obligation to do such work. Goodhumouredly he wrote to Father Cesare:

"That lady, with all her good intentions, is mistaken in this." In October and November 1553 Jeronima sent two letters to Ignatius, now lost. In the following year, too, she had many complaints to make about the frequent changes of personnel among the Jesuits at Modena, and especially of the confessors in her convent. However, she helped them energetically when from 1555 onwards the college in that city, which to the General seemed much more important than the work for penitent women, was in its first humble and poor beginnings.[54]

Only once did a shadow pass over their friendship. The letter of Ignatius to Jeronima, which we owe to this misunderstanding, is an eloquent witness to his profound knowledge of the feminine soul.

The commissioner Father Viola, who represented Ignatius in Northern Italy, was with all his apostolic zeal a sick man who often suffered from nerves. Ignatius always attached great importance to the care of the health, as being a matter of divine ordinance. He had therefore warned Father Viola as early as 1549, when the latter was still in Paris, to take better care of his body. Perhaps the good religious had taken this admonition rather too literally. During his sojourn in Modena he had had himself looked after in a way that scandalized the austere Donna Jeronima. On October 7th, 1553, she sent an indignant letter to Ignatius. Her displeasure with Father Viola had been increased by the fact that the commissioner had had to order the recall of Father Cesare and the Fleming Adrian Witte.

Ignatius evidently read the complaint from Modena with some amusement, for he sent Jeronima's letter by return of post back to Father Viola for the latter to read, adding the following words: "I send you this letter that you may know how the feeling is in Modena. Do not let the writer of it notice anything. The letter has made no particular impression on us here. Do not let such things prevent you from looking after your health. If one must consider the frail virtue of such persons, let it not on any account be in matters that affect the health; for it is much better to care for one's health in God's service than to shut the mouths of such persons – which would in any case be very difficult."

This was on November 11th, 1553. Ignatius thought over his reply to Madonna Jeronima till December 2nd. Then, however, he penned a real lesson to the sharp-tongued sister in Modena.[55]

The sovereign grace and eternal love of Christ our Lord be always with us to our continual favour and help.

I have received by the same post from Your Charity two letters, dated October 7th and November 3rd, and thank you for your very warm affection, out of which I am persuaded you were moved to write what was contained in those letters.

So far as the person mentioned in the letter of October 7th, I have only this one opinion: the persons who so think and speak of him what Your Charity writes to me, know and judge the father badly. It is an easy thing for them to allow themselves to be deceived because they intervene to reprove not only outward things, but even the hidden and secret intentions, of which God alone can be judge. From such a judgment, clearly wrong, it follows that they have defective vision in other things. Some apparent justification there may have been on account of that person being treated as sick — as, indeed, he is. Where there is solid charity and a true spirit, however, one ought not to be considered "fastiduous" and "over-indulgent" in taking whatever medicines are necessary for one's indispositions and those of one's brethren, particularly in a place where all [the Fathers] have been ill through the neglect of the body and a poor standard of living.

In short, I have said what I think. Your Charity should take such representations as temptations of the devil, if they come to you, as you should such suggestions as come from others. I say expressly temptations; and temptations against charity they are, although disguised under the cloak of spirituality. This person is better known to us than to those who have judged him; and so, since we consider him apt for the office entrusted to him, with the divine help, it would be just as right that we should be believed as that they should. Let us say no more of this.

About our brother Master Cesare, he has been recalled (as I understand) from Modena, because he was always ill, relapsing repeatedly, as was also the case with many other of the brethren. Even now, I understand, he is ill. Accordingly I consider it certainly better that another priest should remain in his place. I shall, therefore, write to the Father Commissioner to see what can be done. Whatever he thinks, Your Charity should take as the best course in this matter.

Master Adrian, for the same reason, has been sent away from Modena. If he could have remained there with somewhat better health and strength of body, I should have been glad.

I do not make any reply to other matters, except to pray God our Lord to grant us all the true light of his spirit so that we may always know his holy will and perfectly fulfil it.

Ignatius

From Rome, December 2nd, 1553.

To Madonna Jeronima Pezzani, in Modena.

Jeronima did not take even this reproof amiss. Letters and greetings were still often exchanged. Ignatius' last message to Sister Jeronima is dated November 10th, 1554, as we know from a note in the *Regesta:* "A short answer, because I am so busy and ill."[56]

In Modena, as everywhere else, it was taken for granted among the pious women that they could turn to Ignatius, who was so clever and so ready to help in spiritual matters, with all their troubles. There lived in the city a kinswoman of Jeronima Pezzani, Madonna Barbara Pezzani. The chronicle of the Society calls her "a matron belonging to the highest circles of the city". She had made retreats with the first Jesuits in Modena, and was evidently a deeply spiritual woman; but the ideals of the Spiritual Exercises were perhaps a little too much for her. Her apostolic zeal was especially directed at the members of her not very edifying family, and this without any success, as so often happens in the case of spiritual exhortations coming from pious aunts. Donna Barbara grew melancholic because of her ill-success and began to doubt the value of her own ascetic ideals. She was soon utterly lost in a maze, trying to distinguish between the good and the evil spirit, of which she had heard so much in the Exercises and understood so little.

What could she do when so befogged but turn to the universally revered Father Ignatius? So towards the end of 1554 a request was sent to Rome through Father Leernus for some words of comfort and enlightenment. Ignatius, it must be admitted, did not regard the case as very tragic. He was also at this time a very sick man. On November 10th, therefore, he wrote to Leernus: "You can tell Madonna Barbara that I am answering her more by deeds than by words. May God our Lord let her feel in her soul the graces that I implore for her in some masses and prayers which are being specially offered on her behalf. And if you see that she would like to have a written answer, I will do that too, although I am just now quite ill." Now there again occurred one of those minor psychological miracles: even this laconic reply filled Donna Barbara with profound consolation. Joyfully she thanked her Master.[57]

Very reverend and blessed Father in our Lord,

I have understood all that Your Reverence writes has been done for this poor little unworthy soul of mine and I admit to having suddenly felt the effect and fruit of these prayers and Holy Masses. Thus my troubles are now more manifest and I am now clearer and take particular note of my very great errors and faults, so that I clearly see myself always to have been under illusions in all my acts and works, and that Satan has transformed himself into an angel of light, making me think I was led by a good spirit to do things which were not of my prerogative, namely in seeking to convert souls. I tried to do this not only with prayer, which could not have done harm, but with words, exhortations, letters and in a thousand other useless and unsuitable ways. And what it was necessary that I should do in my own case I have never yet done, namely, that I should mortify my passions, deny my own will and acquire humility and the other virtues. Furthermore, not only will no one ever be converted by me, but I have done so much harm to my soul that it would be impossible to express it. Under the pretence of gaining my blood relations, brothers, nephews and others, I have never detached myself from the world or from the flesh, and go on the same level with them. I have never been of any use to them, and it also seems that, the more I go forward, the less they are disposed to any good. For my sins I lose hope more and more, and reap nothing but sorrow and trouble from this living with them, and even harm in some things. But through not knowing the will of God, either in this or in other things, I do not know what I ought to do, nor which way to turn. Besides this, it greatly increases my suffering that already now for some years I have lost confidence in prayer. I see most clearly fulfilled in myself not only that saying: "When they shall multiply prayers I will not hear" (Isa. 1:15), many other sayings on this head. For this reason I beg you of your charity, reverend and blessed father, that you will not cease from prayer, until you have moved the divine mercy, and the Lord be reconciled with me, and forgive me my wrongs and very great errors, giving me some clear sign. This reply alone will be sufficient for me, for I need no other but God's grace and reconciliation.

Your Reverence's servant and daughter in Christ,
Barbara Pezzani

Modena, December 7th, 1554

To the most reverend father in Christ,
Father Master Ignatius.

328

Teresa Rejadella

THE aspirations of women to place themselves under the rule and obedience of the new Society were not confined to pious ladies living in the world. Because Ignatius had concerned himself from the earliest days in Barcelona with the ascetic reform of the Catalan convents and had pursued this object throughout his life, it seemed an obvious idea to incorporate into the Society nuns who desired reform. We shall see that it was Father Araoz especially who again and again recommended such a step, even after Ignatius' decision of 1546. On this subject the General was torn between natural inclination and well-considered rejection. He could never forget the days in Barcelona when, as early as March 1523, he had, as his own account states, visited "according to my custom all persons devoted to the spiritual life, even when they lived in hermitages far from the city, to hold converse with them". Nor did he ever forget the good portress Sister Antonia Estrada of the Hieronymite convent on the Prado Square, who held in high honour the box with flowers from the Holy Land that he had brought her.[58]

Not far from that convent stood another, which was to play an important part in the spiritual history of the Society and in the Saint's correspondence. This was the Benedictine convent of Santa Clara. In it lived a nun belonging to a noble Catalan family, Teresa Rejadella, or, as she also called herself in her mother-tongue, Rajadell. No doubt Ignatius made her acquaintance during his two years of study between 1524 and 1526 – hardly as early as 1523, for those three weeks in February and March were spiritually disappointing for him: "Neither in Barcelona nor in Manresa could he find, during the whole time that he was there, any persons who would have helped him as he wished. . . . So it came about that after his departure from Barcelona he completely lost his strong desire to visit pious persons." This was true inasmuch as he referred to conversations which might contribute to his own spiritual advancement or consolation; but in the meantime Ignatius had become a man taught by God alone and an apostle to others. We need not wonder then, that when he came to Barcelona a second time he took up with ardent zeal the reform and spiritual direction of those nuns whom he found willing to listen to the things of God.

None of them did Ignatius understand better than Teresa. In her convent, it is true, the question of reform was a matter of special urgency. Santa Clara, founded in 1233 as a house of Poor Clares, had been under the Benedictine rule since 1427. But the rule was not taken too seriously in this aristocratic convent for the unmarried daughters of the Catalan nobility, and the nuns insisted on being addressed as "Señora". Moreover, the convent had for a long time been immediately subject to the Holy See, and on this account the inmates called themselves "Apostolic", so that by invoking this privilege they lived with even greater laxity. At the time when Ignatius was studying in Barcelona there was in the convent a small group of about eleven nuns, who seriously desired a canonical and spiritual reform. The leader of this group was Sister Teresa. Ignatius and one of his earliest companions, Lope de Cáceres, were their advisers, holding long spiritual conversations with them.[59]

In Ignatius Teresa had found her master. Even after the unusual student of Latin had long since left Barcelona and got his master's degree at Paris, she felt a burning desire to speak occasionally with him, at least in letters, about spiritual things. Ignatius had meanwhile reached Venice and was waiting there for his companions. Cáceres was no longer among them, and was soon to return to a life of vexations in the world at his home-town Segovia. In the years around 1536 he was still in Barcelona, advising Sister Teresa on spiritual questions which he also discussed in correspondence with Ignatius.

The first letter which we possess of Ignatius' voluminous correspondence with the nun, an answer to a no longer extant letter of hers, is dated June 18th, 1536, and it is the longest spiritual document in the whole collection. It is as it were an echo of the many hours of spiritual converse in Barcelona. Apparently Teresa had asked the Master to undertake to be her spiritual director in the strict sense, at least from afar: the first sign of that great problem of reform upon which she was to write so much to Ignatius. Perhaps Teresa already knew something of the plan hinted at by Ignatius at the end of this letter, namely to return to Barcelona once more. God, however, ordained otherwise: Teresa never saw Ignatius again in this life. But this first letter will always remain the classic example of Ignatius' basic spiritual teaching; for it is like a commentary on the book of the Spiritual Exercises, especially on the fundamental experiences of the Saint at Loyola and Manresa, and on the doctrine about the influence of the good and evil spirits.

Something else distinguishes this letter from all others, those to Francis Borgia excepted: it speaks from deep experience of the things of the mystical life. Not for nothing does Ignatius refer Sister Teresa at its conclusion to the spiritual direction of the Carthusian Juan de Castro in Val de Cristo, with whom he had the previous year spent eight blissful days in mystical colloquy.[60]

May the grace and love of Christ our Lord be always with us to protect and help us.

When I received your letter a few days ago, it gave me much joy in the Lord whom you serve and desire to serve better, to whom we ought to attribute all the good we find in creatures. As you said he would in your letter, Cáceres[61] has informed me at length about your affairs, and not only about them, but also about the suggestions or guidance he gave you for each particular case. On reading what he says to me, I find nothing else he need have written, although I should have preferred to have the information in a letter from you, for no one can describe sufferings so well as the one who actually experiences them.

You ask me to take charge of you for the love of God our Lord. It is true that, for many years now, his divine Majesty has given me the desire, without any merit on my part, to do everything I possibly can for all men and women who walk in the path of his good will and pleasure, and, in addition, to serve those who work in his holy service. Since I do not doubt that you are one of these, I am pleased to find myself in the position of being able to put what I say into practice.

You also beg me to write to you what the Lord says to me and that I should say freely what I think. What I feel in the Lord I will tell you frankly with a right good will and if I should appear to be harsh in anything, I shall be more so against him[62] who is trying to upset you than against you. The enemy is troubling you in two ways, but not so as to make you fall into the guilt of sin which would separate you from your God and Lord. He does, however, draw and separate you from God's greater service and your own greater peace of soul. The first thing is that he sets before you and persuades you to cultivate a false humility; the second that he strives to instil into you an excessive fear of God with which you are too much taken up and occupied.

As to the first point, the general course which the enemy follows with those who love and begin to serve God our Lord is to set hindrances and obstacles in their way. This is the first weapon with which he tries to wound them – by suggesting "How will you be able to live in such penance all your life without the enjoyment of parents, friends and possessions and in so solitary a life, without even some slight relief? In another way of life you could save yourself without such great dangers". He thus gives us to understand that we have to live a life which is longer, on account of the trials which he sets before us, than that of any man who ever lived, whereas he hides from us the many and great comforts and consolations which the Lord is wont to give to such souls, if the man who has newly embraced the Lord's service breaks through all these difficulties, choosing to want to suffer with his Creator and Lord.

Then the enemy tries his second weapon, namely, boasting or vainglory, giving the soul to understand that there is much goodness or holiness in it and setting it in a higher place than it deserves. If the servant of the Lord resists these darts with humility and lowers himself, not consenting to be what the enemy would persuade him to be, he brings out the third weapon which is that of false humility. That is, when he sees the servant of the Lord so good and humble that, when he does what the Lord commands, he thinks it all valueless and looks at his own short-comings, not at any glory for himself, the enemy puts it into his mind that if he discovers any particular blessing given him by God our Lord, any good deed done, or good intention or desire, he is sinning by another kind of vainglory, because he speaks in his own favour. Thus the enemy strives that he should not speak of the blessings received from his Lord, so that there shall be no fruit either in others or in the person himself, for the recognition of what one has received is always a stimulus to greater things, although such speaking must be practised with restraint and motivated by the greater profit both of others and of the man himself, as opportunity provides and when others are likely to believe what we say and profit by it. When, however, we make ourselves humble, he tries to draw us into false humility, that is, into humility which is exaggerated and corrupt. Of this your words are clear evidence, for after you relate certain weaknesses and fears which are true of you, you say, "I am a poor nun, desirous, it seems to me, of serving Christ our Lord" – but you still do not dare to say: "I am desirous of serving Christ our Lord" or: "The Lord gives me desires to serve him", but you say: "I seem to be desirous." If you look closely, you will easily see that those desires of serving Christ our Lord do not come from you, but are given you by our Lord. Thus when you say: "The Lord has given me increased desires to serve him", you praise him, because you make his gift known and you glory in him, not in yourself, since you do not attribute that grace to yourself.

Thus we ought to be very circumspect and if the enemy lifts us up, humble ourselves, going over our sins and wretchedness. If he casts us down and dejects us, we ought to look upwards with true faith and hope in the Lord, going over the benefits we have received and considering with how much love and kindness he waits for us to be saved, whereas the enemy does not care whether he speaks the truth or lies, but only that he may overcome us. Ponder well how the martyrs, standing before their idolatrous judges, declared themselves Christ's servants. So you, standing before the enemy of the whole human race and tempted in this way by him, when he wants to deprive you of the strength the Lord gives you and wants to make you weak and full of fear with his snares and deceits, do not merely say that you are desirous of serving our Lord – rather you have to say and confess without fear that you are his servant and that you would rather die than separate yourself from his service. If he represents God's justice to me, I bring up his mercy; if he puts God's mercy before me, I reply with his justice. If we would avoid trouble, this is the way wherein we should walk, that the deceiver may in turn be deceived, applying to ourselves the teaching of Holy Scripture which says: "Beware that thou be not so humble that in excessive humility thou be led into folly" (cf. Eccles. 13:11).

Coming to the second point, as the enemy has placed in us a certain fear under the cloak of a humility which is false, and so suggests that we should not speak even of good, holy and profitable things, so he brings in its train another, much worse fear, namely whether we may not be separated and cut off from our Lord as outcasts – in great measure on account of our past lives. For just as through the first fear the enemy attained victory, so he finds it easy to tempt us with this other. To explain this in some measure, I will bring up another device the enemy has. If he finds a person with a lax conscience who passes over sins without adverting to them, he does his best to make venial sin seem nothing, mortal sin venial and very grave mortal sin of small account – so that he turns the defect he finds in us, that of too lax a conscience, to account. If he finds some other person with an overtender conscience – a tender conscience is no fault – and sees that such a person casts far from him mortal sin and as far as possible venial sin – for it is not in us to avoid all – and even tries to cast away from himself every semblance even of small sin, imperfection or defect, then the enemy tries to throw that good conscience into confusion, suggesting sin where there is no sin and defect where there is perfection, so that he may disturb and trouble us. In many instances where he cannot induce a soul to sin and has no hope of ever bringing that about, at least he tries to trouble it.

In order to explain more clearly how fear is caused, I shall speak, although briefly, of two lessons which the Lord usually gives or permits. The one he grants, the other he permits. That which he gives is interior consolation, which casts out all trouble and brings one to the full love of our Lord. To such souls as he enlightens with this consolation, he reveals many secrets, both at the time and later. In short, with this divine consolation, all trials are a pleasure and all weariness rest. In the case of him who walks in this fervour, warmth and interior consolation, there is no burden so great that it does not seem light to him, no penance or other trial so severe that it does not seem sweet. This shows and lays open to us the way we ought to follow, fleeing from the contrary. This consolation does not always remain with us – it follows its due seasons according to the divine ordinance. All this is to our profit, for when we are left without this divine consolation, then comes the other lesson, which is this – our old enemy now puts before us all possible obstacles to turn us aside from what we have begun, and he harasses us unceasingly, everything being the contrary of the first lesson. He often makes us sad, without our knowing why we are sad, nor can we pray with any devotion, contemplate or even speak of or listen to the things of God our Lord with relish or any interior delight. Not only this, but if he finds us to be weak and much dejected by these harmful thoughts, he suggests that we are entirely forgotten by God our Lord and we come to imagine that we are separated from God in everything and that however much we have done and however much we want to do, it is of no value whatsoever. Thus he strives to bring us into distrust of everything and we shall see that our great fear and weakness is caused in this way, for we then make too much of our miseries and are too passive in the face of his false arguments. It is necessary, therefore, that he who fights should look to what condition he is in. If it is consolation we should be humble and lowly and think that afterwards the test of temptation will come. If temptation, darkness or sadness comes, we must withstand it without any irritation and wait with patience for the Lord's consolation which will shatter all troubles and darkness coming from without.

It now remains for me to say something of what we feel when we read about God our Lord, how we must understand what we read and, when it is understood, learn to profit by it. It often happens that our Lord moves and impels our soul to one particular course or another by laying it open – that is, speaking within it without the sound of any voice, raising it all to his divine love, without our being able to resist what he suggests, even if we wanted to do so. In accepting such suggestions, we must of necessity be in conformity with the Commandments, the precepts of the Church, obedient to our superiors and full of complete humility, for the same divine Spirit is in all. Where we can frequently deceive ourselves is that after this consolation or inspiration, while the soul remains in bliss, the enemy creeps in under cover of joy and an appearance that is good, to make us exaggerate what we have felt from God our Lord, so as to make us disturbed and upset in everything.

At other times he makes us undervalue the lesson received, making us disturbed and ill at ease, because we cannot perfectly carry out all that has been shown to us. More prudence is necessary here than in any other matter. Many times we must restrain our great desire to speak of the things of God our Lord. At other times we must speak more than the desire or movement we have in us prompted – for in this it is necessary to think more of the good of others than of our own desires. When the enemy thus strives to increase or diminish the good impression received, we must go forward trying to help others, like someone crossing a ford. If he finds a good passage, that is, if he confidently hopes that some good will follow, he goes forward. If the ford is muddy, that is, if others would take scandal at his good words, then he always draws rein, seeking a more suitable time and hour to speak.

Matters have been mentioned into which it is impossible to enter further without writing at great length. Even then, there would be much which it is easier to feel than to explain, above all in writing. If it thus pleases our Lord, I hope we shall meet soon and then we shall be able to go into these matters more deeply. In the meantime, since you have Castro[63] nearer to you, I think it would be good for you to write to him, for, whereas harm cannot follow, some good may result. Since you tell me to write all I feel in the Lord, I will say that you will be fortunate if you know how to keep all you possess.

I conclude, praying the most holy Trinity through God's infinite and supreme goodness, to give us full grace to know and follow out perfectly his most holy will.

From Venice, June 18th, in the year 1536

Poor in goodness,
Ignatius

To my sister in Christ our Lord, Sister Teresa Rejadella, in Barcelona.

We can see that Ignatius, later so laconic, was still ready to instruct in detail a woman of high courage. Did he not say at the beginning of the letter that God had inspired him for many years past with an ardent desire to be completely at the service of all men and women, if they did but wish to follow the divine will? On September 11th of the same year, then, a second letter was despatched to the convent of Santa Clara at Barcelona. Teresa, evidently very impatient, had, without waiting for the receipt of the first letter, sent to Venice another request for spiritual consolation, almost in the same words – it too has not been preserved in its original text. Therefore the Master, not without gentle reproach, now gave her a much briefer answer.

Nevertheless, this lesson on contemplative prayer, filled with the exquisite naturalness of supernature, is a veritable model of lucid spiritual direction. We can understand why Sister Teresa wished to follow no other leader.

The grace and love of Christ our Lord be always with us, to our favour and help.

At different times, I have received two letters from you. You should already have received my answer to the first, an answer of some length. In your second letter you repeat what was said in the earlier one, except for two or three points with which I will now deal.

You say you find in yourself a great ignorance, great wretchedness, etc. It is a great thing to know this. You add that it seems to you that the various and sometimes rather vague counsels that are given you contribute to this condition of soul. I share your feelings on the matter and I think with you that people who are not definite about things have little capacity for enlightening and directing others; but the divine Master who sees our want of help then comes to our assistance himself.

There can be no meditation wherein the understanding is used without bodily fatigue. There are, however, other meditations, equally God-given, all too often forgotten in these times, which are full of peace as regards the understanding and cause no strain on the interior faculties of the soul. No effort is involved either interior or physical. Meditations of this kind do not weary the body at all. Except in two cases, as I shall now explain, they rest it.

The first is when through such meditations we forget to take the amount of food and recreation that the body needs. I mean food, for sometimes such meditations are so absorbing that we forget to take our meals at the proper times. In referring to recreation, I mean devout recreation, as, for instance, when the mind is allowed to pass freely from one thing to another, provided it is good, or indifferent, excluding only what is bad.

The second case is when such meditations deprive us of the necessary sleep. Many persons given to prayer or contemplation find that because they have been using their minds immediately before the time of sleep, they are so intent upon the things they have been meditating on that day, or preparing for the morrow, that they cannot close an eye. The enemy's tactics then are to present all the good thoughts he can to the mind, his purpose in so doing being to exhaust the body by depriving it of sleep. This is a thing that must be absolutely avoided. Much can be achieved with a healthy body, with a sickly one it is difficult to accomplish anything. A healthy body can be a powerful factor either in the doing of much evil or of much good – evil if the will is depraved and one's habits sinful; good if the will is wholly devoted to God's service and formed to the habit of the virtues.

In your case, as I know what meditations and practices I have recommended you and the time I told you to devote to them, I have absolutely nothing to add to what I have already written. Once more I confirm that you should chiefly dwell on God's love for you which is certain and think only of repaying him love for love. Do not worry about bad, obscene or sensual thoughts, nor about your wretchedness or lukewarmness, when it is against your will that you experience such things. Saints Peter and Paul themselves did not wholly escape such things. By paying no attention to such temptations, one gains much, although, indeed, not everything. Just as I shall not be saved through the good works of the good angels, so I shall not be damned through the bad thoughts and weaknesses suggested to me by the bad angels, the world and the flesh.

God our Lord wants of me one single thing, namely, my soul's entire submission to his divine Majesty. When the soul is thus submitted to God, it causes the body, willingly or unwillingly, to act according to God's will. To bring this about is our greatest difficulty, but it is also the good pleasure of God's eternal and sovereign Goodness. May our Lord by his infinite mercy and grace deign to hold us always by the hand.

Ignatius, the poor pilgrim

From Venice, September 11th, 1536.

A year's silence followed. There can, however, be no doubt that Ignatius was kept informed of what was going on at Santa Clara. Araoz had been visiting there since 1539. Sister Teresa's fellow-nuns must have rejoiced when the news reached Barcelona that Pope Paul III had orally approved Ignatius' Society on September 3rd, 1539, at Tivoli. Isabel Roser was a close friend of Sister Rejadella.

It is understandable that Ignatius had no time to reply to the nun's letters during those busy years when he was founding his Society. Therefore a friend named Juan Pujols wrote to him on August 13th, 1543, asking that he would not entirely forget the convent of Santa Clara. "Not everyone has the patience of Señora Rejadella, who writes two or three times without getting an answer; and the second letter is always as amiable and polite as the first."

No doubt Teresa's letters contained not only news of convent life, as for example the death of one Sister Luisa, one of the group who desired reform, but also the ever more pressing problem of a canonical renewal of the house. No one even knew exactly to what order and to what rule the convent was subject. The other nuns looked askance at the small band of zealots, who had lately dared under Sister Teresa's leadership to receive Communion weekly or even daily.

It was time for Ignatius to write again. Father Araoz, returning to Spain on November 15th, 1543, was able to take a comforting letter to Teresa. Briefly and somewhat impersonally numbered "firstly", "secondly", "thirdly", the required answers were given. The doctrine therein expounded concerning frequent Communion in the early Church is historically and patristically not quite sound. But that Ignatius advised the nuns of Santa Clara to receive Communion daily was excellent spiritual advice.[64]

The sovereign grace and love of Christ our Lord be always with us to our continual help and favour.

Firstly, I understand that it has been the divine will to take away and remove from the present trials of this life your and our sister in the Lord, Luisa, and since we have many reasons or signs to take it for certain that in the other life she enjoys everlasting glory (do not let us forget her in our prayers although they be poor and unworthy), I hope she will favour us and repay us with holy interest. Therefore if, enlarging upon the matter, I should speak words of consolation to you, in some sense I should think I was doing you a wrong since I judge that in all things you conform yourselves (as you ought) with God's supreme and eternal providence, who directs us to his greater glory and to ours.

Secondly, as to custom and observance. Where you have had a definite ruling and, even though you have not had one, where you have con-firmation from the Apostolic See, it is certain that you are in conformity with the divine will and service; for any good rule of the blessed saints can bind under sin just in so far as it is confirmed by the Vicar of Christ our Lord, or by someone else on his authority. Thus the rule of St. Benedict, of St. Francis or of St. Jerome cannot of its own force bind in any sense under pain of sin; but when it is confirmed and authorized by the Apostolic See, it does so bind by the divine power which is infused into such a rule.

Thirdly, as to communicating every day, since in the primitive Church all communicated every day and that since that time there has

338

been no ordinance or any writing of our holy mother the Church (nor of the holy doctors either of scholastic or positive theology), that persons moved by devotion may not communicate every day; and if the blessed St. Augustine says that he neither praises nor blames this practice, saying elsewhere that he exhorts all to communicate every Sunday, he says further on, speaking of the most holy body of Christ our Lord – "this bread is daily. Thus, then, live that each day you may be able to receive". Since matters stand thus, although one might not find in oneself such good dispositions or such holy interior movements, a good and undisputable test on which the matter may be decided is the dictate of one's own conscience. I mean – since all things are lawful to you in our Lord, if you judge that your soul, free from clear mortal sins or what you can judge to be such, is more helped and more inflamed with the love of your Lord and Creator, and with such an intention you communicate, finding by experience that this most holy spiritual food nourishes, quietens and rests you, and preserving you, gives you increase in his greater service, praise and glory, since this is clear, it is lawful for you and will be better for you to communicate every day.

Since, concerning this and other matters, I have spoken at length with Father Licentiate Araoz, who will give you this letter, to him in all things I refer you in our Lord. Thus I write no more, asking God our Lord by his infinite mercy in all things, that you may be guided and governed by his infinite and sovereign goodness.
Poor in goodness.

Iñigo

Rome, November 15th, 1543

To my sister in our Lord, Teresa Rejadella, in Barcelona.

The canonical situation of the convent of Santa Clara now became almost inextricably complicated. In 1546 a new abbess was elected in a patently simoniacal way through the influence of her aristocratic relatives. Sister Teresa and her fellow-nuns who desired reform felt in conscience obliged to refuse her their obedience. All these problems were discussed with the Jesuits, who had founded their first establishment at Barcelona in a small rented house in 1545. Father Araoz as Provincial had shortly before admitted into the Society of Jesus four much respected clerics of the city, among them the kindly Juan Queralt – who was not, it is true, very well-versed in the principles and ideals of Ignatius. The nuns of Santa Clara provided the Jesuits' poor house with food.

It was not long before Father Araoz sent a report to Ignatius, dated March 6th, 1546. He told him about the election of the new abbess and its consequences; and again it was Cousin Antonio who suggested to the General the idea of placing at least Sister Teresa's little group under the obedience of the Jesuits. "Rejadella and a few others wish – since in any case they do not live under a definite rule – to place themselves under the Society's obedience. Sister Roser knows about it already. Many ladies of quality are also in favour of this plan, for there exists here no little envy of Sister Roser and her companions – and quite rightly."

Ignatius, who at this time had not yet finished with Isabel Roser, was placed in a highly embarrassing position; for by the same post he received a letter from Prince Philip, urging him to undertake the reform of the Catalan nunneries. Moreover, Isabel Roser made herself the zealous advocate of the nuns of Santa Clara, so that Ignatius could write to Francis Borgia: "Señora Roser has put before us in terms of urgency her desire for the reform of the convents in Barcelona".[65]

Now Ignatius began one of those campaigns of which he was a master; everybody of rank and influence was mobilized for the work. This was the same Ignatius who, twenty years before when a student at Barcelona, had been beaten and ridiculed. All this happened in the same month in which Ignatius, after the renunciation of Isabel Roser, gave Miguel Torres his memorandum concerning a female branch of the Society of Jesus. Torres was also commissioned to make a special visit to Sister Teresa. The General's attitude was unequivocal. With all his readiness to promote the work of reform, there could be no question of the admission of nuns into the Society. On November 9th, 1546, Bishop Cazador of Barcelona sent Ignatius a description of the corrupt condition of the convents in the Catalan capital. He was in despair: "To reform these nuns would be a real miracle!" In May 1547 Ignatius sent him encouragement; and in August of the same year he received two letters (now no longer extant) from Rejadella, which Father Martin de Santacruz, travelling from Portugal through Barcelona to Rome, brought with him. Therein the nun expounded to her Master not only some personal questions concerning the spiritual life, but also the problem of convent reform. The reply which Ignatius sent her in October was cautious and restrained. Reform, in which even the Prince of Spain took so keen an interest and which had almost become a political matter, was hailed with joy and received every encouragement; but of admission to the Society of Jesus there was not a word.[66]

IHS

The grace and love of Jesus Christ, our God and Lord, live ever in our souls. Amen.

Father de Santacruz brought me two of your letters in which, while you express dissatisfaction on account of both personal and general evils, you also show that you have a just desire given to you by God our Lord that a remedy should be found for both the one and the other. As he himself has said and it is written: The Lord shall hear the desires of the poor.

As to your personal troubles, it is certainly inevitable that whoever knows himself should find troubles and necessities in himself. He will never lack such things in this state of present misery until in the forge of the eternal love of God, our Creator and Lord, all our sinfulness is entirely consumed. Then we shall be penetrated by him, our souls wholly possessed by him and our wills wholly conformed, or rather transformed, into that which is essential holiness and perfect goodness.

May he at least grant all of us his infinite mercy that we may experience his love more each day and abhor all our imperfections and wretchedness without exception. Then we should rather attain to participation in the eternal light of his wisdom, which is inseparable from his infinite goodness and perfection, before which any defects of ours, even slight ones, become perfectly clear to us and are something we cannot tolerate. Then, by crushing them, we weaken and diminish them by the grace of the same God our Lord.

As to the general ills for which you desire God's hand to provide a remedy, hoping that in his goodness he will do so, not only do I desire this, but I even hope so too. I take as a sign that the reformation of this convent will be pleasing to God the fact that the Prince is seen to be so desirous of it and that effective means to bring it about are being sought. That there should be difficulty is nothing new, rather is it the ordinary state of affairs in things of much importance for God's service and glory. The more difficult it is, however, the more this work will be acceptable to, and the occasion of giving God our Lord more heartfelt and unceasing thanks for it.

As to the affairs of our Society, you will find someone in Barcelona who can inform you better. I only ask you for the love of Jesus Christ, who is the head of it, as he is the common lord of all created things and their God, that you recommend us much in your prayers to his divine Majesty, so that each day he may be increasingly served and glorified by it.

As to my bodily health, I have little. May he be blessed who with his blood and life purchased life eternal for us in the sharing in his Kingdom and glory, and may he give us grace so that the temporal state of our bodies, be it well or ill, and all other dispositions which he has placed in his creatures, may always be employed to his greater service, praise and glory. Amen.

(Ignatius)

Rome, month of October, 1547.

The hopes which Araoz and Queralt had held out to Sister Teresa's little group in 1547 were not fulfilled. It must straightway be admitted that not even the reform of Santa Clara, in the shape of a renewal in conformity with the spirit of the founder of the Benedictine order, was accomplished. As late as 1559 a Jesuit in Barcelona wrote to the General Laynez: "Santa Clara is that convent, the reform of which our Father Ignatius once so ardently desired, and in which God has always allowed a number of souls to flourish who had a strong yearning for reform. So far their longing has not been satisfied."

Between those years there took place a hard battle waged by the courageous nuns under the leadership of Sister Teresa and the old Prioress Hieronyma Oluja, not only for reform in general, but also against Ignatius and against the papal bull of 1549, with the object of being admitted to the Society of Jesus as female members in spite of everything.[67]

From 1548 to 1549 Father Araoz lived for more than a year in Barcelona as Provincial of Spain. This he did on the orders of Prince Philip for the express purpose of reforming the Catalan convents. He it was who even then kept alive in Teresa's fellow-religious the desire to win a victory in the end over the unyielding Ignatius. In answer to his representations, the General had in March 1548 to say no once again, with a clear reference to the papal ordinances. But old Prioress Oluja, like the aged Simeon, wished to see salvation before her death, and so on January 10th, 1549, she sent a letter to Ignatius, imploring him that he would even yet take the nuns who desired reform under the holy obedience of the Society.[68]

IHS

The grace and love of the Holy Spirit be always in our souls. Amen.

Most dear and loving Father in Christ our Lord.

I think Your Paternity will already have been informed about our troubles and necessities through the Licenciate, our father [Araoz], whom our Lord in his mercy has willed to be in Barcelona. This has been no small grace to help us to bear them, and from him and through him, we hope, with the help of God and with his encouragement, for a solution. You already know what is happening here and has happened, both in our inmost souls and in outward things.

We hope through the intervention and information given by this father that Your Paternity will in your compassion grant [our request], and interest yourself on behalf of persons so greatly in need. For a long time, indeed, before this great and pressing necessity, the Lord gave us a very great desire of this thing that we are now asking for so reasonably and now he has permitted an opportunity to present itself whereby we derive courage for what we did not dare even to think of but are now asking for with great insistency. Thus I ask and beg for this, for my part on my knees and prostrate at Your Paternity's feet, not without tears, as I have many times asked it from the Lord of all with great insistency. His Majesty who in this as in all else knows my inmost heart, is my witness. If a request is good, it comes from God, and on that ground I think my request is wholly from him. I am under a very deep obligation to God over this matter, merely because he has given us the desire of it. Through his goodness I have sometimes felt a great hope of obtaining this favour, so that at least with it I may make a good death, and the others learn to live well. Moreover, through that same goodness of the Lord, I have felt and do feel that God would be greatly served by the others of us if this request were granted, whereas for me I must not fail to serve God and always remember who I am and the very little aptitude I have for good, and how little I deserve that my request should be granted. This is very clear and can be stated without any hesitation.

I do not want to write at too great a length, although to satisfy myself, despite my unworthiness, I cannot help being importunate in again begging, in the way already mentioned, that you would advise and direct us how we may be able to obtain the favour of being governed, ordered and in all things subject to your obedience and holy Society. This, like Simeon, I desire to see before I die. I should then be freed from so many entanglements and confusions as there are at present, which, since they are so numerous, I will mention none of them, nor should I know where to begin. I have said enough, and commit myself to your charity and tender care and to the reports sent to you. There is no reason to say more and so give you trouble. May the Lord give us all his holy grace and especially to Your Paternity, for he has given you so many graces to distribute for his greater service and the good of our souls. Some of the most devout sisters kiss Your Paternity's hands.

They are among those who very earnestly desire and ask the Lord to have them and all men in his hand. Amen.

Your Paternity's most useless subject
Oluja

From Barcelona, January 10th, 1549.

Father Juan Queralt, who after the early death of Father Martín de Santacruz had most to do with the nuns, had a tactical plan of his own for waging the war; the Secretary Polanco must first be won over. So scarcely had the courier departed with the above letter when on January 14th, 1549, another one was sent off to Rome. Queralt thus described the situation in Barcelona: "Here everyone is so stubborn even the weaker sex must take part in the battle and the victory. It therefore seems absolutely necessary to found in Barcelona a convent or a house of women belonging to the Society of Jesus, to which these influential and exemplary nuns may retire." Of this and nothing less Polanco was to persuade his master. Together with this letter went a joint letter from Sister Teresa and Prioress Oluja to Father Polanco: "Be our procurator, advocate and intercessor with Father Master Ignatius".[69]

IHS

Very dear father in Christ,

May the grace and love of Jesus Christ our Lord be always with us and be felt in our souls. Amen.

From the letters which are accompanying this one, Your Reverence will be advised of our business and necessities. These are many and great, as Your Reverence, with your heart of mercy and goodness, will be better able to appreciate than we to write. We feel them most deeply, and they really deserve help and a remedy. We ask for your help, indeed, for God's honour alone.

Thus we, sailing across the temptestuous sea of these difficulties and desiring to escape without shipwreck, with much reason and cause are obliged to seek every anchor and support for our [spiritual] well-being and holiness.

Moreover, since it was the Lord's will to remove from the troubles of this life to heavenly rest the soul of the good Father de Santacruz, in whom we had great confidence in these matters, knowing Your Reverence's great charity and the desire and great zeal which the Lord has given you for the salvation of souls, and in view of the love which the Lord gives our souls to feel inwardly for that of Your Reverence, he has put it into our minds to think that, since he has willed to give us the said Father de Santacruz as heavenly advocate, so Your Paternity will be our earthly one, for we are given to understand that we have you as such.

Thus, prostrate at Your Reverence's feet, we beseech you, by that infinite charity which the eternal Father has shown us in giving us his only begotten Son as the price of our redemption on earth and as our advocate in heaven, that you would exercise charity towards us, imitating him in the office he performs for us in heaven, by doing this upon earth, being our procurator, advocate and intercessor with Father Master Ignatius, so that he may deign to grant us our request, which is so just and so long desired. We ask you to beseech his Paternity to take pity on our souls, so desirous as he knows of serving the Lord beneath the obedience of the Society, since we judge this to be very much to the Lord's greater glory, and also on our behalf to beg Father Codacio for the love of our Lord to perform the same office for us, together with all our other advisers, in so far as he may judge to be most suitable for the furthering of this business.

It is true that we have no causes in process with Your Reverence nor with Father Codacio, nor with others, who are our advocates, nor, indeed, have we the wherewithal to repay such charity, but we hope in the Lord who is rich in mercies, that he will repay it very abundantly with interest. We shall always remain under the obligation of begging him to increase his gifts and graces to you and the others on earth and in heaven his everlasting glory. Amen. Amen.

The unworthy servants of Jesus and of Your Reverence.

Teresa Rejadella, Jeronyma Oluja
unworthy Prioress

Barcelona, January 14th, 1549

To the most reverend father in Christ, Master John of Polanco, of the Society of Jesus, in Rome.

Yet another letter arrived in Rome by the same post, a detailed report from the Provincial Araoz dated January 15th, 1549. For years, he wrote to Ignatius, he had been daily assailed with the same request, but the position had now become acute. The Abbess of Santa Clara, because her election in 1546 had been tainted with simony, had now been suspended in accordance with canon law. In the event of this suspension's being upheld, eleven nuns of the convent asked to be admitted to the Society of Jesus under the leadership of Prioress Oluja, who was temporarily in charge of the house. In the event, however, of the abbess' being reinstated, contrary to canon law, they simply could not obey her. They were actually (he wrote) neither fully Benedictines nor even less Franciscans; and because they had so long called themselves "Apostolic", they felt themselves to be half Jesuitesses already. A convent of their own could be built for them; money enough was to be had, for the abbess and her supporters would be only too pleased at the departure of the reformed nuns.

Araoz received in reply a sharp and curt reprimand; such plans were contrary to the rules of the Society! However, added Ignatius, he would like to have clear information from the nuns themselves about the canonical position in this conflict. Was he softening? The case of Santa Clara was the first of its kind and undoubtedly required special handling.

A short while afterwards the General received another letter from Spain, this time from a layman and an old friend of his Barcelona days, Mateo Murranos, who had meanwhile become an officer of the crown in Saragossa. This gentleman took up the idea of a house of "Jesuitesses" with ardent enthusiasm. The nuns of Santa Clara, he wrote, knew no higher objective than to live according to the rule of the Society of Jesus, however strict it might be. He regarded such a development as simply unavoidable. (We have heard this before.) With some exaggeration he called the nuns Oluja and Rejadella "two heavenly stars upon earth". We do not know if this poetic language made much impression on Ignatius. In his prompt reply he did, indeed, speak of the sincere friendship in our Lord which he felt for those two women; but in view of his principles the answer could not be in doubt. Ignatius appealed, as he was always to do henceforth, to the Pope's ordinances. The Jesuits "must be ever ready to set out, with one foot off the ground".[70]

His desire for more exact information about the situation at Santa Clara was fulfilled sooner than he expected. On February 24th, 1549, Prioress Oluja sent a report on the progress of the legal battle. As the nuns were regarded as Benedictines, the Abbot of San Cucufat, head of the Catalan Benedictine congregation, took the convent under his authority. The suspended Abbess was reinstated, and a previous ruling directed against her was annulled. But the nuns who desired reform had already, on Father Araoz' advice and with the help of their influential families, taken a legal adviser of their own. Whom were they now to obey, the Abbess or the advocate? The Jesuits had counselled them to let the solution of the problem depend upon the result of an appeal to the Roman curia. The Abbot forbade any such action and summoned the Prioress to appear before his court.

Nevertheless, her supporters signed the document that was necessary for the appeal to Rome. This was a declaration of war, and Ignatius was informed of it.[71]

IHS

May the most holy Trinity be always in our souls.

Very dear Father.

I have earlier sent you a letter with the renewed request for your kind consent. This I also expressed in other letters which went in the folder of our father, the Licentiate [Araoz], who was recently here. He left on the 11th of this month. Afterwards we received a letter from Your Paternity, from which to our regret we did not receive any more news about you. You can imagine how much we long for news. Of our own affairs I will inform you briefly, for there would be so much to say in telling you all, that it would be troublesome to you.

The lord abbot removed the suspension on Saturday, which was the sixteenth of this month. He sent us two short letters by a porter, the one to the lady abbess, the other to me, intimating that he restored her to her office. He wrote nothing more, nor did he want to come himself, showing dissatisfaction with the judges who had given their verdict in this sense. Previously, on the advice of Father Licentiate Araoz, we had sought an understanding with the relatives and with a learned counsellor whom they brought with them, Don Jaime de Queralt. He is married to a sister of someone here called Don Francisco de la Caballería. We sisters were greatly worried and had considerable scruples, having heard from the superior and from others, and from learned men and theologians, that we could not obey such people in good conscience. All the nuns said what they thought and thus declared that the remedy was to appeal and so we appealed, I with five others – Señora Rejadella and the others most devoted to our desires for reform. The five others obeyed, being advised by the same learned men, that this was the best course in the business, although they did not want this but rather felt great repugnance over it. Now, however, they are more loyal and more of one mind with us than before. It can, indeed, be said that tribulation makes them love and greatly desire what in other times they detested. In short God must be thanked that these little handmaids of his have been brave in the matter. On the morning of the restitution came the prohibition and summons of the Lord abbot. The porter brought me the summons in Latin, and at the same hour he sent a similar one to those who have charge of the business. Afterwards I received two or three summonses; our advocates are dealing with them. Now they have come and have made us sign a proxy for the said Don Francisco which it seems to me is taking the law-suit to Rome.

Your Paternity must now do what you think best in the matter, favouring what is most to the service of God our Lord. I say with all truth that the very thought of the law-suit makes me more distressed than all the rest. Each time they tell me to go forward with it, it is a fresh distress. As far as my soul can see there are two grounds for this: firstly, it is against my state in life to have to contradict; secondly, because it causes so much indignation and violent passions and strife are increasing. Now they have appointed rules and have established a somewhat mitigated observance, at least so far as we are concerned. May it please the Lord to permit us soon to find a way by which God our Lord may be better served and our souls more tranquil, for he knows of what sort they are. By the passion of Christ may he have compassion on us, as we trust by that charity for souls with which he has inspired you. To you and to all of us may the Lord grant his holy grace. Amen.

From the most useless,
Hieronyma Oluja

Barcelona, February 21st, 1549

To the most reverend Father in Christ, Master Iñigo de Loyola, General of the Society of the Name of Jesus, in Rome.

To the great sorrow of the nuns, Father Araoz had to leave Barcelona just at this time. Sister Teresa could do nothing about it but add a personal complaint to her prioress's letter. Father Queralt, who also sent a letter by the same post, remarked: "The two of them have written these letters with much weeping and lamentation."[72]

IHS

Very Reverend Father in Christ,

May the most holy Trinity be always with your charity and with us all. Amen.

Most dear and loving Father in Christ.

If it were possible to send tears instead of a letter, I feel more like weeping than writing or expressing our desires. Although I have often written and expressed what we felt, it seems to me that up to the present I have said nothing, although I think your charity has understood me better than I understand myself. Blessed be God our Lord, who gives or allows us creatures whom he so loves the possibility of expression through which it seems increasing strength will be given to us. He is, indeed, even on earth the father of mercies and God of all consolation.

Thus we entreat you by the wounds of Jesus Christ our Lord to show compassion on us and accept us as your daughters — and me as your slave, purchased a thousand times over and not with money alone. This is what I feel and I cannot write it without many tears. Indeed, Father, it seems to me right that I should be received because I am so wretched, just as others are because they are very good. With this I make bold to dare to desire and ask what I know I do not deserve nor am I fitted for so much good, yet God our Lord is kind and has endowed Your Paternity with so much charity that it gives me much heart.

The lady prioress will lay our request before Your Charity in detail. It provides sufficient both for consideration and to be sad about and thus I implore you to have pity on us, since Your Charity is to be our protector.

Ah Jesus! Who could realize or express what good the Father Licentiate Araoz has done, both in this business and in that of my personal needs and those of other sisters. It is a matter for much thanksgiving to God our Lord. He seems to be a father to everyone. Here in Barcelona they much wanted him to preach this Lent in Santa María del Mar. If his duties and his physical health permitted, there would be very great profit from it, by the grace of God. I fear that we do not deserve so great a good, although it was obvious that he was greatly and genuinely desired. The loss of him in our affairs was and is great. Had Father Araoz been here, I do not think they would have dared to do what has been done in the few days since the Licentiate left. May Jesus Christ our Lord keep him always and in everything in his almighty hand. Amen. May he preserve and prosper Your Charity in his greater service as shall be to his greater glory and the profit of souls. Amen, Amen.

> Your Charity's least slave,
> Rejadella

Barcelona, February 21st, 1549

To the most reverend father and lord in Christ our Lord, Master Ignatius of Loyola, General of the Society of Jesus, in Rome.

The subject of all these requests was always the same: to be admitted to the Society of Jesus. From Valencia Father Araoz again put in a word in favour of such a solution. This encouraged the two nuns, now almost in despair, to implore Ignatius in that same month of February 1549, to grant their one and only prayer. Their letter is a veritable outburst of emotion.[73]

IHS

Very Reverend and dearest Father in Christ.

May the most holy Trinity always gloriously inhabit and dwell in Your Paternity as we, although most wretched creatures, entreat and desire, and may God's eternal goodness, having regard to the most sacred and precious blood which Jesus Christ our Lord shed for us and for all, and not to our wretchedness and lack of merit, move and incline Your Paternity's soul to hear us. We are confident that you feel and know what our most poor and worthless souls desire and ask.

Oh Father, do not deny us the mercy and consolation which the God and father of our souls inspires us to desire and ask for even unto death. We well know, dearest Father, that if we were to consider what it is we are asking for, we should be covered with confusion. This is certain. Although, however, we stand before you in confusion, we have confidence in the goodness and charity with which the Eternal and Infinite God has endowed Your Paternity. Indeed, very reverend Father, what can we do if the Lord himself makes us earnestly desire, [this], so that it is impossible for us to do otherwise than demand and seek it unwearyingly? We shall fulfill our part — that of asking, entreating and seeking, hoping in the Eternal Majesty that Your Paternity will fulfil yours — that of giving, responding, consoling. Now, Father and master, we do not say in words what we are asking for because we are already aware, beyond all possibility of doubt, that Your Paternity knows this more and better than we do ourselves. In short, since we are sure by the charity of our great God, that Your Paternity loves us as a father, we should like to be worthy of being placed under your obedience as our lawful and true superior. For with what has now passed, not only we, but many others desire and ask this. We are as the Lord knows we are and we hope that Your Paternity knows us through and through. The Father Licentiate Araoz, who is a good father to us, will do the office of charity in expressing our desires which we, although we dare to desire, do not dare to ask. He has had personal knowledge of our difficulties and has not failed to show us compassion and pity.

And since we hope that our Lord is going to give us our remedy through Your Paternity, all affectionately prostrate at your feet we implore this of you and ask it with tears, begging for compassion. We are certain you will be moved to pity and if at this moment we could send you our souls, instead of this letter, we do not doubt you would give your consent. We trust in the Lord, who gives us these desires with so much intensity that we cannot doubt they come from his great goodness, that, since in his mercy he moves us to desire and ask this privilege, by that same mercy he will move Your Paternity's heart to grant it. May the most holy Trinity, who makes and is wont to make what is impossible and difficult to men possible and easy, work in this as may be to God's greater glory and service. Amen.

It seems that God's uncreated charity has permitted these innovations in this house, so that with increased compassion Your Paternity may be moved to show us mercy. This is our desire and we are completely certain that Your Paternity will not refuse us this great good. For it cannot be that, since we hold you as our father and true superior, Your Charity should not accept us as daughters and subjects, although we are unworthy. If Your Paternity gives consent, all the rest is possible and easy. May the most glorious and blessed Mother of almighty God be our intercessor in so holy a business — that is our hope.

Well then, most dear Father, give ear to our voices, receive our tears, fulfil our desires, that the Lord may fulfil your holy and perfect desires. May all the angels and the blessed in heaven help us in this both in heaven and on earth, particularly Your Paternity's guardian angel. Amen. Amen.

Oh, very reverend Father, pardon our affection which, if we could express it rightly we should want to send back to you. May the most sweet and good Jesus, our Father and Lord, always guide and rule Your Paternity in this and in all things. Amen.

Since, in any event, our souls and those of many others are longing for this thing, do not disappoint us, dearest Father. May Jesus Christ our Lord make us always desire his greater service and love and give us whatever will enable us most to love and serve him, until we obtain himself and possess him without any separation. Amen.

So that you may read this more easily it has been written by another hand.

Your Paternity's most useless subjects,

Oluja   Rejadella
unworthy Prioress

Barcelona, February 1549

To the most reverend and dear father in Christ, Father Master Ignatius of Loyola, General of the Society of Jesus, in Rome.

351

From March to April the spiritual distress of the anxious little group in Santa Clara increased to the point of being intolerable. The nuns could not refrain from making yet once again their request for admittance to the Society, for this appeared more and more clearly to be the solution of every problem. Several of the letters forming part of this concentrated attack on Ignatius' heart have been lost. One, dated March 6th, has been preserved, a single heart-rending appeal for the granting of their prayer.

IHS

Very reverend Father in Christ.

The grace and peace of God our Lord be always in our souls and with all men. Amen.

My dearest and most loving Father in Christ, I do not know how to describe our struggles to you because there is so much to say and such dissensions. Furthermore because a few days ago the Prioress informed Your Paternity of matters at length, I will now say nothing. I desire to learn how to bear suffering, that God our Lord may be more served and praised.

Ah, Jesus! Dearest father. May we not hope from these tribulations that they are the road and door leading to our desires? – although I do not, indeed, deserve even to desire this, how much less to obtain such a great mercy, such a great grace as that Your Paternity should receive me as your subject, and that I should be your slave. May God our Lord not permit that I shall ever cease to be so.

I do not speak of the other sisters, since through the Lord's goodness it is legitimate to think that since they deserve this grace, they will, I hope, obtain it, by the grace of God our Lord and Your Paternity's great charity and kindness. Indeed, how fully do I believe that you know and are aware of our needs and difficulties, I mean the difficulties of our religious life! Indeed, Father, we hope for protection and help from Your Paternity.

I entreat you by the most holy wounds of Jesus Christ our Lord, and on behalf of all those who have received so holy a desire from our Lord, that Your Paternity take pity on all such, for they deserve it, and do not forget my tears and afflictions over this desire for so many years, although very truly in my soul I count them all as nothing, as I do whatever I was able and am able to do; and the proffering of my request now appears to me great boldness. Your Paternity's greatness of soul gives me heart and, finally, it seems to me that you are the father on earth who is to guide and take us to the father in heaven. May it please God in his infinite and supreme goodness to lead Your Paternity always and in all things by the hand, as is best for his greater glory and the profit of souls.

For all that concerns your reverend and very dear Father the Licentiate Araoz I refer you to Father Master Queralt. It does not seem to me that I ought to look so much at the loss of his presence to us as at his contentment at having what he so much desired. May the most blessed Jesus have him always and in all things in his keeping. Amen, Amen.

Your Reverence's servant and useless slave
Rejadella

From Barcelona, March 6th, 1549

To the most reverend father in Christ our Lord, Father Master Ignatius of Loyola, General of the Society of Jesus, in Rome.

The poor women were already working themselves into a kind of pious frenzy. They saw and thought about nothing else but leaving the convent and occupying a house of their own as female Jesuits. Three weeks later another plea for help was sent to Rome, the joint composition of the two leaders of the reform: "We are set in so great a necessity which has no law." Polanco also received a letter addressed to him personally.[74]

IHS

Very reverend and dear Father in Christ

May the most holy Trinity always inhabit and make their abode in Your Paternity's soul. Amen, Amen.
Some days ago we wrote to Your Paternity mentioning and pointing out the desires which for a long time now the Lord has been giving, preserving and increasing in our poor souls. By his secret judgments he inspires us with these desires in such a way that although when we consider our wretchedness, the mere thinking of them seems an impertinence, yet we find we cannot do otherwise than not only to think, but to desire, ask and entreat, remembering that our Lord not only gave us leave to seek, knock and ask, but in various ways urged us to do so.

Because of this and also because we trust in Your Paternity's charity, we take courage to mention these desires and bring them before Your Paternity, together with the almost inevitable needs and difficulties which have arisen. These — and likewise the causes of them — not only, through God's goodness, have not ceased but have in various ways increased and daily continue to do so, giving us occasion of legitimately and even importunately seeking, knocking and asking the medicine and remedy for our infirmities and necessities as persons sick and in need.

So great is the confidence that our Lord gives us in Your Paternity's charity, that we cannot fail to hope that, as a loving father, you will take pity on your unworthy servants, and do them the charity of what with so much reason and just title, although they are unworthy of it, our Lord makes them desire. Thus, dearest Father, prostrate at Your Paternity's feet as humbly as we can by the merits and passion and most precious blood of Christ our Lord, we again implore you to grant what we have been begging for.

We clearly see and know, dear Father, that we are unworthy and undeserving not only of receiving, but even of thinking of and begging for this. However, we do not ask it for our merits or worthiness, but as a favour and special mercy. Since we are set in so great a necessity, which has no law, we ask that we may dare to hope that the Lord in his goodness will work in Your Paternity's soul in such a way that his name will be praised and served and our souls comforted and confirmed in their long-standing desires, in respect of which the Lord has given us the grace that many others are in agreement with and hold the same desires as we do.

We do not doubt that since you are a very living vineshoot set in the true vine, you feel deeply in your heart the troubles and needs of our souls. These, although we suffer and feel them, yet, since they are so many and so great both inward and outward, we cannot express. We will not, therefore, write about them at greater length, but make an end. We continually beg the eternal goodness to preserve and increase his best gifts in Your Paternity's soul.

Your Reverend Paternity's slaves and servants in the Lord,
      Oluja   Rejadella

From Barcelona, April 3rd, 1549

To the most reverend and dear father in the Lord, Master Ignatius of Loyola, General of the Society of Jesus our Lord, in Rome.

The two could not yet know that Ignatius almost at that very time was writing a letter to them, which, while its terms were a clear and inflexible rejection, indicated with calm firmness possible ways towards a solution. Ignatius left it to his secretary Polanco to transmit the details more explicitly. We possess a summary of this letter, dated May 15th, 1549. From this it must be inferred that Ignatius' letter lay undispatched at Rome for a month. The essential point of his instructions is that the reform, which was on no account to be abandoned, must begin within the convent itself and be undertaken in accordance with the directions of the Grand Inquisitor of Spain; that is to say, independently to a certain extent of any religious order. These measures could be supported by a legal adviser in Rome.

May the sovereign grace and eternal love of Christ our Lord be always with us to help and protect us.

By the letters I have received from Barcelona from various persons I see how God our Lord visits them with trials, giving them no little occasion to exercise the virtues which his divine goodness has instilled in them, and to show the solidity of those virtues, for in difficult matters (of which I see there are many in your affairs) an opportunity is given us of true spiritual profit. May it please Jesus Christ, who did and suffered so much for all of us, to give us abundant grace, so that whatever there is to suffer may be suffered fruitfully for his holy love and all that needs remedying may be remedied in the way most pleasing to his divine goodness.

This I hold for certain that what you are now thinking of is not according to the mind of God; for, although in our Society, as one of the many obligations which it holds especially dear in our Lord, there is the whole-hearted will to console and serve you in conformity with our profession, the authority of the Vicar of Christ has closed the door against our taking on any government or superintendence of religious, a thing which the Society begged for from the beginning. This is because it is judged that it would be for the greater service of God our Lord that we should have as few ties as possible in order to be able to go wherever obedience to the Sovereign Pontiff and the needs of our neighbours may call us. This remedy then I do not think would be pleasing to God our Lord in any way and I hope in his infinite goodness that some other more suitable way will be found to arrive at what you and all of us desire in our Lord, his peace and special consolation.

Although I must abide by what seems best in this case you will learn from Master Polanco what my personal feeling about it is. In this I shall not enter into details, merely saying that I should like you to trust me in this matter, believing that in the interests of what we are all aiming at, which is the greater service of God our Lord, it is not fitting for us to do what you wish, although, if responsibility for certain religious persons

355

had to be assumed, it would be to you before any others that our ministry would be offered.

May it please the Eternal Wisdom to grant us all ever to know his holy will, in it to find peace and contentment, and to fulfil it perfectly.

Your servant in our Lord,

Ignacio

From Rome, April 5th, 1549

For the nuns:

1. A few kind words.
2. Show that it is not lawful to make such a request: and that if they persist, they would be the first.
3. That what was represented to our Father Ignatius as Superior as the best means of bringing things to a satisfactory conclusion as soon as possible, would be that they should take the Inquisitor as their superior and that he should appoint some vicar or confessor, and apply reform when and where it should be necessary. Moreover, the said vicar should not be connected with any religious order.
4. About this, it would be good for them to appoint a legal adviser in Rome and from the house of professed fathers here all the help they wish should be given to them whenever they ask for it.

Rome, May 15th, 1549

To Jeronyma Oluja and Teresa Rejadella

Meanwhile the position at Santa Clara had become more acute. The abbess persecuted the recalcitrant reformers in various underhand ways and by withholding food from them. In May 1549 the provincial chapter of the Catalan Benedictines met to settle the matter. On May 14th the abbess was suspended for the second time; it was seriously contemplated that the whole convent should again be placed under the Franciscan rule, and Sister Teresa's group was asked to support this plan. These felt themselves forsaken by Ignatius and his sons, when even Father Araoz backed the General's refusal. Their Father Ignatius had for a long time sent them no word from Rome – the above letter was apparently still on the way. So the plan to carry out the reform on the basis of the Franciscan rule – to which, moreover, Ignatius showed himself wholly favourable a few months later – gave the desperate nuns once more courage to approach the adamantine General in Rome with a request for admittance to the Society of Jesus.[75]

IHS

Very reverend and dear Father,

The sovereign grace and Jesus Christ our Lord be always with us, to our continual help and favour. Amen.

A short time ago we wrote to you and to Father Master Polanco and sent you a power of attorney with a memorandum about our affairs and what we desired, and earlier we wrote sending the same power of attorney and memorandum. For our sins we have received no reply, nor do we even know if any of those letters and documents have been received, for which cause we are no little troubled and worried. For, since these are matters which are so important to us and since necessity constrains us in various ways, and we hope, through our Lord, for the remedy at your hands, we cannot help feeling this very much, and we have several fears: on the one hand, that the letters have been intercepted and in this way our necessities prevented from coming to your knowledge; on the other, that Your Paternity, finding us over bold in asking what our desires impel us to ask, is answering us by silence but it is not right to think this of Your Paternity's charity, of which we are very sure, and we are certain that if only to disillusion us you would be sure to reply.

We are, therefore, tossed about in this sea of troubles as in a mighty storm, without finding any remedy, and if it were not that we hope in the blessed Jesus who commands the winds and the sea and they obey him, we should be expecting every moment to be drowned. However, the Lord in his goodness gives us hope in him that the more the world and other adversaries crush us, so much the more surely will the best remedy come through his most sacred hands.

The worst and most dreadful thing that is happening in our affairs is that the attorneys in Rome whom we appointed on the advice of our relatives may not trouble about our lawsuit, because of a penal warning and summons from Barcelona which they presented to us on behalf of the abbess, that we are bound to obey her. We may, indeed, be condemned and declared excommunicated, however much right we have on our side. On the other hand, we have here in Barcelona many legal advisers and each one treats the business as his own and we see that they bring all the affairs they handle to a speedy conclusion. All this time, however, we have found no remedy. Blessed be the Lord for ever.

In this month of May the province of our Order has held a chapter here in Barcelona, and there was much discussion about this business of

357

ours. We know that they have offered to absolve the abbess from all her faults except simony, if she would renounce all the privileges she had from the Pope and leave all the affairs of the house freely in the hands of the Order. The abbess said she would be content to have a visitation, but not from the president or the theologians who were the canon lawyers in the chapter, nor should the lawsuit which the said president has instituted against her be maintained, but they should absolve her, she claimed, and take a favourable view of matters. If the chapter were satisfied, neither the president nor his theologians would take any action. She did not yield; indeed, upon this, she presented them with an inhibition from Rome, by which the whole chapter was declared incompetent. Afterwards, when the sending of a monk to Rome on behalf of the Order, there to defend the rights of the chapter, was discussed, and a tax for the expenses was to be levied, she presented a further brief which inhibited the chapter from making such a levy.

The conclusion of the chapter was that a monk should be sent to Rome on behalf of the whole Order to petition His Holiness that, since our convent owed no obedience to the chapter, His Holiness should provide us with another superior or should again place us under the obedience of the friars of St. Francis, by whom this monastery was governed previously. Thus the said monk is to leave shortly on this business.

The president has sent us another monk who for his part has told us that even though this be done, the Order will not abandon us, and that we eleven nuns who opposed the abbess should appoint this same monk who will be going to Rome to act for us and petition His Holiness not to give us another superior.

We are determined not to give this proxy, for we want another superior. We think, moreover, that the president of the chapter has only done this to ingratiate himself with us and in his own interests, for we are very certain that he has little desire to find himself involved in such business and it troubles him and he fears with a human fear on account of the past and because he has not acted with due care. Up to now we have only received from him fair words — and unfriendly deeds, and the other side with all their disobedience and rebellion have always done what they wished, both with the president and because they have enjoyed the favour of the viceroy and the Inquisitor to their hearts' content. We on the other hand remain as the Lord sees and knows, for we no longer have anyone to whom we may have recourse except to his divine goodness. Now our relatives, by whose advice up to the present (advice which they took from learned men and theologians) we have done all we have done in the past, are proving very weak, and the one who can do most and ought to do it with the other party, has told us that he sees no remedy for us but obeying the abbess (although up to the present he has been of the contrary opinion) and that he cannot help us with a single céntimo, although we have not even bread to eat or the possibility of working for it on account of our bodily infirmities. In short, very dear Father, troubles press in on us from every side and we do not know where to turn.

Oh God our eternal Lord, look thou to us, thy poor creatures, redeemed by thy blood! O dearest Father — by the most sacred wounds of our Lord Jesus Christ and by all the merits of his most holy passion, we humbly beseech Your Paternity to the utmost of our power, that you would consider with favourable eyes our wretchedness and calamities and the dangers in which we live and have pity on these poor sheep without a shepherd, and send them comfort.

Now, Father, it appears that there is a more favourable opportunity for our petition, since another superior is to be given us, and although we see that we do not merit what we ask, yet if the Lord gives us such long-lasting and strong desires, how can we go against them? We cannot, nor do we find that we ought to resist them and we find them difficult to fulfil; and since they are not being fulfilled, we see ourselves lost and deprived of comfort for the whole of life, and in great danger for our souls and those of others. Consider then, dearest Father, that we cost our Lord much and it is not right that we should perish. Out of charity answer our petitions with consent and comfort us with your favourable answer.

We have written many letters to the Father Licentiate Araoz, and it is a long time since we heard from him, nor do we know anything about his person. We can say in very truth that those who were near to us are now far off and those who are working against our souls are near to us and do us violence. We seek someone to comfort us but find no one. We now fear, since they have taken away from us our earthly bread, that they will take away the sacramental bread, under the pretence and claim that we are disobedient because in some sort we do what another Father wants, for it is so wrong and against our consciences to act according to the advice received. We make an end, beseeching God's goodness to give us all his most holy grace and love.

Your Paternity's subjects and useless servants,

Hieronyma Oluja   Teresa Rejadella

From Barcelona, May 14th, 1549.

From October of that year the whole complicated case was being dealt with not only at Rome but also in the royal courts at Barcelona. It is noteworthy that the lawyers regarded Señora Rejadella as the actual leader of the reforming party and wrote to her as if she were the superioress. Nothing of any effect was accomplished. The abbess remained in office, and the differences of discipline which made community life a torment continued.

From the following letters of Sister Teresa to Ignatius it appears at all events that she and her fellow-nuns had courageously renounced the ideal they had long so hotly striven for – their admittance to the Society of Jesus. All the more, however, did they cling to the mediation of Ignatius – to whom they were still devotedly attached – in the matter of reform, since the lawsuit was meanwhile pending also at Rome. Conditions in the convent were becoming more and more intolerable. However, we can see too from these letters how much such difficulties had formed the soul of this high-minded woman and led her to a truly purified virtue. She had learnt in Ignatius' school never to give up "the desire for higher things" nor to "shun the Cross".

With regard to the reform, the nuns seem to have agreed to remain zealous Benedictines under the direction of the Abbot of San Cucufat. All this Teresa reported to Ignatius in Rome.

IHS

Very Reverend Father in Christ,

The most holy Trinity be with Your Paternity and with us all always and in everything. Amen.

Most dear and loving Father.

My soul has two feelings at the present time: a very great displeasure with myself, but also pity, for having been so long without writing to Your Paternity. This has not been through negligence, God forbid, for, even though I am not worthy, as, indeed, I am not, that my present circumstances should be changed, it seems to me that I very greatly need to keep the longing after higher things with me until I die, always provided it seems good and right to Your Reverence. Not to waste words, I desire to express the poverty of my soul and the great need it has of your blessed spirit. May Jesus crucified have care of you all always and in everything, to his greater praise and glory. Amen.

The lady prioress is advising you of what has happened with this second suspension. We have great confidence in Your Paternity's help, both as regards speaking with His Holiness and in your intervention with the other persons with whom it is necessary to speak.

The Lord Abbot of San Cucufat, president of our Order, is here in this city and a monk whose name is Fray Palmarolla, a gentleman, and a man of great goodness, although young, is taking as much care of our business as if he were our principal representative. It is not he who has our proxy, but Don Francisco de la Caballaría and up to the present he has carried out his responsibilities very well. By his good efforts nothing has been neglected. From now onwards all the diligence will have to be employed here at this court.

Of my own affairs I do not know what to say, since I have already said so much, except to praise the Lord. May he be glorified in all things. In so far as all this is a cross I do not deserve it, although it seems to me that I do not know or feel the great burden I have and it is of such a nature that when its full weight is felt, as Your Paternity will know, one's chief distress is the not being able to do what is fitting or in the way it is fitting. If, however, our Lord were more served in this way, I should rejoice much more in God's having left me with the burden I have borne so long than in its removal. May it please God's mercy to have pity on me and on all. Amen. After all, one cannot shun the cross, nor is it right to do so. Oh Father, for charity's sake I beseech you to excuse my many words.

To-day I have been told by the notary, who is one of those who have good knowledge about this lawsuit of ours, that we have much need of the favour of the Right Reverend Bishop Poggio, the Nuncio, because our case has been brought before the auditor of the tribunal of the Rota, where the notary says there is much need of favour. Your Paternity knows and can do so much more than I can understand or express. May Jesus Christ our Lord by his infinite and supreme goodness always and in all things have you and the whole Society in his keeping. Amen. The latest news of our Reverend Father Provincial I leave to Father Master Queralt.

Your Paternity's most useless slave and servant,

Rejadella

From Barcelona, October 18th, 1549

To the most reverend Father in Christ, Master Ignatius of Loyola, General of the Society of Jesus, in Rome.

The cross which Teresa wished to embrace was almost too heavy for her. Once more she had to complain to Ignatius: "The way in which we live in this convent to-day is no way of living." Three weeks later, she

361

wrote another letter of complaint, feeling utterly forsaken, even by Araoz.

Had not the latter just had to defend himself at Rome against the somewhat sharp-tongued Polanco, because of his "too great attachment to the nuns of Santa Clara"? It is understandable that he was now more reserved.[76]

IHS

Very reverend Father in Christ,

May the most holy Trinity be always with Your Paternity and with us all. Amen.

Most dear and loving Father.

With all the indications and information we sent to Your Paternity, I do not know how I can better make you understand our tribulation and confusion. It seems to me that one should have faith that our Lord will give Your Paternity an understanding of the matter better than I can do with the help of words, although it often seems to us that nobody can understand or imagine how things really are. Jesus! I should like to be counselled as to how to be free of so much disturbance and confusion. God our Lord can do all things but, from what it appears, from those who are responsible for justice here, there is nothing to be expected for us but considerable injustice and obstacles to our receiving justice. This I would not say were it not for having heard it on good authority and there is no passion in my words. For the love of Christ I beseech Your Paternity to commend the matter to God our Lord, that he may give you to understand how he can best be served by us and then do us the charity of giving us your advice.

The way in which we live in this convent to-day is no way of living. It cannot or ought not last long, but we have had and have full trust in Your Paternity's charity. I end my letter beseeching God's goodness to have Your Paternity and all the Society in his keeping always and in all things. Amen. Of our Reverend Provincial the Licentiate, we have no news. May God our Lord be good to all as they desire and as is to his greater service.

Your Paternity's servant and most useless slave,

Rejadella

From Barcelona. November 5th, 1549

To the most reverend father in Christ, Father Master Ignatius of Loyola, General of the Society of Jesus, in Rome.

362

It is not surprising that the zeal of the hitherto loyal friends of the reforming nuns gradually waned. By purely legal means nothing could be done. It is true that the case of Santa Clara had aroused interest even at the court of the Prince of Spain; and his private secretary Gonzalo Pérez sent an occasional comforting letter, signifying nothing, to the "Abbess" Rejadella.

With gentle reproach the faithful Teresa asked her Father Ignatius if he too had forgotten her. Weary and resigned, she no longer dared to make any explicit request. There was nothing now but mute lament.

IHS

Very Reverend Father in Christ,

May the divine power, wisdom and goodness be always and in everything with Your Paternity and with you all. Amen.

Most dear and loving Father, I did not want to give Your Paternity trouble with my importunate letters when they are all of them about our business, disagreements, etc., but after God's favour, we set our hope in that of Your Paternity. Now on our side it seems that all sleep or that we are forgotten or zeal is grown cold. Thus we have to trust all the more in true charity, although Your Paternity has no obligation [towards us] but charity alone. Moreover, because I myself am so much your serving-maid, it seems to me that there remains on me the obligation and right to desire to be the one most subject in every way, as and when it shall give greater glory to God.

His Highness'[77] secretary, Gonzalo Pérez, has just sent a letter in respect of our business bidding us take great hope: he does not say how or in what respect. In his letter he shows that he considers me as abbess, which I do not desire, still less seek, and as much as I can and is lawful, without offending our Lord I shall protest against this. God in his goodness will not permit this for my sins, even though I have more courage for troubles and insults than I have wisdom and strength, but I fear for myself, and rightly so, and for the others. May God our Lord take pity of the great need of this house, little known and less appreciated by those who could provide some help for it. In short, what good can come from a thing in which so many gentlemen have a finger?

Of our Reverend Provincial, the Licentiate, Father Master Queralt can give you news. We are concerned about his bodily infirmities, which I think he has, or has contracted, through his very great charity. May Jesus Christ crucified take him always and in everything by the hand, amen, for God's greater service and the well-being of souls. Amen.

363

The lady prioress and all of us kiss Your Paternity's hands. I conclude, praying to the most holy Trinity always to have Your Paternity and all of you in his keeping. Amen.

Your Paternity's servant and most useless slave,

Rejadella

From Barcelona, January 10th, 1550

To the most reverend father in Christ, Master Iñigo de Loyola, General of the Society of Jesus, in Rome.

Ignatius' views on the solution of the question must evidently have been reported to Barcelona by the legal adviser whom the nuns had appointed at Rome. The General's opinion was that as long as the convent was under Benedictine jurisdiction the only basis of any true reformation was obedience to the lawful superiors. Moreover all had now become quiet in Barcelona. Nobody took the part of Teresa and her sisters. Even Ignatius' old friend from his Barcelona days, Doña Guiomar Gralla y Desplá, who had hitherto been so much in favour of the reform plan, seems now to have retired from the scene; ". . . this blessed business which it seems to me has the support of God our Lord alone". A last glimmer of hope remained; perhaps Ignatius would take up the case with the Roman curia; but even for that the disappointed disciple scarcely dared to beg.[77]

IHS

Very Reverend Father in Christ,

In everything may the most holy Trinity be always with Your Paternity and with all of you. Amen.

Most dear and loving Father. I do not think nor can I believe that Your Paternity's charity forgets us in all our necessities and in all matters that may be for God's greater glory. Particularly would I say this of the case in which we at present stand with this blessed business, which it seems to me has the support of God our Lord alone, for we do not know of anyone here in Barcelona who really works for us, although Don Francisco de la Caballaría still has our proxy and Señor Reposter acts for him now. Doña Guiomar [de Gralla] to whom they turned, does not write with the warmth we expected and we are now doubtful whether what ought to be looked into on our behalf is being looked into. On the other side neither diligence nor favours are wanting. I could say much but I leave matters to truth and justice. God our Lord will himself make provision how he may be best served and what is most for the good of souls. Amen.

We have great hope in Your Paternity's favour although we must not be a burden. Here we are keeping silence about the matter. They have written to us from Rome that Your Paternity wished that in all cases we should obey. With this my soul was at peace, when the blessed election and confirmation took place. Now, when I consider the matter, I have no other wish than to obey and do what seems good to Your Paternity. Ah, Father, answer me, what else could I say? I trust, however, that God our Lord is giving you light to see what should be done and thus I beg you to continue to exercise your care over us in the whole question as you can, and judge it is fitting.

I conclude, begging God our Lord to take Your Paternity and all of you by the hand always and in all things.

Your servant and most useless slave,

Rejadella

From Barcelona, April 11th, 1550.

Two years later Sister Teresa's reform plan received a new impetus. On his way to Rome there arrived from Saragossa that noble Conservador of the Aragonese crown, Don Luis González de Villasimplez, who had, of course, had similar experiences in connexion with disputes concerning matters of canon law. At the same time Ignatius' old friend, Verdolay, was staying in Barcelona. Ignatius had once written him letters from Venice, and he was now himself a Jesuit.

Don Luis knew from what had happened at Saragossa and from his sister Aldonza how beneficial it was to found a house of nuns who were faithful to their rule. He therefore encouraged Sister Teresa's little band to establish a convent with strict enclosure and to withdraw to it with all the nuns who desired reform. Verdolay too supported this plan enthusiastically. There was, indeed, no longer any question of the admission of the projected convent to the obedience of the Society of Jesus. In two letters of June 1552, of which the first has been lost and the second preserved through being carried by a different route, Teresa made bold to lay before Ignatius in detail all these plans, together with the obstacles, great and small, which stood in the way of their realization.[78]

IHS

Very reverend Father in Christ,

May the most holy Trinity be always with Your Paternity and with us all. Amen.

Dearest and most loving Father.

Thinking that the galleons would be leaving I wrote to you many days ago giving the letter to a cleric of His Holiness, named Antonio Olmedo. I think he is leaving now. In that letter I asked for advice and with this one I do the same – as regards our desires. May it please God our Lord that we may be his. If it is to be for his greater service, then the Lord will bring it about.

Don Luis González, the Conservador of Aragón, was here with us before he went away with the galleons. We have spoken not only with him but with Father Master de Verdolay, who is also here. It seemed to him it would be a very good thing for an enclosed house to be erected here in Barcelona for such nuns as had an inclination to transfer to it. I gave him a full account of what I feel about the matter, explaining the pros and cons and everything I could. It seemed to him that all possible diligence should be employed, although one or two of those sisters who have been very determined and greatly desired this thing are now hesitating. One of them is almost determined not to go, the other says she has hope of so doing. God our Lord will enlighten her for up to now she has had a great desire for that life. I do not know about the others, because three of them are not in the house now. There is even more information to give you. I have here in our convent, two nieces, the daughters of my brother. Neither of them has the black veil, only the habit and they are not deeply recollected, but lead a mediocre life, neither bad nor very good. There is no possibility of making them understand enclosure. As to my going away, leaving these or others of those I have in my company and charge, I should like to know Your Paternity's opinion. The liberties of this house are not only such as greatly to tempt souls, but such as to make them cease following after perfection or desiring it. I mean that even this wish for the perfect life must inspire us with the resolution to work for our salvation and all the more so in the case of those who have less experience of spiritual things and are in greater danger. There is something more, although I am not altogether certain of it – it is thought that one sister, if we go away, will withdraw on the pretext of a brief to live in the house of her relatives, who are, indeed, persons of honour. If that happens it may be that the example would spread and all would go, as being the surer course. May God our Lord make his most holy will understood of some one of us who may deserve to understand it.

I think the Lord Conservador will possibly ask Your Paternity for help if he makes up his mind to this course. I do not, indeed, think His Honour can take this letter because I think he is already embarked. I have spoken with him little and in much haste. He must report as he thinks best and relate the matter as he has understood it. May God our Lord with all his power and grace make matters understood for God knows all our needs. May it please him through his infinite and highest goodness always to have Your Paternity and all of you in his keeping, in all things. Amen. With this letter I have merely sought to give you a brief account because of the haste, relying for the remainder on the report which the said Lord Conservador will give to Your Paternity on our behalf and about the whole business. Your Paternity's servant and most useless slave,

Barcelona, June 20th, 1552   Rejadella

This plan too came to nothing. The problem of reforming the convent of Santa Clara remained unsolved. The old Prioress Oluja was evidently long since dead; and only one more year passed before the now weary Sister Teresa Rejadella, at the beginning of July 1553 lay on her deathbed. The faithful Father Juan Queralt assisted her in her last moments. With her dying breath Teresa asked that Ignatius might be informed and lovingly commended the convent to him. Queralt promptly fulfilled Teresa's last request by sending Polanco on July 12th a report of the holy death of Ignatius' loyal disciple[79]:

"As I cannot exactly remember whether I have already told you in another letter about the death of Señora Rejadella or not, and as I promised her on her deathbed that I would, I herewith do so. She died with her mind quite at peace, and with that inner fortitude which she possessed during life. She charged me to write to our Reverend Father Ignatius and to beg him in her name always to watch over this convent and keep a place for it in his heart. She said that the longing for perfection which God the Lord had awakened in some of the nuns of this convent made it worthy to be helped by the Fathers of the Society of Jesus. She begged that this request might be fulfilled for the sake of the sufferings and wounds of our Lord Jesus Christ, and asked for prayers to that end.

"When she was about to die, she spoke with urgency to the abbess and

367

nuns, exhorting them to perfection and to the zealous service of God our Lord. Those nuns, however, who were specially loyal to her she begged to remain true to their holy ideals, and unceasingly to prove their sincerity by good works. She even desired to speak personally to each nun, and with great fervour (as is understandable when such a person is dying) she conjured them to be faithful to their holy resolutions and to persevere unto the end.

"Truly, dear Father, to assist at such a deathbed was enough to convert a Turk! Thus it came about that after her death a few nuns felt urged to make holy resolutions. May God the Lord guide them always by the hand. Amen.

"One of our brethren and myself were present at her decease. I pray you give this note to the Reverend Father Ignatius, for I would like thus to fulfil my promise to the dying woman."

Father Polanco incorporated this beautiful letter in his chronicle of the Society. The rather strong expression about the Turk, not very kind to the unreformed nuns of Santa Clara, he tactfully changed to: "Such a death might have moved the hearts of men strong in the Faith." To Barcelona he wrote on his Master's orders as follows:

"So the reverend Mother Rejadella is gone home from this temporal life into that of eternity. God be praised, that he shortens the labours of this earthly pilgrimage for his servants, that he may the sooner give them in return everlasting life. Our Father Ignatius has caused many holy masses and prayers to be said for her by the whole house; although we all hope to God that she has already reached that place where she can rather help us with prayers, having no more any need of ours."

Ignatius and Teresa Rejadella prayed in Heaven for the beloved convent of Santa Clara. The reform for which they strove in vain all their lives was at last achieved. At the beginning of the seventeenth century the "Señoras" of the convent used to send the Jesuits some loaves of bread every week in thankful memory of Ignatius and his solicitude for the spiritual bread of the nuns.[80]

The Anchoress of Salamanca

IGNATIUS made a slight exception from his strict rule about undertaking the spiritual direction of religious women in 1547, just a year after all his painful experiences with Isabel Roser. He took over the pastoral care of the *Murate* near St. Peter's, those strange "walled-up ones" who lived in the shadow of the Vatican basilica and there, enclosed in a cell in accordance with an ancient Western tradition, devoted themselves entirely to prayer and giving spiritual counsel to visitors. Ignatius accepted this task at the urgent request of Cardinal Farnese. It was for him also a reminder of his own ascetic beginnings, when he was still a student at Salamanca and in prison.[81]

It was this memory that caused him to write a beautiful letter to an anchoress at Salamanca, whose name remains unkown to us. She is thus one of those women who pass as it were anonymously through Ignatius' life, like the mysterious old woman at Manresa, who wished that Jesus Christ might one day appear to the Pilgrim Ignatius and whose advice was sought by the Catholic King himself; like the "Doña María in Paris" whom we have already met; like the *Beata* of Barcelona, of whom Ignatius wrote from Venice to Jaime Cazador and who he knew was safe under the spiritual direction of his friend Juan de Castro; or like that noble lady who visited him in the prison of Salamanca and to whom he said the selfsame words that he used to the young Francisco de Mendoza (later, as Cardinal, his very great friend) "In all Salamanca there are not so many fetters and manacles, that I would not long for more out of the love of God".[82]

In the same city of Salamanca there were at this time near the church of San Juan de los Bárbalos several *emparedadas,* walled-up anchoresses; and Ignatius had apparently become their friend soon after his arrival in the town, in July 1527. This would have been quite in accordance with his psychological state at the period, which (as in Barcelona and Alcalá) constantly urged him to seek spiritual converse with persons who could understand the burning love of God and desire to help souls which filled his heart. It is noteworthy that three years after Ignatius' conversations with the anchoresses of San Juan there set out from that very place the first nuns to be sent to the vast territories of Spanish America.

Later too Ignatius retained his interest in these religious; for in 1544

369

Father Mirón in Valencia told him about such a walled-up anchoress, knowing that his General would be pleased to hear of her. We can then understand when Ignatius writes to the anchoress of Salamanca that "the true and sincere love of your soul in our Lord is never absent from my mind". This he wrote on July 24th, 1541, while in the midst of all the worries and projects involved in his election to the generalship in April of that year. With childlike piety, so much in keeping with the character of the great Ignatius, he sent the anchoress some blessed rosary beads. He also added greetings to her companion.[83]

May the Lord be always with us for our help and favour.

As the true and sincere love of your soul in our Lord is never absent from my mind, but very continually present, I thought I would send you a greater treasure or more precious stone, in my poor opinion, for persons who seek only the love of their Creator and Lord and the salvation of their own souls, than could be found in the whole earth and the whole of human power in so far as it is human. It is that His Holiness granted our Society many and, indeed, inestimable graces on certain blessed rosaries and, as he blessed them, laid his hand upon them. The graces granted to these beads are as follows. When one bead of those thus blessed is put in a rosary, whoever recites such rosary will gain, each time he prays, all the indulgences of all the stations and churches in Rome, as if he had gone there and gained them in person; and since the graces which are gained at those stations are well-nigh countless, so that you may know what they are more in detail, I send them to you with this letter but on a separate sheet. In addition, whoever, from devotion shall recite such rosary thirty-three times for the thirty-three years that Christ our Lord lived upon earth, releases a soul from purgatory. I send you one of such blessed rosaries for your consolation and spiritual profit, and I also send three more – one for your good companion and my dear sister in Christ, our Creator and Lord, whom you ask me to pray much for to our Lord. The other two are for those whom you feel to be most devout among you and who will most devote themselves to the greater praise and glory of God our Lord. May he, in his infinite and supreme goodness be always with us to our help and favour.

From Rome, July 24th, 1541

Yours in our Lord, Iñigo

To my sisters in Christ our Lord, the Anchoresses of St. John's in Salamanca.

So when Ignatius undertook to minister to the *murate* in Rome, it was no unfamiliar duty to him. His secretary Polanco reported on October 31st, 1547, to Araoz in Spain: "Here in Rome our Father has at the request of Cardinal Farnese collaborated in the reform of the anchoresses of St. Peter's by helping to regulate the statutes which they have to observe and by entrusting their spiritual care to a father of our house."

Apparently this form of asceticism was often discussed among those who were nearest to Ignatius; for Doña Leonor Osorio's lady-in-waiting, María de Araujo, who had gone to Sicily with her mistress, seriously thought of having herself walled up somewhere as an anchoress after the death of the Vicereine. Probably she wanted to do this in Rome, so as to be near Ignatius. We still possess the summary of a letter dated September 13th, 1550, in which Ignatius earnestly dissuades the lady from carrying out this plan. Evidently Doña María obeyed, for in April 1556 she was still at the Viceroy's court in Palermo, although a sick woman; Ignatius sent her greetings and good wishes for "that degree of health which is best for her eternal happiness".

It appears that the anchoresses of St. Peter's were subsequently caused much distress through the rebuilding of the basilica. We learn from contemporary sources that there were in 1571 still three of them, two Spaniards and a Sicilian. It was no doubt in memory of their connection with Ignatius that they were finally moved in that year from St. Peter's to the House of St. Martha near the Arco di Camigliano, Ignatius' own foundation. There they must often have prayed before the wooden cross which the Founder had once carried into the enclosure.[84]

Bartolomea Spadafora

IT remains to add an epilogue to the story of Ignatius' fight to prevent the admittance of spiritual daughters to the obedience or direction of the Society.

Near Messina there was an aristocratic convent of Cistercian nuns, Santa Maria dell'Alto, presided over by the Abbess Bartolomea Spadafora, an important figure in the ecclesiastical circles of Messina, who was addressed as "Reverend Excellency". The nuns did not take kindly to discipline and holy poverty, and the senate of the city had long been endeavouring to reform the convent. They applied to Ignatius, whose sons were just then opening a college at Messina, requesting him to undertake the spiritual direction of the nuns. Here indeed there was no question of placing the convent under Jesuit obedience; but the spiritual direction, as a regular thing, of a house of female religious was also against the principles for which Ignatius had secured papal approval.

The city fathers wrote to Ignatius early in the spring of 1549, after the conflict with Isabel Roser, and he replied clearly but politely on May 2nd, pointing out that such a task, however important it might be and however willingly he would like to undertake it out of regard for the senate of the city – to which he was so grateful because of the founding of the college – was entirely contrary to the regulations of the Society. To Father Nadal, however, he sent instructions that "to oblige the municipal government and for the comfort of those reverend ladies" he could allow a Jesuit to hear the confessions of the whole convent, and thus at least to direct the reform along the right path. The best way to bring about a thorough reform (he wrote) was to give the nuns the Spiritual Exercises, at least the meditations of the first week, but only if the abbess approved.[85]

Meanwhile the Lady Abbess had asked the fathers in Messina to send a good preacher. Father Nadal appointed the Fleming Father Cornelius Wischaven to this work – a somewhat odd but holy man, whose spiritual talks, in spite of his bad Italian, were found highly satisfactory by the nuns.

The good Father Cornelius was the victim of some amusing misunderstandings in the convent of Santa Maria dell'Alto. When at the invitation of the Abbess he first came to the door of the convent, he said to the portress that he had been sent for a *colazione*. The etymological equivalent of this word in Flemish means "a short sermon", but the Italian word means "breakfast". Only when the nun was putting the plates on the table did Cornelius realize his mistake. Another time the Jesuit heard a cry of pain and was told that the doctor had taken out one of the Lady Abbess's sound molars (in Italian *mola*) instead of the bad one. Wischaven took the word to be *mula*, "she-mule", and preached a sermon to the Reverend Excellency to the effect that so much crying for the loss of a mule was excessive.[86]

Soon three of the nuns were making the Spiritual Exercises, and then they gave them to their fellow religious. Nadal told Ignatius in 1549 about this unusual method of reform. Wischaven was able to his great joy to convert some of the nuns to the practice of frequent communion and of holy poverty. Abbess Spadafora co-operated enthusiastically and was so pleased with the Jesuits that on January 7th, 1550, she wrote a letter full of praise to the General. Ignatius sent her a polite answer, not without a delicate reference to the inviolable principles which guided him and his sons in the matter of undertaking pastoral work of such a kind.[87]

Very reverend Mother in Christ,
Pax Christi.

The sovereign grace and eternal love of Christ our Lord greet and visit your reverend Ladyship with his most holy gifts and spiritual graces.

By a letter from Your Reverence of January 7th received this week, I have learnt to my consolation in our Lord the holy longing for spiritual things that Your Reverence has, and how this is bound up with the care and solicitude inevitable in the case of one to whom a flock is entrusted.

Because of this longing and pious desire, you ask for someone from the unworthy instruments of God our Lord who reside in this college of Messina, thus showing that in the past their work in these parts has not been unfruitful. Now, thanking God's goodness, from which alone any good from any instrument at all comes to his creatures, for what has been done, I am very pleased that this pious office should be continued in so far as it is compatible with our institute and its necessary occupations. We are of opinion that this is pleasing to the divine Majesty and we have much regard for the great devotion of this holy house of Your Reverence's, you who are the head of it, and also a regard for the sworn fathers of this city whom we always hold in affection, in conformity with our poor profession, which is to do any service for God's honour and glory. Therefore, I have to-day had a letter written to Master Jerónimo

Nadal to see to the matter of consoling you and serving you in our Lord in so far as the fathers can, as has been done in the past.

I say no more, except to commend us all to Your Reverence's devout prayers and those of all your daughters in Christ in that holy house; and to pray God's supreme goodness to give us all his abundant grace to know and carry out perfectly his holy will at the service of Your Reverend Ladyship.

Ignatius

Rome, February 22nd, 1550

To Bartolomea Spadafora, most reverend and venerable in Christ, Lady Abbess of the Monastery of Santa Maria dell' Alto.

All we know of the further progress of this work of reform is that it cost the Jesuits and the Abbess a good deal more trouble. In the summer of 1551 a Turkish fleet threatened the coasts of Sicily. Father Nadal, who at that time was a frequent preacher at the convent of Santa Maria dell'Alto, warned the recalcitrant nuns that the janissaries would get them if they did not accept reform; and that was perhaps just as much use as the Spiritual Exercises. At all events, later the nuns reverently enshrined St. Ignatius' letter to their abbess in a golden reliquary.[88]

PART FIVE

FATHER IN CHRIST

Letters to the Mothers of Fellow-Jesuits

Introduction

IN the government of his Society, which enthusiastic young men flocked to join, Ignatius was constantly faced with the problem which has always troubled Christians when they become aware of the sword of God which separates the son from his father and mother. Perhaps in the case of the Society of Jesus this problem of the right relationship between the religious and their families was especially acute; for through the work of the Jesuits in schools and in education, which soon became their principal occupation, they necessarily came in contact with young men who were filled with enthusiasm by the example of their teachers, and at an age which seems to us unusually early begged to be admitted to the Society. Many mothers wept bitter tears. Ignatius had frequently to comfort parents; but he had also to defend young fellow-Jesuits against possessive mother-love. To this part of Ignatius' work we owe a number of fine letters.

The principles and practice of the General in this matter were dominated by his unequivocal conviction, quietly but passionately defended, that a young man had a Christian right to follow a clearly recognized vocation to the religious life, even against the will of his parents. According to the laws of the Church at that time, and as appears also from the Constitutions of the Society, a young man was considered capable of making such a decision, and free to make it, at the age of fourteen. The General indeed preferred a higher age, eighteen to twenty, and even then he insisted on paying due regard to parents. When in 1551 some youthful students at Louvain were admitted to the Society with undue haste, made their vows and were sent to Cologne and Vienna for further studies, Ignatius expressed himself strongly against such a course of action. In the same breath, however, he defended the right of making so early a choice of the religious life:

"As regards the admittance of young men into the Society's noviciate, one can but wonder how pious and learned men can declare themselves against it. To follow the counsels of Christ and to long for a life of holiness is something so praiseworthy that no opposition of any kind is permissible. Prudent and Catholic-minded men may therefore never doubt that young men who, as you write, are eighteen or twenty years old, are allowed to submit themselves for examination as to their suitability for entering a religious order, and this even in spite of the prohibition of their parents."[1]

To calm the agitation caused by this case among Flemish parents and even in the university of Louvain, Ignatius related two similar cases in which the freedom of choice was defended by the highest authority – by the King of Portugal and by Pope Julius III. One was that of Don Teotonio de Braganza, of which we already know. The other occurred under dramatic circumstances in Rome itself, when the nephew of the Bishop of Tivoli, Lucio Croce, joined the Jesuits at nineteen. We will let Ignatius describe the event himself; it has its echoes in a number of his letters.

"In Rome a young man of noble birth felt drawn by divine grace to the Society of Jesus. He was a nephew of the Bishop of Tivoli and had had bene- fices heaped upon him by the latter. To avoid the unwelcome attentions of his relatives, Lucio himself asked to be sent to some college in Sicily. Thereupon the said bishop and some cardinals who sided with him took a course that was both astonishing and tragic. Three or four cardinals inter- vened with the Pope, urging that the young man might at least return to our house in Rome, so that his parents might speak to him there; but they prevailed nothing with the Vicar of Christ. 'I will not in any way be respon- sible', said the Pope, 'for the spiritual ruin of this young man.' And there the matter rested, despite the pleas of the parents and all the machinations of highly placed persons. A religious should not be exposed to the danger of losing his vocation."[2] The General also defended the vocation of the young Florentine Giovanni Riccasoli against his father and mother, even before the very throne of the Pope.

In 1553 a fresh storm of indignation broke out in Flanders when the gifted Dutchman Theodorich Geeraerts of Amsterdam entered the Society. This was regarded in the Netherlands as a grievous sin against the fourth com- mandment, wrote Father Adriaenssens in great distress to Ignatius. The latter sent him a treatise which Father Oviedo in Naples had written on the ques- tion of allowing youths to enter the Society without the consent of their parents. In Louvain itself the learned chancellor of the university, Ruard Tapper, publicly spoke in favour of the Jesuits, and the holy Abbot Louis de Blois defended, in a conversation at table with the Regent's all-powerful secretary, Viglius van Zwichem, the young students who had entered the Society. All this was carefully noted in the General's curia.[3]

These experiences led Ignatius, when drawing up regulations and in numerous instructions contained in letters, to strengthen the novices' naturally weak powers of resistance. In those college rules drawn up by Ignatius personally a course of action was laid down which we shall often encounter in the following correspondence: "In the case of those who are molested by relatives living near the college, their place of residence will as a rule be changed, and they are to be accommodated in other colleges." The same instruction appears in the Constitutions of the Society, completed soon afterwards.

Father Gonçalves da Câmara has related several amusing cases of this form of protection in his memoirs of Ignatius. To mention but one of them: in the Roman College there was a young scholastic named Mario Beringucci, son of a professor of law teaching at Naples. He was so much molested by his relatives that these had to be forbidden to enter the college and the house of the Jesuits. When, still undeterred, they tried to slip into the lectures attended by Brother Mario with books under their arms like the other students, so that they might at least speak to him thus, Ignatius smilingly ordered the lecturer to subject these "guest students" to a thorough oral examination. This probably proved effective.

The counter-measures taken by mothers who had become alarmed at their sons' enthusiasm for the Jesuits are vividly illustrated by an incident related in Polanco's chronicle. There was in Naples a young man whose mother made him swear an oath never to go into the church of the Jesuits, solely out of fear that he might join them. On the same page the chronicle tells of the scholastic Francesco of Atina, who had been sent home to his mother on account of an illness and there lost his vocation. Polanco notes: "Too young plants should not be put back in their native soil until they have struck deep roots in their vocation."[4]

It was, as we have already seen, no part of Ignatius' policy to go out of his way to be on bad terms with the parents of candidates for the Society. On the contrary: while remaining faithful to his principles he always insisted, even in the Constitutions, that those who asked for admittance should always be subjected to a detailed interrogation as to the duties they owed towards their parents, who might perhaps be in need. Moreover, taught by many painful experiences, he attached increasing importance to the consent of parents to the entry of their youthful sons into the Society. As early as May 8th, 1550, he wrote to Father Nadal that youths, who were actually little more than children, should not on principle be admitted without the permission of their parents.

Two years later a great stir was caused in Rome itself by two desperate mothers. Ignatius reported to all rectors of colleges: "This week two boys disappeared from their parents' house. Their mothers came into our church during Mass, screamed and made a dreadful noise. They did the same in the college and in the palaces of several cardinals, who have told us of it themselves. The ladies said: 'The Jesuits have only built their college in order to rob us of our children, they are hiding our boys', and so on. In fact, neither

379

of the boys entered our house or college. I relate these examples to Your Reverences, that you may be on your guard in similar cases. You are to make it a rule not to accept a single pupil without the approval of the parents, for the damage that arises from the scandal caused and the estrangement of our friends outweigh the advantages of such admissions. We must after all keep the general welfare in view."[5] A reply equally cautious in tone was sent on this subject to Vienna, where Father de Lanoy wanted to admit two very suitable students of fourteen.

The General's final attitude to this question was influenced by his difficult experiences with the mothers of certain novices, about which we are to hear. On March 3rd, 1554, Ignatius wrote to all rectors of colleges throughout the Society: "It seems advisable to inform all rectors and to impress upon them most strongly that no boy who is still under the authority of his parents or guardian may be admitted to the Society, without the express approval of those who are in charge of him. Even less should we by exhortation or advice invite our pupils to join the Society. For however permissible and even praiseworthy it may be in itself to help those whose minds are formed and to advise them to embrace a life of perfection, such things should not be done in our schools, for it would be inopportune, inasmuch as we must always have in view the service of God and the general good of all."[6]

One other characteristic of the founder is of cardinal importance for the understanding of the letters which follow. Whenever Ignatius was assured of the novice's free choice and due regard for the affection of his parents, he displayed a charming kindness towards the mothers of his fellow-religious and missed no opportunity of encouraging young Jesuits to write to their mothers, occasionally to visit them and always to pray for them. There are many examples of this. The way in which Laynez and Polanco, who certainly understood their Father's mind most thoroughly, wrote to their mothers shows how Ignatius felt in this matter.

Even young novices and brothers were often delighted by the kindness with which their mothers, too, were remembered by Ignatius. There was for instance a young scholastic from Siena, Taddeo Amaroni; he did not show much promise, and his superiors in Venice were already thinking of dimissing him for his stubbornness, which bordered on stupidity. Ignatius wrote on May 19th, 1554: "If Taddeo does not do well, send him home at once." Nevertheless, the General generously allowed him to undertake a journey to Siena to visit his mother; and because war was then raging between Florence and Siena, he went to the trouble of taking what amounted to diplomatic action to obtain from Duchess Eleonora a permit for the mother, allowing her to leave beleaguered Siena.

Another Jesuit brother was Master Cesare, a native of Aversa, the humble son of a poor tailor. The father had just died, and the widow was living in straitened circumstances. Cesare was studying at the time in Gandía, and so Ignatius consoled the poor widow with news about her successful son, who had just been ordained priest in Spain.[7]

Ignatius had to deal with a parent of a very different kind in the person of the mother of the three brothers Hannibal, Louis and Claude du Coudray, of Sallanches in Savoy. All three had decided to enter the Society of Jesus. Two remained in it, but Claude left again, to the great sorrow of his brothers. The reason for his leaving the Society had to do with sordid questions connected with inheritance; for the mother had remarried after the death of her first husband. She sent Claude a letter of woe, which he forwarded to Ignatius through his brother Hannibal with the remark: "Show it to Father Ignatius; he will with his usual wisdom judge what is best to be done, especially if you explain our mother's nature to him." The General comforted the brothers, saying that they should not allow themselves to be affected by the troubles at home, and that their mother might without scruple keep the inheritance. Later too he urged Louis and Hannibal never to forget the duty of being loving and just towards their mother.[8]

To the mother of Father Juan de Vitoria of Burgos, mourning for the death of her husband, Father Polanco (himself a native of Burgos) sent on Ignatius' behalf a heartfelt letter of condolence, which the son to his mother's great joy was allowed to carry to Spain himself. The Fleming Father Leernus likewise received a consoling letter on the death of his mother: "Many prayers are being said for the soul of your dear mother."

Ignatius always had a sincere affection for the courageous mothers of his fellow-Jesuits. Upon many a woman to whom he was deeply indebted, such as Leonor Mascarenhas, Isabel Roser, or the nobly-born Marchioness of Priego, he bestowed the beautiful title "Mother of the Society of Jesus"; for he knew what the best of his brethren owed to their mothers, whether they were poor tailor's wives or Spanish duchesses. Perhaps, too, he thought of his own mother.[9]

Catherine of Córdoba, Marchioness of Priego

THE astonishingly rapid development of the young Society in Spain was due mainly to the entry of Duke Francis Borgia. Because of this event members of the higher nobility of Spain at once began to take an interest in it, especially – as we have already shown – the ladies who were related to Borgia. There was also much excitement when another son of one of the first families of Spain – Don Antonio de Córdoba – announced his intention to join the Society of Jesus. No doubt Ignatius listened with attention when this news reached Rome, for he was just at that time defending, in a letter to his friend Gaspar de Dotti, the freedom to follow a religious vocation, and was looking for examples. He therefore immediately added that of the Andalusian count: "He is Don Antonio de Córdoba, son of the Countess of Feria and Marchioness of Priego. He belongs to an exceedingly rich family in Andalusia, with an income of about 80,000 ducats a year, and is of the highest aristocracy of Spain. In spite of her tender love for her son, the Marchioness was remarkably cheerful about his choice."[10]

To show the importance of this event for the Society, we must first give some account of the history of this ancient noble family. The Marchioness Catherine was the granddaughter of Don Alfonso Fernández de Córdoba, who fell in battle against the Moors and who, celebrated in song, bears the title of *el Grande*. Her even more famous great-uncle was the *Gran Capitán*, Gonzalo Fernández de Córdoba, who conquered the Kingdom of Naples for the Spanish sovereigns. For ten years, from 1518 to 1528, the Marchioness was married to Don Lorenzo Suárez de Figueroa; and her family was among the few "first-class grandees" confirmed by the Emperor Charles V when he reorganized the Spanish nobility at Aachen in 1520. Through her mother, Elvira Enríquez, Catherine was related in addition to Duke Francis Borgia. The wealth of this family was almost proverbial in Spain, and a modern genealogist has written of Catherine: "The Marchioness Doña Catalina was one of the greatest heiresses of all time, if not the greatest, in the whole of Andalusia."

Catherine's eldest son, Pedro de Córdoba, Count of Feria, married Ana Ponce de León, daughter of the Duke of Arcos, but died in 1552. His mother's title and property therefore went to Gómez Suárez de Figueroa, her second

382

son. This was the Count and (from 1567) Duke of Feria celebrated in the history of Philip II. The Venetian ambassador Badoaro reported of this nobleman that he would on his mother's death enter upon an inheritance that brought him an income of 100,000 ducats. The third son of the house was Don Antonio, with whose vocation to the Jesuits we are here concerned.[11]

As was almost taken for granted in such families at that time, the younger sons adopted an ecclesiastical career, which held out the prospect of positions of honour. In 1539, when Don Antonio was scarcely twelve years old, he was already a canon of Córdoba cathedral and later he became rector of the College of St. Bartholomew in the university of Salamanca. There in 1549 he made the acquaintance of the fathers of the Society of Jesus. Frequent communion, a practice which the Jesuits taught him, strengthened him in the resolve to forsake the riches and honours of the world. In 1551 he met Father Miguel de Torres at Oropesa in the house of Count Álvarez de Toledo, and his enthusiasm for the new Society crystallized into a firm resolve to join it. Antonio's youngest brother, Don Lorenzo Suárez de Figueroa, was already a member of the Dominican order and was to be for many years, as Bishop of Sigüenza, an ornament of the Spanish hierarchy.

His mother followed this development with joy and was already thinking of founding a college for the Jesuits on her estates at Montilla near Córdoba. A long conversation between the young canon and Father Araoz, whom he met at Salamanca, had the effect, however, of postponing his entry into the Society till the following year, 1552; for at this time his noble relatives and the Emperor Charles V himself (who had once sent condolences to the Marchioness Catherine in 1517 on the death of her father) had quite different plans for him – he was recommended to Pope Julius III as a candidate for the red hat. In March 1552 it became known that the Pope had already appointed Antonio a cardinal *in petto*. But, as the chronicle of the Society notes, Antonio "had by then tasted the Spirit of God", and so the candidate went in May of that year to Oñate in the Basque provinces, where his uncle Francis Borgia was just then spending the blissful days of his eremitical life after having celebrated his first Mass. There the young man made the Spiritual Exercises. His mother was delighted.[12]

Before his departure for Oñate, Antonio had laid before Ignatius in a long letter of March 31st the whole question of his vocation and the danger of his being appointed cardinal. "By blood I am a great man *(grande)*, but in truth I am great only as a sinner", he confessed to the General. With the latter's permission, Antonio was admitted to the Society. He remained at Oñate till September, corresponding from there with Ignatius. The happy mother sent news of her son's vocation to the celebrated Fray Luis de Granada, who with the Blessed Juan de Ávila was cordially attached to the family. Ignatius allowed Don Antonio to be ordained early. The young Jesuit was ordained priest in the cathedral of Burgos and celebrated his first mass there on Corpus Christi day 1553. The Duchess of Frias and the Countess of Osorno decorated the altar, and Ignatius procured from the Roman curia a special jubilee indulgence, which, however, arrived too late. One can see that Rome and Ignatius regarded this event as an important one. After his first mass, Antonio went home to Córdoba, where his mother and the whole city received him with joy. There Ignatius' congratulations reached him; the letter ends with the words: "I kiss the hands of the Señora Marquesa."[13]

After the festivities Antonio returned to Salamanca, apparently to finish his theological studies. He was in poor health, and his mother was worried about him. The chronicle of the Society relates some very edifying examples of humility in the erstwhile grandee, as for instance that, driving an ass through the town, he brought fresh water to the college from the river.[14]

The virtues of mother and priest-son were by no means hereditary in the Córdoba family. The elegant Count Feria, Antonio's brother, led a very different life at court in Madrid and in Flanders; in Badoaro's account his goodness of heart and his truly Spanish sentiments of honour are praised, but it also states that he was on occasion too unbridled in his sensuality, that he was extravagant and contracted many debts. At the same time, however, the Count was a good friend to Father Ribadeneira and helped him, as we have seen, at the court of Brussels to promote the projected college in Flanders. For that reason he was given, simultaneously with the Emperor's daughters, a share in the spiritual riches of the Society.

At Córdoba itself there was yet another member of the great family, Don Juan de Córdoba, a distant kinsman of Antonio's and a prelate of the cathedral. His relations with a woman, who had been his mistress in his youth, caused great scandal in the city. The old catalogue of the nobility by Alonso López de Haro discreetly notes of this prelate: "Don Juan de Córdoba, dean and canon of the holy cathedral of Córdoba, of whom issue exists". The Andalusians knew more details, and modern research has established that the Dean had six children, whom he left well provided for. They were popularly called simply "the Dean's Córdobas".

This worthy kinsman one day received from the Marchioness Catherine a friendly letter, asking that he would out of his ecclesiastical riches place a house at the disposal of the fathers of the new Society. The mistrustful prelate, who up till then had unquestioningly believed all the town gossip against the Jesuits, declared that he was prepared to do so only when he knew these strange religious better; he first wished, as he expressed himself, to "undertake an anatomy of the Jesuits". Father Francisco de Villanueva and a

Brother called Alonso López came to his house, and the prelate was soon won over and converted, but not from his sinful life.[15]

After Don Antonio's first Mass he was moved to offer his own beautiful house in Córdoba for use as a college. This fitted in perfectly with Catherine's plans. The pious gossips of Córdoba, however, took a bad view of the Jesuits' friendship with the prelate whose way of life was so scandalous. "The Jesuits carry Baal together with the Ark of the Lord", they said. But Don Juan was completely converted by the fathers who now moved into his house.[16] In the unpublished history of the Spanish Jesuits by Pedro Ribadeneira this struggle for the soul of the Andalusian prelate is described in some detail; the account closes with the words: "Our Lord gave Don Juan such a mighty and effective impulse, that he at once went to the house where that lady dwelt and publicly broke off his connection with her. He lodged her in a convent, where she ended her life in retirement." Father Antonio hastened to inform Ignatius in a long letter, dated August 12th, 1554, of this transformation. One senses from this letter how the whole of his illustrious family breathed a sigh of relief. Antonio could not refrain from making the somewhat unkind observation: "Don Juan has indeed given the Company of Jesus a house, but hitherto he had in his heart quite different company."

No one was happier at this turn of events than the Marchioness Catherine. To place the new foundations at Córdoba and Montilla on a firm footing, she suggested diverting the rich revenues of the canonry, which Antonio still received, to the Jesuits of Córdoba. Legally this was by no means an easy thing to effect. Ignatius had to seek the advice of canonists in Rome, based on information supplied by the Marchioness in July and December 1553. When all was in order, he wrote to the mother of Don Antonio a charming letter, consoling her on the death of her first-born and congratulating her on Antonio's vocation. Nor did he forget to greet the sorrowing young widow, Countess Ana de Feria, who had buried herself in the convent of Poor Clares at Montilla. To comfort both ladies, Father Francis Borgia was allowed to pay a visit to Córdoba.[17]

My Lady in our Lord,

The sovereign grace and eternal love of Christ our Lord be always with us to our continual favour and help.

I have recently received from Your Ladyship two letters together of July 9th and December 18th. What you have written has not only given me much satisfaction because of the trouble your Ladyship is taking to favour the college of Córdoba, but very special consolation to see the spirit and entire conformity with God's will that is revealed in your Ladyship's letter, and your acceptance of the fact that God our Lord should take for himself two such sons, one to live wholly in heaven, and the other to die at once to the love and designs of earth, disposing himself not to be concerned with any other business than that of guiding himself and many others to heaven and devoting himself entirely to the glory and service of his Creator.

And although this is a very singular benefit that God our Lord has done Father Don Antonio, and all the more so since he had great inducement to allow his affections (at least in part) to rest on things of earth, but now they are all turned to and occupied in things on high – still it is not always the way of mothers to appreciate a blessing of this kind in their sons. Divine grace must be deeply working in and imprinted on your Ladyship's heart, enabling you to appreciate and love eternal good things, so that you may thus console yourself that Father Don Antonio has left temporal things for them.

May it please him who is the source of light and of all well-ordered love, to increase in your Ladyship what he has begun and to communicate to you with his infinite and supreme generosity and give you this true and Christian consolation of seeing all your children, each one in the state to which God shall call him, employing themselves devotedly in his service and praise, always following very closely the path to the final and blessed end which is prepared for them.

As to Don Antonio's business, taking account that we have persons as learned as Andrés Vela and the Licentiate Casarrubios, I do not think there will be much need to trouble you, except to ask God our Lord to reward, according to his infinite riches and generosity, the charity which he himself has given to your Ladyship, and to Father Don Antonio, whom he inspires to bring about this thing, and the other help which your Ladyship gives, so that this work may go forward in his divine service. With this I have already told him that if we can help in any way we shall not fail to do so, at any rate in good will; although it is not our custom to intervene in business of this sort, which does not seem to belong to our vocation.

Concerning what your Ladyship writes about ordering Father Francisco Borgia to come to Córdoba and visit Your Ladyship and the Señora Condesa de Feria, I should have been very glad in our Lord to have had this advice earlier, because previously, at the instance of the Count and Countess of Ribagorza, I offered to let Father Francisco come to Saragossa on his return from Portugal. Thus I wrote to him some months ago now that he should do this, spending a little time there, and I think he is already in that city or on the way to it. Still, I will tell him that since he will have done in some measure what those people and the city wanted, he should give close attention to the work in Córdoba, and to the service and consolation of Your Ladyship and of the Countess.

Of the house that Don Juan de Córdoba gave for the college, with all the rest, we have had advice. May it please the divine goodness to make a dwelling for him in heaven, and to grant him a very abundant share in whatever good may accrue from this work for the divine glory and the help of souls. And certainly, not only there but everywhere, the Society is under much obligation for his service in our Lord, for his great devotion, charity and generosity.

I kiss the hands of the Countess and heartily commend myself, with the whole Society, to her prayers; for, as her example has been and is of so much edification to the world, so I hope her prayers will be the more efficacious before God. I also offer to bring Your Ladyship's name often before God, begging his divine mercy to preserve and greatly increase the gifts he has granted you until you receive the glorious confirmation of them in his holy kingdom.

May he give us all his abundant grace that we may always know his most holy will and carry it out to the full.

(Ignatius)

Rome, May 15th, 1554

To the Marchioness of Priego, Córdoba

During the whole of the following year the enterprises of the Jesuits in Andalusia flourished under the patronage of the indefatigable Marchioness. Already colleges had been founded at Seville and Granada. Catherine's beloved cousin Francis Borgia was still active as the General's representative in Spain, and in Lent 1555 he visited his kinswoman. The reformed prelate Don Juan celebrated the solemn dedication of his foundation. In Granada the bishop welcomed the fathers with open arms. It was a real sorrow for the zealous Marchioness that the Archbishop of Córdoba, Don Leopold of Austria (as in Valencia, the see was held by an illegitimate son of the Emperor Maximilian I), was ill-disposed towards the Jesuits. Had he not had difficulty in getting for himself the wealthy see of Córdoba in 1541, for which Francis Borgia had seriously proposed to the Emperor his own nine-year-old son? It could not then have been pleasant for him to have to discuss the spiritual needs of his diocese with this duke who was now a Jesuit. The Marchioness therefore recommended him urgently to Ignatius' prayers when on August 10th, 1555, she sent an otherwise glowing report to Rome on the progress of the work in Andalusia.[18]

Most illustrious Father,

I have not written to you for some time telling you how the matter of the colleges of Córdoba and Seville was proceeding. Now, however, I can wait no longer. I beg you, moreover, that when you have a moment of leisure, you would do me the favour of sending me a letter, for there is no one whom it would be a greater charity on your part to remember than myself, who am so much in need of it.

My Father Francis [Borgia] was in these parts before Lent; he did not stop in Córdoba more than a week. His reverence left the matter of Seville arranged; he was pleased that that house was so well received and at how much our Lord was beginning to be served there. Since then everything has gone on prospering more, and to all manner of people the profit they receive from the teaching and example of those Fathers seems very great. They are very much edified by their persons and example. Of this there would be much to say in detail and because I cannot be such a good narrator as the matter deserves, I shall say no more of Seville.

Córdoba, blessed be our Lord, has developed very well. Señor Don Juan already has the fathers settled in his house and recently the dedication of it was celebrated, all with such great contentment and joy that to him it seemed a very good thing that our Lord had inspired him to establish the house. Father Doctor Torres whom you know, has been there, and his residing there has been a great good for these parts and for all that falls within his province. The entrance examinations have been very well attended and the students have made good progress, both in manners and in their studies. All the fathers and brothers have given good example: they have persevered in the teaching of Christian doctrine with good success and, therefore, the Father Doctor has not suspended it or the preaching of sermons by which our Lord has been much served. Now Doctor Torres is in Granada founding that house of which they say that the archbishop and all the people there of public authority and weight have received them very gladly and declare their willingness to profit by their preaching. I could wish that we might soon enjoy a better opinon from our prelate here in Córdoba. Pray to our Lord for him and his ministers that they may know the favour God has done them in bringing our Fathers to their diocese for up to now the prelate does not realize this and has great need to understand this and other things, in order to carry out his obligations. . . .

Antonio is in Salamanca and has been in poor health these days. I beg you to remember him and commend him to our Lord that he may have him in his keeping to use him for his service. I commend them all to Your Reverence and ask our Lord to guard and prosper in his service Your Reverence's very illustrious person. I kiss Your Reverence's hands.

August, 10th, 1555

To the most illustrious lord, Don Master Ignatius, General of the Society of Jesus, in Rome

Subsequently, too, the Marchioness Catherine was unsurpassed in her kindness to the Jesuits. The influence of the fathers on the members of her family was a great consolation to her motherly heart. Thus her son-in-law, the second Duke of Arcos, found his way back to God through the Jesuits, and Blessed Juan of Ávila, her friend, was overjoyed. Shortly before Ignatius' death her son, the Count of Feria, wrote to the General from Brussels: "Even were I a Turk, I would always feel bound to her service."

Catherine gave the Jesuits a country house on her estates as a holiday home and retreat house. She provided a new noviciate in Córdoba. It is not, therefore, surprising that she occasionally, with the air of a *grande dame,* interfered in matters which it was proper for the General only to decide. In a long letter to her son Antonio in Salamanca – who was to forward it to Ignatius – the Marchioness waxed very indignant that many "new Christians" of Jewish or Moorish descent were being admitted to the Society of Jesus. Catherine, with aristocratic self-assurance, uttered a warning: through this, the nobility of Córdoba might turn away in disgust from the Jesuits. She would have preferred, as Araoz wrote to Ignatius, only pure-blooded Basques in Córdoba. A short while before, however, Ignatius had made known to Araoz at the royal court of Valladolid his considered opinion about this "nonsense of racial pride". So his answer to the Marchioness was as clear as it was wise: he remained firm that such candidates were certainly to be accepted, but recommended that prudent regard should be had to the understandable aversion – especially strong in Andalusia – for everything that recalled the Arab domination.

His good relations with Catherine remained unaffected. The grateful General caused every Jesuit in Spain to say three masses for the Marchioness.

Father Antonio had meanwhile been leading a truly saintly life in Salamanca. In the same year, 1567, in which the king's favour made his brother a duke, Don Antonio received the crown of eternal life. His sorrowing mother had him buried in the family vault at Córdoba. There were at the funeral some awkward incidents connected with matters of ceremonial, with the smoothing over of which Francis Borgia, now General, had to go to some trouble. The latter sent Marchioness Catherine an extravagant letter of consolation. What a contrast with the laconic and reserved manner in which Ignatius used to comfort his friends in cases of bereavement!

On July 3rd, 1569, the Duke of Feria announced to the General's curia the illness of his mother. The cause of her sickness was said to be the loss of her spiritual director Juan de Ávila. On July 14th, this truly great mother of a Jesuit entered into her heavenly home. With justice St. Francis Borgia called her "mistress and mother of this whole little company of Jesus".[19]

Juana de Valencia

THERE was another vocation which gave the General as much happiness as that of the grandee Antonio de Córdoba and consoled him in the midst of all the cares brought upon him by that eccentric scion of royalty, Teotonio de Braganza. It was that of a member of the Castilian house of Manrique de Lara, which since 1482 had borne the ducal title of Nájera. Ignatius had finished his military career under Don Antonio Manrique, who at the time of the fall of Pamplona in 1521 was Viceroy of Navarre. In a letter of August 26th, 1552, he recalls with pride the days of his service with the ducal house, to which moreover he was related through the counts of Oñate.

In May 1554 the news came to Rome that a young gentleman called Fadrique Manrique had announced his intention of entering the Society. The chronicle calls him "a youth of noble blood". His father was García Manrique of the house of Lara, who held the office of Alcaide and Captain of Málaga, hereditary in the family since the conquest of Andalusia. His mother was Doña Juana de Valencia, who in 1525 at Toledo had married García, a former page of Queen Leonor of Portugal. Her firstborn son Iñigo was a page of the Empress Isabel; and later the second son Don Fadrique also received a good position at court, as was usual in these grandee families.[20]

It may be that Ignatius was especially pleased by the unusual history of this young man's vocation, for it was not unlike his own. At all events, secretary Polanco thought it worth while to relate this edifying piece of news in some detail to Father Nadal. Fadrique was a page at Philip II's court and also a knight of the order of Calatrava with an income of 12,000 maravedís. Taken seriously ill while in Corsica on a military expedition, he made a vow – being then in danger of death – to enter a religious order. The young warrior also somewhat rashly promised to recite the Lord's Prayer an enormous number of times each day.

The sick man was brought by ship to Genoa, where he met Father Laynez, and, though he had scarcely recovered, he decided with ardent enthusiasm to become a Jesuit. On May 17th, 1554, Laynez informed Ignatius that he was travelling with Don Fadrique to Florence, and from there the candidate was riding to Rome to present himself before the General. "We are much pleased at the grace which God has shown to Fadrique", wrote Ignatius in reply; but in his anxiety for the still convalescent novice he added that he should rather wait for the better season in September. Fadrique now made a short retreat at Florence with Luis de Mendoza, Laynez' nephew, and on the feast of the Assumption 1554 – exactly twenty years after Ignatius' great day on Montmartre in Paris – he made the simple vows of the Society. Out of devotion and humility he altered his name on this occasion from Fadrique to "Francisco de Bonaventura". The prosaic Ignatius soon made him give up this form of piety – he remained Fadrique as before. He was also released from the vow concerning the numerous Paternosters. Brother Fadrique now felt himself as if newborn and newly baptized in his vocation, wrote Ignatius.[21]

After Fadrique had settled the legal business of renunciation of his income as a knight of Calatrava and had paid his old student debts in Alcalá, Valladolid, and Medina del Campo – Ignatius wrote him out a special procuration for this – he was to go to Rome. But then the young religious was stricken with the ague. Ignatius was touchingly concerned about his "dearest Brother Francisco de Bonaventura". However, at the end of September Brother Fadrique did arrive in Rome and began his studies at the Roman College. Ignatius was more than usually enthusiastic about him, and in his letters during the months that followed expressions of praise constantly reoccur. Fadrique (he wrote) was like an angel, he had made the Exercises a second time in the most edifying way; the General even used of him the words of the Epistle to the Hebrews (11:38): "Of whom the world was not worthy".

It is understandable that in Spain they were especially delighted at all this, for there the illustrious name of Manrique de Lara enjoyed enormous prestige. Ignatius reported on July 6th, 1555, to Father Bernard Olivier: "Among the Spanish scholastics is one named Don Fadrique Manrique, who was formerly a page to the King of England and then a noble in His Majesty's court. He is as good as an angel and an excellent student." No doubt the news travelled also to Fadrique's distant mother in Málaga, who had been a widow since 1537. The highminded lady therefore wrote Ignatius a letter (no longer extant) in which she expressed her happiness at her son's holy choice. From the reply which the General sent her on September 5th, 1555, we see clearly the love of the house of Lara which Ignatius had retained from his early days.

Such was the occasion of the following letter, intended only to be one of comfort to a loving mother.[22]

JESUS

My Lady in our Lord:

The sovereign grace and eternal love of Christ our Lord be with Your Ladyship, with his most holy gifts and spiritual graces.

Your Ladyship's letter gave me much occasion of consolation in our Lord, since I recognized in it that the same spirit that moved Don Fadrique, your son, to pursue the constitutions and way of life which he follows in our Society also moved you to be pleased at his decision. This is a sign that the great love you have for him is not so much tenderness of flesh and blood as it is of the spirit and from that charity by which we desire true and eternal good for the one we love, rather than the temporal and perishable goods of this life. This I can certainly tell Your Ladyship – that as far as can be judged by experience up to the present, there is much cause for whoever loves Don Fadrique to be consoled at seeing him in the state in which he is; for, apart from his peace and contentment, each day it appears that God our Lord gives him an increase of his grace and virtue. Thereby he gives us all much edification and good hope that his divine Majesty will be greatly served and glorified in him. In the studies also he is initiating himself very well and making more than ordinary progress, so that we are all very satisfied with him. God our Lord be praised.

Because I know it will give Your Ladyship consolation, I have written what we feel about your son. If our Society can serve Your Ladyship in anything, we shall be very glad of the opportunity and you may command us in the fullest confidence.

Thus I will say no more except to pray that God's supreme goodness may deign to give us all his abundant grace so that we may always know his most holy will and fulfil it perfectly.

(Ignatius)

Rome, September 5th, 1555

To the mother of Don Fadrique

On October 31st, 1555, Fadrique sent his mother a letter of greeting, which Father Nadal took with him on his journey to Spain, and in which he begged for alms. Towards the end of the year another letter arrived from the Alcaide's widow, who was anxious about her son; and Ignatius took the opportunity to answer her at the beginning of 1556 with a charming epistle. He knew the feelings in the heart of a mother who had given her

393

son to the Society, and so he consoled her with the joyful prospect that Fadrique on conclusion of his studies would be able to go home to Spain, to gladden his waiting mother "with his bodily presence".[23]

IHS

The sovereign grace and eternal love of Christ our Lord be always with us to our continual help and favour.

After having replied to a letter I received from you in recent months, another has been given to me dated April 10th. The more your letters show us of your maternal love for Don Fadrique, the more edification do we receive from the conformity of your will with God's, so that it appears that the same spirit which drew Don Fadrique from the world to religion has taught Your Ladyship how to be calm and contented with his decision, making up for the fragility of nature with the strength of God's grace. May it please this same God always to increase his light and charity in Your Ladyship's soul, so that each day you may be more consoled to see him whom you love so well employed in the service of him who must be loved above all things, and in whom and for whose glory they must all be loved.

As to the rest, Don Fadrique is now so much, and more than ever, Your Ladyship's son in our Lord; the love of God will perfect the natural love he bears you as a son. When he is further advanced in his studies (which, judging by the ability he has will not be very long), he will be able some day to visit Your Ladyship with his bodily presence. In the meanwhile, because his virtue and religious life and good example are so meritorious, he cannot but be highly satisfactory to us and greatly loved in Christ our Lord by all those with whom he comes in contact. And because Your Ladyship commends him to us so much, special care will be taken of his person.

May God's supreme goodness maintain Your Ladyship in his holy service and may he will to give us all his abundant grace so that we may always know his most holy will and follow it out to the full.

Ignatius

Rome, January 8th, 1556

To the mother of Don Fadrique, Málaga

This is the last letter of the saint's correspondence with the mother of the much-praised Fadrique. It appears that the latter never returned to

Spain. In this records of the Society at Rome dating from the years of Laynez' generalship, his name often occurs. Fadrique was in 1562 prefect of the Jesuits' church, soon to become the magnificent *Gesù*. He was filled with childlike pleasure when he was permitted to use the beautiful chalice employed at Father Juan de Vitoria's profession; and the corporals of finest linen, which the wealthy Ursula Fugger of Trent had presented to the church, delighted him more than all the worldly honours which he had forsaken at the court of the Spanish king.

The great family chronicle of the de Laras is silent about Fadrique's religious vocation: all the more, on that account, was he understood by his mother. In her old age – in 1567 she was still alive – she retired to the peace of an Andalusian convent, leaving behind her the splendours she once enjoyed at the court of the Empress Isabel. Fadrique died after a virtuous life in the year 1588.[24]

Madonna Cesare

THERE is in the early history of the Society a classic case of a vocation which has occupied the attention of recent historians. Much ink flowed because of it in Ignatius' curia. Equally copiously too flowed the tears of a mother fighting for her son who had entered the Society.

As this conflict between the General and the family also produced a special letter to the mother and caused a stir in Rome that lasted till the closing year of the saint's life, we shall describe it in greater detail. It concerned the vocation of a young Neapolitan of sixteen, Ottaviano Cesare. Born in 1537, the third son of the secretary to Duke Ettore Pignatelli di Monteleone, he was his mother's favourite.[25]

At the height of the conflict of which he was the centre, he described in a long letter to Ignatius the early history of his vocation. His pious father had dedicated the child to God from boyhood. Ottaviano had once fallen into the deepest part of Naples harbour, and when he was taken out of the water a Benedictine monk had spoken to him on the subject of vocations. Ottaviano became gravely ill and promised, with his father's approval, to enter the order of St. Benedict. Then he met the Jesuits — Father Bobadilla and soon afterwards Father Salmerón. Quickly making up his mind he begged them to admit him to the new Society. His request was however refused, for besides the agreement of his father, that of his mother was also necessary. This reply was prudent and cautious, as events showed.

The boy was so keen on the Jesuits that he attempted a flight to Rome, in order there to force Ignatius to admit him. But his indignant mother had him overtaken on the way and brought back; she locked him up at first and then banished him to the country, where he was subjected to attack from the skilful tongue of the Duchess of Monteleone. But her tears and entreaties produced the opposite effect from that intended. He successfully escaped a second time, on a ship that was taking some Jesuits to Sicily, then under the jurisdiction of the Viceroy Juan de Vega. This was at the end of 1553. Ottaviano was allowed to begin his noviciate, first at Palermo and afterwards at Messina.

Now began the passionate mother's campaign to recover her child. She first sent two servants of the family to Palermo, to try and force her son to come home; a third soon followed, and when all this seemed of no avail, the father set out for Messina armed with letters from the Duchess of Monteleone to the Viceroy. The chronicle of the Society specially noted that the father did this only under heavy pressure from his wife, for scarcely had Don Pietro reached the noviciate than he had an opportunity to hear his son preach on the text: "The Lord possessed me from the beginning" (Prov. 8:22). The father listened sobbing and returned converted and satisfied to Naples.

His wife, however, was not impressed. Indignant letters were dispatched to Father Doménech in Sicily, threatening that she would come herself next time to fetch her son home. She intended to charter a special mail frigate for the purpose. It was at this time that Doménech wrote laconically in a letter to Rome: "This woman is mad!"[26]

Ottaviano himself expressed a determined refusal to return: "Send me to the ends of the earth", he wrote to Ignatius. The latter was already planning to send the young religious to Spain, so that he might there, free from all molestation, begin his studies; but there was at the moment no ship available.

The centre of the conflict now shifted to Rome. To make an impression, the Duke of Monteleone had to write to Ignatius. The General's answer to this letter has been preserved; it refers, with learned quotations from St. Thomas Aquinas' *Summa theologica,* to the fact that according to canon law Ottaviano was old enough to choose the religious life and was therefore free to do so. Then came letters from Ottaviano's father, again quite obviously written at the instigation of the mother; for Ignatius based his refusal to recall the youth from Sicily on the ground that "his lady mother would leave him as little peace in Naples as in Sicily. She is not the first mother of a religious, and the child belongs more to Jesus Christ than to his mother". The father was again reassured, and in a third letter of the General's to him it is made quite clear whom Ignatius regarded as his real opponent. His words to Don Pietro were: "You must employ different means to persuade your wife to understand the grace of her son's vocation."

This was on December 3rd, 1553. Meanwhile the persistent lady had called upon the services of her confessor, Father Francesco de Medde, a Franciscan, who assailed Ignatius with spiritual arguments, and Madonna Cesare enclosed with his letter of January 1554 one of her own to Ignatius, with the request that he would recall Ottaviano to Naples, because she was in ill health, and to see her son again might contribute to her recovery – the same old maternal psychology. Now the General judged the time was come to give the overwrought mother a lesson on the true understanding of a son's religious vocation.[27]

The sovereign grace and eternal love of Christ our Lord be always with us to our help and favour.

I have received a letter from Your Ladyship dated the twelfth of this month in which you show a desire that your son, Ottaviano, should be moved to Naples, for the sake of your health which you think would be improved by seeing him.

I think Your Ladyship will already have understood that in anything in which I can serve and comfort you without going against the will of God our Lord, I shall be most ready to do so. In this matter, however, it is not fitting that anyone of my profession should show himself more ready to please men than God, a thing which should be alien not only to religious but even to any secular person. Now because I think it would be against the divine will to put that young man in danger, I cannot consent to have him brought to Naples now until he is more resolute and Your Ladyship calmer and more content with your son's choice. I cannot think that for the bodily or spiritual health of Your Ladyship the presence of your son is necessary; because, to believe this, would be not only a slur on Your Ladyship but also on God's high Majesty, for it would then appear that we thought that God had no other way of healing Your Ladyship in body and soul than our falling into disorder and committing sin, for at this time to bring Your Ladyship and your son together would be to bring him into temptation.

You should remember that you are not the first mother whose son has become a religious and that no earthly father or mother has so much part in their children as God has, who has both created them and redeemed them with the blood of his only-begotten Son. Thus we must accept God's holy will and Your Ladyship's consolation depends on this acceptance more than on the visit of your son.

For the rest, in whatever I can give satisfaction and happiness to Your Ladyship according to God, I shall always do so; and so much the more willingly, as the more Christlike and patient do I learn is your submission to the will of God our Lord.

May his divine and sovereign goodness grant us all grace always to know his most holy will and to follow it out perfectly.

Ignatius

Rome, January 28th, 1554

To Madonna Cesare, Mother of Ottaviano Cesare

The letter had the opposite effect to that desired. Madonna Cesare now took up the fight against Ignatius by every possible means, and her willing messenger was again her own husband. Don Pietro had to travel to Rome and there, as Ignatius said, he set the whole world in motion. Cardinals and even Pope Julius III were called upon to take action; and in Cardinal Carafa, whose coolness towards Ignatius was well known in Rome, he found a suitable ally. The chronicle of the Society specially notes that the Cardinal had lately caused to be summarily ejected a father of the Society who sought an audience in connection with Ottaviano's case. An intimidating order was sent by Carafa to Ignatius that Ottaviano was to be sent to Naples at once, "that he might talk with his mother". Pope Julius, however, declared this instruction to be invalid.

Madonna Cesare was now quite furious and travelled herself to Rome. The foreboding which Ignatius had expressed shortly before in a letter dictated to Polanco was fulfilled: "We have heard that Ottaviano's mother is coming to Rome in person to conduct the case. She might easily succeed in winning over the hearts of the ladies, whose favour can effect so much in Rome. I would not then be surprised if fresh vexations arose for us through this."

In fact, Madonna Cesare tried to influence three cardinals with tears and lamentations and even managed to get an audience with the Pope. Ignatius felt something like admiration for this determined lady: "I believe this woman will force the Pope himself to give way and employ all the fire of passion that she is capable of." The Protector of the Society, Cardinal Carpi, suggested a middle course: let Ottaviano come at least to Rome. The Pope set up a commission of cardinals to consider the case. In principle the General was completely right. At the Roman curia they were already weary of the woman's persistent complaints, and at the end of 1554 Ignatius noted the result: "The poor lady at last found all doors closed and returned to Naples." Moreover, the Pope sent her word that she should rather concern herself about her daughters than about her son, who was well provided for.[28]

The moment Ignatius thought the case had been sufficiently defended, he made a tactical concession. In January 1555 Ottaviano did in fact come to Rome, there to continue his studies. The mother seems to have calmed down, at least towards the end of 1555. However, we shall hear later how once in June she gave hospitality in Naples to five Sicilian scholastics whom Ignatius had had to dismiss; they were on their way home, and she showered kindnesses upon them. Ignatius knew why and scented fresh dangers for Brother Ottaviano – not without cause, for since May 23rd, 1555, his opponent Cardinal Carafa had been Pope as Paul IV. So it came about, as was inevitable, that the father again on December 8th requested the return of his son to Naples, because this was alleged to be advantageous for his health. Ignatius allowed this, probably in order to remove at least this stumbling-block out of the Pope's way. On February 2nd, 1556, he announced to Don Pietro Ottaviano's speedy return, adding with gentle irony, by way of a reason for allowing it, that he was sending Ottaviano "in order to satisfy his mother".

Brother Ottaviano went home; and how he was worked upon there can be imagined. It was one of the last disappointments of Ignatius' life when Ottaviano's request to leave the Society reached Rome. It was dated May 31st, 1556. Even in the month of his death, July 1556, Ignatius was trying with touching affection to bring back the young religious to his vocation, but in vain. It was as a task inherited from his Master that Laynez when General continued the attempt for two whole years. Not until October 1558 was Ottaviano finally dismissed from the Society. Perhaps the Duke of Monteleone was right when he wrote to Laynez: "Ottaviano chose the religious life more out of boyish enthusiasm than by the impulse of the Spirit of God." Perhaps we can more truly say that Ottaviano lost his vocation because he was overcome by his mother's possessive love.[29]

AUTOGRAPH COPY OF THE VOW MADE BY ISABEL ROSER

see page 286-287

DRAFT OF A LETTER FROM ST. IGNATIUS TO MIGUEL DE TORRES
see page 289-290

The Widow Johanna Agnes Berze

THINGS were not always as tempestuous in the General's curia as in 1554, when Ignatius had to wage war with the Neapolitan mother. Simpler questions, too, were solved there quietly and in strict accordance with canon law, as in the case of the widow Berze of Goes in South Beveland. Her son Father Caspar Berze, born in 1515, was a gifted boy, but of a somewhat adventurous disposition. At seventeen he obtained at Louvain the degree of Master of Arts; then, however, he joined the army of Charles V, subsequently tried to live for a time as a hermit on the holy mountain of Montserrat, and came after many adventures to Portugal, where he was moved by a Lenten sermon of Father Strada's in Coimbra to request admittance to Ignatius' Society. On April 20th, 1546, Caspar became a Jesuit; he was ordained at Christmas and successfully completed his theological studies in two years. On March 17th, 1548, he set off from Lisbon for India, where Francis Xavier was waiting eagerly for helpers.

Master Barzaeus, as he was henceforth called, was to become St. Francis Xavier's most valiant fellow-labourer in his work for souls. Even during the voyage, in a ship that was full of gentlemen of noble birth and ladies of doubtful repute, he was a true apostle and made himself useful too, as cook and apothecary. The chronicle relates that during a three-days' storm off the Cape of Good Hope Master Caspar sang exultantly in the face of the mountainous waves: *"Christus vincit, Christus regnat"*, and that even the loose women on board confessed to him.

On September 4th, he reached India and began his truly magnificent apostolate, which earned him the commendation of Francis Xavier and the General of the Society. Ignatius and those about him were filled with joy on reading his reports; even the contemplative Carthusians in Cologne received tidings of Barzaeus' astonishing journeys. He became especially famous through the sermon on the Trinity that he preached in 1549 in the synagogue of Ormuz on the Persian Gulf. From there he sent his brethren in Europe a long letter which afterwards circulated widely. He was called simply "the great Kashish of the Franks", and his accounts read like something out of the *Arabian Nights*. Ignatius asked him on August 13th, 1553, to

401

send as exact and detailed reports as possible. It was indeed like a greeting from another world when there came to Rome from the Far East, travelling via Coimbra, a "Yogus", an Indian whom Caspar had baptized with the name of Paul of the Holy Faith and had sent as a messenger to his Father Ignatius.[30]

It must have been in that same year that news reached secretary Polanco from Goes about legal difficulties which had arisen in the home of Master Caspar. Barzaeus had on his superiors' instructions expressly renounced in 1552 his right to all property that might come to him from the inheritance of his father, who had in the meantime died. A doubt now arose as to whether Caspar could really make such a renunciation at all, since he had already made his vows in the Society of Jesus. It was therefore necessary to issue a document to the widow Johanna which unequivocally testified that Caspar had up to that time made no vows in the Society and that his act of renunciation was therefore legally valid. Ignatius was at once prepared to issue such a certificate in view of the modest circumstances of the Flemish widow. On October 4th, 1554, the document was despatched to the widow Berze, signed by the General and his secretary.[31]

Ignatius of Loyola, Master General of the Society of Jesus.

To my beloved sister in Jesus Christ, Johanna, widow of Francis Berze, everlasting health in the Lord.

Since your beloved son and our brother, Master Caspar Berze renounced in your favour all his worldly possessions in the year of our Lord 1552, as can be clearly seen from his will or deed of renunciation transmitted to you; and since we understand that there are some people who question whether the aforesaid Master Caspar was professed at the time, or had, perhaps not the right to make a will – lest anyone dispute the matter with you, his mother, we now give testimony that your son according to the flesh already named did not make profession at any time during the year 1552 or the following year and that according to our Constitutions he was able to make a will or deed of renunciation. Now because he belongs to our Society, whatever he has arranged has to be ratified by me. I, therefore, approve and confirm in the name of the whole Society and my own, his will and deed of renunciation.

In testimony of all this we give these present letters written with our hand, and sealed with our general seal and that of the secretary of the Society.

Given at Rome, at the house of our Society, in the year of our Lord 1554, on the fourth day of the month of October.

Ignatius of Loyola
Juan de Polanco

To Johanna the Mother of Father Berze

This document had a peculiar history. It was with this as with so many letters that Ignatius wrote to Francis Xavier. They were written in Rome at a time when Francis had already died; so it was now with Master Barzaeus. On December 24th, 1553, a large packet was despatched to him, in which was contained the following admonition: "Take more care of your health and do not work so excessively, for you cannot carry on in this way." In February 1554 followed a similar warning: "We hear from Goa that you are ill from overwork. Although I am much edified by this holy zeal, it nevertheless appears to me that you are somewhat lacking in that salt with which God wishes every sacrifice to be mingled, namely 'reasonable service' (Rom. 12:1)."

But these admonitions came too late. On October 18th, 1553, almost a year before the date of the document sent to his mother, Barzaeus collapsed during a sermon. The chronicle of the Society proudly notes of the death of this true son of Ignatius: "Master Caspar died as it were in the pulpit." The finest epitaph of the widow Berze's son was written by Ignatius himself: "Master Caspar has completed his earthly course and is gone home to his heavenly and everlasting fatherland. God our Lord be praised! For He is the true life and salvation of all men."[32]

Magdalena Angélica Doménech

WHAT follows is not the story of a mother who sacrificed a son to Ignatius' Society, but that of the strange career of a Jesuit's sister. It had a profound effect upon the vocation of one of the General's best companions and produced a remarkable letter from the saint.

When Ignatius' two companions, Faber and Laynez, were having their first successes at Parma from June 1539 to the summer of 1540, a young canon of Valencia visited them there at the end of August 1539. He was Juan Jerónimo Doménech, twenty-three years old, already a Master of Philosophy, member of a rich family and the holder of many benefices. At his home in Valencia there lived in the street of St. Vincent his already aged father with a sickly son and the daughter of a second marriage, Magdalena Angélica. In Rome Doménech had an uncle of the same name, who was *Scriptor Apostolicus,* a skilled man of affairs and quite influential. Jerónimo had travelled to Rome in 1538 on his father's business and on the way had made the acquaintance at Bologna of Francis Xavier, whose virtue made a deep impression on him and whose glowing words about the mission to India and the conversion of the infidels he could never forget as long as he lived. In Rome he had met Xavier again and he now wished to go to Paris after settling his affairs and there complete his theological studies. Xavier gave him a letter of recommendation to his two companions in Parma.[33]

Grace had long been at work in the rich and gifted canon, and after a conversation with the two disciples of Ignatius at Parma he resolved, while still staying at the inn, to join their community – the actual founding of the Society had not yet taken place. He made the Exercises and made a written vow on September 24th to join Ignatius' company. Jerónimo had already so well understood the spirit of his Master's Exercises that he was directly afterwards able to give the Exercises to four noble ladies, among whom was the "mystic" Giulia Zerbini, whom we already know. Ignatius said later that Doménech was, together with Faber, the best at giving the Spiritual Exercises.[34]

Jerónimo's uncle, the prelate in Rome, was annoyed at his nephew's choice, for it destroyed all the hopes which the family had placed in the

404

young man. He lost no time in deciding to set out for Parma to rescue Jerónimo from the "Iñiguists". He declared to the Cardinal Legate Ennio Filonardi that these priests were highly suspect on account of their connection with the Spanish pseudo-mystic Francisca Hernández, that many had already left the community, and that he would not, in the name of his family, tolerate it that his nephew should join them. The Cardinal was already better informed about the case: Pietro Codacio, who had become one of Ignatius' companions that same year, had written him a long and detailed letter from Rome. So the disappointed uncle now appealed to a strange authority – he went to Pavia to consult a woman mystic famous in those parts.

The brethren in Parma had meanwhile as it were hidden the young Doménech so that his uncle could not speak to him; Jerónimo was staying at Sissa, ten miles away from Parma. Faber reported all these things to Francis Xavier in Rome and added with gentle humour: "We shall see what happens now when he [the prelate] returns from that woman. If that one is not enough, we will show him another in Parma, who since July 5th has eaten and drunk nothing save the Host in communion." This was that Giulia Zerbini who had just made the Exercises with Doménech and now from her sickbed was giving them to other women and at the same time prophesying great things of Ignatius' new community.

The uncle surrendered after a talk with his nephew and was satisfied when Jerónimo promised in any case to complete his studies in Paris, in order to reassure his father. In 1540 Jerónimo was admitted to the Society by Ignatius in Rome and at the end of the year he departed for Paris. In the spring of 1543 he was again in Rome and acted for two years as the General's secretary. In 1547 he began his great career in Sicily, where he was the best friend of the Viceroy Juan de Vega.[35]

At home in Valencia his old father and his sister Angélica followed all this with loving interest. The house of the wealthy Don Pedro became the centre for the work which Father Araoz began there in 1544, and which was soon being carried on by twelve other Jesuits. They lived in the house in the street of St. Vincent, and Don Pedro provided generously for their support. Araoz could not praise the family enough. He was especially delighted by Angélica. "Angélica is indeed something we must praise God for", he wrote to Ignatius; and to her half-brother Jerónimo he said: "Angélica is, as her name implies, a seraph."

Don Pedro, who was on terms of cordial friendship with Francis Borgia, was already thinking of founding a college. The legal preliminaries, however, were full of difficulties, for they were concerned principally with the estate of Father Jerónimo's long-dead mother. That is why from

405

1548 onwards, Don Pedro in his letters to Ignatius kept on asking for the return of his son. This put Ignatius in an embarrassing position: such a journey could only be made with the express permission of the Sicilian viceroy; meanwhile, he consoled Don Pedro and his daughter with the Jubilee indulgences of the year 1550. After Easter 1551 Jerónimo was at last able to sail for Valencia.[36]

On April 10th he arrived there, to the immense joy of his family. The holy Bishop of Valencia, Thomas de Villanueva, greeted him warmly. Then Jerónimo's elder brother died, and this sad event strengthened Angélica in her resolution to imitate her half-brother and forsake the world. What followed is a story of which the chronicle of the Society remarks ironically: "By this we can once again see how little one can rely on promises, especially when they are made by women."

Angélica had made a vow of virginity and now seriously wished to enter the cloister; but a friend who was already a nun dissuaded her, saying that in a convent she could not lead such a spiritual life as in the world. Angélica now renewed her vow in her brother's presence, but decided to remain with her old father and after his death to retire to a small house with a pious widow. The college was then to be founded with her and Jerónimo's inheritance.

Ignatius was kept informed of these developments in Valencia. On June 4th, 1552, he wrote: "Angélica would rather not go into a convent; one can live safely in the world too, according to individual circumstances, although life in a convent is in itself safer." As if he knew what the near future was to bring, a further instruction to Father Jerónimo followed on July 13th: "I would not dare to advise your sister to enter the cloister, if she feels strong enough with God's grace to continue her chaste and virtuous life in the world, especially in doing works of charity. There seems to me to be no real urge in her towards the religious life."

These letters had evidently reached Valencia when Father Jerónimo left there on August 25th for Rome. He carried in his luggage a letter from his sister to Ignatius, dated August 24th, 1552. This letter is indicative of the hesitation in the mind of Angélica, who after all was no angel. She would and yet would not. From the revered Master's instructions she expected salvation.[37]

IHS

Holy Ghost

Very Reverend Sir and my dearest Father in Christ our Lord.

The grace and peace of the Holy Spirit be always in your blessed soul. Amen.

I have wanted to write this letter if only to thank you and to kiss Your

Paternity's feet for the opinion and advice that you sent me as to the foundations of my life both for soul and body. Thus, then, as Your Paternity's least servant, I beg you to deign to command me in all other things, too, for I am prepared to obey you as a Father given to me on the part of God. You will be informed by my Father and brother Master Jerónimo of the mercies which God has shown me and the knowledge he gave me of my vileness and how right it was that I should give myself wholly to him, since he gave himself wholly to me on the Cross, and also from the example of obedience which he gave us to follow him along the same road. Thus I made vows and gave them in writing to my father and brother. He will give you a fuller account of my soul and the intentions with which God has inspired me he will tell you of. Thereby may my desires for God alone grow stronger and stronger. To him belong both my soul and body and the power I look for in my father.

For, indeed, Father, so great is the mercy that God our Lord has done me in giving me an affection for this holy Society that it seems to me there is nothing which serves God more than this and thus I would like to cut myself in pieces for this holy order, I mean in its service.

Before God I beg you, as humbly as I can, to think fit to send back here my father and brother until all these necessities are passed, until at least Your Paternity should think fit and for as long as is possible. For this, I will tell you of my corporal necessities, wherein God has set me. I place myself at Your Charity's feet, you who, like the father of my dearest soul, wants to remedy my needs in the blood of Christ. I am confident Your Paternity's tender heart will be moved to provide a remedy for me.

I, Father, am a woman and alone in my father's house. He is old and much taken up with many affairs which even in times past he was not able to settle and extricate himself from. If God calls him I have no relative in whom I can have confidence, to whom to entrust myself and my house, but shall have to put myself in the care of people who are strangers and of these there will be found few or none. I fear that the days of my father's life may be few, with the absence of his only son. Now, if he should leave me and I so alone, Father, what shall I do? I was, indeed, hoping and had considered it certain that if my father and brother were here – I thought my father seemed disposed for this – he would very soon have to put his house in order and adopt some kind of life in which he could serve God more perfectly.

Thus, Father, I beg you before God, to remedy my necessities as you see God will be most served. I remain kissing Your Paternity's feet and hands and asking God always to keep your soul full of the Holy Spirit. Amen.

Jhs. Your Paternity's unworthy servant who kisses your hands and feet and desires to serve you,

Magdalena Angélica Doménech,
your servant

Valencia, August 24th, 1552

To the very reverend lord and dear father in Christ our Lord, Father Master Ignatius, General of the Society of Jesus, in Rome

Ignatius laid aside Angélica's letter for a few months. Not till January 27th, 1553, did he answer it in a letter preserved only in the *regesta*, accompanied by a letter of comfort to her old father. In April he wrote again, promising that perhaps Jerónimo would soon come home once more. In September fresh news arrived from Valencia, and Ignatius hastened to forward it to Jerónimo in Sicily. Nadal, he said, had written from Valencia to say that Angélica was indeed persevering in her chosen way of life, but she wished for consolation in the form of letters from Ignatius and her brother. "I will write a few words soon to Angélica", said the General in his reply to Nadal on October 27th.

Father Jerónimo, however, was better acquainted with the facts. Worse tidings had reached him from Valencia, and he promptly communicated them to Ignatius. Angélica (he had heard) was unwell, she was suffering from fits of depression and oppressive melancholy. "She is much in need of prayer, and I ask Your Reverence to pray for Angélica, for the sake of Christ's love."

So once again Ignatius, patient as ever, sat down to write a letter to Angélica, which sounds like a heart-to-heart talk with a headstrong pupil. Lovingly and kindly he expounded to her the old and ever new doctrine of the value of spiritual trials, and attempted to lead the waverer back again on to the path of perfection.[38]

My Lady in our Lord,

The sovereign grace and eternal love of Christ our Lord be always with us to our help and favour. Amen.

Through letters from Valencia I have learned that God our Lord has been visiting Your Ladyship with spiritual and physical trials, showing, by giving so many occasions of merit, the very special love he has for Your Ladyship and his will to reward so much the more abundantly Your Ladyship's good desires and works in his eternal happiness, as in this world and temporal life he shows he wants to reward them less.

It is true, my Lady, that I desire as much contentment and full consolation for your soul as for my own, and I sympathize with your trials as right reason and the law of charity oblige me. In spite of this, however, I cannot but consider as a very special gift of God our Lord the opportunity thus given to Your Ladyship of exercising patience, and faith and hope, being persuaded that the divine and sovereign goodness and charity of the most wise heavenly father provides you with what is most fitting, no less in adversity than in prosperity, and that as much in afflictions as in consolations he shows his eternal love with which he guides his chosen ones to everlasting happiness.

His love and mercy are such that, if it were good for us, he would be more disposed for his part to have us always consoled rather than in distress, even in this world. Since, however, the disposition of our wretchedness in this present state requires that at times, instead of favours, he visits us with trials, in this at least we can see his fatherly and sovereign mercy, which includes the trials in the brief course of this life – and that not without many consolations at the times he chooses – and in the life that is eternal and without end, rewards patience with contentment and inestimable glory, without any admixture of trial, or sadness or any unfulfilled longing, for there is no such thing in heaven but only the complete fulfilment of joy and bliss. Given all this, if Your Ladyship tries to resign yourself into the hands of Christ our Lord, conforming your will wholly to his, and is fully prepared, when it shall please him to send them to you, to follow him in the trials he suffered in this world, in order to follow him afterwards in the glory of the other life, I do not doubt but that the trials will cease in great part and the fortitude to suffer them will increase so much that they will be very little felt.

I for my part shall not fail, with those of us who are here in Rome, to commend Your Ladyship's affairs much to God; and if anything which might be within my power could help to give you comfort, I would do it with a right good will, as someone who loves Your Ladyship much in our Lord. May it please him to give us all abundant grace, so that we may always know his most holy will, and perfectly fulfil it.

(Ignatius)

Rome, January 12th, 1554

To Magdalena Angélica Doménech (at Valencia)

Unfortunately Ignatius could not grant the Doménech family the joy of a reunion with their Jerónimo. The latter (he wrote to Don Pedro) was now too much needed in Sicily, Malta and Barbary; but the General did not forget to add in his letter a few words of comfort to Angélica. He even took the opportunity to commend himself to her prayers.

The building of the church of the new college in Valencia was meeting with difficulties, although old Don Pedro had given his whole fortune towards it. Did Angélica perhaps make difficulties? Matters dragged on for a year. The question of the inheritance, still a problem in Valencia, was solved by the solemn profession of Father Jerónimo before Ignatius on October 20th, 1555. It arose again, however, in another way, inasmuch as at Rome they were still in the dark as to Angélica's actual intentions. Apparently as the idea of entering a convent became less attractive to her, her fear that her own fortune might be used for the Jesuit foundation increased. "All is not yet settled", wrote Ignatius on March 23rd, 1556, to Doménech, "as Angélica is to some extent applying the brake."

Only a month later disturbing news came from Nadal in Valencia. On April 24th Ignatius wrote to Doménech that Angélica had appeared of late to have quite different plans, and it was necessary for Jerónimo to travel to Valencia to see what could best be done. This is understandable, for in January 1556 old Don Pedro had died. Angélica had to come to a decision. In July Ignatius sent a fresh warning to Jerónimo, that it was high time for him to go home on his sister's account. At the end of July, when Ignatius already lay on his deathbed, the bombshell burst — Angélica was married. Her happiness must have been brief, for in November of the same year news reached Rome of the second nuptials of the lady whom even Ignatius had not been able to direct.[39]

PART SIX

FRIENDSHIP IN GOD

Correspondence with Women who were his Friends

Introduction

LETTERS of spiritual converse, in which the secrets of the heart and of the love of God are exchanged, are not to be found among the correspondence of St. Ignatius to women. He was certainly no Francis de Sales; nor could one imagine his embarking on a correspondence with a woman like St. Teresa. Talking about spiritual things came to him no more easily than writing about them – his early efforts in the correspondence with Teresa Rejadella belong to a phase of his inner development that was soon over.

It would be to underestimate the greatness of Ignatius' heart, however, if we saw in him only the man of silence, of renunciation and inflexible logic. He was a Basque, and he was not a man to let all that was in his heart issue like a spring from the rock-like exterior presented to the world. All his life he was shy and reserved in the expression of his affections. "He who measures my love by what I show of it outwardly would be much deceived."

Ignatius was always something more and something greater than what he said or wrote. His friends found no other word that better described the character of this man than *magnanimitas*, "greatness of soul". There was nothing cramped or narrow about him, and the warmth of his spirit won him friends again and again, even in his tempestuous and far from pious youth – friends for whom he cherished a silent but unwavering affection. This strength of friendship kept together the band of companions which gathered about him in Paris. He himself called them "my friends in our Lord". With them he created the new Society, and until the death of their beloved Father this friendship animated all the bonds of rule and obedience which they laid upon themselves at those unforgettable conferences in Vicenza and Rome; the decision of Paris that shaped their lives was the expression of their sole wish – "to follow Ignatius' way of life".[1]

But it was a power restrained and formed by the manly modesty which was one of Ignatius' essential characteristics. He loved without words, and in his correspondence with his fellow-religious we would look in vain for well-turned phrases or easily flowing expressions of affection or friendship. It was precisely those whom he loved most to whom he

413

showed least sign of affection. Ribadeneira even said of him: "To the strongest among them he gave hard bread and manly fare to eat." This very sternness of his love won him the hearts of all. Father Luis Gonçalves da Câmara, who for two years lived in close contact with the General and kept a diary in Spanish and Portuguese during that time, testifies that Ignatius in spite of his severity "was yet so inclined to love that he was, as it were, love incarnate and therefore was so loved by all in the whole Society of Jesus that each one felt especially loved by him".[2]

This mysterious power of restrained affection was shown also in the case of the 'men and women of the world' with whom he came in contact. He was at pains to exemplify in his own life what he laid down in his Constitutions for the rectors of colleges: it was (he said) their sacred duty "to keep their friends in a good frame of mind", to pray for them and "to bring back to friendship" those who were not well disposed towards the Society. With that disarming aristocratic politeness which he had once learnt at court, Ignatius took an interest in his friends. In Father Gonçalves' Portuguese diary it is related how he often invited them to dinner and would greet them with the phrase later made famous by Cervantes: "He invited persons from outside, who were specially influential or friendly towards the Society, and when they came to dinner, he would say: 'Let Your Grace come and sit with us, if you wish to do penance with us.'" To his friends, Ignatius could be quite charming. Gonçalves tells us: "When he received a visitor, he showed such joy, as if he would take him into his very heart."[3]

Much could be told from the saint's voluminous correspondence about the lifelong friendships he had with a remarkably large number of men of his time; and such an account would form a hitherto unpublished chapter of what one might call the intimate Church history of the sixteenth century. A "sincere friendship" with Pietro Codacio began Ignatius' work in Rome. There he soon met Philip Neri, and the two loved one another dearly in spite of the great differences between them. Lattanzio Tolomei, the gifted humanist and friend of Vittoria Colonna, was reverently devoted to Ignatius. The little man with the limp at Santa Maria della Strada numbered some of the cardinals among his best friends, who supported him in his work of reform – Gasparo Contarini, Marcello Cervini and Francisco de Mendoza. In Venice the good Prior Andrea Lippomani could never forget his guest of the far-off days in 1523 and 1536 and remained on affectionate terms with the General till the latter's death. At the imperial court in Flanders Ignatius' best friends were his Basque fellow-countryman Don Pedro de Zárate and the imperial secretary Alexius Fontana, whom he deeply respected. In Italy there was Master Doimo Nauci, in Barcelona the Archdeacon

Dimas Camps, in Rome the physician Dr. Iñigo López – not to mention the two men who had in Paris and Venice investigated the matter of Ignatius' suspected heresy and in doing so become his faithful followers for the rest of their lives – Dr. Ortiz and Gasparo de Dotti. Indeed, the overflowing heart of Ignatius found a loving response in his friends, and if we did not take these friendships into consideration we should be drawing a false picture of the saint.[4]

Ignatius' correspondence with women also contains letters which are evidence of genuine friendship. They are not letters of "spiritual friendship" or even of kindly but non-committal gossip. Although concerned mainly with the promotion of apostolic or charitable works, with spiritual needs and the difficulties of life – and death – they are all written with true affection and cordiality. They differ from the letters to benefactresses or spiritual daughters in the sensitive understanding which the writer shows for the everyday affairs, great and small, of these women, such as only an old and trusted friend would have. Finally, when we have regard to the vicissitudes to which the archives containing St. Ignatius' letters have been subject during four hundred years, we cannot but be struck by the extent of this particular group of letters: to nobody else among his female correspondents did he write more letters, and none – apart from official correspondence – did he preserve more carefully than those which now follow.

Three women enjoyed such a friendship with the undemonstrative Ignatius. The first was Doña Leonor Mascarenhas, whom he had known since 1527 and to whom he wrote shortly before his death a wonderful letter of farewell. The two other women were Doña Leonor Osorio, wife of the imperial ambassador in Rome and her daughter Isabel de Vega, who later became Countess and Duchess of Luna. They were ladies of the highest rank, one of them exercising a maternal omnipotence at the court of Philip II of Spain; the other, when afterwards she became Vicereine of Sicily, Ignatius' most loyal helper in the work of ecclesiastical reform, who bequeathed to her daughter her love and her readiness to help. It is significant for the understanding of the saint's character that even the bestowal of his purified and restrained affection was confined to the class in which he was born and to which by his whole upbringing he belonged. One might almost say that his friendship was a kind of final and transfigured version of that knightly devotion which, as he himself confessed, he had given when a young nobleman at Arévalo to a lady "who was more than a countess or a duchess".

It can be said of the saint's friendship with these women, as Gonçalves in his Portuguese diary wrote of Ignatius: "He was friendly to all, but familiar with none". These ladies knew that between them and him there stood the majesty of God, wherein the hearts of men come closest to one another, by maintaining due distance on earth. It was in this sense only that the saint wrote to Leonor Mascarenhas: "You are written deep in my heart, and I bear you a sincere affection in His Divine Majesty"; and to young Isabel de Vega, for whom he showed until her death such a fatherly solicitude: "Now and for always you are written deep in my heart."[5]

Leonor Mascarenhas

THE unswerving loyalty and constant help, which her high position at the king's court in Valladolid and Madrid enabled her to give to the new Society, earned for Doña Leonor Mascarenhas, as for many others, the title of "Mother of the Society of Jesus". In a contemporary biography it is said of her: "She did all in her power to assist Ignatius in the founding of the Society of Jesus. She was heartily devoted to him and gave him alms all her life; she helped the Jesuits in their first beginnings, when difficulties were always to be expected, and gave them the house in which the college of this city of Madrid was first opened."[6]

She was the daughter of Don Ferdinando Martins d'Almada and Doña Isabel da Veyga, both of the highest nobility of Portugal. One of her kinsmen (their great-grandparents were brother and sister) was afterwards Portuguese ambassador at Rome – Pedro Mascarenhas, who played a part in the history of the Society, especially in connection with the mission of Francis Xavier, and whose wife Helena Mascarenhas was so great a friend to Ignatius that her husband could later write to him: "My wife, a faithful handmaid of the Society, is as devoted to Your Reverence as I am myself."[7]

Leonor was born on October 24th, 1503. In her youth she resolved never to marry, although as lady-in-waiting to King Manoel's second consort María (sister of Joanna the Mad) she had plenty of opportunities. As she was of the same age as the Portuguese Infanta Isabel, she went as the latter's companion to Spain in 1526, when Isabel married the Emperor Charles V. Leonor was a close friend of another young lady of the imperial court, Leonor de Castro, who afterwards married Francis Borgia. From that time on an almost sisterly attachment existed between her and the future General of the Jesuits[8]. Leonor was filled with those ascetic ideals which had already been cultivated at the court of Isabella the Catholic. She wore a Franciscan habit and busied herself with needlework for the Church and clothing for the poor. When the Empress bore her first son Philip, Doña Leonor was soon appointed governess to the Prince, in spite of her youth (she was twenty-four). It was an event of great future significance for the destinies of the Society of Jesus.

In the same year as Prince Philip was born, the pilgrim and student

417

Ignatius de Loyola made the acquaintance of the governess to the heir-apparent. Whether this was at Alcalá, as Ribadeneira appears to believe, at the time when Doña Teresa de Cárdenas visited Ignatius in prison, or somewhat later, when he interviewed the archbishop in Valladolid while travelling to Salamanca, remains uncertain. At all events the birth of the Prince was as it were the pivotal date for Ignatius, when later he dictated his memoirs and discovered some lapses of memory in his own chronology: "While he was in prison at Alcalá, the Prince of Spain was born, and from that time the date of all events can be reckoned, even those of earlier years".[9]

We may presume that Ignatius at once made a deep impression on Leonor, and that he recognized in her one of those courageous souls who can be asked to undertake many works of charity. He wrote to her from Paris almost as a matter of course with the request that she would use her influence at the court of the King of Portugal to obtain a free place in Sainte-Barbe for Callisto de Sa. "Doña Leonor gave Callisto a mule and money for the journey." The gifts, it is true, failed in their object: Callisto did not arrive in Paris, but went "together with a certain religious lady" to Mexico, whence he later returned a rich man to Salamanca.[10]

Ignatius met Leonor for the second time when in 1535 he called at Madrid while on his way to visit the families of his Spanish companions; and there, too, he met the eight-year-old Prince Philip, holding his governess' hand. Ribadeneira was able to write to Ignatius from Brussels on February 20th, 1556, that the King had said in an audience granted to himself and Ruy Gómez at Antwerp, that he (the King) had known Ignatius quite well in the days when "dressed in dark grey clothes he used to come and see Doña Leonor Mascarenhas in Spain".[11] It may have been then that Leonor, on the occasion of Philip's serious illness, changed her intention not to marry into a vow of chastity.

The death of the Empress Isabel deprived her little family, Philip and his two sisters María and Juana, of a mother's love. "No wonder that, like chickens about the hen, the little brood drew closer together under the care of the good Doña Leonor Mascarenhas, whose love and solicitude increased tenfold."[12] Barely a year later, on July 4th, 1540, Father Araoz, Ignatius' first missioner in Spain, reported to Rome – even before the Society had actually been approved – that Doña Leonor Mascarenhas had introduced him to the Infantas at Ocaña in the most friendly way.[13] In 1541 Doña Leonor became friendly with Ignatius' holy son, Peter Faber. Whereas not a single letter from the royal governess to Ignatius has been preserved, we possess a letter of hers to Peter Faber dated February 1542 from Ocaña. From every word we sense that Leonor and Faber were united in their love for Ignatius. "I would with readiness choose the life of perfection, that is, follow you and

Ignatius, if I were a man. But I am only a woman, a sinner making no progress in virtue, and so I may not join you in meditating and speaking about holy things, much less those that concern the Company of Ignatius."

Faber later brought from Cologne the head of one of the 11,000 virgins for the pious lady, who presented it to the college of Alcalá.[14] Enthusiasm for Ignatius – Leonor always called him "Iñigo" without any title – and for his Society was such at the court of the Infantas, that not only the two princesses but also all their ladies-in-waiting, solemnly listed by name, commended themselves to his prayers. Doña Leonor was already looking after the first scholastics at Alcalá; and the two court chaplains of the Infantas, Álvaro Alfonso and Juan Aragonés, entered the Society.[15]

Doña Leonor's life entered a new phase when her beloved foster-son, the sixteen-year-old Philip, married the beautiful Infanta María of Portugal, Queen Catherine's daughter, at Salamanca on November 13th, 1543.[16] It was the first act of that matrimonial tragedy which Ignatius had greeted with words of extravagant praise as more the work of heaven than that of earthly agencies. We know that the fruit of that irresponsible union, brought about by Habsburg political ambitions, was Don Carlos, inheritor of his great-grandmother's madness. Duke Francis Borgia and his wife Leonor de Castro were to have been chosen to preside over the princely pair's household; but they fell into disgrace with Catherine of Portugal – and it was this painful experience which contributed more than anything else to the gradual development in the hitherto elegant and successful courtier of a vocation to the Society of Jesus.[17]

Don Carlos was born on July 8th, 1545. Ruy Gómez, Philip's favourite, who also played an important part in the early history of the Society of Jesus, galloped to Worms to take to the Emperor Charles V the news of the birth of his grandson, who was to bear his name. The message had not reached the Emperor before the unfortunate seventeen-year-old mother died on July 12th. Philip was stricken with grief. Who else was there to turn to but the faithful Mascarenhas? We know from a contemporary source that he placed the feeble infant, his son, in the arms of Doña Leonor and said to her: "My son has lost his mother; now you must be a mother to him. For my sake, treat him as your own." The Emperor's confidence in Doña Leonor appears from the fact that Charles V issued from Brussels on November 15th, 1549, exact instructions concerning the court of Prince Carlos and ordained therein that the child's food and clothing were always to be in accordance with the directions of Doña Leonor.[18]

Ignatius followed all these events from Rome with the greatest interest. Faber and Araoz kept him constantly informed. It is not then surprising that

Doña Leonor, even before the tragic death of Princess María, applied to Ignatius with the request that he would put before the Roman curia some legal questions that closely concerned her.

Throughout his sixteen years in Rome, Ignatius was plagued with such matters; but was it not, after all, by his endless patience that he attained to sanctity? His friend's first request concerned a Dominican in Valladolid, Fray Bernardino de Minaja. This priest intended to establish a house in Valladolid which, like the House of St. Martha in Rome founded by Ignatius, was to be a refuge for fallen or morally endangered girls. He wished to call this house "San Felipe de la penitencia", and in order to conduct it he had evidently to be dispensed from obedience to his immediate superiors. Prince Philip himself had already applied to Ignatius in the same matter, and the latter had actually sent a dispensation from Rome to Valladolid. However, the prince also sent the same petition through the regular channels, the Spanish Dominican authorities, and so things had become involved in such a way that Doña Leonor now undertook to have them sorted out.[19]

The second case which troubled the royal governess was obviously very close to her heart; for as we shall learn, the imperial ambassador Juan de Vega and his wife were also asked to help in the affair, and the fictitious name employed – as canon law required – must have concealed a person of high rank. Be that as it may, the question concerned a lady who for her peace of mind wished to change a vow she had made to become a nun into a permission to live merely as a member of the Third Order of St. Francis. On April 19th, 1545, Ignatius read to the Grand Penitentiary Cardinal Pucci the petition addressed to the Holy See by Doña Leonor through him. The issue of the dispensation was, however, delayed for some time, and so Ignatius' answer to Doña Leonor did not leave till June 28th, 1545. She was then at Alcalá, where she was governess to the Emperor's daughters María and Juana.

IHS

The sovereign grace and eternal love of Christ our Lord be always with us to our help and favour.

About what you told me in our Lord concerning Beatrice Paz, and as she, moreover, declared in her letters, I send you what she asked for for the greater peace of her soul. You will see how matters stand from the petition to the Principal Penitentiary, who is Cardinal Pucci, and from the report I give about it.

It is true, however, that in general I desire, with a view to striving after greater perfection and following one's vocation, to be one more inclined to binding closely in Christ our Lord than to loosing. Thus I should have liked Beatriz Paz not to have waited so long, but offering herself to her Lord in all things, to have fulfilled her vow without delay. Nevertheless, since she failed to do this, and since she has now come to a ripe age, and has no longer sufficient strength for such a life, and since you vouch for her and give such a favourable report on her, I subordinate my judgment to yours. I even rejoice at what has been done, and, considering the present circumstances, believe that it is for the best.

About Father Bernardino Minaja in his case I have had continual and very great difficulties in obtaining the dispensation for him; nevertheless, with what the prince[20] wrote in his letter, and the fact that the ecclesiastical court of Valladolid has pronounced in his favour, claiming for him the privilege of the bull of the Convertidos, I have submitted my judgment, and applied myself to the matter with all the diligence I could in the Lord; and (it seems to me) his business would be already despatched if it were entrusted to me alone. The matter was already proceeding favourably and now I have learnt through Fray Diego de Merlo, who is General Procurator of his Order here, that the Prince sent for Father Bernardino's prior and handed over to him the deed of dispensation which I had sent back to him, but also said that he now handed over the whole matter to the prior. Now the prior sent the document to Rome and the General Procurator has shown it to me. They are both, however, against a dispensation for Fray Bernardino. In this matter, however, I think one should follow the same course as His Highness. If the Prince would write me a few favourable lines of recommendation, for I here have only a very slight influence, I could come to an understanding with the Procurator and prior, as His Highness has done. If they command something different to be done, and it be found acceptable, I desire to be advised of it; if a counter order be given, and were lawful, I ask for instructions, because the negotiations are now moving against the dispensation and any further petition essentially depends on that.

Of things directly spiritual, both because I judge that you will find everything in our Lord as in a universal source, and because I am persuaded that for spiritual converse Master Faber and the Licentiate Araoz will act in my stead, I shall justly be able to excuse myself from writing. I make you, however, a sharer in the grace of indulgences that up to now were not attached to your rosaries, as is explained in the memorandum which goes with this letter.

Please recommend me to the grace and charity of all whom you feel would take comfort from being greeted by me. Commend me to them and greet them for me heartily in our Lord. May he through his infinite

421

and supreme goodness deign to give us his full grace so that we may have an awareness of his most holy will and fulfil it in its entirety.

From Rome, June, 28th, 1545

Ignatius

Doña Leonor Mascarenhas, Alcalá

Memorandum in the matter of Beatrice Paz

I

Beatrice Paz, having a great desire to become a nun, made a vow to do so, and likewise made a vow never to be absolved from the first vow, and again to enter an order within a stated time. From the vow to enter within a stated time, she has been absolved. The aforesaid Beatrice Paz now humbly asks for the dispensation from these vows on condition of her becoming a sister of the Third Order of St. Francis, at all events until a house of nuns with enclosure, which her father, with the help of another person, wishes to erect, be built.

II

THE DISPENSATION

On the nineteenth day of April 1545 I read all the abovementioned petition to the most reverend Cardinal Pucci, Chief Penitentiary, and gave him a very full explanation. His Eminence transmitted to me the responsibility in conscience for this matter and making the holy sign of the cross gave me authority to commute the vows of the said Beatrice Paz in all respects and [to do] whatever seemed to me best in this matter.

Thus I, by virtue of the apostolic authority and power that his most Reverend Eminence gave me, the force of which covers the whole case, I commute to you, the said Beatrice Paz, all the vows named above, into the willingness to become a sister of the Third Order of St. Francis. You may now live in some convent or in a private house but only with persons of good reputation, until your father with the help of some other pious person has built an enclosed convent, which you can enter. This must be done calmly and without scrupulosity. Meanwhile with a safe conscience, in much love of God our Lord you will be able to live as a sister of the said Third Order of St. Francis.

422

As a testimony to the truth of what is written above, I sign here my name.

Given at Rome on the twenty-eighth of June 1545

Ignatius of Loyola

To Doña Leonor Mascarenhas

Leonor received the news with the greatest joy. She was especially comforted by the rosaries which Ignatius enclosed with his letter. The reply in which she expressed her delighted gratitude contained news both good and sad, above all the information that God's providence had now made her foster-mother to the orphaned Don Carlos. Ignatius was not slow to congratulate her on being entrusted with a task so important both in the religious and in the political sense; and with Don Carlos' tragic fate in mind we cannot but read with sorrow what Ignatius here says of the "many nations and souls" which he would have to govern.

IHS

The sovereign grace and love of Christ our Lord be always with us, to our continual help and favour.

At one of your letters I received, I rejoiced much in our Lord, since I saw in it the consolation your soul has received with the present of the beads, which you say you want to have continually close to your person. This is a sign that you do not forget the giver and fount of all good, since for his love and reverence you so embrace his gifts and graces which I hope will be continually increased in your blessed soul by our Lord, for the way to acquire new gifts is to use well those we have already received.

No less have I consoled myself in what I have learned since, and that is that it has pleased our Lord to make use of your person, giving you the charge of the son of the prince as he had before given you that of his father. In this enterprise, I hope in God's divine goodness that he will give you full grace that you may serve him much, serving and helping and setting in the right way the person by whom, if it please God our Lord, so many nations and souls have to be governed in such a way that finally they may be developed and corrected.

Dean de la Roca, Chamberlain to His Holiness, to whom we owe much and who has much affection for us in our Lord, will be able to give you verbally fuller information touching the petition that Father Minaja wishes to put forward. The matter is almost concluded and satisfactorily; although in the preamble to the bull he wanted many stipulations for which I had already obtained a promise from the Cardinal to whom His Holiness entrusted the decision, for instance, the stipulation that whoever should give alms to this new convent for penitents would gain many indulgences and spiritual graces. This, however, has been refused at the Signatura,[21] so that I do not know if he will be satisfied.

For the rest I think it better that, when some opportunity of spiritual affairs presents itself, if you would leave me a free hand, for sometimes what one does, others undo and thus the business and service of our Lord are obstructed and hindered.

May his divine and infinite mercy deign to give us his full grace, so that we may know his most holy will and perfectly fulfil it.

From Rome, September 24th, 1545

(Ignatius)

To Doña Leonor Mascarenhas

Doña Leonor must have read with a smile Ignatius' wise and somewhat resigned final remark. In such affairs there are always some misunderstandings. When Ignatius here had a gentle dig at his "helpers", he was no doubt thinking not only of the two ways in which the Prince of Spain had sent Father de Minaja's petition to Rome, but also of something else: Doña Leonor herself had sent the petition of Beatrice Paz to the curia not only through Ignatius, but also through the imperial ambassador and his wife Doña Leonor Osorio. Thus one day the unsuspecting Ignatius found himself between the two Leonors who were so dear to him and had to try to smooth out the misunderstanding between the two ladies. Ignatius had heard, probably from Father Araoz, who was always well-informed about court gossip at Valladolid and Alcalá, that Doña Leonor Mascarenhas was dissatisfied at the apparently rather casual way in which Doña Leonor Osorio was handling the affair in Rome. The ambassadress, on the other hand, made no secret in conversation with Ignatius, her confessor, of her sorrow at the influential governess' ill-humour. Ignatius could not stand by without taking action. His conciliatory letter to Leonor in Spain is a touching testimony to the friendship which united him with both women and which he wished to preserve.

IHS

Since my last letter, I have spoken with Doña Leonor Osorio, and found her troubled because she had heard that you are not entirely satisfied with what she and Don Juan de Vega have done here in Rome over the matter of Batista [Beatriz] Paz. Now Doña Leonor has explained to me what she and her husband had done, and reported how the whole thing has solved itself to the discharge of good consciences, and I am convinced that you yourself, if you had found yourself in the same case, could have done no more. You are, indeed, acting in all things justly for the greater glory of God our Lord.

For his love and reverence, I ask most earnestly that you will be so good as to write Doña Leonor a comforting letter showing the love and esteem you have for persons so devoted to God's service. For in my opinion, according to what I have been able to gather from hearing Doña Leonor speak of you, her soul has a very special love and affection for yours in our Lord. Thus, I hope that this will be a greater reason for your being always more united with her in the divine Majesty. I have nothing more to say.

(From Rome) January 19th, 1546

Ignatius

To Leonor Mascarenhas

Meanwhile the life of the royal governess and her foster-child continued quietly, first at Alcalá and then at Toro. Peter Faber was asked by her before his departure for Rome to read a gospel over the head of the little prince. Leonor gave to the humble house in which the first scholastics of the Society lived at Alcalá an altarpiece that had belonged to Philip, who had received it from the Empress Isabel. Her page of honour Duarte Pereira joined the Jesuits in 1546.[22] She was often greeted in the letters Ignatius sent to Spain, as for example on May 18th, 1547, when he wrote to Araoz: "To Señora Doña Leonor Mascarenhas I send my most sincere regards."

In the matter of the reform of the Catalan convents, in which he showed such an interest throughout his life, Ignatius asked Doña Leonor to get Philip to write to the viceroy, the Marquis of Aguilar.[23] It is clear that this intelligent woman was becoming a kind of spiritual chargée d'affaires at the Spanish court; so in 1546 Ignatius could apply to Doña Leonor in a very important and difficult question, the favourable solution of which was absolutely decisive for the future progress of the Society in Spain. It concerned the hostile attitude to the Jesuits of Archbishop Siliceo of Toledo, the celebrated "Flint" (for thus his name can be interpreted), who simply could not stand the new Society. Francis Borgia, still Duke of Gandía, had already politely drawn his attention to the scholastics of the Society of Jesus in

Alcalá and asked him to look on them with favour. Soon afterwards Siliceo threatened the Jesuits with a strict visitation.

This problem was, however, connected with another. Siliceo's predecessor, Cardinal Juan de Tavera, had had a legal dispute with the university of Alcalá, which had even been taken to Rome. On the university's behalf a learned theologian, Dr. Miguel de Torres, had gone there in 1540. He was told by the imperial ambassador, the Marquis of Aguilar, about Ignatius of Loyola, who charmed his at first suspicious fellow-countryman at their first meeting. Torres made the Spiritual Exercises in 1542 with Ignatius at the villa of Donna Giulia Orsini and decided, though not without hesitation, to enter the Society. In September 1546 he returned to Spain, without for the time being making his membership known when he got there. Ignatius granted him, as it were, full power of attorney for this important journey and commended him, together with his young companion Cristóbal de Mendoza, to the woman who undoubtedly could be of most service to him at court: Doña Leonor.[24]

The sovereign grace and eternal love of Christ our Lord be always with us to our continual favour and help.

Since Doctor Torres, procurator of the university of Alcalá is, in our Lord, so dear to me in my inmost heart, no less than the Licentiate Araoz, and all the others in our Society, which is more yours than ours, and since he is a living letter and is au fait with all our affairs, which are at the same time yours and his, I need not enlarge upon matters by writing a longer letter from Rome.

Concerning Spanish affairs his intention is very just and holy, namely to establish some means of complete concord and peace between the Archbishop of Toledo and the University. Since the matter is, as I say, so just and holy, and since I regard his person as my own, without any difference whatsoever, in all love and affection in our Lord, I ask you for the love and reverence of that same Lord, to favour him in every possible way, both with His Highness the Prince and everywhere, and by any way in which you could help him, so that all things may come together in perpetual peace, love and concord.

Thus, besides the fact that God our Lord will be much served by this, I shall take the favour as done to myself, as I did another one I received in the matter of Doña Leonor Osorio, who is wholly yours in our Lord.

As to Master Cristóbal de Mendoza, who is journeying to Spain in your company, since he is one of our Society and a person who is very well-conducted, I recommend him much to you in our Lord.

426

May God in his infinite and supreme goodness deign to give us his full grace so that we may know his most holy will and fulfil it perfectly.

Greet their Highnesses the Lady Infantas respectfully on my behalf, with any others you think fit.

(Ignatius)

Rome, September 10th, 1546

To Leonor Mascarenhas

We do not know exactly how often Leonor wrote to the saint during the following ten years until his death. In any case, no letter has been preserved. Nevertheless, we know for certain that Ignatius never broke off contact with his spiritual daughter. Thus in November 1551 Antonio Gou, supplying his Father in Rome with news, reported that Doña Leonor's advice and help had been very valuable to the Jesuits in Alcalá in the still smouldering dispute with Archbishop Siliceo; and we know that Leonor about that time wrote a special petition to the Archbishop.[25]

Of the two Infantas whom Don Carlos' foster-mother also had to care for, María had meanwhile married the Archduke Maximilian and thus later became Empress; in her love for the Jesuits, which was to be so important for religious policy in Vienna, she had followed Doña Leonor. There were now under the latter's care at Toro only the Infanta Juana, soon to be married in Portugal, and young Don Carlos. On the departure of his dear aunt Juana, who left for Portugal in July 1552, the passionate prince gave himself up to continuous weeping for three days. All the more affectionately did Doña Leonor cherish the motherless boy.[26]

At the end of 1551 Father Araoz greeted the governess in the name of Father Ignatius, and "she received him with that affection which, as Your Paternity knows, she has always had towards the Society of Jesus", reported Gou to the General.[27] At the beginning of 1552, however, a problem arose: at the age of seven, according to the law of the Burgundian court, Don Carlos was removed from the care of women and placed under a tutor. With that, Leonor's immediate task at court was at an end, especially as in the same year the Infanta Juana left the parental home. Doña Leonor had wisely foreseen this eventuality and turned to Ignatius in Rome, whether by writing to him herself or through the mediation of Father Araoz we do not know. She now wished to enter a convent. Unfortunately Ignatius' answer to her, dated February 2nd, 1552, survives only in a brief note of Polanco's in the *regesta*: "The Father to Doña Leonor, some spiritual thoughts *(spiritualizando)*, that she might postpone her entry into a convent;

427

and that when the Infanta was taken from her care she might designate one or two convents for her to enter, so that a petition might be addressed to the Pope." We do not therefore know exactly of what such a petition would consist. If it concerned the postponement of her entry into an order, then Doña Leonor must have made a promise or vow to become a nun as soon as her service at court was over; or if it concerned the choice of a convent, it would at least require papal permission to enter another convent than that named in the original promise. However that may be, the contemporary biography of Leonor also states that she wanted to go into a convent when Don Carlos received a household of his own; but even then the king advised her to found her own convent.

At the end of August 1552 Ignatius wrote to Francis Borgia that he had sent Doña Leonor a long letter about her idea of entering the cloister.[28] Moreover, a lively interest was being taken at Ignatius' curia in Don Carlos' new household, for persistent rumours had it that the Jesuit Araoz had been selected as the prince's tutor. Perhaps Doña Leonor was behind this plan and was tactfully trying to let Ignatius know about it. Nothing, indeed, came of this project, but we are already acquainted with the not very creditable role that Araoz was henceforth to play at the royal court.[29]

Leonor obeyed Ignatius at least in so far as she postponed her entry into a convent. Instead she organized in her apartments in the palace at Toro, and soon afterwards at Madrid, an apostolic undertaking which she built up with great zeal and an astonishing grasp of social needs. It was a kind of piecework system for poor girls, whom she paid well for the work they did. She took care of women who were leading evil lives, and to some of them she even gave shelter and the opportunity of reform in her palace apartments. Her life was as strict as that of a nun, yet she remained a motherly friend to the royal family. Through the good offices of Philip II, the Pope gave her permission to have a private oratory with reservation of the Blessed Sacrament. The king, and later too the new queen, Isabel of Valois, the Infanta Juana and Don Carlos often met at her table or for conversation in her apartments. In the summer of 1554 Doña Leonor travelled to Benavente with the nine-year-old Don Carlos, to say farewell to the king on his departure for England to marry Queen Mary.[30]

From the *regesta* we know of another letter from Ignatius to his now slowly aging friend in Toro, dated June 1552.[31] Then follows a long silence. This is apparently to be explained not only by the loss of documents, but also because no doubt Ignatius had less occasion in the last three years of his life to write letters of mere politeness to a lady of whose virtuousness he was assured. Doña Leonor, it is true, did not share this opinion. On April 28th, 1556, Father Diego Carillo reported to Ignatius: "Doña Leonor gently complained that the Father no longer wrote to her as formerly. As we here in Alcalá owe so much to her, I beg Your Paternity to remember her occasionally, especially now when she has just made the Exercises with Father Duarte Pereira, who was once her page of honour."

This was not the only news of the same kind that Ignatius received from Spain. The perceptive Father Araoz noticed Leonor's slight vexation much earlier, but wrote to Ignatius only when he could report a visible improvement in the lady's mood: "Doña Leonor Mascarenhas seems to have found again her old and former love for Your Paternity and the Society. She desires a letter from Your Paternity." Ignatius was, as we know, very ill during the last months of his life. He had long since finished, or rather broken off, the dictation of his memoirs. All the more clearly and lovingly did the dying man's thoughts go back to the beginning of that career to which God's Majesty had called him. He could not then forget her who had once visited him in prison at Alcalá and with whom he had been in correspondence for more than twenty years since their last meeting in Madrid. Just then two letters from the faithful Doña Leonor arrived in Rome, also after a long silence; they had been on the way from November 1555 to April 1556.[32]

Ignatius answered them at once. It was difficult for him in his weak, almost dying condition; nevertheless, he sent two letters to his friend, of which the second has been preserved. Secretary Polanco, an eye-witness, wrote soon afterwards to Francisco de Villanueva at Alcalá, no doubt with the intention that Doña Leonor, who was still a little put out, might hear of it: "Our Father has written to Doña Leonor Mascarenhas with his own hand, and this with great labour, twice within a short space of time, and with the second letter he enclosed an *Agnus Dei*. So I think she might cease her complaining that he does not write to her any more."[33]

It was the last communication between them. Apparently Leonor had asked him again if it would be better for her after all to enter a convent or to continue her maternal care of King Philip and his unfortunate son, both of whom she had brought up. Ignatius still held that God would be better served by her remaining at court. We read with deep emotion what he writes about his prayers for King Philip, the ruler of so many realms; it was just at this time that in distant Flanders the weary Charles V had bequeathed his crown and his territories to his son. An evening light of sad farewell lies upon this letter. The old Emperor retires to his solitude, Leonor longs for the peace of the cloister. King Philip, with concealed horror, watches his heir grow up; and in his humble cell at Rome Ignatius prepares for death. All things pass; only love remains, and friendship founded in God. Never did Ignatius, in his laconic way, write with greater truth than he did at the end of this letter to Doña Leonor: "all yours in our Lord".

IHS

May the sovereign grace and eternal love of Christ our Lord be always with us to our continual help and favour.

I received on the same day, at the end of April, two letters from Your Ladyship dated November and December. From them I see clearly how deeply you stand written in my soul, from the day we first became acquainted in our Lord, and the very deep love and charity we have for each other in his divine Majesty. This, I hope in God's goodness, will always last both on your side and on mine, and will continually increase.

As to the difficulties of your station and your physical sufferings, I have done what you so earnestly recommended to me, namely that I should have recourse to God our Lord in prayer, that he may show you how you can serve him better. You add that I should write you my opinion and advise you what you ought to do. Accordingly, speaking in the presence of God our Lord, I will tell you what I feel within me in his divine Majesty, as if I were in Your Ladyship's place. I should, then, remain firm and steadfast in the same condition and estate in which His Highness had left me until he should ordain some other thing for me; and for this, and for what is most to God's glory, I should write him telling him everything, namely, my desires, my sicknesses and all other things that might occur to me in this connection. If you do this, beyond any doubt, I think that His Highness, looking at the matter all round, will clearly come to see whatever is most for God's glory, and you will be comforted and at peace in our Lord.

In what you commend to me with so much insistence, that I pray much for the Prince who is now by divine grace king of many kingdoms, in my prayers to God our Lord, this, indeed, I do very day, and I hope in God's Majesty in the few days that remain to me I shall do so even more, since he is our prince and we are under a great obligation to him. I also do this on account of Your Ladyship's desire and great devotion in reminding me of a thing so much my duty and that of all this humble Society.

Before I received the letters from you twelve or fifteen days ago, a lady devoted to me in our Lord sent me a certain spiritual present. From it I chose two Agnus Dei, encased, to send to Your Ladyship with my letter, mindful, as I said above, how much I have had you and still have you in my inmost soul and would do so still more in the future if it were possible.

After receiving your letter, other Agnus Dei were sent me from the Pope's palace. Accordingly I thought it well to send with the two just mentioned eight more, so that you can have them encased to your pleasure and devotion, or use them as seems most to God's glory.

May it please him through his infinite and supreme goodness to deign to give us his abundant grace so that we may know his most holy will and perfectly fulfil it.

All Your Ladyship's in our Lord,

Ignatius

To my Lady in our Lord, Doña Leonor Mascarenhas
Rome, May 19th, 1556

When this letter reached Spain, Ignatius was already on his deathbed. Doña Leonor no doubt heard of his death through Father Francis Borgia, who had received the sad news from Ribadeneira in Flanders. A note which Polanco wrote in his chronicle gives some idea of what she felt: "Doña Leonor Mascarenhas, who once had charge of King Philip's upbringing and now does the same for Philip's son Carlos, begged with pious insistence for a memorial of Ignatius; for she revered him greatly (vehementer) even in the days before the founding of the Society of Jesus, and she had supported him and the Society with alms. So Father Francis asked the Father Vicar [Laynez] to send her some part of the clothing of our Father, or some other thing of his."

Leonor now made the promotion of the Society her life's work, in gratitude and reverence towards her never-to-be-forgotten friend and teacher. From 1557 onwards she occupied herself with the foundation of the projected college in Madrid, which in 1560 became feasible through a generous gift from her. The first superior of this house was Duarte Pereira, her former page. In the same year she gave the fathers in Portugal a villa with vineyards and chestnut woods from her mother's estate.[34] With all this, the old pious plans about which she had so often consulted Ignatius were not forgotten. A sincere love of the ideals of Franciscan poverty was always active within her. So in 1563 she reverted to the plan already suggested by King Philip and founded in Madrid in the square of St. Dominic the Franciscan convent of Santa María de los Ángeles. On December 18th, 1563, there took place the solemn clothing of the first nuns, and among the faithful knelt the Infanta Juana.

But even now Leonor did not forget the Society of Ignatius, which at one time she would fain have joined. There was a constant interchange of letters between her and Francis Borgia, General of the Society since 1565. Thus they discussed matrimonial affairs; Doña Leonor related how she had

431

too trustingly lost a sum of money to two questionable Coptic monks; and she was asked to put in a word with King Philip for the college at Messina.[35]

Incidentally, it is interesting to compare the letters which Borgia wrote to Doña Leonor with those of Ignatius. Ignatius was always polite and formal, laconic, deliberate and almost dull; Borgia full of feeling and unction, always ready to give a lesson in asceticism, especially in his letter to "my dearest sister" Mascarenhas on the occasion of Laynez' death. Ignatius could not have written thus. But in one respect the two friends were alike. Doña Leonor was to them both, as Borgia wrote in the letter just mentioned, "mistress and sister of this our Society", or as Father Ribadeneira said, *nuestra devota*.[36]

Another sorrow came into Leonor's life with the tragedy of her foster-son Don Carlos. Many volumes have already been written on this subject; but hardly any historian has made use of the material contained in the archives of the Society of Jesus. Don Carlos was placed in confinement at Christmas 1567. From the correspondence of the General Francis Borgia with his son-in-law the Count of Lerma, who had to guard the captive prince, we know the intimate details of the madman's illness. He died on July 24th, 1568. The letter of comfort which Borgia wrote on November 22nd, 1568, to Doña Leonor on the death of the unfortunate prince and that of Queen Isabel, who died in October of the same year, is deeply moving: "O my sister, what a pledge of a holy death has the person who dies in life in order to live in death!" The royal governess was so deeply concerned in the fate of Don Carlos "that it was a wonder she did not die of all she suffered on this occasion", wrote the nun to whom we owe Leonor's life-story. Perhaps she and Borgia were the only ones who did not forget Don Carlos in their prayers. On June 6th, 1569, the General wrote to her that he had offered the Holy Sacrifice at Loreto for the repose of the soul of the unhappy prince.[37]

It was long before Doña Leonor forsook the strict solitude to which she withdrew in her convent after the death of Don Carlos, in order to devote herself, at least from time to time, to spiritual converse with Ignatius' other disciple, the Infanta Juana. In her rooms adjoining the Franciscan convent she also received Teresa of Ávila, who there met the Infanta Juana and, as we have heard, delighted the ladies with her cheerful talk. That was in November 1567, before the tragedy of Don Carlos. In 1569 Leonor met St. Teresa again, at the foundation celebrations of the Carmelite convent which the hysterical Princess of Éboli had established near her ducal seat of Pastrana. In the list of those present there is mentioned a lady "who is called Doña Leonor Mascarenhas, was formerly the king's governess, and is a great servant of God our Lord".[38]

Until her death Doña Leonor remained under the spiritual direction of the

Jesuits. In 1578 the General Mercurian entrusted the fathers in Madrid with this duty. In her seventieth year she was still in good health; and how much her services and her influence were valued at court appears from the fact that the imperial ambassador Adam von Dietrichstein could propose her in 1565 as lady-in-waiting to her former foster-daughter the Empress María.[39]

During these last years of her life was painted the portrait which still hangs in the Convent of the Angels in Madrid. The inscription reads: "Doña Leonor Mascarenhas, governess of King Philip II and the Prince Don Carlos his son, foundress of the convent of Santa María de los Ángeles el Real at Madrid". In this magnificent picture the unknown artist has exactly caught the features of the noble woman, spiritualized by suffering. Thus she must have stood before the mental eyes of the dying Ignatius.

At last death came to her too. The widowed Empress, who after the decease of Maximilian II had returned to Spain – in her suite was the young Luigi (Aloysius) Gonzaga – visited the sick Doña Leonor several times. In her will Leonor remembered above all the house founded by her at Madrid, from which was to develop the splendid *Colegio Imperial*.[40] On December 20th, 1584, she entered into eternity.

Leonor de Vega Osorio

In the whole of St. Ignatius' extant correspondence the letters which are the most numerous and the most cordial in tone are those he exchanged with the family of the imperial ambassador in Rome, Don Juan de Vega. In view of the importance of this diplomat, who played a significant role in the policy of Charles V towards the Holy See, it is understandable that Ignatius also invoked his services as well as those of Vega's wife and daughter, with whom he was connected by ties of genuine friendship, for the promotion of religious works. Even Karl Brandi, writing of the political role of the ambassador Vega in the negotiations between the Emperor and Pope Paul III about the war against the Protestants, mentions this friendship in his biography of the Emperor Charles: "His wife, an Osorio, was among the first devoted admirers of Ignatius of Loyola."[41]

It was, as we already know, one of the saint's firmest principles to call upon the services of the great ones of the earth, with a kind of ingenuous worldly wisdom, to help him and promote his work. Among these were the imperial ambassadors belonging to the Spanish aristocracy who resided in Rome. With the Marquis of Aguilar, Juan Fernández Manrique, Ignatius was soon on friendly terms; and when that nobleman was recalled in 1542 to become Viceroy of Catalonia as successor to Francis Borgia, Ignatius asked for his co-operation in the projected reform of the Catalan convents.[42] As early as March 1st, 1542, Peter Faber in a letter drew Ignatius' attention to the successor appointed to the embassy in Rome. When we consider what decisive importance his friendship with Juan de Vega had till the end of his life, and what a bond of sincere friendship connected him with the ambassador's wife and daughter, it is interesting to see how Peter Faber became acquainted with this family. He wrote to Ignatius that he had got to know the sister of Juan de Vega, Teresa de Quiñones, Countess of Monteagudo and Lady of Almazán, home of Father Laynez. "The Countess is a blessed creature, spiritual wax, upon which every spiritual seal can be impressed." "But it would also be highly desirable", he went on, "for you to form a spiritual connection with her brother, for he is a gentleman who can be of service to you in every way."[43]

Juan de Vega (1507-58) came of one of the great Castilian families who

434

had placed themselves entirely at the service of Charles V's policy. On his mother's side he was related to the royal family of Aragon. At seventeen he married Doña Leonor de Osorio, daughter of the Marquis of Astorga, who again was connected through her mother (a member of the great Enríquez family) with the kings of Castile. Juan de Vega was the sixth Lord of Grajal de Campos near León, where the church of St. Michael and the magnificent inner courtyard of the palace still bear witness to his wealth and generosity. Of his happy marriage were born four sons and a daughter named Isabel.[44]

From July 1543 Juan de Vega lived in Rome with his family as imperial ambassador, after having accompanied Charles V on his campaign in Tunis and been Viceroy of Navarre. He was, then, highly in favour with the Emperor; and nothing was more natural than that Ignatius should heed Peter Faber's advice and should at once establish friendly relations with the ambassador through the mediation of his pious wife. The earliest information we have of this relationship with the Vega family is contained in the long account of the work of the Jesuits in Rome which the fathers sent to Spain. According to this, Ignatius was confessor not only in the Palazzo Madama, but also in the household of the imperial ambassador's wife – and this in spite of much illness and while he was in the middle of drawing up his Constitutions. Ignatius found among all the ladies of Roman society none who entered into his apostolic plans with more enthusiasm and at the same time with more prudence than the ambassadress. Only a year later he wrote to Rodríguez in Portugal: "Doña Leonor is my spiritual daughter in our Lord."

It was at this time that Ignatius began his great work for the moral reform of the Eternal City, above all the founding of the House of St. Martha. In this he was helped by the ambassadress especially; the following report, sent at the end of May 1545 to the Jesuits in Spain, sounds almost like a spiritual war communiqué:

"Doña Leonor Osorio, consort of Señor Juan de Vega, the imperial ambassador, has formed such an affection for this House of St. Martha that one can only praise God for it; it puts many others to shame. She has specially appointed a woman in her household, whose sole task it is to go into the dwellings of women of immoral life in order to convert them. Not satisfied with this, she herself goes into the churches and on to the streets, talks to the women and takes them back with her to her palace, where she gives shelter to all who wish to be converted until they can be accommodated at St. Martha's or with the Penitents. Just recently she was in Sant' Agostino and there she met one of the most notorious courtesans, spoke to her and persuaded her to leave her life of sin. The woman looked with deep contri-

435

tion upon her miserable wickedness, and so Doña Leonor took her home with her. In this way five or six have already come through her to live at St. Martha's. So great is the love that our Lord has implanted in her soul that she seems intoxicated with the holy service of God. . . . When she saw that the house was getting too small to take in so many women, she boldly went to speak to His Holiness, and on this subject alone, showing him the need of enlarging the house and acquiring some of the adjoining buildings. She asked the Pope to buy these houses, and His Holiness generously agreed to her request. From these and other works of hers you can see the love of God our Lord which enflames her heart. I will say nothing of her frequent confessions, for she confesses every week to our Father, Master Ignatius."[45]

Pedro Ribadeneira noted in his diary:

"At the time when the House of St. Martha was being established at Rome and some leading courtesans were beginning to turn away from their evil business and to confine their activities to works of salvation and pious tears, Ignatius made a habit of accompanying them in the public street – not several at once, but now this one, now that. It was a wondrous sight to see the holy old man – a footman, as it were, running before a young and pretty street-girl, in order to save her from the clutches of the most cruel tyrant and to lead her into safety in the hands of Christ. He went with them either to the newly established convent or to the house of some highborn lady, in which the girls were to be at first accustomed to domestic tasks and then, spurred by the example and admonitions of other girls, to a life of virtue. In this work the pious love and ardent zeal for souls of Leonor Osorio, wife of Juan de Vega, at that time ambassador of the Emperor Charles V to the Holy Father, shone above all others. When some persons objected that such girls were hardened in their vice, and would all too easily fall back into former ways, and that therefore there was no need to be so zealously concerned for their conversion, Ignatius said: 'That is not so. If with all my care and trouble I can persuade but one of them to refrain from sin for a single night for the sake of my Lord Jesus Christ, then I would leave nothing, absolutely nothing, undone in order that she should at least during that time not offend God – even if I knew for certain that she would immediately afterwards return to her former vice.'"

When the papal postmaster Mattia di San Cassiano created a scandal about the House of St. Martha, Doña Leonor used all her influence to pacify the angry gentleman. In a long conversation with Leonor the postmaster declared himself ready to speak favourably of Ignatius everywhere, if necessary "even by putting up a public notice in the Campo de' Fiori". Ignatius did not place too much reliance on these peace-making efforts, however, but insisted on a clearcut legal solution to the matter.[46]

Ignatius' friendship with the Vega family also had a growing political importance. While Vega's wife was zealously working in the House of St. Martha, the tension between the Pope and the Emperor over the duchy of Parma and Piacenza led to the ambassador's secret departure from Rome on May 22nd, 1544, to return in triumph the following November. This tension was felt also between the Emperor's daughter Margaret of Austria and her husband Ottavio Farnese, the Pope's grandson. Margaret, Ignatius' penitent, had impassioned political discussions with Juan de Vega, in which she inveighed against the "brood" of the Farnese. We have already heard how Ignatius smoothed out her matrimonial quarrel, itself a result of political circumstances; and the reconciliation was no doubt effected through the influence of Doña Leonor, whom he held up as a model to the unbridled Madama.

All the letters during the years 1544–46 are full of news about the increasingly cordial collaboration between the General of the Jesuits and the wife of the imperial ambassador. Thus Doña Leonor asked for a Sunday sermon in Spanish; she stood godmother to a converted Turk whose baptism was solemnly celebrated, and when she had him baptized Ignazio, Ignatius with a chivalrous gesture added the name Osorio. Leonor appeared as a witness in the unfortunate lawsuit with Isabel Roser; she wrote a letter of recommendation for the Society of Jesus to Duke Cosimo of Florence; she took the deepest interest in everything that concerned the prosperity of the new Society. In October 1546, when Ignatius was occupied with the patriarchate of Ethiopia, which was to be taken over by a Jesuit, he wrote: "Doña Leonor Osorio said to me one day with much warmth that she would rather lose all her possessions than see a father of our Company accept a bishopric." Leonor really was, as a modern historian has said of her, "one of those great Spanish ladies who were as noble as they were pious, and Ignatius rightly called her a blessed soul and the model of all virtue".[47]

On April 11th, 1547, however, Don Juan de Vega left Rome, destined for a more important office. For political dealings with Paul III it was better to replace that too outspoken diplomat by the more obliging Diego de Mendoza, whom Ignatius already knew from his Venetian days. In the same month of April, Doña Leonor, together with Father Doménech and the Roman Jesuits' old friend Dr. Iñigo López, left for Sicily. The travellers halted at Gaeta, and here the zealous Vicereine lost no time in initiating the reform of the local convent of Cistercian nuns, which had become very lax.

For Ignatius in Rome her departure was a real loss. Doña Leonor had been a welcome advocate with the Pope, and before she left she had asked the Holy Father for a number of spiritual favours. As early as June 10th, she wrote a long letter to Ignatius about herself and the health of her sons, and about all the good works she intended to undertake in Sicily. With this letter begins the actual correspondence with Doña Leonor, of which a few letters have been preserved.[48]

The reply which Ignatius sent to Palermo, probably at the end of July 1547, suggests the tangle of spiritual and political relationships among which he and his helpers had to carry out their apostolic works. We learn that Ignatius' relations with the Theatine cardinal, the future Pope Paul IV, were not of the best. The lawsuit with the angry papal postmaster was not yet over. Old Cardinal Agostino Trivulzio, who held seven South Italian bishoprics, was well-disposed. At the end of the letter Ignatius commended to her Don Juan Rodríguez de Figueroa, who had once condemned him in Alcalá and whose political career in the Emperor's service Ignatius was now promoting with his influence. Doña Leonor will have been most pleased at the news about the House of St. Martha, for she was already planning similar institutions in Messina and Trapani.[49]

My Lady in our Lord.

May the highest grace and eternal love of Christ our Lord greet and visit Your Ladyship.

Last week I received a letter from Your Ladyship dated June 10th, with that spiritual joy which the daily memory and letters or news of Your Ladyship generally bring to my soul. May God our Lord be praised for all and especially that his divine Majesty has deigned to give Your Ladyship your full health again as also to Señor Hernando de Vega and Don Álvaro, with all the others who have been visited by his divine hand.[50] Now by his infinite mercies may it please him to preserve and bless them more abundantly for his greater service, praise and glory.

As to the reform of the convent of Gaeta, the same order of St. Bernard has sent to notify all the nuns there that, under pain of excommunication, within forty days they must be enclosed, setting new grilles in different parts. As the nuns are pleading excuses, proceedings are being taken so energetically and with so much support from His Eminence Cardinal Trivulzio that I found Master Jerónimo Gastaferro very pleased with things, and I am satisfied with the means that are being taken to reach the desired objective. I am writing about the matter in greater detail to Master Jerónimo Doménech if Your Ladyship would find it useful to have fuller information about the whole affair.

As to the Agnus Dei that Your Ladyship wants to give me as a present, God our Lord will be pleased – and so also am I. I give unceasing thanks to his divine Majesty for this and also to your Ladyship. I was hoping, indeed, to receive some Agnus Dei from the most reverend Theatine Cardinal and I begged them so earnestly that Don Juan Bautista, his nephew, told me with a kindly smile that he had the charge of collecting them and that it would not be necessary to remind him again. However, as he did not send me any, I ceased troubling him, for it seemed to me I had expended enough diligence over the matter – especially now that the expected Agnus Dei are coming through Your Ladyship. I have not said anything to him on your part more than that since his Eminence offered to send them, Your Ladyship would be very pleased to have them.

As to the affair of Matía, the matter is at the same stage as before. I think that to achieve what we desire for the greater glory of God, it would be advisable for Your Ladyship to send me a letter signed with your hand, giving testimony as to what Don Galeazo Rótulo said to Your Ladyship on Matía's behalf. This, however, I only ask because it was agreed with Señor Juan de Vega.

The Papal Vicar will do everything possible to give testimony how Matía himself unsaid everything in his presence. I think with two such testimonies, even if there were no other reason, it would be more than just that sentence should be given.

As to the convent of St. Martha, by the grace of God our Lord, the work is growing to the greater service and praise of his divine Majesty and to the greatest satisfaction of all. Since the contradictions have outwardly ceased, a company of noble Roman ladies has been formed to favour and serve this pious work. Thus to three of them we have given all three keys with which the doors of the monastery of St. Martha can be locked, so that no man or woman can go in or out without their leave and by their hand. These ladies are very pleased to have this work and their numbers increase daily, thus promoting the work to the greater glory of God.

I would ask Your Ladyship, for the service of God our Lord, always to show favour to certain relatives that Master Francisco Banuzo has in your neighbourhood. He has written to them that they should pay Your Ladyship the respect of a visit. The good man does not fail to do all he can to promote this holy work of St. Martha's, as is his wont.

About the business the Pope's Vicar had in mind concerning Don Figueroa and the Emperor, my great wish in our Lord is that Don Figueroa should be asked to give some new token of goodwill, or some word of encouragement that would be a good help, although he himself is utterly devoted to Your Ladyship, and to all Your Ladyship's undertakings.

439

Of the great progress in holy and pious works which is afforded Master Jerónimo through Señor Juan de Vega, I can never think enough, and I am persuaded that he will to the greater glory of God continue to find increasing favour with His Grace. I commend myself heartily to him in our Lord and greet him. I also commend myself to your two sons who are also mine in our Lord and to your whole household.

Rome, July [or August], 1547

To the Lady Doña Leonor Osorio

Doña Leonor took the keenest interest, from the first moment of her sojourn in Sicily, in all the works which the Jesuits undertook in the territories of her husband's viceroyalty, which from the religious point of view were in a state of sad neglect. Polanco, in his *Summarium Italicum* on the Society's beginnings in Italy, was later to sing loudly the praises of Vega and his wife, and to relate how the Vicereine, by the promotion and foundation of orphanages and colleges and by the reform of convents, contributed "to remove great abuses". The first Jesuit who went to Sicily was the Belgian Jacob Lhoost. Ignatius wrote in June 1546 to Canisius that he had sent him at the request of Cardinal Rodolfo Pio de Carpi, Bishop of Agrigento. Lhoost was an enthusiastic young man of twenty-seven, who had not long been a Jesuit, and from what the chronicle of the Society relates of his work in darkest Sicily his tactics closely resembled those of Ignatius in Rome: spiritual ministrations to the sick and to children, to the Saracens and to ignorant priests, and above all – here too – the reform of nunneries.

All this met with the full approval of the Vicereine. To her great sorrow Ignatius had to recall Lhoost in August 1547 to Rome. The latter duly took leave of Doña Leonor in Palermo, and she gave him a long letter for Ignatius. This has unfortunately been lost; but we still possess a note from the lady, impatient for an answer. It has been preserved in the original among more important papers – a charming evidence of the loving solicitude with which Doña Leonor followed the Jesuits' journey through the heat of Southern Italy and Naples seething with revolt. The Vicereine was, alas, soon to hear that her dear Father Lhoost had died a holy death at Bologna, while on his way to Flanders, on November 30th, 1548.[51]

Very reverend lord and Father,

I greatly desire to know how Your Reverence is and if Master Jacob who was having such a difficult time, both through the rebellion at

Naples and on account of the ill-health I fear for him, has arrived back in Rome. God grant that he has arrived safe and sound. I gave him a long letter for Your Reverence.

All I would say now besides what is already said, is to commend myself to Your Reverence's prayers, which I greatly need both for body and soul and each day feel [the need of] more. May our Lord remember me.

With this I conclude, asking God to guard Your Reverence's very revererd person.

At Your Reverence's service,
Doña Leonor

Messina, August 17th, 1547

To the most reverend father, Father Master Ignatius, General of the Society of Jesus, in Rome

The General's secretary Polanco could therefore write with a certain degree of pride to Spain: "The Viceroy, his consort and their whole family are very devoted to the Society." Less agreeable for Ignatius was the fact that these great personages had always to be handled with a prudence that bordered on anxiety.

A typical example is the letter of late 1548, in which Ignatius told Laynez that the return of Father Doménech was being demanded in Spain at the express wish of Prince Philip and also at the request of his old father – Father Doménech, who had become so dear and so indispensable to the viceregal pair in Palermo. It was necessary to proceed with the utmost caution; the Viceroy must not be offended. "Speak then first to Doña Leonor, and then Her Excellency will speak with Señor Juan de Vega", advised Ignatius, versed in the manners of courts. Apart from this, Ignatius' patience was sorely tried by Doña Leonor's habit of asking favours from the Pope, and from time to time he had to act as mediator.[52] Nevertheless, Doña Leonor was an ideal person to work with. Letters passed to and fro between them, as for instance the Vicereine's long report of July 9th, 1548, from Messina, where the Society's undertakings were flourishing. Under the leadership of Father Nadal ten chosen Jesuits had been sent by Ignatius to Messina, where they had begun work in the newly established college on April 24th, 1548. Among them was Peter Canisius. Doña Leonor was delighted. Her plans to found four orphanages at Messina, Palermo, Trapani and Agrigento were about to be realized; and the Roman curia was actively interested in the work of monastic reform. In brief, things were going forward in Sicily, and it was

441

already nearly as it had once been at Rome, when with Madama de Austria and her lady-in-waiting María Mendoza de Guzmán she laboured for the girls of St. Martha's, or with the financier Dr. Villanueva carried out charitable works, while Ignatius sparingly bestowed eagerly longed-for praise upon the ladies.[53]

Doña Leonor also had the spiritual and domestic cares peculiar to a woman. Someone had privately told her that the Pope had withdrawn the indulgences once granted to her for her rosary beads. Who could better assist her than Ignatius? She asked him to get an audience and clear the matter up. Then there were the usual troubles with her charity cases. Ignatius through the mediation of Doña Leonor had asked the Viceroy for a recommendation to the government for a certain Zuazola, probably one of his Basque relatives. The lady duly dealt with the case. She was after all under some obligation to Ignatius, for shortly before one of her court tailors, a married man called Salzedo, had run away from his wife and gone with his boy to Rome, where Ignatius had helped him, and even offered to accommodate both in the Jesuit house. What Doña Leonor wished from Ignatius in regard to the poor tailor is written all in the same breath, as it were, with the request that he would send Father Laynez to Sicily – a truly feminine medley of important and trivial affairs. Everything, absolutely everything could be told to Father Ignatius.[54]

Then there was the problem of all mothers: young Isabel, of whom Ignatius was so fond, must be married off, and already a web of matrimonial strategy was being spun that reached across to Spain. The prospective bridegroom was a son of the Marquis of Alcañices, to whom Doña Leonor was related through the family of Enríquez. Ignatius had to pray for the marriage – for what, indeed, had he not to pray! But he did so. Doña Leonor was not destined to see the outcome; but Ignatius' lifelong friendship with Isabel proved that the mother had commended her daughter to the right hands.

The valuable consignment of Sicilian wax candles for Holy Week at Santa Maria della Strada, which Doña Leonor sent and for which Ignatius thanked her specially in a now lost letter dated June 9th, was as it were, a symbol of the Vicereine's love for the Jesuits. An eyewitness, Benedetto Amarone, was to write many years later an account of this generous gift. There were green, yellow and white candles, beautifully gilded, for use in the chapel; and a great quantity of sweetmeats, preserves and biscuits. Ignatius was evidently embarrassed at the sight of all this and was reluctant to accept the good things; so he picked out only a few candles and made a present of the preserves (as the witness expressly states) to some of the cardinals. Leonor's letter to Ignatius is as full in content as her gift-chest.[55]

Very Reverend Father,

I have received Your Reverence's letter of July 9th. In the first place
I give thanks to our Lord that he has given you the health to write it; may
it please his divine Majesty always to give you health for his service.
As to the rest, it seems to me that the altar candles arrived just at the right
time, since I sent them off so that they should arrive in Rome for Holy
Week and this it seems they did.

As to the Papal Brief for the house of the orphan boys, Master Jerónimo [Doménech] tells me that he sent you the names of the [houses in
the different] dioceses; and as to the other Brief for the reform of the
monasteries, I greatly desire that this should now arrive, since Your
Reverence knows how great the need is in this kingdom for these
monasteries to be reformed. Would that it might please God that the
Brief reach Your Reverence's hands soon, for I really think that in this
connection something drastic must happen in the whole of Christendom
and much more so in Sicily. I still hope in our Lord that if Your Reverence deals with the matter God will surely send us a good remedy
soon.

Father Master Nadal and his companions are very well. They are so
full of burning zeal here that wherever they are what they do clearly
appears to be the work of God. They are hurrying on as much as possible
the building of the house which I think will be handsome and well
designed. As I have written to Your Reverence in another letter, I am sure
that in Palermo and in other places in this kingdom, they envy the people
of Messina and I cannot but importune Your Reverence and that in a
very special way that we go to Palermo, if it please God, for there another
college is very necessary.

Doctor Villanueva has no right to complain so much of me as you
write; for, although I know I am to blame for not having written as
often as is reasonable and as is due to his goodwill and his work, I am
certain I have written him two or three times since I came to Sicily in
reply to letters of his. Thus I ask Your Reverence to clear me of blame
with him on this point, and certainly there is nothing he might order me
that I would not do, as if he were my own Father. I have written to him
in this sense. Will Your Reverence kindly give him my letter?

Here they have told me that His Holiness, Paul III, has withdrawn the
indulgences on my rosaries. I cannot believe it. Your Reverence would
be doing me a great favour if it were possible, to try and see if you could
speak with His Holiness and kiss his foot on my behalf and tell him how
they have told me this here and that I am relying on the favour His

443

Holiness did me and bestowed on me when I left and that he told me he would never withdraw a favour he had given me. Thus I would again beseech His Holiness to deign to grant me anew all the graces he has given me, both for the rosaries and for the candles for the mortuary. With what Your Reverence will say verbally, I do not need to take any other action. I am writing to Doña María de Mendoza, begging her on my behalf to tell Don Lope de Guzmán to try and obtain an audience with His Holiness for Your Reverence; although if Your Reverence could have it through some other means I should not want to give these people this trouble.

The letter of recommendation for the nephew of Zuazola my husband, Juan de Vega, wrote in the best form he could and in this I refer you to Father Master Jerónimo.

The care Your Reverence has taken of Salzedo and the affection you have shown him in order to help him I am deeply grateful for. Since he is now all right, there is no further need for Your Reverence to take any more trouble, since he will be able to come back, or do what he wishes, although if what he said to me when he left is true, that he was married, it would seem better that he should go back to his wife. If, however, he should come back here, it will not be possible to refuse him what he had before although, as I have written to Your Reverence, I now have a tailor in the house who serves me.

I have no more to say, except that I shall take it as a very great favour if Your Reverence sends Father Master Laynez here, as my husband, Juan de Vega, is writing you; for I am sure that his coming here will do much good and great service to our Lord.

My daughter kisses Your Reverence's hands and, thanks be to God, is well; so are her brothers. It is days since we had a letter from Suero and we expect news from day to day. To all the Fathers in the house please give my remembrance, especially to Father Peter Codacio and Master Mirón.

At Your Reverence's service,
Doña Leonor

In regard to our daughter there is a question of a certain marriage in Spain, which was beginning to be dealt with in Rome. I informed Your Reverence of this. Now it appears that the matter is nearer its conclusion. I beg Your Reverence to commend it to our Lord. This is an affair which Don Graviel Sarmiento spoke to us of, when he was [engaged] in the legal business; and as Varvarán was intermediary nothing was done. Now they have returned to it through the Admiral.

I ask you as a favour that the letters which accompany this you would kindly give to those for whom they are intended.

Messina, July 9th, 1548

Ignatius must have sighed as he read this letter, in spite of his joy at the good news. For once again it meant that he would have to make many fruitless journeys to the Vatican or San Marco in order to fulfil the wishes of the Vicereine, who was on such friendly terms with the Pope. On Saturday August 4th, Ignatius was clearly in desperation, and in a letter to Doña Leonor (unfortunately lost) he represented to her the innumerable difficulties he encountered on his visits to the pontifical anterooms. A day later, however, the situation had completely changed: Ignatius at last had a personal audience with Paul III, and was able to win a victory for her. The report of this diplomatic engagement sounds like an advocate's account of a successful case.

Ignatius thought out this letter carefully, as he did every communication that left his desk. We know this because the original draft in Ignatius' handwriting has been preserved. Neatly and with care he had made his corrections by means of various signs in the margin for the secretary who had to prepare the fair copy.[56]

To Doña Leonor,

The sovereign grace and eternal love of Christ our Lord be with Your Ladyship. May he fill you with his most holy gifts and spiritual graces.

After I wrote to Your Ladyship last Saturday of the difficulties that had been put in my way over the indulgences for the rosaries, etc., on the following Sunday, August 5th, I spoke to the Pope personally, and the victory is Your Ladyship's – to the greater glory of God. For after I had given some account of the Society and had spoken of the Señor de Vega and of Your Ladyship as seemed to me fitting, His Holiness praised you – to my way of thinking affectionately. I then touched on the point, namely, as to whether His Holiness had withdrawn the privileges granted to Your Ladyship in connection with the rosaries, etc. His Holiness answered me graciously and, indeed, emphatically,

445

that he had never withdrawn them, and he again confirmed them, giving me his blessing with the sign of the cross.

I then, kissing his foot once more, also spoke to him about the four towns where houses for orphan children might be erected and of the petition we thought of making to have the Papal signature as confirmation and that His Holiness might order the business to be expedited. To this he also agreed with a very good will.

Afterwards I went to speak with Cardinal Crescenzi and his Eminence showed himself very well disposed. The petition has already been handed to a lawyer and I think the business will soon be dispatched for the whole matter was dealt with after careful consideration, to the greater glory of God.

Commend me much in our Lord to the good graces of Doña Isabel and of her brothers, with the whole household, as devoted to them all in our Lord.

May God in his infinite and sovereign goodness give us all his graces and favours. The most reverend Bernardino de la Cruz wishes to be kindly remembered to Your Ladyship and also to Señor Juan de Vega.

Rome, August 11th, 1548

The effect of this letter might have been foreseen: the two Vega ladies, mother and daughter, were delighted at Ignatius' readiness to help, and so their requests for his good offices did not cease. Nor did the good and often nourishing gifts which arrived from Sicily at the humble house next to Santa Maria della Strada.

The kind of requests that Ignatius had to deal with can be seen from a letter in which Father Doménech defends himself against the reproach that he had not supported the Vicereine's petitions strongly enough. On February 8th, 1549, he wrote to Ignatius:

"We have already written in other letters that the Lady Vicereine is by no means being presumptuous in requesting permission to enter monasteries. She only desires permission *vivae vocis oraculo,* and with the agreement of the monks, to be able to pass through the monastery of San Benito at Monreale, as it would be convenient for her, inasmuch as she could get to church from the house where she lives through a garden belonging to the monks. . . The Vicereine told me she wished to send Your Reverence I know not what kind of sweetmeats; she was relying on Don Juan de Vega in the matter, as he was going to send some present to a cardinal, and the gift for Your

446

Reverence could then be sent at the same time, as well as one for Monsignor Vicario [Archinto] and thirty *scudi* in wheat or in money for St. Martha's. I will make it my business to remind her of this, although she has a good memory in such matters."[57]

Soon afterwards another list of similar requests appears to have arrived in Rome. Clearly they were now at the end of their patience in the curia of the Society, and Polanco sharpened his pen to write to Doménech for the attention of all the fathers in Sicily:

"Moreover, you are to inform all the brethren: when our Father saw the list of favours asked for by Doña Leonor he observed that even if he were the Pope he would not dare to grant such favours. Nevertheless, he preferred the judgment of highly-placed persons before his own and undertook to obey her. He went often to and fro between here and St. Peter's to speak to one or another of the cardinals, so that it has certainly injured his health. And it appears that some think – as indeed one cardinal said to him – he takes the matter too seriously, because he 'has his heart in it'. For does not everyone know that it is characteristic of him to perform energetically all things that he undertakes?"

It can be seen that Ignatius was not to be restrained, even by the gossip of the papal court, from doing everything possible for the Vicereine of Sicily; and he had a right to, for he knew how to send a negative answer, gently but firmly, to the proud Vicereine when the occasion required. There was, for instance, at Messina a boy of thirteen who had since his fifth year been the object of wonder as a kind of infant prodigy in the pulpit. Doña Leonor too was among his enraptured listeners, and she now wished that the Jesuits would take him into their college. The fathers were highly embarrassed, whereupon the Vicereine sent an imploring letter to Ignatius. A polite "no" was the answer from Rome. Ribadeneira has noted this in his memoirs as an example of the General's unshakable firmness even towards his dearest friends.

A few months before his visits to St. Peter's on Doña Leonor's behalf, he had sent her, at the beginning of Advent 1548, an instruction about the value of the spiritual life, which flowed quite spontaneously from his pen in the midst of business communications. We can savour its exquisite immediacy in his own draft, in which the crossed-out and corrected sentences at the end no longer quite fit together. Ignatius' letters are always distinguished more by their love of God than by their grammar. Ignatius also sent Father Laynez to her after the latter had been quietly and cautiously released from the service of the Duchess of Florence. The announcement of this great preacher's coming was the best of Christmas presents for the Vicereine. She never forgot this letter.[58]

To Doña Leonor

I have received the letter from Your Ladyship telling me about the discussions and the points of disagreement and also the bill of exchange for five hundred ducats. In order not to seem importunate with my letters and my advice, which can contribute so little to the furthering of the great and good works which God is bringing about through Your Ladyship to his greater glory, I have left answering until I could see something begun or brought to achievement for the divine glory. I have, however, advised Master Jerónimo each week of what has been done up to now so that Your Ladyship should be informed of everything. In this connection we ought to long for such favours just as far as we can have hope of profiting by them, to the greater glory of his divine majesty. And because, without the gift of God's grace, all our thoughts, words and works are very half-hearted, slothful and of little or no value, we ought always very diligently to seek after it and desire to obtain it for with God's grace which gives us facility in what we do, all our deeds will be found pleasing and acceptable in the presence of the divine Majesty, as I hope will be the case with Your Ladyship, so that you may ascend from step to step and from good to better, and so will find yourself continually more acceptable in the presence of his divine goodness.

Doña Isabel must take this letter as also written for her. In reply to what she wrote me about a certain pious work, I replied at once. If anything should transpire in which my very little worth can help, it will be for Your Ladyship to command and for me to obey, in everything that is possible to me in our Lord.

Master Laynez indeed is leaving here, and that with no little opposition, as you will be able to learn from Master Jerónimo. Moreover, the season is unfavourable on account of the winter. He goes to Naples, and thence to Palermo. Remember him continually in your devout prayers for the service of God our Lord, as I ask Doña Isabel and Doña María de Arujo also to do, with all the other ladies there who are leading a spiritual life, that he will do good in the service of God our Lord. To the favour of this prayer I recommend myself and all the fathers of the house of professed in our Lord.

Rome (end November or beginning October, 1548)

In the middle of January Laynez reached Palermo. Doña Leonor received him with joy, though her tears were soon to flow, for Laynez had been entrusted with the task of preparing the way for Father Doménech's departure.

The plan of founding a college at Palermo was progressing well; and although the Vicereine's health was deteriorating, she was always there when Laynez, with magnificent success, delivered his Lenten sermons in the cathedral. Leonor sent enthusiastic letters to Rome; but Ignatius was sick unto death and was at this time beginning to think seriously of resigning from the Generalship.

Leonor had besides a grave disappointment in the matter of her daughter's projected marriage. The old Marquis of Alcañices was dead, and apparently his son was now looking round for another bride who would bring him a larger dowry than Isabel. Juan de Vega was always of a thrifty disposition, and the Spanish marriage plan evidently foundered on the negotiations concerning the amount of the dowry. Probably the bridegroom Doña Leonor wanted was that son of the Marquis of Alcañices who in the following year married the daughter of the Duke of Gandía, Francis Borgia. She received a dowry of fifteen *cuentos,* as we know from the marriage contract.

Of this sorrow too the disappointed mother had to tell Ignatius. To add to all this there was the Viceroy's gout, which is the concluding subject of the last letter from Leonor's hand to Ignatius that we possess.[59]

Very reverend Señor,

I have written Your Reverence two or three times since Father Master Laynez has been in Sicily, but we have never received a reply. I hope to God that Your Reverence is well and that some illness has not been the cause of your not writing. For this reason, I beg Your Reverence to let me know how you have been and are.

From here I can say that Master Laynez' preaching this Lent has been extremely profitable, as I think the fathers have advised Your Reverence. The business of the college also, with the help of our Lord, is going very well. I can say that it is almost finished, because the whole city is well disposed towards the project, as I think they have written at some length to Your Reverence. This also will be a great service to our Lord. I give him deep thanks that each day he is more served, for we all know the great fruit that this holy Society of Jesus is producing.

Of myself I must tell Your Reverence that I have continued to be not very well, but I give thanks to our Lord for all. Juan de Vega, my husband, is not too well either. I beg Your Reverence to commend us all to God.

Your Reverence will already know that my daughter's marriage did not take place, because Juan de Vega, my wedded lord, did not want to give the thirteen *cuentos*.[60] I still thought it would come about through the good will there was on the other side, but it pleased our Lord to take to himself the Marquis of Alcañices. Our Lord knows best; to him be thanks given for all.

May Your Reverence recommend me to God in your prayers, for I have much need of this; for to see Juan de Vega, my husband, ill, and other troubles I have which, indeed, I deserve, robs me of the peace I desire. Juan de Vega, God keep him, has the gout, and this is my chief trouble. May God be served in it all and with this I conclude.

At Your Reverence's service,
Dona Leonor

Palermo, August 6th, 1549[61]

At the end of 1549, Laynez wrote to Ignatius that he had visited the Vicereine, and observed: "We found the poor lady so downcast and ill that we cannot find words to express her condition." At once Ignatius wrote her a letter of comfort, the manuscript draft of which, with its innumerable small corrections, we still possess – a document written by one who was great even in little things, and who after all the profound words of spiritual consolation did not forget to mention the case of the poor tailor Salzedo, who wanted to go home to Sicily.[62]

Doña Leonor,

By Your Ladyship's letter of August 6th, I have learnt of certain indispositions of Don Juan de Vega and also of Your Ladyship. I cannot do otherwise than feel them inwardly, and this still more in our Lord than in myself. In the meantime, I have assured myself with relief, by letters from Master Jerónimo, that you are both better. May it please the most holy Trinity that the improvement continues for a long time to come, for the grace and glory of God and the universal good of the souls redeemed with his most precious Blood. Before his divine presence, as Your Ladyship commands me, I cannot forget in my poor but continual prayers to remember you both frequently, asking his divine Majesty for all that is to his greater glory, and for what Your Ladyship most desires for his greater service and praise.

When Salzedo received the money and I showed him what Your

Ladyship wrote to me about him, namely that I can tell him that he can go to Sicily when he likes, he was very pleased and immediately determined to go there. Thus afterwards they sent to tell me that he will set out immediately after the first rains and that I can write this to Your Ladyship.

Rome, end December 1548 [1549]

To Leonor de Osorio

This is the last complete letter that we possess of Ignatius' correspondence with Doña Leonor. But a summary dated March 29th, 1550, suggests what these two, neither of whom rested as long as they lived, had to write about to one another. Doña Leonor sent the fathers through Master Codacio (who meanwhile had died on December 7th, 1549) two hundred ducats and a gift of Sicilian cheese. In return Ignatius reassured her in the matter which had been the subject of a previous request of hers, namely the validity of the papal favours which had now to be renewed under Julius III, and promised that he would make a number of visits for her. On Palm Sunday, March 30th, 1550, the noble lady died a holy death at Palermo. The chronicle of the Society thus reports her death:

"The Lenten sermons which Father Laynez was preaching, to the great satisfaction of the Viceroy, the nobility and all his hearers, had to be interrupted towards the end of Lent because the Vicereine, Doña Leonor, was dangerously ill. When death became imminent, she desired Father Jerónimo [Doménech] and Father Laynez to assist her, which they did. On Palm Sunday it pleased the Divine goodness to call her to a happier life. Her death was as her life had been – full of faith, devotion, love, humility and contempt for the world, of kindness and solicitude for her children and her whole household, especially for her husband, to whom she had always been respectfully submissive. She always displayed open and unlimited charity and compassion towards the poor, the oppressed and sinners."[63]

Such was the end of a true friendship in God. Ignatius transferred all his affection from the mother to her daughter Isabel.

Isabel de Vega

FROM Ignatius' first letter to Isabel de Vega it is clear that the young daughter of the imperial ambassador at Rome took an active part in her mother's charitable works. The friendship which Ignatius bestowed upon her while he lived dates from those days. Isabel was the youngest child of Doña Leonor, the only daughter, and for that reason the darling of all. We know already that in 1547, shortly before her parents' departure for Sicily, plans had been made for Isabel's marriage in Spain. Nothing came of them. In Messina and Palermo Isabel energetically supported her mother in all her undertakings. Here too she was linked by close ties of friendship and memory with Rome, and often she added greetings or enclosed letters of her own when her mother wrote to Ignatius. Thus in November 1548 he had to reply to a letter from Isabel that was evidently very detailed. He took great trouble over the matter, for we still possess a draft of his answer in his own handwriting. Its date can only be presumed from that of his letter to Doña Leonor written at the same time, at the end of November 1548, and the stereotyped concluding formula is not given in full.

Isabel's letter concerned the case of a young girl named Clara belonging to the Spanish colony at Rome – a case the details of which are obscure. Evidently Isabel had already helped her. We are hardly wrong in supposing that the girl had been seduced by a man of rank; in any case, a person who remains unknown had given Doña Isabel 20.000 *maravedís*, with the request that she would convey this sum to Clara by way of compensation. This is where the patient Ignatius came in. First he spoke to the notary and registrar Blas de Casarrubios, who had done him such good service in the lawsuit with Isabel Roser; but there he sought the girl in vain. So the weary apostle set out to look for her, limping through the streets of Rome and climbing stairs – merely to fulfil the wishes of young Isabel. At that very time Ignatius was seriously ill; but that did not prevent him from writing to Doña Isabel, thanking her with chivalrous courtesy for letting him share in her charitable work.[64]

To Doña Isabel.

I have received a letter from Your Ladyship which gave me much joy in our Lord, because in it I perceived that things were well with you, both as to bodily and spiritual health (although in your humility you are not convinced as to the second point), and also that you are engaged in so many pious works for the greater glory of God and that you give me a share in them. May it please God our Lord always to increase his grace in you, so that you may proceed from good to greater good in his service and praise.

Now I have literally applied all the diligence I could in the following manner. Firstly, I spoke to Señor Casarrubios and understood from him that there was not in his house nor had there been a girl called Clara. Secondly, I learnt there that this girl had been living in the house of Don Álvaro de Herrera and so I went to speak with him. I found him in bed, suffering from a broken leg. I gathered from him that Clara had been in his house and that in the month of March last he had sent her, together with her mother and two little brothers, that is, one little brother and one little sister, and also a certain husband and wife who were natives of Barcelona, to Naples and there they embarked for Zamora. He told me letters had been received from Barcelona to the effect that they had arrived there in perfect health, and that the husband of the couple from Barcelona would have to accompany Clara, and her mother, brother and sister, to Zamora.[65]

You write me about a certain person who for the discharge of his conscience would give 20,000 *maravedís*, which Your Ladyship would take charge of for the girl, and that I could arrange the matter whether she were in Rome or not, and that you would send the money to me. In this matter one should proceed carefully, for the girl is living in good circumstances in the family who have taken her in. Therefore, for greater secrecy, I have said that a lady, in order to do a work of mercy, etc., will give 20,000 *maravedís* to marry her, for I am certain that you are moved because it is a work of mercy. In the one house, when they asked me who this lady was, I replied that I was not free to say etc. They all remained so completely without suspicion that they urged me and asked, since Clara was not here, that I should plead with the lady in question to give that alms to another girl who was living in their house and much in need, and they pointed her out to me, for they think that in any case it concerns someone living in Rome. I replied that I must first ascertain the intention and will of the lady.

Since matters passed thus, Your Ladyship will now see for yourself if it is better that such compensation in money be sent to Zamora or here. The matter, if it is to be expressed plainly – and naturally we cannot lie – seems to be somewhat delicate, chiefly on account of the absence of the person concerned. However, if it seems to Your Ladyship that I can serve you in anything, to God's greater glory, it will be for you to command and me to obey in all things, for I consider it a very signal favour that Your Ladyship may be served at any rate by my whole-hearted desires, when in works I cannot do so, through my insignificance and little worth in our Lord.

Rome, November 1548

To Isabel de Vega

Meanwhile Isabel took an interest in everything that her mother wrote about to Ignatius. Another consignment of wax candles and other gifts had just been despatched to Rome for Lent 1550, when Doña Leonor fell ill and, to the immeasurable grief of her daughter, died at Palermo on March 30th, 1550. The news of the death reached Rome almost immediately after the arrival of the presents. Ignatius too was deeply affected, and it was by no means merely the obligation of gratitude but the impulse of a loving heart which now prompted him to write one of the most beautiful of his letters of consolation. His secretary Polanco still remembered it in later years: "Father Ignatius wrote letters of condolence to the Viceroy and his daughter, which contained more religious teaching and spiritual comfort than mere official politeness, and which were always greatly treasured by both."[66]

IHS

My Lady in our Lord

The sovereign grace and eternal love of Christ our Lord greet and visit Your Ladyship with his most holy gifts and spiritual graces.

I was on the point of writing about the arrival of the wax candles and many other things which Doña Leonor with her accustomed and generous charity had sent us, when we learnt that God, our Creator and Lord, has called her from the trials and miseries of the present life to the rest and bliss of the life that is everlasting, a thing which, if we were to consider it humanly and not with the eyes of faith would cause in all of us the greater sorrow, as her presence and company were the more pleasant and indispensable, and also for the greater love that her good works and her considerable virtue deserved.

Looking, however, as we ought, to the reward which God our Lord has prepared in his holy kingdom for those who live and die in his service and for whom the ending of this brief and toilsome life is the beginning of that which is blessed and eternal, this should be looked upon as an occasion of praising and blessing our Creator and Lord, Jesus Christ, our life and all our good, and of rejoicing at the glory and bliss which he communicates to those he takes to himself, rather than of grieving at the lack of help or comfort we feel through such a death. For although the flesh feels this, because it is flesh, our spiritual knowledge of what is best ought to mean that we do not grieve so much for our own loss but are moved by the gain of the person to whom we owe so much, and by what is more pleasing to God our Lord, to whose service, praise and glory, life and all things ought to be ordained.

May it please the most Holy Spirit and true comforter of the faithful to console Your Ladyship with the abundant inflowing of his grace. Thus, I think, from heaven Doña Leonor will obtain grace and comfort for you, and will help us all humbly to accept the dispensation of God's sovereign Majesty, for now that she has no need to take care for herself, since she has come to the term and fulfilment of all her desires and the everlasting good is communicated to her with perfect fulness, so she will have all the greater solicitude about those whom she left here on earth, to help them until they obtain the same joy.

All of us in our house here have already begun to offer Masses and prayers and we shall continue commending her soul to him who created and redeemed it and endowed it with so many special graces. Instructions have been given that the same be done in different religious houses in Rome and in all the places to which our Society extends. It is true, none the less, that I am persuaded that it is rather we who are in need of being helped and favoured by Her Ladyship before God our Lord. May it please him to give us grace to employ the whole of this life in his holy service, so that at the end of it we may rejoice, like those who from the trials and peril of the sea reach the harbour of rest and safety; and may he give us all his abundant grace so that we may always know his most holy will and perfectly fulfil it.

Ignatius

Rome, April 12th, 1550

To Isabel de Vega

After the death of her mother, the daughter retired at first to the Dominican convent, where Fathers Laynez and Doménech had to minister to her spiritual comfort, often till far into the night. Most of all, however, Isabel sought comfort from the distant Ignatius. Letters had already been exchanged between them in May and June; but Isabel wanted more. To this unquenchable grief of Isabel's – she was evidently inclined to melancholy – we owe the second letter of consolation on her mother's death. It must have been at this time that the saint, favoured with mystical experience, became ill as a result of all the strain to which the celebration of Mass subjected him. At all events, Father Nadal said later in one of his instructions at Coimbra: "For a fortnight Ignatius was ill after having said three Masses at the request of the daughter of Juan de Vega."[67]

My Lady in our Lord.

The sovereign grace and eternal love of Christ our Lord greet and visit Your Ladyship with his most holy gifts and spiritual graces.

As I have already answered one letter I received from you, I have not hastened to write again, but I have not neglected to commend your affairs very frequently to God our Lord, as one who in his divine Majesty greatly desires the continual increase of God's gifts in your soul. If God give such increase, it will follow that, with greater light and relish for spiritual things, those which are corporal and temporal will make less impression on you. Not only will Your Ladyship find your loss diminished in the taking by God our Lord from this world to the other of the blessed soul of Doña Leonor – for you will find consolation in the fact that her Ladyship is at rest – but you will even see that this cannot be called a loss for you, since from where your mother is she will be able to help you all the more to obtain the bliss that she possesses, inasmuch as her prayers and desires will be more efficacious before God's presence. Moreover, Your Ladyship will feel the absence even of her company upon earth so much the less, as with the consideration and love of heavenly things, you will hold your converse more in heaven. May it please Jesus Christ, our God and Lord, to lift up your soul so close to himself and to possess it so completely with his holy love, that, in whatever state he finds it, it may be a chosen vessel and full of his spiritual treasures. Amen.

As to the rest, I hope that the good and holy inspirations and desires that God our Lord has given Your Ladyship and will give you continually, will not be ineffective and that you will always be ready and prepared to follow his divine will and calling and in it will greatly serve and glorify his holy name. May it please his infinite and sovereign goodness to direct you always and with very special providence in all things and much more in those which are so important for the whole of life. I for my part shall not fail to beg this continually from the divine Majesty.

As to the Masses which you instructed me should be said at privileged altars, I have taken steps that this should be done, and more than three hundred others we have said here in the house. So much so that it already seems to me almost a shameful thing to commend so much a soul which for some time has been in glory and helps us by her intercession. Thus I have appointed that all the Masses and prayers of the house be changed into desiring and asking the divine favour for Señor Juan de Vega and his fleet. I am having letters written in this sense to the other houses of the Society.

May it please God our Lord to grant our prayers as much as shall be for his greater glory and service, so that we may always know his most holy will and fulfil it perfectly.

Ignatius

Rome, July 19th, 1550

To Isabel de Vega

The Viceroy had not long to indulge his grief. In June 1550 he was assembling a Spanish fleet which, together with papal, Maltese and Florentine ships, was to attack the Turkish fortress of Aphrodisia near Tunis. Juan de Vega was in command – and in Rome the heart of the old soldier Ignatius was stirred. In his own way at least he wanted to take part in the expedition. In July 1550 he despatched to the Viceroy and the armada the solemn Latin document in which was proclaimed the indulgence he had obtained from the Pope for all the participants in the 'war for the glory of Christ and the spread of the Holy Faith'. Father Laynez sailed with the fleet as spiritual assistant, in spite of the fact that his presence was urgently demanded by the Duchess of Florence. On September 10th, 1550, he delivered a brilliant victory sermon in the mosque of Mahedia (Aphrodisia); and the triumph over the Turkish pirate Dragut made Sicily and all Italy resound with joy.

In the midst of the celebrations came the news that Hernando de Vega, eldest son of the Viceroy, had succumbed at the end of September 1550 to a strangely swift sickness. A Jesuit, Father Paolo d'Achille, was at his deathbed and at once sent a detailed report to Ignatius about the young man's saintly death. He was the late Doña Leonor's firstborn and Isabel's favourite brother. Pedro de Ribadeneira preached a moving panegyric. The grief was general, and the Pope himself sent a letter of condolence to the Viceroy. Ignatius, who had just read the news of the victory at Tunis, was much affected when the report of Hernando's death reached Rome, and at once he sent a letter of consolation to the young man's father. But he knew that there was another to be comforted in Sicily. So on November 1st he sent by the same post a letter to Isabel also.[68]

IHS

My Lady in our Lord.

May the sovereign grace and eternal love of Christ our Lord be always with us, to our continual help and favour.

Although not by any letter from Palermo, we have heard rumours of how God our Lord, having given the father such a triumph on earth, has willed to give the son a more complete one in heaven. There, all contrary things having been overcome, both in the case of the frail body and of the soul, Señor Hernando de Vega will, despite his few years, attain to and enjoy in security the highest good which we are all aiming at in this life, whether we have many years or few.

I do not doubt that the tenderness of natural love will have done something of its work in you. I hope, however, that grace, with which God our Lord supplies and perfects the weaknesses of nature, will have given you such conformity with the divine will and so much remembrance and love of eternal things, that you will rather have a desire to find yourself with such a mother and brother in the heavenly country – if this would serve God our Lord – than to draw either of them back to the troubles of this pilgrimage or exile. For it is certainly to be hoped from the life and death of Don Hernando, and much more from what Jesus Christ suffered for him, that the supplication that has been made for his soul to God's sovereign goodness, both here in Rome and in other places, will have been accepted, anticipating our prayers or a great part of them.

May it please God to give all of us who remain here his full grace, so that we may always know his holy will and fulfil it perfectly, and thus may rejoice in his most holy presence for ever.

I desire to be remembered very kindly to the Señores Don Álvaro and Don Suero.

Ignatius

Rome, November 1st, 1550

To Isabel de Vega

In this bereavement too Isabel was almost inconsolable. She was indeed busily occupied from the beginning of 1551 in helping the Jesuit fathers in Messina to establish their first noviciate there. The novices used to greet the young noblewoman with Greek and Latin verses. Isabel made them deliver practice sermons before her; and in the viceregal palace the learned Father Nadal gave lectures to her and her ladies on the life of Jesus. She assumed the patronage of a house of St. Martha in Trapani, modelled on that in Rome; she helped to save a beautiful courtesan; and it was a great vexation to her when a young cousin called Hernando de Vega had no liking for the life of a novice and returned to the world.

All this, however, was not enough to comfort her. Various theological problems concerning predestination and the salvation of the soul came to confuse her mind still more. So on January 11th, 1551, she sent Ignatius, together with the customary Lenten gifts inaugurated by Doña Leonor, a somewhat desperate letter. His answer has been preserved.[69]

My Lady in our Lord.

May the sovereign grace and eternal love of Christ our Lord visit you with his most holy gifts and spiritual graces.

I received your letter of January 11th, and the gifts which you sent us with it for this coming Lent. May he who gave you such a kindly thought accept it and reward you with a very full increase of well-being in this life and with the perfection of charity in his eternal glory. About what you write to me, that on the one hand you envy Señor Hernando de Vega, who is already in glory, because you see him out of the danger of offending God our Lord in this evil world, and, on the other hand, you cannot help being anxious about him since his call has come at such an early age, I tell you that such envy is holy and good, and your anxiety also – provided that in the case of the envy there is no lack of conformity with God's will, to remain on this pilgrimage, although it is full of trouble, as long as is fitting for God's greater service, and provided that in the case of the anxiety there is not lacking the very certain hope that God, our Creator and Lord, has Don Hernando in his holy glory, or that he is on the way to reaching it very soon. For before God, indeed, as old age does not increase, so youth does not diminish the merits of eternal life. Rather at whatever age, that one is the richest who most participates in the [merits] of Christ with the charity that God gives, and many make up with their intense will to serve God for the much time and many works they would like to have given

459

to his service. Thus I trust in God's infinite mercy that Don Hernando de Vega will have done, for both his conduct in this life and his death justify us in thinking this.

Finally, we have such a good God and so wise and loving a Father that we ought not to doubt his kindly Providence which removes his children from this life at the best moment there is for them to pass to the other. Thus I will say no more of this.

As to Don Juan de Vega, you say with truth that it is not necessary for there to be much reminding in letters for me, to have him present in my poor prayers and at Mass. May it please God's sovereign goodness to grant what I continually beg for His Highness and all his household and affairs.

Master Laynez has already left (with the Duke)[70] for Florence. I will have what you tell me in your letter written to him.

We are well (although I have been ailing these past few days), by the grace of God our Lord.

May he by his infinite and sovereign goodness grant all of us his full grace so that we may always know his most holy will and perfectly fulfil it.

Ignatius

Rome, February 21st, 1551

To Isabel de Vega

One would like to know why Isabel so longed for death. The answer should not be difficult: she was in love and faced with a painful choice. As she was a somewhat pensive girl and inclined to melancholy, all this caused her double anguish. She had long been accustomed to take her troubles to Ignatius; and troubles of this kind, too, could be told to the good and inexhaustibly patient Master Ignatius. The above reply had not yet come into her hands before two more letters of hers had been despatched to Rome. They have not been preserved, but from the prompt answer which Ignatius gave them we can guess at their contents: they concerned the great conflict of conscience involved in the choice between inclination and duty, between the love of the heart and the obedience of a daughter. Evidently Isabel still hankered after that Spanish marriage of which her mother had already written to Ignatius; but according to the custom of Spain her father, quite inexorable in such matters, had already made his choice. Isabel's marriage, he intended, should strengthen the Sicilian connections of the family; and she was thus faced with two possible suitors, the Marquis of Gerace and the

Count of Luna. There was, however, a third possibility, and it is not surprising that Isabel, in her grief for the loss of her mother and brother, thought of that too. Should she not enter a convent? Her father was quite opposed to such a solution – he knew Isabel too well; but she was in such a state of depression that she seriously thought of forsaking the world and taking the veil. It was this no doubt that even the young scholastic Benedetto Palmio noticed, when he wrote about this time in 1551 to Ignatius: "Doña Isabel shows so many signs of unusual piety that in this she wholly resembles her mother. She often gives me subjects for sermons. And what subjects? Indeed, my father, only things which lie close to the hearts of men of perfection: contempt of the world, self-denial, the Cross, death, love of God, humility. From this I conclude that she is hiding some secret within her, which will come to light in due season".[71]

Ignatius saw clearly from her letters that in Isabel's mind everything was now at stake, her whole life's happiness. Therefore, in his reply he referred with almost fatherly tenderness to the special affection which he had always felt towards Isabel. His letter was despatched on March 7th, 1551, together with some information, apparently to do with her charitable works, which he had collected for her in Rome and which has been lost; and we see from these lines that Ignatius was already seeking a solution to the problem based upon Isabel's submission to her father's will.

May the sovereign grace and eternal love of Christ our Lord be with you and visit you, with his best gifts and spiritual graces.

A letter from you to which I replied a few days ago was followed afterwards by two of the same tenor, from which I see the very praiseworthy care and solicitude that you exercise in matters touching the discharge of conscience. May God our Lord preserve and increase in you his holy love, from which diligence in striving after the things which are to his service, proceeds.

As soon as I received your first letter, I immediately sought the information for which you asked me. Herewith the result. I have prayed over the important matters which you have entrusted to me, asking me to pray to God our Lord to direct them as may be most for his glory and the greater satisfaction of Señor Juan de Vega and yourself. The affectionate care I have always had and shall always have for you is unfaltering, quite apart from any other considerations, such as the fact that this care is my duty and that I find in myself a very special love for serving you in our Lord.

461

In regard to these important questions, may your Ladyship preserve the good and holy disposition which I have always known you to have, that of saintly indifference to what God our Lord shall ordain. May his divine love and Providence rule and direct your affairs better than we know how to ask or desire. Thus may it please God's sovereign goodness and may he give us all his abundant grace, so that we may always know his most holy will and fulfil it perfectly.

Ignatius

Rome, March 7th, 1551

To Isabel de Vega

The original of the above letter is to-day at Villarejo de Fuentes in Spain, and we can still read the somewhat damaged superscription which says: "To my Lady in our Lord, Doña Isabel at Trapani." The letter reached her there while she was occupied with the house of St. Martha.

It was apparently a long time before the hesitant Isabel could force herself to make a decision. Things did not really begin to move until June 1552, when the energetic Father Nadal came to Messina and took the question of Doña Isabel's marriage into his own hands. Now the matter proceeded according to Ignatius' wishes. First the possible religious vocation of the young lady had to be tested. For this, Nadal appointed one of the most remarkable of his fellow-Jesuits, the Fleming Cornelius Wischaven, an enthusiastic defender of the religious state. Isabel could not refrain from laughing at Nadal's proposal; but she entered into the spirit of this pious game. One summer's day in 1552, there was a meeting with Fathers Nadal and Wischaven at which she had to defend herself in a battle of words lasting three hours against all attempts to make the religious life attractive to her. Isabel won all along the line. Cornelius Wischaven endeavoured to represent this spiritual contest in a literary essay in the form of a conversation between the royal maiden Basilissa, the angel Felicianus and the worldly devil Cosmus. Fortunately the work remained unfinished.

Isabel, however, once again faced with the choice of suitors, now became seriously ill, and Ignatius read with anxiety the news coming from Nadal. A letter to Isabel was quite unequivocal. We possess, it is true, only the decisive fragment preserved in the unpublished life of Cornelius Wischaven: "Your Grace having decided, as your letter states, to marry, I advise you to be obedient in this matter to the will of your father the Viceroy." Triumphantly Isabel showed this letter to Father Cornelius, who still wished to entice her into a convent.

Now she had to obey. It is a great pity that we no longer have the exact words of the letter in which Ignatius induced Isabel to give her hand to the suitor preferred by her father. [72]

Nadal, who was sent to Sicily early in the summer, was the bearer of this important letter of comfort and advice, as well as a communication obtained by Ignatius from the Pope for the Viceroy, to reassure his conscience about the use of the so-called *Monarchia Sicula*. The chronicle of the Society reports as follows:

"On June 10th [1552], Nadal arrived in Messina. The Viceroy felt the greatest joy when Nadal informed him of the contents of the message about the *Monarchia Sicula*. The permission to celebrate the jubilee, which had been granted by the Holy Father, also caused the Viceroy great satisfaction. Doña Isabel, on the other hand, was at this time in the deepest spiritual distress, and was so to speak without any human assistance. Then the letter which Father Ignatius sent her called her back to life again, for it concerned her marriage. Her heart was strongly disinclined towards a marriage in Sicily; in particular her disinclination was towards the Count of Luna and the Marquis of Gerace, but her father intended to give her as wife to the former. Through Father Ignatius' letter, however, she was so strengthened inwardly and moved to obedience towards her father, that, being much comforted and filled with spiritual peace, she decided to accept as suitor him to whom her father intended to give her. And so she married the Counts of Luna The latter then together with Doña Isabel expressed his thank to Father. Ignatius, and the Count offered him every assistance." [73]

The affair did not end as simply as is here described. There were apparently all kinds of difficulties, even just before the wedding, and Isabel must have applied once again to Ignatius; but by now even his patience was exhausted, and through his secretary Polanco a somewhat laconic message was sent to Nadal, for transmission to Doña Isabel: "It would seem to be acting improperly towards her father, if I wrote again to Doña Isabel." This was on August 20th, 1552. Now the ever-hesitating Isabel obeyed the advice of her friend in Rome and at once all became easy and simple. Isabel married her count, and in mid-September, 1552, the splendid wedding took place at Messina.

Pedro de Luna was, as Nadal reported to Ignatius, "one of the first lords of the Sicilian kingdom", with rich estates at Bivona and Caltabelotta in the centre of the island. Isabel was happy, and she celebrated the day of her wedding in the spirit of her late mother and their common father, Ignatius. Father Antony Vinck knew with what news about the wedding he could give Ignatius special pleasure, and so he wrote on September 20th, 1552: "I believe Your Paternity knows already that Doña Isabel, the daughter of the Viceroy, has lately been married to the Count of Luna. On the occasion of the wedding there was, at Father Nadal's instigation, no poor person that did not experience several days' happiness. So much was distributed in alms, that not only on the wedding day itself did all the poor receive abundantly, but for nearly two weeks each one got as much as he needed."

The bride's father, too, was more than delighted, and he knew well what support for him and his paternal authority Ignatius' letter had brought. The men's little conspiracy had succeeded so well that the Viceroy wrote the following testimony to the efficacy of that letter: "What Your Paternity wrote to my daughter came so opportunely and was so full of the grace of the Holy Ghost, that matters were soon quickly settled, and she is to-day already married, as Your Paternity will no doubt have heard. She is now highly content, and there are indeed reasons enough why she should be so. For all we must thank God our Lord, for it is he who has so arranged everything." Ignatius sent an official letter of congratulation to the young couple on October 8th, 1552. [74]

From that time on, good news arrived regularly at Ignatius' curia from Sicily concerning the matrimonial happiness of the Countess of Luna. Father Paolo d'Achille especially could not say enough in praise of the virtuous Isabel. On the first Sunday of each month, he reported to Ignatius, Father Nadal preached in Sant' Antonio at Palermo to the ladies of the nobility, and the Countess was always at their head. Isabel helped him to obtain better food for the prisoners, medicines and proper doctors for the hospitals.

Then Father Doménech, who was so dear to her, was recalled by Ignatius, who wished to appoint him Provincial in Sicily and wanted to test him thoroughly first. On February 4th, 1553, Doménech arrived in Rome, and in his baggage was a letter from the Countess Isabel to Ignatius. It evidently radiated nothing but happiness and satisfaction, for when Doménech got back to Messina again on March 12th, 1553, he carried with him an answer from the delighted Ignatius, who took a sincere interest in the matrimonial happiness of the young wife. The usually so laconic Ignatius did not hesitate to admit in this letter that he had Isabel written deep in his heart, now and for ever. Carefully and with due knowledge of courtly etiquette he now altered the form of address to the married Countess, who was no longer entitled "Your Ladyship" but "Your Excellency". [75]

DONA LEONOR MASCARENHAS

see page 433

DRAFT OF A LETTER FROM ST. IGNATIUS
TO DONA LEONOR DE VEGA OSORIO
see page 445-446

My Lady in our Lord.

The sovereign grace and eternal love of Christ our Lord be always with Your Excellency, with his highest gifts and spiritual graces.

I received the letter that Master Jerónimo Doménech brought from Your Excellency and I have understood what you instructed him to tell me by word of mouth.

Although I am using him as a living letter to reply to you about many things, I want to say now that I shall send Father Doménech back as quickly as possible and in such good company that I shall thereby satisfy the wishes of Señor Juan de Vega and also of Your Excellency, whom I have and always shall have so deeply written in my soul that there is nothing that might be of service and the least consolation to Your Excellency, that I should not wish or could fail to do in the measure of my poor capacities.

For the company in married life that God our Lord has given to Your Excellency, and for the satisfaction and fruit that will follow from it, we ought all to give deep thanks to the Author of all good. May it please him to give us his most holy blessing and preserve and increase his holy grace in Your Excellencies, and in all your household and estate, so that in all things his holy name may be more greatly served and glorified.

During the last few days I wrote to the Count and now I beg Your Excellency to take this letter for yourself.

Relying on Master Jerónimo for the rest, I shall say no more, except that I pray God our Lord to deign to give us all his abundant grace, so that we may always know his most holy will and fulfil it perfectly.

> Your Excellency's most humble servant in our Lord,
> Ignatius

Rome, March 4th, 1553

To the Countess of Luna

Ignatius meanwhile could not, in his government of the Society, consider merely the spiritual life of the Countess of Luna. He had to recall from Sicily Father Nadal, whose sermons Isabel liked so much. As early as January 1553 Nadal had written to Ignatius: "It is a glory to God and a real consolation to see with what deep interest Juan de Vega follows everything that concerns the Society of Jesus." Now came like a thunderbolt Nadal's recall to Rome. He was to go to Spain and Portugal to promulgate the completed Constitutions of the Society; that was more important than preaching to ladies in Palermo. From Nadal's answer to Ignatius we can see that the Viceroy agreed, "as if", he added, "he had taken the Society's vow of obedience". It was otherwise with the self-willed Doña Isabel. The Countess was sulking. Her note to Ignatius, which Nadal took with him on his departure, has been preserved.[76]

Very Reverend Señor,

Father Master Nadal leaves us in so much loneliness, and me particularly, that if I did not remember that it is a thing that you have commanded, you whom we must all obey, I do not know how I should be able to bear it. I have discussed matters with his Reverence and, relying on him, I will not say more, except that I beg you to remember the Count and myself in your prayers.

Your servant kisses Your Reverence's hands. May our Lord guard your very reverend person.

At Your Reverence's service,
Doña Isabel de Vega y de Luna
Palermo, March 11th, 1553

At Easter 1553 Father Doménech was at Bivona, the residence of the noble pair, about forty miles south of Palermo. There he heard the confessions of Isabel and her ladies, and a report was duly sent to Ignatius. Doña Isabel was happy in the expectation of a child; she intended with Father Doménech's help soon to draw up a will, and she earnestly requested Father Ignatius to pray for her safe delivery.[77]

There was, however, something else which occupied the indefatigable Countess Isabel. A year before she and her husband had already asked Ignatius to send two fathers to minister to the people on the Count's extensive estates at Bivona. The chronicle of the Society describes their pagan and strangely savage customs in a few pages that are of great interest for their bearing on the history of civilization. Now the project was being enlarged. Isabel eagerly desired to establish a college of the Society at Bivona with a well-appointed school. The Countess had evidently approached Ignatius in order to get things moving, and with an eye to the practical had offered all that was necessary, for on August 21st, 1553, Ignatius was able to write to Nadal in Spain: "We have received the offer of the foundation of a college at Bivona, and we can no longer withstand the insistence of Doña Isabel.

She is giving a suitable house, bread, meat and everything else necessary for the support of ten or twelve persons, as well as a hundred *scudi* for clothes, not to mention beds and the rest; and the Countess will pay for all this – indeed, she seems prepared to give even more."

Countess Isabel had in the meantime given birth to a daughter. Scarcely had she recovered than, with the help of the equally enthusiastic Father Doménech, she threw herself once more into the plan for a college.[78] Her demands to Ignatius became more and more insistent; and in this connection the General, who seems after all to have somewhat lost his patience, sent Doménech through Polanco one of those reprimands, administering a sound rebuke, which the members of the Society dreaded so much – in this case because Doménech had not calmed down the enthusiasm of Doña Isabel. From all over the world requests and petitions for priests, professors, teachers and missionaries were reaching Ignatius. Was Bivona in darkest Sicily, of all places, to be the most important? Yet he could refuse nothing to the irrepressible Isabel.

In May 1554 the foundation stone of the new college at Bivona was laid, "in a charming spot", as Ignatius joyfully announced to Alcalá. Isabel was afire with enthusiasm, quite her mother's daughter, and Ignatius secretly delighted in her zeal. "Just as others seek to create an entail, I will make it my business henceforth to place this college on a secure financial basis", she said one day. This indeed caused the Viceroy to frown, for his son-in-law had considerable debts. Moreover, the Count of Luna had in the same year 1554 been made a duke by Charles V, expressly "as a mark of favour to his consort "– more precisely, as a manifestation of imperial gratitude towards the ever loyal Viceroy. This involved higher expenses and a truly luxurious way of living. But Isabel only said: "Then I will pay for the foundation of the college out of my own fortune"; and so it was done. The following letter from Isabel to Ignatius dates from the early days of the Bivona project. In it she at the same time announces the birth of her daughter.[79]

Very reverend Señor,

Many times would I write to you, for the consolation it is to me to see a letter from you in reply, if it did not seem to me that, with the many occupations you must have, this would be to give you trouble. This, however, I do beg of Your Reverence, that when there is an opportunity you will always keep me informed about your well-being.

With the confidence Master Jerónimo Doménech has given me as to

467

the favour Your Reverence will do us namely, that some of the Society will come here, the Count, my husband, and I have decided to erect a college in Bivona, as Master Jerónimo will write and explain to Your Reverence at greater length. I think as great service will thus be done to our Lord in Bivona as in any other part of this kingdom, since the people here are very lacking in instruction. Since I have the confidence I have mentioned, I shall say no more of this, except that, although I have always been content that God has given me a husband like the Count, my lord, now I am very much more so, to think that out of his wealth he is to do so much good as to erect a house of the Society.

Your Reverence will already know how our Lord was pleased to give me a daughter. I beg you to give her your blessing from where you are, and to remember in your prayers the Count, my husband, and myself, for truly we consider ourselves as much part of the Society as those who are members of it. Thus in every possible way we can serve it, it is for us a matter of duty and also a very great blessing.

May our Lord guard your very reverend person as you desire.

At Your Reverence's service,
Doña Isabel de Vega y de Luna

To the most reverend Señor, Master Ignatius of Loyola, General of the holy Society of Jesus.

Ignatius had meanwhile decided, in spite of all other demands, to send the required number of Jesuits to Bivona. He could not after all risk offending the influential family of the Viceroy, he was too fond of Isabel; and besides, her brothers Álvaro (who had called himself Hernando since his elder brother's death) and Suero were occupied in establishing colleges for the Jesuits in Catania and Syracuse. About a year later Ignatius, in a letter to the Viceroy, sang the praises of this family which had been of decisive importance for the young Society:

"For I know the great charity which has been given by the most High and Divine Goodness to Your Excellency and your whole illustrious house, to the profit of so many good works; and I know, too, how well disposed you are towards our Society as being something which is wholly attached to you. And of the same disposition are not only the Lady Duchess of Luna but also your sons Hernando and Suero de Vega, as I see proved by their actions".

So Ignatius answered Isabel's letter by return, in spite of his sickness.[80]

My Lady in our Lord.

May the sovereign grace and eternal love of Christ our Lord be with Your Excellency, with his most holy gifts and spiritual graces.

Although I do not write to Your Excellency frequently, on account of my little health and because I do not judge it to be necessary, I do not doubt that you are certain that each day I shall remember Your Excellency in my meeting with God, since neither my duty nor the affection which God our Lord has given me for Your Excellency's service, to the honour and glory of his divine Majesty, would allow of anything else.

The devotion which I see Your Excellency has to establishing a college in Bivona is not a new thing to me, for I know that, like Señor de Vega and Doña Leonor of holy memory, Your Excellency also considers our whole Society as yours in our Lord, as, indeed, it is. Thus we could not fail to have a special desire for the erection of this college in Bivona, since it is so particularly the affair of the Count and Your Excellency. And although I shall entrust the matter to the care of Father Master Jerónimo, I shall not fail to exercise due care myself that the work proceed in a way that is fitting and wholly satisfactory.

I had already known of and given thanks to God for the firstfruits that have been given to Your Excellencies.

May it please God's infinite goodness to give you his blessing, which is always accompanied with his graces and spiritual gifts, and may he give it to us all, that we may always know his most holy will and perfectly fulfil it.

Ignatius

Rome, November 5th, 1553

To the Countess of Luna

For nearly two years work continued on the building of the college at Bivona under Duchess Isabel's directions. Its progress was observed as joyfully and as carefully in Ignatius' office as was the promotion of the noble couple, and Polanco writes of the zeal of the "former Countess, now Duchess of Luna". On Easter Day 1554 the Lady of Bivona gave the whole Jesuit community at Palermo a magnificent banquet. Father Nadal, who had meanwhile returned to Sicily, told all his fellow-religious (as we know from a still unpublished instruction) to pray specially for the following persons: for Ignatius, for King Philip II, for the Viceroy, and for Duchess Isabel. Occasionally the pious lady could be a nuisance even to her Father Ignatius, as when she once asked for "a specially good confessor", who was to be appointed for the purpose from Rome. The answer to Father Domén-ech, through Polanco, was very brief: the "best fathers" were then busy attending the Council of Trent and therefore could not go to Bivona.

This did not affect the good relations of Isabel with the Jesuits, however, and Father Nadal was delighted with the charming situation of the new college, which Doña Isabel was furnishing. It lay in the most beautiful spot in Sicily; in the middle of the garden was a fountain, the cool waters of which could be led into the refectory. The building could almost be called magnificent, and the zealous Duchess was busy all day with the interior arrangements and the clothing of the fathers who were soon to arrive. For the kitchen and the dining-room she had procured utensils of English pewter. "Even if I have to sell all my jewels", she said, "the college must be established!"[81]

At this period of friendly relations between the Luna family and the General of the Jesuits, a painful event occurred which might have seriously disturbed them. A cousin of Duke Pedro named Hasdrubal de Luna had entered the Society at Palermo in the summer of 1550. For a time all went well; but when the restless Hasdrubal was due to begin his studies in the college of Monreale his enthusiasm evaporated, and he literally ran away. The Duchess was indignant at this scandal, and her persuasions at length induced the fugitive to return; indeed, at her express wish the young Jesuit was now sent to Rome, for Isabel wanted to place him under the discipline of Father Ignatius. On February 7th he arrived in Rome, bringing with him a letter from the Duchess. Ignatius at once changed the wild Sicilian's somewhat exotic name of Hasdrubal into a pious John and sent him after a period of trial to the Roman College, where he was to continue his studies. Ignatius, a shrewd judge of men, had been sceptical from the beginning, and subsequent developments proved him right. In the college Hasdrubal met other young Sicilians, five in number, and his improvement was short-lived. Ignatius continued to look on with angelic patience – after all, this was a cousin of the Duchess of Bivona. Then the good lady sent her usual gifts from Sicily for Lent 1555, this time cheese, honey and semolina. Ignatius thanked her heartily and took the opportunity to add some news about Hasdrubal.[82]

JESUS

My Lady in our Lord.
The sovereign grace etc.

Although I write but seldom, on account of the little opportunity my infirmities give me, and because there has been nothing that required much attention, Your Excellency already knows that God our Lord has inscribed the memory of you upon my soul in the fairest hand, with the desire that his holy love and grace may always be preserved and may increase in Your Excellency, to his glory.

Now the gift and alms Your Excellencies have given to this house have given me occasion to write this present letter to Your Excellency. This is no new thing for the Duke and Your Excellency, neither are the charity and special love towards us whence the gift proceeds, and which are valued much more than all the rest, new. May he who is charity and perfect love reward what he has inspired Your Excellency to do, according to his infinite and supreme goodness. I beg the most illustrious Duke to take this letter as written to him, too, and that you will both consider all of us as wholly yours, as we are in our Lord.

Recently I replied to a letter which Don Hasdrubal, whose name has been changed into John, brought me from Your Excellency. Now that he has spent some time in the house here, with very great edification to us all, we have sent him to the college to pursue his studies. Your Excellency takes a very great interest in him, and since there could be no better recommendation, I hope that his good behaviour will justify this trust, with the help and favour of God, our Lord and the Author of all good. May it please him to give us his abundant grace, so that we may always know his most holy will and perfectly fulfil it.

Ignatius

Rome, March 26th, 1555

To the Duchess of Bivona

One can sense from this letter how Ignatius beneath all the polite phrases was foretelling what was to come. It was as in the affair of Teotonio de Braganza, which was going on at the same time. In May Father Salmerón wrote Hasdrubal a friendly letter, exhorting him to be faithful to his vocation; but it was already too late. On June 2nd, 1555, Ignatius had to tell Duke Pedro that Hasdrubal wanted to get back to Sicily at all costs. So five Sicilians, discharged from the Society, travelled southwards via Gaeta. They were royally entertained at Naples by Donna Cesare, of whom we have already heard, and who was furious with Ignatius. On Hasdrubal's arrival at Messina there were distressing goings-on, until the turbulent young man again disappeared. On New Year's Day 1582, Hasdrubal was murdered in Palermo[83]; but Isabel did not live to see that.

Once more the pious insistence of Leonor de Osorio's daughter was to cause Ignatius embarrassment by a similar request to admit a candidate, such as she had made in the cases of young Hernando de Vega and Hasdrubal de Luna. Close to the person of the Viceroy was an official named Don Juan Osorio de Silva, a near kinsman of his late wife. This gentleman was captain of the guard to the Viceroy and later royal *Conservador* in Sicily and the Viceroy's agent at the imperial court – an important person, therefore, who had besides supported the colleges at Messina and Palermo and to whom in that connection Ignatius had written a letter of thanks. Don Juan Osorio de Silva had a nephew called César Ramírez, aged thirteen. The duchess, in her not always enlightened piety, wished to make of her small kinsman a great Jesuit; and as Father Doménech considered the boy too young to be admitted to the noviciate, Doña Isabel again applied direct to Ignatius on March 14th, 1555, expecting in her aristocratic way that he would accede to her request.[84]

Just at that time the Pope had died, Ethiopia was being opened up, and Ignatius was dictating his memoirs. Now the duchess came importuning him with her pious wishes – *pia quadam impudentia*, St. Augustine would have said of her. Ignatius' reply is a gem of diplomatic seriousness, developing, distinguishing and finally courteously deciding the question.

JESUS

My Lady in our Lord.

The sovereign grace and eternal love of Christ our Lord be with Your Excellency, with his most holy gifts and spiritual graces.

Recently, after having written to Your Excellency, I received a letter from you of the fourteenth of last month, in which you indicate that you would be pleased if César Ramírez, nephew of the Captain of the Guard to Señor Juan de Vega, could be received into our Society – which is wholly yours in our Lord – despite the fact that Master Jerónimo was unwilling, since Ramírez is not of sufficiently mature age.

Our opinion about this is that since we are certain that Your Excellency's charity is well-ordered, you will look more to the universal than to the particular good, and thus be content that we observe our Constitutions, which do not allow boys below the age of fourteen to be received. On account, however, of the much we owe Your Excellency in our Lord, we have thought out what can be done in this case without prejudice to our Constitutions – namely, that the said César should be received in our house for one year, not as admitted to the Society but on probation. By this means he will make trial of our institute and the Society of his behaviour. When the year is over, we shall both be free, he to go away

472

or remain and we to receive him or otherwise. I am, therefore, writing to Master Jerónimo to receive him on this condition and that he should arrange for him to be treated and governed in all other respects like any of the other young men already incorporated in the Society. In other details I stand by what I wrote to Master Jerónimo.

With this I conclude, recommending myself to Your Excellency's favour and that of the Duke, whose most illustrious persons may Christ guard and prosper in his holy service. May he deign to grant us all his abundant grace to know and fulfil his most holy will.

Ignatius

Rome, April 25th, 1555

To the Countess of Luna

Another letter was sent on the same day, April 25th, 1555, to Father Doménech, settling the details of young César's provisional admittance. There was nothing that could disturb Ignatius' unruffled calm; and if he should be the patron saint of anything, it should be that of Christian patience in the thousand little – and for that very reason great – trifles of daily life. We do not know what became of César Ramírez; in any case he did not stay with the Jesuits, and so the pious duchess had no luck with this candidate either.[85]

The progress of the college building at Bivona was therefore all the more a source of joy to her, and her married happiness was unclouded. In 1554 she bore a second daughter, which among the Sicilians indeed was not considered a good omen; but Isabel was pleased, since she had the spiritual assistance of Father Nadal during her confinement. In November 1556 a son was born to her. All the time, Ignatius received good news from Isabel. The duchess went to every Jesuit sermon at Messina when she was there and she went publicly to confession with her ladies – previously she had confessed only in her private chapel. She was a real heroine, prevented neither by bad weather nor by sickness from attending Lenten sermons. Once, in the greatest agitation, she caused a whole flotilla to search for Father Doménech when he was missing after a shipwreck. She was already planning another college on her estates at Caltabelotta. To celebrate the return of England to the Catholic faith when Prince Philip married Queen Mary, Isabel led the ladies of the nobility to confession, in order to gain the papal indulgence. She had a newly baptized Moor among her servants. In short, an abundance of news, and Ignatius could be satisfied with his spiritual daughter. His secretary Polanco praised her in his report on the state of the

473

Society at the beginning of 1555, written for the information of all members, in which he also noted the Emperor Charles V's lack of interest in it:

"The Emperor indeed has taken no special notice of this Society, but he did nevertheless show favour to the colleges in Sicily when he was asked to do so; and it was Señor Juan de Vega, Viceroy of that realm, who asked him. The foundation of the colleges in Sicily is due to this gentleman's favour and truly Christian zeal to help the kingdom – his and that of his children who have imitated him in this, most especially the Lady Duchess of Bivona and Don Suero de Vega."

It seemed as though the whole Vega family with its ramifications now belonged to Ignatius' Society. The duchess could therefore always turn to her spiritual comforter whenever family cares oppressed her. In the summer of 1555 a cousin of hers on her mother's side, Don Hernando de Silva, died a sudden death in the prime of his manhood. Evidently Isabel was always greatly frightened by death, and at once she was filled with religious anxiety. At the same time her dearly loved uncle, Don Hernando de Vega, was preparing to follow the call to a political career at the court of Philip II in Brussels. Isabel's letter prompted by these manifold worries was the last that she sent to Ignatius.[86]

Very reverend Señor,

Not to give Your Paternity trouble in replying to my letters, I do not write often, though God knows the consolation it is to me when I see a letter from Your Reverence.

Recently a first cousin of mine has died here, very young and very much of the world, and the death was so sudden that he had no time to make his confession – a Father had to be sent for in haste, for he asked to make his confession, but when the priest arrived he had already expired. His death, being so sudden, has caused me much grief. Thus I wanted to tell Your Paternity, so that you might be good enough to commend his soul to God and instruct those in the house to do the same and to arrange for some Masses to be said at privileged altars. Since this is a work of great charity, I am certain that Your Paternity will do me this favour and thus I shall say no more of this.

The Duke kisses Your Paternity's hands and is as devoted to the Society as I am. We are all well and in our affairs everything is going prosperously, thanks be to God. I take it as very certain that this and the daily increasing contentment I have with the Duke's person is due to your prayers and those of the Society; thus I beg Your Paternity to ask our Lord to preserve this in me and to guard the Duke my lord, and to give us both his grace that we may serve him more. Although I know it is unnecessary to remind you of it, I ask Your Paternity to be kind enough to remember Juan de Vega, my lord – for it gives me pain to see him with such little health – and his affairs. Señor Hernando de Vega, brother of Juan de Vega, my lord, I love much and I owe him a great deal; it does not seem to me that I can repay him in any way, except by begging Your Paternity to commend him to God and to get those in the house to do so, especially now that he has certain business of importance. Among other things he has to choose a state of life, which is what it is so important not to make a mistake about. He is very devoted to the Society, for when he was here in Sicily, he knew the Fathers well.

The building of the college of Bivona is making good progress. I think it will be a very fine house, and that our Lord will be greatly served by the Fathers who will come there. I say no more, because Father Master Jerónimo has charge of everything. He has told me how good Your Paternity is in devoting yourself to this house. I merely entreat Your Reverence that among the Fathers there may be a preacher who is pleasing to the people.

Of myself I would have Your Paternity know that each day I am more of a sinner and have less feeling for the things of God, so that, since I know the great benefits that he confers on me in particular, I am filled with confusion; and although I know that it will be an added burden for Your Paternity, I wanted to tell you this so that you would commend me to God.

I beg Your Paternity to greet Father Master Nadal and Master Laynez for me; they have told me that Juan de Vega, my lord, and the city of Messina have asked Your Paternity for Father Master Laynez to come here this Lent. I desire this most earnestly.

May our Lord guard Your Paternity and give you much health.

Your Paternity's servant,
Doña Isabel de Vega y Luna

Polizzo, August 10th, 1555

To the most reverend Señor, Master Ignatius of Loyola, general of the holy Society of Jesus in Rome.

The reply followed as quickly as the increasing sickness of the exhausted Ignatius permitted. In Rome, rumours were circulating that the Sicilian Viceroy was soon to be recalled. There was some ground for them; for at this time the Emperor Charles, his great patron, abdicated, and Juan de Vega was not in favour with Philip II, as we know from the diplomatic reports of the Venetian ambassador. A lawsuit which Doña Isabel's husband was fighting in the royal courts distressed her very much and made the Viceroy think of retirement; he was attracted by the Emperor's example to a life of solitude and contemplative repose. He wanted to go home to Spain, and Father Doménech was to accompany the body of the ever-remembered Doña Leonor to Grajal.

All this meant parting and sorrow for Isabel. One comfort only remained to her: "God knows the consolation it is to me when I see a letter from Your Reverence." Thus she received the last letter she was to have from her dear Father Ignatius, who had something important and infinitely kind to say in answer to all her questions.[87]

IHS

My Lady in our Lord.

The sovereign grace and eternal love of Christ our Lord be with your Excellency, with his most holy gifts and spiritual graces.

Your Excellency's letter of 10th August I received somewhat late, and, since my health has not been good, I have delayed even more in sending a letter in reply, although not in what Your Excellency recommends to me – prayers and Masses for the soul of Señor Don Hernando de Silva, whom may God have in his glory. Although death did not give him the opportunity of the help of the most holy Sacraments, we must hope in divine Providence who will have supplied the efficacy of them from the depths of his infinite mercy, from which comes the whole power of the sacraments and the other means of spiritual health for us. Moreover, besides the fact that I know he went to confession in Genoa on his way through, generally to Master Laynez, the desiring and asking eagerly for confession is a sign of the interior contrition which God our Lord gives to those towards whom he wills to use his mercy.

Again, the remembrance which Your Excellency bids me have of the Lord Duke and his affairs is so much a duty that it would be a great fault if I were to neglect it. May it please him who is the Author of all good to communicate himself to you both with most abundant grace, as I desire and entreat God.

Of Señor Juan de Vega and his well-being, not only ought our Society to take much count because he has been such a father and lord to all of us, but very specially because it is so important for the general good and for the glory of God in which he has used his gifts for so many years now so zealously and with such remarkable fruit. And if what is rumoured in Rome now should come to pass, namely that his transfer is imminent, so much the more shall we all have to persevere in commending his well-being to him who is the true health of all men. May his infinite wisdom also deign to direct Señor Hernando de Vega in the very important decision of which Your Excellency writes and that is what we shall pray for in this house.

As to the college of Bivona, what Master Jerónimo Doménech tells us of it shows clearly the devotion and charity with which it has been erected and through this I hope in God our Lord that he will be served much by it. As to the Fathers beginning there some exercise such as is usually practised in our colleges, Master Jerónimo knows that all that is possible is being done, although not all that we should desire if we had greater strength. May God our Lord increase our strength in his holy service, and it will soon be seen from the effects that all of us have the appreciation due to a work begun with so much charity and continued for God's service.

Of other things, relying on Master Jerónimo, I need not write, only asking God our Lord that he will continually increase in Your Excellency, with a growth in purity and abundant communication of his light and love, the despising of self and esteem of the benefits of the divine goodness and generosity. May it please God to give us all his grace always to know his most holy will and perfectly fulfil it.

Rome, October 28th, 1555   Ignatius

A word about the end of this lifelong friendship. The darkness of death fell upon this bright and charmingly human part of the earthly pilgrimage of Ignatius and of Isabel, whom he loved like a daughter. The Master himself was the first to enter eternity. When at the beginning of August 1556 the news of his death reached the Viceroy and the Duchess, their grief was as great as their love for Ignatius had been.

"The news of Father Ignatius' death caused the Viceroy and his daughter the deepest sorrow. But when the letter arrived that brought more exact information about the manner of his death, the Duchess and the Viceroy experienced great consolation in the midst of their tears. How the Viceroy thought of Ignatius he expressed in his letter of condolence to Father Laynez in the restrained language of an officer. The Duchess told Father Laynez that she was wholly and entirely devoted to the Society of Jesus and dedicat-

477

ed in obedience to it." Thus the chronicle of the Society. Laynez, who was to be Ignatius' successor, knew well enough how dear Isabel was to the great saint, and so he hastened to write on August 7th, 1556: "The whole Society of Jesus will always regard you as its mistress in our Lord, and every General in future will always imitate that readiness to serve the Lord Duke and Your Excellency which was shown by our blessed Father Ignatius."[88]

In the same month of August 1556 Juan de Vega was relieved of his post as Viceroy, and he spent a carefree period occupied with pious exercises at Trapani with his daughter and grandchildren. The son of his Isabel was his especial pride. He wrote all this to Master Laynez in Rome, where the fathers had assembled to elect a successor to Ignatius. Then he set out on his return to Spain. Father Doménech accompanied him and the coffin of Doña Leonor to Grajal, where Ignatius' friend in God rests among the relics which Pope Paul III once gave her in the happy Roman days, when she and Ignatius were together engaged in works of Christian charity.[89]

Alone of the family, Duchess Isabel remained in Sicily; for her brother Suero too now lived in Spain, where the distressing affair of the annulment of his marriage was soon to occupy the Jesuits and Doña Leonor Mascarenhas, who enjoyed sorting out such problems. In the year of Ignatius' death a beautiful church arose in Bivona, and classes could begin in the new college, to the great satisfaction of the Duchess. It was the last happiness of her life. On January 3rd, 1558, she died, while still young, of the consequences of a difficult childbirth. The rector of the college assisted at her deathbed, and in the Jesuit church founded by her at Bivona a beautiful monument was erected to her memory. Vestments were made from her rich dresses. In the same year her little son followed her in death, and on December 21st died her father, Juan de Vega, whom the king, as a last earthly consolation, had made president of the council of Castile.

Pedro de Ribadeneira, who had been so intimate with Ignatius, wrote from Brussels to Juan de Vega a long letter of condolence on the occasion of his daughter's death. He had in mind the feelings of inalterable friendship which Ignatius had shown towards this family. In the name of the Society he wrote: "Our hearts sincerely sympathize with you in your sorrow, for we too have lost in the Duchess a peerless lady and patroness of the whole Society of Jesus."[90]

EPILOGUE

In his memoirs, the dictation of which was completed in October 1555, Ignatius looked back to the "primitive church" of his life, Manresa, where the mysteries of God had been revealed to him. Of that time he said: "Even then many noble ladies had a great veneration for him." When his dead body lay in the church of Santa Maria della Strada on the morning of August 1st, 1556, it was especially the noble ladies of Rome (as is noted particularly in the documents) who hastened to show their love for their revered Master and spiritual director.

After the magnificent church of the Gesù had been erected over his tomb, not a day passed on which pious women did not pray there for the early beatification of their never-forgotten Master Ignatius. What happened in 1599 in the Gesù at Rome on the anniversary of Ignatius' death is as it were a beautiful symbol of this almost obstinate love. The Duchess of Sessa, wife of the Spanish ambassador to the Holy See, Don Antonio Fernández de Córdoba – of the same family as the Marchioness of Priego whom we already know – had in the excess of her veneration for Ignatius caused a silver lamp to be hung over his tomb. The General of the Society, Claudius Acquaviva, quietly had it removed. But on the eve of July 31st a servant came and brought a new lamp: the noble lady would not be put off even by the canonical prudence of the successor of her beloved Ignatius.

The solemn beatification of Ignatius of Loyola soon justified this veneration. In the process that preceded the ceremony, the evidence of women also played an important role. They were the successors of all his faithful friends with whom we have become acquainted through the saint's correspondence; it is as though the generations that came after wished to have a part in the deep gratitude which their mothers and grandmothers felt towards Ignatius. There were the nuns of Barcelona with their edifying stories, which were still being told in the convent after half a century. There were the grandchildren of the women of Manresa. The great ladies, too, were not missing. The daughter of the Duchess Giovanna Colonna, whose marriage had once caused Ignatius so much anxiety, appeared in Barcelona as a witness. She was Donna Girolama Colonna, wife of the Duke of Monteleone. Her daughter, Giovanna di Aragona e Pignatelli, Duchess of Terranova, was healed of a malignant cancer of the breast through the intercession of Father Ignatius.

479

It was all just as when Ignatius was on earth: in every care that can trouble a woman's heart, one could turn to the great and good heart of Ignatius. Nothing had changed since he entered into his glory.[91] The two intervening centuries of baroque art have surrounded the Saint of Loyola with magnificence and enlarged him to heroic stature, so that his humanity has become almost inaccessible to us. As far as an understanding of the subtleties of hagiographical psychology is concerned, it is significant to record that women retained a truer idea of the real nature of this great man. St. Ignatius remained until the beginning of the nineteenth century, among the common folk of Catholic lands, a patron of expectant mothers and women in childbirth. Having read these letters, we shall not regard this as strange or incomprehensible. True piety has a sense for the truth. Women forgot the human kindness of Ignatius less quickly than the men who wrote his biographies.

It is too, so to speak, another symbol of this feminine loyalty that it was often women who preserved for us the originals of Ignatius' letters. The original of the famous letter to Portugal on obedience was in the possession of a certain Doña Aloisia González de Echevarri. The Archduchess Isabel Clara Eugenia, Governor of the Netherlands, gave to the noviciate at Malines a letter that Ignatius had written to King Philip II. The letter in which Ignatius announced to his family at Loyola the news of his first Mass at St. Mary Major was given as a present to Countess Anna von Galen, wife of the Prussian ambassador at Madrid, who took it back reverently to her Westphalian home. In the convent of the Augustinian nuns at Frenegal de la Sierra in Spain, there hangs framed behind glass a letter of the General to Francis Borgia. The signature has been gilded by a pious hand.[92]

The correspondence of Ignatius with women of his time has indeed shown us that the picture of him as a man needs no gilding. It is luminous from within; for his heart was filled with the radiance of the humanity of Christ our Lord, who shone before him "like a great golden sun". His whole earthly life was a fulfilment of what the holy woman in Manresa once wished for him: "O that my Lord Jesus Christ may one day appear to you!" We have caught a reflection of this radiance in his letters.

NOTES

In the historical commentary on the Correspondence we have had two considerations in mind. Firstly, we have consulted the contemporary documents contained in the *Monumenta Historica Societatis Jesu* as fully as possible, in order to show how important for the study of the sixteenth century is this monumental collection, so little used by professional historians. Secondly, we have consulted other relevant sources and the historical literature on our period only in so far as seemed necessary for the explanation of the letters.

The seventy-five volumes of the collection *Monumenta Historica Societatis Jesu* that have appeared up till now are indicated by the following abbreviations:

MI	*Monumenta Ignatiana* in the following four series:
	MI I: *Epistolae et Instructiones S. Ignatii*, 12 vols. (Madrid, 1903–11). Letters and instructions of St. Ignatius.
	MI II: *Exercitia Spiritualia S. Ignatii eorumque Directoria*, 2 vols. (Madrid and Rome, 1919 and 1955). Spiritual Exercises.
	MI III: *Sancti Ignatii Constitutiones Societatis Jesu*, 4 vols. (Rome, 1934–8). Consitutions and rules of the Society of Jesus.
	MI IV: *Scripta de Sancto Ignatio*, 2 vols. (Madrid, 1904, 1918). Contemporary evidence about Ignatius and documents concerning his canonization.
FN	*Fontes Narrativi de Sancto Ignatio*, 2 vols. (Rome, 1943, 1951). New and enlarged critical edition of contemporary documents on Ignatius.
Chron.	*Chronicon Societatis Jesu auctore Joanne de Polanco*, 6 vols. (Madrid, 1894–8.) Early history of the Society.
Pol. Compl.	*Polanci Complementa*, 2 vols. (Madrid, 1916, 1917). Letters and notes of Fr. Juan de Polanco.
Mixt.	*Epistolae Mixtae ex variis Europae locis* (1537-56), 5 vols. (Madrid, 1898–1901). Mainly letters to Ignatius.
Quadr.	*Litterae Quadrimestres*, 7 vols. (Madrid and Rome, 1894–1932). Four-monthly reports of 1546–62 to the government of the Society in Rome.
Doc. Ind.	*Documenta Indica*, 3 vols. (Rome, 1948-55). Letters from India.
M. Bob.	*Monumenta Bobadillae*, 1 vol. (Madrid, 1913). Letters of Fr. Nicholas Bobadilla.
M. Borg.	*Monumenta Francisci Borgiae*, 5 vols. (Madrid, 1894–1911). Letters, diaries and instructions of Fr. Francis Borgia.

M. Broet	*Monumenta Broeti, Jaji, Codurii et Simonis Rodericii,* 1 vol. (Madrid, 1903). Letters and documents of Ignatius' first companions, Paschase Broët, Claude Jay, Jean Codure and Simon Rodríguez.
M. Fabr.	*Monumenta Fabri,* 1 vol. (Madrid, 1914). Letters and diaries of Peter Faber, Ignatius' early companion.
M. Lain.	*Monumenta Lainii,* 8 vols. (Madrid, 1912–17). Letters of Fr. Diego Laynez.
M. Nad.	*Monumenta Natalis,* 4 vols. (Madrid, 1898–1905). Letters and instructions of Fr. Jerónimo Nadal.
M. Rib.	*Monumenta Ribadeneirae,* 2 vols. (Madrid, 1920, 1923). Letters and notes of Fr. Pedro de Ribadeneira.
M. Salm.	*Monumenta Salmeronis,* 2 vols. (Madrid, 1906, 1907). Letters of Fr. Alonso Salmerón.
M. Xav.	*Monumenta Xaverii,* 2 vols. (Madrid, 1898, 1912). Letters of St. Francis Xavier.
Ep. Xav.	*Epistolae S. Francisci Xaverii aliaque ejus scripta,* 2 vols. (Rome, 1944–5). New and enlarged critical edition of the letters and other writings.

The principal constantly quoted documents on Ignatius and the early history of the Society are abbreviated as follows:

Astráin	A. Astráin, *Historia de la Compañia de Jesus en la Asistencia de España,* i and ii (Madrid, 1902, 1905).
Cartas	*Cartas de San Ignacio de Loyola,* 6 vols. (Madrid, 1874–89).
Creixell	J. Creixell, *San Ignacio de Loyola. Estudio crítico y documentado de los hechos ignacianos relacionados con Montserrat y Barcelona,* i (Barcelona, 1922).
Karrer	O. Karrer, *Der heilige Franz von Borja, General der Gesellschaft Jesu (1510–72),* (Freiburg, 1921).
Larrañaga	V. Larrañaga. *Obras completas de San Ignacio de Loyola,* i, *(Auto-biografía y Diario Espiritual),* (Madrid, 1947), *Biblioteca de Autores Cristianos,* 24.
Rodrigues	F. Rodrigues, *História da Companhia de Jesus na Asistência de Portugal,* i, 1 and i, 2 (Oporto, 1931).
Schurhammer	G. Schurhammer, *Franz Xaver, Sein Leben und seine Zeit.* 1 vol: *Europa 1506–41* (Freiburg, 1955).
Tacchi-Venturi	P. Tacchi-Venturi, *Storia della Compagnia di Gesù in Italia,* 2 vols. (New edition, Rome 1950–1).

General Introduction

[1] Letter to Peter Faber dated March 10th, 1542: *MI* I, i, 237.

[2] The earliest edition of a selection from the Correspondence (in a Latin translation) is: R. Menchaca, *Epistolae Sancti Ignatii Loyolae* (Bologna, 1804), 17 letters; second

edition (Bologna, 1837), 132 letters. More recent editions of selected letters are: C. Genelli, *Das Leben des hl. Ignatius von Loyola* (Innsbruck, 1848), Appendix pp. 423–519, sixty-nine letters in the original; M. Bouix, *Lettres de saint Ignace de Loyola* (Paris, 1870); A. Goodier and D. O'Leary, *Letters and Instructions of St. Ignatius Loyola* (London, 1914); O. Karrer, *Des heiligen Ignatius von Loyola Geistliche Briefe und Unterweisungen* (Freiburg, 1922); P. Bondioli, *Sant' Ignazio di Loyola, Lettere e Scritti scelti* (Milan, 1928); P. Dudon, *Saint Ignace de Loyola, Lettres spirituelles choisies* (Paris, 1933); J. Casanovas, *Cartas espirituals de San Ignasi de Loyola*, 2 vols. (Barcelona, 1936); I. Isern, *Cartas selectas de San Ignacio* (Buenos Aires, 1940); O. Karrer and H. Rahner, *Ignatius von Loyola, Geistliche Briefe* (Einsiedeln-Cologne, 1942) (new edition: Einsiedeln-Cologne, 1956); A. Macía, *Cartas espirituales de San Ignacio de Loyola* (Madrid, 1944); C. de Dalmases and I. Iparraguirre, *Obras completas de San Ignacio de Loyola (Biblioteca de Autores Cristianos 86), Cartas e Instrucciones* (Madrid, 1952), 631–957.

[3] Three letters which Ignatius received from women are found only in Menchaca (Bologna, 1837), two from Doña Juana Cardona and one from Margaret of Austria (pp. 316–21 and 503). Of letters written by Ignatius to women, thirteen are found in Menchaca, six in Genelli, ten in our edition of 1942, out of a total of seventy; in Iparraguirre's latest selection there are sixteen.

[4] *Obras completas, Cartas (Introducción)*, p. 633. Cf. B. Schneider, "Der weltliche Heilige. Ignatius von Loyola und die Fürsten seiner Zeit" in *Geist und Leben* xxvii (1954) 35–58.

[5] A. Huonder, *Ignatius von Loyola. Beiträge zu seinem Charakterbild* (Cologne, 1932), 296; P. de Leturia, *A propósito del 'Ignatius von Loyola' del P. Huonder: Arch. Hist. S.J.*, ii (1933), pp. 310–16.

[6] The following letters are in the *Regesta*: to Violante Gozzadini (*MI* I, ii, 725); to Guiomar Coutinho (ibid., 294); to Maria de Salinas (ibid., 355); to Leonor Osorio (ibid., 155 et seq., 371 et seq., 429, 526, 721); to Isabel Agustín (ibid., iii, 345); to Juana de Borja, Marchioness of Alcañices (ibid., 284); to María de Araujo (ibid., 173); to Elvira de Mendoza (ibid., 268); to Jacoba Pallavicino (ibid., 268); to Beatrice Rangoni (ibid., 626); to Isabel Roser (ibid., 161); to Duchess Pignatelli of Monteleone (ibid., iv, 607); to Demoiselle de l'Aigle or d'Acheville (ibid., iii, 139, 211); to Jacoba Pallavicino (ibid., v, 73, 140). A letter dated July 19th, 1556, to Martia Marramalda (ibid., xii, 147–9) has been preserved in its entirety, but on account of Ignatius' mortal sickness it was written wholly by Polanco. We therefore include it here. The same applies to the letter of January 22nd, 1556, to the mother of Fr. Juan de Vitoria (ibid., x, 542 et seq.), which was also written entirely by Polanco.

[7] A. Huonder, *Ignatius von Loyola*, 297.

[8] Testimony of Ribadeneira in *FN*, ii, 494. The expression "empty chatter" occurs in the canonization documents, *MI* iv, ii, 902. Testimony of Gonçalves in *FN*, i, 732. For Ignatius' imperfection of style see I. Iparraguirre, *Obras completas*, 633.

[9] For the correspondence of Michelangelo with Vittoria Colonna, see E. Ferrero and G. Müller, *Carteggio di Vittoria Colonna* (Turin, 1892) and A. von Reumont,

Vittoria Colonna (Freiburg, 1881), 164–77, 229 et seq.; also K. Pfister, *Vittoria Colonna. Werden und Gestalt der frühbarocken Welt* (Munich, 1950), 106–54. For Ignatius' relations with St. Philip Neri, see the introduction to chapter six, note 4. For the correspondence of St. Teresa, see *The Letters of St. Teresa,* trans. E. Allison Peers (London, 1951). We possess altogether 450 of the saint's letters, of which fourteen are to women in the world, mostly ladies of the Spanish aristocracy.

¹⁰ Polanco's correspondence with women: *Pol. Compl.,* i, 71–80, 42 et seq., 46–8, 402–5. Ribadeneira's correspondence with women: *M. Rib.,* i, 103–13, 243 et seq., 335 et seq., 721–3; ii, 204 et seq., 216–20, 221–4. Borgia's correspondence with women: *M. Borg.,* iii, 211 et seq., 296–8, 605 et seq. (to Queen Catherine of Portugal); ii, 552 (to the Infanta María of Spain); iv, 677, v, 99 et seq. (to Leonor Mascarenhas). The letters of Laynez to nearly all the ladies with whom Ignatius had already been in correspondence are strongly influenced in style by Polanco: *M. Lain.,* i, 41–8, 135–8 (to his mother); iii, 633 (to Queen Catherine); ii, 311 et seq. (to Queen María of Bohemia); iii, 416 (to Madama Margarita); ii, 259 et seq. (to Duchess Eleonora of Florence); i, 483 et seq., 642; ii, 600 et seq., iii, 335 et seq. (to Maria Frassoni del Gesso), i, 643 et seq., ii, 611 et seq. (to Margherita Gigli).

¹¹ For the character of Ignatius as revealed in his letters, see *Cartas,* i (Madrid, 1874), pp. ii et seq., xvi, xix, and V. Baesten, "St. Ignace d'après sa correspondance" in *Collection de précis historiques,* 24 (1875), 401 et seq.

¹² M. Mir, *Historia interna documentada de la Compañia de Jesus,* ii (Madrid, 1913), 172–202; P. von Hoensbroech, *Der Jesuitenorden. Eine Enzyklopädie,* i (Bern–Leipzig, 1926), 382–9; E. Gothein, *Ignatius von Loyola und das Zeitalter der Gegenreformation* (Halle, 1895), 304–9; L. Koch, *Jesuitenlexikon* (Paderborn, 1934), 602–5; A. Huonder, *Ignatius von Loyola,* 285–300; L. von Pastor, *History of the Popes* (English translation ed. by F. Antrobus and F. Kerr [London, 1891-1938], XII, ch. 1 & 2; R. Blunck *Der schwarze Papst. Das Leben des Ignatius von Loyola* (Berlin, 1937), 78–87, et seq., 273–5; H. Böhmer, *Ignatius von Loyola* ed. H. Leube (Stuttgart, 1941), 79 et seq. 82–90.

¹³ On the relations with women unmentioned by earlier hagiographers, see H. Böhmer, *Studien zur Geschichte der Gesellschaft Jesu,* i (Bonn, 1914), 316 et seq. Ribadeneira in his *Vita,* i, 14 (Cologne, 1602, 83–92), omits Ignatius' experiences as spiritual director of women in Alcalá. The reference to "affairs with women" is in *FN,* i, 154. For Ignatius' account of his vision of Our Lady, see *ibid.,* 374 et seq. Consult also G. Lomer, *Ignatius von Loyola. Vom Erotiker zum Heiligen. Eine pathographische Studie* (Leipzig, 1913).

¹⁴ Testimony of the first biographical sketch *(Epistola Lainii,* n. 13) in *FN,* i, 84. For the nickname "Iñigas" see *MI* iv, ii, 369; Astráin, i, 41, note 2; P. de Leturia, *Arch. Hist. S.J.,* x (1941), 28, note 44.

¹⁵ For "the nobility of Barcelona" see *MI* IV, ii, 89. For Sister Antonia see *ibid.,* 275, 334. There is a picture of the box, which was destroyed in the attack on the convent in 1909, in Creixell, i, 288. It bore the inscription in French, *Prenez en gré.* For the story of the beating see *MI* IV, ii, 77 et seq., 90 et seq., 275 et seq., 306 et seq.

¹⁶ *Beata:* a woman living under religious rule in her own house. – Trans.

[17] The documents of the trial in Alcalá are in *MI* IV, i, 598–622. For María del Vado see *FN*, i, 444; María de la Flor's confession, *MI*, IV, i, 613; hysteria of Mencia de Benavente *ibid.*, 617. Ignatius' account of Alcalá is in *FN*, i, 440 et seq. For Doña Teresa Enríquez de Cárdenas cf. Ignatius' account in *FN*, i, 446–7, note 25; Larrañaga, i, 270, note 32; C. Bayle, *La Loca del Sacramento, Doña Teresa Enríquez* (Madrid, 1922). The Confraternity of the Blessed Sacrament in Rome, which Teresa promoted, erected to her memory in the church of San Lorenzo in Damaso a marble tablet to the left of the entrance, which still exists. For the instruction to Portugal see *MI* I, xii, 677 et seq. and II, ii, 112.

[18] Faber's letter is in *M. Fabr.* 128 et seq.; the commission to Torres in *MI* I, i, 423.

[19] For the "Devota" of Salamanca see *FN*, i, 452; the Lady's visit to Ignatius in prison, *ibid.*, 460. For Magdalena de Mendiola see *MI* IV, ii, 185, 220, 242 et seq.; I, i, 145 et seq.

[20] For Ignatius' admonition on arrival in Rome see *FN*, i, 498. For Faustina de'Jancolini, cf. Tacchi-Venturi, ii, 1, 323–8; Schurhammer, i, 481–5; her will is in Tacchi-Venturi, i, 2, 224–9. For Girolama Orsini Farnese, see *MI* I, i, 268, 316 et seq. The letter from Parma, see Tacchi-Venturi, i, 2, 198–200; cf. H. Stoeckius, *Parma und die päpstliche Bestätigung der Gesellschaft Jesu* (Heidelberg, 1913), 20 et seq. The reference to "women's patronage" is in *MI* I, xii, 277. Nominal list of the *Compagnia della Grazia* in Tacchi-Venturi, i, 2, 296–307. "He who rejects. . . ." in *MI* I ii, 481; cf. Karrer and Rahner, *Ignatius von Loyola*, 149–53.

[21] Villa Orsini, *MI* I, i, 183, note 2. Sale of Giulia Colonna's house, *ibid.* xi, 378; *Chron.*, vi, 14, 37. For the "mendicants' road" see *MI* I, xii, 659. For Costanza Salviati, see *ibid.*, xi, 380, 546 et seq.; xii, 154. For Don Torrano's complaint see Tacchi-Venturi, i, 2, 273–7. Complaint of Teofilo da Tropea, *ibid.*, 278–81. Excuses to Zárate in MI I, xi, 19. For the rings of elk-horn see *ibid.*, 122, note 3; 196, note 2. Ignatius' letter to Zárate, *ibid.*, 196. Polanco's report to Zárate, *ibid.*, 197.

[22] For the history of the House of St. Martha cf. Polanco's memorandum of 1551 in *Pol. Compl.*, i, 63–5; Tacchi-Venturi, L'azione di S. Ignazio nella vita italiana del 500 in *Atti dell' Accademia degli Arcadi* 1930, 8–13; *ibid.*, ii, 2, 160–82. For Ribadeneira on Rome, see *Vita Ignatii*, iii, 9, 267. The bull *Divina summaque* is in Tacchi-Venturi, i, 2, 284–8. Ignatius' words: "If no one . . ." are in Ribadeneira, *Vita*, iii, 9, 269. The sale of the marble sculptures, *MI* IV, i, 357, *FN*, ii, 348 et seq., Tacchi-Venturi, ii, 2, 164 et seq. Statutes for St. Martha's *ibid.*, i, 2, 288–94. Report to Francis Xavier, *MI* I, i, 269 et seq.; the number of inmates *ibid.*, 250, 305; *FN*, i, 199. The note from St. Martha's in *MI* I, xii, 390 et seq.; two others *ibid.*, 384 et seq. The document of Cardinal Farnese is in Tacchi-Venturi, i, 2, 311–13; *ibid.*, ii, 2, 175 et seq. (with wrong date).

[23] The contents of Fray Barbarán's complaint, now lost, are to be inferred from a letter of Ignatius, *MI* I, i, 447; his answer to Barbarán, *ibid.*, 408 et seq.; cf. *FN*, i, 310, note 26. Documents of the lawsuit against the postmaster are in *MI* IV, i, 659–66. Other houses of St. Martha in Italy are given in Tacchi-Venturi, ii, 2, 174; the house in Valladolid in *MI* I, iii, 108 et seq. Ignatius' instruction on the treatment of the penitents, *ibid.*, v, 69, *Chron.* iii, 154 et seq. The questionnaire for St. Martha's

in Tacchi-Venturi, i, 2, 294 et seq. Memorandum for the *Miserabili, Chron.*, i, 169; cf. Tacchi-Venturi, ii, 2, 184, note 4. Ferrao's letter in *MI* I, i, 373.

²⁴ Ignatius' instruction to d'Achille is in *MI* I, IX, 220; *Chron.*, v, 202; to Patarino in *MI* I, vii, 39. Ignatius and the House of St. Martha in 1547, *ibid.*, i, 613. The encyclical letter to confessors, *ibid.*, v, 253. For the case of Lippomani, see *ibid.*, 290; *Chron.*, iii, 122; for a similar case in Padua, see *ibid.*, ii, 211. Women's confessions in Venice, *MI* I, ix, 172; *Chron.*, v, 169. Rebuke on account of visits to women in *FN*, i, 564; cf. the encyclical letter to rectors in Italy, *MI* I, vii, 588 et seq. Rebuke to Adriaenssens, *ibid.*, ii, 670 et seq.; to Leernus, *ibid.*, vii, 66. On retreats for women, *ibid.*, vi, 521; I. Iparraguirre, *Historia de los Ejercicios espirituales*, i (Bilbao, 1946), s.v. *Mujeres ejercitantes*. For Beatrice Carafa see *Chron.*, iv, 190. Instruction to J. Vitoria, *MI* I, xii, 46. Letter of Araoz, *Mixt.*, i, 246. M. Cano's reproach, *ibid.*, v, 665. On the malicious talk of the Duchess of Alba see *Chron.*, vi, 257. Ignatius' expression "smoke and flame" is in Ribadeneira, *Vita*, v, 11, 658; in Bartoli, *Vita di S. Ignazio*, iv, 37 (Naples, 1856, p. 250), the words are as follows: "If one is on too familiar terms with women, even if they are in religion, it is seldom that there does not arise a flame which burns or smoke which blackens."

²⁵ Instruction to Galvanello in *MI* I, iv, 629; *Chron.*, iii, 126. The letter to Fr. Tavoni in *MI* I, ix, 175 et seq.; to Araldo *ibid.*, viii, 336 et seq.; to Ferrarese *ibid.*, ix, 266 et seq. The report from Lisbon in *Mixt.*, iii, 320 et seq. For the ladies' guild in Naples, see *Chron.*, iv, 174; v, 174.

²⁶ Judgments on Ignatius' skill in spiritual direction, see *FN*, I, 84, 166, ii, 379; *MI* IV, i, 565, I, i, 614. The marriage of the Jew to the courtesan, *ibid.*, 181–4. The matrimonial quarrel of Nicolá, *ibid.*, vi, 317, 659, 589.

²⁷ Gonçalves' report is in *FN*, i, 645 et seq., 719; Ribadeneira's *ibid.*, ii, 328 et seq.; *MI* IV, i, 407 et seq.; cf. B. Wilhelm, "Die Stigmatisierte von Bologna" in *Zeitschrift für Askese und Mystik*, v (1930), 176–8; A. Huonder, *Ignatius von Loyola*, 298 et seq. For Magdalena de la Cruz, see Ribadeneira, *Vita*, v, 10, 631–3. The attitude of Ignatius in *MI* IV, i, 460.

Part One

THE COURTIER OF HEAVEN

Introduction

¹ The standard life of Charles V is that of K. Brandi, *Kaiser Karl V*. (Munich, 1937); notes and commentary, 1941. (Eng. translation, *The Emperor Charles V* [London, 1949]). By way of introduction see also B. Schneider, "Der weltliche Heilige. Ignatius von Loyola und die Fürsten seiner Zeit" in *Geist und Leben (ZAM)*, xxvii (1954), 35–58. For Charles V's relations with the Jesuits see also K. Eder, *Geschichte der Kirche im Zeitalter des konfessionellen Absolutismus* (Vienna, 1949), 60. The Emperor's letter to Paul III has been published by Tacchi-Venturi in *Studi e Documenti di storia e diritto*, xxii (1901), 173. For the affair of Bobadilla in connexion with the Interim proclaimed at the "armed Diet" of Augsburg on

June 30th, 1548, see *M.Bob.*, 137 et seq., 143, 154 et seq. (where Bobadilla's letter of September 20th, 1548, from Rome to King Ferdinand is given); *Mixt.*, i, 503–5; *MI* IV, i, 467; *Chron.* i, 293 et seq. Cf. also B. Duhr, *Geschichte der Jesuiten in den Ländern deutscher Zunge,* i (Freiburg, 1907), 31 et seq. Years later, Viglius still remembered the behaviour of Bobadilla; in his remarks opposing the admission of the Jesuits to Flanders (cf. p. 43), he accused them of having *"facultas discurrendi et vagandi sine socio et arbitro, uti Bobadilla qui erat in mensis omnium et disquirebat nova"* (in L. Delplace, *L'établissement de la Compagnie de Jésus dans les Pays-Bas* [Brussels, 1887], 451). For Charles V's letter permitting Francis Borgia to enter the Society, cf. Karrer, 115 et seq. Polanco's observation in *Pol. Compl.*, i, 114. Ignatius' letter of February 24th, 1551, was to Fr. Jay, who was at Augsburg (*MI* I, iii, 333). Soon afterwards Ignatius sent to the Emperor copies of the bull *Exposcit debitum,* of the book of the *Exercises* and other documents (*ibid.,* 386), at which Charles expressed his satisfaction (cf. *Chron.* ii, 233). The letter of March 3rd, 1554, that was never sent is in *MI* I, vi, 421 et seq.

² That is, Philip II married to Mary Tudor. – Trans.

³ For Ignatius on Charles V's abdication, see *MI* I, x, 269 et seq.; xi, 5, 23. For Francis Borgia's conversations with Charles see Atráin, ii, 105–9; Karrer, 162–4; M. Gachard, *Retraite et mort de Charles-Quint au monastère de Yuste. Lettres inédites* (Brussels, 1854–5), i, 74, 235; ii, 145, 253–7, 368 et seq. It was by no means only religious questions that were discussed at these conversations; they had also for their subject a highly political matter, the Spanish succession in Portugal, in which Borgia was employed as an agent; cf. Brandi, 578. Borgia's report to Laynez is in *M. Borg.,* iii, 271 et seq., dated December 28th, 1556 (not 1557, the year given in the letter itself, because at that time the new year in Spain began at Christmas; cf. Astráin, p. 107, note 1); the first conversation took place at Jarandilla(cf. Brandi, p. 545).

⁴ Polanco's letter to Salmerón dated July 3rd, 1557, is in *M. Salm.,* i, 182 et seq., being a reply to Salmerón's enquiry of June 3rd, 1557 (*ibid.,* 180).

⁵ For M. Cano's attitude towards the Society of Jesus, cf. Astráin, i (1902), 321–40. The Emperor's confessor was in correspondence with Cano, whose letter is in *Cartas,* ii (Madrid, 1875), 500. The Marquis of Tavara here mentioned was a great friend of the Society and especially of St. Francis Borgia *(Chron.,* V, 436 et seq.; cf. also *ibid.,* 553 et seq.; vi, 654; *MI* I, ix, 365; *Mixt.,* i *passim*). Prayers and Masses were afterwards ordered for the deceased Emperor (*M. Bob.,* 245, 265).

⁶ For the birth of Philip and the accident with the gunpowder, cf. L. Pfandl, *Philipp II* (Munich, 1938), 35 and *Acta Sanctorum,* July, vii, 446. This event became for Ignatius in his memoirs a date from which he reckoned that of others (No. 73; *FN,* i, 464). For the meeting with Leonor Mascarenhas, see Ribadeneira, *Vita,* i, 14 (Cologne, 1602, p. 89) and below p. 418. The meeting with Philip in Madrid, *FN,* i, 31 and 105, note 20; cf. also Larrañaga, i, 429 et seq. Here also is the account of the event of 1586. Altogether thirteen letters of Ignatius to Philip II have been preserved. Thus on February 15th, 1556, Ignatius calls him *Señor natural* (*MI* I, x, 712 et seq.); the first letter (*ibid.,* i, 299 et seq.) was written when Ignatius was still unaware of the death of the Princess María. Ignatius' joy at the English marriage

and the return of England to the Catholic faith: February 23rd, 1555 (ibid., viii, 305 et seq.); the letter of July 1548: ibid., ii, 149 et seq.; on the reform of the Catalan convents: December 26th, 1546 (ibid., i, 455 et seq.) and June 3rd, 1552 (ibid., iv, 268 et seq.); in this letter Ignatius also expresses his thanks for protection against the attacks of Archbishop Siliceo; on the Council of Trent: February 17th, 1546 (ibid., i, 360 et seq., 732 et seq., xii, 238); the request in favour of the Roman College: July 1st, 1555 (ibid., ix, 267 et seq.); Philip's letter of recommendation is in Mixt., iv, 151–3; on the admission of the Jesuits to Flanders Ignatius wrote to Philip on July 23rd, 1555(MI I, x, 32–4); the "spiritual instruction" of February 18th, 1549, in which it states: "For many years we have remembered Your Majesty daily in our prayers": (ibid., ii, 344 et seq.). Philip's goodwill towards the new Society had already been remarked by Araoz in 1546 (Mixt., i, 271 et seq.).

⁷ The correspondence with King Ferdinand begins in 1546 with the affair of Fr. Jay, whom the king had proposed as Bishop of Trieste (MI I, i, 450), and continues till the year of the saint's death; the last letter to Ferdinand is dated February 12th, 1556 (ibid., x, 681 et seq.). For a letter written by the king's Spanish secretary, see e.g. ibid., xii, 423. For the influence of Philip's sister, the future Empress María, in Vienna, cf. below, note 9.

⁸ Further details of the Lady of Ignatius' affections are in the section on Queen Catherine of Portugal. The princesses here named are dealt with in the sections that follow.

⁹ For the Infanta María cf. Pfandl 168, 172–4. Her esteem of Fr. Araoz: MI I, iii, 76; Chron., i, 248, 304. During her regency in Spain her goodness was especially praised (ibid., ii, 129 et seq.). On her journey to Vienna she took with her among others the pious lady-in-waiting Doña María Manrique de Lara (MI I, iv, 333; Chron., ii, 570). For her return journey to Spain, which lasted from October 1581 to March 1582, and on which the young Luigi Gonzaga accompanied her as a page, cf. the report of the Venetian envoys Michele, Soranzo, Tiepolo and Correr, who welcomed María in the name of the republic and escorted her through Venetian territory, November 18th, 1581. See J. Fiedler, "Relationen venezianischer Botschafter über Deutschland und Österreich im 16. Jahrhundert" in Fontes rerum austriacarum, 2nd part, vol. 30 (Vienna, 1870); J. M. March, Niñez y juventud de Felipe II (Madrid, 1941), i, 439 et seq. and the painting of Juan van der Beken at the Descalzas reales (reproduced ibid., 97). The Venetian Tommaso Contarini relates of her closing years in Madrid in 1593: "The Empress María lives a very retired life near the convent of the Discalced Franciscans, which one of her daughters has entered. She keeps a modest household and has not much money at her disposal; she might very well be dissatisfied with such a mode of life. Nevertheless, she is highly respected by His Majesty, who never leaves Madrid or returns thither without waiting upon her." Cf. M. Gachard, Relations des ambassadeurs vénitiens sur Charles-Quint et Philippe II (Brussels, 1856), 227, note 1. The Venetian Vendramin notes two years later: "The Empress still lives in Madrid, but she enjoys little consideration, although she is a lady of singular goodness" (ibid., 246, note 4). Pfandl summarizes her situation thus: "The unfortunate victim of disgraceful neglect and court jealousy." The Empress María lived till her death in

1603 mostly with the *Descalzas reales;* her daughter, born in 1567, who came with her in 1582 from Vienna, entered this convent on January 21st, 1584, and died there on July 5th, 1633. The life of sister Margarita de la Cruz (her name in religion) was written in 1658 by Fray Miguel Abelán; cf. F. Fita, *Boletin de la Real Acad. de Hist.,* xviii (1891), 61 et seq. Her help for the Jesuits in Vienna: *Chron.,* vi, 351-3; sermons of Canisius and Salmerón before the queen and her court, *ibid.,* iii, 244; vi, 342. For her influence on her husband Maximilian, see Pfandl, 174; *Chron.,* ii, 571. The Venetian Michele reports of her in 1571 that she led a truly saintly life, like a real nun, and that she was the deciding factor in the preservation of the Catholic faith in Germany, cf. Fiedler, 282 et seq. Ignatius' letter to Ribadeneira of July 20th, 1556, is in *MI* I, xii, 157.

¹⁰ The congratulatory letter to Philip that arrived too late is in *MI* I, i, 299; the Princess María had already died on July 12th, 1545. Araoz' communication about the new marriage plan is in *Mixt.,* ii, 269, dated August 28th, 1549; Ignatius' answer in MI I, iii, 10 et seq. Ignatius wrote to Fr. Queralt on August 20th, 1553, that María had promised to found a college in Barcelona if she married Philip (*ibid.,* 366 et seq.). The expression "complete silence" occurs in the reply, dated October 19th, 1553 (*Mixt.,* iii, 536). The "forsaken bride" remained a great friend of the Jesuits (*Chron.,* iii, 407; iv, 540); Francis Borgia often met her (*Mixt.,* iii, 505, 543; *Chron.,* iii, 359). The expression "sovereign courage" is in *Mixt.,* iii, 500, note 1. Maria died unmarried in 1577. For the "forsaken bride" see also Schurhammer, i, 584 et seq.

¹¹ For the English marriage see Brandi, 538 et seq.; Pfandl, 230-79. Ignatius' letter of August 5th, 1553, is in *MI* I, v, 288. The expression about the "open door" occurs in a letter of August 7th, 1553, to Cardinal Pole (*ibid.,* 304). Shortly afterwards Ignatius wrote concerning the same event: "God be eternally praised for it!" (*ibid.,* 354). An indulgence was proclaimed on the occasion of this change in the situation (*Chron.,* iii, 43). In April 1554 Queen Mary sent a Latin letter expressing her loyalty to Pope Julius III, who read it aloud five times before the Consistory with tears of joy; Ignatius reported this to all Jesuit superiors (*MI* I, vi, 665, 706; cf. also *Chron.,* iv, 19). Ignatius wished to send Fr. Araoz to England (*MI* I, vi, 713), who, however, considered the time not ripe, whereas Borgia and Nadal were of the contrary opinion (*Chron.,* iv, 35, 492 et seq.). But King Philip, who at this time intended to make Araoz tutor to Don Carlos (*ibid.,* 387), was against the proposal; (*MI* I, vii, 113, 287) and so no Jesuit accompanied Philip to England (*ibid.,* 573). Delightedly Ignatius wrote on August 21st, 1554, to Fr. Adriaenssens: "We have already heard that the Prince has landed in England; may Christ direct all this to his glory and the general good of the Church" (*ibid.,* 433). Letter to the Spanish superiors of January 2nd, 1555, *ibid.,* viii, 221; the congratulatory letter to Philip of January 23rd, 1555, *ibid.,* 305 et seq.; that to Cardinal Pole of the same date, *ibid.,* 308 et seq. In the latter he also expounds his apostolic plans. Joy in Rome on the occasion of the English embassy of obedience, (*ibid.,* ix, 181; *Chron.,* v, 35). For Charles V's will of 1554, cf. Brandi, 539 et seq. Cardinal Pole's letter about the expected birth of an heir to the throne is in *MI* I, xii, 509; the quotation from the Chronicle of the Society is in *Chron.,* v, 316.

¹² For Jeanne d'Albret, see Pfandl, 50–3. For Gérard Roussel, who is also called Gerardus Rufus, cf. Herzog-Hauck, *Realenzyklopädie für prot. Theologie und Kirche,* xvii, 178–80; he is there described as a "conciliatory reformer"; the year of his death, given as 1550, should be corrected to 1555 (cf. O. Raynaldi, *Annales ecclesiastici,* xxxiii [Paris, 1878], 541). For Roussel's activities as bishop cf. *Gallia Christiana,* i (Paris, 1715), 1277 et seq., where the year of his death is wrongly given as 1559. Ignatius' Paris memories of him are in a letter of Martin Olave (*MI* I, v, 174–6). Requests for information about Roussel on behalf of the Inquisition in letters to various superiors dated July 8th, 1553 (*ibid.,* 170 seq.). Cf. Schurhammer, i, 113, note 2.

¹³ For help given by Margaret to the fathers in Paris see H. Fouqueray, *Histoire de la Compagnie de Jésus en France,* i (Paris, 1910), 199. Ignatius' answer to Fr. Broët's double request is in *MI* I, xi, 213. On the day on which Margaret of Valois married Duke Emmanuel Philibert of Savoy her brother King Henry II (1547–59) lost his life in a tournament; for the latter's passion for the tournament see the account of the Venetian Matteo Dandolo in M. A. Baschet, *Les princes de l'Europe au XVIᵉ siècle d'après les rapports des ambassadeurs vénitiens* (Paris, 1862), 433. *Ibid.,* 489 et seq. is a flattering character-sketch of Margaret. For the Duchess of Valentinois, cf. the acute observations of the Venetians, *ibid.,* 431, 438–40.

¹⁴ For Princess Renée of France, see B. Fontana, *Renata di Francia,* 3 vols. (Rome, 1889–99); E. Rodocanachi, *Reneé de France, Duchesse de Ferrare* (Paris, 1896); G. Buschbell, *Reform und Inquisition in Italien* (Paderborn, 1910); C. Hare. *Men and Women of the Italian Reformation* (London, 1914). Renée had married Hercules of Ferrara in 1528; in 1536 Calvin stayed at her court (Fontana I, 283–333), and she remained in correspondence with him. Beza dedicated his *Opuscula* to her. Because of the early connexions of the new Society of Jesus with Ferrara – the duke was the first prince who supported the Society in its beginnings (cf. *Chron.,* i, 225; *MI* I, i, 142 et seq., 567 et seq.) – references to the Duchess Renée are exceedingly numerous in the *Mon. Hist.* The most important events of her career there mentioned are as follows: In 1547 the duke asked Ignatius to send a Jesuit, French if possible, having regard to the duchess, of whom the secretary wrote in a postscript that she was reputed to be infected with the doctrines of Luther – a matter on which, however, he had no definite information (*MI* I, i, 570; cf. *Chron.,* i. 224 et seq.). Fr. Jay came to Ferrara in August, but the duchess was not very well disposed towards him (*ibid.,* 278 et seq.); in 1549 he was sent to Germany (*ibid.,* 441 the reason is given: "As there was no longer scarcely any hope of bringing the duchess back to the Catholic faith"). Jay was succeeded in 1551 by Frs. Broët and Pelletier, at whose first audience in the ducal palace Renée again appeared very reserved (*ibid.,* ii, 189; the instructions given to the two fathers by Ignatius are in *MI* I, iii, 542–50). *Chron.,* iv, 68–81 gives a detailed report of Renée's dramatic conversion, which occupied the year 1554. Pelletier advised the duke to dismiss the Protestant members of his consort's court and to resume married life with her – she had been living separate from him at Castel Consandolo near Ferrara. From France came the Inquisitor of Paris, the Dominican Matthieu Ory; at the same time Calvin sent François Morel to support the duchess. The latter was arrested and her court dissolved. Ignatius spoke of the

"pestilence" in that palace (*MI* I, vi, 562) and called it an "asylum of the Lutherans" (*ibid.*, 663); the duchess' daughters were separated from her. She made a recantation before Dr. Ory, went to confession on September 22nd and two days later received Communion. Ignatius followed all these phases of the struggle for "Madama" (*ibid.*, vii, 35, 234, 340, 469, 707) and caused Masses and prayers to be said for its successful outcome. Pelletier's reports are in *Mixt.*, iv, 119–21, 337–9, 350 et seq. At the news of the happy result Ignatius' joy was great (*MI* I, vii, 591). The news, together with Pelletier's report of September 24th, 1554 (*Mixt.*, iv, 360–2) was sent to all superiors (*MI* I, vii, 616–18, 632, 645, 650), as well as to Cardinal Mendoza in Brussels (*ibid.*, vii, 664) and to Francis Borgia (*ibid.*, viii, 10, 253). In November there were difficulties again (*Mixt.*, iv, 443 et seq., *Chron.*, iv, 80); however, Pelletier was able to report at the end of the year that now all was going well (*Mixt.*, iv, 484 et seq.). The example of the duchess, he said, was a model for the whole court (*Chron.*, v, 136, 139). Calvin wrote to her with annoyance on February 2nd, 1555, "that the devil could celebrate this triumph" (Fontana, ii, 399–401), and remarked with resignation in a letter to Farel, "constancy is rare among princes" (J. Bonnet, *Lettres de Jean Calvin*, ii, Paris, 1854, 4). Subsequently, too, Ignatius took a great interest in the duchess (*MI* I, viii, 10, 202). His letter of September 21st, 1555, to Pelletier still shows some uncertainty about her. Describing the precarious situation of the Roman College, he suggests that Pelletier might show her the letter, "to see if God has chosen her to help us" (*ibid.*, ix, 640). After the death of her husband in 1559 Renée returned in 1560 to France, where together with Jeanne d'Albret she remained for fifteen years the protector of the Calvinists.

[15] For Bona Sforza, see N. Ratti, *Della famiglia Sforza*, ii, (Rome, 1795), 69–86; A. von Reumont, *Vittoria Colonna* (Freiburg, 1881), 26, 32 et seq.; L. von Pastor, *History of the Popes* (Eng. trans.), xiv, 212. For Salmerón's journey see *Chron.*, vi, 537 et seq.; O. F. Tencajoli, *Principesse italiane nella storia d'altri paesi* (Rome, 1933), 189–200. Salmerón's letter is in *M. Salm.*, i, 130. Ignatius' instruction to Salmerón in Warsaw in *MI* I, ix, 376–8. Letter to Fr. Vignes, *ibid.*, x, 295.

Queen María of Hungary

[16] For biography see T. Juste, *Les Pays-Bas sous Charles-Quint. Vie de Marie de Hongrie, tirée des papiers d'État* (Brussels, 1855). L. Pfandl has a short character-sketch in *Philipp II.* (Munich, 1938), 166–8, 210–12. The expression "Charles V in petticoats" and the quotation from Brantôme, *ibid.*, 164.

[17] For Viglius, see Pfandl 43 and *MI* I, ii, 247 252 et seq.; for Granvelle, *ibid.*, 416 et seq. Viglius is described as a suspected heretic and Lutheran in a report to Philip II of 1564 (M. Gachard, *Correspondance de Philippe II sur les affaires des Pays-Bas*, i [Brussels, 1848], 319 et seq.); Granvelle, on the other hand, regarded him as irreplaceable (*ibid.*, 205, 219), and Margaret of Austria protected him against the above accusations (*ibid.*, 318 et seq.). The remark about Philip's relations with his aunt is in Badoaro's report of 1557 (M. Gachard, *Relations des ambassadeurs vénitiens sur Charles-Quint et Philippe II* [Brussels, 1856], 17, note 1).

[18] The beginning of this affair is in *Chron.*, ii, 68; the attempt of Fr. Adriaenssens and the opinion of the theological faculty of Louvain, *ibid.*, 85; text of the latter, *ibid.*, vi, 436 et seq.; the refusal and its reasons, *ibid.*, ii, 289. Words of Viglius, *ibid.*, iv, 282 and elsewhere. For the allegedly large number of Jesuits in Brussels, cf. also *MI* I, vi, 227; viii, 283; this was a constantly repeated complaint. For the whole affair, see the account in A. Poncelet. *Histoire de la Compagnie de Jésus dans les anciens Pays-Bas,* i (Brussels, 1927), 76–110.

[19] Fr. Jay had to take a letter of recommendation from King Ferdinand to his sister (*MI* I, iii, 375), which the former, however, at first regarded as impracticable (*M. Broët.,* 369 et seq.); nevertheless, the king and Cardinal Truchsess did write (*Chron.*, ii, 274, 289). Fr. Adriaenssens, who was commissioned by Ignatius to attempt to negotiate with the queen (*MI* I, iv, 91, 156), handed the letter to Viglius, who suggested, when they were at dinner together, that the Pope should write to the Emperor (*Chron.*, ii, 289 et seq.). For the carrying out of this suggestion and its negative result see *ibid.*, 468 et seq. The instructions to Fr. Jay to find ways and means of winning over "my Lord of Arras" (Granvelle was bishop of that city) are in *MI* I, iii, 333 et seq.; here also is the reference to the services rendered to the Emperor by Ignatius' ancestors. Repetition of the request to Ferdinand, also through Fr. Jay, *ibid.*, iv, 75. Salmerón summoned to Innsbruck, *Chron.*, ii, 468. The two copies of the petition were sent to him for forwarding (*MI* I, iv, 202–4).

[20] In *Chron.*, ii, 469; the foregoing also *ibid.*, 468 et seq. For the fruitlessness of this affair cf. also *Chron.*, iii, 281 et seq. For the political situation at that time, cf. Pfandl 221 et seq., and Brandi, *Kaiser Karl V.* (Munich, 1937), 518.

[21] Ignatius' letter to Fr. Adriaenssens of December 27th, 1552, is in *MI* I, iv, 576. Letter to Araoz of July 28th, 1553, *ibid.*, v, 250. The hint to leave the Emperor out of the matter, *ibid.*, vi, 362. Reply of Araoz in *Mixt.*, iii, 602. Petition to the Emperor, *MI* I, xii, 257–9. For the text of the letter to the Emperor that was never sent, see p. 30

[22] The Archdeacon of Liége, Guillaume de Poitou, used his influence with María (*Chron.*, iii, 262 et seq.; iv, 280), Cardinal Pole spoke with her (*MI* I, viii, 282; *Chron.*, iv, 296); Gonzalo Pérez and Ruy Gómez were prepared to support the project (*MI* I, viii, 282); Louis de Blois, who had made the Spiritual Exercises (*Chron.*, iii, 277 et seq.), would intercede with Viglius (*ibid.*, iv, 281 et seq.; *Mixt.*, iv, 114). He also wrote a letter to the secretary defending the Jesuits, of which the text is in *Cartas*, ii, 507–9 (cf. L. Delplace, *L'établissement de la Compagnie de Jésus dans les Pays-Bas* [Brussels, 1887], 5); *ibid.*, 451 et seq., is Viglius' memorandum. Intervention of Pedro de Soto, in *Chron.*, iv, 283–5; *Mixt.*, iv, 113 et seq. Cardinal Pole and Louis de Blois agreed on concerted action (*Chron.*, iv, 286). All was in vain (cf. *ibid.*, v, 301).

[23] The first rumour to reach Rome of María's impending departure is mentioned in a letter of December 7th, 1555 (*MI* I, x, 268). Shortly after followed an instruction that the Jesuits should refrain from preaching until the queen was out of the country (*ibid.*, 273); in fact, she did not leave till September 15th, 1556. For Charles's abdication and María's departure, cf. Brandi, 542 and Pfandl, 289–93. Ribadeneira's letter to Ignatius of December 11th, 1555, is in *M. Rib.,* i, 127). The courtly pun "Ruy-

Rey Gómez" is mentioned in Badoaro's report of 1557 (M. Gachard, *Relations des Ambassadeurs vénitiens*, 47, note 1). Philip's answer to Count Feria in *Chron.*, vi, 441.

[24] The new petition, drawn up by Ribadeneira, of February 14th, 1556, is in *MI* I, x, 704–9; cf. also *Chron.*, vi, 437 et seq. That María was misinformed had already been emphasized (*MI* I, x, 243), and the Jesuits were not admitted to her presence (*Quadr.*, iii, 268). Indicative of the coolness of the Regent María towards the Jesuits is the remark in *Chron.*, vi, 633 about a rumour current at the court of Valladolid to the effect that now the Emperor and his sister María were there, the activities of the Jesuits were at an end, and they were no longer permitted to enter the palace of the Infanta Juana. Ribadeneira's communication to Ignatius is in *M. Rib.*, i, 172, dated June 21st, 1556; *ibid.*, also is mentioned the letter of the Infanta Juana, which Ribadeneira handed to the Queen of Hungary together with one from Francis Borgia of the July 22nd, 1556 (*ibid.*, 198 et seq.) Ignatius' instruction to procure the intervention of the Queen of Bohemia (María, Philip's sister) with her aunt, whose very presence still formed an obstacle (cf. *Chron.*, vi, 440), dated July 20th, 1556, is in *MI* I, xii, 156 et seq., for the journey of the royal pair, Maximilian and María, to Flanders cf. M. Koch, *Quellen zur Geschichte* des *Kaisers Maximilian II* (Leipzig, 1857), i, 2 et seq.

[25] Report on the decisive negotiations on July 30th, 1556 is in *M. Rib.*, i, 180. Philip's verbal approval and Nadal's interpretation in *MI* IV, i, 474; the matter was finally settled on August 8th and 20th (cf. *Chron.*, vi, 444, 448); the text of the permission is in *MI* I, xii, 201–5. Spiritual community granted to Juana and María (Count Feria also received the same favour) in *M. Rib.*, i, 215.

[26] Laynez' letter is in *M. Bob.*, 245. Borgia's letter of October 18th, 1558, was addressed to Laynez (*M. Borg.*, iii, 405).

Queen Catherine of Portugal

[27] For biography see F. De Llanos y Torriglia, *Contribución al estudio de la Reina de Portugal, hermana de Carlos V, Doña Catalina de Austria* (Madrid, 1923); by the same author, *Santas y Reinas. Apuntes biográficos* (Madrid, 1943), 253–315; A Rodríguez-Villa, *La Reina Doña Juana la Loca* (Madrid, 1892), 186 et seq., 270–4. The report of the eye-witness Lorenzo Vital has been published in M. Gachard and Piot, *Collection des voyages des souverains des Pays-Bas,* iii (Brussels, 1875), 1–114. For the Cortes, see F. Fita, "S. Ignacio de Loyola en la Corte de los Reyes de Castilla" in *Boletín de la Real Acad. de Hist.*, xvii (1890), 492–520. For King Ferdinand's visits cf. Rodríguez and Villa, 233 et seq., 238.

[28] For the abduction of the Infanta, cf. Rodríguez and Villa, 272 et seq. For the court festival at Valladolid, cf. F. de Leturia, *El gentilhombre Inigo López de Loyola en su patria y en su siglo* (Barcelona, 1949), 97–9. Proof that Ignatius had already seen the Infanta previously, *ibid.*, 56 et seq. The eye-witness account again comes from L. Vital. For the "Lady of his heart" see *FN*, i, 370. Leturia decides for Catherine, 72 et seq., 302 et seq., where he summarizes his *Notas críticas sobre la Dama del Capitán Loyola* (*Arch. Hist. S. J.*, v [1936], 84–92), and so does Larrañaga, i, 130–3;

and we follow them. Llanos y Torriglia, on the other hand, in *Santas y Reinas,* 319–56, takes Doña Leonor de Austria, Catherine's elder sister, to be the "Lady of his heart".

[29] For the rising of the *Comuneros,* cf. Rodríguez and Villa, 300–10; the regaining of Tordesillas, *ibid.,* 340. The victory at Villalar, *ibid.,* 363. Report of Count de Haro of May 24th, 1521, to Charles V about the threatening situation in Navarre, *ibid.,* 364–7. Catherine's letter of justification of August 19th, 1521, *ibid.,* 371–4. For the plan to move to Arévalo, cf. *ibid.,* 380; M. Danvila, *Historia crítica de las comunidades de Castilla,* iv (Madrid, 1898), 393; F. Fita in *Boletín de la Real Acad. de Historia,* xvii (1890), 6. For the departure of Catherine from her mother see Contarini's report to the Signoria of Venice (*Venetian Calendar,* iii, 398); E. Gossart, *Charles-Quint, roi d'Espagne* (Brussels, 1910), 231 et seq.

[30] Report of Rodríguez' audience in *Ep. Xav.,* i, 33; Xavier's report of the audience granted to him, *ibid.,* 41. For the queen's help for the Indian mission cf. *ibid.,* 33; *Doc. Ind.,* ii, 611; iii, 588.

[31] L. Pfandl, *Philipp II* (Munich, 1938), 64 et seq. Ignatius' letter of March 8th, 1543, is in *MI* I, i, 245.

[32] Request to all superiors for prayers for the royal family of Portugal in *MI* I, v, 125 et seq. M. de Torres was appointed visitor of the Portuguese province of the Society on January 1st, 1552; see Astráin, i, 209 et seq. Ignatius left the decision concerning the queen's wish to have Fr. Torres as confessor to Fr. Borgia (*MI* I, ix, 167), who agreed (*M. Borg.,* iii, 211 et seq.). For her spiritual exercises see *Chron.,* iii, 408 and *Mixt.,* iii, 713. Faber's letter of condolence dated July 13th, 1545, is in *M. Fabr.,* 333; Fr. Araoz' letter of May 3rd, 1546, from which the quotation in the text is taken, is in *Mixt.,* i, 271. Pfandl's statement that these two Jesuits attended the princess on her deathbed is wrong, cf. *M. Fabr.,* 334. The crisis caused by Simon Rodríguez is summarily described in O. Karrer and H. Rahner in *Ignatius von Loyola. Geistliche Briefe* (Einsiedeln, 1942), 257–65; but the number of those dismissed, given there as 130, should according to the latest research be altered to about 30 (Rodrigues, i, 2, 137 et seq.). A more detailed description is in the new edition (Einsiedeln-Cologne, 1956).

[33] For Faber's gift of relics see *M. Fabr.,* 679 et seq. Permission for Ignatius to collect is in *MI* IV, i. 558 et seq.; the authentication of the relics collected in *MI* I, iv, 184. Directions to Torres to take them to the queen, *ibid.,* 171. Report of her goodwill from Nadal in Lisbon in *M. Nad.,* i, 172 et seq.

[34] Dated February 19th, 1555, in *M. Borg.,* iii, 191 et seq. Relations between the queen and her former page of the years 1523–5 (cf. Karrer, 8 et seq.) had become strained, so that Catherine refused the ducal pair the place at court intended for them on Philip's marriage. Cf. the cold letter of the Portuguese sovereigns to Borgia (*M. Borg.,* ii, 676–8), in contrast with the latter's heartfelt letter of consolation to Philip II (*ibid.,* 508 et seq.). The letter of 1555, however, indicates a renewal of good relations.

[35] The instruction to Fr. Gonçalves da Câmara is in *MI* I, x, 506 et seq. For Catherine's activities as a ruler, cf. *Chron.,* vi, 741 et seq. Pfandl's judgement of da Câmara (403 et seq.), whom he calls "an extravagant eccentric" is utterly false; cf. Karrer,

416–18 and P. de Leturia, "Luis González de Cámera, maestro del rey D. Sebastián. Notas a un memorial inédito" in *Arch. Hist. S. J.*, vi (1937), 97–106.

[36] Thus Pfandl, 85. The text of the papal letter of mediation between Catherine and her grandson is in O. Raynaldus, *Annales ecclesiastici*, xxxvii (Paris, 1883), 341–6.

Princess Juana of Spain

[37] For the history of the period see the works mentioned in the Introduction on Charles V and Philip II. There is a short biographical notice on Juana in M. Serrano y Sanz, *Apuntes para una biblioteca de escritores españoles desde el año 1401 al 1833* (Madrid, 1903), i, 76–8; *Enciclopedia española* (Espasa), 28, 2, col. 3039; J. M. March, *Niñez y juventud de Felipe II* (Madrid, 1942), II, 447. The opinion there expressed (*ibid.*, 448), that Leonor Mascarenhas (cf. p. 417 et seq.) was also formally admitted to the Society, seems to us to be without foundation; the fact that Borgia addressed her as "mistress and dearest sister in Christ" (*M. Borg.*, iii, 743) means little in itself. Cf. M. Bataillon, *Études sur le Portugal au temps de l'humanisme* (Coimbra, 1952), 257–83.

[38] For Doña Catalina de Toledo, daughter of the Count of Oropesa, see *M. Fabr.*, 151. Araoz' sermon before the Infantas is in *Chron.*, i, 89; *Mixt.*, i, 45; *FN*, i, 242. For his relations with the court of the princesses at that time cf. also *Mixt.*, i, 289, 358–62; *M. Fabr.*, 431; March, ii, 394 et seq. For the court chaplain who entered the Society see *FN*, i, 613, note 32; *Mixt.*, i, 122; *M. Fabr.*, 506; *Ep. Petri Canisii* (ed. Braunsberger), i, 98, note 2. Araoz calls him in *Mixt.*, i, 200 "a very edifying man"; there are two of his letters *ibid.*, 513–20, 559–63; cf. also Tacchi-Venturi, ii (1st ed. Rome, 1922), 406–8; *M. Fabr.*, 141.

[39] Ignatius' enthusiastic congratulations on the marriage projects are in *MI* I, i, 245; Francis Borgia wrote in similar terms to the imperial secretary Francisco de los Cobos (*M. Borg.*, ii, 430 et seq.; cf. also Karrer, 56). Araoz' words are in a letter of April 26th, 1544, *Mixt.*, i, 164. For John Emmanuel (1537–54), who was heir to the throne from March 30th, 1544, cf. *MI* I, i, 322. Recommendations to Juana through Leonor Mascarenhas, e.g. *ibid.*, 415.

[40] For Araoz' sermon in Toro see *Mixt.*, ii, 628, 654. The two daughters of Borgia at the court of the Infanta were the Countess Isabel Lerma and the Marchioness Juana Alcañices. Ignatius' report to G. de Dotti is in *MI* I, iv, 428 et seq.; for Juana's spiritual exercises see also *Chron.*, ii, 609 et seq.; iii, 360; *Mixt.*, iii, 502. For the fight against card-playing cf. *Chron.*, ii, 610; iii, 357; the Venetian Badoaro observes in his report of 1557 that the Spaniards' passion for play was greater than that of any other people. See M. Gachard, *Relations des ambassadeurs vénitiens sur Charles-Quint et Philippe II* (Brussels, 1856), 71, note 1; cf. also Karrer 127.

[41] As early as January 1552 Fr. Luis da Câmara was commissioned by Ignatius to take over the duties of confessor to the Portuguese heir apparent, *MI* I, iv, 66 et seq.; in spite of his humble refusal (*Mixt.*, ii, 707–9), Ignatius insisted (*MI* I, iv, 363–6). At the end of November 1552, Juana arrived in Portugal (*Mixt.*, ii, 801, 848); in *Chron.*, iii, 340 there is an account of an Englishman in her suite who

profaned the Eucharist in her presence (cf. also *M. Borg.*, iii, 131 et seq.). For the wedding preparations in Almeirim and Lisbon see *Chron.*, ii, 686 et seq. For Borgia's sojourn in Lisbon cf. *Chron.*, iii, 354–9; *ibid.*, his communion sermon before the princess and his other religious ministrations at court; yet he still feared the *inconstantia sexus foeminei*.

[42] For the invention of the religious card-game cf. the medieval moralizings on chess and cards in the 13th, 14th and 15th centuries, as e.g. Br. Johannes, O. P., *Ludus cartularum moralisatus* (1377 probably at Basle); quoted by W. Wackernagel, "Das Schachspiel im Mittelalter" (*Kleinere Schriften*, i [Leipzig, 1872], 122–5). Bustamente's report is in *Mixt.*, iii, 502–5; Polanco's first answer in *MI* I, vi, 435 et seq.; his later answer after receipt of the specimen *ibid.*, viii, 228. Juana's sister, the future Empress María, afterwards introduced this game at Vienna (*Quadr.*, vii, 280). At this time Borgia also invented the game of lotto with the virtues (*Chron.*, iii, 357).

[43] There is a report of the events of January 1554 in *Chron.*, iv, 543–5. Before the birth of her son Juana made a will leaving 500 *scudi* for a college in Jerusalem and 500 for one in Peru (*MI* I, vii, 28). Ignatius' letter of condolence on the death of the heir apparent, *ibid.*, I, vi, 422; 570 et seq. For her son's subsequent fate, cf. Karrer 416 et seq., 419 and L. Pfandl, *Philipp II*, 403 et seq. Ignatius' letter to Nadal is in *MI* I, vii, 143.

[44] For Juana as Regent, cf. the description in the archives of Simancas in M. Gachard, *Correspondance de Philippe II sur les affaires des Pays-Bas,* i (Brussels, 1848), pp. xcvii–cii; her correspondence with Charles V in M. Gachard, *Retraite et mort de Charles-Quint au monastère de Yuste. Lettres inédites* (Brussels, 1854–5). Accounts of the Venetian ambassadors of 1557 and 1572 in M. Gachard, *Relations des ambassadeurs vénitiens,* 62, note 4; 174, note 1. For the portrait, which after the Infanta's death was valued at 22,550 *maravedís* (Prado, no. 2112) cf. March, II, 446 et seq.

[45] Reports of Juana's illnesses in 1555: *MI* I, ix, 170; *M. Borg.*, ii, 220; 1558: M. Gachard, *Retraite et mort de Charles-Quint*, i, 308; ii, 447; 1568: *M. Borg.*, iv, 649; 1569: *ibid.*, v, 168, 249. In each case the sickness was the ague. O. Pfülf, "Die Geschichte eines unglücklichen Fürstensohnes" in *Stimmen aus Maria Laach*, 47 (1897), 140, asserts that Juana had inherited insanity, which afflicted her for years at a time until her death. Without mentioning any period, G. Turba (*Venezianische Depeschen vom Kaiserhof* [Vienna, 1895], iii, 447, note 4) likewise speaks of "raving madness", and M. Büdinger (*Don Carlos' Haft und Tod insbes. nach den Auffassungen seiner Familie* [Vienna-Leipzig, 1891], 258) of "madness and delirium". The only contemporary report is in a letter to the Duke of Alba, written after the death of Don Carlos (in *Documentos escogidos del archivo de la Casa de Alba. Los púdlica la Duquesa de Berwick y de Alba, Condesa de Siruela* [Madrid, 1891], 410). That this sickness was only temporary is proved both by the Venetian ambassador's report of 1572 already mentioned and by the events of the closing years of the Infanta's life described below, which definitely exclude the possibility of madness lasting for years. The sudden attack seems to have been due to mental shock on the death of her nephew Don Carlos, to whom she was deeply attached: at their separation in 1552 they had both wept for days. As regent she directed his educa-

tion (Büdinger, 135); later, there was even talk of a marriage between aunt and nephew (cf. below, note 65).

[46] The Venetian's report is in M. Gachard, *Relations des ambassadeurs*, 62, note 4.

[47] Juana had already written from Portugal to Borgia, asking him to place himself at her disposal (*Chron.*, iv, 585); she received him immediately after her return (*ibid.*, 586 et seq.). For her visit to Tordesillas, see *ibid.*, 437. Bustamente's words are in *Mixt.*, iv, 618 et seq. (likewise in *Quadr.*, iii, 120, 124, 408 et seq.; iv, 34; v, 40, 456, 707; *Chron.*, v, 424 et seq.; iv, 580). For the co-operation between Juana and Borgia from the beginning of the regency cf. *Quadr.*, iii, 22 et seq.; *M. Nad.*, i, 240, 253. Sojourn at court described as exile in Egypt in *M. Borg.*, iii, 637 (cf. also *Chron.*, iv, 590, 592). Ignatius' commission to Borgia of May 28th, 1555, in *MI* I, ix, 79 et seq. Pious exercises at court in *Chron.*, v, 427, 431 (here it is related that the Infanta repeated word for word a sermon of Bustamente's). Visit of Borgia to Joanna the Mad on her deathbed, *ibid.*, 546–9. He had already paid a visit to Tordesillas with Philip II before the latter's departure for England (*ibid.*, iv, 487 et seq.). *Ibid.*, v, 436 is mentioned the bread which Borgia gave the Infanta. The fact of her vow is established by what follows; nothing can be said with certainty about its date.

[48] For Araoz' attitude, cf. pp. 296 et seq., 299, 308, 342. His sermon on St. Sebastian's day in *Chron.*, v, 459.

[49] For the negotiations see *Chron.*, v, 47; the possibility of marriage at some future time mentioned in *MI* I, viii, 220. The pseudonym Mateo Sánchez is used up till the end of 1556 (cf. *M. Borg.*, iii, 271, 301) and then replaced by Montoya (cf. note 56). There are brief biographical notices of the five authors of the memorial in *FN*, i. For the precedent mentioned at the beginning of the document, cf. the section on Isabel Roser, p. 262 et seq.; the difference consists in the fact that then (1545) it was a question of founding a "Second Order" (a female branch of the Society), whereas the admission of Juana was to be an unique exception and she was thereby actually to be received into the existing community. The form of vow given here follows more or less Text A of the Constitutions (about 1550), cf. *MI* III, ii, 514, col. 1, whereas the later and definitive text differs principally in placing the promise to enter the Society after the three religious vows. The reference to the "sixth part of the Constitutions" in the text of the memorial is an error; it should read "fifth part", which even in the earlier version of 1550 deals with the various degrees of membership of the Society.

[50] The bull of the Apostolic Penitentiary. – Trans.

[51] For the alteration of the regent's earlier vow, cf. *MI* I, vii, 684 et seq.; viii, 21, 88; *Chron.*, v, 47. The communication concerning the admission of the Infanta and the conditions to be observed is in *MI* I, viii, 198, 219 et seq.

[52] The infanta's words are in *Quadr.*, iii, 387; cf. *M. Borg.*, ii, 226. The fact that in 1556 Juana received the *bonorum communicatio* of the Society at the same time as her sister María (*M. Rib.*, i, 210, 215) is a proof of the strict secrecy with which her admission to the Society was kept, for that would in itself have made the conferring of such a favour superfluous.

[53] For her intervention in the persecution of Saragossa see *Chron.*, v, 397 et seq.,

402, 404. Ignatius' request for her support, *MI* I, x, 513; *Chron.*, vi, 531. Her directions to the archbishop and the viceroy, *ibid.*, 536, 626 et seq. For her attitude to M. Cano cf. *Mixt.*, iv, 548; *Chron.*, vi, 630 et seq. Talk of "jesuitical practices", *ibid.*, 633. For Borgia's conversations with Charles V cf. *M. Borg.*, ii, 462 et seq.; *M. Rib.*, i, 225. The Infanta's joy at their success in *M. Borg.*, ii, 271; cf. also introductory section to Part one, note 3. Juana's statement that she would like to be a preacher is in *M. Borg.*, iii, 259 et seq.; she had already written previously to the Emperor in the matter of the Louvain college (*Chron.*, vi, 463, 466).

[54] Concerning help for the Roman College cf. *MI* I, viii, 197; ix, 136, 162, 615; x, 78 et seq.; *Chron.*, vi, 524; she was also approached on behalf of the college in Naples (*MI* I, viii, 103; x, 114). Gift to the college of Valladolid: *M. Borg.*, ii, 452; *MI* I, viii, 199, 217, 345; *Chron.*, iv, 438. On convent reform cf. *MI* I, x, 222. *Ibid.*, ix, 162 Borgia is asked to get Juana to be the Society's intermediary with Pope Paul IV. Similarly the princess is asked to write to the Pope requesting special favours for the pilgrimage to Our Lady of Aránzazu (*ibid.*, vii, 423; viii, 196).

[55] For the affair of Fr. Doménech's inheritance, cf. *Chron.*, vi, 508. The question of Fr. de Córboda's estate, see *MI* I, viii, 25. Polanco's words are in *Pol. Compl.*, i, 114. Ignatius' words, *MI* I, ix, 139. Juana's letter of recommendation to Paul IV dated February 10th, 1556, is in *Mixt.*, v, 186. For Juana's influence in preventing Borgia's being made a cardinal, see *Chron.*, iv, 590, 592. In recognition of all these services the princess received blessed rosaries from Ignatius (*MI* I, ix, 86); likewise later from Laynez, with "almost infinitely great indulgences" (*M. Lain.*, v, 55), and a holy picture from Borgia in May 1568 (*M. Borg.*, iv, 602). Juana for her part requested permission through Ignatius to read the Bible in her mother tongue (*Chron.*, iv, 591; 5, 541); the reply is in *MI* I, viii, 21, with the brief qualification: "it must be a really good translation" (*ibid.*, 87), and furthermore it must not be the Ferrara Bible, published in 1553 in Ferrara by Jerónimo de Vargas and Duarte Pinel (*ibid.*, 194).

[56] Borgia's letter to Laynez is in *M. Borg.*, ii, 406 (cf. also *ibid.*, 415). Words of the novice-master of Simancas, *ibid.*, 226. Borgia to Nadal in *M. Nad.*, iii, 414; the same pseudonym is used in *M. Lain.*, i, 335; ii, 263.

[57] The remark about the college of Valladolid comes from Fr. de Ribera (Astráin, ii, 484). For the suspicions concerning the relations between Borgia and the Infanta, cf. Astráin, 118 and Karrer, 184. Borgia as executor of Charles V, see Astráin, 109.

[58] Juana acted as matchmaker on other occasions, cf. *M. Lain.*, v, 268. For Pedro Galcerán de Borja cf. *M. Borg.*, i, 432 et seq., 455-7; in 1540 he became, owing to the renunciation of his half-brother Errigo (who in December became a cardinal at 21), Comendador of the Order of Montesa at the age of twelve (*ibid.*, 413); for the election of 1544 cf. *ibid.*, 435-7, 439 et seq. For the personal appearance of the bride cf. *ibid.*, 445, 450 et seq., 457. Pedro's letter to Ignatius, *ibid.*, 444.

[59] Araoz. – Trans.

[60] In 1557 Pedro was made Marquis of Navarrés by Philip II (*ibid.*, 733-7). Borgia's words to Laynez, *M. Borg.*, iii, 462 et seq. For Philip's displeasure with

Francis Borgia, cf. Astráin, 116; F. Cereceda, *Diego Lainez en la Europa religiosa de su tiempo,* ii (Madrid, 1946), 11 et seq. The quotation from a contemporary historian is in *M. Borg.,* i, 445. For the final settlement of the question in 1588, cf. *ibid.,* 451. Birth of a son in 1560, *M. Borg.,* iv, 272; on the latter's early death in 1568 Ribadeneira wrote a letter of condolence (J. M. Prat, *Leben und Wirken des R. P. Peter de Ribadeneira* [Regensburg, 1885], 233–6); Pedro had besides, an illegitimate son (*M. Borg.,* i, 461). Details of Borgia's efforts to obtain the dispensation are to be found in *M. Borg.,* iii, 273, 366, 414, 462–4; *Chron.,* vi, 648; *M. Nad.,* ii, 66 (here also is a reference to Borgia's disgrace with Philip caused by this affair); Laynez pushed the matter with the Spanish ambassador in Rome (*M. Lain.,* i, 592 et seq.). In 1559 Borgia, in a letter to Laynez, called the case of his stepbrother "a scandal" (*M. Borg.,* ii, 462 et seq.). Cervantes' verses on Don Pedro are in the *Galatea* (*ibid.,* i, 461).

[61] Cf. I. E. Nieremberg, *Vidas exemplares y venerables memorias,* iv (Madrid, 1647), 632 et seq. For the spiritual decline of Fr. Araoz, cf. Astráin 483–8.

[62] The contemporary remark about Araoz, *ibid.,* 487. Juana was on the side of Araoz against Borgia (*M. Borg.,* iv, 190, 201); Araoz had already previously become indispensable to her (*MI* I, x, 244, 249; xi, 250). Duarte Pereira's letter is in *M. Nad.,* i, 797.

[63] For the founding of the convent see *Chron.,* iv, 433, 438 et seq.; Elias Tormo, *En las Descalzas Reales. Estudios históricos, iconográficos y artísticos* (Madrid, 1915–17). For the first abbess see *M. Borg.* i, 503–5. For the visit of the great St. Teresa to the "Royal Discalced" cf. M. Auclair, *Das Leben der hl. Teresa von Avila* (Zürich, 1953), 189. Eng., *St. Teresa of Avila* (London, 1953).

[64] These details are from the Venetian ambassadors' reports (M. A. Baschet, *Les princes de l'Europe au XVIe siècle d'après les rapports des ambassadeurs vénitiens* [Paris, 1862], 243; M. Gachard, *Relations des ambassadeurs vénitiens,* 164) and from those of the imperial ambassador von Dietrichstein (M. Koch, *Quellen zur Geischichte Kaiser Maximilians II* [Leipzig, 1857], i, 124, 133, 194, 196); cf. also *M. Borg.,* v, 603. In 1568 Juana was again considered for the post of Regent, when Philip II was thinking of going to Flanders (*M. Nad.,* iii, 359, 512).

[65] Projected marriages for Juana occur again and again in diplomatic reports. The earliest plan for her remarriage concerned the Archduke Ferdinand (Turba, *Venezianische Depeschen,* 136 et seq.); about the year 1560 marriage with the son of the Duke of Florence was being considered, a plan favoured by the Pope (*ibid.,* 177 and note 7); the French project was under consideration for several years (*ibid.,* 384, note 2; Koch, *Quellen,* i, 133, 137, 146, 150, 169, 191). Simultaneously there was a plan to marry her to her nephew Don Carlos, which she herself wished; on this see esp. Dietrichstein (Koch, *Quellen,* i, 119, 123, 125 et seq., 130, 218–20) as well as Nadal's letter to Borgia as early as the end of 1561 (*M. Nad.,* i, 581 et seq.); cf. besides M. Gachard, *Don Carlos et Philippe II* (Brussels, 1863), i, 180–3. How devoted the Spanish princesses were to their House and especially to their brother Philip can be seen from a report of the Venetian Michele (J. Fiedler, "Relationen venezianischer Botschafter über Deutschland und Österreich im 16. Jahrhundert" in *Fontes rerum austriacarum,* 2nd part, vol. xxx [Vienna, 1870], 283). This justifies the

interpretation here given of "dynastic heroism". Later further matrimonial projects were aired, with the Archduke Charles (Turba, *Venezianische Depeschen*, 447, note 4) and finally in 1571 with the Archduke Rudolph (*ibid.*, 548, note 3).

[66] Reports about Juana to Borgia in *M. Borg.*, v, 249, 292. Entries in his spiritual diary, *ibid.*, 826, 829, 883. The announcement of the victory of Lepanto in D. C. Rosell, *Historia del combate naval de Lepanto* (Madrid, 1853), 209 (quoted by M. Gachard, *Relations des ambassadeurs vénitiens*, 62, note 3). In the last year of her life we hear also of a dispensation granted to Juana by the Pope (despatch of the Spanish ambassador in Rome dated May 22nd, 1573, in *Colección de documentos inéditos para la historia de España*, cii, 136); this was a permission to enter all convents without restriction. Borgia's death was specially reported to Juana: *M. Borg.*, v, 716. The day of her death is given in March, ii, 449. Juana was buried at the *Descalzas Reales*, where a statue by Pompeio Leoni was erected to her memory.

Infanta Isabel of Portugal

[67] For her family history see A. C. de Sousa, *Historia genealógica da Casa Real portugueza*, v (Lisbon, 1749), 592. For Dom Duarte cf. Schurhammer, i, 584, 633–6. Eulogy of the Braganza family in *Chron.*, i, 446. For the relations between Isabel and Teotonio cf. also *Mixt.*, iv, 18, 288; *MI* I, ix, 549. For Teotonio see *FN*, i, 620, note 2; also J. M. Aicardo, *Comentario a las Constituciones de la Compañia de Jesús*, v (Madrid, 1930), 576–89 and Rodrigues, i, 2, 210–20.

[68] His studies in Coimbra and entry into the Society, see *Chron.*, i, 446. His fellow-Jesuits' opinion of him in *Quadr.*, i, 471. Polanco's later judgment in *Chron.*, ii, 375.

[69] Thus in *MI* I, iv, 93.

[70] Continuation of his studies on the orders of the Visitor, Dr. Torres; *Chron.*, ii, 621. His dissatisfaction at the "Castilian exile", *ibid.*, 712. Letters of Teotonio to Ignatius from Salamanca dated September 28th, 1552: *Mixt.*, ii, 790; and from Alcalá dated December 8th, 1552: *ibid.*, 862–5. Ignatius' answer of January 7th, 1553, is in *MI* I, iv, 588 et seq. Rodríguez' arrival in Alcalá, see *Chron.*, iii, 322; reference to the "tragedy of Teotonius", *ibid.*, 436. Rodríguez' return to Portugal, *ibid.*, 393; for Teotonio's intended journey and his sudden change of plan see *Mixt.*, iii, 508, 535 et seq.; on September 30th, 1553, King John III wrote to Gonçalves that Teotonio was at Villaviciosa with his mother for the sake of his health (*Doc. Ind.*, iii, 28; cf. *FN*, i, 620, note 3). Ignatius' two letters are in *MI* I, v, 168 et seq., 620; for the exception to the rule of obedience cf. *M. Nad.*, i, 205–9. Mirón's report is in *Mixt.*, iv, 17–23. Ignatius' patient letters to Teotonio in *MI* I, vi, 130 et seq., 572; the latter's readiness to go anywhere, see *Mixt.*, iv, 101 et seq.; his letter of April 18th, 1554, *ibid.*, 146 et seq. Ignatius' order to Teotonio dated April 6th, 1554, is in *MI I*, vi, 572; *ibid.*, 568 his letter to Mirón of the same date. Mirón gave an account of the roundabout journey to Rome on August 2nd, 1554 (*Mixt.*, iv, 288); Borgia's reasons for this route in *Chron.*, iv, 547; fear of a family disgrace, *ibid.*

⁷¹ For Teotonio's arrival in Venice on Sept. 9th, 1554 (cf. *Mixt.*, iv, 379, note 5); his letter from there to Ignatius, *ibid.*, 339–41; Ignatius' intention of preventing a meeting with Rodríguez: *MI* I, vi, 121; only after the latter's departure from Rome was Teotonio to arrive there (*ibid.*, vii, 295). Ignatius' letter to Venice, *ibid.*, 555–7; the three letters to Teotonio, *ibid.*, 562–4.

⁷² For the journey from Venice to Rome cf. *MI* I, vii, 683; *Pol. Compl.*, ii, 577. Teotonio's friendly reception there: *Chron.*, iv, 129. Good behaviour at first: *ibid.*, v, 39. Sickness of Teotonio and gossip in Portugal: *MI* I, viii, 444. Duke Teodosio's letter is in *Mixt.*, iv, 532 et seq., dated January 24th, 1555. Celebration at the departure of the Indian missionaries, *Chron.*, v, 608 et seq.; one of the missionaries called the Infanta in 1556 "our dearest mother and sister in Our Lord" (*Doc. Ind.*, iii, 521), Ignatius' reply to the Duke dated April 11th, 1555, is in *MI* I, viii, 662; letter to the Infante Luis, *ibid.*, 478. Teotonio's request for forgiveness and renewal of vows, February 1555, *ibid.*, 493. For the conversation between Ignatius and Teotonio in August 1555 cf. *MI* IV, i, 385 et seq., 416.

⁷³ In *M. Salm.*, i, 125. *FN*, i, 740 et seq. For the conference of twelve, cf. *MI* IV, i, 388, 416 et seq.; *Pol. Compl.*, ii, 581.

⁷⁴ Polanco's remark is in *Chron.*, v, 39 et seq. Ignatius' words to Mirón about a "desperate case" on August 22nd, 1555: *MI* I, ix, 488. There is a detailed account of the difficulties *ibid.*, 501–5 (August 26th and 29th, 1555). Report of September 1st, to Mirón, *ibid.*, 525 et seq.; For the scandal on the same day cf., also *Pol. Compl.*, ii, 581. The letter of September 3rd is in *MI* I, ix, 544 et seq.; the Portuguese ambassador, his son and Fr. Olave talk to Teotonio, *ibid.*, 546; *Chron.*, v, 39 et seq.; *M. Nad.*, ii, 32.

⁷⁵ For Teotonio's departure see *Pol. Compl.*, ii, 581. The quotation from the letter to Mirón is in *MI* I, ix, 547. Letter to King John III, *ibid.*, 550; letter to Duke Teodosio, *ibid.*, 547 et seq.

⁷⁶ Directions for the journey are in *MI* I, ix, 565 et seq.; the order to Rodríguez, *ibid.*, 571. Details that became known subsequently, *ibid.*, 570. Events of the journey in the report of his companion Fr. Fernández in *Mixt.*, iv, 867 et seq.; v, 22 et seq. Report on Teotonio's sojourn in Paris in *MI* I, x, 260; instruction to Broët dated October 30th, 1555, *ibid.*, 75; likewise that of Laynez to Broët in 1557, *M. Lain.*, ii, 18 et seq.

⁷⁷ Gonçalves da Câmara speaks to the Duke of Braganza and the Infanta Isabel; his report is in *Mixt.*, v, 277 et seq.; cf. also *Chron.*, vi, 742; request for repayment of the 250 ducats is in *Mixt.*, v, 750. For the talk in Flanders see *M. Rib.*, i, 147. Hostility of the Marchioness of Elche, *M. Nad.*, ii, 41; in her house Nadal met Teotonio in 1561 (*ibid.*, 83).

⁷⁸ Concerning this Maria of Portugal cf. L. van der Essen, *Alexandre Farnèse, prince de Parme, gouverneur général des Pays-Bas* (Brussels, 1933), i, 98 et seq.; 105 et seq. Teotonio, too, was involved in the marriage negociations, *ibid.*, 101. The statement of van der Essen, 106, repeated by G. Drei, *I Farnese, grandezza e decadenza di una dinastia italiana* (Rome, 1954), 118, that Ignatius was once confessor to Maria, is false; both in Lisbon and later in Parma her confessor was Fr. Sebastian Morales, cf. *M. Borg.*, v. 580. At Parma Maria died on July 8th, 1577 (van der

Essen, 195). Teotonio became in 1578 coadjutor to Cardinal Enrique, in 1579 his successor cf. *M. Salm.*, ii, 688; *Mixt.*, ii, 505, note 4. For his correspondence with St. Teresa – he complains especially of distractions at prayer while travelling – cf. M. Auclair, *St. Teresa of Avila*, (London 1953), 308, 359. *Letters of St. Teresa*, trans. E. Allison Peers (London, 1951), 114–18, 155–6, 168–172, 511–18, 676–80.

Margaret of Austria

[79] L. Pfandl, *Philipp II* (Munich, 1938), 416; cf. also 318. The standard biography is by F. Rachfahl, *Margareta von Parma, Statthalterin der Niederlande* (Munich-Leipzig, 1898). For the promotion of the Jesuits in Flanders by her son Alexander cf. O. Manaraeus, *Exhortationes super instituto et regulis S.J.* (ed. Brussels, 1912), 8.*

[80] Thus Tomás Armenteros (for him see *M. Borg.*, v, 19) to Gonzalo Pérez on January 11th, 1566: M. Gachard, *Correspondance de Philippe II sur les affaires des Pays-Bas* (Brussels, 1848) i, 391; there is further material on the regency in the first two vols. of the above collection and especially in M. Gachard, *Correspondance de Marguerite, duchesse de Parme, avec Philippe II* (Brussels, 1867–81).

[81] Thus Rachfahl, 3 et seq.; details about what is here related, *ibid.*, 1–4; cf. also K. Brandi, *Kaiser Karl V.* (Munich, 1937), 142. Strada's account of Margaret's origins is in *De bello belgico* (Leyden, 1643), i, 40–8.

[82] For the political background to the marriage see Rachfahl, 4–6 and A. von Reumont, *Geschichte Toskanas seit dem Ende des florentinischen Freistaates* (Gotha, 1876), 64; there is a description of the wedding to the Pope's grandson in L. von Pastor, *History of the Popes*, xi, 324–6; F. de Navenne, *Rome, le Palais Farnèse* (Paris, 1914), 237–49.

[83] There is an account of this event in Peter Faber's letter dated November 23rd, 1538 (*MI* I, i, 132).

[84] Cardinal Lenoncourt's words, in a letter to the Constable of Montmorency, are in Rachfahl, 14; instruction of Charles V to his daughter, *ibid.* The opinion of Margaret's reply is her father's (*ibid.*) Cf. also the account of the matrimonial tragedy in C. Capasso, *Paolo III* (1534–1549) (Messina, 1924), ii, 62–74. This does not say a single word about Ignatius' activities as mediator.

[85] For the Jesuits named as confessors to Margaret see *FN,* ii, 94, 105, 265; *MI* I, i, 184, 290, where Ignatius is called "confessor to the house of Madama"; *M. Lain.,* vi, 340. The opinion of Codure is in Nadal, *FN,* ii, 105.

[86] E. Gothein, *Ignatius von Loyola* (Halle, 1885), 129.

[87] Meeting with the knight of Santiago in *FN,* ii, 327. The expression "characteristically Habsburg devotion" is in *MI* I, i, 182; *ibid.,* she is called *nuestra Madama.* For the privileges gained through her see *FN,* ii, 105. Ignatius' protest against alleged help in getting the Society approved in *MI* I, xii, 277.

[88] Thus Ribadeneira in *FN,* ii, 374 et seq. The previously mentioned event concerning the gift of money, *ibid.,* i, 413; ii, 483.

[89] Thus Brandi, 428. For Laynez' journey to Lucca with Madama see *MI* I, i, 184; her arrival there, Pastor, xii, 126 Letter to Francis Xavier about the founding of

the house of catechumens: *MI* I, i, 268. For her co-operation with the House of St. Martha, *ibid.*, 306. Her presence at the baptism of the convert Jew, *ibid.*, 182 et seq.

⁹⁰ Madama's intervention with the Pope on several occasions: *MI* I, i, 210, 219, 240, 373; ii, 71, 204, 220, 560 et seq. For the sojourn of the Pope at that time in Bologna and Rimini cf. *ibid.*, i. 272, note 3.

⁹¹ Strada's account is in Rachfahl, 27 et seq. The latter, ignorant of the material in the archives of the Society, publication of which in the *Mon. Hist. S. J.*, had begun several years before he wrote his biography, also makes the criticism of Strada quoted in the text.

⁹² This letter, with which *FN*, i, 41 is to be compared, supplements the account of the birth of the twins in L. van der Essen, *Alexandre Farnèse*, i, 10 et seq. In Navenne, 280 and G. Drei, *I Farnese*, 41 there is likewise no mention of Ignatius in this connexion. The solemn baptism of the second child, at which he received the name of Alexander, took place on November 30th, 1545.

⁹³ *MI* I, ii 240. For Ignatius' mediation in the quarrel between Tivoli and the Castel cf. *Chron.*, i, 266 and *FN*, i, 45.* For the lady-in-waiting María de Mendoza-Guzmán see *MI* I, i, 306 and *Mixt.*, v, 660. For Margaret's help in the affair of Fr. Jay: *MI* I, i, 464–6; *FN*, i, 749–51; *Chron.*, i, 91.

⁹⁴ The pilgrimage to Loreto: *MI* I, i, 227. The quotation about her devotion to the Society, *ibid.*, ii, 52. Polanco's words, *ibid.*, iii, 178.

⁹⁵ Cf. Rachfahl, 21–4; lost letters to Madama are mentioned in *MI* I, iii, 139, 222.

⁹⁶ Quotation from the Pope's letter in Pastor, xiii, 95; for the war between the Pope and Ottavio see *ibid.*

⁹⁷ For the foregoing reply of Madama cf. *Chron.*, iv, 143 et seq. Question of founding a college at Parma: *MI* I, xi, 318; *Chron.*, vi, 240 et seq. For the Rainaldi affair see the detailed account in our chapter on Duchess Eleonora of Florence. Margaret's letter on this matter is no longer extant.

⁹⁸ The Duchess' letter to Polanco is in *MI* IV, ii, 35 et seq. Polanco's letter has not been preserved.

⁹⁹ Laynez' letter of July 23rd, 1558, is in *M. Lain.*, iii, 416 et seq. Borgia's greeting dated March 17th, 1568, in *M. Borg.*, iv, 592 et seq. For Madama's friendship with Bobadilla cf. *M. Bob.*, 577 et seq.; for the rosary of agate see *ibid.*, 593; her burial at Loreto, *ibid.*, 584. Her "unloved husband" (thus Rachfahl, 272) died eight months after Margaret; cf. *ibid.* their common tomb at Piacenza.

Eleonora of Florence

¹⁰⁰ For the general history see A. von Reumont, *Geschichte Toskanas seit dem Ende des florentinischen Freistaates* (Gotha, 1876); E. Heyck, *Florenz und die Medici* (Bielefeld-Leipzig, 1909), Ignatius' letter to Laynez is in *MI* I, i, 400.

¹⁰¹ For Bronzino, who as court painter to the Duchess decorated her chapel in the Palazzo Vecchio, cf. H. Schulze, *Angelo Bronzino's Werke* (Strasbourg, 1910). L. von Ranke on the Spanish grandees in *Die spanische Monarchie im 16. und 17.*

Jahrhundert (Works, vols. xxxv and xxxvi), (Leipzig, 1877), 180–2. For the political background to Cosimo's marriage with Eleonora see Reumont, 138 et seq. Purchase and extension of the Pitti Palace, *ibid.,* 253. The Venetian Fedeli describes the Duke in 1561 as "paterfamilias", and represents him as popular and affable; M. Baschet, *Les princes de l'Europe au XVIᵉ siècle d'après les ambassadeurs vénitiens* (Paris, 1862), 137 et seq. Charles V's political testament is in K. Brandi, *Kaiser Karl V.* (Munich, 1937), 501. For Eleonora as ancestress of the princes of Europe cf. F. Fernández de Béthencourt, *Príncipes y caballeros* (*Obras* I) (Madrid, 1913), 122.

[102] For Eleonora's family cf. *Mixt.,* i, 310; A. de Burgos, *Blasón de España,* vi, 234; J. Raneo and E. Fernández de Navarrete, "Libro donde se trata de los virreyes lugartenientes del reino de Nápoles" in *Colección de documentos inéditos para la historia de España,* xxiii, 106–39. The contemporary acount is in the MS *Diario di Firenze dal 1536 al 1555,* cf. Tacchi-Venturi, ii, 2, 282. The last quotation is from Reumont, 253.

[103] For Bobadilla and Araoz in Naples see *M. Bob.,* 20; *MI* I, i, 400, note 4. Polanco's letter in *Pol. Compl.,* i, 19. After the death of her father the Duchess asked Ignatius to remember him in his prayers: *Mixt.,* iv, 380–2.

[104] Polanco's memorandum, in which Lucrezia Borgia is set up as a model, is in *Pol. Compl.,* i, 20–9. Friendly reception on the part of the Duchess, *Quadr.,* i, 38; cf. *Chron.,* i, 209, 222. Ignatius' rebuke is in *MI* I, i, 458; cf. also Karrer and Rahner, *Ignatius von Loyola. Geistliche Briefe* (Einsiedeln, 1942), 123–6. Defence of Polanco to the Duke in *MI* I, i, 471 et seq. For a judgment on the whole affair cf. Tacchi-Venturi, ii, 2, 269 et seq., and the introduction to *Pol. Compl.,* i, pp. xvi-xx, as contrasted with the account in Pastor, xii, 87 and Astráin, i, 582.

[105] Laynez' mission to Florence: *M. Lain.,* i, 61 et seq. The Duke's words and the Duchess's expression of her readiness to help, *ibid.,* 75. Projected college in Pisa, *ibid.,* 76. Resigned observations on the state of things: *MI* I, iii, 704 et seq. (cf. *Chron.,* ii, 177) and later in *MI* I, vii, 126, 162 (cf. *Chron.,* iv, 165). For Borgia's visit to Florence see *MI* I, iii, 261, 346, 355; *Chron.,* ii, 12 et seq.; *M. Lain.,* i, 180 et seq.

[106] Ignatius' letter to the secretary is in *MI* I, iii, 347. Instructions to scholastics, *ibid.,* 718 et seq.; account of the audience, *ibid.,* iv, 33; the expression about "not getting on the lady's nerves", *ibid.,* 77. The decision to found a college, *ibid.,* iii, 589, 638, et seq.; cf. also *Chron.,* ii, 174–9, 249. Communication of the news to Francis Xavier is in *MI* I, iv, 132 et seq.

[107] Ignatius wrote in January 1554 to Laynez that the Duchess was not keeping her high-sounding promises (*MI* I, vi, 211). The reference to the example of the Infanta Juana (whose mediation on behalf of the Florentine college had already been asked for: *M. Lain.,* i. 600) is in *MI* I, vii, 28. The Duke's opinion of the riches of the Jesuits is in *Chron.,* vi, 150. Ignatius' reply to Coudray, *MI* I, iv, 158, 205, 288. Account of Salmerón's audience with the Duchess, *Chron.,* vi, 151.

[108] There are biographical notes on Tarquinio Rainaldi in *FN,* i, 569, note 4, and 570, note 8; information about him in *Chron.,* iii, 63 et seq.; iv, 140, 340; vi, 187, 507 et seq.; *Pol. Compl.,* ii, 116 et seq.; *MI* I, v, 180, 193, 505–8; vi, 491, ix 397 et seq., 400 et seq.; *Mixt.,* iv, 88–95; *M. Lain.,* i, 233–5, 492–4. For the Marquis of Marignano cf. Pastor, xv, 67–74

[109] The expression "tragi-comedy" is in *M. Lain.*, i. 233; an account of the scene in the Palazzo Pitti is in *Chron.*, iii, 63; *FN*, i. 570. The opinion of Ignatius' reply is taken from Tacchi-Venturi, *Una lettera inedita di S. Ignazio di Loiola alla Duchessa Leonora di Toscana* in *Civiltà Cattolica*, 17, iii (1898), 152.

[110] For the great impression that his fidelity to his vocation made upon the Duchess see *MI* I, viii, 85. Judgment on this in Tacchi-Venturi, *Una lettera inedita*, 151. Tarquinio was at his own wish (*Mixt.*, iv, 88–95) sent from Rome to Spain (*MI* I, vi, 491), where he arrived at Pentecost 1554 (*Chron.*, iv, 340). Ignatius' letter to him is in *MI* I, viii, 551. In the autumn of 1555 his brother, Canon Annibale de Rainaldi, followed him to Spain in order to persuade Tarquinio to return (*ibid.*, ix, 64, 613; *Chron.*, vi, 508); he did not succeed, but in October 1556 Tarquinio went back to Italy on the advice of his physicians (*Mixt.*, v, 514; *Chron.*, vi, 187).

[111] Prelude to Laynez' mission to Genoa, see *MI* I, v, 288, 313, 344, 402; Ignatius' letter to the Cardinal of Santiago, a brother of the Viceroy of Naples Pedro de Toledo, *ibid.*, 428. His instruction to Laynez to maintain good relations, *ibid.*, 409 et seq. The latter's release for two months, *ibid.*, 475, 544, 649. Instruction to write a letter of thanks to the Duchess, *ibid.*, 650. For Laynez' stay in Genoa cf. *ibid.*, vi, 51, 65, 82, 146, 596; instruction to give way, *ibid.*, 668. The letter about the Duchess' threat is in *Mixt.*, iv, 870. For her change of temper and the resultant possibility of recalling Laynez to Rome see *MI* I, vii, 126, 394, 411 et seq.

[112] For Laynez' journey to attend the Imperial Diet at Augsburg, cf. Pastor, xiii, 226 et seq. F. Cereceda, *Diego Laynez en la Europa religiosa de su tiempo* (Madrid, 1945), i, 514–20. Encyclical letter asking for prayers for Germany is in *MI* I, viii, 266. Order to Laynez to set out, *ibid.*, 270.

[113] For the Duchess' protest see *MI* I, viii, 423; her letters to the Pope and cardinals, *ibid.*, 368, 405.

[114] Ignatius' alarm at the election of Carafa is referred to by Gonçalves da Câmara, *Memoriale*, No. 93 (*FN*, i, 581 et seq.). For Mudarra cf. D. Cantimori, *Eretici italiani del Cinquecento* (Florence, 1939), 74 et seq.; Tacchi-Venturi, i, 2, 77 et seq.; *FN*, i, 132, note 11. The quotation from the memoirs No. 98 *ibid.*, 502; the final judgment of November 18th, 1538, is in *MI* IV, i, 627 et seq.; Schurhammer, i, 417 et seq.

[115] Mudarra suspected of heresy: *MI* I, viii, 648; measures taken by the Inquisition, cf. *FN*, i, 309, 708 et seq. Mudarra's flight to Florence, *Mixt.*, iv, 843. Ignatius' letter of November 1554 in *MI* I, vii, 728; that of February 1555, *ibid.*, viii, 366 et seq.; that of April, *ibid.*, 673 et seq.; cf. also *Chron.*, iv, 166; v, 100; vi, 62.

[116] Mudarra's letter of thanks is in *Mixt.*, iv, 843 et seq.; Fr. Gonçalves' remark in *FN*, i, 708 et seq. Ignatius' letter to de Vega in this connexion, *MI* I, x, 482; the rebuke to Doménech, *ibid.*, xi, 419. For the action in July 1556 cf. *ibid.*, xii, 91, 124.

[117] The extract from the Duchess' letter to Cardinal del Monte is in Tacchi-Venturi, *Una lettera inedita*, 152, note 1; cf. *Chron.*, iii, 93. Ignatius' instruction to Laynez, *MI* I, ix, 20; letter to Florence saying that Laynez could not leave Rome, *ibid.*, 617. The Duchess' displeasure, cf. *Chron.*, v, 34.

[118] Anger of the Duchess: *Chron.*, v, 102; cf. also *MI* I, x, 164, where her letter

of complaint is mentioned. Ignatius' final decision, *ibid.*, 45, 167. The letter of congratulation, *ibid.*, 108. Instructions to Guzmán, *ibid.*, 193; the letter of November 9th, 1555, *ibid.*, 106.

[119] New instructions to Guzmán, *MI* I, x, 405. For the change for the better, cf. *ibid.*, 402; *M. Lain.*, i, 457; *Chron.*, vi, 148. For Juan de Mendoza's audience cf. *MI* I, x, 411. The Duchess' words about Guzmán are in *Chron.*, vi, 157.

[120] The Duchess's request to Guzmán is in *Chron.*, vi, 153; the latter's anxiety, *ibid.*, 157. Occasional gifts from the Duchess to the college, *ibid.*, 142. Ignatius' instruction to Coudray, *Mixt.*, i, 12, 138, 181. For the case of Truxillo, cf. *Chron.*, v, 94; vi, 147 et seq.; *Mixt.*, v, 240 for the report of the Duchess' words.

[121] The communication on the death of Ignatius is in *FN*, i, 777 (almost the same word for word as the corresponding letter to Cardinal Mendoza in Burgos: *Cartas*, vi, 380 et seq.). Laynez' instructions to Guzmán, *M. Lain.*, i, 457; letters of Laynez to the Duchess, *ibid.*, 259 et seq., 312 et seq. Her offer in connection with the first General Congregation is in *Chron.*, vi, 157; her congratulations to Laynez on his election, *M. Lain.*, iii, 411. In January 1560 Laynez asked the Duchess to intercede on behalf of the Society with the new pope, *M. Lain.*, iv, 611 et seq.

[122] For the Duchess' journey to Rome see Pastor, *History of the Popes*, xvi, 344. Her confession to Laynez is mentioned in *M. Lain.*, v, 351. Report of the conversation between him and the Duchess, *ibid.*, vi, 604. Polanco's letter is in *M. Lain.*, i, 317. Requests for medicines for Laynez, *ibid.*, 457, 541 et seq., 629; cf. also *Chron.*, vi, 160.

[123] For the death of her two sons see Reumont, 235 et seq. The Duchess' presentiments of death, *Quadr.*, IV, 152. Laynez from Trent asked Strada for news about the Duchess' sickness and death (*M. Lain.*, vi, 598 et seq.); Strada assisted the Duchess on her deathbed (*ibid.*, 636, 661). She left 200 scudi of income to the college in her will, and is therefore called its "part-foundress" (*ibid.*, 673). Letter of condolence to the Duke, *ibid.*, 602–6.

Part Two

God's Cavalier

Introduction

[1] The expression *noble caballero* is used in the introduction to the Exercises, dictated by Ignatius (MI, II, ii, 96).

[2] For Ignatius' family see. P. Leturia, *El Gentilhombre Inigo López de Loyola en su patria y en su siglo* (Barcelona, 1949). Ignatius himself proudly stresses the racial purity of the Basque people, cf. *FN*, i, 174. Navagero's words are taken from I. C. de Guerra, *Estudios de heráldica vasca* (San Sebastian, 1928), 6.

[3] For the circle of ladies in Barcelona cf. Creixell, i, 262-5. List of the ladies' committee for the House of St. Martha in Tacchi-Venturi, i, 2, 296-307.

[4] In Ignatius' other correspondence there are mentioned, for example, the follow-

NOTES

ing ladies of the Spanish nobility; Catalina de la Cerda, daughter of the Duke of Medina Celi (*M. Fabr.*, 128); Beatriz de Figueroa, Countess of Pálamos (*Mixt.*, i, 204); the Duchess of Medina Sidonia (*M. Lain.*, i, 377; *Mixt.*, iv, 689 et seq.) For the lost letters to Catarina de Velasco cf. *MI* IV, ii, 472; i. 1, 705; *Mixt.*, v, 653.

⁵ From M. Auclair, *St. Teresa of Avila* (London, 1953).

Women of the House of Loyola

⁶ The letter to the Duke of Nájera is in *MI* I, iv, 386; letter to his sister Magdalena, see page 117; the letter of June 1532 is in *MI* I, i, 79–83. Letter giving news of his first Mass, February 2nd, 1539 *ibid.*, 145–7. His brother had died on November 29th, 1538. The letter of September 1539 to Beltrán, *ibid.*, 148–51; here the other letters, no longer preserved, are mentioned.

⁷ For the mother of Ignatius and for the other women of the house of Loyola see esp. P. Leturia, "Damas vascas en la formación y transformación de Iñigo de Loyola" in *Revista Internacional de Estudios vascos,* xi (1949), 7–24. The marriage settlements have not so far been published (cf. meanwhile *FN*, i, 153, note 4). For the piety of Ignatius' mother cf. *MI* IV, ii, 529, 799, 869.

⁸ Cf. P. Leturia, *El gentilhombre Iñigo López de Loyola* (Barcelona, 1949), 42 et seq.; P. Dudon, *St. Ignace de Loyola* (Paris, 1934), 220 et seq.

⁹ For Magdalena's family see Leturia, *El Gentilhombre,* 28 et seq.; *MI* I, i, 82, note 11. The marriage took place on September 2nd, 1498 (cf. Leturia, *Damas vascas,* 17 as opposed to *FN,* i, 153, note 5). For her position at court see *Chron.,* i. 545 et seq. The concluding quotation is from P. Leturia, *Damas vascas.*

¹⁰ For the books read by Ignatius cf. P. Leturia, *El Gentilhombre,* 149–60, 304 et seq. For the payment to the doctor see *FN,* i, 369, note 9. The account of the Belgian Balduin de Angelis is in *MI* IV, ii, 435.

¹¹ Magdalena's children mentioned in her husband's will: *Chron.,* i, 497–515. For Millán cf. *MI* I, i, 77, 148 et seq., 167; *Mixt.*, i, 167; Astráin, i, 257; Leturia, *Damas vascas,* 23, note 45; J. Malaxechevarría, *La Compañía de Jesús por la instrucción del pueblo vasco en los siglos XVII y XVIII* (S. Sebastian, 1926), 4–7. Letter of her daughter Catarina in *Mixt.*, i, 204.

¹² Letter of Araoz in *Mixt.*, i, 35, 38; Ignatius' answer in *MI* I, xii, 215 et seq.

¹³ For the family of Recalde cf. *MI* I, i, 151, note 4. Respects to Doña Juana in the letter to her husband, *ibid.*, 190. For the marriage of her daughter, see page 121 et seq.

¹⁴ Doña Maria's words are in Henao-Villalta, *Averiguaciones de las antigüedades de Cantabria,* vii (Tolosa, 1894), 183. For the family of the Guevaras, Counts of Oñate, see *ibid.*, vi, 344 and vii, 169, 179 et seq.

¹⁵ For Magdalena's husband see *FN,* i, 381, note 3; *Mixt.*, ii, 643, note 3. Ignatius at Anzuola after being wounded: *FN,* i, 366, note 7. His visit after his recovery, *ibid.*, 380. For her son Beltrán cf. *Mixt.*, ii, 643; *Chron.,* ii, 310.

¹⁶ Letter from Ignatius' nephew is in *Mixt.*, ii, 641–3. For Borgia's visit in 1571 cf. *FN,* i, 366, note 7.

¹⁷ For the later history of Loyola cf. R. Pérez, *La santa casa de Loyola* (Bilbao, 1891), 145–53. For the last male descendant, see G. Manso de Zúñiga, "Los Loyolas del Perú" in *Boletín de la Real Sociedad Vascongada de Amigos del Pais*, vii (1951), 203–13; F. A. Encina, *Historia de Chile*, ii (Santiago, 1941), 135–56.

Women of the House of Borja

¹⁸ For the family history of the Borjas cf. O Karrer, *Der hl. Franz von Borja* (Freiburg, 1921). In August 1552 Ignatius still knew nothing of the marriage (cf. *MI* I, iv, 385 et seq.); his displeasure, *Chron.*, ii, 613, 671; for the rumours see *ibid.*, 712. Araoz' letter is in *Mixt.*, ii, 848–51. Fr. Enríquez' defence of the General is in *Chron.*, ii, 712. News of the Infanta Juana's satisfaction is in Araoz' letter.

¹⁹ The commission to Torres, *MI* I, i, 422. Ignatius's letter to Don Carlos, *ibid.*, 79 et seq.

²⁰ For Isabel's marriage cf. *M. Borg.*, i, 624. Ignatius' congratulatory letter is in *MI* I, ii, 321. For Teresa Cárdenas see *FN*, i, 496. Position of Count Lerma, cf. *Mixt.*, ii, 157; *Chron.*, iv, 387, note 1. For Leonor Osorio see page 434 et seq.

²¹ For the death of Countess Lerma see *M. Borg.*, iii, 363; i, 626. The behaviour of her father is mentioned by Ribadeneira, *Vida del P. Francisco de Borja*, iv, 6 (*M Borg.*, i, 627.)

²² Wedding of Juana: *M. Borg.*, i, 648; iii, 56–61; *Chron.*, ii, 11. The report to Ignatius in *M. Borg.*, ii, 572. The poem on Juana, cf. Larrañaga, 127–9; F. González-Olmedo, "Tres bellezas de la Casa de Borja" in *El Español*, ii, (1944), 7. For the reference to "Don Iñigo de Loyola" cf. *FN*, i, 370. For Isabel de Vega see page 452 et seq.

²³ For the tragedy of Ana Enríquez cf. *M. Borg.*, iii, 508 et seq., 617; M. Menéndez y Pelayo, *Historia de los heterodoxos españoles*, ii (Madrid, 1881), 322 et seq., 343; *Realenzyklopädie für prot. Theologie und Kirche*, xviii (1906), 583. For Juana's meeting with her father see *Chron.*, ii, 608; Bustamente's report is in *Quadr.*, i. 580. Ignatius' letter of January 1st, 1551, is preserved only in the *Regesta* (*MI* I, iii, 284); for the dispensation from fasting dated June 1st, 1551, cf. *ibid.*, 526 et seq., note 7.

²⁴ For Doña Luisa cf. J. Nonell, *La santa Duquesa* (Madrid, 1892). For the attack on the Jesuits in Saragossa cf. page 243 et seq. The matrimonial scandal, *M. Borg.*, i, 421; for the husband's absence cf. *Chron.*, v, 401, note 2; vi, 463. Borgia's letters to his sister: *M. Borg.*, iii, 126 et seq., 228 et seq.

²⁵ Borgia's letter to Ignatius in 1546: *M. Borg.*, ii, 526. Disappointment of his sister at his silence, *ibid.*, 576. For Cardinal de la Cueva cf. *MI* I, vii, 103. For the rebuilding of the Gesù by Michelangelo cf. *ibid.*, 100, 136, 257; P. Pirri, "La topografia del Gesù di Roma" in *Arch. Hist. S. J.*, x (1941), 177–217. For Ignatius' answer to the Count of Ribagorza, written at the same time, see *ibid.*, 5, 367 et seq.

²⁶ Araoz called Doña Luisa in 1547 "the true sister of the Duke" (*Mixt.*, i, 387); P. Román called her in 1555 "the blessed countess" (*ibid.*, iv, 809). As early as 1547 she asked for Jesuits for the "New Christians" (*MI* I, i, 481); for the work among the *Moriscos* cf. *ibid.*, x, 219, 64 et seq. For Igantius' meeting with the Moor cf. *FN*, i,

382–4. The Countess' will is in *M. Borg.*, i, 721–33. For the marriage of her son cf. *ibid.*, 722, note 2. Her epitaph, *ibid.*, 732.

²⁷ For the family of Juana de Meneses see *M. Borg.*, i, 567. Her stay in Barcelona, *ibid.*, ii, 16, 21, 42, 47. Ignatius' letter of the end of 1545 is in *MI* I, i, 342; Araoz' report of January 16th, 1546, in *Mixt.*, i, 250. For Isabel Roser see page 262 et seq. Project of founding a religious house mentioned in *Mixt.*, i, 250. *Chron.*, i, 185. Ignatius' refusal in *MI* I, i, 421 et seq. Juana's gifts to the Society, *M. Borg.*, ii, 504; *MI* I, ii, 201, 248. Oviedo's letter of February 20th, 1547: *Mixt.*, i, 338 (cf. *ibid.*, 493).

²⁸ For the death of her sister Leonor cf. *MI* I, i, 380; *Chron.*, I, 185; *M. Borg.*, i, 605, 738–40. Her care for the children of Duke Francis, *ibid.*, ii, 549; iii, 58–61. He announces that he is a Jesuit, *ibid.*, 573.

²⁹ Borgia's letter to Ignatius of April 23rd, 1551, is in *M. Borg.*, iii, 84, 90.

³⁰ Araoz' announcement of Juana's death is in *M. Lain.*, viii, 161. Her wish to be buried in the college church: *MI* I, ii, 498 et seq.

Women of the House of Colonna

³¹ For the Colonna family see A. Coppi, *Memorie Colonnesi* (Rome, 1855); Reumont, *Beiträge zur italienischen Geschichte*, v (Berlin, 1857), 3–117; L. Ross, *Die Colonna. Bilder aus Roms Vergangenheit* (Leipzig, 1912); Prince Colonna, *I Colonna dalle origini all'inizio del secolo XIX* (Rome, 1927); for Vittoria Colonna see the bibliography given in note 9 to the Introduction; also A. Luzio, "Vittoria Colonna" in *Rivista storica mantovana*, i, (1884). For J. Valdés and his activity in Naples see F. Caballero, *Alfonso y Juan de Valdés* (Madrid, 1875); M, Carrasco, *A. et J. de Valdés. Leurs vies et leurs écrits* (Geneva, 1880); M. Menéndez y Pelayo, *Historia de los heterodoxos españoles*, ii (Madrid, 1881), 96 et seq., 149 et seq. L. Amabile, *Il Santo Officio della Inquisizione in Napoli*, i (Città di Castello, 1892), 125; B. Amante, *Giulia Gonzaga Contessa di Fondi e il movimento femminile nel secolo XVI* (Bologna, 1896). For B. Ochino see K. Benrath, *Bernardino Ochino von Siena. Ein Beitrag zur Geschichte der Reformation in Italien* (Brunswick, 1892); also in *Realenzyklopädie für prot. Theologie u. Kirche*, xiv, 258; P. Cuthbert *The Capuchins* (London, 1928) i, 75, 121 et seq.; Tacchi-Venturi, i, 2, 115–17; R. H. Bainton, *Bernardino Ochino. Esule e riformatore senese del cinquecento (1487–1563)* (Florence, 1940).

³² Rodríguez' account is in *M. Broët.*, 496, 682; cf. U. Boncompagni-Ludovisi, *Roma nel Rinascimento*, iv (Albano, 1929), 389–93; H. Böhmer, *Studien zur Geschichte der Gesellschaft Jesu*, i (Bonn, 1914) 216 et seq. In 1538 Vittoria also made the acquaintance of Bobadilla (Tacchi-Venturi, ii, 1, 261). For Renée of Ferrara see note 14 to the introductory section of Part 1.

³³ For the projected pilgrimage to Jerusalem cf. Tacchi-Venturi, "Vittoria Colonna, fautrice della riforma cattolica" in *Studi e documenti di storia e diritto*, xxii (1901), 154; for the permission to go on a pilgrimage see Ferrero-Müller, *Carteggio*, 131 et seq. The permission for Ignatius and his companions is in *M. Fabr.*, 9–11; cf. *FN*, i, 40, note 37. Vittoria's letter to Cardinal Gonzaga is in Ferrero-Müller, 144.

Ochino's letter to her, *ibid.*, 247–9. For the effect of his apostasy cf. Bainton, 56 et seq.; Reumont, *Vittoria Colonna*, 209.

[34] At the beginning of Sept. 1540 Araoz returned from his first journey to Spain (cf. *MI* I, i, 184); then he worked in Naples (*ibid.*, 203). At Christmas 1541 he celebrated his first Mass at Rome (cf. *FN*, i, 243, note 16), and shortly after February 19th, 1542, he returned via Naples to Spain (*ibid.*, 243 et seq.).

[35] For the friendship between Vittoria and Michelangelo see H. Grimm *Leben Michelangelos*, ii (Berlin, 1907), 273–309. Her intercession for Ochino is mentioned in *MI* I, i, 343 et seq. Her name on the list of patronesses of the House of St. Martha: Tacchi-Venturi, i, 2, 306 (No. 161). Account of her activities: *MI* I, i, 372. Her request for sermons, *ibid.*, 306 et seq.

[36] L. Tolomei performs the Exercises: *FN*, i, 196; Larrañaga, i, 531. Vittoria's letter to her brother: Ferrero-Müller, 314. Her sonnet on Ignatius of Antioch is in *Rime della divina Vittoria Colonna* (ed. B. Arndts, ii [Schaffhausen, 1858], 214); J. J. Wyss, *Vittoria Colonna* (Frauenfeld, 1916), 197. Michelangelo's words in H. Grimm, 308.

[37] We agree with Tacchi-Venturi (ii, 1, 40) against Böhmer (i, 72, note 2) that the city not named by Ignatius (*FN*, i, 414) was Fondi. Ignatius on Isabella di Capua: *MI* I, x, 524 (cf. *Chron.*, v, 93; vi, 95). Isabella Gonzaga's request for Fr. Salmerón: *MI* I, viii, 382; Ignatius mentions her, *ibid.*, 304, 330 et seq., 384 et seq.; 11, 475; cf. *Chron.*, v, 174. For Giulia Colonna cf. *MI* I, xi, 378; *Chron.*, vi, 14. His last conversation at table, *ibid.*, 37.

[38] For Joanna see besides the books mentioned on the Colonna family: J. W. Imhof, *Historia Italiae et Hispaniae genealogica* (Nuremberg, 1701), 80–7. Vittoria's sonnet is in Arndts, i, 228.

[39] For Cardinal Bibiena see Pastor, *Hist. of the Popes*, viii, 110 et seq.; his French legation, *ibid.*, 152 et seq. For the painting cf. G. Vasari, *Vita de Giulio Romano* (ed. Milanesi), v (Florence, 1880), 525; A. Springer, *Raffael und Michelangelo* (Leipzig, 1878), 349, 516. Contemporary poets, e.g. Aug. Niphus, *Ad Ill. Joannam Aragoniam de Amore liber* (Leyden, 1541); Ruscelli, *Tempio alla divina Signora D. Giovanna d'Aragona* (Venice, 1558). The modern historian is A. Coppi, 312 et seq. For the life by F. Alicarnasso (Costantino Capriota) cf. Reumont, *Vitt. Colonna*, 253 et seq. The MS is Bibl. Barberini Cod. Lat., 5053 et seq., 1–27^v.

[40] For the betrothal see A. Bertoletti, "La prigione di Ascanio Colonna (1553–7)" in *Atti e memorie delle disputazioni di storia patria per le province Modenesi e Parmesi*, III, 2 (Modena, 1883) 28 et seq. For the wedding see Wyss 22.

[41] For the family of Avalos cf. J. W. Imhof, *Corpus Historiae genealogicae Italiae et Hispaniae* (Nuremberg, 1702), 145–52. The quotation from the most recent family history is from Prince Colonna, *op. cit.*, 187.

[42] The attack on Rome: Pastor, ix, 328; Ascanio's part in the Sack of Rome: Reumont, 86 et seq. Remark from the family history: Colonna, 187.

[43] Account in the Chronicle of the Society: *Chron.*, iii, 171 et seq. For Bobadilla's mission see Tacchi-Venturi, ii, 1, 261 et seq.; Schurhammer, i, 502–4. His letter to Duke Hercules: *M. Bob.*, 16; quotation from the autobiography, *ibid.*, 618. His account of Valdés' lecture, *ibid.*, 19.

[44] For the "Salt War" see Pastor, xi, 337 et seq. Juana's letter to the Pope has been

published by Reumont in the *Archivio storico italiano,* Series II, vol. v, 143–5. One of Vittoria's sonnets is in Reumont, *Vitt. Colonna,* 187. For Araoz' mission to Naples in 1541, cf. *Chron.,* i, 97; *MI* I, i, 203. For the journey in 1543 cf. *FN,* i, 243 et seq.

⁴⁵ Ignatius' letter to Ascanio is in *MI* I, i, 254 et seq.

⁴⁶ This is a small island in the territory of Naples. – Trans.

⁴⁷ Remark of F. Alicarnasso, *op. cit.,* f. 2ᵛ; cf. Ferrero-Müller, 373 et seq. (Appendix by D. Tordi). Ascanio's dispute with Cardinal Pole, cf. Reumont, *Vitt. Colonna,* 243 et seq.

⁴⁸ Ignatius' illness: *MI* I, ii, 296, 301; the legation to Germany: *ibid.,* 342; Laynez as Visitor, *ibid.,* 279; *FN,* i, 288. Joanna's letter to Ignatius is no longer extant. Her solicitude for the sea voyage: *Chron.,* i, 384. For Bobadilla's mission cf. *ibid.,* 389, note 1 and *MI* I, ii, 332, 335.

⁴⁹ For the political opposition see *Chron.,* v, 23, 314; Reumont, *Vitt. Colonna,* 245 et seq., and *Beiträge,* 92–6.

⁵⁰ For Ascanio's reproaches see Tacchi-Venturi, ii, 1, 262, note 2. The recent historian: A. Bertolotti, 28 et seq. Crimes imputed to Ascanio *ibid.,* 30.

⁵¹ For the relations between Ignatius and Ascanio cf. *Quadr.,* i, 534. For Alvito see G. P. M. Castrucci, *Descrizione del Ducato d'Alvito nel Regno di Napoli in Campagna Felice* (1st ed.: Alvito, 1632). (We used the 4th edition, ed. by Comm. Stanislao d' Aloe [Naples, 1863].)

⁵² Ribadeneira's account is in *FN,* ii, 414; cf. Tacchi-Venturi, ii, 1, 262; Ferrero-Müller, 373 (App. by D. Tordi).

⁵³ There is a direct account of the journey by Polanco in *MI* I, iv, 534 et seq.; cf. *Chron.,* ii, 427 et seq.; *MI* I, v, 504.

⁵⁴ Ignatius to Araoz: *MI* I, v, 334. Ascanio's will is in Bertolotti, 44–9.

⁵⁵ The quarrel between Ascanio and Marcantonio: *Chron.,* v, 23, 314. Ascanio's arrest: Bertolotti, 8 et seq.; Reumont, *Vitt. Colonna,* 245.

⁵⁶ Ignatius to Mendoza: *MI* I, vii, 654 et seq.; for the Prince of Salerno here mentioned (Ferrante Sanseverino) cf. *Chron.,* v, 354; *Quadr.,* ii, 11. The reply is in *Mixt.,* iv, 431 et seq. Ignatius' letter of comfort is in *MI* I, viii, 159 et seq. Testimony of the Duke of Termoli, *Chron.,* iv, 188. For the excommunication cf. *ibid.,* vi, 260; Pastor, xiv, 121. The text of the Bull is in A. Caracciolo, *Vita e gesti di G. P. Carafa,* ii, 4 (MS in the library of the Historical Institute of the S.J. at Rome) f. 27ʳ–38ᵛ. Alba's march on Rome: Pastor, xiv, 165. The records of the Vatican state about Ascanio's death: "Thus died the Lord Ascanio Colonna and set free his wife and his son from many vexations." (Cf. Ferrero-Müller, 373 et seq.)

⁵⁷ Navagier's report of October 9th, 1555, is in Bertolotti, 51. For Joanna's flight see *ibid.,* 34, 54–6; Colonna, 208 et seq.; Caracciolo f. 26ᵛ. For the Peace of Cave see Pastor, xiv, 167 et seq.; *ibid.,* xv, 141 et seq., xv, 176 et seq., the return of Joanna and the restoration of her property.

⁵⁸ Laynez' letter is in *M. Lain.,* iv, 30. Borgia's letter to Joanna: *M. Borg.,* v, 594, 636–8, 676; he prays for her: *ibid.,* 741, 770, 820, 826. Founding of the noviciate, *ibid.,* iv, 348. Borgia to Marcantonio: *ibid.,* 127; Borgia intercedes for him: *ibid.,* v, 63, note 3. Statement of the Duchess of Monteleone at Ignatius'

canonization process is in *MI* IV, 2, 662–5; for Vittoria cf. *Quadr.*, vi, 770; the epitaph is given in Coppi, 313.

[59] For Catalina cf. Schurhammer, i, 432, note 9; 503, note 4.

[60] Catalina's epitaph is in V. de la Fuente, *Historia de las universidades en España,* ii (Madrid, 1885), 615 et seq.

Doña Catalina de Zúñiga, Marchioness of Denia

[61] For the Denia family see L. Pfandl in the introduction to G. Marañon, *Olivárez* (Munich, 1939), 10–14; P. Sandoval, *Historia del Emperador Carlos V,* iii, 12 (ed. Madrid, 1846: i, 372). For the Zúñiga family cf. *F. N.,* i, 105, note 20; Larrañaga, i, 345–7; M. March, *Niñez y juventud de Felipe II* (Madrid, 1942), i, 226–9; Creixell, i, 301–7. Kinship with *la Loca del Sacramento : MI* I, v, 466, 492; *Mixt.,* ii, 649 et seq.; with the Braganza family: *Mixt.,* ii, 863. For Cardinal Gaspar de Zúñiga: *Chron.,* i, 424; ii, 253, 668; vi, 634 et seq.; C. Gutierrez, *Españoles en Trento* (Valladolid, 1951), 530–7.

[62] Relations with Gandía: *Mixt.,* ii, 157. Borgia's visit to Tordesillas in 1552: *Chron.,* ii, 609. Borgia's report to Philip on his second visit: *M. Borg.,* iii, 161–73. His mediation in the matter of the dispensation from fasting: *MI* I, i, 382.

[63] Borgia attends the dying Joanna: *Chron.,* v, 546–9; *Mixt.,* iv, 612–22. Denia writes to the Emperor: Rodríguez-Villa *La reina Doña Juana la Loca* (Madrid, 1892), 403; Cf. also *Chron.,* v, 548, note 3. Borgia to the Emperor: *M. Borg.,* iii, 210 et seq. He wrote a similar letter (now lost) to Queen Catherine of Portugal: cf. *M. Borg.,* iii, 212. See also L. P. Gachard, "Jeanne la Folle et S. François de Borja" in *Bulletin de l'Acad. Royale de Belgique,* 29 (1870), 290 et seq.; Karrer, 158 et seq.

Doña Catalina de Mendoza, Countess of Melito

[64] For the Mendoza family see G. Coronel, *Historia de la casa de Mendoza*(MS in the *Arch. histórico nacional,* Madrid, Fondo Osuña 3408); C. de Arteaga, *La casa del Infantado Cabeza de los Mendozas* (Madrid, 1940–4); G. Muro, *Vida de la Princesa de Éboli,* (Madrid, 1877), 2–11; C. Gutierrez, *Españoles en Trento* (Valladolid, 1951), 264, note 528. Ignatius and Cardinal Mendoza: *FN,* i, 460 et seq., 777, 293, note 15; *Chron.,* ii, 428 et seq.; iv, 139; *MI* I, ii, 108; viii, 319; *Mixt.,* v, 252 et seq.; Larrañaga, i, 296, note 19; A. Volpicella, *Il Cardinale Francesco Mendoza y Bobadilla* (Rome, 1946), 17 et seq., 23–5. For Andrés Hurtado see *Mon. Peruana,* i, 28 et seq. For his son: *Mixt.,* iv, 428 note 3; A. de Burgosa, *Blasón de España,* ii (Madrid, 1854), 149. For Andrés' wife: *Chron.,* vi, 602. For Juan de Mendoza, castellan of Naples: *FN,* i, 551, 765. Ignatius' letter to Philip: *MI* I, x, 666 et seq.; the King's answer: *ibid.,* xi, 138.

[65] For the Melito family see *Chron.,* ii, 126, 640 et seq.; iii, 327–30, 337; iv,

364–70; v, 387–90; I. M. March, "Sobre la Princesa de Éboli" in *Razón y Fe*, 143 (1951), 495–504. Project of a college at Alcalá: *Chron.*, ii, 335 et seq.; *Quadr.*, i, 296 et seq. Melito's help against Siliceo: *Chron.*, ii, 337 et seq.

[66] Request for the book of the Exercises: *MI* I, xii, 427–9; *Chron.*, ii, 640 et seq. Marriage of Ana Mendoza: G. Muro, *Apéndices*, 7 et seq. Remark from the Chronicle: *Chron.*, iv, 484.

[67] News from Saragossa: *Chron.*, iv, 364 et seq.; iii, 330. Popular opinion on the bishops of the house of Aragon: *M. Borg.*, i, 139.

[68] Ignatius' report: *MI* I, vii, 255–66, 274 et seq. For the pious practices see *Mixt.*, iii, 121, 247. The Frenchman set free: *Chron.*, iv, 370. Rumour about Fr. Araoz: *Mixt.*, iii, 252 et seq. The Viceroy's debts: *Chron.*, iv, 370, 384; *Mixt.*, ii, 569; *MI* I, iii, 530, 564.

[69] Count Melito made a duke: *Chron.*, v, 390; *Mixt.*, iv, 637 et seq. Ignatius' prayer: *MI* I, ix, 109. For the Princess of Éboli: *MI* I, xii, 428; ix, 109, 269; for her pride cf. Muro, *Adición a los Apéndices*, 17; L. Pfandl, *Philipp II* (Munich, 1938), 474 et seq.; relations with St. Teresa: G. Papasogli, *Santa Teresa d'Avila* (Rome, 1952), 438 et seq.

Jacqueline de Croy

[70] Family origins: *Biographie nationale de Belgique*, i (Brussels, 1866), 221–31. Ignatius and the two Croy bishops: *MI* I, vi, 652; vii, 47, 182, 303; x, 71, 243; *Chron.*, iv, 286–8, 303–5, 312–4; v, 310–15; *Acta Sanctorum*, July, vii, 548.

[71] For the parish of Bergen see *Chron.*, i, 295. For Nicholas Floris: *Ep. Canisii* (ed. Braunsberger), i, 139 et seq., 260; *Chron.*, i, 294 et seq.; A. Kleiser, *Ein Seelen-eroberer. Lebenserinnerungen des ersten flämischen Jesuiten Kornelius Wischaven* (Paderborn, 1930), 91–3. The Marchioness' first letter is lost, cf. *Chron.*, i, 295; *Mixt.*, v, 675. For Ruard Tapper see *MI* I, ii, 101.

[72] Letters to the chancellor and chapter of Bergen: *MI* I, xii, 234–6. Instructions to Louvain, *ibid.*, ii, 210.

[73] Jacqueline's urgent requests: *Chron.*, i, 416 et seq. Goudanus' mission to Poland: *MI* I, ii, 507, 709. Goudanus in Venice: *ibid.*, 704 et seq., 709; *Chron.*, ii, 60–4.

[74] Warning against Erasmus: *MI* I, iii, 26. Goudanus' profession: *FN*, i, 64*; *MI* I, iii, 96, 100 et seq. Ignatius to Duke Albert: *ibid.*, 143 et seq. Goudanus in Ingolstadt: *ibid.*, 53, 129 et seq., 145 et seq.

[75] Further career of Goudanus: *FN*, ii, 212 et seq.; *M. Lain.*, iii, 14, 133, 202. His stay in Bergen: *ibid.*, 553, 568 et seq.; Arch. Rom. S.J. *Germ., 104, 9ᵛ. Jacqueline's letter to Laynez is in *M. Lain.*, iii, 602–4. Letter from Anna of Bergen, *ibid.*, 606 et seq. For the Marquis John see M. Gachard, *Correspondance de Philippe II sur les affaires des Pays-Bas*, i (Brussels, 1848), 207, 214, 233. For Bishop Robert see *ibid.*, 214, 301. Suspicions of the family, *ibid.*, ii (Brussels, 1851), pp. xxxvi, 61. Goudanus and Mary, Queen of Scots: G. Schneemann, "P. Goudanus am Hofe Maria Stuarts" (an unpublished diplomatic report of the year 1562) in *Stimmen aus Maria-Laach*, xix (1880), 83–108; J. Brodrick, *The Progress of the Jesuits* (London, 1946), 182–203. For quotation from Queen Mary's letter, see *Revue des questions historiques*, ii (1867), 617.

Part Three

Begging for the Kingdom of God

Introduction

[1] See the corresponding sections of the Pilgrim's Book (new ed. by B. Schneider, Freiburg, 1956), in which Ignatius himself describes his way of poverty; and the Spiritual Diary (ed. by A. Feder, Regensburg, 1922). The principles governing the foundation of colleges are laid down in a letter to Araoz, December 1st, 1551 (*MI* I, iv, 5-9).

[2] Ribadeneira's words are in his collection *Dicta et Facta*, No. 75 (*FN*, ii, 492); the letter of March 18th, 1542, is in *MI* I, i, 192; The repetition of 1555 is in Fr. Gonçalves' *Memoriale* (*FN*, I, 742). The last quotation is from the Exercises, No. 233.

[3] The draft of 1547 is in *MI*, III, ii, 170-2; the final text in the Constitutions, part IV, ch. 1, No. 1 (*ibid.*, 386); The detailed directions about the founder's candle, *ibid.*, 387-91; iii, 101-4. The list of benefactors is in the Roman Archives of the Society, Hist. Soc. 42 fol. 136-45; cf. I. Iparraguirre, *Historia de los Ejercicios espirituales de San Ignacio*, i (Bilbao, 1946), 119, note 84.

Inés Pascual

[4] The account of the way from Montserrat to Manresa is in *FN*, i, 388; Juan Pascal's statement in the beatification process is in *MI* IV, ii, 83 et seq. and *Acta Sanctorum*, July, vii, 428 et seq.

[5] For the family circumstances of the widow Pascual cf. Creixell I, 222-5.

[6] The recollection of Manresa is in *FN*, i, 388; the documents of the beatification process are in *MI* IV, ii, 355 et seq.

[7] The expression "ladies of fashion" is in *FN*, i, 408; account of the two serious illnesses, *ibid.*, 406, 408. For the Amigant family cf. Larrañaga, i, 190 et seq., 196.

[8] For Ignatius' sojourns in Barcelona cf. *FN*, i, 29*-31*, 34*, note 102; 81, note 16; 488, note 14. Juan Pascual's account is in *MI* IV, ii, 90.

[9] The Carmelite de Rocaberti's statement is in *MI* IV, ii, 680 et seq. For Isabel de Josa see pages 296 et seq. Ignatius' opinion of the Cardona family in *FN*, i, 410.

[10] For the Requeséns family cf. Creixell, i, 301-7. They were on the best of terms with the first Jesuits in Spain [cf. M. March, *Niñez y juventud de Felipe II* (Madrid, 1942), i, 218; *Mixt.*, i, 203, 212, 225.] For Guiomar Gralla cf. *MI* I, i, 91, note 3; her husband was one of the highest treasury officials of Catalonia (cf. *M. Borg.*, ii, 215, 277, 519, 598).

[11] For the lost letter cf. *FN*, i, 1-4; for Ignatius' change of costume in Barcelona see *Acta Sanctorum*, July, vii, 441.

[12] For Callisto cf. *MI* I, i, 88, note 6 and *Chron.*, i, 33; on the question of the letter's date cf. Larrañaga, 252.

[13] Account of Ignatius' studies in Alcalá and Salamanca in *FN*, i, 440–62. For the "tearful departure" see *MI* IV, ii, 93. The bill of exchange is mentioned in *FN*, i, 464.

[14] It is possible that Juan Pascal in his account (*MI* IV, ii, 93 et seq.), confused Ignatius with Francis Borgia, for the surname Melo occurs among the latter's kindred, cf. *M. Borg.*, ii, 18; *M. Fabr.*, 109; *Chron.*, iii, 361. For the Empress' stay at Barcelona see Karrer, 16. Faber's words about Beatriz are in *M. Fabr.*, 144. She was one of the few ladies who had to accompany the body of the Empress Isabella (d. 1539) to Granada, cf. M. March, *Niñez*, etc., ii, 357.

[15] Ignatius' financial difficulties in Paris: *FN*, i, 464.

[16] Ignatius' begging journeys: *FN*, i, 466; the course of his studies: *ibid.*, 476; cf. also Larrañaga, i, 361–4. The other letters mentioned here are lost.

[17] For the taking of vows on August 15th, 1534, and departure from Paris see Larrañaga 377–86; Schurhammer, 233, 558 et seq.

[18] Araoz was actually in Barcelona in April 1548. (*MI* I, ii, 98, 122–4). Account of the widow Pascual's death *ibid.*, IV, ii, 309 et seq.; cf. also *ibid.*, 400, note 21. The reply has not been preserved. In the beatification process, however, its contents are attested many times, cf. *ibid.*, 79, 96, 278 et seq., 292, 310, 325, 345, 400 et seq., 584. In Aquaviva's time the Jesuits were still supporting Juan in his poverty, out of veneration for his mother (cf. Creixell, i, 283).

Doña María in Paris

[19] The reference to the pious woman of Manresa is in *FN*, i, 392, 412.

[20] For the early weeks of Ignatius' sojourn in Venice see *MI* I, i, 94. The letter to Guzmán, *ibid.*, 109–11.

[21] For the premature departure of his companions from Paris see *FN*, i, 480; *M. Fabr.*, 496. In August 1536 war had again broken out between Charles V and Francis I of France; in the south the Spaniards advanced as far as Avignon, while an attack led from Flanders caused alarm in Paris itself. Therefore only the way through Lorraine and Germany remained open to the little party. A detailed account is in Schurhammer, i, 253–8, 265–83.

Donna Maria Frassoni del Gesso

[22] The rules about poverty that apply to the colleges of the Society are laid down in the *Examen Generale* of the Constitutions.

[23] For the life of the Fattora see Count F. Pasini-Frassoni, "Donna Maria Frassoni e i Gesuiti in Ferrara" in *Riv. del Coll. Araldico*, ii (1904), 585–94; what follows is taken from this work unless otherwise noted. By the same, *I Conti Frassoni, memorie storiche-genealogiche* (Rocca S. Cassiano, 1895). Cf. also *Chron.*, iv, 57, note 2 and *M. Lain.*, ii, 28, note 4. For correspondence with Ignatius see Tacchi-Venturi, ii, 2, 396 et seq. Ignatius' stay in Ferrara in 1524: *FN*, i, 430; cf. also *Chron.*, i, 30. For

the activities of the three companions in 1537–8 cf. *ibid.,* 62 et seq., and Tacchi-Venturi, ii, 2, 127–33. For Vittoria Colonna and her recommendation at court cf. *M. Rodr.,* 496; *MI* IV, i. 118; Tacchi-Venturi, ii, 2, 132, note 2.

[24] Ignatius' letter of thanks to the Duke is in *MI* I, i, 257 et seq. Sending of Fr. Jay to Ferrara: *Chron.,* i, 224 et seq. For the personality of the Duchess Renée cf. page 36. Ignatius' instructions to Fr. Jay are in *MI* I, i, 568–70. The latter's account of the problems he was faced with in *M. Broët.,* 336, 341 et seq.; he wrote: "I feel more comfortable at the hospital [Sant' Anna, where he had taken up residence] than I do at court" (*ibid.,* 337); cf. also *Chron.,* i, 278 and ii, 495 for his activities. The beginnings of his ministrations to the *Conversae*: *M. Broët.,* 340; *Chron.,* i, 407; later there was formed a special guild of noble ladies under the direction of the Jesuits (*MI* I, vii, 203; *Chron.,* iv, 61; *Quadr.,* iii, 180). There is high praise of the deceased Minister in *Chron.,* iv, 64.

[25] For the beginning of the college project see *Chron.,* ii, 185 et seq. Correspondence between Ignatius and the Duke: *MI,* i, 3, 480 et seq., 482, 574 et seq.; cf. also *Chron.,* ii, 186 et seq. Sending of Fr. Broët: *M. Broët.,* 65 et seq. Summary of the letter to the Fattora in *MI* I , iv, 291.

[26] For Borgia's visit to Ferrara cf. *M. Borg.,* ii, 577, 705; *Chron.,* ii, 12. Pelletier's activities, *ibid.,* 187. Plans of the Fattora for a new building and her complaint on the recall of Fr. Broët: *ibid.,* 495–7. Pelletier mentions her having performed the Exercises in *Quadr.,* i, 514 (cf. I. Iparraguirre, *Historia de los Ejercicios,* i [Bilbao, 1946], 242).

[27] For an account of the majordomo's vocation cf. *Chron.,* ii, 500; his admission allowed: *MI* I, iv, 375. The gift of alum declined, *ibid.,* 567; instruction to Pelletier, *ibid.,* 427. The letter of Nov. 1552 is preserved only in summary form (*ibid.,* 515).

[28] Ignatius to Pelletier concerning the foundress's patent: *MI* I, iv, 603, 651. For Fr. Viola see *FN,* 57★, note 403; as "commissioner", he was a kind of direct representative of the General in addition to the Provincial Laynez.

[29] Quotation from *Chron.,* iii, 139; *ibid.,* also the news of the Fattora's illness and the importunity of her kinsmen. The instruction to Viola is in *MI* I, v, 48; *ibid.,* 58, the letter of May 6th to Pelletier; that of June 3rd, *ibid.,* 95. The assurances to be conveyed by Pelletier, *ibid.,* 291; extract from the letter of Sept. 2nd, *ibid.,* 430 et seq.

[30] Report of renewed illness is in *Chron.,* iv, 56 et seq. Ignatius' letter to Pelletier (also dated January 20th, 1554), in *MI* I, vi, 226.

[31] The family legend is to be found in H. Silvieri, *Memorie storiche di Casa Frassoni* (MS of ca. 1750); Polanco's account in *Chron.,* iv, 57.

[32] The whole year 1554 was filled with this anxiety about the financial security of the Roman College; cf. Tacchi-Venturi, ii, 2, 597–601.

[33] Polanco's list of the gifts is in *MI* I, vi, 468 et seq.; his letter of the same date to Pelletier, *ibid.,* 466.

[34] The first quotation is from a letter to Pelletier of January 27th (*MI* I, vi, 244); the second from one of February 10th (*ibid.,* 310). For the Fattora's loan see *ibid.,* vii, 127, 153, 203; the question of the interest, *ibid.,* 233. For the purchase of the new building cf. *Chron.,* iv, 63.

[35] Directions concerning the outward signs of gratitude towards founders of colleges are in the 4th part of the Constitutions (*MI* III, iii, 101–4). The first proposal is in *MI* I, vii, 372; the second (foundress *incognita*), *ibid.*, 470; the final agreement, *ibid.*, 590.

[36] Prayer for the Fattora: *MI* I, ix, 439; request for help: *ibid.*, 640; Pelletier remains in Ferrara: *ibid.*, 642. Sale of the estate: *ibid.*, 736; cf. *Chron.*, v, 138 et seq. Quotation from the letter of October 1555 in *MI* I, x, 47. Joy at the Fattora's improvement in health: *ibid.*, 498. Pelletier's complaints of the lady's peculiarities: *ibid.*, 645.

[37] The question of singing vespers: *MI* I, xi, 326. Laynez' letter in *M. Lain.*, i, 642 et seq.

Donna Costanza Pallavicini Cortesi

[38] Perhaps the Cavaliera was related to the Benedictine Gregorio Cortese of Mantua, who in 1541 had to investigate heresy in his native town of Modena; cf. a brief of Paul III of December 10th, 1541, and Tacchi-Venturi, i, 2, 131. For the conflict between Salmerón and the Bishop cf. Tacchi-Venturi, ii, 2, 225–35. For Fr. Landini's success in Modena see *Chron.*, ii, 196 et seq.; *Mixt.*, ii, 718; *MI* I, iv, 300. For the convent of penitent women in that city cf. *Chron.*, iii, 155; for the Pezzani ladies see pages 323 et seq.

[39] Details of Landini's further activities: *Chron.*, ii, 199 et seq., 449 et seq.; *Mixt.*, iv, 199 et seq. The Bishop planned to found later a kind of Early Christian guild of widows under the direction of the Cavaliera (*Chron.*, iv, 97 et seq.) The Cavaliera is first mentioned in a letter of Ignatius to Landini (*MI* I, iv, 294); summary of the letter of greeting, *ibid.*, 568. On the projected college cf. *Chron.*, ii, 453 et seq.

[40] Account of the beginning of the college in *Chron.*, ii, 455; *ibid.*, 460 states that the Cavaliera was "solicitous as a mother". For the bad living conditions and Ignatius' decision see *ibid.*, iii, 157; cf. also Tacchi-Venturi, ii, 2, 465–72. Ignatius' instructions for Modena are in *MI* I, iv, 408–14.

[41] The physician's opinion is in *Chron.*, iii, 158; its repetition to the Bishop, *MI* I, v, 554.

[42] Despatch of Fr. Leernus to Modena: *Chron.*, iii, 158 et seq. (He later changed his name to Fabro, cf. *MI* I, vii, 724.) His report on the situation, *Mixt.*, iii, 475. Efforts of Fr. Palmio: *Chron.*, iii, 161; for the new rented house see *ibid.*, iv, 93, 106.

[43] For the change of superiors see *Chron.*, iii, 154, 158. There is an account of the apostolic zeal of the ladies of Modena in *Quadr.*, ii, 277. Rebuke to Aversa because of his strictness in *MI* I, v, 214; he is ordered to remain in Bologna, *ibid.*, 636; complaints of the *devotae*, *ibid.*, 684; among them the Cavaliera was the leader (*Mixt.*, iii, 475). Aversa had previously been warned not to concern himself too much with the *Convertite* (*MI* I, v, 116).

[44] Fr. de Aversa's return to Modena, *MI* I, v, 697; list of his mistakes, *ibid.*, 703 et seq. Ill-success in the year 1554, see *Chron.*, iv, 100. Leernus' letter, *ibid.*, 99; Polanco's reply, *MI* I, vii, 468.

[45] On the admission of small children to the school see *Chron.*, iv, 101; permis-

sion given in this special case: *MI* I, vii, 377. Recall of Master de Patarinis in *Chron.*, iv, 101; his replacement: *MI* I, viii, 29 et seq.

[46] Plans for building a new college in *Chron.*, v, 151 et seq.; Fr. Nadal's remark in *M. Nad.*, i, 330. The report of success is from Leernus (*Mixt.*, iii, 475). For the help of Card. Morone cf. *ibid.*, v, 520 et seq.

Donna Margherita Gigli

[47] The account of Ignatius' journey to Bologna is in *FN*, i, 488. *Ibid.*, and in *MI* I, i, 94 his stay in the city is described. For his plan to continue his studies there see *FN*, ii, 572.

[48] The sending of his two companions to Bologna and the success of their labours: *FN*, i, 122. Testimony of the magistrate of the city concerning their work in *M. Xav.*, ii, 133 et seq. For their acquaintance with Donna Margherita cf. *Chron.*, i, 63. The MS referred to is in the Archives of the Society at Rome (*Ven.*, 112, 4).

[49] For Tommaso Gigli see *Chron.*, i, 361; his efforts to obtain the bull of 1549 (text in *MI* III, i, 357–71): *MI* I, ii, 718. For his relations with Ignatius cf. *ibid.*, 135, 206, 350, 402, 460, 697. The patent signed by him is in *MI* IV, i, 559. His brother Giovanni also helped the Society (*Chron.*, vi, 184; *MI* I, vii, 418). The latter's son joined the Jesuits (*ibid.*, iii, 694); for the son's studies in Florence see *Chron.*, vi, 152; his letters to Ignatius in *Quadr.*, i, 602–6; iii, 260–2; 534–7; iv, 147–9. Ignatius' answer about the youngest nephew is in *MI* I, x, 459.

[50] For Fr. Jay's work cf. *MI* IV, i, 274; Palmio's and Salmerón's activities in *Chron.*, i, 175–7. For Donna Margherita's will see below note 59. Purchase of the house in *Chron.*, i, 276 et seq. (cf. *MI* IV, i, 292).

[51] Report on the year 1550 in *Chron.*, ii, 52 et seq.; the text quoted is *ibid.*, 193 et seq. Margherita communicated twice or thrice weekly (*MI* IV, ii, 479).

[52] For the poverty of the house see *Chron.*, ii, 58.

[53] Palmio's account of the beginnings of the college: *M. Xav.*, ii, 114–18 (cf. *FN*, i, 300); also *Chron.*, ii, 502 et seq.

[54] The letter to Palmio is in *MI* I, vi, 694 et seq.

[55] Polanco's letter to Bologna: *MI* I, vii, 338.

[56] The report of the interview is in *MI* I, ix, 320 et seq. Criticism of Palmio's letter, *ibid.*, x, 43 et seq. News of the daughter's death: *M. Lain.*, iv, 271.

[57] Plan for a removal: *Chron.*, v, 127.

[58] Failure of the plan and the gift of money: *Chron.*, v, 128 (cf. *MI* I, vi, 314). Letter to Palmio, *ibid.*, x, 400; greetings to the Gigli family, *ibid.*, 396 et seq.; in February 1556 they were addressed as founders (*ibid.*, 588, 653 et seq.). Letter of May to Palmio, *ibid.*, xi, 317. Report of favourable developments: *Chron.*, vi, 179. For the miraculous apparition of the Saint see *MI* IV, ii, 478 and *ibid.*, 542, 859; for the enquiry *de integritate vitae et veracitate Dominae Margaritae Lilii*, cf. *ibid.*, p. xix et seq.

[59] The words about the ever-sufficient alms are in *Chron.*, vi, 185. On the sub-minister and on the measures taken to assure the financial position of the college

see *ibid.*, 187 et seq. In December 1556 Laynez wrote Margherita a letter of condolence on the death of her brother (*M. Lain.*, i, 643 et seq.); a month later he wrote another letter (*ibid.*, ii, 611 et seq.). For her will, see *ibid.*, iv, 271. In the same month she received from Laynez the *communicatio bonorum* (*Arch. Rom. S. J., Ven.*, 112, fol. 6ᵛ).

Madonna Violante Gozzadini

⁶⁰ For family history see Tacchi-Venturi, ii, 2, 243–50; there is an unpublished account of the lady by Fr. Palmio in the Society's Archives at Rome (*Ven.*, 112). For her relations with Francis Xavier cf. *M. Xav.*, i. 30 et seq.; Schurhammer, i, 367–9.

⁶¹ The lady is first mentioned in 1546 in the correspondence with Palmio (*Mixt.*, v, 638 et seq.; *MI* I, i, 375); cf. also *Chron.*, i, 174 et seq. where under the year 1546 her urgent desire for help from the Jesuits is mentioned and she herself is called *nobilis et magnae pietatis matrona*. Summary of the letter of 1550 in *MI* I, ii, 725. For Camillo see *Chron.*, iv, 114. Promise of prayers: *MI* I, viii, 131. Letter of condolence dated December 15th, *ibid.*, 170.

⁶² The first mention of the will is in *Mixt.*, iv, 478 et seq. For the cartoon cf. Tacchi-Venturi, ii, 2, 249.

⁶³ Ignatius' instructions to Palmio are in *MI* I, viii, 170, 188. Palmio sent a summary account of the conclusion of the affair of the will to Laynez in November 1556: *Mixt.*, v, 516 et seq.; *Chron.*, vi, 183 et seq.

⁶⁴ For the change of parishes that was not carried out cf., besides page 216 et seq., *Mixt.*, iv, 719 and *Chron.*, v, 127, where reference is made to the great number of requests that reached Ignatius in this matter. The lady's letter of April 2nd is no longer extant; there is a reference to it also in *MI* I, ix, 23.

⁶⁵ The Jesuits remain in the same house: *Mixt.*, iv, 719; *Chron.*, v, 127. Report of the lady's death and verdict upon her: *ibid.*, vi, 183: *Mixt.*, iv, 478 et seq., 719; v, 516.

Donna Lucrezia di Storento

⁶⁶ For the projected college in Naples and its foundress see *Chron.*, iv, 175. A certain amount of scandal was caused because a pious lady named Feliciana and seven companions occupied the house opposite and thus could see into the windows of the college; a Jesuit, who was going to give these women the Exercises in their own house, was sharply rebuked (*MI* I, vi, 521; *Chron.*, iv, 174). Donna Belotta is first named in *MI* I, vi, 493 (March 18th, 1554); *ibid.*, 680, her pilgrimage to Loreto is mentioned – Ignatius sent her his respects through Mercurian. His greetings were repeated in July, "in case Madonna Belotta should still be there" (*ibid.*, vii, 347). The letter to Geronimo, in which mention is made of the letter to his mother, *ibid.*, 571. Salmerón's letters to her are in *M. Salm.*, i. 117–19, 193 et seq., with the request: "Pray for me at S. Maria degli Angeli", (i.e. at Assisi), 207 et seq. In February 1557, there is news of her financial difficulties: *Mixt.*, v, 546. For her death see

M. Salm., ii, 80, 100. Ignatius told Salmerón in January 1555 of her son's entry into the Society: *MI* I, viii, 303. After the lady's death there were long negociations with her son, who had meanwhile left the Society, cf. *M. Salm.*, ii, 796–8, until the house was finally sold, cf. *ibid.*, 171.

[67] The visit and the request are mentioned in *MI* I, xi, 274; cf. *Chron.*, vi, 264.

[68] For the contents of the letter cf. *MI* I, xi, 295. Refusal on the part of the rector in Naples: *Chron.*, vi, 264. Negative result of the whole project: *ibid.*, 265.

Aldonza González de Villasimplez

[69] For the family background see *Chron.*, i, 309. Ignatius' letter to the father is in *MI* I, i, 590 et seq. Cf. also for the whole matter, Astráin, i, 438–64.

[70] For further developments see *Chron.*, i, 318, 442. Let it be remarked here that we have made some unimportant cuts in the correspondence of Aldonza González with Ignatius, in order to make more intelligible this highly complicated legal case.

[71] Polanco's letter to the Conservador is in *MI* I, ii, 180. Instructions to Oviedo, *ibid.*, 238. For Fr. de Roja's negotiations see *M. Borg.*, ii, 33–5.

[72] The steps taken in Rome are reported in two letters of October 1548 and January 1549 (*MI* I, ii, 249, 310). Letter to Borgia, *ibid.*, 323.

[73] Efforts of Araoz, *Mixt.*, ii, 266. Summary of the letter of May 15th in *MI* I, ii, 415.

[74] For Aldonza's dissatisfaction see *MI* I, ii, 501. Araoz' words are from his letter of August 28th, 1549 (*Mixt.*, ii, 266). The no longer extant letter of July to Aldonza is mentioned in the following letter (*ibid.*, ii, 282).

[75] The foregoing letter of October 11th, 1549, has been wrongly published as being addressed to Doña Ana; in fact the addressee is Doña Aldonza (cf. *Cartas*, ii, 194, note 2), The news of January 1550 is in *MI* I, ii, 654. That of June *ibid.*, iii, 82. Polanco's letter of July *ibid.*, 119 et seq. Summary account of the events of 1550 in *Chron.*, ii, 9.

[76] For the principal opponents in Saragossa cf. *Chron.*, ii, 103, et seq. See *ibid.*, 355 for the lawsuit brought by Doña Ana, which pervades the correspondence of the whole year: cf. *MI* I, iii, 244, 286, 438, 522, et seq. 627, 710.

[77] Don Luis' letter to Polanco is in *Mixt.*, ii, 584 et seq. The Governor of Aragon, Don Francisco de Gurrea, added a petition of his own to Philip II (*ibid.*, iii, 450–3).

[78] Doña Ana's journey to Rome and the attempt to persuade her to turn back: *MI* I, iii, 438. The statement that the affair was Ignatius' daily topic of conversation, *ibid.*, 681; the lawsuit an intolerable burden, *ibid.*, iv, 69; request for a legal represen-tative, *ibid.*, 164 et seq. In July 1552 it is stated that Doña Ana is still in Rome, *ibid.*, 324 et seq. Arrival of Don Luis, *ibid.*, 475; departure in August 1553, *ibid.*, v, 357; after further difficulties (*ibid.*, 511 et seq.; vii, 13) the Roman lawsuit ends favourably, *ibid.*, viii, 13. Summary account of the year 1552 is in *Chron.*, ii, 674 et seq.

[79] For the year 1553 cf. *Chron.*, iii, 387. Letters of comfort to Aldonza mentioned in *MI* I, iii, 681; iv, 475, 620. Polanco's remark on the conclusion of the affair, *ibid.*, viii, 13 (to Fr. A. Román).

[80] For the need of a new house see *Mixt.,* iv, 799. Detailed account of the attack on the Jesuits, *ibid.,* 799–814. Fr. Queralt's report, *ibid.,* 767–73.

[81] The Duchess' support and the events in Pedrola are also mentioned by Fr. Román (*Mixt.,* iv, 814). The Regent Juana's letters in connexion with this matter, written between June 25th and August 24th, 1555, *ibid.,* 706–9, 709–12, 743 et seq., 766 et seq., 773 et seq., 819–21. The Bishop of Huesca too, Pedro Agustín, wrote on behalf of the Jesuits to his sister, the Duchess of Cardona (*ibid.,* 874). For the excommunication of the Conservador see *Chron.,* v, 397; an account of the scene in the cathedral is in *Mixt.,* iv, 728.

[82] Loyalty of Doña Aldonza, *Mixt.,* iv, 768; *Chron.,* v, 402. Laynez's renunciation, *M. Lain.,* vii, 19 et seq. Further proceedings by Ana, *ibid.,* vii, 194, 256, 285.

The widow Boquet

[83] Ignatius' letter to Cazador: *MI* I, i, 96. For Juan Boquet see *ibid.,* vii, 410, note 4. Araoz' account: *Mixt.,* i, 159 et seq.; cf. *Chron.,* i, 140. Hospitality of the family: *Mixt.,* i, 235, note 4.

[84] Boquet's letter: cf. *MI* I, i, 493. Commission to Torres, *ibid.,* 418. Ignatius' letter to Boquet, *ibid.,* 494 et seq.

Part Four

THE INEXORABLE COMFORTER

Introduction

[1] Some indications are given in P. Dudon, *S. Ignace de Loyola* (Paris, 1934), 640 et seq.

[2] Mascarenhas' words are from the letter on page 418. For the Infanta Juana see pages 55 et seq. The quotation from Murranos is taken from a letter dated February 3rd, 1549, *Mixt.,* i, 65; for the writer see *Cartas,* i, 331, note 2; ii, 172, 194. Ignatius' answer, *MI* I, ii, 345–7.

[3] For the beginnings of convent reform in Catalonia see Creixell, i, 226–9, 263–8; *MI* IV, i, 756 et seq. Reform in Siena: *Mixt.,* i, 20, 29; *Chron.,* i, 80. In Parma: *ibid.,* 83, 90; Laynez' letter im *M. Lain.,* i, 4 et seq. His later accounts from Reggio: *ibid.,* 18 et seq.; from Venice: *ibid.,* 29 (cf. *Chron.,* i, 111); from Padua: *M. Lain.,* i, 33 et seq.; from Brescia: *ibid.,* 38. Fr. Jay's work in Faenza: *Chron.,* i, 92; Broët's work in Reggio: *ibid.,* 128: *M. Broët.,* 32; in Faenza: *ibid.,* 39. Araoz in Barcelona (his three journeys to Spain: 1539–41, 1542, 1543 onwards): *Chron.,* i, 103, 118, 120, 140; *Mixt.,* i, 263.

[4] The draft of 1546 is in *MI* III, i, 180 (cf. *ibid.,* 200, 229). Letter to the Duke of Ferrara in *MI* I, iii, 575; to Messina *ibid.,* ii, 391; to Torres *ibid.,* i. 421; to Murranos *ibid.,* ii, 346.

[5] The petition of 1547 is in *MI* III, i, 181 et seq.; its favourable answer, *ibid.*, 183–5; for the relevant passage in the bull of 1549 see *ibid.*, 363.

[6] Constitutions p. vi, cap. 3, n. 5: *MI* III, iii, 190; for the carrying out of this in practice cf. the references *ibid.*, ii, 551, note 5.

[7] To Louvain: *MI* I, ii, 101 et seq.; to Valladolid: *ibid.*, 505 (cf. i, 299); for Ferrara see *ibid.*, iii, 482; *Chron.*, ii, 186 et seq.; Ignatius' refusal: *MI* I, iii, 574–6; to Florence: *ibid.*, ix, 39; to Genoa: *ibid.*, 420, 489; to Modena: *ibid.*, v, 69 et seq., 49, 116; to M. Botello: *ibid.*, xii, 176. Other similar instructions: to Nadal, *ibid.*, ii, 338, 440, et seq.; to Mercurian: *ibid.*, iv, 345; vi, 168; to Palmio: *ibid.*, vii, 157; to Navarro: *ibid.*, ix, 210; to Adriaenssens: *ibid.*, iv, 575; ix, 301; x, 66, 637; to Leernus: *ibid.*, 145; to Viola: *ibid.*, iii, 323; to C. Gropillo: *ibid.*, iv, 528 et seq.; to d'Achille: *ibid.*, ix, 220.

[8] For convent reform in Barcelona cf. Creixell, i, 358–88. Beginning of reform by Borgia in 1539: Karrer 44–6; quotations from Borgia's letter, *M. Borg.*, ii, 516–21 (cf. also *ibid.*, 596 et seq.) Ignatius' letter to Faber: *MI* I, i, 333 et seq.; Philip's letters in *Mixt.*, i, 260 et seq., 263; v. 640 et seq.; cf, *FN*, i, 41*. Letter to Borgia: *MI* I, i, 382–5; account of the steps taken: *ibid.*, 417 et seq. (cf. *ibid.*, 425 et seq., 433 et seq., 487). Cazador's report in *Mixt.*, i, 321–3. Ignatius' admonitions to Araoz: *MI* I ii, 16, 73 et seq., 247, 309. Philip's letter to the Pope in *Mixt.*, v, 648 et seq.; for the brief cf. *MI* I, i, 693. As late as June 7th, 1556, the Visconde de Rocaberti applied to Ignatius in the matter of monastic reform in Catalonia (*MI* I, xii, 481 et seq.). For his attempts to reform the convent of Sta. Clara cf. the report of April 22nd, 1559 (*M. Lain.*, iv, 303–5).

[9] Efforts to obtain a brief for Sicily: *MI* I, ii, 70. Instruction to Landini: *ibid.*, iv, 367; to Palmio: *ibid.*, v, 206 (cf. *Chron.*, iii, 135). Bustamente's report is in *Mixt.*, v, 427; Kessel's in *Quadr.*, i, 287, 464, 670. For Cogordan's work see *Chron.*, v. 9 and *MI* I, viii, 375, 391–4. Report on the radical reform in Messina: *Chron.*, iii, 226–8; iv, 194; vi, 298; cf. also *MI* I, vi, 23, 45–8 (Ignatius' opinion of the excessive severity used), 70 et seq., 190; vii, 89, 195, 353, 356, 359, 390 et seq., 441; *Quadr.*, ii, 528–33, 702–5.

[10] Sor Angela's request: *MI* I, vi, 183, 255, 318, 373, 423, 493, 549, 589; for Sister Armellina see *ibid.*, x, 594. For Sor María cf. *ibid.*, viii, 475; *Mixt.*, ii, 745 et seq., 865 et seq.; for Sor Livia: *MI* I, vii, 441; viii, 45; for Feliciana's convent see *ibid.*, vii, 527, 569 et seq., 595, 652, 713; *Chron.*, iv, 189 et seq.

[11] Oviedo's letter is in *Mixt.*, i, 287. Letter to Torres in *MI* I, i, 421 et seq. For the contents of the lost memorandum cf. *Cartas*, i, 266, note 13; Creixell, i, 367–75.

Isabel Roser

[12] For the departure from Manresa see page 175. For Isabel's family background cf. Creixell, *S. Ignacio en Barcelona* (Barcelona, 1907), 113–17; *MI* I, i, 187. Juan Pascual's statement is given in *MI* IV, ii, 396 (cf. *FN*, i, 413, note 35). For the first meeting with Ignatius see Ribadeneira, *Vita*, i, 10 (Cologne ed. 1602, 65 et seq.); cf. also *MI* I, i, 83, note 2; IV, i, 733 et seq. The conversation with the lady:

FN, i, 410. Ignatius saved from shipwreck: *MI* IV, i, 338: Ribadeneira *Vita* I, x, 66 et seq.

¹³ For his period of study in Barcelona see *FN,* i, 434–8. The quotation from Widmanstadt, *ibid.,* 791. Isabel's complaints of her disorders are to be inferred from Ignatius' reply. For help to him while studying cf. *Chron.,* i, 41. For the group of ladies in Barcelona see P. Dudon, *S. Ignace de Loyola* (Paris, 1934), 130.

¹⁴ Ignatius to Cazador: *MI* I, i, 96. For the legend of St. Marina see Honorius Augustod., *Speculum Ecclesiae* (*PL,* 172, 1053 et seq.); *Acta Sanctorum, Julii,* iv, 283 et seq.; H. Usener, *Acta Marinae et Christophori* (Bonn, 1886), 15–46; H. Günter, *Legendenstudien* (Cologne, 1906), 128; H. Delehaye, *Légendes hagiographiques* (Brussels, 1927), 188–93; L. Clugnet, *Vie et Office de Ste. Marine* (Paris, 1905).

¹⁵ Money sent to Bologna, see *MI,* I, i, 94, 96.

¹⁶ For the persecutions of 1538 cf. *FN,* i, 201–3, 502; Tacchi-Venturi, ii, 153–69. To Cazador was sent a report similar to that received by Señora Roser: *MI* I, i, 144.

¹⁷ For Araoz' journey see *Mixt.,* i, 32; Schurhammer, i. 500 et seq.; Creixell, i, 311; *FN,* i, 242.

¹⁸ Death of her husband: Creixell, i, 289 et seq. For Cazador cf. *Mixt.,* I, 321–3; *MI* I, i, 382, 425 et seq., 487. For L. García cf. *ibid.,* 15 et seq.; *FN,* i, 8, note 14, 125, note 32; *M. Fabr.,* 40, 157; Schurhammer, i, 405, 433.

¹⁹ Faber's letter is in M. *Fabr.,* 156. Francis Borgia sent greetings to Isabel Roser in 1546; evidently he knew her well from the days of his viceroyship (*M. Borg.,* ii, 527).

²⁰ P. Santacruz' report is in *Mixt.,* i, 94; for the summer stay in the country see *ibid.,* 96; for the project of entering the cloister see Dudon 97; Creixell, i, 323. For Araoz' sojourn in Barcelona see *Mixt.,* i, 95, 113. Instruction to him in *MI* I, xii, 216 et seq., (cf. *Mixt.,* i, 112, note 1).

²¹ Millán de Loyola visits Isabel: *MI* I, i, 189. Isabel's countermeasures are related in *Mixt.,* i, 96, 98, 124.

²² Statement in court: *MI* IV, i, 653. The journey was made by sea (*ibid.,* 2, 335). She arrived in Rome in August: Tacchi-Venturi, ii, 2, 79, note 2; cf. *Mixt.,* i, 118. The nun's statement of 1606 is in *MI* IV, ii, 696. For her luggage see *MI* I, i, 491. *Ibid.* also the report on Eguía. The greetings and statements of Araoz are in *Mixt.,* i, 150, 156, 247, 256, 263, 282, 311; *ibid.,* ii, 142 and *MI* I, i, 440 words in praise of Cruyllas.

²³ For the beginnings of the House of St. Martha cf. *FN,* i, 198; *MI* I, i, 269; *Chron.,* i, 128; Tacchi-Venturi, ii, 2, 288–307. Roser's letter to Madama: *ibid.,* 307–9. For her language see Creixell, i, 327.

²⁴ For Lucrezia Bradine cf. *MI* I, i, 246, 335; *Mixt.,* i. 29, 246, 335; *M. Fabr.,* 23; Schurhammer, i, 481, note 3. The petition to the Pope: *MI* IV, ii, 12.

²⁵ Letter to Rodríguez: *MI* I, i, 329 et seq. Isabel's bequest of her property: *MI* IV, i, 645–7; Ignatius' renunciation, *ibid.,* 647 et seq. The words of the vow are in the Society's Archives in Rome: *Cod. Ital.,* 59, f. 11 (the forms used by Cruyllas and Bradine, *ibid.,* f. 11ᵃ and f. 12). For conditional acceptance of the vows see *MI* I, i, 439.

²⁶ Nadal's account: *Scholia in Constitutiones* (Prati, 1883); the remark about her

food is in *M. Nad.*, i, 22. Palmio's words are from Tacchi-Venturi, i, 2, 251–3; Cogordan's letter, *ibid.*, 355 et seq. Isabel's letter to Cazador is mentioned in *Mixt.*, i, 321. Interview with Card. Ardinghelli: *MI* I, i, 438. For the lawsuit cf. also Pastor. *Hist. of the Popes*, xii, 52–54. The list of presents is in *MI* IV, i, 648–51; Ignatius' statement: *ibid.*, 654. Account of the negociations: *MI* I, i, 439.

[27] The brief is in *Acta Sanctorum, Julii*, vii, n. 416. Details in the two letters to Torres: *MI* I, i, 488–93. Documents of the case in *MI* IV, i, 656–9. For the further career of Cruyllas see Creixell, i, 374; for Bradine see *MI* I, i, 440, 493; ii, 342.

[28] I. Roser's declaration in *MI* IV, i, 652 et seq. Petition to the Pope *MI* I, i, 515–19. Circulation of calumnies, see *ibid.*, 493. Ignatius' letter to Boquet, *ibid.*, 494 et seq. Even Araoz was in agreement with the way the matter was settled (*Mixt.*, i, 373).

[29] Her return to Barcelona: *Mixt.*, ii, 54. The convent was founded in 1494 and was considered very faithful to the rule (cf. *ibid.*, iv 150, note 13).

[30] There is a summary of the reply in *MI* I, iii, 161. The nun's testimony is in *MI* IV, ii, 696.

[31] *MI* I, viii, 343.

Isabel de Josa

[32] For Isabel see Creixell, I 292–6; Schurhammer, i, 501, note 2; Gothein (*Ign. von Loyola* [Halle, 1895], 306) confuses her with Isabel Roser. Letter to I. Pascual, see page 182 (*MI* I, i, 91). Information about the family in *MI* IV, ii, 89, 289. Isabel's intellectual gifts praised, *ibid.*, 92, 289 et seq., 309, 397.

[33] I. Josa's letter exists only as a compilation of different items serving as a basis for an encyclical (*Mixt.*, i, 125).

[34] For the journey to Rome see *MI* IV, ii, 335: Palmio names her together with I. Roser and the latter's two companions (Tacchi-Venturi, i, 2, 252, 255); Araoz greets her not as *Hermana* like the other three, but as *Señora Doña* (*Mixt.*, i, 247). The information about her preaching before the Pope is in *MI* IV, ii, 348; *ibid.*, 275, praise of her virtue and learning.

Sebastiana Exarch

[35] Partly published in *Geist und Leben*, xxiv, (1951) 181–5. For Castro see Ignatius' account in *FN*, i, 468, 486; cf. also Larrañaga, i, 431 et seq. The letter itself gives an account of Araoz' stay in Valencia. Mirón's first report of 1544 is in *Mixt.*, i, 176; the enquiry of July 1545, *ibid.*, 216. Mirón's account of the ladies of Valencia dated October 20th, 1547, *ibid.*, 413. Mirón gives them the Exercises: I. Iparraguirre, *Historia de los Ejercicios*, i (Rome, 1946), 133, 190, 305. Araoz' conversation with the Archbishop is reported in a letter to Fr. Doménech of January 21st, 1546: *ibid.*, 257.

[36] Instruction to Torres in *MI* I, i, 419. Note about promotion of the college in *Chron.*, ii, 656; for its earlier history cf. Astráin i, 268–73.

Juana de Cardona

[37] Extracts have already been published in *Geist und Leben,* xxiv (1951), 185–90. For Juana see Alvarez, *Historia de la provincia de Aragón,* i, 4 (MS in the library of the *Arch. Hist. S.J.,* Rome); G. Escolano, *Decadas de la Historia de Valencia* (ix, 47), (Valencia, 1610), ii, 1388 et seq.; *MI* I, xii, 379; *Cartas de S. Ignacio,* i, 267, note 14, 464, 470. For the meeting with Faber see *M. Fabr.,* 130. Sebastiana Exarch's letter, see page 300 et seq. Mirón to Ignatius: *Mixt.,* i, 216. For Juana's Exercises see I. Iparraguirre, *Hist. de los Ejercicios,* i (Rome, 1946), 36 et seq., 133; Creixell, i, 368–71.

[38] For Juana de Meneses see pages 126 et seq. Ignatius' answer to J. Cardona is mentioned in *MI* I, xii, 377 (cf. *Mixt.,* i, 315). Faber reports her journey to Madrid: *M. Fabr.,* 427 et seq. Araoz' letter is in *Mixt.,* i, 281 et seq. The example of I. Roser: *MI* I, i, 419.

[39] Memorandum for Torres in *MI* I, i, 419–21. Ignatius' deliberations on his sickbed: *FN,* i, 372. For the composing of the dispute in 1535 see *FN,* i, 34★.

[40] The account of the end of her life is in *Chron.,* i, 251 et seq. Oviedo's letter in *Mixt.,* i, 350 (cf. *MI* I, xii, 379).

Guiomar Coutinho

[41] Araoz' letter from Evora: *Mixt.,* i, 200 et seq. For Coutinho see Rodrigues, i, 2, 14, 150–3.

[42] Ignatius' greetings to the lady: *MI* I, i, 353, 413. Araoz' relations with her: cf. his letter to Faber in *M. Fabr.,* 430. The despatch of the tract is mentioned in *Chron.,* I, 185; cf. also Karrer, 79.

[43] Fr. Aragonés' report is in *Mixt.,* i, 561 et seq. Reverence for Rodríguez: see *M. Rodr.,* 586. Summary of Ignatius' letter to the lady in *MI* I, ii, 294.

[44] For the conflict with Rodríguez cf. Karrer and Rahner, *Ignatius von Loyola* (Einsiedeln, 1942), 257–65. The number of those who left the Society amounted to about 33. (Compare F. Rodrigues, i, 2, 140 et seq., with Astráin, i, 608).

[45] G. Coutinho's letter to the Legate is mentioned in the summary of the reply to Lisbon: *MI* I, v, 29. Greetings were still being sent to her in 1557 (*Doc. Ind.,* iii, 636).

Jacoba Pallavicino

[46] For the work of the two Jesuits in Parma see *FN,* i, 42 et seq., 128. Laynez' report, *ibid.,* 212 et seq. For G. Zerbini cf. Tacchi-Venturi, ii, 1, 235, 367. Faber's report in *M. Fabr.,* 34. For the senators' letter cf. Tacchi-Venturi, i, 2, 198 et seq.

[47] The refusal of 1546 is in *MI* I, i, 358, 375; Pezzana's labours: *ibid.,* 417; his entry into the Society: *ibid.,* 477. Rebuke to him and fresh refusal to the city: *ibid.,* ii, 273, 289. Refusal to the *Convertite*: *ibid.,* 423 (cf. *Chron.,* i, 489). Instructions to Pezzana: *ibid.,* 575.

[48] For Madama Margarita de Austria cf. pages 84 et seq. The senate's letter is in *Mixt.,* v, 708–11.

[49] Ignatius' answer is preserved only in summary form: *MI* I, iii, 268. Fresh refusal to the senate: *ibid.*, 409 et seq. Commendation of Jacoba in a letter-summary, *ibid.*, iv, 435 et seq. Repeated refusal to assume spiritual direction of women: *Chron.*, iii, 6. Instruction to Ugoletti: *MI* I, v, 70; news of his transfer (summary only) to Jacoba: *ibid.*, 73. For his companion see *Mixt.*, iii, 380. Letter of comfort to Ugoletti: *MI* I, v, 77. For him see *Chron.*, i, 82, 405; *MI* I, ii, 421.

[50] Letter to Ugoletti: *MI* I, v, 139 et seq.; summary of a letter to Jacoba, *ibid.*, 140. The Fleming's report is in *Mixt.*, iii, 381; Ugoletti's report, *ibid.*, 386 et seq.

[51] Ignatius' letter (summary only) is in *MI* I, v, 173.

[52] For the founding of the college see *MI* I, xi, 318; *Chron.*, vi, 240. Jacoba's death, see *FN*, i, 219, note 30.

The Pezzani Ladies

[53] For Bishop Foscarari see *MI* I, iv, 294, 300; *Chron.*, ii, 452; *Mixt.*, ii, 718. Castelvetro: *MI* I, iv, 238; *Chron.*, ii, 453 et seq. Polanco's remark, *ibid.*, 449 et seq.

[54] Ignatius' letter to Aversa: *MI* I, vi, 16 (cf. *Chron.*, iii, 155). The lost letters are mentioned *ibid.*, iv, 106; *MI* I, vii, 723. For the beginnings of the college at Modena see pages 203 et seq.

[55] Cf. J. de Laburu, *La salud corporal y S. Ignacio de Loyola* (Montevideo, 1938). Admonition of 1549: *MI* I, ii, 339. Ignatius' letter of Nov. 11th, 1553, *ibid.*, v, 685; cf. also *ibid.*, vi, 445–7.

[56] The note in the *regesta*: *MI* I, viii, 31.

[57] Remark in the chronicle: *Chron.*, iv, 107 et seq. Ignatius' letter to Leernus is in *MI* I, viii, 30 et seq. A month earlier a letter from Barbara (now lost) had already been brought to Ignatius by Fr. Lorenzo de Patarinis: cf. *ibid.*, vii, 723. Cf. also *Geist und Leben*, xxiv (1951), 177–9.

Teresa Rejadella

[58] This correspondence has already been published in part by H. Rahner in *Ignatius von Loyola und sein geistlicher Briefwechsel mit Frauen* (*Geist und Leben*, xxiv 1951, 257–74). Ignatius' words are in *FN*, i, 412. For the portress see Creixell, i, 228; Larrañaga, i, 202 et seq. Even in 1559 these Hieronymites were still called "more ladies than nuns" (*M. Lain.*, iv, 302).

[59] For the Rejadella family see *MI* I, i, 100, note 2. Ignatius' account of his experiences during his first stay in Barcelona: *FN*, i, 412. For Lope de Cáceres cf. *FN*, i, 170, note 9, 439, 472; *MI* I, i, 170.

[60] Ignatius' plan to go again to Barcelona is also mentioned in a letter to Cazador: *MI* I, i, 96. For de Castro cf. *FN*, i, 486; *MI* I, i, 96, note 8; L. le Vasseur, *Ephemerides Ordinis Cartusiensis*, ii (1890), 447–52.

[61] This would seem to refer to Lope de Cáceres, a native of Segovia, who joined St. Ignatius at Alcalá and had belonged to the suite of the viceroy of Catalonia.

After Ignatius went to Paris, he abandoned the saint and returned to his native city. In Paris St. Ignatius won over another Cáceres, Diego by name, a distinct person from this one. – Trans.

[62] That is, the devil. – Trans.

[63] Dr. John Castro (1488–1556), doctor of the Sorbonne, to whom St. Ignatius gave the Exercises in Paris. He eventually became a Carthusian. – Trans.

[64] Araoz' stay in Barcelona in 1539; *FN*, i, 242. For T. Rejadella's friendship with I. Roser cf. *Mixt.,* i, 110. Pujol's letter, *ibid.,* 119. For Ignatius' teaching on frequent communion cf. *Zeitschrift für Aszese und Mystik,* xvii (1952), 65.

[65] For the election see Araoz' account in *Mixt.,* i, 263. The Jesuits' first establishment at Barcelona and Fr. Queralt: *FN,* ii, 112, note 194; *Mixt.,* i, 159, 235; Astráin, i, 276. The Prince's letter is in *Mixt.,* i, 260 et seq., being an answer to Ignatius' letter, *MI* I, i, 299; the latter to Borgia, *ibid.,* 382–5.

[66] Instruction to Torres in *MI* I, 418. Cazador's letter in *Mixt.,* i, 321–3; Ignatius to him, *MI* I, i, 487.

[67] The report to Laynez is in *M. Lain.,* iv, 303.

[68] For Araoz' activities see *Chron.,* i, 439; *Mixt.,* ii, 37; Ignatius' letter to him in *MI* I, ii, 47. At the same time as the following letter one from Araoz was despatched to Rome: *Mixt.,* ii, 37–41.

[69] Santacruz died on October 27th, 1548 (*Mixt.,* i, 529). Queralt's letter, *ibid.,* ii, 50.

[70] Araoz' report: *Mixt.,* ii, 51–7. The rebuke to Araoz is mentioned in *Chron.,* i, 439. Murranos' letter (for him see *Mixt.,* i, 499–503), *ibid.,* ii, 63–6. Ignatius' answer is in *MI* I, ii, 345–7.

[71] Ignatius' desire for more exact information: *Chron.,* i, 439.

[72] Queralt's letter: *Mixt.,* ii, 84.

[73] Araoz' support of their request: *Mixt.,* ii, 87.

[74] The nuns' letter to Polanco: *Mixt.,* ii, 163–5.

[75] Ignatius on the reform of the nuns to A. Gou, December 31st, 1549: *MI* I, ii, 623.

[76] Araoz justifies himself: *Mixt.,* ii, 310.

[77] For Doña Guiomar Gralla see page 176.

[78] For Don Luis González see page 242. For Verdolay see *Chron.,* ii, 658 et seq.; *MI* I, i, 118–20, 283–5; xii, 320–3.

[79] Queralt's report: *Mixt.,* iii, 390 et seq.

[80] The account with somewhat altered wording is in *Chron.,* iii, 387. Polanco's reply: *MI* I, iv, 471. The final remark is from G. Alvarez, *Historia de la provincia de Aragón,* 38 et seq. (MS in the library of the *Arch. Hist. S.J.,* at Rome.)

The Anchoress of Salamanca

[81] For Ignatius' undertaking the spiritual direction of the walled-up anchoresses of St. Peter's, see *MI* I, i, 613. Cf. on this subject P. M. Baumgarten, "Die Inklusen bei Sankt Peter in Rom" in *Hist.-polit. Blätter,* cxli (1908), 6–15; there is here no mention of Ignatius.

[82] The holy woman of Manresa is mentioned twice in the memoirs (*FN,* i, 392, 412), the *Beata* of Barcelona in *MI* I, i, 96. For the lady who visited Ignatius in prison at Salamanca see *FN,* i, 460.

[83] For the sending of nuns to South America cf. *MI* I, i, 172, note 1. The anchoress of Valencia: *Mixt.,* v, 633. The election took place on the 8th and again on April 13th, 1541 (*FN,* i, 16 et seq).

[84] The text of Polanco's letter is in *MI* I, i, 613. For María de Araujo and her desire to become an anchoress, cf. *ibid.,* ii, 260; iii, 94, 173; Ignatius' last greetings to her, *ibid.,* xi, 283. For the subsequent fate of the anchoresses of St. Peter's see Baumgarten, *op. cit.,* 8. Cf. also O. Doerr, "Das Institut der Inklusen in Süddeutschland" in *Beiträge zur Geschichte des alten Mönchtums und des Benediktinerordens,* xviii (Münster, 1934), 26, note 7.

Bartolomea Spadafora

[85] Request of the senate: *Chron.,* i, 369; Ignatius' reply, *MI* I, ii, 391 et seq. Instruction to Nadal, *ibid.,* 338, supplemented in June, *ibid.,* 440 et seq.

[86] For Wischaven's difficulties with the language cf. A. Kleiser, *Ein Seeleneroberer. Lebenserinnerungen des ersten flämischen Jesuiten Kornelius Wischaven* (Paderborn, 1930), 126–8.

[87] Nadal's account: *M. Nad.,* i, 75 et seq. The Abbess's letter is lost.

[88] For Nadal's later activities see *M. Nad.,* i, 754.

Part Five

FATHER IN CHRIST

Introduction

[1] *Constitutiones* p. i, cap. 3, decl. K (*MI* III, iii, 55). *MI* I, iv, 92 et seq.

[2] *MI* I, iv, 93; cf. for the Croce case *ibid.,* ii, 603–6, 682, 688 et seq., 710; iii, 31, 617–19; iv. 164; *Chron.,* ii, 16–9; iv, 337–9; *Mixt.,* i, 586; *FN,* i, 571, note 10.

[3] For Riccasoli see *MI* I, vii, 671, 726 et seq.; *FN,* i, 572, note 11; *Quadr.,* v, 543, note 1. For Geeraerts see *Ep. Canisii* (ed. Braunsberger), ii, 307; *Quadr.,* ii, 309 et seq.; A. Poncelet, *Histoire de la Compagnie de Jésus dans les anciens Pays-Bas,* i (Brussels, 1927), 83. Adriaenssen's report: *MI* I, v, 739. Sending of the treatise, *ibid.,* 233; cf. *ibid.,* vi, 227. Tapper's intervention: *Chron.,* iv, 288. Defence by Louis de Blois: *ibid.,* 281; *Mixt.,* iv, 114.

[4] The first ruling is in the *Constituciones de los colegios:* *MI* III, iv, 227; the same text occurs in the Constitutions, p. iii, cap. 1, decl. A and B (*ibid.,* iii, 76). Account of the Beringucci affair: *FN,* i, 568; other examples: *ibid.,* 568–74. The two cases mentioned by Polanco are in *Chron.,* iv, 176.

[5] The questions to candidates are in the *Examen Generale,* cap. 3, n. 2 and decl.

B and n. 3 (*MI* III, iii, 11). Ignatius' letter to Nadal: *MI* I, ii, 710; to the rectors: *ibid.*, iv, 111 et seq.; cf. *Chron.*, ii, 421.

⁶ Lanoy's enquiry: *Mixt.*, iv, 319 et seq.; reply in *Chron.*, iv, 252. Encyclical letters to the rectors: *MI* I, vi, 410.

⁷ Laynez' letters to his mother: *M. Lain.*, i, 41–8, 136; cf. also *MI* I, ii, 581. Polanco's letters to his mother: *ibid.*, iv, 615; cf. *ibid.*, 552; for the story of his vocation see *FN*, i, 572–4. For Amaroni cf. *Mixt.*, v, 580; *M. Lain.*, iii, 657, 689; v, 511; *MI* I, v, 691; *Quadr.*, i, 186. Opinion of the superiors in Venice about him: *Mixt.*, v, 737; Ignatius' reply: *MI* I, vii, 30; permission to visit his mother: *ibid.*, vi, 107; approach to the Duchess Eleonora, *ibid.*, viii, 98. For Aversa cf. *Mixt.*, i, 433; *Chron.*, ii, 346. Ignatius' letter to his mother (preserved only in summary): *MI* I, iii, 578.

⁸ For the mother of the Coudray brothers see *Mixt.*, ii, 352–4. Her letter to Claude with the latter's remark, *ibid.*, 404. Claude leaves the Society: *MI* I, iii, 323, 584. Ignatius' letter of comfort: *ibid.*, ii, 682, 723; later instruction, *ibid.*, v, 427 et seq.

⁹ Polanco's letter to Vitoria's mother: *MI* I, x, 542; cf. *ibid.*, 550, 554. Letter of comfort to Leernus: *ibid.*, 145.

Catherine de Córdoba, Marchioness of Priego

¹⁰ Ignatius to Dotti: *MI* I, iv, 429.

¹¹ For the Marchioness' family see Burgos, *Blasón de España*, v, 115 et seq. For the Gran Capitán see *Chron.*, ii, 618; F. Nicolini, *Aspetti della vita italo-hispanica nel cinque e seicento* (Naples, 1934), 11–46; *Biblioteca de autores españoles* (ed. Rodríguez-Villa), x (Madrid, 1903); A. Morel-Fatio, *Historiographie de Charles-Quint* (Paris, 1913), 119. For the family connexions of the Enríquez cf. *M. Borg.*, i, 235–43; *Cartas*, iv (Madrid, 1887), 149, note 2. The modern genealogist is F. Fernández de Béthencourt, in *Historia genealógica y heráldica de la monarquía española*, vi (Madrid, 1905), 175; *ibid.*, are further details concerning the family history. For Ana Ponce cf. M. de Rosa, *Vida de Doña Ana Ponce de León, Condesa de Feria* (Seville, 1615), (2nd ed., Madrid, 1883); *Chron.*, iii, 350; *Mixt.*, ii, 701. For the death of the eldest son, cf. *Mixt.*, ii, 790; iii, 285. Badoaro's remark is in Gachard, *Relations des ambassadeurs vénitiens sur Charles-Quint et Philippe II* (Brussels, 1855), 55 et seq.

¹² For an account of Antonio's youth see Béthencourt, *op. cit.*, 185. For his earliest connexion with the Jesuits see *Chron.*, i, 428 et seq. Meeting with Torres, *ibid.*, ii, 326. On the youngest brother see Béthencourt, 186–8. Project of founding a college, *Mixt.*, ii, 695. Meeting with Araoz, *Chron.*, ii, 340; *Mixt.*, ii, 440. Danger of Antonio's being made a cardinal, *Chron.*, ii, 618; cf. Karrer, 125. His admittance to the Society, *Chron.*, ii, 612; *FN*, ii, 211.

¹³ Antonio's letter of March 31st, 1552: *Mixt.*, ii, 697. Further correspondence with Ignatius: *MI* I, iv, 398; *Mixt.*, ii, 788–90. His mother's letter to Luis of Granada, *ibid.*, 698 note 1. Permission for his ordination: *ibid.*, iii, 284 et seq. For his first Mass see *Chron.*, iii, 321 et seq., 343; the indulgence that came too late: *MI* I, v, 324. Ignatius' congratulations: *ibid.*, vi, 434 et seq.

[14] His studies at Salamanca: *Chron.*, iii, 324. Account of his exemplary virtues: *ibid.*, vi, 573.

[15] For the Count of Feria cf. *Chron.*, iii, 330, 349; *Mixt.*, v, 344. For the uncle see Béthencourt, vii (Madrid, 1907), 73–6; A. López de Haro, *Nobiliario genealógico de los reyes y títulos de España* (Madrid, 1622), 359. The expression about the "anatomy" is in Ribadeneira, *Historia de la Compañía de Jesús de las Provincias de España* I, 23 (MS in the possession of the Society I, f. 61ʳ).

[16] For Don Juan's conversion cf. *Chron.*, iv, 443 et seq., 454 et seq.; *MI* I, vi, 445; Karrer, 137.

[17] Ribadeneira, *Historia* f. 63–5. Antonio's report in *Mixt.*, iv, 306. For the employment of the revenues see *ibid.*, 795; *MI* I ix, 151, 190; x, 122.

[18] Founding of colleges see *Chron.*, iii, 350 et seq., 362 et seq.; Astráin, i, 413–18; *Quadr.*, v, 561–3. For the Bishop of Córdoba cf. *M. Borg.*, ii, 213; *Chron.*, iv, 460; v, 524 et seq., 531 et seq.; vi, 675 et seq.; Eubel and von Gulik, *Hierarchia catholica,* iii, 194.

[19] For her son-in-law see *Mixt.*, iv, 305 et seq., 798 et seq.; joy of Juan de Avila in *Chron.*, iv, 470, note 3; Count Feria's letter, *Mixt.*, v, 344. Gift of the country house: *Chron.*, iv, 451 et seq. Solicitude for the noviciate: *ibid.*, v, 530. The Marchioness' letter to Antonio: *Mixt.*, v, 758 et seq.; cf. *Chron.*, v, 527. Araoz to Ignatius: *Mixt.*, iii, 556. The latter's remark about the "nonsense of racial pride" in *MI* I, v, 335. Instruction to Córdoba: *ibid.*, viii, 24. Mass for the benefactress: *ibid.*, ix, 146; x, 131; cf. *Chron.*, vi, 652. Antonio's death: *M. Borg.*, iv, 402; for the burial see *ibid.*, 587, 623 et seq.; v, 870. Borgia's letter of condolence, *ibid.*, iv, 434–6. The Duke of Feria's letter, *ibid.*, v, 115. Death of the Marchioness: *ibid.*, 134. Comment of St. Francis Borgia: *ibid.*, iii, 754.

Juana de Valencia

[20] For the family history see Salazar y Castro, *Historia genealógica de la casa de Lara* (Madrid,1696), i, 587 et seq.; ii, 721–30, 736–8. Ignatius' letter of 1552 is in *MI* I, iv, 385 et seq.; cf. *FN,* ii, 428, note 4, 430. Remark on Fadrique: *Chron.*, iv, 36.

[21] Polanco's report on the history of Fadrique's vocation: *MI* I, vii, 138. Fadrique's income, *ibid.*, 217; ix, 140. His vow, *ibid.*, 126, 160; *Chron.*, iv, 36. Laynez' letter to Ignatius is in *M. Lain.*, i, 256. Ignatius' reply, *MI* I, vii, 27, 60. Sojourn at Florence, *Mixt.*, iv, 210 et seq.; *Chron.*, iv, 163 et seq.; *MI* I, vii, 504. Ignatius' words about Fadrique, *ibid.*, 415 et seq.

[22] Payment of his student debts, *MI* I, vii, 254. The power of attorney, *ibid.*, 455. Ignatius' solicitude for the sick Fadrique: *ibid.*, 446. His words of praise: *ibid.*, 603, 640; viii, 7, 639; cf. *Quadr.*, iii, 261. Ignatius' letter to Oliver: *MI* I, ix, 278.

[23] Fadrique's letter is mentioned in *MI* I, x, 77 et seq.

[24] For his subsequent activities see *M. Rib.*, i, 379, 459, 516, 590, 609; *M. Lain.*, vi, 7, 310, 697 et seq., &c. His delight over the chalice of Vitoria, *ibid.*, v, 525; over the corporals, *ibid.*, vi, 351 (cf. *Ep. Canisii,* [ed. Braunsberger] iii, 653 et seq.) For his death see *MI* I, ix, 552, note 3.

Madonna Cesare

[25] For the story of Ottaviano's vocation cf. H. Stoeckius, *Ottaviano Cesare. Ein Rechtsstreit zwischen Gesellschaft Jesu und Elternhaus* (Heidelberg, 1914); M. Reichmann, "Die Geschichte eines Ordensberufes" in *Stimmen der Zeit*, c (1921), 222–9; J. M. Aicardo, *Comentario a las Constituciones de la Compañía de Jesús*, ii, 2, 694–716.

[26] Ottaviano's letter to Ignatius: *Mixt.*, iv, 365–71; cf. also *MI* I, vii, 674 et seq. For his second flight see *Chron.*, iii, 169, 190. His mother's efforts: *Mixt.*, iii, 241, 400 et seq. His father's journey: *ibid.*, 489; iv, 369; *Chron.*, ii, 191. The mother's threats and Doménech's words: *Mixt.*, iii, 242.

[27] Ottaviano's letter of July 21st, 1553: *Mixt.*, ii, 402. Ignatius' reply to the Duke of Monteleone is in *MI* I, v, 167; to the father, *ibid.*, 326 et seq., 418–20; vi, 21 et seq.; to the mother's confessor, *ibid.*, 252 et seq.

[28] For the father's journey to Rome see *MI* I, vi, 536, 548 et seq., 563, 700; cf. *Chron.*, iv, 17 et seq., 212. Carafa's instruction and the Pope's judgment: *MI* I, vii, 92–5. Notification of the mother's approaching arrival: *ibid.*, 483 et seq. Her activity in Rome: *ibid.*, 670; viii, 85. Ignatius' opinion of the mother: *ibid.*, vii, 672. Proposal of Card. Carpi: *Chron.*, iv, 212. There was a fruitless conversation between Ignatius and the mother, cf. *MI* I, vii, 734. Ignatius' remark on her failure: *ibid.*, viii, 44; *ibid.*, 105 are given the words of the Pope.

[29] Ottaviano's removal to Rome: *MI* I, viii, 263, 386. Journey of the five scholastics through Naples: *ibid.*, ix, 240. The lady calms down: *ibid.*, x, 435. Ignatius' reply to the father: *ibid.*, 321; cf. *ibid.*, 577. Statement that Ottaviano was leaving the Society: *Mixt.*, v, 337 et seq. (cf. *ibid.*, 263 et seq.); *Chron.*, vi, 253. Ignatius' further efforts: *MI* I, xi, 516; xii, 113. Laynez' attempts: *M. Salm.*, i, 633 et seq. Ottaviano's final dismissal: *ibid.*, 251 et seq. Letter from the Duke of Monteleone: *M. Lain.*, iii, 594.

The Widow Johanna Agnes Berze

[30] For the biography of Caspar Berze cf. *Doc. Ind.*, I, 49*–51*; *Ep. Xav.*, ii, 36, note 4; N. Trigault, *Vita Gasparis Barzaei Belgae* (Antwerp, 1610); E. Lamalle in *Dict. d'histoire et de géographie eccl.*, vi, 1059–61; G. Schurhammer, *Die zeitgenössischen Quellen zur Geschichte Portugiesisch-Asiens und seiner Nachbarländer zur Zeit des hl. Franz Xaver* (Leipzig, 1932), No. 4713 et seq., 6056; Countess E. Vitzthum, *Die Briefe des Francisco de Xavier* (Leipzig, 1939), 313–15. His vocation to the Society: *Mixt.*, i, 267; *Chron.* i, 193. Voyage to India: *ibid.*, 321, 338 et seq. His letters from India: *Doc. Ind.*, i, 597–638; ii, 66–71, 241–4, 246–67; cf. *Chron.*, ii, 398–401, 580–603. G. Schurhammer, "Die Trinitätspredigt Mag. Gaspars in der Synagoge von Ormuz 1549" in *Arch. Hist. S.J.* ii (1933), 279–309; cf. *FN*, i, 757, note 5. The modern historian is Schurhammer, *op. cit.* 281. Ignatius' instruction to Berze: *MI* I, v, 331. For the baptized Indian's coming to Europe see *Chron.*, ii, 157; iii, 398, 409, 481; iv, 398, 409; v, 652, 668 et seq.; *Doc. Ind.*, ii, 622–5.

[31] Cf. the list of vows in *FN*, i, 63*–6*.

[32] The letter of December 24th, 1553, is in *MI* I, vi, 87–92; the admonition of February 1554; *ibid.,* 357–9; cf. *Doc. Ind.,* iii, 63. For the death of Barzaeus see *Chron.,* iii, 486. Ignatius' remark: *MI* I, viii, 482.

Magdalena Angélica Doménech

[33] For the history of Fr. Doménech's vocation see *FN,* i, 43, note 45. Meeting with Francis Xavier in Bologna: *ibid.,* 382; i, 252 et seq.; *M. Rib.,* ii, 160–4; Schurhammer, i, 370 et seq.

[34] Doménech in Parma: *FN,* i, 212 et seq.; *M. Fabr.,* 19, 33 et seq., 37; Schurhammer, i, 509–14. Opinion of Ignatius: *FN,* i, 658. For Giulia Zerbini cf. *ibid.,* 213, note 8, 217.

[35] For Francisca Hernández cf. *M. Fabr.,* 16, note 7; Menéndez y Pelayo, *Hist. de los heterodoxos españoles,* ii, 316–56; E. Böhmer, *Francisca Hernández und Fray Francisco Ortiz* (Leipzig, 1875); Schurhammer, i, 513, note 3. Codacio's letter is published *ibid.,* 511 et seq. Faber's report in *M. Fabr.,* 14–20. Journey to Paris: *Mixt.,* i, 52–6; *Chron.,* i, 102. His work as secretary: Schurhammer, "Die Anfänge des römischen Archivs der Gesellschaft Jesu (1538–1548)" in *Arch. Hist. S.J.,* xii (1943), 89–118.

[36] Araoz in Valencia: *Chron.,* i, 140 et seq. Don Pedro's support of the Jesuits: *ibid.,* ii, 353. Araoz praises the sister to Ignatius: *Mixt.,* i, 246; to her brother: *ibid.,* 255. Ignatius' reply to the father's request: *MI* I, ii, 283. Sending of the jubilee indulgence: *ibid.,* iii, 82, 104. Instructions to Fr. Doménech for his journey to Valencia: *ibid.,* ii, 504; he was to work there for the founding of the college: *ibid.,* 573, 651, 679.

[37] Arrival and reception at Valencia: *Chron.,* ii, 347 et seq. Angélica's intention of entering the cloister: *ibid.,* 652 et seq. Ignatius' letter of June 4th, 1552: *MI* I, iv, 279; of July 13th: *ibid.,* 322.

[38] Ignatius' reply: *MI* I, iv, 618; letter of April: *ibid.,* v, 36. His letter to Fr. Doménech: *ibid.,* 466; to Nadal: *ibid.,* 622. Report from Jerónimo to Ignatius: *Mixt.,* iii, 663.

[39] Ignatius' letter to the father: *MI* I, vi, 277–9. He commends himself to Angélica's prayers: *ibid.,* 670; vii, 148, 609; viii, 20, 581. Difficulties with the building of the church: *Chron.,* iii, 375. Doménech's profession: *Chron.,* v, 42; *FN,* i, 65*. Ignatius' letter of March 23rd, 1556: *MI* I, xi, 166; of April 24th: *ibid.,* 293; of July 14th: *ibid.,* xii, 123. For the father's death see *ibid.,* xi, 30, 53; *Mixt.,* v, 169; *Chron.,* vi, 319. Marriage of Angelica: *ibid.,* 325, 508, 515. Her second marriage: *Mixt.,* v, 509, 542. Further mention of her in *M. Lain.,* vi, 397.

Part Six

FRIENDSHIP IN GOD

Introduction

[1] Ignatius' words, "He who measures my love" etc. have been recorded by Ribadeneira (*MI* IV, i, 392, 424; *FN*, i, 588). For his *magnanimitas*, cf. *FN*, i, 72 (Laynez), 154–6 (Polanco), 305 (Nadal); Ribadeneira devotes a special chapter to it in his *Vita*, v, 9 (Cologne ed. 1602, 604–19). "My friends in Our Lord": e.g. in *MI* I, i, 119. The expression "Ignatius' way of life" occurs e.g., in *FN*, ii, 56, 82, 183.

[2] Ribadeneira's words are in *MI* IV, i, 424. Ignatius' friendship: "friendly but never familiar": *FN*, i, 580; universal love and veneration towards him, e.g. *MI* IV, i, 195. Fr. da Câmara's words: *FN*, i, 579.

[3] Quotations from the Constitutions: p. iv, cap. 10, decl. C and p. vii, cap. 4, n. 3 (*MI* III, ii, 459, 597); p. x decl. B (*ibid.*, 725). Invitations, see *FN*, i, 640; the polite Spanish phrase, *ibid.*, note 10. Fr. da Câmara's words: *ibid.*, 637.

[4] Friendship with Codacio: *MI* IV, ii, 98. For St. Philip Neri: *ibid.*, i, 513; ii 425 et seq., 499; cf. also Tacchi-Venturi, ii, 1, 301–4; L. Ponnelle and L. Bordet, *S. Philippe Neri et la société romaine de son temps* (Paris, 1929), 51–4; For L. Tolomei: Tacchi-Venturi, II, i, 106 et seq.; Schurhammer, i, 394 et seq. For G. Contarini: *MI* IV, ii, 872 et seq.; Schurhammer, i, 395; Larrañaga, i, 535–41. For M. Cervini: *MI* I, i, 261 et seq., 300–2, 378 et seq.; v, 406, 591 et seq.; xii, 383; *Mixt.*, v, 767 et seq.; *FN*, i, 362, 714 et seq., 716. For F. de Mendoza: *FN*, i, 460; *Cartas*, vi, 380 et seq. For G. Quiroga: *MI* IV, i, 761–3; ii, 110 et seq., 393, 403, 822, 855; *FN*, ii, 376, note 101. For A. Lippomani: *MI* I, i, 94, 366; ii, 361 et seq., 596; xi, 118–20; *Mixt.*, i, 571–4; *Chron.*, i, 275; *Cartas*, VI, 526 et seq.; Schurhammer, i, 286–8. For P. de Zárate: *MI* I, xi, 195–7, 545–7; xii, 154–6; *Chron.*, ii, 668; iii, 5; iv, 134 et seq.; v, 48 et seq. For A. Fontana: *MI* I, vi, 140, 502; xi, 5–7, 190, 550; *Mixt.*, iv, 115, 785; V, 592 et seq. For D. Nauci: *MI* I, i, 408 et seq.; vi, 343; viii, 238, 307, 323, 379; xii, 44 et seq., 176 et seq.; *Chron.*, v, 43; *Mixt.*, V, 446–50. For D. Camps: *MI* I, iii, 274; vi, 721; ix, 507, 510 et seq.; *Chron.*, ii, 658; iv, 357, 595; *Mixt.*, iv, 660–4. For I. López: *MI* IV, i, 646 et seq.; *Ep. Xav.*, i, 88, 260; *M. Broët.*, 268, 522, 542; *M. Salm.*, i, 14; *Mixt.*, i, 30, 41, 255, 311; ii, 316; *Chron.*, i, 240, 242, 289; Tacchi-Venturi, ii, 1, 107; Larrañaga, i, 532–7; Schurhammer, i, 394, note 14. For Dr. Ortiz: *FN*, i, 44, note 48; *MI* I, i, 577 et seq., 699 et seq.; *Mixt.*, i, 475 et seq.; Schurhammer, i, 129, note 2, 395 et seq. For G. de Dotti: *FN*, i, 11; *Chron.*, i, 56, 69; iii, 120; *Mixt.*, i, 456 et seq.; Schurhammer, i, 291, note 7; Larrañaga, i, 447–9.

[5] For the reference to the "Lady of his heart" see page 46. Fr. da Câmara's words in *FN*, i, 580. The quotations are from the letters printed on pp. 430 and 465.

Leonor Mascarenhas

[6] J. M. March, *El Aya del Rey D. Felipe II y del Príncipe D. Carlos, Doña Leonor Mascareñas. Su vida y obras virtuosas. Relación de una religiosa su contemporanea.*

Off-print from *Boletín de la Sociedad Española de Excursiones, Arte, Arqueología, Historia,* 46 (Madrid, 1942), 12. This contemporary account is the principal source, except where otherwise noted, for what follows. There are short accounts of her life in March, *Niñez y juventud de Felipe II* (Madrid 1941), i, 226–9; Rodríguez I, i 200–4. For the honorary title "Mother of the Society of Jesus" cf. *Ep. Canisii* (ed. Braunsberger), i, 99, note 6.

[7] On October 15th, 1553, (*Mixt.,* iii, 519); further information on Pedro Mascarenhas and his wife Helena in *MI* I, vi, 157–9; viii, 442.

[8] Thus Borgia writes to her e.g. on February 14th, 1565: "to my Lady and dearest sister in Christ" (*M. Borg.,* iii, 742–4).

[9] *FN,* i, 465. For Leonor's activities as governess to the Prince see L. Pfandl, *Philipp II* (Munich, 1938), 41. "In the nursery there held sway besides the mother the lady-in-waiting Doña Leonor de Mascarenhas, her close friend from the days of her youth; she was, like her mistress, a Portuguese, and was devoted to the family with touching fidelity. On her, Prince Philip bestowed the greater part of his childish affection, which he could not give to his absent father; and even when she was old he retained a tender devotion to her as long as she lived." For the first meeting between Ignatius and the governess cf. *FN,* i, 447, note 25; Larrañaga, i, 428 et seq.; March, *Niñez* etc., I, 220; Rodrigues, i, 1, 10, 200–4.

[10] *FN,* i, 472.

[11] Ribadeneira to Ignatius, February 20th, 1556: *M. Rib.,* i, 154; cf. also *Chron.,* vi, 443.

[12] Pfandl, 48.

[13] *Mixt.,* i, 45.

[14] The letter to Faber: *M. Fabr.,* 143–5; the gift of the relic is mentioned in Faber's diary (*ibid.,* 666). It was given to the college of Alcalá in 1556 (*Chron.,* vi, 590 et seq.). Faber gives an account of his first visit to Leonor in a letter of November 17th, 1541, to Ignatius (*M. Fabr.,* 136–9).

[15] The ladies who sent their respects to Ignatius were: Doña Beatriz de Melo, of whom it is specially mentioned that she was very devoted to Ignatius; Catalina de Roble, Isabel Osorio, María de Castro, the Marquesa de Duarte, the Condesa de Faro, Ana de Zúñiga, Isabel de Silva, the sister of the Infanta's master of the household. This Faber wrote to Ignatius on March 1st, 1542 (*M. Fabr.,* 150 et seq.). Care for the scholastics in Alcalá: *ibid.,* 327, note 10, 398, 431 et seq.; *Mixt.,* i, 229, 290. For the two court chaplains cf. *M. Fabr.,* 164, 225.

[16] Ignatius' opinion of this matrimonial policy has already been mentioned, cf. page 48.

[17] Cf. Karrer, 57 et seq.

[18] Cf. M. Gachard, *Don Carlos et Philippe II* (Brussels, 1863), i, 5–8.

[19] Cf. *Mixt.,* v, 652 et seq.

[20] Philip II. – Trans.

[21] A department of the Roman courts. – Trans.

[22] For the prayer over Don Carlos see *Chron.,* i, 163 et seq. Gift of the altarpiece: *ibid.,* 190. For Duarte Pereira cf. *Mixt.,* ii, 636.

[23] The letter to Araoz: *MI* I, i, 513. For the reform of the nunneries see *ibid.,* 422.

²⁴ For the conflict with Abp. Siliceo cf. Pfandl, 44 et seq., who always speaks of him as "Archbishop Flint *(Kieselstein)*". Borgia's letter to the archbishop: *Chron.,* i, 187; the latter's threat of a visitation: *ibid.,* 300. For M. de Torres, his sojourn in Rome and his return, see *MI* I, i, 183, 196, 414: *Chron.,* i, 169; *MI* I, i, 422.

²⁵ A. Gou's letter is in *Mixt.,* ii, 616; for Mascarenhas' letter to Siliceo see *ibid.,* 632.

²⁶ The leave-taking is described by Gachard, *Don Carlos,* i, 9.

²⁷ On November 19th, 1551 *(Mixt.,* ii, 628); for her stay in Toro at that time see *ibid.,* iii, 218, note 1.

²⁸ The note in the *regesta* is in *MI* I, iv, 145 et seq. For Philip's suggestion cf. M. Gachard, 6. Letter to Francis Borgia: *MI* I, iv, 382.

²⁹ Rumours about Araoz: *MI* I, iv, 127; vii, 230 et seq.; *Mixt.,* iv, 80; *Chron.,* iv, 386 et seq.

³⁰ Related in *Chron.,* IV, 493.

³¹ *MI* I, iv, 273.

³² Carillo's letter is in *Mixt.,* v, 301; cf. also *Chron.,* v, 590; Araoz' letter of January 13th, 1556: *ibid.,* 164. For Ignatius' sickness during the last months of his life cf. the chronology in *FN,* i, 60*.

³³ Letter of July 13th, 1556 (*MI* I, xii, 118).

³⁴ Quotation from the chronicle: *Chron.,* vi, 665. For Leonor's interest in the projected college at Madrid, cf. Borgia to Laynez, *M. Borg.,* iii, 316; for her gift cf. *Chron.,* vi, 591, 644. For the handing over of her property in Portugal cf. *M. Lain.,* iv, 655 et seq.; v, 292.

³⁵ *M. Borg.,* iii, 625 (on matrimonial affairs); Ribadeneira to Borgia on February 5th, 1563 (the two Coptic monks): *M. Rib.,* i, 487; Laynez to Borgia, July 13th, 1564 (the college of Messina): *M. Lain.,* viii, 93; cf. also *M. Rib.,* i, 545.

³⁶ Letter of Borgia's, February 14th, 1565 (*M. Borg.,* iii, 742–4); Ribadeneira's remark: *M. Rib.,* i, 487.

³⁷ Correspondence between Borgia and the Count of Lerma in *M. Borg.,* iv, 585 et seq., 649 et seq. Letter of consolation from Borgia to Leonor: *ibid.,* 677. His account of prayers at Loreto: *ibid.,* v, 99 et seq.

³⁸ Meetings between Leonor and St. Teresa are mentioned in the latter's work, *Las fundaciones (Obras,* ed. P. Silveiro de S. Teresa, v, 133); cf. also M. Auclair, *St. Teresa of Avila,* London 1953.

³⁹ For her loyalty to the Jesuits cf. *Chron.,* vi, 591, note 2; Mercurian's recommendation is in *M. Rib.,* i, 810. Dietrichstein's proposal: cf. M. Koch, *Quellen zur Geschichte Kaiser Maximilians II* (Leipzig, 1857), i, 142.

⁴⁰ For her portrait see March, *Niñez y juventud,* I, 354 et seq. (It is reproduced *ibid.,* 129). For her will cf. *Chron.,* vi, 591, note 2.

Leonor de Vega Osorio

⁴¹ For the biography of Juan de Vega see Marqués de Saltillo, *Juan de Vega, embajador de Carlos V en Roma (1543-1547)* (Madrid, 1946); K. Brandi, *Kaiser Karl V.* (Munich, 1937), 460.

[42] For Ignatius' relations with the Marquis of Aguilar cf. *MI* I, i, 183, note 4, 240, 290. His activities in connection with the reform of Catalan nunneries: *ibid.*, 418, 422, 433 et seq.; *Mixt.*, i, 235; *Chron.*, i, 140, 170; ii, 104, 314.

[43] *M. Fabr.*, 152 et seq.

[44] For the family of Juan de Vega cf. *MI* I, i, 290; F. Cereceda, *Diego Lainez en la Europa religiosa de su tiempo* (Madrid, 1945), i, 160. For his wife's descent cf. J. W. Imhof, *Historia Italiae et Hispaniae genealogica* (Nuremberg, 1701), i, 41, 105; A. López de Haro, *Nobiliario genealógico* (Madrid, 1622), 289. The marriage contract is in Saltillo, *op. cit.*, 281–92.

[45] For the beginning of her work in Rome cf. Pastor, *Hist. of the Popes*, xii 42. De Vega lived in the house next to S. Apollinare, called *domus oratoris Hispanici* in Bufalini's plan, cf. Tacchi-Venturi, ii, 2, 169. Ignatius soon asked for the new ambassador's help in the matter of convent reform already mentioned: *MI* I, i, 433 et seq.; *M. Fabr.*, 396. The first mention of his relations with the ambassador's family, at the beginning of 1554, is in *MI* I, i, 290. The words to Rodríguez are in a letter of November, 1545 (*ibid.*, 322); the report of May, *ibid.*, 305 et seq.; cf. also *FN*, ii, 436. At that time Leonor Osorio received permission from Cardinal Crescenzi to spend five days of each month in a convent (Tacchi-Venturi, i, 147 et seq.).

[46] Ignatius' words are in *FN*, ii, 346 et seq. The affair with the postmaster: *MI* I, i, 436; cf. *ibid.*, 494, 564; Tacchi-Venturi, ii, 2, 181 et seq.

[47] For the tension between Pope and Emperor see Pastor, xii, 189; E. Gothein, *Ignatius von Loyola und das Zeitalter der Gegenreformation* (Halle, 1895), 566; the word "brood" is also found in Pastor, *loc. cit.* For the political background to the temporary recall of the ambassador from Rome, which was equivalent to a breaking off of diplomatic relations, cf. Pastor, xii, 193 and C. Carpasso, *Paolo III* (Messina, 1923), ii, 353 et seq., 387 et seq., 391. Leonor's request for Spanish sermons: *MI* I, i, 305; account of the Turk's baptism, *ibid.*, 371; Leonor as a witness in the lawsuit with Isabel Roser: *ibid.*, 446, 438, 493; letter of recommendation to Duke Cosimo mentioned: *ibid.*, 471; her words about the acceptance of ecclesiastical dignities: *ibid.*, 435. At the end of 1545 Leonor gave Ignatius some relics in precious settings as a present for the Heir Apparent of Portugal (*MI* I, i, 322). The modern historian from whom the last quotation is taken is F. Cereceda, *op. cit.*, i, 161.

[48] For what preceded Vega's recall cf. Carpasso, ii, 561, note 4; for an appreciation of his work in Rome see Pastor, xii, 282, 290. Ignatius' acquaintance with Mendoza: *MI* I, i, 135; he too had to help with convent reform (*ibid.*, 694, 715). For Leonor's departure and her travelling companions cf. *ibid.*, 483: *Chron.*, i, 236.

[49] For Figueroa cf. *MI* I, i, 148; *FN*, i, 203, 444; *Chron.*, i, 69; Larrañaga, i, 264 et seq., note 23.

[50] That is, by sickness. – Trans.

[51] Polanco's report: *FN*, i, 287. Ignatius' letter to Canisius: *MI* I, i, 393; cf. also *FN*, ii, 206. For Lhoost and his work in Sicily cf. *Chron.*, i, 198 et seq.; A. Poncelet, *Histoire de la Compagnie de Jésus dans les anciens Pays-Bas*, i (Brussels, 1927), 48; for the unrest in Naples at that time, see Adriani, *Istoria de' suoi tempi* VI, 226 et seq. Lhoost's death is reported in *MI* I, ii, 207 et seq.; *Chron.*, i, 238.

[52] Polanco's letter to Araoz: *MI* I, i, 612. Cautious instructions to Laynez concerning the recall of Fr. Doménech, *ibid.,* ii, 283.

[53] The Vicereine's letter of July 9th, 1548, follows below. For Canisius' activities in Messina cf. J. Brodrick, *Peter Canisius,* (London 1935) 118 et seq. For Dr. Villanueva cf. *MI* I, ii, 251; *Mixt.,* iii, 56; v, 133, 224. For the Vicereine's first successes cf. *FN,* ii, 208.

[54] For Zuazola and Salzedo here mentioned cf. the summaries of letters to Doménech dated June 2nd, and August 4th, 1548 (*MI* I, ii, 128, 174 et seq.).

[55] Amarone's account is in *MI* IV, i, 564. The lost letter of thanks dated June 9th is mentioned in that of August 11th, 1548. The following letter is partly written in Leonor Osorio's own hand.

[56] The postscript of the letter has been omitted in *MI*; it concerns the Bishop of Como (cf. *MI* I, ii, 188, 560 et seq.; *Mixt.,* v, 659 et seq.).

[57] Doménech's letter is in *Mixt.,* ii, 75.

[58] Polanco's letter: *MI* I, ii, 384. For the infant prodigy cf. *ibid.,* IV, i, 438; *FN,* ii, 495; *Chron.,* i, 288. For Laynez' journey to Sicily cf. *ibid.,* 279 et seq.

[59] Laynez' account of the ladies' complaints is in *M. Lain.,* i, 103, 110 et seq. Marriage contract between Francis Borgia's daughter and the son of the Marquis of Alcañices: *M. Borg.,* i, 648; iii, 59. By way of comparison with the sums here mentioned: Charles V gave Eleonor de Castro 8 *cuentos* on her betrothal to Francis Borgia; while María of Portugal, wife of Philip II, received 800,000 *cruzados* (=300 *cuentos maravedís*), A *cuento* was a million *maravedís,* roughly equivalent to £1,000. (Cf. L. Pfandl, *Philipp II,* 65).

[60] 13,000,000 *maravedís.* – Trans.

[61] In the Spanish edition, this date is given as May 1549. – Trans.

[62] Laynez' report on his visit to the Vicereine is in *M. Lain.,* viii, 355 et seq.

[63] The summary of the letter of March 29th, 1550, is in *MI* I, ii, 721. Eulogy of the dead Vicereine in *Chron.,* ii, 40. Account of Laynez' panegyric at the funeral: *ibid.,* 41. Leonor's will, dated February 13th, 1550, is in Saltillo, *op. cit.,* 293–301.

Isabel de Vega

[64] The sum here mentioned, which Ignatius was to deliver, is a very modest dowry. Ignatius was then (towards the end of 1548) very ill (cf. *MI* I, i, 279). For the notary and *actor causarum* (*ibid.,* IV, i, 647) here named, whose name is also written Casas-Rubias (thus in *M. Lain.,* v, 625), cf. *MI* I, ii, 695; v, 18, 58; vi, 710; *Mixt.,* ii, 316. For Isabel de Vega cf. Tacchi-Venturi, ii, 1, 361, note 1.

[65] Presumably via Barcelona. – Trans.

[66] *Chron.,* ii, 41. Laynez preached the panegyric *(ibid.)*; Ignatius' letter of condolence to Juan de Vega: *MI* I, iii, 15-7.

[67] *FN,* ii, 158.

[68] For the expedition to Africa in 1550 cf. Brandi, *Kaiser Karl V.,* 511; *MI* I, iii, 27, 72, 111. Promulgation of the indulgence: *ibid.,* 113. News of victory: *ibid.,*

190. In *Chron.*, ii, 45 et seq., there is a synopsis, in which Laynez' part in the affair is also described. Aphrodisia is the modern El Kef (cf. *FN*, ii, 210 note 20). For the sickness and death of Hernando de Vega cf. *MI* I, iii, 153; *Chron.*, ii, 51; *Quadr.*, i, 233 (report of Fr. d'Achille); the Pope's letter of condolence is in Raynaldus, *Annales ecclesiastici*, xiv, 394. Ignatius' letter to the father: *MI* I, iii, 219 et seq.

[69] For the noviciate in Messina cf. *Chron.*, ii, 221. Nadal's lectures: *ibid.*, 220 et seq., and 232. For the courtesan and the house of St. Martha cf. *ibid.*, 233 et seq. Story of cousin Hernando's vocation: *ibid.*, 543.

[70] That is, Francis Borgia. – Trans.

[71] For the two suitors cf. *Chron.*, ii, 554. Her mental anxiety even made Isabel ill (*M. Nad.*, i, 100). Palmio's letter is in *Quadr.*, i, 437.

[72] For the testing by Wischaven cf. A. Kleiser, *Ein Seeleneroberer* (Paderborn, 1930), 134–6. As early as March 1552 Ignatius had referred Isabel to Nadal (*regestum*: *MI* I, iv, 180).

[73] The account is in *Chron.*, ii, 554. De Vega's thanks for explanation with regard to the *monarchia sicula* (i.e. the extensive rights in ecclesiastical matters which the rulers of Sicily claimed by virtue of a privilege granted by Urban II in 1098 and confirmed by Paschal II in 1117, and which had been insisted upon even more strongly since the time of Ferdinand the Catholic): *MI* I, xii, 438.

[74] Polanco's remark to Nadal: *MI* I, iv, 377; quotation from Nadal's letter to Ignatius: *M. Nad.* i, 89. The prospective bridegroom was governor of Messina (*ibid.*, 93). Vinck's report is in *Quadr.* ii, 27 et seq.; cf. also *Chron.* ii, 537. The Viceroy's letter to Ignatius: *MI* I, xii, 438 et seq. The latter's congratulations: *ibid.*, iv, 450.

[75] There is news of Isabel in e.g. *Quadr.*, ii, 154, 159, 323, 348 et seq. (cf. *Chron.*, iii, 238). For Nadal's monthly sermons cf. also *ibid.*, ii, 557. Fr. Doménech's arrival in Rome: *MI* I, iv, 632; his return to Messina; *Mixt.*, iii, 150; *FN*, i, 583, note 46. For the gradation of titles cf. L. Pfandl, *Spanische Kultur und Sitte* (Munich, 1924), 207 et seq.

[76] Nadal's recall: *MI* I, iv, 607; his letter of Jan. 1553: *M. Nad.*, i, 140. He went as commissioner to Spain and Portugal [cf. M. *Nicolau, Jerónimo Nadal. Sus obras y doctrinas espirituales* (Madrid, 1949) 41]. His answer of February 10th, 1553: *M. Nad.*, 141 et seq.

[77] Doménech's report is in *Mixt.*, iii, 236; cf. *Chron.*, iii, 219.

[78] The first request for Jesuits for Bivona is in *M. Nad.*, i, 137 (cf. *Chron.*, iii, 235). Description of conditions there: *ibid.*, vi, 305 et seq. The Countess's project for a college, May 1553: *Quadr.*, ii, 323; report of it to Nadal: *MI* I, v, 382. Mention is made *ibid.*, vi, 513 of all that the Countess was doing for the college.

[79] Rebuke to Doménech: *MI* I, vi, 73. Laying of the foundation stone: *ibid.*, vii, 90 (cf. *Chron.*, iv, 228); likewise *MI* I, vi, 708. The Countess's words are given in *Chron.*, iii, 235 et seq. Financial difficulties: *ibid.*, 236 et seq. Her husband made a duke: *ibid.*, iv, 212.

[80] Ignatius' praise of the Vega family: *MI* I, viii, 145. In 1555 Fr. Elpidio Ugoletti was sent with others to Bivona (*Chron.*, v, 204).

[81] The quotation from Polanco's letter: *MI* I, vi, 716. The Duchess' Easter gift: *Chron.*, iv, 211. Nadal's instruction: Nicolau, *op. cit.*, 75. Polanco's reply to the request for a special confessor: *MI* I viii, 262. News of progress on the college building: *ibid.*, ix, 216, 339; x, 236, 449, 466. Nadal's opinion of the almost completed building: *Chron.*, v, 222; more detailed description: *ibid.*, iii, 236 et seq. The Duchess' readiness to sell even her jewels: *ibid.*, iv, 229.

[82] News of cousin Hasdrubal's entry into the Society: *M. Nad.*, i, 89. Family relationships: *MI* IV, i, 458. Stay at Monreale and flight: *Chron.*, iv, 226 et seq. (cf. also *MI* I, viii, 104). News of his arrival in *Rome*: *ibid.*, 386, 420. For the Lenten gift cf. *ibid.*, 422, 604.

[83] Admonitory letter from Salmerón: *M. Salm.*, i, 124 et seq.; letter to the Duke of Luna: *MI* I, ix, 103 et seq. Doménech informed of the Sicilians' departure: *ibid.*, ix, 239 et seq.; cf. *FN*, i, 721 et seq. For the party's stay at Naples cf. *MI* I, ix, 339. Trouble at Messina on their arrival there: *Chron.*, v, 192.

[84] For Osorio de Silva cf. *MI* I, iii, 460, note 2; *M. Lain.*, II, 9; *Chron.*, vi, 318. The letter referred to from Ignatius to him is in *MI* I, iii, 460.

[85] Letter to Doménech: *MI* I, ix, 25 et seq.

[86] Birth of the second daughter: *Chron.*, iv, 222. Report of the birth of an heir: *Mixt.*, v, 543. Account of Isabel's piety: *Quadr.*, iv, 123, 216 et seq. Her solicitude for Doménech: *Chron.*, v, 193 et seq. Celebration of the jubilee: *ibid.*, 198. The Moor in Isabel's service: *Quadr.*, iii, 515 (cf. *Chron.*, v, 202). Polanco's praise of the family: *Pol. Compl.*, i, 114. For the uncle Hernando de Vega, a friend of the Society, cf. *M. Fabr.*, 152, 368; *Mixt.*, i, 226, 273; v, 135; *Chron.*, iv, 324, 459 et seq. In the latter his death soon afterwards at Brussels is related; thereupon Ignatius sent a letter of condolence to his brother, the Viceroy (*MI* I, xi, 496 et seq.).

[87] The news of Juan de Vega's disfavour with Philip is in Badoaro's report of 1557 (Gachard, *Relations des ambassadeurs vénitiens*, 40 et seq., note 1, 61). In *Chron.*, vi, 321-3 are mentioned the Viceroy's difficulties and his plans for retirement.

[88] The impression made in Sicily by the death of Ignatius: *Chron.*, vi, 326 et seq.; the report on his death sent to Juan de Vega: *Cartas*, vi, 373. Laynez' letter expressing devotion to the Duchess: *M. Lain*, i, 292. Isabel offers Bivona for the holding of the General Congregation: *Chron.*, vi, 327.

[89] The Viceroy relieved of his office: *Chron.*, vi, 326. Vega remained in office until December; his successor was the Duke of Medinaceli: *ibid.*, 329. Vega's letter to Laynez: *M. Lain.*, iii, 217-9. For the return journey to Spain cf. *MI* I, xii, 27; *Chron.*, vi, 324 et seq. For the relics received from Paul III cf. *M. Nad.*, i, 56 et seq.; *Chron.*, vi, 321, note 8; *M. Rib.*, i, 506; *Ep. Canisii* (ed. Braunsberger) i, 295.

[90] For the history of the marriage of Suero, whose wife was Ana Enríquez, and the part played by Leonor Mascarenhas in connection with it, cf. Araoz' letter to Laynez of August 11th, 1560 (*M. Nad.*, i, 779). For the new church at Bivona cf. *M. Rib.*, i, 505 et seq. The account of the Duchess' death is in *Quadr.*, v, 556 et seq., 560; for the death of her little son see *M. Lain.*, iii, 599 et seq.; for that of her father: *M. Nad.*, i, 355. Ribadeneira's letter of condolence: *M. Rib.*, i, 275-81. The Duke of Luna died on August 8th, 1575 (*Pol. Compl.*, ii, 360).

Epilogue

[91] The expression "primitive church" is found in *FN,* ii, 344. Veneration of the women of Manresa: *FN,* i, 408. The noble ladies of Rome pay their respects to the dead body of Ignatius: *MI* IV, ii, 839; *Acta Sanctorum,* Julii, vii, 610. The Duchess of Sessa's silver lamp: *MI* IV, ii, 485. Testimony of the Duchess Girolama Pignatelli: *MI* IV, ii, 662–5. Cure of the Duchess Juana de Aragón y Pignatelli Terranova: *MI* IV, ii, 666–9.

[92] Ignatius as patron saint of expectant mothers: *Acta Sanctorum,* vii, 642 (for Cologne), 619 (for Naples), 620 (for Innsbruck and Donauwörth); cf. G. Schreiber, *Deutschland und Spanien. Volkskundliche und kulturkundliche Beziehungen* (Düsseldorf, 1936), 144–9; A. Schüller, "Ignatiusverehrung in der niederdeutschen Jesuitenprovinz" in *Annalen des Hist. Vereins für den Niederrhein,* 115 (1929), 297 et seq. Original letters of Ignatius preserved by women: the letter on obedience: *MI* I, iv, 670; Archduchess Isabel Clara Eugenia: *MI* I, x, 32; Countess Anna von Galen: *MI* I, i, 126; the letter with the gilded signature: *MI* I, ii, 494 et seq.; other letters of Ignatius kept by women: in the chapel of the Duchess of Villahermosa: *MI* I, v, 8; in a reliquary belonging to the Abbess of Santa Maria dell'Alto in Messina: *MI* I, ii, 691; by Doña Eustaquia Ortés de Velasco: *MI* I, i, 188, note 1; letter to the town of Azpeitia preserved by Doña Maria Ignacia de Aguirre, Countess de la Torre: *MI* I, i, 161, note 1, and *MI* I, xii, 695. Words of the female mystic of Manresa: *FN,* i, 392.

INDEX

A

Achille SJ, Paolo d', 20 457 464
Acquaviva SJ, Claudio, 479
Agnus Dei given to ladies, 429–31 439
Aguilar, Juan Fernández Manrique, Marquis of, 425 426 434
Alba, Dukes of, 93
Alba, Fernando Alvarez de Toledo, Duke of, 146
Alba, María Enríquez, Duchess of, 22 31
Albert V, Duke of Bavaria, 164 165
Albret, Jeanne d', 35
Alcalá, 5 11 12 13 14 31 32 69 112 126 149 153 155 418 419 420 425 426
Alcañices, Juan de, Marquis of, *see* Enríquez
Alcañices, Juana de, Marchioness of, *see* Borja, Juana de
Alexander VI, Pope, 115 122
Alicarnasso, Filonico, 134
Almeirim (Portugal), 54 74 121
Álvarez de Toledo, Juan de, Card., 104
Álvaro SJ, Alfonso, 419
Alvito (Naples), 139 140
Amarone, SJ, Benedetto, 442
Amaroni SJ, Taddeo, 380
Amigant, Ángela de (Manresa), 175
Amigant, Paula de, 174
Amigant, Pedro de, 174
Anchoresses: Rome, 369 370 371; Salamanca, 13 369–71; Valencia, 370
Angela, Sister (Naples), 259
Antonia, Sister (Barcelona), *see* Estrada.
Anzuola (Guipúzcoa), 119 120
Aphrodisia (Tunis), 457
Appiani, Beatrice, Countess, 133
Aragón, Fernando de, Archbishop of Saragossa, 154 227 241 244
Aragón, Juan de, Archbishop of Saragossa, 124
Aragón, Juana de (Joanna of Aragon), wife of Ascanio Colonna, Duchess of
  Tagliacozzo, 15 24 113 131; *133–48;* origins and name, 134; painted by Raphael,
  133; marriage 134; matrimonial quarrel, 134–5 138 145–6; relations with
  Ignatius, 145–6; he instructs her on her conjugal duties, 141–5; flight from Rome

541

B

C

D

E

K

L

N

V